Information Security in Research and Business

IFIP – The International Federation for Information Processing

IFIP was founded in 1960 under the auspices of UNESCO, following the First World Computer Congress held in Paris the previous year. An umbrella organization for societies working in information processing, IFIP's aim is two-fold: to support information processing within its member countries and to encourage technology transfer to developing nations. As its mission statement clearly states,

> IFIP's mission is to be the leading, truly international, apolitical organization which encourages and assists in the development, exploitation and application of information technology for the benefit of all people.

IFIP is a non-profitmaking organization, run almost solely by 2500 volunteers. It operates through a number of technical committees, which organize events and publications. IFIP's events range from an international congress to local seminars, but the most important are:

- the IFIP World Computer Congress, held every second year;
- open conferences;
- working conferences.

The flagship event is the IFIP World Computer Congress, at which both invited and contributed papers are presented. Contributed papers are rigorously refereed and the rejection rate is high.

As with the Congress, participation in the open conferences is open to all and papers may be invited or submitted. Again, submitted papers are stringently refereed.

The working conferences are structured differently. They are usually run by a working group and attendance is small and by invitation only. Their purpose is to create an atmosphere conducive to innovation and development. Refereeing is less rigorous and papers are subjected to extensive group discussion.

Publications arising from IFIP events vary. The papers presented at the IFIP World Computer Congress and at open conferences are published as conference proceedings, while the results of the working conferences are often published as collections of selected and edited papers.

Any national society whose primary activity is in information may apply to become a full member of IFIP, although full membership is restricted to one society per country. Full members are entitled to vote at the annual General Assembly, National societies preferring a less committed involvement may apply for associate or corresponding membership. Associate members enjoy the same benefits as full members, but without voting rights. Corresponding members are not represented in IFIP bodies. Affiliated membership is open to non-national societies, and individual and honorary membership schemes are also offered.

Information Security in Research and Business

Proceedings of the IFIP TC11 13th international conference on Information Security (SEC '97): 14–16 May 1997, Copenhagen, Denmark

Edited by

Louise Yngström
Department of Computer and Systems Sciences
Stockholm University
Sweden

Jan Carlsen
Data Security Institute,
a subsidiary of Coopers & Lybrand
Denmark

SPRINGER-SCIENCE+BUSINESS MEDIA, B.V.

First edition 1997

Originally published by Chapman & Hall in 1997
MyCopy version of the original edition 1997

DOI 10.1007/978-0-387-35259-6

A catalogue record for this book is available from the British Library

∞ Printed on permanent acid-free text paper, manufactured in accordance with ANSI/NISO Z39.48-1992 and ANSI/NISO Z39.48-1984 (Permanence of Paper).

www.springer.com/mycopy

CONTENTS

Preface

Dear Friends and Colleagues in IT Security!

Sincerely welcome to the IFIP/TC 11, 13th International Information Security Conference, *IT Security in Research and Business - Maturing Towards the Future*, and to Royal and Wonderful Copenhagen. Denmark is one of the oldest monarchies in the world but also a modern bustling society with IT profilerating all aspects of life - business and pleasure, trade & industry and government, healthcare and medicine, education and research - the list of where IT influences the mere being and living of humans has no end, all based on the fundamental assumption that IT Security is in place in the present and will be in place in the future. This is the theme our Conference addresses: knowledgeable and maturing use, applications, developments and research of IT Security in order to provide individuals, companies and societies with a reliable, safe and secure, and changing world.

The call for papers attracted some fifty submissions from nineteen countries, out of which were chosen thirtyone papers from fourteen countries, all appearing in this publication. A special position paper produced during the latter half of 1996 by a task force within the International Federation for Information Processing, Technical Committee No 11 on Cryptopolicies is also included here, as are the statements of six specially invited international key-note speakers. In addition, the programme of the conference will include special business presentations and panel discussion on current topics of international interest which will appear in the Danish IT Security magazine. During the conference two awards will be presented: the Best Student Paper Award, BSPA, and the Kristian Beckman Award, KBA. The BSPA will be chosen amongst papers in this publication written by mature students of IT Security, and the KBA, commemorating the first chairman of the International Federation of Information Processing, Technical Committee No 11, will be awarded an individual who made outstanding international contributions to the field of IT Security. Certainly, none of this had been possible had there not been many devoted members of special committees - the names of all involved appear on the previous pages.

This book aims to present, demonstrate, discuss and scrutinise IT Security phenomena through the words of international key actors. They will lay out tools and methodologies usable in modern IT Security environments, standards, standardisation, harmonisations, bridging techniques and methodologies, and international guidelines, current and future prospects in technology, architecture, techniques and methodologies, paradigm shifts, maturing use and understanding, future risks - as well as present IT Security in retrospective: the use of resources, achievements of efficiency and effectiveness, criteria of success and failures, and worth while inheritance. The material is structured into eleven topics, of which some appear more than once: *Secure Information Systems, Secure Databases, Management of Information Security and Risks, Secure Group Communication, Secure*

Commercial Systems, Tools for Intrusion Detection, Privacy and Education, Assessment and Evaluation of Secure Systems, Cryptopolicies, Security in Healthcare Systems, and Secure Communications and Networks.

Special efforts were made to make the final conference programme attractive to practitioners as well as to academics. This influenced the choices of invited speakers and their topics, and made us include more people with practical experiences in the international referee committee. Each of the papers published here were reviewed individually by three referees, but the conference will also present some more business oriented papers. In all, about half of the presentations at the conference and one third of the reviewers were classified as focussing practical use of IT Security.

The Conference will be preceded by three workshops, organised by the TC11 working groups:

- 11.1 Information Security Management: The Future,
- 11.2 Small Systems Security: Components of a Secure Infrastructure
- 11.8 Information Security Education: Current and Future Needs

which papers are published elsewhere.

We offer you the knowledge and wisdom of many included in this publication and trust it will further the international mature use and developments of IT Security. In addition, attendees of the conference, will certainly enjoy the flavour of good Scandinavian design and organisation - joined with the famous Danish smile.

Finally we wish to thank all involved and devoted individuals and sponsor organisations who made this experience possible.

Dear Friends around the world, welcome to IFIP SEC '97.

Louise Yngström
Department of Computer&Systems
Sciences, Stockholm University
Electrum 230
S-164 40 Kista
Sweden
Phone: +46 - 8 - 16 16 10
Fax: +45 - 8 - 703 90 25
E-mail: Louise@dsv.su.se

Jan Carlsen
Data Security Institute of 1977
Coopers & Lybrand
20, Lyngbyvej, PO Box 2709
DK-2100 Copenhagen O
Denmark
Phone: +45 - 39 - 27 88 55
Fax: +45 - 39 - 27 33 22
E-mail: coopjacl@inet.uni-c.dk

IFIP SEC '97 Conference Committees

Conference General Chair

Jan Carlsen, Coopers & Lybrand, Denmark

Programme Committee

Louise Yngström, Stockholm University, Sweden (Chair)
Mads Bryde Andersen, University of Copenhagen, Denmark
William J Caelli, Queensland University of Technology, Australia
Hilary H. Hosmer, Data Security Inc., USA
Sokratis Katsikas, University of the Aegean, Greece
Svein Knapskog, University of Trondheim, Norway
Kaisa Nyberg, The Finnish Defence Forces, Finland
György Papp, Prime Minister's Office, Hungary
Reinhard Posch, Graz University of Technology, Austria
Sebastian von Solms, Rand Afrikaans University, South Africa
Gerard Tan Wee Seng, Coopers & Lybrand, Singapore

Referees

Nikos Alexandris, University of Piraeus, Greece
Mads Bryde Andersen, University of Copenhagen, Denmark
Ab Bakker, HISCOM, The Netherlands
Barry Barber, NHS/IMC, United Kingdom
Richard Baskerville, Birmingham University, USA
John Beatson, New Zealand
Vesselin Bonchev, FRISK Software Int., Iceland
Klaus Brunnstein, Hamburg University, Germany
Michael Burmester, University of London, United Kingdom
Jan Carlsen, Coopers & Lybrand, Denmark
Vassilis Chrissikopoulos, University of Piraeus
Ed Dawson, Queensland University of Technology, Australia
Lynette Drevin, Potchefstroom University, South Africa
Jan Eloff, Rand Afrikaans University, South Africa
Simone Fischer-Hübner, University of Hamburg, Germany
Viiveke Fåk, Linköping University, Sweden
Sara Gordon, Command Software Systems, USA
Dimitris Gritzalis, Athens University of Economics & Business, Greece
Sushil Jajodia, George Mason University, USA
Erland Jonsson, Chalmers University of Technology, Sweden
Jorma Kajava, University of Oulu, Finland

Referees (cont'd)

Sokratis Katsikas, University of the Aegean, Greece
Dipak Khakhar, Lund University, Sweden
E. Kiountouzis, Athens University of Economics & Business, Greece
Svein Knapskog, University of Trondheim, Norway
William List, The Kingswell Partnership, United Kingdom
Sead Muftic, Stockholm University, Sweden
Kaisa Nyberg, The Finnish Defence Forces, Finland
Torleif Olhede, SPRI, Sweden
George Pangalos, Aristoteles University of Thessaloniki, Greece
Ahmed Patel, University College Dublin, Ireland
György Papp, Prime Minister's Office, Hungary
Günter Pernul, University of Essen, Germany
Andreas Pfitzman, Technische Universität Dresden, Germany
Reinhard Posch, Graz University of Technology, Austria
Karl Posch, Graz University of Technology, Austria
Bart Preneel, Katholieke Universiteit Leuven, Belgium
Gerald Quirchmayr, University of Vienna, Austria
Kai Rannnenberg, University of Freiburg, Germany
Juha Miettinen, Telecom, Finland
Pierangela Samaranti, University of Milan, Italy
Peter Sanders, University of Plymouth, United Kingdom
Leon Strous, De Nederlandsche Bank, The Netherlands
Gerard Tan Wee Seng, Coopers & Lybrand, Singapore
Rossow von Solms, Port Elizabeth Technikon, South Africa
Sebastian von Solms, Rand Afrikaans University, South Africa
Miquel Tuset, IBM, Spain

Student Paper Award Committee

Louise Yngström, Stockholm University, Sweden (Chair)
Jan Carlsen, Coopers & Lybrand, Denmark

Kristian Beckman Award Committee

Sebastian von Solms, Rand Afrikaans University, South Africa (Chair)
Louise Yngström, Stockholm University, Sweden
Jan Carlsen, Coopers & Lybrand, Denmark

Organising Committee

Jan Carlsen, Coopers & Lybrand (Chair)
Tony Franke, Danish Data Association
Stig Folkmar Andersen, Kommunedata
Knud E. Kristiansen, SDC
Aage Melbye, Danish Data Association (Treasure)

PART ONE

Secure Information Systems

Information security - challenges for the next millennium

A. K. Stanley
Managing Director
European Security Forum
Plumtree Court, London EC4A 4HT, England
Tel: +44 171 213 4671, Fax: +44 171 213 4813,
E-mail alanstanley@securityforum.org

Abstract

This paper looks at the key challenges in information security in the years ahead from the perspective of a leading business organisation. Four particular areas are addressed - awareness and management commitment, risk analysis, security architecture and cryptography. For each area the current status, issues and challenges are discussed.

Keywords

Information security, awareness, management commitment, security architecture, cryptography.

1 INTRODUCTION

Information security is a challenging topic at the best of times. It is a complex, wide ranging subject that has to deal with a computer and network environment which is developing very rapidly. In a business context, information security has to support key business processes and those involved with information security need a good grasp of how businesses operate. Information security also has great depth as it covers subjects from high level principles and policy right down to the very detailed calculations in encryption algorithms. It covers computers, networks, system software, application software and information itself. Its practices and procedures cover physical security, access control, continuity planning, secure systems development, cryptography and much more. It is, in short, one of the most intellectually challenging topics I know.

We are at the dawn of a new age - the 'Information Age'- which is likely to change and challenge may of our current practices and business processes - an age of exciting and far reaching developments. And the key factor that will underpin these developments is information security. It is information security that will provide the trust necessary for the information age to blossom.

There are exciting opportunities and challenges ahead in the field of information security - challenges for user organisations, suppliers, governments and for all individuals involved with information security. However, I am going to focus my talk on the business world and look at topics from the perspective of the user organisation.

Much of my thinking is based on my time with the European Security Forum and the work the Forum has conducted over the last eight years. I will be drawing statistics from the information security status survey conducted by the Forum amongst its Members. In my presentation at the conference, I will provide more detailed charts and statistics. But firstly, what is the Forum? The European Security Forum is an association of leading organisations, currently numbering over 150 organisations from 13 countries, dedicated to clarifying and resolving key issues in information security and developing security solutions that meet the needs of its members. It is independent and non-profit making in the sense that any surplus of income over expenditure is ploughed back in to support the next year's programme. Members of the Forum agree a work programme and collaborate and participate actively in Forum projects. Over the last eight years the Forum has spent over ECU 6.5m ($13m) on addressing issues in information security.

2 CHALLENGES

In looking ahead and determining what challenges will be faced by those associated with information security as we enter the next millennium, I have chosen four areas as follows:

- **awareness and management commitment** which form the foundation of any serious approach to information security;
- **risk analysis** which builds on awareness and commitment and plays a key part in ensuring that business managers understand information security risks and what to do about them;
- **security architecture** which focuses on the management of security in a distributed environment;
- **cryptography** which, although not used widely today, will form the basis of secure electronic commerce and the development of the information society.

3 AWARENESS AND MANAGEMENT COMMITMENT

Achieving a high level of security across an organisation is very dependent on staff awareness at all levels and on the commitment of top management. While progress has been made in this area and awareness about information security has risen, partly due to concerns about the security of the Internet, there is still room for improvement. In the Forum survey, over 90% of members have a corporate information security policy although only three quarters of them were ratified at board level. Yet, when asked about top management's commitment to chairing key working groups, only 30% of members were rated strong or very strong. In many organisations, senior individuals pay lip service to information security or do not fully accept their responsibilities by saying 'I've got someone who looks after that'.

I believe that a major reason for this is to do with security metrics. In information security there is a scarcity of good information about such things as security incidents, likelihood of occurrence and the effectiveness of controls. In the Forum's survey the worst rated area was 'monitoring performance and plans' and within this area, the weakest sections were to do with establishing performance indicators and the fact gathering process. Very few organisations have a coherent process for measuring security at a detailed level and reporting on it at, for example, a department, business unit, company and group level.

The challenge in this area is to keep the level of awareness growing and to gain a real commitment from top management. In support of this, significant work is needed in the area of security metrics. In addition, the development of best practice for top management could be of substantial help. For example, if the board of an organisation reviewed the organisation's security status twice a year, it would demonstrate the importance of information security and provide a real incentive to fix any problem areas.

4 RISK ANALYSIS

One of the ways that business managers can become more aware of the issues in information security is by using risk analysis. A formal, well-structured process for looking at information security risk can enable business managers to understand the risks involved and agree what measures to control risks are worthwhile.

Although progress in this area has been made, it remains an area where there is significant room for improvement. In the Forum's survey it is one of the weakest areas both in terms of identifying and valuing information assets and in conducting the risk analysis process itself. However, there are signs that improvements are being made.

The Forum has done considerable work on risk analysis including:

- a report on how to establish a satisfactory risk analysis process
- SARA, a risk analysis methodology for critical business applications
- OSCAR, which captures risk analysis information
- SPRINT, a simplified version of SARA for important, but not critical, systems
- a report on how to build security into the systems development process.

Many Forum members are using the above tools and reports and it is encouraging that members have made risk analysis a priority over an extended period.

The challenge in this area is to make risk analysis part of every day practice so that every new or significantly modified application has a risk analysis conducted as a matter of course. Ideally business managers should see it as part of their responsibility to instigate the process. Perhaps one of the security metrics reviewed by senior management could be the number of risk analyses conducted by the organisation. A further challenge is to make the analysis of risk in information systems consistent with the processes the organisation uses to evaluate risk in other areas such as insurance or credit risk. Real progress will have been made when information security risk is dealt with alongside other business risks.

5 SECURITY ARCHITECTURE

Managing security across a distributed, multi-vendor environment is a difficult task made more difficult because of a lack of standards and tools. A coherent security architecture describing how users can be given access, in a controlled way, to applications, transactions and data would be a considerable step forward. However, currently there is little or no agreement on where and how control should be excercised - at the operating system level? using the access control software? via the database? in the application itself? or in the communications network?

In the Forum's Status Survey, only half the members say they have a security architecture. Of those that do, 40% do not have a common user ID and 75% do not have single sign-on to corporate systems. Clearly there is much to be done!

The topic of security architecture is complicated further by issues such as:

- single sign-on
- distributed security administration
- client/server applications
- groupware
- emerging standards such as X/Open's distributed computing environment (DCE) and their Baseline Security Standard (XBSS)
- a lack of user input into the standards process.

Also, I believe, a major reason why progress has not been more rapid is the difficulty of explaining to senior business managers exactly what the problem is and why a security architecture is a key element of the solution. The timeframe for a solution tends to be outside a business manager's horizon and therefore not something to which funds can be allocated now.

In addition, solutions need to be agreed by many parties (users, suppliers and standards bodies) internationally and this takes time.

Without a well-thought-through, coherent, practical security architecture, managing security in a distributed environment will become an increasingly difficult and time consuming task and one which is likely to result in errors and security weaknesses. The challenge in this area is to recognise the current situation, to communicate with business managers and to ensure that resources are allocated and to work with others towards a solution. User organisations can play an important role in raising the importance of this topic and helping to develop a practical solution.

6 CRYPTOGRAPHY

The use of cryptography across the business community is currently quite small. In the Forum's Status Survey, only 6% of Forum members use digital signatures, only 9% use message authentication codes and two thirds do not encrypt sensitive information. However, it is likely that the use of cryptography will grow substantially as electronic commerce, homeworking/teleworking, direct customer interfaces and automated supply and delivery channels develop.

The security features or services needed to provide trust in this electronic marketplace can be summarised as follows:

Table 1

Security service	**What it provides**
• confidentiality	ensuring information can only be seen by authorised individuals
• integrity of data	ensuring that information cannot be maliciously modified
• authenticity of data	ensuring that it is possible to identify the originator of information
• non-repudiation of electronic messages	ensuring that neither the sender nor the recipient of a message can subsequently deny the fact
• proof of originality	ensuring that an electronic document is the original version and not a copy
• proof of identification	ensuring that an individual is who they claim to be when accessing electronic systems

Currently, the only effective way of providing these services is by using Cryptography which will therefore become the key technology for establishing a secure network infrastructure.

But dealing with cryptography is not a simple process:

- most organisations have little or no experience of using cryptography (banks are, of course, the exception);
- managing cryptographic keys can be very complex;
- many countries impose import, export and/or use controls on cryptography;
- a global approach to cryptography policy is just emerging via the OECD;
- new terminology and processes are emerging such as trusted third party, key escrow and certification authority;
- new laws may be required governing such things as digital signatures.

The challenges ahead in cryptography will be significant. Individual organisations will need to learn where and when to apply cryptography. They will also need to develop a corporate policy on the use of cryptography and establish a framework for managing cryptography across their organisation and with their trading partners. Business and Governments will have to work together internationally to develop common, practical procedures so that cryptographic processes can support electronic commerce in the global marketplace. Individuals will be challenged to keep abreast of developments and to play a part in ensuring that solutions are practical and effective.

7 BIOGRAPHY

Alan Stanley is the Managing Director of the European Security Forum, an independent non-profit making association of leading organisations from 13 countries with some 150 members. He has been working in the area of information security for man years and was coauthor of a major £1m study on information security in commercial organisations, cofunded by the European Commission and 40 major organisations. Subsequently he was responsible for establishing and managing the Forum which, over the last eight years, has spent over £9m undertaking research into information security and providing practical authoritative information to its members. Alan has over 20 years experience in information technology and has a degree in mathematics from Manchester University in England, and an MBA from York University in Canada. He has lectured and conducted consulting assignments in Europe and North America.

2

Selection of secure single sign-on solutions for heterogeneous computing environments

C.P.Louwrens and S.H. von Solms
Department of Computer Science, Rand Afrikaans University,
P.O. Box 524, Auckland Park, Johannesburg, 2006, South Africa.
Telephone: +27 011 489 2843
Fax: +27 011 489 2138
E-mail : buks@icon.co.za, basie@rkw.rau.ac.za

Abstract

Secure Single Sign-on (SSSO) is the concept of minimizing the number of different userids and passwords required to access various host systems in a distributed computing environment, while providing a consistently secure environment which also provides confidentiality and integrity services. In its purest form, Single Sign-on (SSO) allows a user to sign -on once to the enterprise computing environment and be granted access to participating host systems across the enterprise. In a wider context, extending the concept to SSSO, it impacts on the enforcement of security policies, security management and administration, security services, and overall productivity. Selecting and implementing SSSO solutions may present interesting challenges, and may lead to increased risk, if not done carefully and properly.

This paper discusses the concepts of SSSO, user requirements, and presents a reference framework for selection of Secure Single Sign-on solutions in heterogeneous computing environments, which can assist in SSSO requirements specification and product evaluation.

Keywords

Secure Single Sign-on, Authentication, Access Control, Integrity, Confidentiality, Security Management, Heterogeneous Environments.

1 INTRODUCTION

In today's heterogeneous computing environments, end users frequently need to access applications and network resources running on multiple platforms to perform their day-to day responsibilities. This typically requires that end users use different sign-on routines, userids and passwords creating a cumbersome management problem for themselves as well as systems administrators and security managers. The same end users often depend on the note-posting technique, trivial passwords or password sharing to contend with multiple sign-on procedures and passwords. (Computer Associates, 1996)

Whilst it is vital to ensure that data remains secure, traditional approaches can make systems unusable, requiring users to learn and navigate through different layers of passwords and log-on routines. Current research estimates that usability issues cost the average organization some 10% of the potential productivity gains enabled by IT systems. (ICL, 1996)

1.1 Impact of Single Sign-on

Gaining access to disparate systems, without single-sign-on impacts businesses in three ways :

- **Dissatisfied users.** Users experience security as a burden and foster an attitude of security being an impediment to performing day-to-day business activities.
- **Reduced efficiency.** Users can lose significant productive time by multiple sign-on's, changing and maintaining passwords and duplication of the administration effort.
- **Weakened security.** Faced with the need to remember a series of sign-on data, users are more likely to select passwords that are easily remembered, and thus easily guessed, share them or write them down. (Stanley, 1996)

1.2 Single Sign-on (SSO) versus Secure Single Sign-on (SSSO)

Single Sign-on (SSO) is a concept that provides the user with a single userid and password for access to all the resources on the enterprise network. The problem is, that in many cases, passwords and data are sent in the clear over the network, making it susceptible to interception and abuse. The concept of Single Sign-on must thus be extended to Secure Single Sign-on (SSSO) by also ensuring aspects of confidentiality and integrity. (Louwrens, 1996)

Secure Single Sign-On is thus defined as the ability to provide principals (users), after being authenticated once, with transparent access to a variety of services through a defined set of credentials from trustworthy certification authorities, via authorized applications, while maintaining end-to-end confidentiality, integrity and auditability.(Open Horizon, 1996; Louwrens, 1996)

SSSO, to be implemented successfully, requires a carefully architected security design, consistent security policy enforcement and a single view of security management and auditing. The challenge is to apply these requirements to heterogeneous and distributed computing environments.

When an organization is faced with the dilemma of selecting or building a solution for its SSSO requirements, there are very few, if any, standards to assist in making the right choice. Off -the -shelf products are generally immature and seldom cater for all circumstances. It is, therefore, essential to be able to measure products and in-house solutions against a common standard. The aim of this paper is to provide such a reference framework, against which SSSO solutions can be evaluated.

This paper is structured as follows: Section 2 gives an overview of the concept of Secure Single Sign-on; Section 3 sets out the requirements for SSSO; Section 4 introduces a Reference Framework for Evaluating SSSO solutions; and Section 5 the Conclusion.

2 OVERVIEW OF SSSO

2.1 Security Services Required for SSSO

In order to implement SSSO, as previously defined, the total or partial integration of the following security services into the solution is essential: Authentication, Authorization/Logical Access Control, Security Management and Administration, Auditing, Cryptographic services, Key management, Integrity, Confidentiality and Availability. (Louwrens, 1996) The required components of a comprehensive SSSO solution as defined by Pfleeger (1989), are briefly discussed below:

- **Authentication.** This requirement is essential to confirm the identity of a communicating party, ensuring that only authorized people are allowed access. It is also essential that authentication happens on an individual level, i.e. any action can be uniquely linked to a specific subject or object, enforcing total accountability.
- **Authorization and Logical Access Control.** Authorization is enforced by logical access control. **Logical access control** ensures that only **authorized** users (subjects) get access to those resources (objects) they are authorized to access.
- **Integrity.** Data Integrity means that assets can be modified only by authorized parties. This is implemented using message authentication codes (MAC's), to prevent it from being undetectably tampered with.
- **Confidentiality.** Confidentiality or secrecy means that the assets of a computing system are accessible only by authorized parties. This is usually implemented through encryption.
- **Availability.** Availability means that assets are available to authorized parties. An authorized party should not be prevented from accessing those objects to which he or she or it has legitimate access.

- **Non- repudiation.** This means proof that a message received was not fabricated by someone other than the declared sender. This is implemented using digital signatures.
- **Security Management.** Effective management is the basis of any Information Security system. Full management facilities are needed. These include:
- **Administration.** User friendly administrative tools to administer logical access control through profiles.
- **Auditing.** For effective management of Information Security, full and proper auditing facilities should be available on all levels of the Environment. These auditing facilities include the logging of all relevant (selected) actions, and the proper tools to investigate the audit logs. On-line exception reporting should be possible.
- **Cryptographic Services and Key Management.** To implement Confidentiality and Non-repudiation and Strong Authentication, cryptographic services are needed.

2.2 New vulnerabilities introduced by SSSO

While single sign-on reduces the likelihood of users compromising their passwords, it can also introduce new vulnerabilities. These are:

- **Single-point-of-failure.** Some single sign-on solutions rely on dedicated authentication servers to support users. Multiple users may be inconvenienced if a server goes down. This can be addressed by introducing back-up (fail-over) servers, as well as alternate access paths to these servers. (Deloitte & Touche, 1996)
- **Multiplied access.** The risk of unauthorized access may be increased rather than reduced where single sign-on solutions are introduced, which if a user's password is disclosed, permit unauthorized access to all systems accessible to the user. The use of secure physical tokens for authentication can mitigate this vulnerability.
- **Insecure storage.** Sign-on data enabling access to multiple systems is exposed to unauthorized disclosure if stored insecurely by target systems, workstations or servers. Critical sign-on data should be stored in encrypted format where possible.
- **Insecure transmission.** Sign-on data is exposed to unauthorized interception if transmitted in clear, particularly when transmission is across networks using broadcast protocols which expose sign-on data to interception at all network nodes. Sign-on data should be encrypted when transmitted over networks. (Stanley, 1996)

2.3 Obstacles and Pitfalls to be considered

Without a proper design, implementing a SSSO system can create pitfalls for users and administrators. There are several obstacles and pitfalls to be considered:

- **Immaturity of Products.** The latest generation SSSO products are generally immature. No product as yet offers a perfect solution and there are obvious dangers in installing fast-moving technology which may be subject to bugs or unforeseen limitations, or obsoleted by further advances.
- **Lack of experience.** The limited number of successful SSSO implementations, plus lack of first-hand experience leaves information security managers, IS strategic planners and system developers uncertain about when and how to introduce single

sign-on, and which solutions to specify. Uncertainties are compounded because the capabilities of single sign-on products, and the ease with which they can be introduced , are frequently oversold.

- **Uncertainty about Costs.** The relative immaturity of the field as a whole and the pace of change mean that there is widespread uncertainty about the costs and benefits of single sign-on. Costs are difficult to assess without detailed study. They vary depending on the nature of the single sign-on solution selected, method of implementation, number of users and the number and diversity of target platforms and applications, and can be substantial for implementations supporting many users. (Stanley, 1996)
- **Scalability.** Scalability of the solution seems to be another major concern, both in capability of handling peak demands, such as concurrent sign-on's in the mornings and manageability across the enterprise.
- **Dependence on Architecture.** SSSO solutions are dependent on the enterprise systems architecture, e.g. dumb terminal - host, client- server, two- or three-tier architectures, etc. Therefore, not every SSSO solution would be compatible with a given enterprise architecture.
- **Catering for future requirements.** There are few, if any, software solutions that accommodate all of the top operating system environments. So tailoring the right mix of solutions to the enterprise's information technology architecture and strategic direction is essential. Achieving technical integration across multiple platforms and applications is a major challenge, particularly when target systems and applications are themselves subject to constant change. Not all SSSO solutions are capable of meeting this challenge. Some entail significant change to platforms, applications and overall system architectures.
- **Cost of features not required.** Most SSSO software packages include more features than just SSO, thus the price paid for SSO includes other capabilities, which may be redundant with existing controls and management tools.
- **Key Management.** Good Key management is essential to ensure secure key generation and distribution. This should be done from a trusted key management center or Certification Authority.
- **Establishing Single Userids.** Establishing single userids in an enterprise is not a trivial management and administrative task. It is essential that implementation can be done in a phased manner. (Deloitte & Touche, 1996)

2.4 SSO Solution Types

There are several software products on the market that facilitate the implementation of single sign-on strategies. Available solutions fall into five main types:

- **Synchronization solutions.** These set a user's sign-on data to a consistent value on all target systems which he or she is entitled to access. (Stanley, 1996)
- **Scripting solutions.** Another technique for implementing single sign-on is scripting. This does not require changes to a user's existing sign-on data. A script is a string of commands and values that would normally be entered into the system. The script organizes these commands and values into a single module. So instead of executing

each command individually, the script is executed by the SSO server to provide the user with the requested access. (Deloitte & Touche, 1996)

- **Proxies and Trusted Hosts.** Another technique, using Proxies and Trusted Hosts, does not require any additional software. By setting up trust-relationships between hosts, and using proxy mechanisms, trusted users are logged on to any host in the trust-relationship without having to enter a userid or password. (Gregory, 1994)
- **Trusted Authentication Server solutions.** These provide a more secure, encryption-based authentication. With trusted authentication servers, a common database is built containing a list of users and cross-references to valid host systems, userids and passwords. When a user accesses the network, they sign -on through the trusted authentication server and are granted access to the host systems. This type of solution normally requires applications and systems to be specially adapted to enabled the security features to be utilized, i.e. implementation of DCE, or Kerberos.
- **Hybrid solutions.** These combine a trusted authentication server solution with one or more of the other types to allow single sign-on to be achieved across both specially adapted and unadapted systems. This allows new systems to utilize the benefits of trusted authentication, while using scripting for legacy applications. (Stanley, 1996)

Of the above, only **Trusted Authentication Server** solutions fit squarely into the SSSO concept. **Hybrid solutions** contain all of the SSSO functionality, but the extension of functionality with other methods, may actually reduce the level of security to some applications and systems.

3 REQUIREMENTS FOR SSSO

3.1 General Considerations

When selecting a SSSO solution, numerous requirements can be considered. These must include functional requirements as well as other requirements like product maturity, installed base, supplier stability, level of support available, introduction of new vulnerabilities and, obviously, cost. Only functional requirements and the introduction of vulnerabilities are considered in the list below.

The list of requirements was compiled from various sources, including the list compiled by the Georgia RACF User's Group (1995), and added to by the authors, from practical experience in assisting with the selection of a SSSO solution for a major bank. This list is not exhaustive and some variation could be expected for specific computing environments. For brevity's sake, 'Nice to Have' features have been omitted.

Requirements are grouped according to the security services required as identified in 2.2 above. Furthermore requirements are ranked as **Essential** or **Recommended** and are uniquely identified by a code which indicates the type of security service it provides. (Refer to section 4).

3.1.1 Authentication

- **Single Sign-on (AUTH E01).**The product should enable authentication by a single logon to all enterprise resources, by a single userid and password, or token/biometric plus password. Re-authentication should only be required if considered necessary for a enhanced level of security.
- **Support common Password Rules (AUTH E02).** All common password rules should be supported.
- **Support a Standard Primary USERID Format (AUTH E03).** All common USERID syntax rules should be defined by the administrator. The product should include features to translate unlike USERIDs from different platforms so that they can be serviced.
- **Auto Revoke after a number of invalid Attempts (AUTH E04).** Users should be revoked from system access after a specified number of invalid attempts. This threshold should be set by the administrator.
- **Capture Point of Origin Information (AUTH E05).** The product should be able to capture telephone caller ID or phone number for dial-in access information if needed.
- **Support Sign -on's from Variety of Sources (AUTH E06).** The product should support signons from a variety of sources, like LAN/WAN, workstations, Laptops/Notebooks, Dial-in, and Dumb terminals without compromising the level of security.
- **Ensure USERID Uniqueness (AUTH E07).** The product should ensure that all USERIDs are unique, so that no two USERIDs can be the same.
- **Authentication Server should be Portable (AUTH R08).** The product should provide for the authentication server to reside on any platform that the product can control to ensure portability.
- **Support Public/Private Key technology (AUTH R09).** The product should support asymmetric encryption technologies such as RSA. This can be used for strong authentication and non-repudiation services.
- **Support Tokens/Biometrics (AUTH R10).** The product should support the use of security tokens such as smart cards, challenge-response tokens and biometrical devices to enable their use on any platform.

3.1.2 Access control and Authorization

- **Differentiated administration Privileges (ACL E01).** The product should support differentiated administration privileges at the different levels of control.
- **Default Protection unless specified (ACL E02).** The product should provide for the protection of all resources and entities as the default, unless the opposite protection for only those resources is specified.
- **Ability to support Scripting (ACL E03).** The product should support the use of scripting for legacy applications and systems.

- **Physical Terminal/Node/Address Control (ACL R04).** The product should have the ability to restrict or control access on the basis of a terminal, node, or network address.
- **Single Point of Authorization (ACL R05).** All authorizations should be made via a single point, i.e. an authentication server. This provides not only a single point of administration for the product, but also reduced network security traffic.
- **Support Standard Ticket/Certificate Technologies (ACL R06).** The product should support standard ticket or certificate technologies such as IBM's RACF Pass Tickets, Kerberos certificates or SESAME Privilege Attribute Certificates (PAC's), ensuring that the product can reside in an environment using ticket / certificate technology to provide security authentication and authorization. (IBM, 1994; SESAME, 1996)
- **Support Masking/ Generics (ACL R07).** The product should support security profiles containing generic characters that enable the product to make security decisions based on groups of resources as opposed to individual security profiles.
- **Allow Delegation Within Power of Authority (ACL R08).** The product should allow an administrator to delegate security administration authority to others at the discretion of the administrator within his/her span of authority.

3.1.3 Data Integrity/Confidentiality/Availability

- **No Clear-text Passwords (DICA E01).** At no time should any password be available on the network or in the security database in clear, human- readable form. The only exception is the use of dumb terminals where the terminal does not support encryption techniques. Where dumb terminals have to be used, 'one-time' passwords should be considered, possibly together with challenge-response tokens.
- **Integrity of Security DB(s) (DICA E02).** The database used by the product to store security information and parameters should be protected from changes via any source other than the product itself.
- **Failsoft Ability (DICA E03).** The product should have the ability to perform at a degraded degree without access to the security database. This enables the product to at least work in a degraded mode in emergency in such a fashion that security is not compromised.
- **Inactive User Time -out (DICA R04).** All users who are inactive for a set period of time during a session should be timed out and signed off all sessions.
- **Commercial Standard Encryption (DICA R05).** The encryption used in the product should be standard.
- **Option for Single or Distributed Security Databases (DICA R06).** The product should support the option of having a single security database or several distributed security databases on different platforms.
- **Inactive User Revoke (DICA R07).** All users who have not signed on within a set period of time should be revoked. The period should be configurable by the administrator.

- **Optional Application Data Encryption (DICA R08).** The product should provide the optional ability to interface to encrypted application data if the encryption techniques are provided.
- **Key Management (DICA R09).** A Trusted Key Management Center / Certificate Authority is essential when dealing with cryptographic keys. This is especially true if asymmetric encryption is to be used.

3.1.4 Security Administration Management and Auditing

- **Single point of Administration (SAMA E01).** The product should provide for full administration from a single point, if required.
- **Role - profile based (SAMA E02).** The product should enable the grouping of like Subjects (users) and Objects into role based profiles, using Discretionary Access Control. This will enable more efficient administration of access authority.
- **Full Audit Trail (SAMA E03).** All changes, modifications, additions, and deletions to the security database should be logged. The audit trail for all systems should be configurable to suit different security requirements and reduce overhead. The degree of logging should be controlled by the administrator.
- **Single Revoke/Resume for All Platforms (SAMA E04).** The product should support a single revoke or resume of a USERID regardless of the platform.
- **Ability to Enforce Enterprise Security Rules (SAMA E05).** The product should provide the ability to enforce security rules over the entire enterprise regardless of platform. This will ensure the implementation of a single security policy and consistent security over resources on all protected platforms.
- **Ability to Trace Access (SAMA E06).** The product should enable the administrator to be able to trace access to systems regardless of system or platform.
- **Scoping and Decentralization of Control (SAMA E07).** The product should be able to support the creation of spans of control so that administrators can be excluded from or included in certain security control areas within the overall security setup.
- **Synchronization Across all Entities (SAMA E08).** The product should synchronize security data across all entities and all platforms. This ensures that all security decisions are made with up-to- date security information.
- **Real-Time and Batch Update (SAMA E09).** All changes should be made on-line /real-time. The ability to batch changes together is also important to enable easy loading or changing of large numbers of security resources or users.
- **Customize in Real -time (SAMA E10).** The ability to customize or make changes to those features which are customizable without re-initializing the product, is important.
- **User Defined Fields (SAMA E11).** The product should have a number of user customizable/ user-defined fields.
- **Support Customized Reporting (SAMA E12).** The product should have the ability to create customized reports using SQL query or similar reporting tools to produce security setup reports/queries.

- **Support User Exits/Options (SAMA R13).** The product should support the addition of user exits/options that could be attached to the base product at strategically identified points of operation.
- **Customizable Messages (SAMA R14) .** The product should support the use of customized security messages.
- **Common Control Language Across All Platforms (SAMA R15).** The product should feature a common control language across all serviced platforms so that administrators do not have to learn and use different commands on different platforms.
- **Ability to Recreate from Logged Information (SAMA R16).** Information logged by the system should be able to be used to "backout" changes to the security system. Example: used to recreate deleted resources or users. This enables mass changes to be "backed out" of production or enables mass additions to be made based on logged information.
- **Administration for multiple Platforms (SAMA R17).** The product should provide for the administration of the product for any of the supported platforms.
- **Ability to Create Security Extract Files (SAMA R18).** The product should have the feature to produce an extract file of the security structure and the logging/violation records.
- **Test Facility (SAMA R19).** The product should include a test facility to enable administrators to test security changes before placing then into production.

3.1.5 General Functionality

- **Backward Compatible (GFR E01).** All releases of the product should be backward compatible or release independent. Features of new releases should co-exist with current features and not require a total reinstallation of the product.
- **Conformance to Standards (GFR E02).** The product should be able to interface with existing application, database, or network security by way of standard security interfaces. This will ensure that the product will mesh with existing security products installed. Where possible, the product must conform to the known and accepted international standards. This will go a long way in ensuring that the product is flexible and "future proof".
- **Phased Implementation (GFR E03).** The product should be able to be selectively implemented for individual users, systems or resources to enable ease of implementation and migration for legacy systems. This will also allow the product to be 'phased in'.
- **Consistent User Interface (GFR R04).** The product should have a common and familiar procedure for users to gain access to their systems and applications.
- **Ease of Use (GFR R05).** The product should make use of a standard GUI interface that is both consistent and intuitive to use. The interface may vary slightly between platforms (i.e. Windows, OS/2, Xwindows, etc.) but should retain the same functionality. This ensures operating consistency and lowers training needs.(CKS, 1996)

- **Flexible Cost (GFR R06).** The cost of the product should be reasonable. Several cost scenarios should be considered such as per seat, CPU, site licensing and MIPS pricing. Pricing should include disaster recovery scenarios.
- **Certification (GFR R07).** The product should be certified in terms of acknowledged international standards, i.e. ITSEC E2 Level , C2 level of the US Orange Book. This will give a more accurate measurement of the security level obtainable if the product is properly installed and configured.
- **One Single Product (GFR R08).** The product should be a single product, not a compendium of several associated products. Modularity for the sake of platform-to platform compatibility is acceptable and favored.
- **Software Release Distribution (GFR R09)**. New releases of the product should be distributed via the network from a single distribution server of the administrator's choice. This enables an administrator to upgrade the product on any platform without physically moving from platform to platform.

4 FRAMEWORK FOR EVALUATING SSSO SOLUTIONS

4.1 Essential Functionality

Table 1 below indicates the functionality considered Essential for a Secure Single Sign-on solution. These are the requirements that **must** be satisfied.

Table 1 Essential Functionality for a Secure Single Sign-on solution.

Reference	*Essential Functionality*
AUTH	*Authentication*
AUTH E01	Single Sign-on
AUTH E02	Support common password rules
AUTH E03	Support a Standard Primary USERID Format
AUTH E04	Auto Revoke after a number of Invalid Attempts
AUTH E05	Capture Point of Origin Information
AUTH E06	Support Sign- on's from Variety of Sources
AUTH E07	Ensure USERID Uniqueness
ACL	*Authorization and Access Control*
ACL E01	Differentiated Administration Privileges
ACL E02	Default Protection unless specified
ACL E03	Ability to support scripting
DICA	*Data Integrity/Confidentiality/Availability*
DICA E01	No Clear Text Passwords
DICA E04	Integrity of Security DB(s)
DICA E05	Failsoft Ability
SAMA	*Security Administration Management and Auditing*
SAMA E01	Single point of Administration
SAMA E02	Role profile based
SAMA E03	Full Audit Trail
SAMA E04	Single Revoke/Resume for All Platforms

SAMA E05	Ability to Enforce Enterprise Security Rules
SAMA E06	Ability to Trace Access
SAMA E07	Scoping and Decentralization of Control
SAMA E08	Synchronization Across all Entities
SAMA E09	Real-Time and Batch Update
SAMA E10	Customize in Real-Time
SAMA E11	User Defined Fields
SAMA E12	Support Customized Reporting
GFR	*General Functionality*
GFR E01	Backward Compatible
GFR E02	Conformance to Standards
GFR E03	Phased Implementation

4.2 Additional Recommended Functionality.

Table 2 below lists the additional functionality recommended for a Secure Single Sign-on solution. Although these items are not essential, much value can be added to the eventual successful implementation of a solution.

Table 2 Additional Recommended Functional Requirements for a Secure Single Sign-on solution.

Reference	*Recommended Functionality*
AUTH	*Authentication*
AUTH R08	Authentication Server should be Portable
AUTH R09	Support Public/Private Key technology
AUTH R10	Support Tokens/Biometrics
ACL	*Authorization and Access Control*
ACL R04	Physical Terminal/Node/Address Control
ACL R05	Single Point of Authorization
ACL R06	Support Standard Ticket/Certificate Technologies
ACL R07	Support Masking/ Generics
ACL R08	Allow Delegation Within Power of Authority
DICA	*Data Integrity/Confidentiality/Availability*
DICA R02	Inactive User Time -out
DICA R03	Commercial Standard Encryption
DICA R06	Option for Single or Distributed Security Databases
DICA R07	Inactive User Revoke
DICA R08	Optional Application Data Encryption
DICA R09	Key Management
SAMA	*Security Administration Management and Auditing*
SAMA R13	Support User Exits/Options
SAMA R14	Customizable Messages
SAMA R15	Common Control Language Across All Platforms
SAMA R16	Ability to Recreate from Logged Information

SAMA R17	Administration for multiple Platforms
SAMA R18	Ability to Create Security Extract Files
SAMA R19	Test Facility
GFR	*General Functionality*
GFR R04	Consistent User Interface
GFR R05	Ease of Use
GFR R06	Flexible Cost
GFR R07	Certification
GFR R08	One Single Product
GFR R09	Software Release Distribution

For detailed explanations of the requirements listed above, refer to section 3 of this paper.

4.3 The SSSO Reference Framework

As stated previously, this paper does not concern itself with selection criteria other than the functional requirements for a Secure Single Sign-on solution. It assumes that the other related criteria like product maturity, installed base, supplier stability, level of support available, introduction of new vulnerabilities and cost, will be investigated.

The proposed reference framework for selection of Secure Single Sign-on solutions consist of two main aspects, namely:

- Firstly, considering the essential requirements. These requirements are not weighted. The decisions are binary and should the solution not conform to every one, it should not be considered further.

- Secondly, after the essential requirements have been satisfied, the additional recommended functionality should be considered. Unlike the essential requirements, these requirements should be weighted. The individual weights must reflect the individual needs of the enterprise environment.

Having completed the two steps above, an objective comparison of the available Secure Single Sign-on solutions can be made. The best candidate can then selected for piloting. Bearing in mind the possible pitfalls for the prospective buyer, it is prudent to pilot the SSSO solution with a selected group of users in a well defined computing environment, after which full implementation can follow. Refer to figure 1 below.

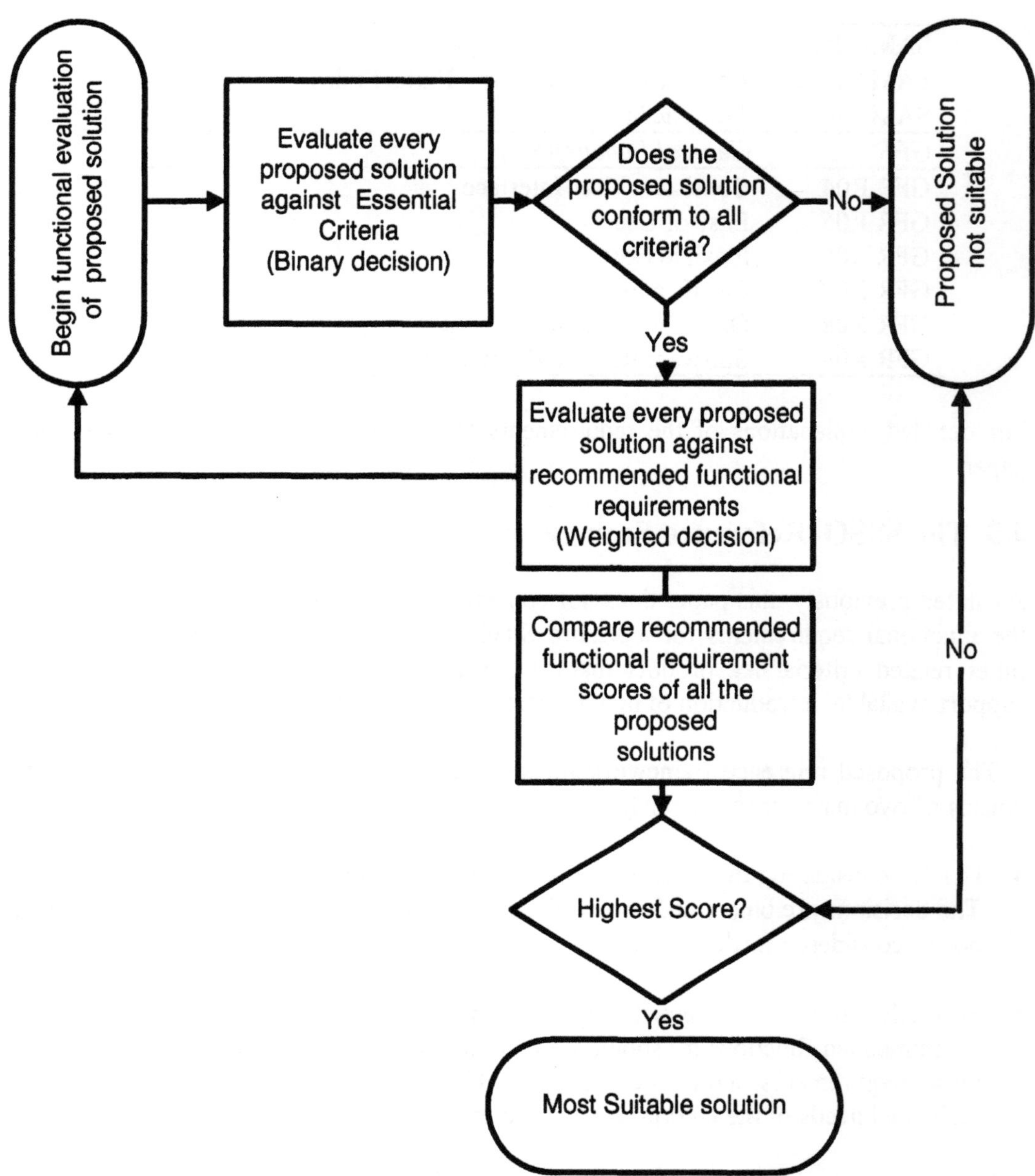

Figure 1 The SSSO Evaluation Flowchart.(Louwrens, 1996)

5 CONCLUSION

Using traditional security approaches with today's heterogeneous computing environments can make systems unusable, lead to reduced productivity and potentially compromise the security of the systems. By introducing single sign-on functionality alone, some of the security issues, like sharing of passwords and enhance productivity may be addressed, but it may introduce other vulnerabilities like single points of failure, multiplied access, insecure storage and insecure transmission of sign-on data. These vulnerabilities can only be addressed by taking a holistic view of the total enterprise security environment and implementing a properly architected Secure Single Sign-on (SSSO) solution. Of the five identified types of solutions, only Trusted Authentication Server and Hybrid solutions can provide Secure Single Sign-on if properly implemented. By following the approach as illustrated in the Reference framework for the Evaluation of a SSSO solution as presented in this paper, an objective decision on the most appropriate SSSO solution can be made.

Nevertheless, it is clear that a well designed and architected SSSO solution can provide added levels of security and substantially reduce security administration and security management workloads.

6 REFERENCES

Pfleeger, C.P. (1989) *Security in Computing*, Prentice-Hall.

Louwrens, C.P. (1996) *Single Sign-on in Heterogeneous Computing Environments*, MSc Dissertation, Rand Afrikaans University.

International Business Machines Corporation (1994),*Secured Single Signon in a Client/Server Environment,* International Support Organization, Poughkeepsie Center, NY 12601-5400.

Stanley, A. et al, (1996) *Position Paper Single Sign-on*, European Security Forum.

Georgia RACF Users' Group, *Single Signon Functional Requirements,* September 18, 1995, http://widow.mindspring.com/~ajc10/sso.html

Deloitte & Touche (1996) *Taking the Mystery out of .. Single Sign On,* http://www.dttus.com/dttus/publish/mystery/singsign.htm

ICL Access Manager Business Unit, *AccessManager*, Eskdale Road, Winnersh, Wokingham, Berkshire, RG11 5TT, http://www.icl.com/access

CKS (1996), *CKS MyNet, MyNet Concepts and Facilities*, Publication reference : MyCF0.01

Computer Associates (1996) *CA-Unicenter/Single Sign-On,* Concepts and Facilities v.1.0.

Gregory, N. (1994) *One Click, Many Services, Security- Single Signon using Proxies &Trusted Hosts,* ACO User Forum, http://www1.psi.ch/www_aco_hn/documentation/uf940525.html.

Open Horizon (1996) *Enterprise Client/Server Secure Single Sign-On*, Open Horizon White Paper, http://www.openhorizon.com:80/whtpaper/sso/sso0369.htm.

SESAME (1996), *Secure European System for Applications in a Multi-vendor Environment*, http://www.esat.kuleuven.ac.be.80:sesame3.html.

7 BIOGRAPHY

Cecil (Buks) Louwrens is currently an MSc student at the Department Of Computer Science of the Rand Afrikaans University in Johannesburg, South Africa. The contents of this paper forms part of his MSc studies on Single Sign-on in Heterogeneous Computing Environments.

Prof Sebastiaan (Basie) von Solms is Head of the Department of Computer Science at the Rand Afrikaans University in Johannesburg, South Africa. He is also the South African representative on Technical Committee 11 [Information Security] (TC11) of the International Federation for Information Processing (IFIP), and is present Chairman of TC11.

Prof von Solms has published numerous research papers on Information Security, and had spent 1995 on a 12 month industry sabbatical at IBM Development Laboratory at Hursley in the UK. He is presently also a consultant on Information Security to IBM South Africa. He is also a member of the Review Panel of the journal Computers and Security, as well as a member of the Editorial Board of the South African Computer Journal.

A Formal model to aid documenting and harmonizing of information security requirements

Jussipekka Leiwo and Yuliang Zheng
Monash University
Peninsula School of Computing and Information Technology
McMahons Road, Frankston, Vic 3199, Australia
Tel. +61-(0)3-9904 4287, Fax. +61-(0)3-9904 4124
E-mail: {skylark,yzheng}@fcit.monash.edu.au

Abstract
A formal top down model shall be presented to aid documentation and harmonization of information security requirements. The model formalizes layered development of information security, where top level abstract objectives, strategies and policies are step by step refined into concrete protection measure specifications. The model consists of static and dynamic parts, where static part refers to the organization, and dynamic part to the refinement of requirements. Major functions are horizontal and vertical harmonization functions used to transfer requirement into lower levels of abstraction, and to identify requirements of secure inter-operation of systems on each layer. Application of the model then consists of two parts: specification of the organization and specification of requirement harmonization functions.

Keywords
Information security development, harmonization of information security, organizational modeling

1 INTRODUCTION

A formal top down model to harmonize and document information security requirements shall be presented. Development of information security within an organization is seen as a specification and enforcement of vertical and horizontal information security harmonization functions that are used to step by step refine abstract top level information security requirements and objectives into more concrete protection measure specifications. The model formalizes layered information security development, where the organization is divided into layers, each consisting of a set of administrative units. Based on upper layer requirements, unit specific requirements and layer specific requirements, total requirements on a given unit are specified by harmonization functions. Information security requirement here is any formal or informal statement about information security that the system should satisfy. The common approach shall be adopted, where information security refers to protection of three properties of information (ISO7498-2 1988, ITSEC 1992):

Confidentiality Information being accessible only to authorized entities.
Integrity Information being altered or removed only upon an authorized request.
Availability Information being accessible always when requested by an authorized entity

The fundamental goal of the model is to support specification and documentation of protection measures and operational procedures to enforce secure application of information systems. Components and functions of the model shall be specified formally to enable automated analysis of the target system. Formal specifications can be used to specify and verify each refinement to assure from the enforcement of higher level policies (Williams & Abrams 1995). Formal analysis is desirable also to follow the evolution of specification of protection measures from check lists to formal models (Backhouse & Dhillon 1996, Baskerville 1993). Formal presentation also supports the two major requirements of models in the development of trusted systems (Bell 1988): Faithful presentation of the situation of interest, and formal analysis of the model. Several formal access control models exist for database security (see, for example, (Castano, Fugini, Martella & Samarati 1995) for a summary) but the model presented in this paper attempts to adopt a wider perspective towards information security by considering any information security requirement as input for the model taking into account that real life security requirements originate from many different sources and are not always clarly structured. Also, no exact grammar is given to the specification of an information security requirement. At this stage, an assumption is made that any requirement, whether presented formally or informally, can be analyzed according to the model.

Due to the layered nature, the model is strongly related to hierarchies of information security policies. Layered information security policy concept shall be introduced in section 2. Based on layered security policies, the hierarchical development of information security, that the model formalizes, shall be discussed in section 3. This is also where an example is used to highlight the role of different layers. Formal specification for the model shall be given in section 4. Finally, conclusions shall be drawn and the directions for future research summarized in section 5.

2 LAYERS OF SECURITY POLICIES

The idea of establishing a harmonized framework for the development of information security within corporations started when studying the requirements that legislation should satisfy to provide an adequate protection against computer network crime (Leiwo 1995*a*, Leiwo 1995*b*). The need for a harmonized legislation in several nations, as for example the European Union is attempting to establish, lead to the identification of fundamental components of the hierarchical information security development. The model was first described by a case, where the development of information security is divided into five major layers, further divided into three categories, as illustrated in figure 1. Characteristics of categories are as follows:

Strategic Decision Category International and national objectives, standards, decisions, and guidelines establishing a harmonized framework for the information security development in several organizations. Requirements set at these layers are those that the operational environment sets to organization concerning protection of sensitive data and privacy of humans, or required or minimum level of security required in different transactions.

Organization Administrative Category Strategies and policies specific to each organization, adapting international and national framework for the organization specific needs and establishing a systematic approach for the development of information security within the organization. Requirements at this level are organization specific and contain all requirements that are concerned with storage, processing and transmission of information within the organization or to external parties.

Implementation Category Specifying and implementing mechanisms to guarantee the adequate level of protection for systems to satisfy the corporation information security objectives. This is where required protection measures are implemented and operated. Requirements include requirements on implementation methods and tools and may require changes on upper level requirements in order to improve cost efficiency of protection and to ensure secure interoperation of different systems.

The division into categories is influenced by the layered security policy concept (Abrams & Bailey 1995, Olson & Abrams 1995, Sterne 1991) where information security policy consists of three layers each representing different views to the system: Corporate Security Policy, Organizational Security Policy, and Technical Security Policy that can be further divided into sub policies according to the organization. Fundamental layers of policies can be described as follows:

Corporate Security Policy Laws, rules, and practices that regulate how assets including sensitive information are managed, protected, and distributed within a user organization. This level represents top management's view of the system.

Organizational Security Policy Laws, rules and practices that regulate how an organization manages, protects, and distributes resources to achieve specifies security policy objectives. At this level, criteria should be defined for conditions under which entities are allowed to access resources. This level represents system users view on the system.

Technical Security Policy Laws, rules, and practices regulating the processing of sensitive information and the use of resources by the hardware and software on an IT system or product. This level represents system builders view of the system.

This layer security policy approach is then considered in association with the conceptual information system meta model, named PIOCO (Iivari 1983). The meta model divides development of an information system into three levels that are used to analyze different levels of abstraction of the becoming system. The three levels of the meta model are pragmatic level (P), info-logical/organizational level (IO) and constructive/operational level (CO). Within this paper, these levels of abstraction have been adapted into the development of information security by roughly mapping them to fit the categories where requirements of different abstractions of information security requirements are created, so that pragmatic level refers to strategic decision category, info-logical/organizational level refers to organization administrative category, and constructive level refers to implementation category.

As establishment and enforcement of layered security policies refers mostly to the vertical harmonization within our terminology, the justification of horizontal harmonization is still open. Assume two separate secure systems, that need to inter-operate in a secure manner. As studied by, for example, (Gong & Qian 1994), decision about security of interoperation is a computationally complex task. Due to this complexity, assurance of the security of interoperation shall be provided by enforcing harmonized refinements of security requirements at each layer of different systems security development by horizontal harmonization functions. Secure interoperation is approached by analyzing interoperability at each level of abstraction, and then harmonizing requirements between different units that need to inter-operate.

3 HARMONIZED DEVELOPMENT OF INFORMATION SECURITY

Within this section, the harmonized development of information security shall be described. Figure 1 illustrates a five-layer case, that this analysis is based on. First two layers provide an external coordination, that shall be studied in section 3.1. Next two layers, Organization Layer and Business Unit Layer, are where the security management

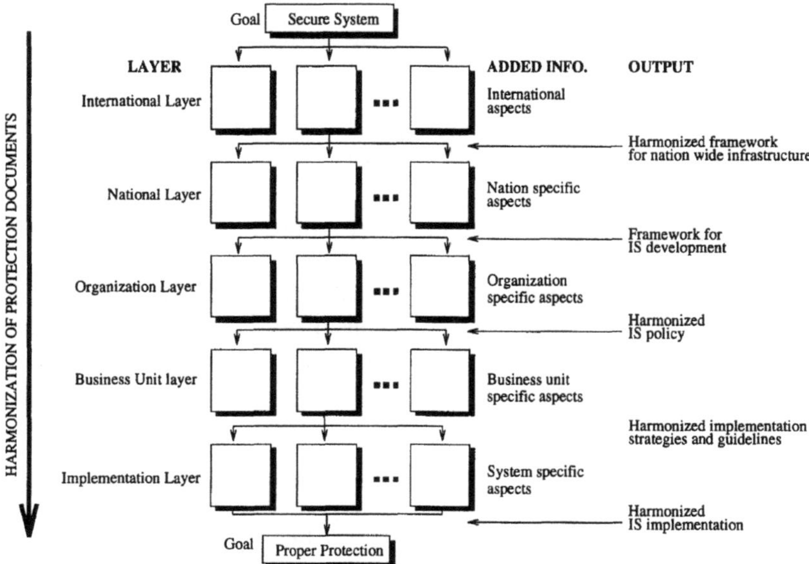

Figure 1 Harmonized development of information security

within an organization is enforced and shall be studied in section 3.2. Lowest layer, implementation of protection measures shall be studied in section 3.3. During the analysis, an example shall be given on the application of the approach into the European Union Directive concerning the protection of individuals in relation to the processing of personal data (EC-C277 1990). Requirements of the directive shall be transferred throughout the development organization to highlight different tasks at each layer.

3.1 External coordination

Most information systems get their security requirements from outside, from, for example, laws and governmental decisions. These documents also provide organizations a base for security work. When developing information security within an organization, international and national standards, strategies, laws and other decisions must be taken as a starting point. They are needed to establish a framework for the corporation information security management. International strategies, for example, set components of information security, classification and evaluation of information security, general guidelines on the goals and requirements of security work and so on. When the security of global systems, where physically distributed components are located across national borders, the importance of international coordination of law increases. International coordination is required to avoid situations, where weaknesses and inconsistencies of nationally different juridical environments can be exploited either to use logical connectivity to commit a criminal act from a country having a weak legislation or use logical connectivity and target a system in a country having inadequate legislation.

The example directive specifies contents of law that each member nation should implement according to nation specific characteristics. A generic specification is given on the contents of the required law with regard to acceptable processing and storage and required protection of personal data. Upper level requirements for nations are here the requirements set by the directive, that provides each country a harmonized base to establish their national law based on country specific special features. Each of the high level requirements set by the directive must be considered nationally within each member country. This provides international organizations with the assurance of the critical topics being addressed by each member nation.

3.2 Organizational coordination

The management level, Organization Layer and Business Unit Layer within figure 1, is where the corporation information security work is coordinated. Based on the operating environment, the top management of the organization is responsible for specifying corporation security policies and strategies. Top management is responsible of the organization information security violations but is also authorized to establish policies and procedures that concern the entire organization. Management has to face two factors (Anderson, Longley & Kwok 1994): The probability that the threat will eventuate, and the potential financial outcome of the business impact. As it is not the responsibility of the security staff to make business decisions in the risk environment, it is essential that the management contributes actively to the security work.

Information security management within organization operates between those who set responsibilities and those who fulfill these requirements. Requirements are set by corporation (or business unit) management and fulfilled by system users and developers. Two major obligations of the security management to the general management are to ensure that security requirements imposed on the system will adequately protect the organization's resources and data, and to ensure that the system is operated in a manner that satisfies its security requirements (Bailey 1995).

Corporations dealing with personal data must then set their security strategies and policies to take into account the requirements set by national laws concerning protection of personal data. As required by example directive, protection measures must be implemented against different threats against the data and guidelines must be established and enforced to control the flows of the information under the law. The protection requirements by law are the minimum requirements. It may be, that at some level, other measures required are stronger than those required by law. In this case, layer or unit specific requirements over ride the upper level requirements, and a stronger security results. In the case of stronger requirements set by a specific unit, horizontal harmonization is required to identify other units that co-operate with the unit with higher requirements. Requirements at these units must then be aligned with the unit having highest requirements to guarantee secure interoperability.

3.3 Implementation of protection measures

To guarantee consistent approach to the information security development, security mechanisms must be aligned with the corporation policies. Mechanisms must guarantee satisfaction of corporation general goals as well as satisfaction of the specific information security requirements of different systems. Implementation layer is the final step in the development of information security. It includes definition, implementation and monitoring of the information security mechanisms. Two major requirements can be set for implemented controls and protection measures. They should be selected so that they can adequately counter the threats found during risk assessment, that means they enforce the security policy, and they should be implemented in a cost-effective manner. Important factor is to not overestimate protection measures, security measure is efficient when it costs less than alternatives, including doing nothing.

Combination of several factors affecting cost of protection results as a graph where costs are high now and in the far future, but as minimized as possible during the optimal time frame (Cohen 1995). An important factor reducing security of information systems is the lack of integration of security measures from the very early stages. No single design element, that may be operating system, application, or network, alone is capable of providing adequate security. Another controversial issue in the implementation layer is how to guarantee, that all informal requirements set at higher layers of the model, shall be transformed into the actual implementation of information security measures, that is enforcement of corporate information security policy.

When different requirements are harmonized at upper levels, different domains can be identified. Once implemented, the cost-effectiveness can be improved by identification of similar functionalities and using same design and implementation documents in each case. Also, at this point similar requirements between different units can be horizontally harmonized to simplify the implementation, and hence improve cost efficiency.

4 THE MODEL

The harmonized development model for information security shall be studied in detail in this section. Static components of the model shall first be specified in section 4.1. Based on these components, harmonization functions can be specified to provide comprehensive requirements of each unit. Section 4.2 studies harmonization functions in detail. Situations, where the model needs to be refined, shall be studied in summarized 4.3.

4.1 Components of the model

The model can be presented as a 4-tuple (L, U, I, S) where L refers to layers, U to units, I to layer specific requirements and S to unit specific requirements. $L = \{L_i | i = 1, 2, \ldots N\}$ is layers L_1 to L_N, L_1 being the top layer. Each layer L_i consists of $count(i)$ units $U = \{u_{i,j} | i = 1, 2, \ldots, N; j = 1, 2, \ldots, count(i)\}$, where function *count* refers to the number of units on a given layer. $I = \{I_i | i = 1, 2, \ldots, N\}$ are the layer specific requirements of a layer L_i. Unit specific requirements are the set $S = \{s_{i,j} | i = 1, 2, \ldots, N; j = 1, 2, \ldots, count(i)\}$. All these components, L, U, I, and S are static, whereas other components of the model, requirements R, and harmonization functions τ and ρ are dynamic.

Each unit $u_{i,j} \in U$ on a given layer has its total requirements $R_{i,j} \in R$ that are based on the previous layers' output, layer-specific requirements, and unit-specific requirements. An exact specification shall be given in equation 5, in section 4.2. The output from upper layers and identification of similar requirements within each layer establishes the harmonized approach for the information security development.

Vertical harmonization within each unit $u_{i,j}$ is enforced by two related sets, $Parent \subset U$ and $Child \subset U$. They are specified so that the set $Parent(u_{i,j}) = \{u_{i-1,j'}\}$ is the set of all those units $\{u_{i-1,j'}\}$ that set requirements for the unit $u_{i,j}$. Similarly, $Child(u_{i,j}) = \{u_{i+1,j''}\}$ where the unit $u_{i,j}$ sets requirements for each unit in $\{u_{i+1,j''}\}$. For each layer L_i, layer-specific requirements, I_i, can be specified to set requirements for each unit at that layer.

To be adequately established, the model should satisfy three conditions: First, the division into layers should be complete, as specified in "Completeness of Layers" condition 1. Intuitively, this means that each unit $u_{i,j} \in U$ should belong to a layer. Second, each layer should be unique, that means no unit can belong to more than one layer. This is determined by condition 2, "Uniqueness of Layers". The model should also satisfy is the "Uniqueness of Units" (condition 3) that says, that the the forming of units should be unique.

Condition 1 (Completeness of Layers) $\forall u_{i,j} \in U | u_{i,j} \in \bigcup_{n=1}^{N} L_n$

Condition 2 (Uniqueness of Layers) $\bigcap_{n=1}^{N} L_n = \emptyset$

Condition 3 (Uniqueness of units) $\forall u_{i_1,j_1}, u_{i_2,j_2} \in U | (u_{i_1,j_1} = u_{i_2,j_2}) \Rightarrow ((i_1 = i_2) \wedge (j_1 = j_2))$

4.2 Harmonization functions

The two major functions within the model are vertical and horizontal harmonization of requirements. In the very essence, vertical harmonization means transformation of abstract upper layer requirements into more concrete lower layer requirements. Horizontal harmonization refers to the identification and harmonization of requirements that need to be similar within each unit on a given layer. The nature of vertical harmonization is interaction between units at different layers, whereas horizontal harmonization is interaction between units at same layer. Vertical harmonization, therefore, is the enforcement of the hierarchical development of information security, whereas horizontal harmonization is the enforcement of secure inter-operation of systems.

Each unit $u_{i,j} \in U$ gets requirements $R_{i,j} \in R$ as a result of requirements originating from upper layers $\{R'_{i-1,j'} | u_{i-1,j'} \in Parent(u_{i,j})\}$, from unit-specific requirements $S_{i,j} \in S$, and from layer-specific requirement $I_i \in I$ (see equation 5). Let $\tau : \{R \times S \times I\} \rightarrow R$ be a set of vertical harmonization functions, specified in equation 1. Function $\tau_{i,j}$ specifies the harmonization of requirements from unit $u_{i,j}$ to all units $u_{i+1,j'} \in Child(u_{i,j})$. Vertical harmonization within the model refers to the identification of functions τ in a top-down fashion. The top down approach is required to provide an integral and formal approach to the specification or high level abstractions of requirements that can then be formally refined.

$$\tau_{i,j}(R_{i,j}, S_{i,j}, I_i) = R'_{i+1,j'} | u_{i+1,j'} \in Child(u_{i,j}) \quad (1)$$

As each unit may have more than one parent-units, and each unit may have several child-units, some of the requirements within each layer must be similar. Horizontal harmonization within the model is required to guarantee secure interoperability between units at same layer. Typically, different systems need to communicate between each other. Horizontal harmonization is required to guarantee that none of the links in the communication flow weakens the level of security under requirements set at the upper level. The basic form of horizontal harmonization is specification of layer-specific requirements I, but in addition to that, identification of similar requirements originating from upper layers within a given layer may be required. A simple example of horizontal harmonization is specification of password protection of systems. The requirement to have password protection (if considered adequate) is a reasonable high level decision. Anyhow, it is not the duty of high level management to specify requirements on length, expiration, required structure, storage method, and other properties of passwords. For example, let us assume, that two different systems S_1 and S_2 need to inter-operate, and they have got a top level requirement of password based protection. If, for example, required length of a password in system S_1 is greater than required length at system S_2, the communication requirement may violate the security level of S_1.

To prevent such a violation, horizontal harmonization is a function to identify all requirements providing with requirements on same properties, like password length in the previous example and provision of horizontal harmonization function ρ_i at each layer L_i. As the requirement is not specified, an assumption is made, that a requirement consists of two parts: identity and the actual requirement. Let the notation $R_{i,j}^{id}$ be used to indicate the identity of a requirement $R_{i,j}$. Also, let the set $ID_i = \{id_n\}$ be a set of n different identities of requirements at a given layer L_i. Horizontal harmonization on a given layer L_i is identification of sets $\{H_i^{id} | id \in ID_i\}$, where $\forall id \in ID_i | H_i^{id} = \{R_{i,j} | R_{i,j}^{id} = id\}$. Function $\rho_i : R \rightarrow R$ on a given layer and id can be specified as in equation 2, where $R'_{i,j}$ is specified as in equation 1.

$$\rho_i(R'_{i,j}) = R_{i,j} | R'_{i,j} \in H_i^{id} \tag{2}$$

Each unit $u_{i,j} \in L_i, i > 1$ has specific security requirements $R_{i,j}$ that are combination of requirements from parents of that unit $\{R_{i-1,j'} | u_{i-1,j'} \in Parent(u_{i,j})\}$, layer-specific requirements I_i and requirements specific for the unit, $S_{i,j}$ when harmonized by a vertical and horizontal harmonization functions $\tau_{i,j}$ and ρ_i. Function $\tau_{i,j}$ generates vertically harmonized requirements $R'_{i,j}$ as illustrated in equation 3. These vertically harmonized requirements are then harmonized horizontally by ρ_i function. It should be noted, that in the case $i = 1$, requirements, $R_{i-1,j'} = \emptyset$.

$$R'_{i,j} = \bigcup_{u_{i-1,j'} \in Parent(u_{i,j})} \tau_{i-1,j'}(R_{i-1,j'}, I_{i-1}, S_{i-1,j'}) \tag{3}$$

Horizontal harmonization is harmonization of requirements $R'_{i,j}$ that are similar at all units within a given layer to guarantee secure interoperability between units. Similar requirements can be identified based on the identity of requirements. An assumption is made, that each requirement $R'_{i,j}$ can be uniquely identified by the requirement identity $R_{i,j}^{\prime id}$. Horizontal harmonization on a given layer L_i is identification of sets H_i^{id} for each $id \in ID_i$, where $H_i^{id} = \{R'_{i,j} | R_{i,j}^{\prime id} = id\}$ and specification of horizontal harmonization functions $\rho_i : R' \rightarrow R$ that harmonize vertically harmonized requirements $R'_{i,j}$ to actual requirements $R_{i,j}$ as specified in equation 4. ID_i refers to a set of different identities on a given layer L_i.

$$R_{i,j} = \rho_i(R'_{i,j}) \tag{4}$$

Comprehensive harmonization, where total requirements R are specified, is done in two phases. First, vertical harmonization of upper layer requirements is carried out, and the

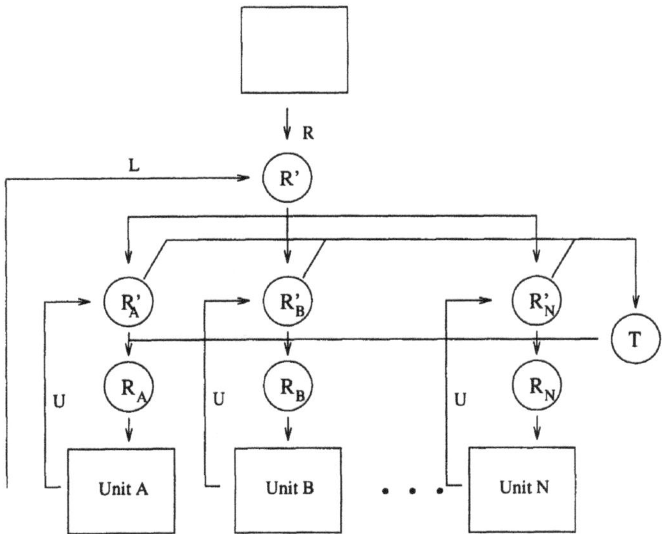

Figure 2 Harmonization of requirements

output is then horizontally harmonized layer wise. The specification is given in equation 5. This is also illustrated in figure 2.

$$R_{i,j} = \rho_i(\tau_{i-1,j'}(R_{i-1,j'}, I_{i-1}, S_{i-1,j'}) | R_{i-1,j'} \in Parent(u_{i,j})) \quad (5)$$

4.3 Refinement of the model

Application of the model includes two tasks: modeling the organization, and specification and enforcement of harmonization functions. The organization is expected to be static whereas harmonization functions change more often. The following cases, are where the model should be refined in order to maintain its validity:

1. Organizational change, for example appearance or disappearance of some units in organizational restructuring.
2. A change has occurred in some layer specific requirements, requiring refinement of harmonization functions from that layer downwards.
3. A change has occurred in unit specific requirements, requiring refinement of harmonization functions from that unit downwards.
4. Within the periodical refinement of information security within the organization.

The cost of change can easily be calculated according to the amount of changes needed to maintain the model. Obviously, organizational changes cost most since most factors of the model need to be refined. Major refinements, like within periodical refinement of information security within organizations, the cost may be reasonable small but the frequency may increase the total cost. Again, automation can be used to reduce the cost of chances in static parts of the model.

5 CONCLUSIONS AND FUTURE WORK

A formal model has been presented to aid in documentation and harmonization of information security requirements. The model assumes a hierarchical, layered, information security development organization and specifies vertical and horizontal harmonization functions in order the establish cost effective protection. Information security requirements originate from many different sources, and may be fragmented. Vertical harmonization provides each layer a common view of requirements established at upper layers, so protection measures can be as identical as possible. Horizontal harmonization identifies similar requirements at each layer to provide a common approach towards them to simplify the implementation and maintenance, and to guarantee secure interoperability of different units within that layer.

The model itself acts as a starting point for further work. Once the formal model is established, different automation of specification and verification of requirements is enabled. There is a need to specify tools and methods to support harmonization, and to test the strength of the model in real life environments. Even though not done here, the model also enables formal analysis of different properties of the information security management itself, like the security of security management. If the organization can be modeled, then established access control and information flow models can be applied to give a formal specification for security properties of the organization.

Another essential topic of research is analysis of requirements. At this stage, no exact specification is given to the contents of requirements, rather the focus has been on the harmonization tasks. To get the most out of the formalism, an exact specification should be given to an information security requirement and refinement and dependencies should be analyzed according to the specification.

REFERENCES

Abrams, M. D. & Bailey, D. (1995), Abstraction and refinement of layered security policy, *in* M. D. Abrams, S. Jajodia & H. J. Podell, eds, 'Information Security - An Integrated Collection of Essays', IEEE Computer Society Press, Los Alamitos, CA, USA.

Anderson, A., Longley, D. & Kwok, L. F. (1994), Security modelling for organisations, *in* '2nd ACM Conference on Computer and Communications Security', Fairfax, Virginia, USA.

Backhouse, J. & Dhillon, G. (1996), 'Structures of responsibility and security of information systems', *European Journal of Information Systems* **5**, 2–9.

Bailey, D. (1995), A philosophy of security management, *in* M. D. Abrams, S. Jajodia & H. J. Podell, eds, 'Information Security - An Integrated Collection of Essays', IEEE Computer Society Press, Los Alamitos, CA, USA.

Baskerville, R. (1993), 'Information systems security design methods: Implications for information systems development', *ACM Computing Surveys* **25**(4), 375–414.

Bell, D. E. (1988), Concerning "modeling" of computer security, *in* 'IEEE Symposium on Security and Privacy'.

Castano, S., Fugini, M., Martella, G. & Samarati, P. (1995), *Database Security*, ACM Press.

Cohen, F. B. (1995), *Protection and Security on the Information Superhighway*, John Wiley & Sons, inc.

EC-C277 (1990), 'Proposal for a council directive concerning the protection of individuals in relation to the processing of personal data', Official Journal of the European Communities No C277.

Gong, L. & Qian, X. (1994), The complexity and composability of secure interoperation, *in* '1994 IEEE Symposium on Research on Security and Privacy'.

Iivari, J. (1983), Contributions to the theoretical foundations of systemeering research and the PIOCO model, Acta Universitatis Ouluensis A150, University of Oulu, Oulu,Finland.

ISO7498-2 (1988), 'International standard ISO 7498-2. information processing systems - Open systems interconnection - Basic reference model - Part 2: Security architecture'.

ITSEC (1992), 'Information technology security evaluation criteria (ITSEC). Provisional harmonized criteria, version 1.2', Commission of the European Communities COM(92) 298 final, Brussels, Belgium.

Leiwo, J. (1995*a*), Deterrence of computer network crime: The international coordinative level approach towards legislation, Working Papers Series B 35, University of Oulu, Department of Information Processing Science, Oulu, Finland.

Leiwo, J. (1995*b*), Deterring computer network criminals with legislative methods: The need for international harmonization, *in* 'GRONICS'95 International Information Technology Conference for Students', University of Groningen, Groningen, the Netherlands.

Olson, I. M. & Abrams, M. D. (1995), Information security policy, *in* M. D. Abrams, S. Jajodia & H. J. Podell, eds, 'Information Security - An Integrated Collection of Essays', IEEE Computer Society Press, Los Alamitos, CA, USA.

Sterne, D. F. (1991), On the buzzword Security Policy, *in* 'IEEE Symposium on Security and Privacy'.

Williams, J. G. & Abrams, M. D. (1995), Formal methods and models, *in* M. D. Abrams,

S. Jajodia & H. J. Podell, eds, 'Information Security - An Integrated Collection of Essays', IEEE Computer Society Press, Los Alamitos, CA, USA.

BIOGRAPHIES

Jussipekka Leiwo received his M.Sc. in computer science from the University of Oulu, Finland, in 1995. From March 1995 to April 1996 he was employed by Nokia Telecommunications in Helsinki, Finland. Since April 1996, he has been enrolled in Ph.D. studies at Monash University, Peninsula School of Computing and Information Technology, focusing on information security management.

Yuliang Zheng received his B.Sc. degree in computer science from Southeast University (formerly Nanjing Institute of Technology), Nanjing, China, in 1982, and the M.E. and Ph.D. degrees, both in electrical and computer engineering, from Yokohama National University, Yokohama, Japan, in 1988 and 1991 respectively. From 1982 to 1984 he was with the Guangzhou Research Institute for Communications, Guangzhou (Canton), China, and from February 1991 to January 1992 he was a Post-Doctoral Fellow at the Computer Science Department, University College, University of New South Wales, in Canberra, Australia. From February 1992 to January 1995 he was a Lecturer of the Computer Science Department, University of Wollongong. Since February 1995 he has been a Senior Lecturer at the Peninsula School of Computing and Information Technology, Monash University, in Melbourne. His current research interests include information security, cryptography, computational complexity theory and information theory. Dr. Zheng is a member of IACR, ACM and IEEE. He has a homepage at http://pscit-www.fcit.monash.edu.au:/~yuliang/.

PART TWO

Secure Data Bases

A Compile-time Model for safe Information Flow in Object-Oriented Databases

Masha Gendler-Fishman and Ehud Gudes
Department of Mathematics and Computer Science
Ben-Gurion University
Beer-Sheva, Israel
e-mail: masha,ehud@bengus.bgu.ac.il

Abstract

Security is an important topic for Object-oriented databases (OODB). Discretionary authorization models do not provide the high assurance provided by Mandatory models, the latter ones, however, are too rigid for commercial applications. Therefore discretionary, information-flow control models are needed, especially when transactions containing general methods invocations are considered.

This paper first reviews existing security models for object-oriented databases with and without information-flow control. Previous models relied on the run-time checks of every message transferred in the system. This paper uses a simple transaction model and a **compile-time** approach and presents algorithms for flow control which are applied at Rule-administration and Compile times, thus saving considerable run-time overhead. A proof for correctness is given, and the performance implications are discussed.

keywords

Object-oriented Databases, Authorization, Information flow, Transactions, Compile-time checking.

1 Introduction.

Security is an important topic for Databases in general and for Object-oriented databases (OODB) in particular [Kim(90), Kemper(94)]. Commercial multi-user Database Management Systems (DBMSs) thus provide authorization mechanisms supporting the definition and enforcement of authorization rules. In general, authorization mechanisms provided by commercial DBMS are *discretionary*, that is, the grant of authorizations on an object to other subjects is at the discretion of the object administrator.

The main drawback of *discretionary* access control is that it does not provide a real assurance on the satisfaction of the protection requirements, since discretionary policies do not impose any restriction on the usage of information by a subject who has obtained it legally. For example, a subject who is able to read data can pass it to other subjects not authorized to read it. This weakness makes discretionary policies vulnerable to attacks from "Trojan horses" embedded in programs. Access control in *mandatory* protection systems is based on the "no read-up" and "no write-down" principles [Castano(95)]. Satisfaction of these principles prevents information stored in high-level objects to flow to lower level objects. The main drawback of mandatory policies is their rigidity which makes them unsuitable for many commercial environments.

There is the need of access control mechanism able to provide the flexibility of discretionary access control, and at the same time, the high assurance of mandatory access control. A first attempt to do it in the context of OODBs was made by [Samarati(96)]. The main problem with the model in [Samarati(96)] is that all the checks are done at *Run-time* which increases considerably the overhead in the system. Many DBMSs rely on protection which is checked at compile time! For example, Query modification in Ingres [Stonebraker(76)] or View-based mechanisms in System R [Griffith(76)] in Relational systems, or the model suggested by [Fernandez(94)] for OODBs. In this paper we investigate the problem of ensuring safe information flow for OODBs by performing the checks at *Compile time* or at *Rule-definition time*, thus saving considerable overhead at run-time. A very important assumption of the paper presented here is that the run-time of the Query-language and the DBMS can be trusted. That it, if one composes its transactions only from well-defined Queries and Update, (the exact model for transactions is discussed later), one can rely on the Query translator and on the Access validation associated with it. Clearly, this cannot include an OODBS with the most general *methods*, since some of these methods may not be trusted. (see [Gudes(97)]). In the rest of the paper we assume therefore that transactions contain queries with basic Read/Write (or other trusted methods) operations.

As this paper relies heavily on the two previous papers [Samarati(96)] and [Fernandez(94)], these papers are first reviewed briefly in Section 2 and the definition of safe information flow is given. In Section 3 we present our compile-time model and some examples. The main algorithms and their performance analysis are presented in Section 4. Section 5 is the Summary.

2 Background.

2.1 Fernandez et. al

This model uses the following well known concepts:

Object: A real-word entity with unique identifier.

Attributes & Methods: The components of an object which define its behavior.

Class: Hierarchically structured sets of objects with the same methods and attributes. We can say that an object is an instance of a class or *object instance*.

Generalization: The classes are partially ordered, the relation "*subclass-superclass*" exists (we denote $t_1 \preceq t_2$ if t_1 is subclass of t_2). Both attributes and methods are inherited by subclasses from superclass.

Encapsulation: The only way to access data values of an object is through the methods in its interface. It is assumed that for every attribute there are built-in read/write methods.

This model assumes a simple discretionary Rules-based authorization. The model deals mainly with the impact of inheritance on security and enforces the following basic policies:

P_1 (*inheritance*) – a user that has access to a class is allowed to have similar type of access to the corresponding subclasses attributes inherited from that class.

P_2 (*class access*) – access to a complete class implies access to the attributes defined in that class as well as to attributes inherited from a higher class (but only to the class-relevant values of these attributes).

P_3 (*visibility*) – an attribute defined for a subclass is not accessible by accessing any of its superclasses.

In following papers, policies were proposed for negative authorization, content-dependent restrictions, and for resolving conflicts between several implied authorizations (see [Larrondo(90)]). Another paper extended the basic model to include treatment of general methods [GalOz(93)]

To enforce the above policies an *Access Validation* algorithm was presented. The validation algorithm is applied at *Compile-time* in that it works after the Query translator and its output is entered to the Optimizer and run-time system (see Figure 1.). The Access-validation algorithm accepts two major inputs:

- The original query after translation in form of a tree. This query is further extended using the inheritance hierarchy to something called *Authorization Tree (AT_yes)*. (the AT_yes will be redefined in the next section, therefore we do not detail its structure here). Initially, all the AT_yes's nodes are set to authorized. After the validation algorithm, the AT_yes contains only the nodes and the attributes to which access is allowed.

- The rules which are relevant to this query are extracted from a tree called the *Security Graph* which is an extension of the AT_yes upwards and downwards to include all relevant rules.

The algorithm scans in parallel the query nodes and security graph nodes, applies the three policies mentioned above and produces the final AT_yes which defines the allowed access. Briefly, for each node and attribute in the AT_yes, the algorithm searches for rules authorizing them. If such an explicit rule is not found, an implicit rule authorizing a node at a higher level is searched for. If such a rule is not found, then a rule authorizing partial access for a node in a descendant of the AT-node is looked for. If no rule is found, then no authorization is given. [1]

[1] the algorithm above assumes the class-hierarchy is a tree, but it can be generalized easily to acyclic graphs and multiple inheritance. It is not a central point in this paper and therefore will not be discussed further.

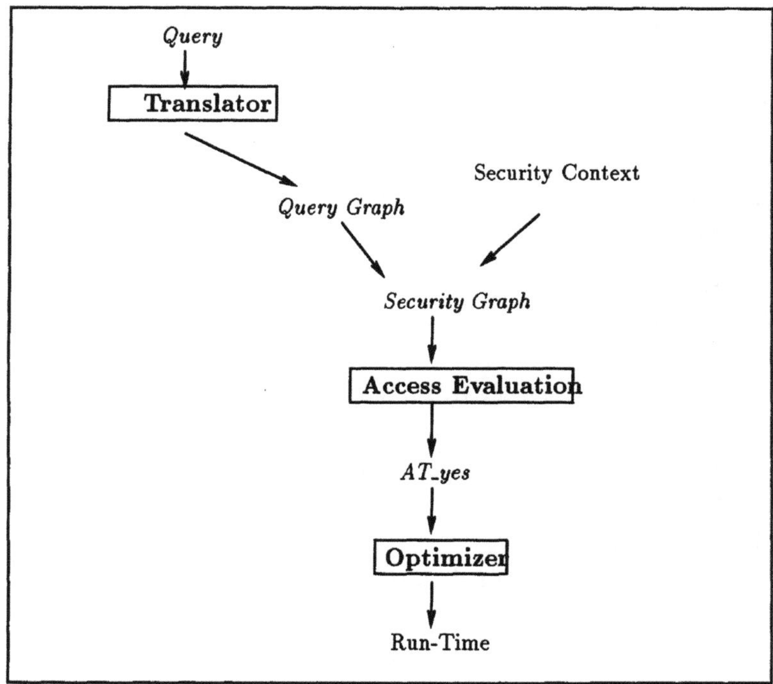

Figure 1: Architecture of access evaluation

2.2 Samarati et. al

The model includes the following main entities:

- **Objects** Objects are identified by a unique identifier, an ordered set of attributes, and an ordered set of methods.
- **Messages** A message is an ordered pair *(name,pars)* Where *name* is the name of the message, and *pars* is its parameters. There may be *Read*, *Write* or *Create* messages.
- **Transaction** A transaction is a sequence of methods invocations caused by a user sending a message. The first message invokes a method which invokes other methods by sending messages to it and waiting for replies. The invoking method may in turn wait for the reply (synchronized) or can defer its waiting (deferred). A user executing a transaction is called the *Transaction initiator* .
- **Access lists** There are several access lists associated with each object including
  RACL(o) - the list of users which can read from object o,
  WACL(o) - the list of users which can write into object o.

- **Forward and Backward Transmission** Since one method may invoke another method, information may be transferred forward (from the invoker to the invokee) or backwards (from the invokee to the invoker). Computing this information is important for the purposes of computing Information Flow.
- **Information flow** There exists a flow between O_i and O_j in a transaction if and only if a write or create method is executed on O_j, and that method had received information (via forward or backward transmission) on O_i. When a method A sends a message to another method B, then all the information which flowed into A is assumed to flow into B. Similarly, if a method A receives a reply from B, the information that flows into B is assumed to flow into A.
- **Safe Information flow** Information flow is safe only if there is information flow from O_i to O_j and all users which can read O_j can also read O_i, i.e. RACL(O_j) is contained in RACL(O_i).

To enforce only safe information flows, [Samarati(96)] suggests the construction of a *Message Filter* component which intercepts each and *every message* in the system. For each such intercepted message, the Message filter keeps track of:

1. The information that the execution has received from its invoker, through the message parameters.
2. The information that the execution has received from the execution it has invoked through the message replies
3. The RACL of the relevant objects

Using all this information it is possible to enforce safe information flow and **disallow** transferring of information which may cause an unsafe flow (i.e an empty reply is returned in that case...)

Although the above algorithm is very general and works for various types of methods and executions, it requires the check and filtering of every message in the system. This is a considerable overhead! In the next section, we present a simpler model with a compile-time algorithm.

3 The Object and Transactions Model

Our model include the following concepts:
Object Model The object model is similar to the one in [Fernandez(94)]
Authorization Model - The authorization model is also similar to the one in [Fernandez(94)]. Authorization rules are in the form of triple $(U, A, O.attr.)$ where U - a user or a user group, A - is a basic access type like READ/WRITE, *O.attr* - stands for an attribute of a class O.
Authorization rules reference Classes, although the model carries over when we

deal with Objects, i.e class instances. In the sequel we will use O to denote classes, and will not make the distinction to objects unless necessary. We also adopt the *inheritance* policies described in Section 2 above.

Transactions A transaction in our model is simpler than in [Samarati(96)]. It consists of two types of methods calls only, i.e Read and Write (we call both of them queries below) and both are called from the transaction level:

Read query. $val = read(O.Attr)$ where O is database object/class , $Attr$ is an attribute and val is the variable that stores the result.

Write query. $write(O.Attr, val)$ where O and $Attr$ are as before and val is the value (or variable) to be written to the object attribute.

For every write query all read queries executed before are considered.

Access Lists.

In [Fernandez(94)] the main administration structure was the *authorization rule.* For purposes of flow control we need to define also for each attribute of each class a list of all users authorized to read it. We maintain the structure called *read access list*(RACL) containing the list of users who are allowed Read access to the attribute. The RACL of-course can be obtained using the inheritance policies mentioned above:

$$\text{RACL}(O.Attr) = \{u : (\exists\, O' | O \preceq O' \text{ and } \exists \text{ rule } (u, R, O'.Attr))$$
$$\wedge\ (\nexists\, O'' | O \preceq O'' \preceq O' \text{ and } \exists \text{ rule } (u, -R, O''.Attr))\}$$

i.e. this list contains users that are authorized to read the attribute either explicitly or via the inheritance policies specified above. [2]

Information Flow Using the concepts of Transactions and Access list we can define information flow. The main idea here is to collect information about read queries: what attributes were read and who may read these attributes. With the aid of this information we can decide whether a write method causes a non-safe information flow. The information flow from object o_i to object o_j is safe if the set of users who can read object o_j is contained in the list of users who can read o_i, i.e.

$$\text{RACL}(o_j) \subseteq \text{RACL}(o_i)$$

As an example, let us consider the transaction T:

$v_1 = read(O_1.Attr_1)$
$v_2 = read(O_2.Attr_2)$
...
$v_n = read(O_n.Attr_n)$
$write(O_j.Attr_j, v_j)$

[2] there may be some rules for some users which negate access to descendants of the current attribute, thus this RACL actually represents the list of users who have either complete or partial access to this attribute.

For this transaction, the flow of information is safe if and only if the union of all lists belongs to RACL($O_j.Attr_j$).

$$\cup RACL(O_i.Attr_i) \subseteq RACL(O_j.Attr_j)$$

However, this is only a strong sufficient condition. A particular user when issueing $Query_i$ gets only part of the query authorized by the AT_yes structure. We can therefore find a better bound for this transaction using Compile-time analysis! In order to apply our compile-time algorithms we need to define several types of Authorization trees:

Authorization Tree Each query of the type above is validated against the initiator (U) authorization rules using the model and algorithm presented in [Fernandez(94)]. The result of such validation is the set of objects (classes) and their attributes which is authorized for this query. Basically, this set is a sub-tree of the query graph rooted at $O.Attr$ and is called *authorization tree*, denoted AT_yes($u, A, O.Attr$). In the sequel we will only use the authorization-trees for Read access, and therefore denote them as: AT_yes($u, O.Attr$). Also, in the following, we will use AT_yes(i) to denote the authorization tree of the read query number i in the transaction above. Now we define for any user the structure which is his visible part of database .

User Access Tree (UAT) The set of attributes in the entire database [3] that user u is allowed to access for reading is called *user access tree.*

$$\text{UAT}(u) = \{(O.Attr) : u \in \text{RACL}(O.Attr)\}$$

The above UAT is computed from the additional data structure $RACL$, but, obviously, it is also true that

$$\text{UAT} = \cup_{i,j} AT\_yes(O_i.Attr_j)$$

Common User Access Tree(CUAT). We introduce a new measure for each attribute A_j: the intersection of UATs of all users who are permitted to read it. This intersection expresses the set of all attributes which is allowed to be read by all users who are allowed to read attribute A_j.

$$\text{CUAT}(O.Attr) = \bigcap_{\forall u \in \text{RACL}(O.Attr)} \text{UAT}(u)$$

Safe Information Flow.

Using the definitions above we are now ready to express the criteria for safe information flow. Intuitively, we know that every read query after validation can only read the objects and attributes contained in the query authorization tree. Therefore, the union of these trees expresses all the information to which this transaction has read access. We must make sure that the users who have access to the object into which this transaction writes, are allowed to access that union of information.

[3] the term "entire database" is used here for purposes of definition and correctness, it is not used in this way in the algorithm

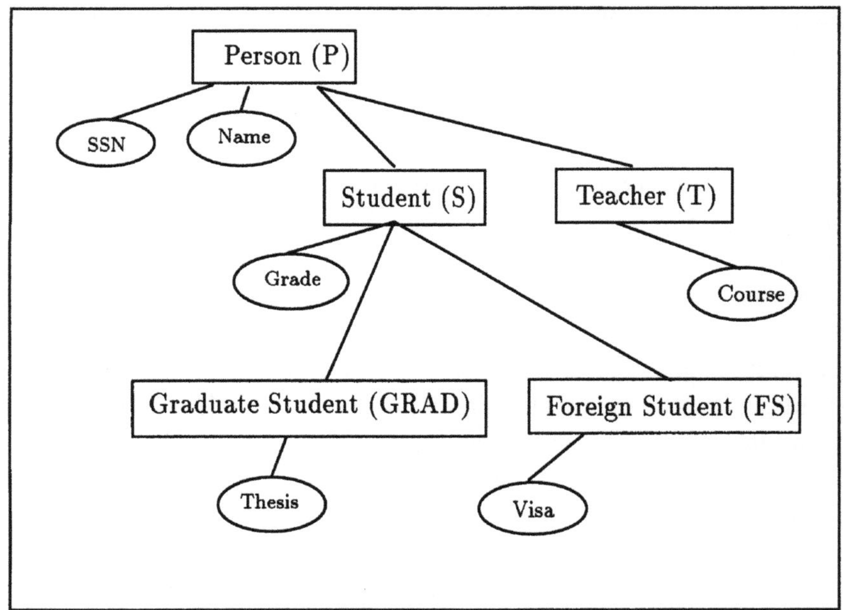

Figure 2: University database

Theorem 1 (Safe Information Flow) The information flow to the attribute $O_k.Attr_j$ caused by the write access $write(O_k.Attr_j, v)$ in transaction is safe if and only if the common users access tree of the attribute $O_k.Attr_j$ contains the union of the authorization trees of all previous read queries.

$$\bigcup_{i=1}^{j-1} \text{AT\_yes}(i) \subseteq \text{CUAT}(O_k.Attr_j) \iff \text{the information flow to } O_k.Attr_j \text{ is safe.}$$

Proof. $\Rightarrow$ If CUAT contains the union of AT_yes then there is no user u and attribute a such that u was not authorized to read a and could read the value of a from $O_k.Attr_j$ after write access.
$\Leftarrow$ If the information flow to $O_i.Attr_j$ is safe then there is no way of transmitting secret information to $O_k.Attr_j$. So all data that may be transferred to $O_k.Attr_j$ is accessible for all users of $O_k.Attr_j$. So $\bigcup_{i=1}^{j-1}$ AT_yes$(i) \subseteq$ CUAT$(O_k.Attr_j)$ exists.
[4]□

3.1 Example.

Consider the university database shown in Figure 2. Assume the following authorization rules are defined:

(u_1,R,S.SSN) (u_1,R,T.SSN)
(u_2,R,P.SSN) (u_2,-R,T.SSN)
(u_3,R,P.SSN) (u_3,-R,GRAD.SSN) (u_3,W,FS,SSN)

[4]as stated in the introduction the query optimizer and run-time system is trusted and only those accesses allowed at compile time are actually executed

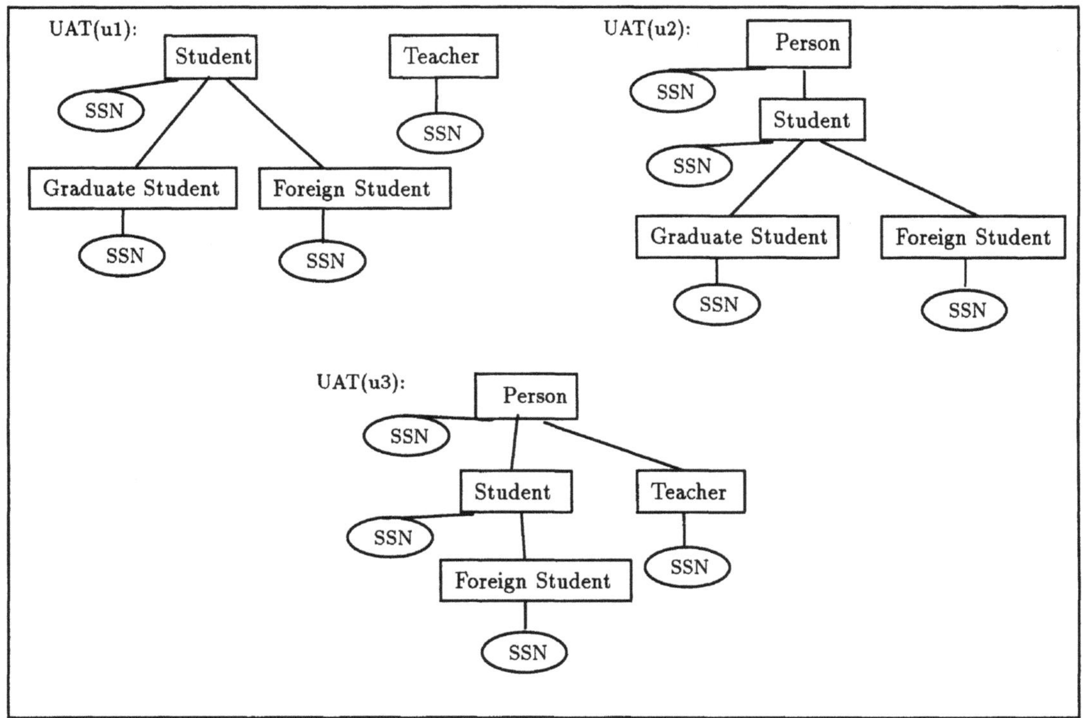

Figure 3: UAT example

The user access trees for users u_1,u_2,u_3 are shown in Figure 3. Now consider the following transaction T_1:

$$v_1 = read(S.SSN)$$
$$v_2 = read(T.SSN)$$
$$\ldots$$
$$write(FS.SSN)$$

Assume that T_1 is executed with u_3 privileges (i.e u_3 is the initiator.) The Authorization trees for the two read queries are shown in Figure 4. Now consider the RACL of the attribute of the last write query:

$$\text{RACL(FS.SSN)} = \{U_1, U_2, U_3\}$$

The CUAT for this attribute (which is the intersection of the 3 UATs in Figure 3) is shown in Figure 5. Now let us look at the situation that can happen after the transaction execution. Intuitively, the attribute FS.SSN is accessible to more users than T.SSN. Therefore the SSN value of a teacher may be read during the transaction and written to the SSN attribute of foreign student. The user u_2 has now access to the value previously unaccessible to him. So unsafe information flow may occur during the transaction execution. As can be seen from the figures, the union of the authorization trees is not contained within the relevant CUAT, as the theorem requires.

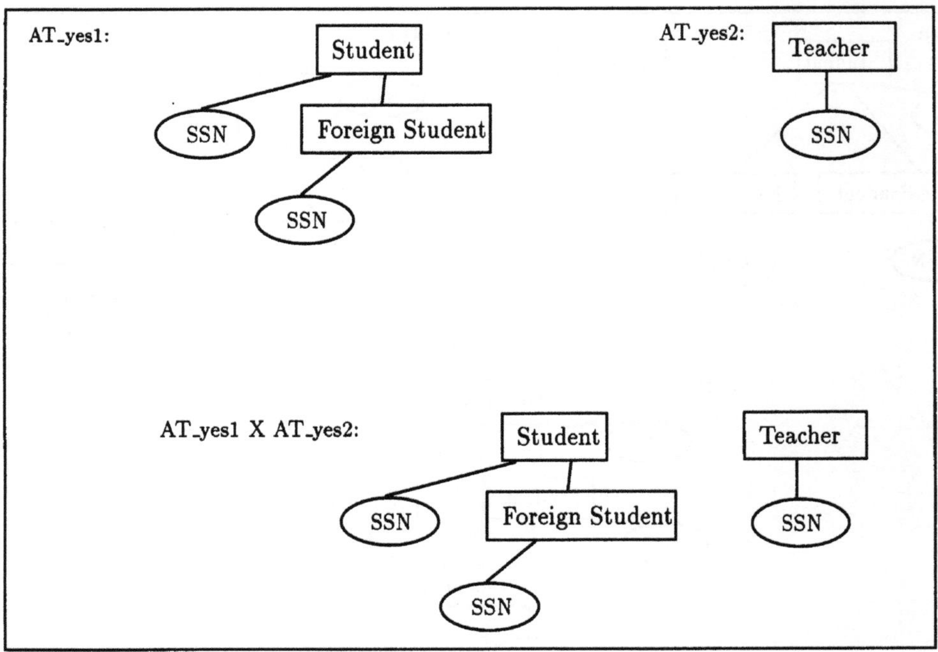

Figure 4: Example Authorization Trees

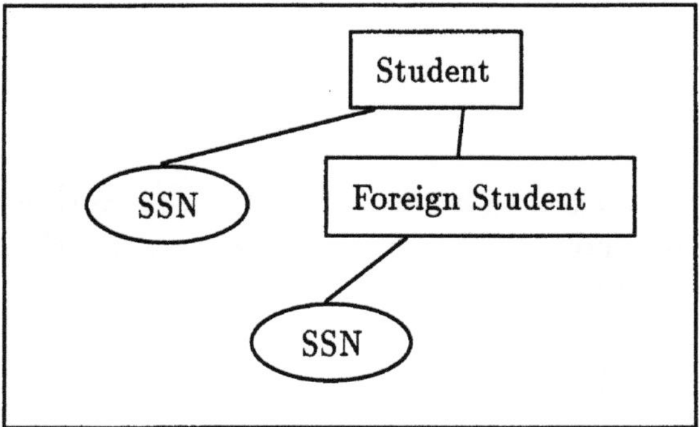

Figure 5: CUAT example

4 The Algorithms.

4.1 The CUAT management algorithms.

There are two possibilities to construct and manage the CUAT structures: to calculate CUAT at compile-time or to store and maintain all the CUAT global structures in the system. We first consider the second method because it allows to update the necessary structures without complex calculation. Once the CUATs are created, we must update them only at the moment of adding/removing of authorization rules. Note, that the system must maintain the CUAT structures of only those attributes which may be accessed for writing. A similar approach, i.e that of storing data structures at Rule Administration time, is suggested in [Bertino(96)].

First, consider an adding rule situation. Assume we add a new rule : $(w, R, O.Attr_1)$. What is $CUAT(O.Attr_1)$ now? Recall that it is equal to the intersection of all UAT's of all users who are granted read access to $(O.Attr_1)$.
Formally,

$$\mathrm{CUAT(O.Attr_1)} = \bigcap_{\mathrm{u \in RACL(O.Attr_1)}} \mathrm{UAT(u)} = \bigcap_{\mathrm{u \in RACL'(O.Attr_1)}} \mathrm{UAT(u)} \cap \mathrm{UAT(w)} =$$

$$= \mathrm{CUAT'(O.Attr_1)} \cap \mathrm{UAT(w)}$$

where RACL' and CUAT' are the corresponding structures before adding of the authorization rule. Therefore, it is quite easy to compute the new CUAT in this situation. The new CUAT depends on the new RACL list , which is the old list plus the user w. So we just need to intersect the old UAT's of all users from the old RACL with UAT(w).
The rule adding algorithm also tries to update the CUAT structures of attributes from existing UAT tree. There is the chance for expanding of CUAT by adding attribute $O.Attr$ if all users of some attribute except w had access to $O.Attr$.

```
AddRule(w, R, O.Attr)
   /* first, check chance for expanding of existing CUAT structures */
  for each Oi.Attrj ∈ UAT(w)
   common := O.Attr
   for each v ∈ RACL(Oi.Attrj), v ≠ w
    common := common ∩ UAT(v)
   CUAT(Oi.Attrj) := CUAT(Oi.Attrj) ∪ common
    /* calculate CUAT */
  UAT(w) := UAT(w) ∪ O.Attr
  for each node o.Attr ∈ O.Attr
   if (RACL(o.Attr) = ∅)
    CUAT(o.Attr) := UAT(w)
   else
    CUAT(o.Attr) := Intersect(UAT(w),CUAT(o.Attr))
```

RACL($o.Attr$) := RACL($o.Attr$) ∪ w

The removal of an authorization rule is more complex. The only case when the CUAT structure must be changed after deleting an authorization rule is that all users except w may read some attribute $Attr_{all}$. After deleting user w from RACL($Attr_1$) the attribute $Attr_{all}$ will belong to CUAT($Attr_1$) (while before it didn't). But the implementation of this property requires to keep the information about all *candidates* to a new CUAT and the storage of this information is too large. We therefore prefer the simpler implementation, that of re-building the CUAT from scratch - i.e. calculating the intersection of UAT of all other users. (a reasonable assumption is that deletion of authorization rules occur much less often than adding new ones...). The algorithm is as follows:

```
RemoveRule(w, R, O.Attr)
 UAT(W) := UAT(W) - O.Attr
 for each O_i.Attr_j ∈ UAT(w)
  CUAT(O_i.Attr_j) := CUAT(O_i.Attr_j) - O.Attr
 for each node o.Attr ∈ O.Attr
  RACL(o.Attr) := RACL(o.Attr) - w
  if (RACL(o.Attr) = ∅)
   CUAT(o.Attr) := ∅
  else
   begin
    CUAT(o.Attr) := Ω      /* universal set - all OODB */
    for each v ∈ RACL(o.Attr)
     CUAT(o.Attr) := Intersect(UAT(v),CUAT(o.Attr))
   end
```

Both the above two algorithms require the intersection of two authorization trees, such intersection algorithm is presented in [Gendler(97)] **Comment**. A problem may arise, when a rule authorizing a Read access to a user U on an object O is added after a transaction is completed. The transaction may have updated the object and caused information flow into it. This flow was valid before the rule was added. However, with the addition of the rule, that past flow may not be valid anymore! There is no easy solution to this problem (it will also occur in [Samarati(96)]...). The best way is to verify before adding rule that allows access to object O, that object O does not contain any unsafe information as far as user U is concerned.

4.2 Compile-Time Algorithm

Now, after the CUAT trees are constructed, we are ready to check for information flow. The information flow control is processed after the compilation of each transaction. First, each query is validated using the transaction initiator privileges, [5] and constructing the AT_yes trees. Then the FlowControl algorithm is applied to verify that the privileges of the transaction initiator are sufficient for all read/write queries within the transaction.

```
FlowControl(transaction, initiator)
 AT_all := ∅
 for ∀ method meth invoked by the transaction
  if meth is read primitive: read_i(O.Attr_i)
   AT_i is query graph of meth with regards to initiator
   AT_all := AT_all ∪ AT_i
  if meth is write primitive: write(O.Attr_j, val)
   if not Contain(AT_all,CUAT(O.Attr_j))
    return FALSE
 return TRUE
```

Both the *Union* and *Contain* algorithms of authorization-trees are quite simple and can be found in [Gendler(97)].

Comment The algorithms above assumed that the UAT is constructed for the entire database and is stored that way. Such a structure is associated with every user in the system and may take considerable space, and also the intersection of two such UATs may be quite long. In practice though users work within a particular *view* or *context* [Fernandez(94)]. Therefore, the UATs are usually constructed from distinct trees, and within a specific view or context, only the portions of the tree relevant to that context need to be managed (or intersected). This will require much less overhead.

4.3 Analysis

Considering the worst-case scenario of a CUAT containing all nodes in the database, the complexity of our compile-time algorithm is in the worst case $\mathbf{O}(r * n + w * n^2)$ where r is the number of the read queries in the transaction, w is the number of write queries and n is the number of attributes of all nodes in AT_yes tree (in the worst case the number of attributes in the entire database schema).

The complexity of the CUAT managing algorithm is: adding a rule is performed in time $\mathbf{O}(n^2)$ - complexity of intersection algorithm , while rule deleting is performed in $\mathbf{O}(u * n^2)$, where u is a size of RACL list, in the worst case , the number of users.

On the other hand, the message filter algorithm described in [Samarati(96)] analyses forward information (i.e. the objects that were read) after each write access, so its performance is strongly dependent on the huge number of database

[5]It is assumed that a transaction is associated with an initiator. If another user executes the same transaction, at some other time, the transaction needs to be recompiled and validated with the new user's privileges.

objects (not object *types*) accessed. Therefore the performance of run-time message filter algorithm is in the worst case $\mathbf{O}(R * u^2 + w * R * u^2)$,
where R and w are the *number of database objects* accessed for reading/writing, and u - as before is the size of the RACL list - i.e. number of users. Usually, $R >> n^2$ which shows the clear advantage of the compile-time approach. The advantages of our approach are even larger considering the average case (and the comment on contexts above).

5 Summary

The problem of Information-flow in object-oriented databases was discussed. It was argued that the approach suggested by Samarati et. al. [Samarati(96)] which requires the checking and storing information for every message in the system carries too much overhead at run-time. Instead, another model was suggested, where some data structures are constructed and maintained at Rule-administration time, and the rest of the checks are done at compile-time only, no Run-time checks are needed. This saves considerable overhead, and also potential information flow problem are discovered earlier.

The problem with the model presented here is that the methods called within each transaction are *trusted*!. This does not constitute a problem for the common Read/Write methods, but may be a problem with more complex methods. Furthermore, if a transaction contains control structures such as: Loop or If/Then/Else then our approach is too conservative and can be improved. Both problems can be addressed by looking at techniques for Dataflow analysis [Denning(86)] or program verification (see, e.g. the approach advocated by Java [Java(96)]). These are issues of our current research [Gudes(97)].

References

[Bertino(96)] Bertino, E., Bettini, C., Ferrari, E., Samarati, P., "A Temporal Access Control Mechanism for Database systems," IEEE Trans. on Knowledge and Data Engineering, Vol 8, No. 1, pp. 67-80.

[Castano(95)] Castano, S., M. Fugini, G. Martella, P. Samarati, *Database Security*, Addison-Wesley, 1995.

[Denning(86)] D.E.Denning *Cryptography and Data Security*, Addison-Wesley, 1983.

[Fernandez(94)] E.B.Fernandez, E.Gudes, H.Song "A Model for Evaluation and Administration of Security in Object-Oriented Databases.",*IEEE Trans. on Knowledge and Data Engineering*, Vol.6. No.2., April 1994, pp. 275-292.

[GalOz(93)] N.Gal-Oz, E.Gudes and E.B.Fernandez "A Model of Methods Access Authorization in Object-Oriented Databases.",*Proc. of the 19th VLDB Conference*, Dublin,Ireland,1993.

[Gendler(97)] Gendler, M. "A Model for secur Information-flow in Object-oriented databases," MSc Thesis, Ben-Gurion University, 1997.

[Griffith(76)] Griffith, P., Wade B., "An Authorization Mechanism for a Relational Database System," ACM Trans. on Database Systems, Vol 1, No. 3, September, 1976.

[Gudes(97)] Gudes E., Gendler, M. "Compile-time Flow analysis of Transactions and Methods in Object-Oriented Databases," submitted.

[Kemper(94)] Kemper A., G. Moerkotte, *Object-oriented Database Management*, Prentice-Hall, 1994.

[Kim(90)] Kim W., *Introduction to Object-Oriented Databases*, The MIT Press, 1990.

[Larrondo(90)] Larrondo-Petrie M., Gudes E., Song, H., Fernandez E B., "Security Policicies in object-oriented databases," *Database Security IV: Status and Prospectus*, D. L. Spooner C. E. Landwehr (Ed.), Elsevier Science Publishers, 1990, pp. 257-268

[Samarati(96)] Samarati P., E.Bertino, A.Ciampichetti and S.Jajodia "Information Flow Control in Object-Oriented Systems," to appear in IEEE Trans. on Knowledge and Data Engineering, 1996.

[Stonebraker(76)] Stonebraker, M., Wong, E., Kreps, P., Held, G., "The Design and Implementation of Ingres", ACM Trans. on Database Systems, Vol 1, No. 3, September, 1976.

[Java(96)] F.Yellin "Low Level Security in Java", Unpublished Report, Sun corp, 1996.

5

Deriving Authorizations from Process Analysis in Legacy Information Systems

Silvana Castano [1] *Maria Grazia Fugini* [2]

[1] *Universitá di Milano*
Dipartimento di Scienze dell'Informazione
Via Comelico 39/41, 20135 Milano, Italy
Email: castano@dsi.unimi.it

[2] *Politecnico di Milano*
Dipartimento di Elettronica e Informazione
P.za Leonardo da Vinci 32, 20133 Milano, Italy
Email: fugini@elet.polimi.it

Abstract

The problem of analyzing security requirements is to be addressed in legacy systems when planned restructuring interventions involve also security aspects. In this paper, we propose a three-level model for authorization analysis and an associated method to extract authorizations from legacy systems. The model allows the security administrator to analyze process authorizations for database accesses at different granularity levels of the involved data. The connection between processes and user roles within organizational units of the legacy system are discussed. The initial results of an experimentation of the approach on a set of processes and databases of the Italian Public Administration information systems are presented.

Keywords

Discretionary access control, Authorization analysis, Legacy information systems.

1 INTRODUCTION

Security of data in distributed and heterogeneous systems, such as Public Administration organizations, has received much attention and has been tackled in the last few years with different focuses, such as database security, communications security, standardization of procedures and devices, individual privacy insurance [ISS95,Jon94]. Public Administration information systems are legacy systems characterized by thousands of co-existing processes and applications, spread among several heterogeneous systems [Aik94]. Ad hoc methods and techniques are required to identify security requirements in legacy systems, with capabilities to take into account also security aspects peculiar of distributed and heterogeneous systems [She90]. In fact, legacy systems can have been developed without security requirements in mind and / or without documenting how security requirements have been implemented. In addition, the personnel with the knowledge required to understand these systems and how they work may be no longer available, making the identification of security authorizations a crucial activity to be performed with information actually available.

In this paper we present a method for organization-oriented analysis of security in legacy Information Systems of the Public Administration. The analysis aims at making evident existing authorizations of processes on data, in order to verify their consistency with the current organization security requirements.

The method is illustrated basing on the results of a study being conducted in cooperation with the Italian National Consortium for Informatics (CINI) and the Italian National Research Council. The study is aimed at devising methods and tools for evaluating existing security measures, and possibly developing new measures, in Information Systems of some key organizations in the Italian Public Administration.

In particular, the study is being performed with the Labour and the Justice Ministries also through the coordination of the "Information Systems Authority for Public Administration" (AIPA). Starting from a large set of data made available by AIPA, we have analyzed *processes*, *Organizational units*, and *databases* belonging to the Labour Ministry. The legacy Information Systems thus considered allowed us to perform an analysis of security of *business procedures*, and of *data* stored in the Ministry databases. The purpose of the study is to analyze the *security requirements* in a Public Administration Information System and to propose a business security model able to fulfill a twofold objective:

- to express the authorizations of the analyzed legacy systems, thus allowing security designers to match them against security requirements and possibly modify some authorizations;
- to be a reference model for the Public Administration in the development of security of its systems.

In this paper, we present the results of the first part of this study, regarding the analysis of authorizations of Public Administration processes on databases. The organizational units are identified; their analysis using a role-based model is a subsequent phase of the project and, hence, is not discussed here. Issues of data distribution and database federation have been studied in a preliminary approach in [Cas96]; they are planned to be integrated within the project together with role and organizational unit analysis.

The paper is organized as follows. In Section 2, we describe the application context of our approach. In Section 3, we illustrate the analysis method adopted for identifying process authorizations in our legacy systems. In Section 4, we describe possible uses of our method in the framework of the Public Administration domain. Finally, in Section 5, we give our concluding remarks.

2 APPLICATION CONTEXT

The elements characterizing our application context are described by means of an ER schema, shown in Fig. 1 [Bat96]. In particular, in the schema we identify:

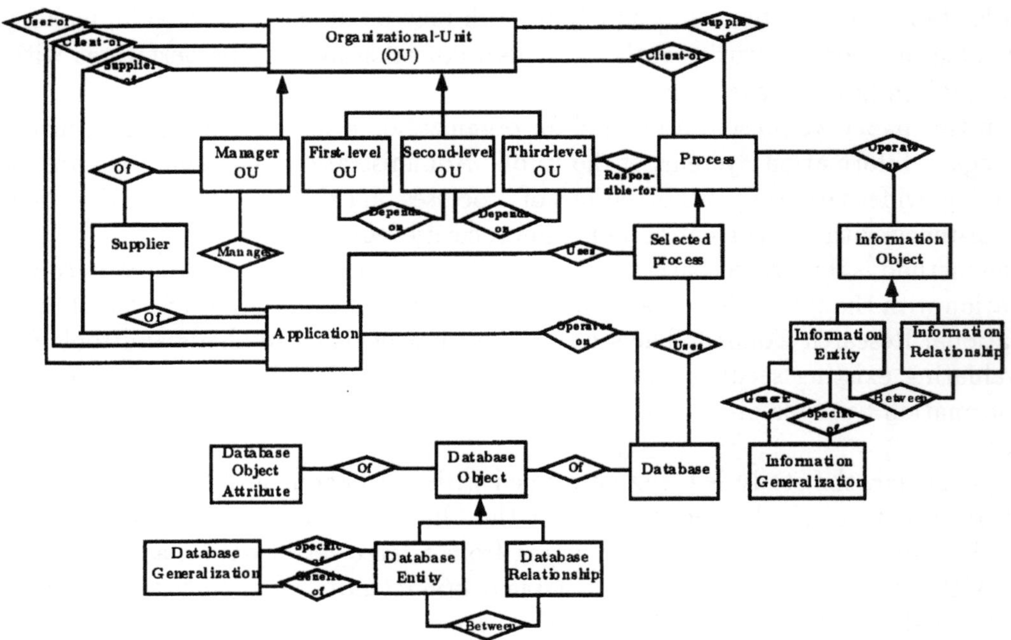

Figure 1 Model of the organizational units and related processes

- *Organizational units*, that is, the users of the information systems. Three levels of organizational units are distinguished, namely Ministries, Divisions, Offices to reflect their hierarchical/functional placement in the organization chart of the Public Administration (PA).
- *Processes*, that is, groups of activities (partly manually executed, partly computer supported) performed to provide services to internal and/or external users of the PA. Organizational units can be responsible for, clients or suppliers of work processes. Processes have an associated ER schema describing the information manipulated by the process in terms of entities and relationships between entities.
- *Applications*, which are computer based and are managed by the EDP manager organizational units; they have client, supplier and user organizational units associated with them.
- *Information objects* exchanged and manipulated by processes, distinguishing between paper based information objects and computer based information objects, all together represented in terms of ER conceptual schemas.
- *Databases*, which are used by the applications. An ER schema is defined for each database describing database structure at the conceptual level.
- *Database objects*, corresponding to the computer based information objects manipulated by the processes.

The data selected for the analysis of security requirements are provided by the Ministry of Labour through AIPA and consist of:

- the description of organizational units of the Ministry of Labour;

- the description of about 100 application processes executed by these organizational units on data;
- the description of 9 databases given as schemas and subschemas according to the Entity-Relationship (ER) model [Chen76].

Our analysis on these descriptions has the purpose of identifying which organizational units can execute which processes and therefore can access which data items; this analysis is performed by coupling the descriptions of the ER process schemas with the ER database schemas. Then, by identifying which organizational unit executes which processes, the aim is to *derive* the existing authorizations between processes and data. These authorizations will be expressed as a triplet $\langle s, op, o\rangle$ where s is a subject, op is a type of access or operation, and o is an object. Initially, the *type of access* is expressed in terms of *transactions* on database schemas and subschemas; subsequent refinements lead to identify process authorizations in terms of basic privileges (read, write, create) on schema elements and eventually on data items.

For the analysis, in the following section we illustrate the three-level authorization model and the associated methodology to identify the existing access modes from processes onto databases.

3 ANALYSIS MODEL AND METHODOLOGY

The three-level authorization model is depicted in Fig. 2 (adapted from the ER security model proposed in [Oh95]). A special type of relationship, called *security relationship* (shown in grey in the figure) is introduced to represent at the conceptual level the privileges that can be executed by a subject on a given object. In our context, privileges are associated with processes. In fact, since we deal with legacy systems, it is very difficult to specify data access privileges directly for user roles, because this would require an in-depth analysis of work procedures in each involved PA office. In legacy systems, role privileges on data can be derived from the authorizations of processes that roles are authorized to execute. Roles which, in an organizational unit, are authorized to execute one or more processes (*process authorizations* in Fig. 2) will, consequently, acquire data access privileges associated with these processes. Issues related the definition of process authorizations are not discussed here, since this task will be performed in a subsequent phase of the project, on the basis of the role hierarchies defined within every single organizational unit.

A *refinement* method is defined for the analysis, leading to show existing authorizations of processes on single data items in terms of elementary access operations (read, write, create). A refinement method is necessary since, dealing with legacy systems, security authorizations are not explicitly stated, but rather, are implicit in the system workflow. Consequently, identification of authorizations for single data items can only be derived starting from a higher level analysis of process functionality and required accesses to existing databases. According to this refinement method, first we identify authorizations for processes to access database schemas (Fig. 2(a)), called *database authorizations*. Then we refine database authorizations

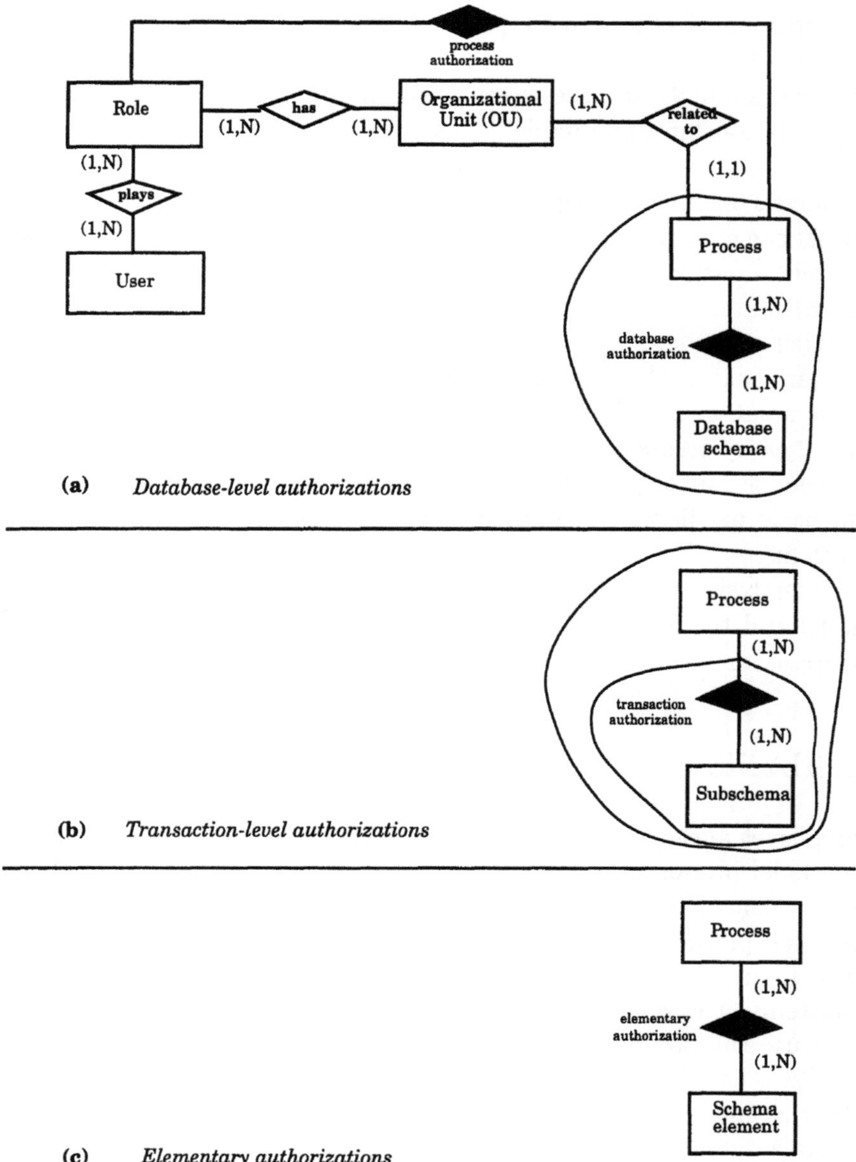

Figure 2 Three-level authorization model

into authorizations for processes to perform operations on subschemas (Fig. 2(b)), called *transaction authorizations.* Eventually we obtain, through a further refinement, authorizations for processes to perform elementary operations on schema elements (Fig. 2(c)), called *elementary authorizations.*

The methodology we propose for the analysis of security requirements is articulated in the following phases:

1. *Identification of database authorizations.*
   In this phase, we identify which databases are accessed by which processes and

organizational units. The analysis is performed by exploiting the ER schemas associated with processes and databases. We describe this phase in Section 3.1.

2. *Identification of transaction authorizations.*
   In this phase, we analyze the functionality of processes in order to identify which *transactions* are executed by a given process on the involved databases. The analysis is performed by exploiting a textual description of process functionality and the involved database schemas. We describe this phase in Section 3.2.
3. *Identification of elementary authorizations.*
   In this phase, for each process transaction identified in the previous phase, we derive the elementary operations involved in the execution of the transaction. The analysis is performed by exploiting the query associated with a transaction and the corresponding database schema(s). We describe this phase in Section 3.3.

3.1 Identification of database authorizations

The goal of this phase is to identify: i) which databases can be accessed by each process of a given OU, and ii) which databases can be accessed by each OU. To this end, we analyze ER schemas associated with processes and ER database schemas to find a match between them. The analysis is performed separately for each OU and, within a given OU, for all processes pertaining to it. In particular, for a given process P_i, starting from elements (e.g., entity, relationship) specified in its corresponding schema, we analyze database schemas to select those containing elements matching P_i's schema elements. A process P_i can access a single database or several databases, depending also on the type of process, namely elementary process or macroprocess. Elementary processes perform an elementary task, with a well defined objective. Macroprocesses perform complex activities whose objective is pursued by means of the coordinated execution of a set of constituent (elementary) processes.

As the result of analyzing ER schemas, we identify a set of *database authorizations*, $DBAUTH = \{\langle s, op, o\rangle\}$, where:

- s can be a process P_i or an organizational unit OU_j;
- *op* is *access-DB*;
- o is a database DB_k.

A database authorization $\langle P_i, access - DB, DB_k\rangle$ specifies that process P_i is authorized to access database DB_k, because it performs at least one operation on data stored in DB_k.

For example, let us consider the process `Statistics Elaboration for Employment Analysis` (P_1) which belongs to the organization unit `DIII` (OU_1) of the Ministry of Labour and is responsible for producing statistics regarding companies and related employees. Process P_1 accesses the `MC` database (DB_1) whose schema is shown in Fig. 3, to retrieve necessary company and employee data. As a consequence, we can derive the database authorization $\langle P_1, access - DB, DB_1\rangle$ shown in Fig. 3, according to the authorization model illustrated in Fig. 2.

Authorizations of the form $\langle OU_j, access - DB, DB_k\rangle$ can be derived specifying that organization unit OU_j is authorized to access database DB_k. An authorization $\langle OU_j, access - DB, DB_k\rangle$ can be derived in the set $DBAUTH$ only if at least one

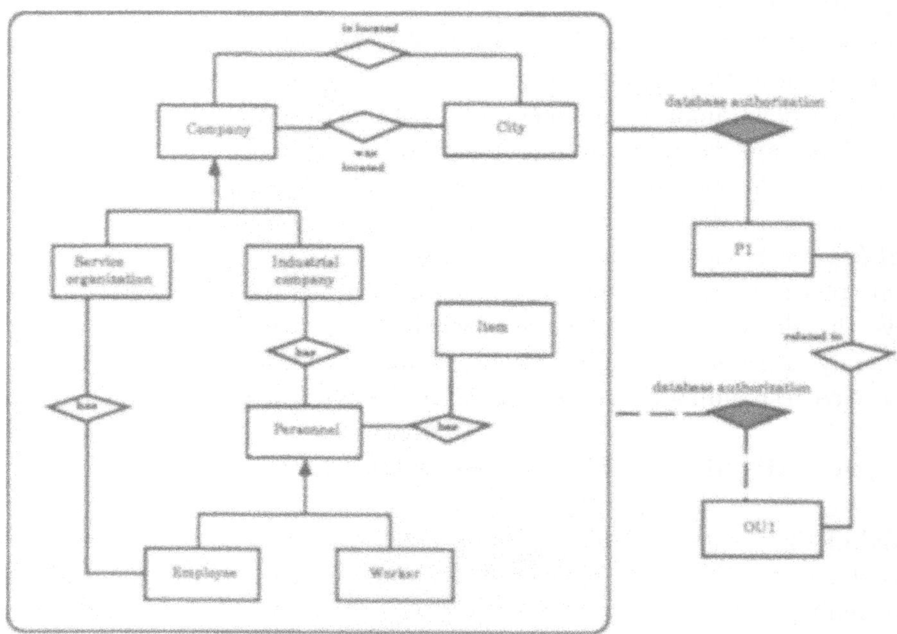

Figure 3 Example of database authorizations

authorization $\langle P_i, access - DB, DB_k \rangle$ is defined in the set $DBAUTH$, where P_i is a process related to OU_j. Database authorizations for OUs are derived in order to perform the security organizational analysis which will be one of the goals of future work. In Fig. 3, the derived authorization $\langle OU_1, access - DB, DB_1 \rangle$ is shown with dashed lines.

3.2 Identification of transaction authorizations

In this phase, we are interested in identifying the groups of operations (transactions) performed by a given process P_i on the database subschemas associated with P_i in database authorizations. For this purpose, the process functionality must be analyzed. For such analysis, a textual specification of process functionality is available in our project, describing the main characteristics of process activity. Referring to available data, we manually identify the main operations performed by the process on a corresponding database(s) by isolating relevant information. In particular, verbs and names of database elements are isolated, denoting the type of operation and the involved data. For each verb and associated database elements, we define a SQL query on the corresponding database subschemas.

One or more SQL queries can be defined for each process P_i, depending on the complexity of the activity performed by P_i. Each defined query corresponds to a *transaction*.

As an example, let us consider process P_1 performing a transaction T_{11} `Company size analysis` to produce an aggregated report giving the number of the industrial companies grouped by size (small, medium, large). The SQL query corresponding to $T_{11}$is the following:

T_{11}:

```
SELECT COUNT(*)
FROM Company, Industrial Company
WHERE Company.Code=Industrial Company.Code
GROUP BY Company.Size
```

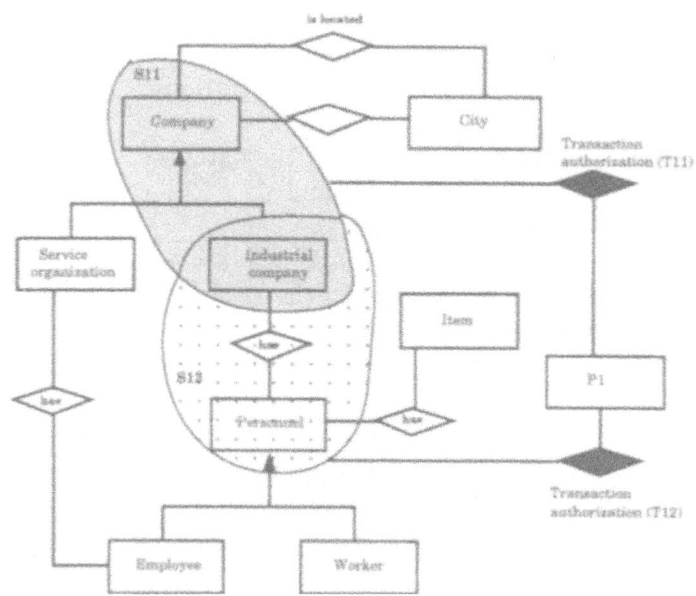

Figure 4 Example of transaction authorizations

As a result, we define a set of *transaction authorizations*, $TAUTH = \{\langle s, op, o\rangle\}$, which is a refinement of the set $DBAUTH$ of database authorizations defined in the previous phase. In particular, for each database authorization $\langle P_i, access-DB, DB_k\rangle \in DBAUTH$ we define one or more transaction authorizations $\langle s, op, o\rangle \in TAUTH$ where:

- s is the process P_i;
- op is a transaction T_{iq} executed by P_i, with $q = 1, \ldots, n$, being n the total number of transactions performed by P_i;
- o is a subschema S_{kt} of the schema S_k associated with database DB_k. S_{kt} contains element(s) of S_k specified in the SQL query associated with T_{iq}.

A transaction authorization $\langle P_i, T_{iq}, S_{kt}\rangle$ specifies that process P_i is authorized to perform operation T_{iq} on (sub)schema S_{kt} of database DB_k.

For example, with reference to process P_1, we define the following transaction authorizations: $\langle P_1, T_{11}, S_{11}\rangle$, where S_{11} denotes the subschema of DB_1 on which T_{11} operates (evidenced by the grey area in Fig. 4), and $\langle P_1, T_{12}, S_{12}\rangle$ where T_{12} is another transaction, named `Personnel/Industrial Company analysis` operating on the subschema S_{12} (dotted area of Fig. 4 according to the following SQL query:

T_{12}:
```
SELECT COUNT(*)
FROM Personnel, Industrial Company
GROUP BY Industrial Company.Code
```

3.3 Identification of elementary authorizations

In this phase, we further refine transaction authorizations to identify elementary operations performed by a given process P_i on database elements during each transaction T_{iq}. We consider the following elementary operations:

- *create*, to create an instance of an element in the database,
- *read*, to read an (attribute of an) element, and
- *write*, to write an (attribute of an) element.

The *read* and *write* privileges are defined to the level of ER attributes. The *create*, *read*, and *write* operations correspond to the *insert* privilege on a relational database table, and to the *select* and *update* privileges on single table columns, respectively.

For a process P_i, we analyze each of its associated transactions together with the corresponding database schema. For each transaction T_{iq}, elementary operations performed by T_{iq} on each schema element are identified by exploiting the SQL query for T_{iq}.

As the result of transaction analysis, we define a set of *elementary authorizations*, $EAUTH = \{\langle s, op, o\rangle\}$, which is a refinement of set $TAUTH$ of transaction authorizations defined in the previous phase. In particular, for each transaction authorization $\langle P_i, T_{iq}, S_{kt}\rangle \in TAUTH$ we define one or more elementary authorizations $\langle s, op, o\rangle \in TAUTH$ where:

- s is the process P_i;
- op is an elementary operation, that is, $op \in \{create, read, write\}$;
- o is an element or an element attribute of S_{kt}.

An elementary authorization $\langle P_i, op, o\rangle$ specifies that process P_i is authorized to perform the elementary operation op on the corresponding schema element o of database DB_k.

With reference to transaction T_{11} of process P_1 previously specified, we define the following elementary authorizations (see Fig. 5):

$\langle P_1$,*read*, *Company.Code*$\rangle$
$\langle P_1$,*read*, *Industrial Company.Code*$\rangle$
$\langle P_1$,*read*, *Company.Size*$\rangle$

For the sake of simplicity, in Fig. 5, we show elementary authorizations on entities rather than on entity attributes.

The notion of authorization implication [Rab91] is now adopted to relate elementary authorizations. Let e_p be an element (i.e., an entity or a relationship) of

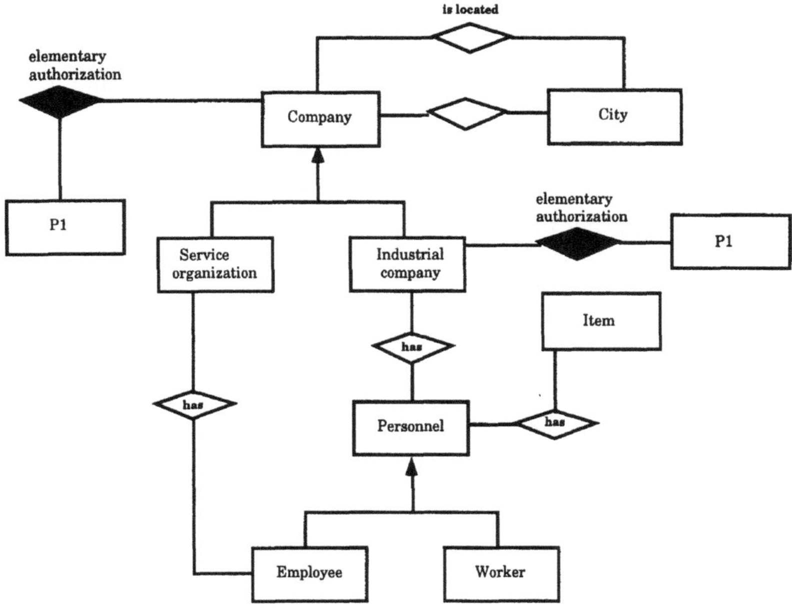

Figure 5 Example of elementary authorizations

a (sub)schema, and $e_p.a_i$ an attribute of e_p. We define the following authorization implications (denoted by symbol "$\rightarrow$"):

- $\langle s, op, e_p \rangle \rightarrow \langle s, op, e_p.a_i \rangle$, with $op \in \{read, write\}$ and $i = 1, \ldots, N$, being N the total number of attributes of the considered element e_p.
- $\langle s, create, e_p \rangle \rightarrow \langle s, write, e_p.a_i \rangle$, for a subset or all attributes of the considered element e_p.

Authorization implication allows one to simplify both the specification and the analysis of authorizations by reducing the number of authorizations of a database. Further implications are under study, together with algorithms for their use.

4 APPLICATIONS OF THE APPROACH

In this section, we discuss the main applications of the analysis methodology presented above. In particular, the methodology and the associated authorization sets can be employed to:

- Derive the existing authorizations of processes on data at different granularity levels, from database level to data item level. This allows the security administrator to identify the security-relevant data items in existing databases.
- Match derived authorizations against the security requirements and policies of the organization. In particular, by aggregating authorizations *by process* the method can show whether a given policy about data access and administration is fulfilled or not. For example, if the minimum-privilege policy [Cas95] must be enforced, the analysis can highlight the data accessed by each process. The security

administrator can then evaluate the adequacy of reported authorizations against the ones required by the policy. Furthermore, by aggregating process authorizations *by organizational unit*, the administrator can check the policy enforcement considering also user roles.

- Support the analysis of role privileges. In order to be effective, the *process-oriented* analysis methodology should be coupled with an *organization-oriented* security analysis in terms of roles and organizational units [Hol95,ISS95]. To this end, Role-Based Access Control models (RBAC) are generally used [San96]. In these models, a role is a job function within an organization describing the authorization conferred to users and is, therefore, suitable to focus the organization structure and its connection to permissions. Moreover, RBAC are a flexible and application-independent paradigm able to accommodate various policies and different applications with minimal customization; it seems therefore a good candidate to become a reference framework for security. RBAC can then be interpreted either into a mandatory or a discretionary access control, depending on the particular organization and on existing mechanisms. Finally, RBAC are based on graphs and hierarchies enabling one to analyze the existing and desired permissions. RBAC is available in some commercial DBMSs and is therefore accessible for experimentation.
  The main advantages of RBAC for our purposes is the ability to represent the roles of users in organizational units, according to the existing organization chart. This allows the security administrator(s) to study the user hierarchies and their actions upon data, through authorization to execute processes.

5 CONCLUDING REMARKS

In this paper, we have presented a methodology for deriving authorizations to access data at different granularity levels on the basis of process analysis. The method described in the paper is intended to be an analysis tool for deriving existing authorizations in legacy information systems and for verifying their adequacy to organization security policies. The method has been illustrated with reference to our experience with some Italian Public Administration information systems.

An environment to support the analysis method previously illustrated has been developed, based on a repository developed by AIPA for storage of ER schemas and other data associated with processes in different organization units. The implementation environment is PC-based, using Access 7.0. The AIPA repository provides functionalities for visualization of process and database schemas and associated information, both with textual information format and with a simple graphical editor for ER schemas. Our analysis method has been experimented on a sample of 30 process specifications related to the Labour Ministry. On top of the AIPA repository, a *toolkit* of SQL queries has been developed to support the three-level based authorization analysis.

Future research work will be devoted to the analysis of user roles in organizational units to identify connections between roles and processes. Experimentation using commercially available DBMS packages will be performed. In addition, security requirements and policies will be collected through interviews to selected Public

Administration offices in order to match them against the authorizations derived by our method. A further issues to be investigated regards the applicability of a finer analysis of process functionality, based on workflow modeling techniques to consider also aspects of data distribution and heterogeneity [Geo95].

Acknowledgments
This work has been partially supported by the Italian Consortium for Informatics (CINI) and by the Italian National Research Council in the framework of "Progetto Strategico Informatica nella Pubblica Amministrazione - DEMOSTENE Project". We thank doctoral students who contributed to test the method and to implement support tools.

REFERENCES

[Aik94] Aiken, P., Muntz, A., and Richards, R.. (1994) DoD Legacy Systems - Reverse Engineering Data Requirements. *Communications of the ACM,* **37**(5).

[Bat96] Batini, C., Castano, S., De Antonellis, V., Fugini, M.G., and Pernici, B. (1996) Analysis of an Inventory of Information Systems in the Public Administration. *Requirements Engineering Journal,* **1**(1).

[Cas95] Castano, S., Fugini, M.G., Martella, G., and Samarati, P. (1995) *Database Security*, Addison-Wesley.

[Cas96] Castano, S. (1996) An Approach to Deriving Global Authorizations in Federated Database Systems. In *Proc. of 10th Annual IFIP WG 11.3 Working Conference on Database Security,* Como, Italy.

[Chen76] Chen, P.P. (1976) The Entity-Relationship Model: Towards a Unified View of Data. *ACM Trans. on Database Systems,* **1**(1).

[Geo95] Georgakopoulos, G., Hornik, M., and Sheth, A. (1995) An Overview of Workflow Management: From Process Modeling to Workflow Automation Infrastructure. *Distributed and Parallel Databases,* **3**.

[Hol95] Holbein, R., Teufel, S., and Bauknecht, K. (1995) The Use of Business Process Models for Security Designs in Organisations, in [ISS95].

[ISS95] (1995) *Information Systems Security - Facing the information society of the 21st Century,* Proc. of IFIP /SEC'95, 12th Int. Information Security Conference, S.K. (Eds. Katsikas S.K. and Gritzalis, D.), Chapman&Hall.

[Jon94] Jonscher, D., and Dittrich, K.R.. (1994) An Approach for Building Secure Database Federations. In *Proc. of the 20th Int. Conf. on Very Large Databases,* Santiago, Chile.

[Oh95] Oh, Y.C., and Navathe, S.B. (1995) SEER: Security Enhanced Entity-Relationship Model for Secure Relational Databases. In *Proc. of OO-ER'95, Int. Conf. on the Object-Oriented and Entity-Relationship Modelling,* LNCS n.1021, Gold Coast, Australia.

[Rab91] Rabitti, F., Bertino, E., Kim, W., and Woelk, D. (1991) A Model of Authorization for Next-Generation Database Systems, *ACM-Trans. On Database Systems,* **16**(1).

[San96] Sandhu, R.S., Coyne, E.J., Feinstein, H.L., and Youman, C.E. (1996) Role-Based Access Control Models. *IEEE Computer,* February.

[She90] Sheth A.P. and Larson, J.P. (1990) Federated Database Systems for Managing Distributed, Heterogeneous, and Autonomous Databases, *ACM Computing Surveys,* **22**(3).

PART THREE

Management of Information Security and Risks (II)

The Role of Government in creating the IT security infrastructure

Builder or bystander?

by Mads Bryde Andersen
Professor of Law, dr.jur.
University of Copenhagen
Denmark

Abstract

The author of this paper has been the chairman of the Danish IT Security Council since it was established in 1995. He has also worked closely with the Ministry of Research and Information Technology on a Danish draft act on Digital Signatures. The paper reports of some *political* experiences in creating an IT security infrastruture; experiences which might very well also be envisaged by other countries. It does not necessarily reflect the views of the IT Security Council or the Danish Government.

The need for an information infrastructure

To implement certain information security solutions you need an information security infrastructure. In an open environment, encryption and digital signatures can only be applied on the basis of a trusted third party infrastructure consisting of certification authorities, key centres etc. Furthermore, certain security measures will only be trusted, if users have confidence that they are using systems which have been okayed by public entitites.

This opens the question of what roles Governments shall have. Broadly speaking, Governments can either play an active role in *building* up such an infrastructure, or they can sit passively as *bystanders*.

First and foremost, Governments can play actively as *law-makers*, setting up the substantial and procedural rules for communicating parties and for the private entities who want to undertake the jobs as certification authorities. As a part of such schemes,

Governments could also be *controlling entities* that authorize private entities to undertake certification authority functions. Government entities could even undertake the role as *trusted third party*. By doing so, Governments play the job of a *builder* of the information infrastructure.

But Governments could also chose a more passive role as a *bystander*, waiting to see what solutions are brought forward by industry, and only interfering if substantial risks are at stake. Indeed, this role appears to be the easiest one, at least in the short run. Due to its immaterial nature and to the complexity of information technology, information is one of the most complicated issues to regulate by law. Politicians are often confused when it comes to questions of "information legislation" (be it data protection laws, "decency" legislation or encryption policy), and information policy processes are therefore difficult to manage and predict. When it comes to personal information - which most information is - the questions also touch upon fears of the unknown. This is mainly due to the unpredictable ways by which information can be used against individuals. Therefore, it is easy to understand why some politicians prefer the role of a bystander; a role which may even be justified by the modern trend of market control and competition in the information industry.

The Danish experience - an example

Denmark presents an example that other countries might be able to learn from when it comes to discussions on the Government's role in building an IT information infrastructure. Denmark is a rather small country with approximately 5 million citizens, but Denmark has a relatively large public sector which has made extensive use of computer technology for decades. Denmark also has a financial sector with a strong tradition for co-operation on IT issues. Within this sector, it is the general attitude not to compete on IT security matters. All Danish citizens have a unique personal identification number (the CPR-number, Central Personal Register) which is used to identify individuals both for governmental purposes (taxation, social security etc.) and for private purposes.

To add to this, Denmark has substantial expertise in the field of the technological applications and the legal implications of cryptology. The Danish company Cryptomathic A/S, founded by Professor Peter Landrock, has provided cryptographic solutions both to public entities and private enterprises for a number of years. In law schools at the universities of Aarhus and Copenhagen, legal scholars are working with contractual and other issues regarding the use of digital technology.

This explains, at least partly, why Denmark also has an early history of considering public key infrastructure issues. As early as 1989, a Danish Teletrust group was created on a private basis by the Danish Data Association to discuss how a Danish "Teletrust" scheme could be established. The group presented its findings in 1991: A government-based control key centre authority, referred to as a CCA - Centre Certifying Authority, should be formed for key centres. The CCA should certify and control key centres and thereby provide a more solid legal basis (e.g. in relation to liability issues) for that new and hitherto unknown kind of business.

Based on the Teletrust proposals, The Danish Telecommunications Agency appointed a working group in the beginning of 1992 to consider how to implement the Teletrust proposal into real life, cf. my article in The EDI Law Review, vol. 1, no. 1, 1993, pp. 43-53. However, the subsequent development proved to be less visionary and certainly more reluctant. It became difficult to gain the Government's support for the proposal: Why should the Government be engaged in the creating of new regulatory infrastructure when the involved industries had not taken any initiatives. Could the intended results not be reached by other means?

As indicated in my above article, it is easy to see the arguments against setting up such a framework. One argument put forward was that the time has not come yet for a small country like Denmark to enter that path. Another, that there were already legislation in force that would make certification of privately held key centres possible, namely the rules providing for a general certification and accreditation scheme dealing with the accreditation and certification as part of a quality assurance concept (however, without specifying the basis for such accreditation and certification).

The political winds around this issue changed dramatically in 1994. Since then, the Danish Government has put information policy and IT security on the top of the political agenda. The idea of creating infrastructures for public key-based communications was invoked in 1994 when a report by the Danish Government was published, "Info-Society 2000". In this visionary report, a long list of proposals for bringing Denmark into the Information Society was made. Subsequently, the Danish Ministry of Research and Information Technology has worked intensively to implement the suggestions from the Info-Society report, and other suggestions have been made and implementing, among them the setting up of a Danish IT Security Council and the proposals for Danish digital signature legislation.

The various roles of Government

As this short presentation indicates, Governments *can* take various different attitudes towards building the IT security infrastructure. Governments do not necessarily have to act as builders. They may very well chose the role of the bystander, while at the same time supporting the very notion of having such an infrastructure. Before we go deeper into the topic of what particular role, Governments *should* play, it may be useful to take a quick glance backwards in history.

Although the role of Governments has changed dramatically over the last centuries, some functions have remained the same. One of them is the task of providing security for citizens against various *threats*. Most activities Governments engage in concern the safety and well-being of individuals and enterprises. Health care, environmental protection, traffic regulation, product safety regulations, food and drug administration not to mention criminal investigation and military security are just a few examples of such security functions.

> It is somewhat of a paradox that one of the threats that Government shall protect citizens against, is Government itself! When personal data on citizens are

processed, a clash of interests occur. The processing itself seems - at least to someone - to turn Government into a "Big Brother". This privacy concern has been the basis for the severe European rules on data protection (cf. European Directive no. 96/46/EC of 24 October 1995). Even though from the outset these rules were aimed at the processing of personal data for purposes of public control, taxation or the like, they also apply in regard to IT solutions provided for computer security infrastructures. A clash between various data protection policies also occurs in the encryption debate. On one side, encryption is one of the most powerful tools to obtain confidentiality of data (and thereby privacy of personal data). Nonetheless, the privacy issue is also raised *against* encryption technologies, because the use of computers to implement encryption solutions implies registration of personal data.

Another important task for Governments concerns the Government as an *organizer*. Governments have a certain obligation to provide for "traffic rules" between individuals and enterprises. Just as important it is to have rules for road traffic, any civilized state must have some basic principles on how citizens shall act towards each other when entering into contracts or other binding relations. Up until now, such rules have mainly been derived from the business practices of a "common law" nature. But presently there is a widespread feeling that in order to foster the use of electronic commerce, specific rules are needed on how to establish legal obligations by means of digital technology.

Last, but not least, in a state with a substantial public sector, there is a demand to provide administrative functions in the most efficient way in order to reduce taxation. Since most public sector activities are financed by taxes, every Government has a natural obligation to apply the most efficient technology in order to reduce costs and enhance services. And obviously, information technology is an important tool to achieve that.

The following three examples will indicate some of the problems faced by the Danish Government in its endeavours to implement new security framework to public administrations and electronic commerce.

The citizen chip card experience

Among the proposals from the Info-Society 2000 report was a proposal already presented by the Ministry of the Interior to create an identification card ("Citizen card") based on public key encryption technology but with other possible features. As the proposal was made, no clear indication was given as to the use of that card, but it was obvious that one of its main features would be to support communication between citizens and Government. The card should provide for digital signature functions and for encryption for confidentiality purposes.

The proposal was met with substantial opposition among people of the kind often referred to as "ordinary citizens" (many of whom saw the proposal as a new way for Government to collect personal data on individuals) and by some politicians (of whom even a significant amount had apparently not understood what the project was about).

The criticism was so substantial that the otherwise technology-favouring Danish Government decided to postpone the final decision on the project.

In September 1995, a new citizen card proposal was introduced. In a new report form the Ministry of the Interior, the chip card should only work as a key combining knowledge on the social security number of the holder and his/her PIN-code. It was strongly stressed that this card would not provide further registration on the card and that no new registers would be made within Government (apart from a log to enable users to *prove* their communication). The main idea was that citizen cards should support communication between individuals and Government, but the card would also be based upon an open architecture allowing for common standards and a coherent infrastructure that might support implementation of digital signatures on a broader scale.

It took only one year before that proposal was also taken back.

In October 1996, the Minister for the Interior decided to postpone the citizen card project. Officially, two reasons were given. One reason was that the operating systems for chip cards of the kind that should be applied in the citizen card were not yet available. It would therefore take considerable time, effort and money to develop the necessary technology for the card. Secondly, it was mentioned that the expected law on digital signatures would have a hampering effect on the citizen chip card project, since the proposal for a digital signature legislation was expected to allow private entities to provide for security solutions for digital signatures. In other words, since the citizen chip card should not be the only technique to provide for this important function, why should the Ministry of the Interior invest such a substantial amount in its implementation?

As it is now, the citizen chip card project is on the "shelf". It is interesting to note, however, that the postponement of this project has effected one of the concerns raised *against* the citizen chip card, namely the concern for the "weak" citizens. In the citizen chip card proposal, citizens would be in a position to obtain a Government sponsored card at a lower cost, if not for free. Now they will face a market of private companies that will offer their services on a profit oriented basis.

The digital signature experience

In the 1996 IT-action plan from the Danish Government, a proposal was included to put forward legislation on digital signatures. Over the summer of 1996, a first outline of a Digital Signature Act was drafted and in the fall of 1996, various hearings were convened to discuss this proposal (and subsequent proposals) with interested parties and industry representatives.

When the question of Government roles is raised, one might ask whether there is a need for such legislation at all. Is it not so, that businesses and individuals who want to communicate by digital means can do so on the basis of contracts?

Under Danish law, the answer to that question is *yes*, if we talk about the relationship between private individuals and if there is no specific obligation to use paper or paper signatures. But when it comes to questions relating to public entities, the power of contracts is limited. If the law requires or assumes that a particular application shall be filed on paper and signed, such a requirement can only be adjusted by way of new legislation. The same problem occurs in areas where regard must be taken to third parties, for example in relation to rules on negotiable instruments.

One of the difficulties in making digital signature legislation is standardization. Digital signatures are made on the basis of digital documents, but digital documents are only used between parties who have already agreed on ways of communication. Without commonly accepted standards for digital communication, it gives no meaning to attach special legal consequences to the digital signatures as such.

This dependency on standards and "codes of conduct" create a circular problem: Without certainty of the legal consequences of digital signatures, it is difficult to implement standards for digital communication on a wide scale. But without such standards, any attempt to draft digital signature legislation runs the risk of vanishing into thin air.

In the first versions of the Danish draft on digital signatures, this "vicious circle" was broken by a proposal that any governmental initiative should be under the obligation to receive digital communication. Such an obligation can only work in relation to public entities. It would not only be politically problematic, but indeed practically difficult to implement. This proposal has not yet been subject to discussions on a broad scale, mainly because its first versions have been restricted. It remains therefore to be seen whether the proposal - that any initiative of the Government should be under the obligation to receive digital communication - will find acceptance.

One might very well assume that this problem has obstructed the digital signature project. Not so. As it appears when this paper is submitted (January 1997), the introduction into Parliament has been delayed by other reasons, namely the problems regarding encryption policy:

The role of investigation authorities

When encryption is used for confidentiality purposes, problems of quite a different nature than those related to communication security arise. Whereas encryption may be used to conceal information, law enforcement and perhaps essential parts of government intelligence activities may be obstructed. Investigating authorities often face difficulties when suspects have locked written communication by encryption, as it is already the common practice among hackers. If encryption is allowed - as it is now in Denmark - criminals and criminal organisations deprive the investigation authorities of one of their most important tools. Therefore, the need for businesses and individuals to secure communication by encryption and the need for Governments to be able to intercept communication have created a confrontation between two valid interests.

The balancing of these fundamental interests has already given rise to political discussions in various international fora as well as to some legislative initiatives. In December 1996, an ad hoc group of experts on cryptographic policy guidelines finalised its work on cryptographic policy guidelines. The December meeting concluded one year of work within that working group, and the proposal will now be brought forward to other fora within the OECD before its final adoption, probably in the middle of 1997.

The Danish IT Security Council has recommended that Denmark should maintain the free use of encryption technology, and that "escrow solutions" should not even be built into those security applications that might be available as a public service (like the former citizen card proposal). Up until now, no formal decision has been taken yet by the Government.

The political marketing issue

Security professionals may find it easy to agree on how to create an IT security infrastructure. But when their conclusions are brought forward in a political process, it often shows that the general public have quite different attitudes. For "ordinary citizens", the very notion that facts are registered within computer systems is subject to much concern. For investigating authorities the need to intercept communication is obviously of high concern.

There is a great risk that the possible roles of Governments in creating an IT security infrastructure is affected by concerns that security people might find less adequate. Therefore, it seems to be an important but somewhat disregarded task for the data security environment to explain things in a direct and clear way to provide for the necessary public support for building an IT infrastructure. This job also includes talking to politicians and Government official to make sure that specific Governmental concern does not lead to unreasonable restrictive policies.

Code of Practice: A Standard for Information Security Management

Lam-for KWOK[1] *and Dennis LONGLEY*[2]
[1]*City University of Hong Kong, Tat Chee Avenue, Kln., HONG KONG*
Tel:+(852)27888625 Fax:+(852)27888614 cslfkwok@cityu.edu.hk
[2]*Queensland University of Technology*
GPO Box2434, Brisbane Q4001, AUSTRALIA
Tel:+(61)7-38645358 Fax:+(61)7-38641507 longley@fit.qut.edu.au

Abstract

The rapid development of networks has caused senior management to reconsider the vulnerabilities of their organisations to information security incidents. Such reconsideration often reveals that the fundamental vulnerabilities lie not with the emerging technology but rather with the lack of an information security infrastructure within the organisation. Appointing a security officer is a common reaction to this situation but the new appointees often find that there is a lack of immediately apparent support form senior management for additional budgets or organisational change and an agreed authoritative source of information security guidelines. The situation has to some extent been addressed by emerging Information Security Management standards such as the *BS 7799*. This paper discusses the manner in which a security officer may best employ such standards to enhance the level of information security in an organisation. The paper also discusses the fact that the application of the standards reveals the requirements for an organisational security model that may be employed to assist in standards conformance and auditing.

Keywords

Information security management, information security standards

1 INTRODUCTION

Surveys and statistical evidence suggest that many senior management have not traditionally given a high or even moderate level of priority to information management. The rapid development of networks, particularly the Internet, has now caused senior management to reconsider the vulnerabilities of their organisations to information security incidents. Such reconsideration often reveals that the fundamental vulnerabilities lie not with the emerging technology but rather with the lack of an organisational information security infrastructure. A common reaction to this situation is to appoint a security officer, or to give an existing employee information security responsibilities.

Discussions with staff given information security responsibilities indicate that a common prime concern lies with a lack of an infrastructural framework for their roles and responsibilities. In recent years senior management have become aware of the potential deleterious impacts of inadequate information security, and have also succumbed to the pressures for the development of visible forms of quality assurance. However, information security management has, to date, lacked a universally recognised framework.

In the late 1960's risk analysis was postulated as the means to assist organisations to formulate their security requirements. The US Federal Government required its departments to undertake a Courtney style of risk analysis (FIPS 65,1979) and subsequently there were formal requirements to report on the implementation of security plans.

The public service managers did not react enthusiastically to these edicts and such practices were not thereafter widely adopted in the private sector. Nevertheless the traditional approach to information security management was based upon a risk analysis study, normally using some proprietary methodology, leading to a set of recommendations on countermeasures, security plan etc. For example, the UK government commissioned the development of the CRAMM methodology (Moses and Glover, 1988), for risk analysis, in an attempt to ensure a degree of uniformity in security management within government data processing units.

The pioneering work of the National Computer Security Centre (NCSC) in the development of TCSEC (Trusted Computer Security Evaluation Criteria) (DoD, 1985) represented an important initial step in the development of a framework for computer security. The significance of these criteria lies in the concept that organisations were required to demonstrate conformance to official guidelines of computer security. The Bell LaPadula security model provided a firm theoretical basis for the criteria. The criteria were extended in the Rainbow Series, to include risk analysis, trusted networks and databases, but the context of the criteria was always limited to the design of multilevel security systems and was therefore primarily directed to the military and government applications.

Subsequent developments of information security evaluation were undertaken by a number of European countries and then harmonised into ITSEC (Information Technology Security Evaluation Criteria)(CEC, 1991). This effort is now being incorporated into international standards, and the Orange Book has been replaced by a large volume of standards documents on CDROM.

The European criteria incorporated the Orange Book concepts of multilevel security but extended the granularity of evaluation assurance and range of system functionality. The criteria thus extended into specific and general purpose security products, intended for a universal market. The criteria also incorporated the evaluation of systems; the essential difference between a product and a system being that the security environment of the system, and hence the security threats, could be more precisely enunciated.

The evolution of the Orange Book into the current set of draft of international standards, coupled with the experience of formal security evaluation over the past decade, have indicated the substantial complexity and costs of such exercises. Such costs may be justified for security products which will generate significant revenue. However, even large organisations are unlikely to include a formal security evaluation of their systems in the security budget.

The security manager therefore is not substantially assisted by the developments in formal security evaluation criteria developed over the past decade. Moreover none of the various risk analysis methodologies or packages appear to have gained universal acclaim or acceptance. Large consulting firms offer substantial risk analysis studies but the cost of such exercises is usually well outside the budget of the average security manager. Thus the security manager could often only glean recommended information security practices from various reference books, or best practice adopted by some organisation. However, if this approach were taken the subsequent proposals from the security manager lacked the credibility of a regulatory framework, and would often fail to gain complete acceptance from senior management.

The publication of a code of practice for information security management by the British Standards Institute (1995) therefore represented a major advance in organisational security management. This document has formed the basis of Australian and New Zealand standards, and is in the process of adoption as an international standard ISO (1995).

The standards are based upon recommendations of security professionals and thus represent a statement on best practices. The document contains recommendations on all facets of information security and hence provides a set of recommended controls and valuable checklists. The most significant aspect of the standards, however, is that they exist; a security manager can now warn recalcitrant senior management that the organisation does not conform to national or international standards of information security management. Such lack of conformance may have consequences for senior management in terms of fiduciary responsibilities, relationships with other departments or organisations etc.

The introduction of the information security management standards thus represents an important advance for the security manager, but the effective use of such standards requires some careful consideration, planning and tools.

2 SECURITY OFFICER AND THE STANDARDS

The emerging Information Security Management Standards (BSI, 1995)(SA/SNZ, 1995) provide an important framework for the role of the security officer, but the standards need to be interpreted and introduced in a structured manner, in order to ensure that they have maximum benefit in terms of organisational information security.

The phases of the implementation may thus be structured:

- development of local set of standards;
- decision from senior management on the policy of conformance to standards;
- evaluation of current level of conformance;
- development of a security plan;
- development of a security model;
- auditing of conformance.

As will be shown in the next section, the standards require careful interpretation and customisation to ensure relevance to a particular environment. At first sight some sections appear to be designed for large computer centres. Upon more careful reading, however, it becomes clear that this experience can be exploited in the current distributed computing systems and the electronic office. The first stage will therefore require a considered review and interpretation of the standards to produce a version for the local organisation.

One of the major advantages of the standards is that they simplify the problem of gaining management commitment. The standards and the localised version can be submitted with a request for a decision after a commitment in principle to conformance to published standards. Senior management's acceptance of the policy of conformity to the proposed standards is an essential condition for the success of the subsequent stages.

Once the principle of conformance is established, i.e. assuming that the whole project is not to be abandoned, the next stage is to determine the current level of security vis-→-vis the standards. This is, to some degree a replacement, or at least a deferment, of the risk analysis activity that normally precedes the establishment of a security plan. At this stage the organisation is effectively evaluating itself at a baseline security level. At the conclusion of the whole exercise, the security manager needs to develop a security plan.

The effort of checking conformance is significantly reduced with use of a software tool such as CoP-iT™ (SMH, 1995). This package allows users to set the level of conformance with the *BS 7799* standard and then provides a series of screens seeking information on the current level of security, in accordance with the standards requirements. Users enter their estimates of the degree of compliance to each topic presented. Upon completion of the dialog the package produces a managerial report with graphs and details of the current level of compliance.

The major advantage of the package is that it provides a detailed and disciplined approach to the collection of security relevant data; effectively producing a series of checklists similar in manner to risk analysis packages such as CRAMM. The advantage of CoP-iT™ over many proprietary risk analysis methodologies is transparency; it is easy to correlate the screens with the printed version of the standards and hence place the questions etc. in a given context.

The second major advantage of tools such as CoP-iT™ is that they maintain the momentum of the process. Having obtained the approval in principle from management, the initial report can be produced and submitted within a couple of weeks. This assumes, of course, that the necessary data to answer the questions is readily available. In many cases the questions may require a search amongst organisational documentation, and/or interviews with operating staff, computer and network managers etc. The package can facilitate the conduct of such interviews by effectively providing a series of checklists.

The desired outcome of the dialog with senior management, following the submission of the initial conformance report, is an agreed security plan. If the report indicates an unacceptably low level of conformance then the first priority will focus upon the current detected deficiencies. The security plan will also address the security requirements beyond the baseline level as discussed in the next paragraph.

The standards emphasise that they primarily address the baseline security requirements. If the evaluation indicates a satisfactory level of conformance at a baseline level then the question of security requirements beyond the baseline level needs to be addressed. This phase will require some forms of risk analysis. It is suggested that the conduct of the risk analysis should be preceded by the formation of a risk model as described by Anderson, Kwok, Longley (1994). This approach overcomes some of the criticisms of current risk analysis methodologies which require extensive data collection in a form dictated by the methodology and the results may become quickly outdated.

Even if a risk analysis is not deemed necessary the formation of the proposed model is recommended for follow up security reviews but more importantly for predicted requirements on auditing of conformance. The initial evaluation using CoP-iT™, as described above, is adequate for its purpose but it assumes that the required information is readily available, and it does not require any evidence of the correctness of the responses. In future reviews the information collected for the initial review should be available in a convenient form. Moreover, if, as is to be hoped, the standards gain widespread acceptance then it is likely that internal or external security auditors will require evidence of the degree of conformance. The proposed model will greatly facilitate such conformance auditing.

3 INFORMATION SECURITY MANAGEMENT STANDARDS

3.1 Overview

The British Standards Institute published A Code of Practice of Information Security Management, the *BS 7799* (BSI, 1995). Standards Australia based the draft Australia and New Zealand Standard on Information Security Management (DR 95305) (1995) on this code of practice and formally adopted it in 1996. An International Standards Organisation document ISO/IEC DIS 14980 (1995) is similarly based upon *BS 7799*.

The standard is an important advance in information security management because it provides security managers with an authoritative statement on good information security practice plus a very helpful set of guidelines and checklists for their security plans. The document makes it clear that its contents require careful interpretation, in the light of the security environment of the organisation. The recommendations are aimed at baseline security and the proposed security measures will require enhancement in areas of high risk.

The standard provides a general section on information security management in which advice is given on the establishment of security requirements and the assessment of security risks, indicating its importance to organisations. The critical success factors are listed as:

- security objectives and activities being based on business objectives etc.;
- visible and commitment from top management;
- good understanding of security risks;
- effective marketing of security to all managers and employees;
- distribution of comprehensive guidance on information security policy and standards to all employees and contractors.

Many organisations develop their own guidelines based upon their individual circumstances but the standard recommends that any such guidelines should be cross-referenced to the standard for the use by future business partners or auditors.

The main body of the document comprises ten sections which will be discussed in the following sections. Each section commences with an objective and the key controls are highlighted within the appropriate sections.

3.2 Main Sections

3.2.1 Security Policy

This section emphasises the requirement for senior management to 'set a clear direction and demonstrate their support for and commitment to information security policy through the issue of an information security policy across the organisation'.

The section suggests the issues that should be addressed in the policy include definition of information security; statement of management intention supporting the goals and principles of information security; explanation of the specific security policies, principles, standards and compliance requirements; definition of general and specific responsibilities for all aspects of information security; explanation of the process for reporting suspected security incidents; and concludes with a recommendation for regular reviews.

Although such a policy must be blessed with the authority of senior management it would be optimistic to think that it will be originated by them. The development of the first policy, or updating of current policies, is an extremely important task for the security officer. It is also likely to be very demanding and time consuming task at the development stage. Although feedback from senior management is essential during this process, it is important not to get bogged down in an excessive number of draft versions due to comments on phraseology etc.

Security officers may find it helpful to study existing security policies from other departments or organisations as a starting point, and to provide a checklist of potential items. Cresson Wood's book (1996) on information security policy can prove to be extremely useful in this regard, particularly since it has an accompanying floppy disk allowing sections to be transferred into organisational documents.

3.2.2 Security Organisation

The topics of the Standard in this section include information security forum; information security co-ordination; allocation of information security responsibilities; authorisation process for IT facilities; specialist information security advice; co-operation between organisations; independent review of information security; and security of third party access.

The useful role of the standard as a checklist is apparent here. For example, in the section co-operation between organisations, there is a mention of appropriate contacts with law enforcement agencies. Many organisations may never be subject to a serious hacking attack, or computer fraud, hence if such an event occurs there will be a dearth of experience of the actions to be taken: logs maintained, evidence collected etc. prior to calling in the police. Discussions with staff endowed with security responsibilities indicates that they readily appreciate the suggestion that a member of staff be given responsibility to liaise with law enforcement agencies and seek advice on the correct procedures.

Upon first reading the standard consistently gives the impression that it is designed for computer centres in large organisations. However, upon further study its relevance to small organisations, distributed environments and the electronic office become apparent. For example, the section on authorisation process for IT facilities is of increasing concern as users install powerful communication software on PCs and laptops, and third party access arrangements are as important today for dealings with electronically linked partners, and Information Services Providers (ISPs), as they were with mainframe maintenance companies.

3.2.3 Assets Classification and Control

This is a very short section containing only three items: inventory of assets; classification guidelines; and classification labelling. In this case the translation of the recommendations from traditional to current computing environments is fraught with difficulty. Physical computing assets have become smaller, more mobile and have proliferated throughout the organisation - and beyond to homes, hotel rooms and airport lounges.

The information assets are likewise widely scattered, and often under the direct control of organisational staff at many levels of responsibility. Classification guidelines are often non-existent and hence highly confidential material may be stored on unlabelled diskettes or transmitted over insecure networks. Most managers would be completely oblivious of the route taken by their messages, or the multifarious nodes that would have handled their highly confidential company documents.

The standard does however make the important point that even when classification schemes are used, difficulties can arise in the absence of universal guidelines on information classification. Hence care must be exercised when exchanging information with other organisations since difficulties could arise from varying interpretation of document labelling.

3.2.4 Personnel Security

The objective of personnel security is given as 'to reduce the risks of human error, theft, fraud or misuse of resources'. These risks increased dramatically as computing was first moved from the computer centre to the office worker's desk, and even more so when organisations linked their computers with networks. There is now a much higher proportion of organisational staff with access to information processing facilities and assets. Moreover although traditionally information security is dominated by CIA (Confidentiality, Integrity and Availability), organisational connections to the Internet open up potential costs arising from misuse of access to the many consumer features of the superhighway.

The areas treated in this section include security in job descriptions; recruitment screening; confidentiality agreement; information security education and training; reporting of security incidents; reporting of security weaknesses; reporting of software malfunctions; and disciplinary process.

Each of these sections now apply to virtually all members of the organisation, and involve a much higher degree of complexity than hitherto. For example, confidentiality agreements need to be extended into codes of conduct covering usage of computing and communication facilities: guidance on email usage, avoidance of harassment on email, legitimate use of the Internet facilities etc.

3.2.5 Physical and Environmental Security

The contents of this section give an emphasis to the security of computer centres, but the introductory paragraph recognises the need for interpretation of the recommendations in other environments. The section deals with physical security perimeter; physical entry controls; security of data centres and computer rooms; isolated delivery and loading areas; clear desk policy; removal of property; equipment siting and protection; power supplies; cabling security; equipment maintenance; security of equipment off premises; and secure disposal of equipment.

The standard refers to the situation of the electronic office and, for example, the problems of security of laptop computers. It is recommended, for example, that personal computers processing sensitive data should be protected with key locks. However, the security officer faced with the managers imbued with the concept of **personal** computers, i.e. not subject to external control, will not find a great deal of assistance from this section.

3.2.6 Computer and Network Management

The objective of recommendations in this section is to 'ensure the correct and secure operation of computer and network facilities'. The introduction to the section emphasises that although there will be wide variations of environment 'in principle, the same security processes should be applied, with appropriate interpretation'. This is a very sensible statement but the reinterpretation of erstwhile computer centre procedures to the electronic office is no mean task.

The areas covered in this section include operational procedures and responsibilities; system planning and acceptance; protection from malicious software; housekeeping; network management; media handling and security; and data and software exchange.

The operational procedures and responsibilities recommendations emphasise the need for the allocation of responsibilities and the documentation of procedures for the secure operation of information processing systems. Although the wording is more apposite to the computer centre it provides a very useful checklist for current distributed environments: security reporting, segregation of duties, separation of operational and development environments, etc.

System planning and acceptance is becoming increasingly significant in the electronic office as packages make increasingly heavy demands on workstation storage and communication software soaks up network bandwidth. Change control is an important issue in large offices as customisation of workstations, development of templates for word processing, etc. by users, can impact upon the portability of electronic documents, and recovery situations where workstations have to be replaced.

Virus control appears to be one area in which management have been convinced to purchase appropriate defensive software. However, the emerging macroviruses and associated vulnerabilities introduced by integration of workstation software systems may require a much greater awareness of the need for an integrated approach to workstation security since such viruses are transmitted by electronic documents rather than software.

The importance of backup facilities is emphasised in the housekeeping section and the security of such backup media requires careful consideration, particularly when it involves user's confidential material that is normally protected by encryption or server password access. The network management section deals briefly with some aspects of the security of networks and it does highlight some common concerns in office environments, e.g. the security of servers located in remote offices.

Media handling and security was normally the responsibility of the tape librarian in the computer centre but this discipline does not seem to have been carried over to the ubiquitous office floppy disks. Clearly floppy disks holding highly sensitive data need to be administered in terms of labelling, receipts, minimisation of distribution, disposal etc., with as much care as the erstwhile magnetic tape. The final section deals, *inter alia*, with the electronic office and some of the security factors of email etc., in fact this section does not give a good indication of its contents.

3.2.7 System Access Control

Access control will play a significant role in baseline security for most organisations. However, in many cases responsibilities for access control are spread around the organisation and the procedures are neither well co-ordinated nor documented. Such a situation can easily reduce the level of security attained; thus this section of the standards is extremely valuable in the formulation of a security plan and promulgation of procedures.

The headings of recommendations include business requirements for system access; user access management; user responsibilities; network access control; computer access control; application access control; and monitoring system access and use.

The standard emphasizes that access control must be defined on the basis of business requirements. Information flows are essential for the smooth operation of the organisation. However, most applications will require control of access to the associated information and it is important that consistent guidelines and policies are established based upon legislative requirements, need to know, organisational responsibilities etc. The use of standard access policies for defined organisational roles can facilitate this task.

The sections on user access management and user responsibilities provide invaluable checklists for the auditing of current procedures and an authoritative source for the introduction of new procedures. Network access control is a significant feature for most organisations, given the fact that many managers and the majority of users will be completely oblivious of the paths that their data will travel. This section deals with user and node authentication, inhibition of network roaming, design and segregation of networks to minimise security problems etc. Similarly the computer access control recommendations provide an excellent checklist of security measures relating to password management, secure log on procedures, terminal security etc.

Application access control is a significant feature now that users may be given access to extremely powerful software and communication facilities. When organisational workers were provided with a dumb terminal and a limited set of menu selections the potential for accidental or malicious damage to information assets was limited. The consumer computing market may now provide office workers with pentium processors, hosting massive software packages, connected to international networks. The need to control the facilities and software packages made available to users is now an important issue, particularly when it comes into conflict with the **personal** computer ethos.

Monitoring system access and use can impact upon areas other than technical, e.g. personnel issues are involved with questions of employee email privacy; monitoring of work performance and harassment; legal issues may be involved if the monitored data is to be used in evidence for disciplinary or criminal procedures etc.

3.2.8 Systems Development and Maintenance

There will be wide variations in the applicability of recommendations of this section. In the early days of commercial computing the possession of a computer automatically implied the existence of programming development team. Currently many organisations rely upon off the shelf software, or outsource their development effort. Nevertheless much of the material in this section requires a careful study by security officers to determine whether or not the recommendations need a re-interpretation in their environment. The detailed sections are security requirements of systems; security in application systems; security of application system files; and security in development and support environments.

The importance of the security officer's role in the planning of new systems is emphasised in 'security requirements of system' because retrofitting security is inevitably difficult and costly. A similar argument applies when new applications are to be commissioned for current systems, and in particular the questions of audit trails and monitoring need to be addressed at this stage.

3.2.9 Business Continuity Planning

Business continuity planning is an obvious component of a security plan and in this area it is essential that the security manager negotiates clear policy statements from senior management. Many of the activities associated with business continuity plans will impact upon operational staff and are likely to be given a low priority. For their own protection security managers need to ensure that they have gained, and documented, agreement and authority from senior management to undertake the recommendations in the standard. The recommendations cover business continuity planning process; business continuity planning framework; testing business continuity plans; and updating business continuity plans.

3.2.10 Compliance

Information security is not necessarily an option that can be accepted or rejected by senior management of an organisation. Increasingly there are legislative and regulatory requirements that require an information security infrastructure for compliance. This section highlights the need to ensure that all such legislative and regulatory requirements are met, and that conformance can be convincingly demonstrated. The section also deals with the need to ensure compliance with internal policies and regulations and concludes with a discussion on the mechanisms to audit such compliance and the protection of the auditing tools. The headings within this section include compliance with legal requirements; control of proprietary software copying; safeguarding of organisational records; data protection; prevention of misuse of IT facilities; compliance with security policy; technical compliance checking; system audit controls; and protection of system audit tools.

4 CONCLUSION

The published standards provide an invaluable tool to the security officer, in terms of comprehensive checklists, but more importantly they provide an authoritative source of information security procedures that should be accepted by senior management.

The standards represent the starting point for the development and implementation of a security plan. They cover baseline security requirements and must be complemented with some form of risk analysis to determine those areas, if any, of sufficiently high risk that warrant additional protection.

The starting point should be an interpretation of the detailed sections to the environment of the organisation, or organisational department, under consideration. This is followed by a survey to report upon the current level of conformance with the agreed interpretation of the standards. Following submission of the report and recommendations to senior management a security plan is then developed. Subsequently the actions may comprise:

- implementation of recommendations to achieve agreed level of baseline security;
- conduct of a risk analysis study to determine any level of risks that cannot be contained by baseline security;
- enhancement of security plan to include the results and agreed recommendations of the risk analysis;
- implementation of risk analysis recommendations; and
- review and auditing of security plans.

5 ACKNOWLEDGEMENTS

This study was conducted under the auspices of the ARC Collaborative Research Grant: An Information Security Model for Finance and Banking Sector, Reference No.: C195301033.

6 REFERENCES

FIPS 65 (1979) *Guidelines for Automatic Data Processing Risk Analysis*, Springfield:National Technical Information Service.

Moses, R.H. and Glover, I. (1988) "The CCTA Risk Analysis and Management Methodology (CRAMM) - Risk Management Model". *Proc. First Int. Computer Security Risk Management Model Builders Workshop*, Denver, Colorado, 24-26 May 1988.

Department of Defense (1985) *Trusted Computer Systems Evaluation Criteria.*

CEC (1991) Commission of the European Communities. *Information Technology Security Evaluation Criteria (ITSEC)*, Provisional Harmonized Criteria, Version 1.2.

British Standards Institute (1995). *BS 7799: Code of Practice for Information Security Management.*

Standards Australia / Standards New Zealand (1995) *Draft Australian / New Zealand Standard: Information Security Management*, DR95305.

International Organization of Standardization (1995) ISO/IEC DIS 14980 *Information Technology - Code of Practice for Information Security Management.*
SMH Associate plc. (1995) CoP-iT™ *User Guide.*
Anderson, A., Kwok, L.F., and Longley, D. (1994) "Security Modelling for Organisations". *Proc. Second ACM Conf. on Computer and Communications Security*, CCS'94, Fairfax, Virginia, USA, 2-4 Nov 1994, ACM Press, 241-250.
Wood, C.C. (1996) *Information Security Policy,* Baseline Software.

7 BIOGRAPHY

Lam-for Kwok gained his degree in Computer Studies in 1983 and an M.Phil. in 1986. He is an Assistant Professor in the Department of Computer Science at City University of Hong Kong and is currently reading a PhD at Queensland University of Technology. His research interests is in information security modelling for organisations.

Professor Dennis Longley was Dean of Faculty of Information Technology and is now Director of Information Security Research Centre in the School of Data Communications at Queensland University of Technology. His main information security research interest is in the field of cryptographic key management for electronics funds transfer networks. He has performed consultancy studies in this field and is joint author of the books *Dictionary of Data and Computer Security* and *Information Security for Managers*.

8

Can Security Baselines replace Risk Analysis?

R. von Solms
Department of Information Technology
Port Elizabeth Technikon
Private Bag X6011
Port Elizabeth 6000
South Africa
Tel: +27 41 504 3604
Fax: +27 41 504 3313
email: rossouw @ml.petech.ac.za

Abstract

To protect the information systems of an organization an appropriate set of security controls need to be installed and managed properly. Many organizations that can afford it conduct either a risk analysis exercise themselves or outsource the process to some consultant. Through such an exercise, the most effective set of controls are recommended. Organizations that cannot afford a risk analysis exercise or cannot conduct it themselves, install controls on an ad hoc basis, with the result that many important business areas might be under protected and vice versa.

Security baselines have provided some guidelines to these organizations on which controls are, under general circumstances, the most effective to install to provide an acceptable level of protection. If an organization requires a higher level of protection in certain areas, a risk analysis can be conducted in those particular areas. As security baselines improve, the need for a further risk analysis will obviously decrease. Will a situation arise where security baselines are so extensive that no need exists for any further risk analysis exercise?

Keywords

Security controls, information security policy, risk analysis, security baselines

INTRODUCTION

Risk analysis has traditionally been the dominant technique to identify and assess risk levels within the various business areas in an organization. From this assessment, a set of security controls is proposed to provide adequate security within the different business areas. Unfortunately, this technique is quite complicated and resource intensive, with the result that many organizations do either nothing or bypass risk analysis and propose and implement security controls based on ad hoc thoughts. The result is that many high risk areas might be under protected or vice versa.

According to an information security breach survey (Information security breaches survey, 1996), most small to medium sized organizations do not perform a risk analysis. Possible reasons for this are; firstly, usually most small to medium sized organizations do not have the required expertise to conduct a proper risk analysis and cannot afford the services of a consultant and secondly, the awareness of information security is usually very low at these organizations.

A relative new development has been the establishment of information security baselines, an approach that suggests a minimum set of security controls that should be installed under most circumstances. Thus, any organization can obtain an accepted minimum level of protection that should be adequate under general conditions without going through an expensive risk analysis exercise. This is obviously not the ideal solution, but a lot better than ad hoc approach or doing nothing at all in connection with information security.

The question that will be addressed in the rest of this paper is, to what extent can the clever application of various security baselines, replace risk analysis to a large extent or probably completely.

THE RISK ANALYSIS APPROACH

Traditional risk analysis is based on a well-defined methodology (Guidelines for Information Security Management, 1996). This methodology basically includes the following steps. Firstly, a boundary is defined for delineating the analysis. All assets are then identified and grouped according to their physical location. Next, all possible threats and vulnerabilities are identified. For each of the threats, a possible rate of occupance is estimated and similar the potential impact is estimated for the loss of each asset. Based on these estimations, risk values are calculated and ordered in descending order. Security controls can now be recommended, based on the risk value and the associated cost. The 'best' controls can now be selected to provide the most cost effective solution. Thus, to determine the most effective set of security controls, a complete analysis is performed to identify and prioritize the various risk areas and to suggest controls to minimize these risks to acceptable levels.

Risk analysis is a very complex, resource intensive process. The main objective of any risk analysis exercise is to recommend a 'best' set of security controls to provide the most appropriate level of information security in the organization. If an organization can identify this set of security controls, using another technique, risk analysis can be abandoned.

THE SECURITY BASELINE APPROACH

Security baselines are a well-established concept that won a lot of ground lately. Baselines can be seen as a bottom-up approach, where a generic set of controls is defined for most organizations or business areas under normal circumstances. By installing these baseline controls, an organization can be sure that the most common and serious risks have been addressed adequately under normal, generic circumstances. It must be stressed clearly, that the objectives of security baselines are to provide a minimum level of security.

One of the problems associated with security baseline catalogues is the lack of guidance on which of the controls are applicable to the specific organization or business area under consideration. Such a set of baseline controls address the full information systems environment, from physical security through personnel and logical security. Many of these listed controls might not be applicable to a specific organization, because an organization does not operate in certain areas, for example, if an organization does not allow access to networks by third parties, those controls can be ignored. Baseline catalogues do not provide clear and definite guidelines on how to choose the applicable controls from the set of controls that will provide an acceptable level of security. This can be dangerous as an organization might decide to ignore some controls that were actually required. Traditionally, if an organization decided not to perform a risk analysis, no real acceptable alternative existed to suggest an acceptable set of security controls. Security baselines definitely provide this alternative to identify security controls that cover most risks satisfactory.

RISK ANALYSIS vs SECURITY BASELINES

Risk analysis is based on a very mathematically sound methodology and certainly the output of a detailed risk analysis exercise is the result of a very thorough process. But, notwithstanding the thoroughness of the methodology, many subjective decisions are made during a risk analysis exercise. For example, decisions must be made whether a threat is of small, medium or large intensity, or a scale of one to five is used to decide on the potential impact of a threat on an asset or group of assets. Thus, although the risk analysis methodology is very sound, the accuracy of the results can be queried, because of possible subjective input decisions into the process.

Many authors doubt the trustworthiness of a risk analysis exercise, because of this reason, for example (Jacobson, 1996), risk analysis is:

- tedious - many decisions to make and lots of data to collect;
- suspect - critics claim results are 'subjective';
- inconsistent - results cannot be repeated;
- useless - senior managers ignore the results;
- in short - painful.

On the other hand, most security baselines available today, are based on either some risk analysis exercise performed on a generic environment or alternatively on a general consensus reached between a number of organizations. Thus, by introducing any security baseline will provide nothing more than minimum protection under very general circumstances. Security baselines and risk analysis can supplement each other under certain circumstances. For example, if an organization, introducing some baseline set of controls, identifies any specific threat or an abnormal high potential impact if certain risks materialize, it is definitely advised that a risk analysis is performed in those business areas to ensure that these risks are assessed properly and to propose and implement more stringent controls to provide adequate protection in these high risk areas.

As seen from above, security baselines provide a minimum level of protection, and to provide further protection to some high risk areas or to ensure that some unique situations are covered, a risk analysis is recommended to cover the extraordinary situations, not covered by the baseline set of controls. Obviously, if security baselines cover more and more, previously unique, situations and/or certain high risk business areas, the need for a further risk analysis will decrease. The ultimate solution is obviously if all situations and high risk areas area included in some security baseline and an organization must merely choose the appropriate baseline or set of baselines.

VARIOUS LEVELS OF SECURITY BASELINES

Many different security baselines are already available to industry. Some baselines are devised for general, discipline independent organizations. Other baselines concentrate more on some specific disciplines. Further, some baselines not only suggest controls for minimum protection, but also for medium-level protection requirements.

One of the better known baselines is probably the Code of Practice for Information Security Management (Code of Practise, 1995). The Code of Practice addresses all types of organizations generically and only aims at minimum protection requirements. It is divided into ten categories, each including a number of proposed controls. Amongst these controls are ten *key* controls. These ten key controls will always, under all circumstances are applicable to all organizations and need to form part of the set of installed security controls in every organization. The rest of the controls also provide minimum level of protection, but might not always be applicable to every situation. An organization must determine themselves which of these non-key controls are applicable to their situation.

The German IT Baseline Protection Manual [IT Protection Manual, 1996) is a much more comprehensive document. The Baseline Protection Manual addresses low-level up to medium-level protection requirements. Unlike the Code of Practice, the Baseline Protection Manual provides guidance on how to determine specific protection requirements for an organization. It also suggests that if high or very high level of protection is required, a detailed risk analysis should be performed.

Some discipline specific security baselines are beginning to evolve, for example, a security baseline for the medical discipline has already been developed. Many of the environment specific risks, experienced in the medical world, are addressed with this set of baseline controls. Any hospital, for example, introducing this set of baseline controls will obviously cover much more risks, more adequately, than by introducing a general baseline, like the Code of Practice.

From these different approaches to baseline security, as discussed above, it can be concluded that security baselines do not provide only minimum security protection any more and further, with more environment or discipline specific baselines appearing, the need to perform a risk analysis, following the introduction of some applicable security baseline, will decrease. Only in really abnormal situations this might still be required.

HIERARCHICAL ORGANIZATION OF SECURITY BASELINES

Controls proposed in different security baselines cover different protection requirements. These requirements vary from the ten key controls in the Code of Practice, which is the absolute minimum that needs to be installed, to more general controls in the rest of the Code of Practice to controls providing medium-level protection. Discipline specific security baselines can also provide a further level of protection.

If all security baselines can be organized in a hierarchical structure, varying from absolute minimum protection, for example the key controls, to more stringent security requirements many new options arise. An organization can then determine which level of protection is required and if any discipline specific security requirements need to be addressed. Once these decisions have been made, the organization can merely work their way down the hierarchy until the required level of protection is obtained.

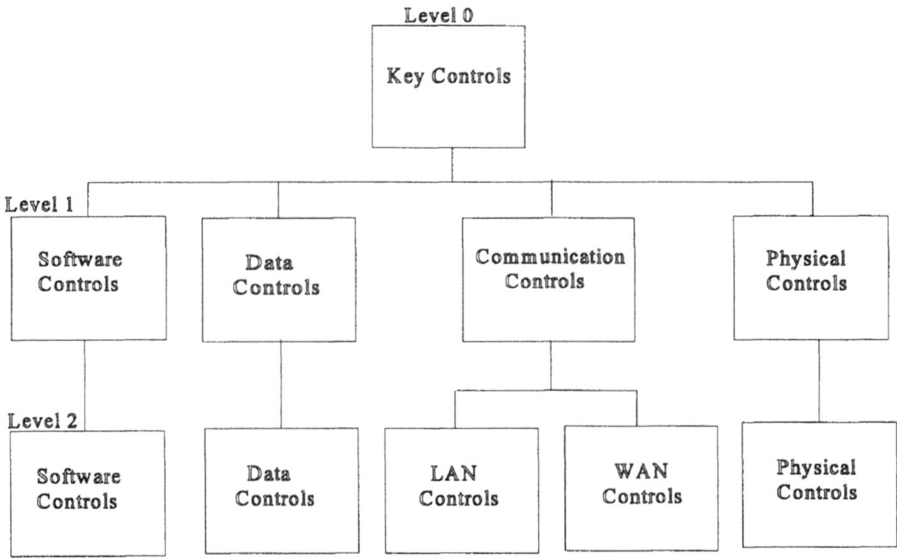

Figure 1 Hierarchical arrangement of security controls

Figure 1 represents an example of a baseline hierarchy, where the individual controls are grouped under the different categories to be protected.

To include discipline specific controls in the hierarchy, a further dimension can be added to the baseline hierarchy. At a certain level in the hierarchy, a specific area, e.g. physical, may provide various discipline specific alternatives. Figure 2 represents this further dimension graphically.

By integrating various, more stringent security baselines, higher levels of protection can be obtained without having to revert to a risk analysis exercise.

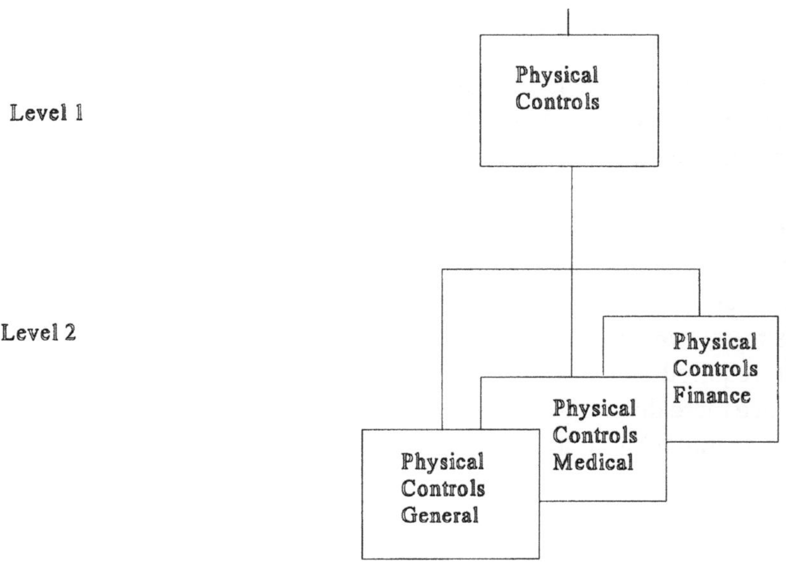

Figure 2 Discipline specific security controls

SEARCH TECHNIQUE THROUGH THE BASELINE HIERARCHY

As mentioned before, one of the shortcomings in most baseline catalogues is the fact that little guidance is given on which controls need to be selected and will be applicable in a specific situation. If baselines are ordered hierarchically, a definite technique will have to be established to guide the user through the various controls and to determine which controls are applicable and which ones not.

A high level analysis needs to determine which level of the baseline will be appropriate. This high level analysis must consider the business values of all IT systems and the risks from the organization's business point of view.

Once the appropriate level of a security baseline has been determined, a further selection or search technique needs to help the implementor to determine the appropriate controls recommended to obtain the predetermined level of security. Once these controls have been identified, the controls can be installed, managed and monitored.

CONCLUSION

All organizations are exposed to many different risks. These risks need to be controlled by the installation of appropriate security controls. To determine the most effective set of controls is not a straightforward exercise. Traditionally, these controls were suggested following a risk analysis exercise. Unfortunately, risk analysis is a very complex, resource intensive exercise and therefore many organizations choose not to perform such an exercise. This is specifically true in the case of small to medium sized organizations. The result is that organizations are either under protected or some ineffective controls are installed.

A security baseline consists of a set of controls that will provide an adequate level of security to most organizations against the general, most common risks. If an organization wishes to install a higher level of security in a specific, very sensitive or important area, a risk analysis can be preformed in that area to address the specific risk situations. As these baselines start to address higher levels of security as well and/or specific discipline environments, the needs for a further risk analysis will decreases. Ultimately, security baselines will be so effective that the need for any further risk analysis will disappear. One prerequisite to the effective implementation of such a technique, is the establishment of an effective search or selection mechanism that can help the user to select an appropriate level of security and the associate controls.

Certainly, such a bottom-up approach will not replace the traditional approach easily. The birth of security baselines has already motivated many more companies to implement security controls, because it is easy to determine which controls need to be installed to provide well-balanced protection. But the intelligent manipulation of security baselines may eliminate the complex, tedious, inconsistent risk analysis exercises completely.

REFERENCES

Code of Practice for Information Security Management (1995), BS 7799, BSi, UK.

IT Baseline Protection Manual (1996), BSI, Germany.

Guidelines for Information Security Management, Part 3 (1996); PDTR 13335-3, ISO/IEC JTC 1 SC27.

Jacobson R.V. (1996), CORA Cost-of-Risk Analysis, IFIP '96 WG 11.2, Samos, Greece.

The Information Security Breaches Survey 1996; NCC, dti, ICL & [UK]ITsec

BIOGRAPHY

Professor Rossouw von Solms is the head of the department of Information Technology at the Port Elizabeth Technikon since 1989.

Rossouw holds a PhD from the Rand Afrikaans University in Johannesburg. He is the author of many papers in international journals and have presented a number of papers at international and national conferences. A number of students have completed research qualifications in the area of information security under his leadership.

Rossouw is also the Chairman of Working Group 11.1 of the International Federation for Information Processing (IFIP), that deals with Information Security Management.

PART FOUR

Secure Group Communication

9

gGSS–API: a group enhanced generic security service

A.C.M. Hutchison
Data Network Architectures Laboratory,
University of Cape Town,
Private Bag, Rondebosch, ZA-7700 South Africa.
Telephone: +27 21 650 4058. Fax: +27 21 650 3726.
email: hutch@cs.uct.ac.za

Abstract

The Generic Security Service Application Programming Interface (GSS–API) offers a common interface to mechanism and protocol independent security. The contexts defined by GSS–API only support point-to-point interactions, and no support is provided for the interaction of multiple parties. This document describes *group* GSS–API (gGSS–API), an extension to support secure group contexts. As demonstration of one possible manner in which the group security features of such an extended API can be achieved, a sample protocol realization is outlined. Concerning deployment of gGSS–API, its use together with a secure IP multicast service is described as evidence that there are multiple ways in which, and layers at which, a group generic security service can be useful.

Keywords

Group security, GSS–API, generic security services

1 INTRODUCTION

Software supporting group interaction has received growing interest in recent years, and as commercial organizations have started embracing this technology so security for group applications has become a critical requirement. The Generic Security Service Application Programming Interface (GSS–API) (Linn, 1993; Linn, 1996) provides *contexts* as instances of secure communication. These contexts are currently limited to two-party interaction, taking no account of group scenarios. This paper proposes that these associations of GSS–API should be enhanced to enable group (multi-party) contexts, in addition to the two party contexts currently supported. Such an extension, to create a *group* GSS–API (or *g*GSS–API) would enable deployment of GSS–API in environments where secure group interaction is required.

In principle it would be possible to construct a co-ordinating layer on top of the existing GSS–API, to establish and maintain a secure meta-context amongst multiple parties. This adds an extra level of indirection, however, and does not provide an integrated solution.

A preferable approach, and that taken by gGSS-API, is to extend the existing GSS–API, allowing multiple parties to create group contexts with the same mechanism and protocol independence that the existing definition achieves.

Enabling group contexts in GSS–API requires several modifications to the API, and these are described. While mechanism independence is achieved, specific mechanisms (Hutchison and Bauknecht, 1996) can be used to achieve secure group contexts in the case where a shared group cryptographic key is established.

2 OVERVIEW OF GSS–API

Four design goals are outlined for GSS–API:

- **Mechanism independence**: The GSS–API defines only an *interface* to cryptographically implemented authentication and other security services. The definition is at a generic level and is independent of particular underlying mechanisms.
- **Protocol environment independence**: The GSS–API is independent of any protocol suites with which it is employed. This allows it to be used in a wide range of protocol environments.
- **Protocol association independence**: The GSS–API's security context is independent of communications protocol association constructs. This allows a single GSS–API implementation to be used by a variety of invoking protocol modules.
- **Suitability to a range of implementation placements**: GSS–API clients are not constrained to reside within any Trusted Computing Base (TCB) perimeter defined on a system where the GSS–API is implemented.

2.1 Credentials

A set of *credentials* is acquired by a particular application, and is used as a proof of identity for presentation to other processes. It is through the use of these credentials that a pair of communicating applications establishes a joint *security context*. A security context is described as a pair of GSS–API data structures that contain shared state information.

2.2 Tokens

To establish and maintain the shared information constituting a security context, certain GSS–API calls return a *token*. A token is a cryptographically protected, opaque data type. The responsibility for transferring tokens to a peer application is left with the caller of the GSS–API routine. Tokens can be distinguished as *context level tokens*, which are exchanged in order to establish and manage a security context between peers, and *per message tokens* which are exchanged (in conjunction with an established context) to provide protective security services for corresponding data messages. The transfer of tokens can be either *in-band* or *out-of-band* at the discretion of the GSS–API caller.

2.3 Stages of use

The presentation of credentials and tokens can be summarized with an exposition of their stages of use:

- *Credential acquirement* is the phase during which a set of GSS–API credentials is established.
- *Security context establishment* occurs between a pair of communicating applications making use of their credentials. Tokens are returned by GSS–API calls and these are exchanged. As part of the security context establishment, the context initiator is authenticated to the responder (and may require that the responder is authenticated).
- *Per message service invocation* occurs according to the security context, and may apply integrity and data origin authentication (through calls to *getMIC* and *verifyMIC* functions * at the sender and receiver, respectively) or confidentiality, integrity and data origin authentication (through calls to *wrap* and *unwrap* functions † at the sender and receiver, respectively).
- *Security context deletion* occurs at the completion of a communication session.

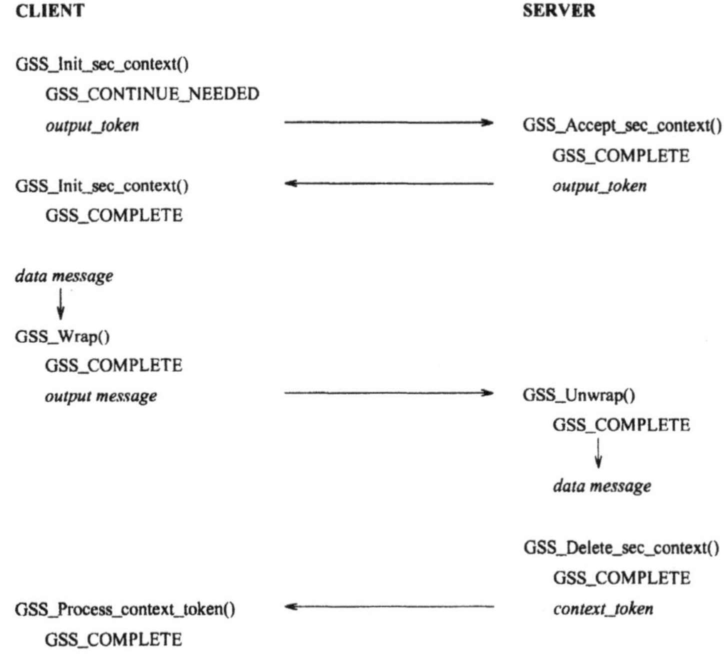

Figure 1 GSS–API example usage

*These are referred to as *sign* and *verify* functions in (Linn, 1993) but these terms are deprecated in current Internet Draft revisions (Linn, 1996).

†These are referred to as *seal* and *unseal* functions in (Linn, 1993) but these terms are deprecated in current Internet Draft revisions (Linn, 1996).

Figure 1 shows the calls which might occur between a client and a server to establish a security context and transfer wrapped messages between them. GSS–API C bindings are proposed in (Wray, 1993). Design of a management interface has was considered in (McDermott and Kamens, 1994), and functions **GSS_Add_Mechanism, GSS_Delete_Mechanism** and **GSS_Replace_Mechanism** have been advanced for the dynamic addition, deletion and replacement of new mechanisms by privileged users.

Figure 2 presents a GSS–API implementation of Kerberos-like (Steiner, Neuman and Schiller, 1988) authentication. This example is provided as a reference point for the subsequent discussion on how GSS–API can be extended for group protocols.

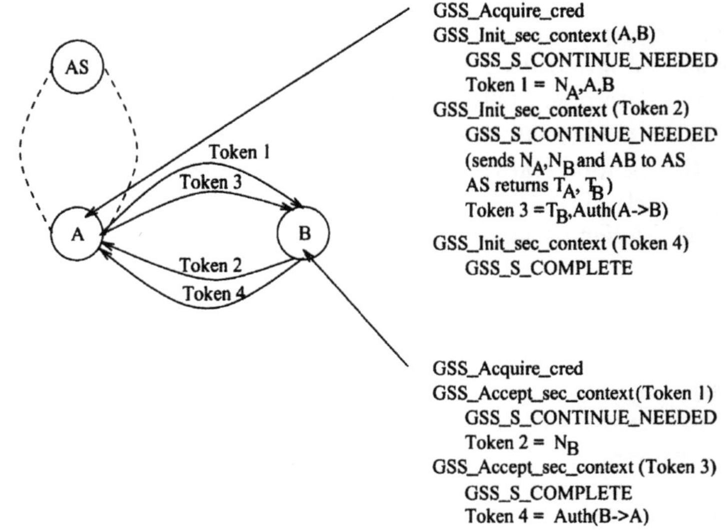

Figure 2 GSS–API implementation of Kerberos like authentication

3 gGSS-API: GROUP SUPPORT EXTENSIONS

In the context of group support, it is conceivable that the use of multicasting‡ would be the most attractive and efficient means of transferring tokens to n peer applications. But since one of the design goals identified was 'protocol association independence' the group solution should not necessarily make this assumption.

It is considered that in the context of extending GSS–API for group support it is still necessary to have an *originator*. In order to initiate a multiparty security context, one or more exchanges with each group member is required. The exact number and manner of exchanges between a group originator and group members is not prescribed by the API but in Section 3.3 one possible implementation is described.

By mapping the specifics of these techniques to gGSS–API tokens, and extending certain GSS–API functions to accommodate group contexts, a generic security service for groups can be achieved.

‡Whereby a single message is sent to a group of recipients, in the manner of a *selective broadcast*.

3.1 Changes to context level calls

In the following paragraphs specific changes required for the gGSS–API functions used to establish a security context are described.

Principal naming

When a multi-party security context is required, a means of listing the communicating parties in **GSS_Init_sec_context** is required. Similarly, it is necessary to return multiple tokens which also require identification. Returning tokens in an order corresponding to the principal naming allows the initiator to demarcate the tokens. Distribution of the returned tokens remains the responsibility of the calling process. The calling process is also responsible for collecting (multiple) reply tokens and submitting these to subsequent **GSS_Init_sec_context** calls.

Channel bindings

The **channel_bindings** used in two party communication can be extended in at least two ways. The first is to replace the **acceptor_address** with a group address, if an address such as Internet Class D [§] can be supplied. The second approach, in a non-multicast type environment, would be to provide a list of channel bindings associated with each of the supplied communication partner identities and in this manner to build specific channel information into each of the returned tokens. This can be achieved by creating a list of acceptor addresses (replacing the **gss_buffer_desc** type with with the **gss_OID_set_desc** type). This provides greater security than simply giving a single multicast group address, but requires more coordination and necessitates individual message delivery or the addition of per-member information into a multicast message.

3.2 Changes to per-message calls

The gGSS–API calls which are called on a per-message basis enable a sender to deliver a signed and/or 'wrapped' message to a receiver who is able to verify and/or 'unwrap' the message. The goal of the group extension concerning these calls, is that the functions should also provide security for messages destined for multiple recipients.

The invocation of **GSS_GetMIC** and **GSS_Wrap** is determined by the manner of group key which is applied. If a single group session key is being shared amongst the communication partners and a single signed or wrapped message is distributed to other parties then no changes to the parameters of the per-message calls are required. If different keys are used between different communication partners (which may be the case according to the implementation) then it may be necessary to accept a list of output messages from the **GSS_GetMIC** and **GSS_Wrap** routines with different messages bound for different recipients. No changes are required in the **GSS_VerifyMIC** and **GSS_Unwrap** routines since the manner of decoding is unaffected by the number of messages returned by the encoding functions.

Processing of **GSS_VerifyMIC** and **GSS_Unwrap** may be different in a group context, for example if a session key is encrypted with each recipient's public key then the

[§] Class D IP addresses are those with '1110' as their high-order four bits. In Internet 'dotted decimal' notation, host group addresses range from 224.0.0.0 to 239.255.255.255.

recipient has to be able to find the offset of the expression relevant to them in a list of expressions.

3.3 Group cryptographic keys and authentication

Having introduced an extended gGSS–API for the purpose of providing secure group contexts, we now turn to the actual realization of the additional group security features. The whole generic security service philosophy is that its use is implementation independent, but in proposing a new aspect of support (for groups) it is also important to demonstrate how an underlying implementation *could* be provided.

For secure group interaction, a set of group authentication protocols is necessary. An overview of such protocols is given in (Hutchison and Bauknecht, 1996). In particular, these protocols for secure group authentication and key distribution can be distinguished by *complete* or *selective* interaction amongst group members and can also be implemented using either *public/private key pairs*, if these are available, or a trusted third party¶ in the form of an *authentication server*. In a *complete* authentication interaction, each member of a group authenticates each other group member. *Selective* authentication refers to cases where interaction is with a single group custodian (or 'gatekeeper') only, or cases where a member joining a group authenticates with all existing members of the group (but these members do not authenticate one another again). Depending on the security requirements, different authentication models may apply. In subsequent discussion in this paper a complete group authentication is applied.

To conduct group authentication via gGSS–API there has to be a mapping from an authentication protocol to the gGSS–API tokens. We can use a complete group authentication protocol, based on the presence of an authentication server, to illustrate a mapping from protocol to tokens. The process of mapping such a group authentication protocol is analogous to the mapping of two-party Kerberos-like authentication which resulted in Figure 2.

Using the notation of:

- $\rightarrow$ to represent a unicast from one principal to another
- G to represent all members of the group
- AS to represent an *authentication server*
- N_X to represent a random number (nonce) generated by principal X
- T_X to represent a ticket (cryptographic token) for principal X and
- Auth(X $\longrightarrow$ Y) to represent a token containing information by which principal X can authenticate itself to principal Y‖

we can generalize a complete group authentication and key distribution protocol as consisting of the following rounds:

¶Or more precisely '$(n+1)$–th party' with n participants.

‖Description of the complete structure of the tickets and authenticator tokens is beyond the scope of this paper.

1. $A \rightarrow X:$	N_A, G	$(\forall X \in (G - \{A\}))$
2. $X \rightarrow A:$	N_X	$(\forall X \in (G - \{A\}))$
3. $A \rightarrow AS:$	N_X, G	$(\forall X \in G)$
4. $AS \rightarrow A:$	T_X	$(\forall X \in G)$
5. $A \rightarrow X:$	$T_X, Auth(A \rightarrow X), N_Y$	$(\forall X \in (G - \{A\}), \forall Y \in (G - \{A, X\}))$
6. $X \rightarrow A:$	$Auth(X \rightarrow Y)$	$(\forall X \in (G - \{A\}), \forall Y \in (G - \{X\}))$
7. $A \rightarrow X:$	$Auth(Y \rightarrow X)$	$(\forall X \in (G - \{A\}), \forall Y \in (G - \{X, A\}))$

In Figure 3 a mapping of this ***initiator coordinated complete group authentication*** protocol to a gGSS-API type implementation is shown. The gGSS-API calls of A (coordinator) and B (group member) are shown. The calls of C and D are analogous to those of B. The token contents are given as an indication of how the rounds of a protocol such as that above can be realized in a gGSS-API context.

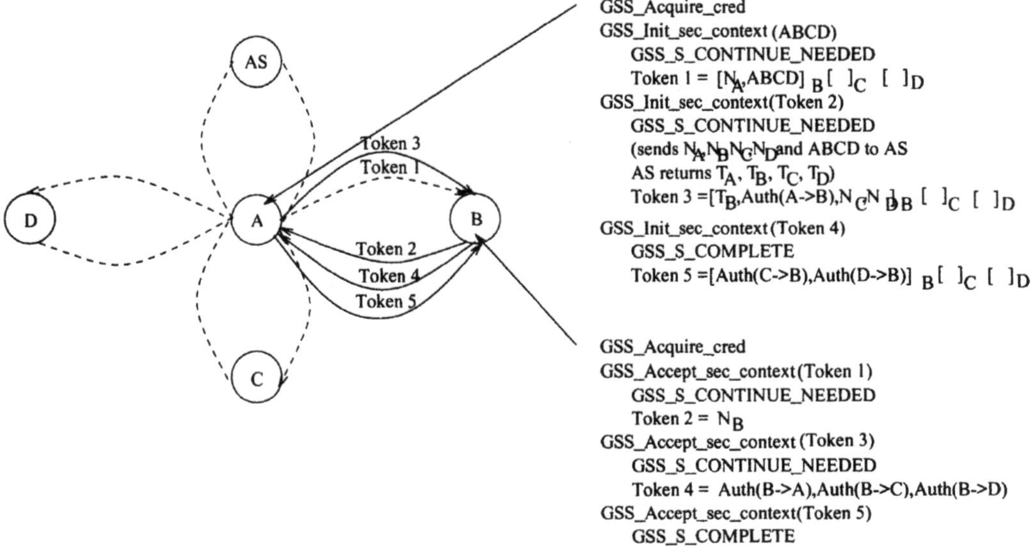

Figure 3 gGSS-API calls in establishing a group context

4 gGSS-API DEPLOYMENT: SECURE IP MULTICAST

At the start of this paper it was implied that (group) security is typically implemented at the *application* level. To demonstrate that gGSS-API can be deployed to complement lower layer security deployment, its use together with a secure IP multicast is described here.

IP multicast allows point-to-multipoint communication via a Class D multicast address which identifies a destination group. Figure 4 shows a conceptual layering together with

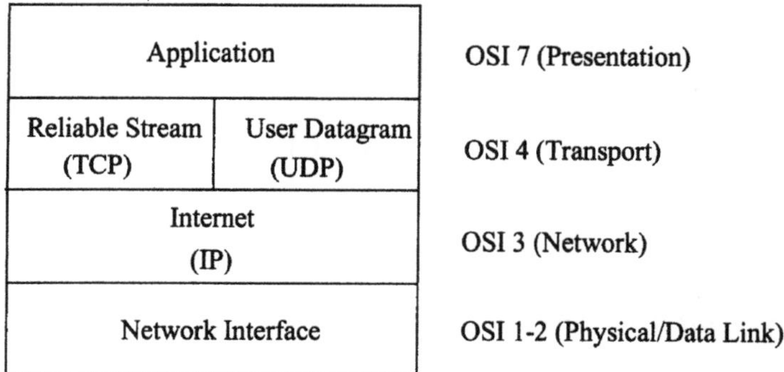

Figure 4 Conceptual communication layering

associated OSI layers (Comer, 1992): a *secure* IP multicast suggests that at the IP layer, multicast (and unicast) IP messages can be processed to achieve confidentiality, integrity, replay detection, etc. according to a caller-specified *quality of protection* (QoP).

The advantage of providing security mechanisms at the IP level is that it is then not necessary for each application requiring secure communication to go about implementing this. The desire for and appropriateness of security being implemented at this level has been advocated in discussions of IPng (Bellovin, 1994) and also in (Cheng, Garay, Herzberg and Krawczyk, 1995) where it is argued that the IP layer is an appropriate place to secure data since the secrecy and integrity of data can be protected in an internetwork environment without affecting higher-layer protocols and applications. Another argument in favor of security at the IP level is that IP headers can be protected using cryptographic techniques with the result that packet filtering can be done based on authentic information (which is very useful for Internet firewalls).

For an IP level secure multicast group implementation, one or more cryptographic keys would be provided to the multicast service by the calling application. Key origination and distribution are typically outside the scope of a secure IP multicast mechanism *but* a library like gGSS-API complements IP level security by allowing groups of application level processes to establish group keys which can then be used in conjunction with a secure IP multicast.

The approach taken is that the key(s) is/are provided to the IP service interface, together with an indication of the QoP desired. According to the QoP requested, packets emanating from the host to the group addressed will be secured using one of the group keys provided. Similarly, packets received from a particular group will be processed in accordance with the required QoP.

Figure 5 shows the interaction of a secure IP multicast and gGSS-API, and how they can be integrated to provide application programmers with a secure environment which requires very little effort on their part if the IP multicast can be secured using the cryptographic keys which multicast group members hold. The gGSS-API is used amongst the processes $P_1, P_2, \ldots, P_n$ to authenticate each other and distribute one or more group keys (represented by K_G) which is/are then passed to the secure IP multicast layer allowing the IP module to perform the security processing function on packets leaving from and arriving at process sockets.

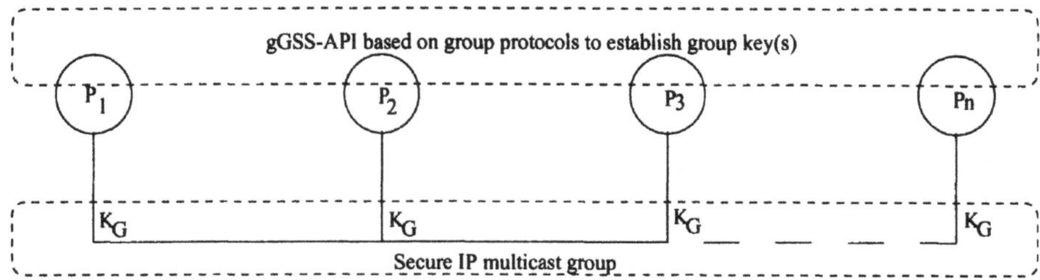

Figure 5 Interaction of gGSS-API and secure IP multicast

The steps which an application program goes through to implement this integrated solution to the problem of secure group communication are the following:

- Call gGSS-API to perform authenticated key distribution. This results in all processes holding the group key(s).
- Initialize socket communication for multicast.
- Initialize socket communication for secure multicast. This includes the provision of quality of protection parameters.
- Perform group multicast communication using the usual UDP **sendto** and **recvfrom** functions for IP multicast.

This example of gGSS-API deployment shows that in addition to native usefulness at the application layer, a group generic security service can be used when group authentication and key distribution are conducted at a higher layer. In this model group cryptographic information is passed to lower layers where support for a service like secure IP multicast is provided.

5 CONCLUSION

GSS-API is a well defined, mechanism and protocol independent, solution to key distribution and authentication problems. The use of GSS-API is good for application developers since the actual realization of the GSS-API can be substituted transparently. gGSS-API, an extension of GSS-API to provide group support, enables n communicating parties to manage secure interaction. While introducing group functionality, it still retains support for all the usual two-party features of the original GSS-API and so is backwards compatible.

gGSS-API achieves the same goal that the security service achieved for two party interaction: freeing the application developer from having to do a security implementation and neatly abstracting the security processing – requiring only that applications transfer opaque tokens. The 'add-on' that gGSS-API provides, is that group support is provided and this is seen as increasingly important with the growing entrenchment of groupware and CSCW type applications. The interaction of gGSS-API with a secure IP multicast was described as an example of gGSS-API deployment spanning conceptual security implementation layers: its usefulness is not limited to the application layer.

Current work comprises implementation of a prototype library which provides a realization of the proposed group support. Consideration is also being given to whether gGSS–API could be used in a Java-like context to provide security for groups of applets interacting to provide CSCW type functionality.

6 REFERENCES

Bellovin, S. (1994) RFC1675: Security Concerns for IPng. *AT&T Bell Laboratories*

Cheng, P-C., Garay, J., Herzberg, A. and Krawczyk, H. (1995) Design and Implementation of Modular Key Management Protocol and IP Secure Tunnel on AIX. *Proceedings of the 5th USENIX UNIX Security Conference, Salt Lake City, Utah.*

Comer, D.E. (1992) Internetworking with TCP/IP: Principles, Protocols and Architecture. Prentice-Hall, Englewood Cliffs, New Jersey, 1992.

Hutchison, A. and Bauknecht, K. (1996) Cryptographic Key Distribution and Authentication Protocols for Secure Group Communication. *Proceedings of the Twelfth International Information Security Conference (IFIP/SEC '96), Samos, Greece*

Linn, J. (1993) RFC1508: Generic Security Service Application Program Interface. *Geer Zolot Associates.*

Linn, J. (1996) Generic Security Service Application Program Interface, Version 2. Internet Draft Document <draft-ietf-cat-gssv2-08.txt> (Work in Progress). *Open Vision.*

McDermott, E. Kamens, J. (1994) GSS–API Extensions for Multi-Mechanism Support. *Draft Document.*

Steiner, J., Neuman, C. and Schiller, J. (1988) Kerberos: An Authentication Service for Open Network Systems. *Proceedings of USENIX Winter Conference.*

Wray, J. (1993) RFC1509: Generic Security Service API: C-bindings. *Digital Equipment Corporation.*

7 BIOGRAPHY

Andrew Hutchison obtained an MSc in Computer Science from the University of Cape Town, South Africa in 1991, and a PhD in Computer Science from the University of Zürich, Switzerland in 1996. While studying in Switzerland he worked at the IBM Zürich Research Laboratory. He is currently a Senior Lecturer in the Department of Computer Science at the University of Cape Town. His research interests include computer networks, network security and performance evaluation.

PART FIVE

Secure Commercial Systems (I)

10

Electronic Document Exchange in Sweden — the legal aspects

Per Furberg
Associate Judge of Appeal
Pl. 9205
S-444 97 Svenshögen, SWEDEN
Phone/Fax +46 303 77 55 54
Mobile tel +46 10 206 25 32
E-mail per.furberg@mailbox.swipnet.se

Abstract

The legal issues which have arisen due to computer based handling of documents may be addressed by following the examples provided by the international standardisation of digital signatures and related services. A generally accepted definition of a digital document should be elaborated, founded upon the underlying legal principles and basic technical routines of electronic information handling. By these means questions concerning legal obstacles may be replaced by the creation of a legally unified regulation of traditional routines and IT-routines, with security maintained.

Keywords

Electronic record, digital document, legal aspects, public administration, electronic commerce.

1 INTRODUCTION

Swedish public administration and businesslife are extensively computerised. The main body of legislation in this area comes however from the 70's, when for example the Swedish Data Act and provisions in the Swedish constitution concerning public electronic records were introduced.

The Swedish Administrative Procedure Act has in the 80's been designed to provide legal principles applicable to both paper-based and electronic handling of cases.

However, the legislation reflects a view of computers and databases originating from a different technical culture. The many special cases, with different technical solutions for different sectors of public administration, has led to extensive laws and regulations that are inconsistent with the general approach.

2 DIGITAL DOCUMENTS

2.1 Documents in the public administration

2.1.1 The Swedish approach

In 1989 the Swedish work in the area of *electronic records with digital signatures* began with the establishing of a committee whose task it was to suggest new regulations for customs procedures.[1] They then observed the possibility of:

— linking the legal efforts to the principles behind the international standardisation of digital signatures and related services,

— creating a base for the legally *unified regulation* of paper-based and electronic routines.[2]

These questions have been further analysed in other areas such as criminal law (document forgery), taxation law (electronic tax returns), electronic mortgages, and eventually the totally electronic handling of cases and proceedings.

In the following I will introduce the Swedish approach, by giving a short presentation of the substantive problems from a legal point of view, created by computer based handling of documents. Then I will describe Swedish laws and bills concerning documents with digital signatures. In conclusion, a description will be provided of the task of *seeking general legal concepts* for digital documents and electronic files, a subject that contains EDI as well as E-mail and transfer of electronic files.

2.1.2 Substantive problems

The use of documents in public administration is — from a legal perspective — mainly constructed on the same notion of "document" as the protection in criminal law against document forgery. The concept document, in administrative as well as criminal law, is built on presumptions that a traditional document obviously possesses certain qualities. These qualities makes it needless to discuss some security aspects, that legal demands are built on. However, these qualities are partly missing in digital documents.

The *paper document* consists of three aspects:

— the carrier (the sheet of paper)

— text and pictures (the physical representation of the information)

— information about the originator (usually a written signature).

The connections among carrier, text and signature are self-evident. The carrier gives border-lines and structure to one finalised representation of the content. However, these qualities are partly missing in an digital document, where all information is broken down to a pattern of digital signals. It is important to address the legal problems that these new objects confer to the notion "document".

I will briefly mention the following aspects:

It is an implicit qualification within the document that it shall give *self-dependent existence* to the information, and via its physical bounds provide a clear distinction from other objects. Data representing a particular digital document, however, is stored together with data representing other information.

One additional demand is the *durability* of a document. The transportation of data via the telecommunication infrastructure or transitory text upon a computer screen will hardly fulfil these demands.

The need for *trust in the authenticity* of a document is central. The document shall give the reader reason to believe that the text originates from the individual who, according to the record, is seen to be the originator. Therefore a traditional document, as carrier of the information, is often furnished with stamps, printed logotypes, attestation of signatures etc., enabling the *examination* of a paper document to find out *if it has been manipulated.*

Until recently most methods used to produce the equivalent functionalities in electronic handling of documents relied on the system being regarded as a secure domain. The users were identified during some log-in procedure. From a legal perspective, however, this provides an unacceptable level of security, leading to the development of new methods for creating digital documents with digital signatures.

However, the function of a paper document to transmit authority as a physical example — an original — can not be recreated digitally in a simple way. Certain applications, such as shipping documents, demand some form of registration in the IT-environment (confer the functionalities within the EU-project Bolero).

The discussed "document problem" leads to the delineation of the term "data". The word data, by concentrating on the representation, has — according to international standardisation — been given a concrete meaning while information is seen as something abstract, namely knowledge.

The difficulty in understanding the nature of data depends on the fact that we are moving in the borderland between concrete and abstract objects, where some of the self-evident presumptions that a traditional viewpoint is built upon do not exist. This confers to the "document problem" new dimensions.[3]

There may be different methods available to solve the legal problems in this area. The Swedish approach, however, has in principle been to follow the example from the international standardisation of digital signatures and related services. The legal system should in this way be capable of supporting adjustments towards a more secure IT-milieu.

2.1.3 The Swedish customs act and succeeding legislation

A basic assumption for the Swedish legislator has been that the digital document needs to provide the same evidence as a paper document, and must be able to be linked to a specified originator. Therefore, the password method was not accepted. A document definition was constructed instead, which was centred on the need for verification of the documents themselves.

It was not appropriate to lay a detailed technical description as a foundation for the construction of the rules since new security methods in accordance with technical advances might arise. The legislation should instead be tied into the developmental work which is continuing for electronic authentication. Therefore the phrase "electronic document" was introduced in the Swedish Customs Act of 1990, and defined as *"a record, the content and originator of which, should be able to be verified by a certain technical procedure."*[4]

The same document definition has been adopted
— in 1993 in a law concerning the registration of mortgages,
— in 1995 in taxation law, and
— in 1995 in the regulations concerning recovery of debt by enforcement orders.[5]

2.1.4 Swedish bills

These problems have been analysed, also from criminal and procedural viewpoints, by *a Swedish governmental committee on computer related crime*. In a report from December 1992[6] the committee has suggested a unified regulation for traditional documents and digital documents with regards to document forgery, according to the Penal Code. The following definition has been suggested: *"By document in this chapter is meant [a written original record or] a defined set of data for automatic information processing, if it is possible to ascertain that the contents originate from the designated issuer."*[7]

This Bill is under consideration in the Ministry of Justice. The demand for authentication according to the definition implies that there shall be a technical procedure providing for the possibility of verification of both the text and the issuer.

The Swedish government established in 1994 *the IT-committee,* whose task was to consider suggestions for the legal redefinition's that are necessitated by the replacement of traditional and established routines of document transmittal and verification by digital documents and services. In March 1996 the committee presented its report Electronic Documents.[8] One of the main features of the committees' findings were the following definitions;

> *electronic record:* a defined set of data, which can be viewed, listened to or otherwise apprehended only by electronic means,
> *digital document:* an electronic record with a digital signature or a digital stamp,
> *digital signature:* the result of a transformation of an electronic record, by means of a unique key, making it possible to ascertain if the contents originate from the individual designated as issuer,
> *digital stamp:* the result of a transformation of an electronic record, by means of a unique key, making it possible to ascertain if the contents originate from the legal person or authority designated as issuer.[9]

2.1.5 Natural legal solutions

The aforementioned definitions of "document" are built on the same concept, and with this kind of definition it has been natural to solve the various legal questions that arise on the basis of the rules which are already established for paper documents. Questions concerning legal difficulties which arise from digital documents and signatures are thereby replaced by the possibility of creating a legally unified regulation of traditional routines and IT-routines. The functions of a paper document are then replicated within the framework of useful applications of a digital signature, with security maintained and without the general principles of legal procedure being affected.

The attainment of a sufficient level of security has been judged as being primarily a technical problem, with the presuppositions that both the contents and the originator should be possible to be verified, as when the demands of a digital signature according to international standards are fulfilled.

2.1.6 Requirements of hand-written signature or the like

The IT-committee also addresses certain practical questions arising from a legal viewpoint due to the rapid transition to electronic document handling. A relevant act, in a case involving legal procedures, may prescribe something which precludes the usage of electronic documents, such as the requirement of a hand-written signature. The committee recommends that the government be allowed to stipulate that digital documents (or, if that is deemed to be sufficient, electronic records without a digital signature or stamp) may be used.

Also recommended is the right of agencies to require confirmation by the originator when a message lacks the originator's hand-written signature, as well as to commission a third party — when needed — for the technical conversion of electronic messages so that they may be read or otherwise comprehended.

2.1.7 Incoming documents

Furthermore, the committee has suggested new provisions concerning the establishment of the point in time when incoming electronic records are deemed to have been received by an agency. In a traditional environment, a document is deemed to have been received by an agency the day upon which the document is delivered to the agency. This rule may also be applied when a diskette is mailed via the postal service to an agency.

In those cases where messages are transmitted via an electronic network, the principle applied is that the document is deemed to have been received by the agency when the data which represents the document have reached the agency's mail-receiving function. This is seen as being applicable whether this receiving function is physically located in the agency's information system or has been relegated to a mediating company which furnishes a service in which the "mailbox" is physically located on the mediating company's premises. These provisions are complemented by certain stipulated exceptions which primarily correspond to current legal practice.

> A document that is transmitted electronically is deemed to have arrived to an agency that day when the document
> 1. has arrived at the agencies electronic address,
> 2. has been received by a qualified employee, or
> 3. may be assumed to have arrived at the agencies electronic address, if it has come into the hands of a qualified employee on the following working day.

2.2 Documents in business life

2.2.1 New patterns of commerce

Similar questions occur within civil law concerning the creation of security in contract formulation, etc. However, IT has not been limited to the conversion of traditional routines to their electronic equivalents. Instead, the entire pattern of commerce is transformed, and the focus of change becomes automatic *processes*, rather than *products* such as bids, contracts, invoices, bills of lading, etc.

An example of this is the concept "Business Process Reengineering", where even such demands that have been perceived as obvious from a legal point of view may be questioned. Striving to utilise the entire potential for rationalisation that IT offers has led to a balancing between effectivity and security that, in some cases, may need to be re-evaluated.

2.2.2 *EDI-agreements*

The private sector has attempted to solve the legal questions that arise by constructing model contracts on how contracts should be entered into, such as the so-called EDI agreements. Among other things, these contracts deal with questions that arise when involved parties enter into agreements automatically, i.e. when computers generate and transmit messages that result in a binding agreement.

Electronic commerce will most likely, at least in certain areas, attain such dimensions that it will hardly be possible to initiate and preserve written EDI agreements with every business associate. Therefore, there is a need for a functioning legal structure even within civil law concerning the creation of predictable and secure information in electronic contract formulations.

2.2.3 *The IT-committees' findings*[10]

The committee has nevertheless found that most of the questions that arise may be answered within the framework of current contractual law. Not every detailed question can be answered in advance, but contract law is formulated at a general level and is limited to basic principles which are appropriate for agreements of varying type. Questions that do not directly fit under any of the prevailing regulations should still be able to be dealt with in close relation to the principles upon which contract law is based.

Regarding the question of whether or not electronic manifestations of a party's "will", generated automatically without direct human involvement, can result in binding contracts, a parallel can be drawn with such traditional "mass" transactions that occur frequently and in large volume in daily practice. Typical contracts that fall into this group are such things as small, simple purchases in stores or a bus trip paid in cash. It may also be cited from Swedish jurisprudence that a contract regarding parking is deemed to be entered into by simply placing the car in a parking place.

In a similar manner, the individual that electronically and automatically makes an offer or an acceptance is bound by the offer or reply. The purpose of the entire procedure is to create binding agreements when certain exterior circumstances combined with one another function as the direct establishment of a contract. The legal text is sufficiently accommodating to allow a non-prejudicial application of contract law, while at the same time avoiding a new construction that departs from traditional civil law.

However, certain provisions in contract law lose their purpose when contracts are entered into completely automatically. These are the provisions that presuppose human behaviour patterns, such as those dealing with coercion, deceit and usury. A computer, for example, cannot threaten another computer. However, this does not necessitate any amendments in contract law since irrational results may be corrected through the so-called general clause, which is completely free from subjectivity.

Also in other areas current contract law should be applicable to the IT area. For example, this is true concerning provisions regarding liability because a transmitted message is delayed or never received, as well as provisions dealing with "written" and "oral" communication.

The committee suggests, however, an amendment in contract law concerning the question of who is liable when an electronic message has been corrupted during transmission. A complementary addition to the current provisions concerning assignment of risk due to the delay or disappearance of a message is recommended. This provision should also be applicable when a message is corrupted during transmission to the receiver (Section 40 of the Contract Law). The Contract Law will then correspond to the present Law of Contract of Sale of Goods, which came into force in 1990.

3 CLOSING LINES

The legal problems concerning computerbased documents are of a general kind and exist in all countries. The character of these objects needs to be examined and legal definitions expanded to include the new dimensions in the field of IT. To preserve a traditional point of view that is partly antiquated will lead to differences in praxis between traditional and digital documents that are hard to understand. It would also most likely hinder an effective regulation.

Primarily, a discussion of whether or not a uniform definition is possible should be considered. A generally accepted document definition, founded in the basic principles of electronic handling of information, would most likely facilitate international harmonisation in this area. Secondly, the possibility of finding a uniform view on the category of objects needs addressing.

As a starting point, the same principle point of view could be adopted concerning paper documents and computer data. Further analysis of the new infrastructure will however probably show a need for adjustments to IT. In this area it is important to address the connection between digital signatures and general improvements of information security as well as consistency with the legal system.

---

[1] The governmental committee with the task to consider the need for legislation in customs computerisation (TDL-utredningen).

[2] See also the aforementioned committees report SOU 1989:20 (SOU is Statens offentliga utredningar; the Governmental Committee Reports).

[3] This Swedish description may be found in the Green Book of Information Security and in the Council of Europe Recommendation Concerning Problems of Criminal Procedure Law Connected with Information Technology, adopted by the Committee of Ministers on September 11, 1995.

[4] Proposition 1989/90:40 p. 4, 27 f. and 50 (proposition means in this instance the governmental bill containing the motivation for the legislation).

[5] Prop. 1993/94:197, prop. 1994/95:93 and prop. 1994/95:168.

[6] SOU 1992:110.

[7] SOU 1992:110 p. 22.

[8] SOU 1996:40.

[9] SOU 1996:40 p. 39.

[10] SOU 1996:40 p. 117-138. These report has also been discussed on the 34:th Nordic Assembly of Lawyers, Stockholm, August 21-23, 1996.

PART SIX

Tools for Intrustion Detection

11

An attack detection system for secure computer systems - Outline of the solution

Ioanna Kantzavelou[1] *and Sokratis K. Katsikas*[2]

[1] *Department of Informatics,*
Technological Educational Institution (T.E.I) of Athens,
Ag. Spiridonos St., Aegaleo, Athens 12210, Greece
tel.: +30-1-6437918, fax: +30-1-6437918
e-mail: ioanna@hol.gr

[2]*Department of Mathematics,*
University of the Aegean,
Karlovassi 83200, Samos, Greece
tel.: +30-273-35482, fax: +30-273-35483
e-mail: ska@aegean.gr

Abstract

The spread of distributed information technology has increased the number of opportunities for crime and fraud in computer systems. Despite the fact that computer systems are typically protected by a number of security mechanisms, attacks continue to occur. In addition, it seems infeasible to close all the known security loopholes of today's systems. No combination of technologies can prevent legitimate users from abusing their authority in a system. Thus, new lines of defence are required to ensure safe operation of computer systems as well as data protection. Attack Detection Systems are an approach to enhancing the security of a computer system. The Attack Detection System (ADS) which is the subject of this paper, is a real-time attack detection system which allocates points to users who are attempting to attack the target system, detects attacks by examining the number of points each user has been given, and takes countermeasures according to this number of points. The outline of the solution that implements the ADS is described in detail in this paper.

Keywords

Attack Detection, Event Analysis, Security Relevant Events, Security Relevant Errors, Risk Levels.

1 INTRODUCTION

In the last few years, many organisations have adopted the use of *auditing systems*. Auditing systems capture all events that occur on a computer system, and keep logs of the audit data in special files for security analysis. In the beginning, the analysis of log files was carried out by the security officer of the system, who had to search all the printed audit data to detect security violations. The large volume of data made this difficult. The need for tools for automated security analysis of audit data became evident. Such a system is called an *attack* (or *intrusion) detection system* and must have the following goals: to provide a trail of computer system events; to determine how the system was breached; to determine who was responsible for a breach; and to take action to prevent further breaches.

In conclusion, there is a need for an attack detection system that can provide protection to a computer system by detecting security violations in real-time. Therefore, the problem to be solved was defined as stated in the next paragraph.

1.1 Problem Definition

The overall goal of the work carried out was to provide a real-time attack detection system which will detect attacks on a computer system and will instruct the computer system to take action to prevent further security violations.

The problem to be solved was the design and implementation of a real-time attack detection system for secure computer systems which could: monitor all events that occur on a computer system, log the events, analyse each event in order to determine whether it is of potential relevance from a security point of view, store the security relevant events separately, examine security relevant events against rules stored in a rule base, decide (in real-time) if an attack is taking place, send a signal to inform the security officer of a system when an attack occurs, and finally take action to prevent further attacks.

These requirements define the problem that was solved by the implementation of the Attack Detection System. The next paragraph presents the essential results of this implementation.

1.2 Results

An attack detection system for secure computer systems, called the *Attack Detection System* (ADS), has been implemented. This system is a real-time rule-based system which provides an audit trail for all computer system events, detects attacks by analysing audit data, and takes measures to prevent additional attacks when an attack occurs.

This attack detection system uses a novel method for detecting attacks, the *point allocation method* (Kantzavelou 1996). According to this method, the ADS allocates points to users who are attempting to attack a computer system. Based on these points, the ADS takes countermeasures to protect the computer system.

Furthermore, the Attack Detection System is modifiable. This allows the administrator of the attack detection system to improve its effectiveness. The concept of the Attack Detection System is described in the next paragraph.

1.3 The Concept of the Attack Detection System (ADS)

The Attack Detection System (ADS) which is the subject of this paper aims at providing enhanced security in a computer system called the *target system*. The ADS carries out the main functions described below in order to fulfil its goal. Figure 1 depicts these functions and the inter-function communication within the ADS (Kantzavelou 1994). The ADS modules are discussed extensively in (Kantzavelou 1996).

Event Collection

The Attack Detection System monitors all target system activities called *events*, and logs these events in a data base called *Event Data Base* (EDB). Furthermore, it examines each event in order to filter the events which are of potential relevance from a security point of view.

Attack Detection

Analysis of the audit records and detection of attacks in real-time. The ADS applies a rule-based technique to detect attacks, which implies the use of a rule base called *Rule Base* (RB). When the ADS detects that a user is acting suspiciously, it counteracts by automatically deciding upon an action and instructing the target system to take this action.

Attack Detection System Access

The ADS informs the Security Officer (SO) of the target system about attacks detected and suspicious users. It also gives to the SO a picture of all events that have occurred on the target system.

Rule Base Access

This function allows the administrator of the ADS to modify the Rule Base in order to adjust the ADS to the target system.

Event Data Base Maintenance

The ADS provides this special function to maintain the Event Data Base (EDB) which is the collection of the audit data files. In particular, the purpose of this function is to retrieve and store records in the EDB.

Rule Base Maintenance

The ADS provides also a function to maintain the Rule Base (RB) which consists of rules. In particular, this function retrieves, stores, updates, and deletes records from the RB.

2 OUTLINE OF THE SOLUTION

The Attack Detection System is a rule-based system (Kantzavelou 1994). In particular, a rule base has been defined to characterise the state of audit data which constitutes an attack. The method of the examination of audit data is an important part of the design of this system. This section is divided into two parts to describe two methods of examination of audit data: the *examination of commands* and the *examination of service points*. It also gives reasons why the second method has been chosen as the most appropriate for the design and implementation of the Attack Detection System.

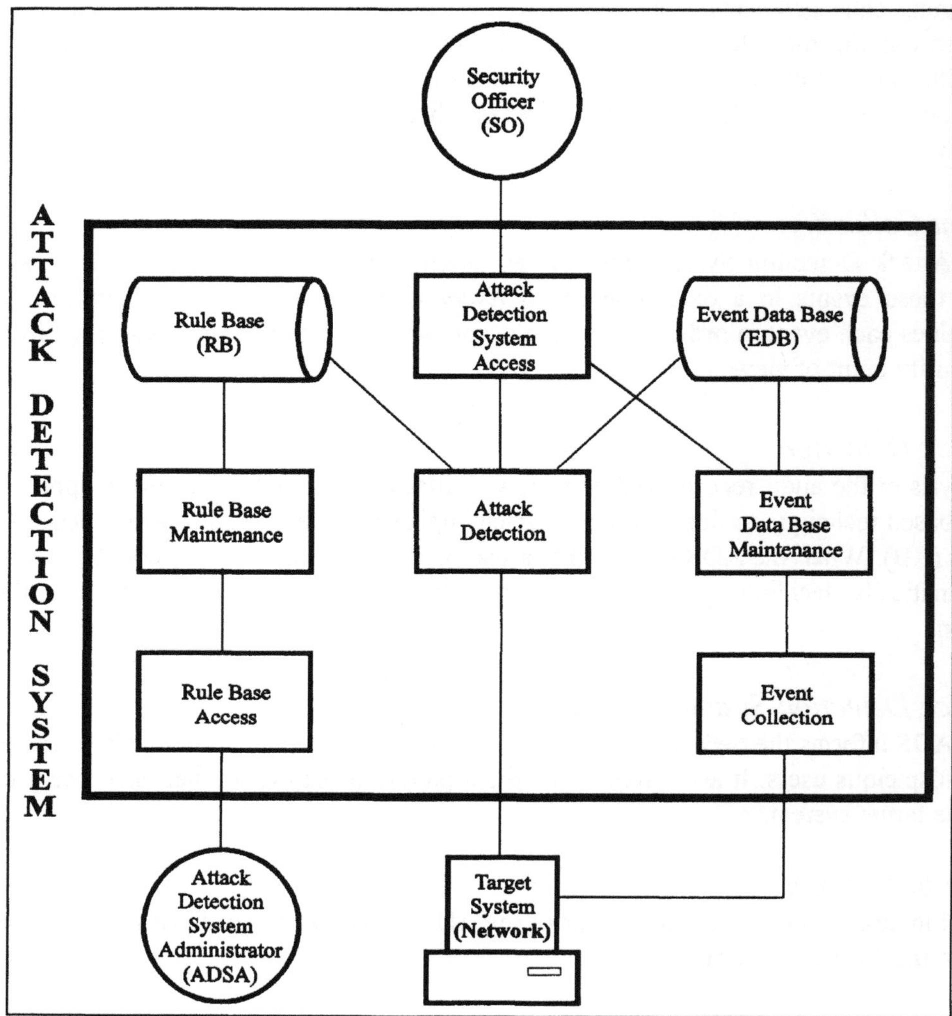

Figure 1: The Main Functions of the Attack Detection System

2.1 Examination of Commands

When a user requests the execution of a command (or a program) from the Target System (e.g. a UNIX[1] -based system), the Event Reception Module collects data about this activity and stores it in the Event Data Base. The key information of each collected activity is the command line which shows the actual event that took place on the Target System and its results. Therefore, a possible method for the examination of audit data would be analysis of the syntax of each command a user types. An approach to implement this method might be the following:

[1] UNIX is a trademark of AT&T Bell Laboratories

- The Event Data Base will include the command line and the status of its execution, as well as information about the user such as his login name, his host machine name, the date and the time of his activity, etc. An example of an Event Data Base record could be the following:

date	time	user	tty	host	command	status
27/4/93	18:26:35	ioanna	tty0	hobbes	cat > /myfile	Permission denied

- According to the above example, user *ioanna* attempted the creation of a file which failed because the user had no write permission for the accessed directory. The reason of the command failure is indicated by the *status* field.
- The Rule Base will consist of sets of rules. Each set of rules will refer to one command type and will include as many rules as there are possible syntaxes and status of this command. An example of the Rule Base construction could be the following:

set	syntax	status	volume	preventing action
cat	cat > filename	Permission denied	3	logout
cat	cat > filename	File exists	4	lock screen
cat	cat filename	Unreadable	4	logout

- According to the above example, the first rule refers to the creation of a file using the *cat* command. It defines that if a user attempts three times to create a file without write permission on the accessed directory, then the ADS will take the action *logout* to prevent the user from further attacks. The volume specified in a rule indicates the expected number of attempts of the associated command that will trigger the rule. This number is the command risk level and derives from risk analysis of the target system commands.
- When the Attack Detection Module (ADM) - which is responsible for analysing and examining the audit data (Kantzavelou 1996) - retrieves records of activities from the Event Data Base which belong to the same user and refer to one syntax of a command, then it will get the rule which matches the syntax of the typed command and the command status. In the above example, the ADM will examine the activity against the first rule, and will take the preventing action that has been defined, if the user has failed three times to execute this command.

Unfortunately, this method has a number of disadvantages and weaknesses:

- The implementation of the rule base requires the analysis of all possible syntaxes and reasons of failure of each command. Considering that the UNIX system for instance supports more than 400 user commands, such an implementation demands too much effort and the ADS effectiveness might prove the lack of rule base completeness.
- A user may rename a command. In this case no rule can match such a command, so that an attack would pass through the Attack Detection Module undetected.
- The rule base cannot include rules for individual user programs. This means that an attacker who uses his own program to damage a system will evade detection.

- The use of an editor would only show that a user called the editor to edit a file. Information about the file status (the file was changed or not) would be available only if the Attack Detection System performs additional examination of the file characteristics (date and time last saved).
- Detection of attacks will be in non-real time because the Attack Detection Module will expect a number of commands (volume) in order to characterise an activity as an attack.

The mentioned disadvantages and weaknesses of this method show that this method is incapable to fulfil some of the primary requirements stated in the problem definition paragraph. Therefore, another approach is required for the examination of audit data. The chosen method for the design and implementation of the Attack Detection System which is analysed in the next paragraph provides the required alternative solution.

2.2 Examination of Service Points

The alternative solution for the examination of audit data, is based on the design of operating systems. All operating systems provide *service points* (Peterson 1985) through which commands and programs request services from the kernel for their execution. These service points are elementary functions which are traditionally defined in the assembler language of the machine in older operating systems, whereas, recent operating systems define them in C language. Thus, in most operating systems, for each service point there is a C function which names the service point.

The UNIX system uses the term *system call* for a service point (Sun Microsystems 1990), the DOS system names it *software interrupt* (Keller 1988), etc. Although the names differ, the basic philosophy is held in common. The term *system call* will be used throughout the rest of this paper, because the implementation platform was UNIX-based. This term is also equivalent to the term *event* in the context of the ADS. In addition, the term *activity* is used here to describe the attempted execution of a command or program.

2.2.1 Service Points Under UNIX

When a command (or program) is requested by a user, then a number of system calls are requested by the command from the kernel. Each of these system calls is responsible for performing an elementary operation required for the execution of the command, and might be called more than once. Given that a system call is actually a function, a value that indicates the exit status of this function is returned when a system call is requested. This value might be:

- *'-1'* if an error occurred and the system call failed.
- *'0'* or greater than zero if the system call succeeded. The number in this case is associated with the requested system call, e.g. a successful *read()* system call will return the number of bytes read.
- *'?'* if the system call never returns a value

When an error occurs, the execution of the relevant command stops, and the associated system call fails returning an error code. This code indicates the reasons of the system call failure. There are a total of 128 system calls and 90 system call errors(Kantzavelou 1994) currently supported by the Sun operating system Release 4.1.3. An example of the list of system calls that are required for an attempt to view the contents of a file without read permission using the 'cat *filename*' command is presented in Figure 2.

System Call	Return Value	Error Code
open()	3	---------
read()	32	---------
mmap()	0	---------
mmap()	0	---------
open()	4	---------
getrlimit()	0	---------
System Call	**Return Value**	**Error Code**
mmap()	0	---------
close()	0	---------
getuid()	82	---------
getgid()	10	---------
open()	3	---------
fstat()	0	---------
mmap()	0	---------
close()	0	---------
open()	3	---------
read()	32	---------
mmap()	0	---------
mmap()	0	---------
close()	0	---------
open()	3	---------
read()	32	---------
mmap()	0	---------
mmap()	0	---------
close()	0	---------
close()	0	---------
fstat()	0	---------
open()	-1	EACCES
write()	7	---------
writev()	25	---------
close()	0	---------
close()	0	---------
close()	0	---------
exit()	?	---------

Figure 2: List of System Calls Required for a 'cat *filename*' Command

Among the system calls requested for the execution of this command, only the *open()* system call failed once returning the *EACCES* error code to indicate that the user had no read permission for the accessed file.

The method chosen for the design and implementation of the Attack Detection System examines system calls instead of commands for the following reasons:

i) The list of system calls in all operating systems is limited. This fact allows the implementation of a complete rule base which assures the effectiveness of the ADS.
ii) System call names cannot be changed by a user, because system calls belong to the operating system.
iii) Individual user programs rely on system calls for their execution. Therefore, auditing of the system calls of a program will permit detection of an attacker who attempts to damage the target system using his own program.
iv) Auditing of editing a file will make available information of the file status.
v) A system call might be requested more than once for the execution of a command. Thus, a number of system call request records may exist after the execution of a command. This fact may allow the characterisation of a single command (which may constitute an attack) thus facilitating real-time detection of attacks.

2.3 Filtering of Security Relevant Events

The Event Reception Module (ERM) is responsible for collecting all target system events (Kantzavelou 1996). Due to the fact that the volume of collected audit data is large, the examination of all events by the Attack Detection Module (ADM) becomes difficult. Filtering of audit data aims to reduce the large volume of audit data collected by the ERM. Thus, security relevant information is retained, while the bulk of innocuous event data is ignored by the ADM.

The principle of filtering security relevant events described below was based on the following criteria:

- A successful security relevant system call is a security relevant event
- An unsuccessful system call that has returned a security relevant error is a security relevant event.

Thus, the filtering of events requires the filtering of system calls and errors. The basic steps that were followed to determine which system call errors and system calls are of potential relevance from a security point of view, are described below (Pfleeger 1989):

1. Filtering of system call errors

As described in the previous section, a system call might fail if an error occurs. In this case, the error indicates the reasons for the system call failure. In particular, a system call error might indicate one or more threats that could endanger the target system. Therefore, filtering of the system call errors was based on the following criteria:

- what is the impact of the action indicated by a system call error on the target system
- what is the frequency of a system call error, i.e. how many system calls might have a specific error.

Among the list of these errors, only ten errors related to security were found. These security relevant errors are described below (Sun Microsystems 1990):

EACCES
An attempt was made to access a file in a way forbidden by the protection system.

EADDRNOTAVAIL
An attempt to create a socket with an address not on this machine was made.

EBADF
Either a file descriptor does not refer to an open file, or a read (or write) request is made to a file that is open only for writing (or reading).

EDQUOT
A *write()* system call to an ordinary file, the creation of a directory or symbolic link, or the creation of a directory entry failed because the user's quota of disk blocks was exhausted, or the allocation of an inode for a newly created file failed because the user's quota of inodes was exhausted.

EEXIST
An existing file was mentioned in an inappropriate context, for example, **link**.

EFAULT
The system encountered a hardware fault in attempting to access the arguments of a system call.

ENOMEM
During an *execve()*, *sbrk()*, or *brk()* system call, a program asks for more address space or swap space than the system is able to supply, or a process size limit would be exceeded.

ENOTEMPTY
An attempt was made to remove a directory with entries other than '.' and '..' by performing a **rmdir()** system call or a **rename()** system call with that directory specified as the target directory.

EPERM
Typically this error indicates an attempt to modify a file in some way forbidden except to its owner or super-user. It is also returned for attempts by ordinary users to do things allowed only to the super-user.

EROFS
An attempt to modify a file or directory was made on a file system which was mounted read-only.

Figure 3 shows the type of threat(s)(Kantzavelou 1995) that each of the security relevant system call errors indicates.

Error Nam Error Name	Disclosure of Information	Corruption of Information	Unauthorised Use of Resources	Misuse of Resources	Unauthorised Information Flow	Denial of Service
EADDRNOTAVAIL				*	*	
EFAULT						*
ENOMEM				*		
EDQUOT				*		
EEXIST		*		*		
EBADF	*	*	*			
ENOTEMPTY		*				
EACCES	*	*	*		*	
EROFS		*				
EPERM		*	*			

Figure 3: Security Relevant System Call Errors - Types of Threats Map

Due to the fact that not all the system call errors are equally serious, a risk level was assigned to each system call error to rate them. The scale used for this rating was 1 to 10, as it is presented in Figure 4. Risk level '1' refers to the lowest risk whereas risk level '10' refers to the greatest risk.

Error Name	Risk Level
EADDRNOTAVAIL	1
EFAULT	2
ENOMEM	3
EDQUOT	4
EEXIST	5
EBADF	6
ENOTEMPTY	7
EACCES	8
EROFS	9
EPERM	10

Figure 4: Risk Levels of System Call Errors

2. Filtering of system calls

The filtering of the system calls was based on the following criteria:

- what is the impact of a successful system call on the target system
- what is the frequency of a system call, i.e. how many commands might request a specific system call for their execution
- what is the *total risk level* of a system call. The total risk level was calculated by adding up the individual risk levels of the security relevant errors that a system call might return. Due to the fact that not all the system calls are equally serious, the total risk level was used to rate them.

	successful system call	non successful system call	security relevant system call	security irrelevant system call	security relevant error	security irrelevant error
successful system call			Y	N		
non successful system call		N	N	N	Y	N
security relevant system call	Y	N	N		Y	N
security irrelevant system call	N	N		N		N
security relevant error		Y	Y		Y	
security irrelevant error		N	N	N		N

Figure 5: Decision Matrix for Filtering of Security Relevant Events

Among the list of system calls, there were 79 found related to security. The security relevant system calls and errors that they might return are listed in (Kantzavelou 1994). Furthermore, the assigned total risk levels of the above system calls are also presented in (Kantzavelou 1994).

Finally, the rationale of the decision as to whether an event is security relevant or not was defined. Figure 5 depicts a decision matrix which presents this rationale. The shadowed boxes represent impossible cases; the symbol *'Y'* represents cases of security relevant events; and the symbol *'N'* represents cases of security irrelevant events.

Upon the determination of the security relevant events that are to be examined by the Attack Detection Module, a list of monitoring actions was specified to represent these security relevant events. This list is provided in (Kantzavelou 1994).

3 CONCLUSION

This paper has addressed the problem definition of the design and implementation of an attack detection system for secure computer systems, called the Attack Detection System (ADS). In comparison with other attack detection systems, the ADS described herein is a real-time system which provides flexibility in order to be more effective in detecting attacks.

More specifically, this paper defined the problem which was solved, presented the most significant results of this work and the overall concept of the ADS. The outline of the solution was extensively discussed by example and other solutions presented in comparison to the chosen one, to show the reasons that the method chosen for the design and implementation of the Attack Detection System was the most appropriate.

4 REFERENCES

Kantzavelou, I *An Attack Detection System for Secure Computer Systems*, M.Sc. Thesis, 1994.

Kantzavelou I, Patel A *'Issues of Attack in Distributed Systems - A Generic Attack Model', Proc. of the Joint Working Conference IFIP TC-6 TC-11 and Austrian Computer Society*, September 20-21, 1995, Graz, Austria, pp. 1-16.

Kantzavelou I, Patel A *'An Attack Detection System for secure computer systems - Design of the ADS', Proc. of the 12th International Information Security Conference (IFIP SEC '96)*, May 21-24, 1996, Samos, Greece, pp. 337-347.

Keller, L *Operating Systems: Communicating with and Controlling the Computer*, Prentice Hall (1988).

Peterson, J and Silbverschatz, A *Operating System Concepts*, Addison-Wesley Publishing Company, Second Edition (1985).

Pfleeger, C *Security in Computing*, Prentice-Hall International Editions (1989).

Sun Microsystems, Inc. *'System Calls' SunOS Reference Manual*, Vol II, Printed in USA, Revision A (1990).

5 BIOGRAPHIES

Ioanna Kantzavelou holds a B.Sc. in Informatics from the Technological Educational Institute of Athens, Greece, and a M.Sc. in Computer Science (by research, on security in computer networks) from the University College Dublin, Ireland. She has been involved with many European R&D projects in the area of security, in particularly medical information systems security. She currently is Visiting Assistant Professor with the Department of Informatics of the Technological Educational Institute of Athens, Greece.

Sokratis K. Katsikas (Dip. Eng., M.S., Ph.D) was born in Athens, Greece, in 1960. He received the Diploma in Electrical Engineering degree from the University of Patras, Greece, in 1982, the M.S. in Electrical & Computer Engineering from the University of Massachusetts at Amherst, USA in 1984, and the Ph.D. in Computer Engineering from the University of Patras, Greece, in 1987.
He has held teaching and research positions with the University of Massachusetts at Amherst, the University of Patras, the Computer Technology Institute, Patras, Greece, the University of La Verne Athens Campus, the Office of Naval Research, Hellenic Navy and the Technological Education Institute of Athens. In 1990 he joined the Department of Mathematics of the University of the Aegean, Greece, where he now is Associate Professor of Informatics and Associate Head of the Department.

He has been involved with many CEC funded R&D projects in the areas of computer security, robotics, and artificial intelligence. He has authored or coauthored more than 65 technical papers and conference presentations in his areas of research interest, which include computer security, estimation theory, adaptive control, and artificial intelligence. He has served as chairman or member of program and organizing committees of many international conferences and is a reviewer for several technical journals.

He is a member of IEEE, of the ACM, of the Greek Computer Society (Vice-President), of the Technical Chamber of Greece and of the Hellenic Association of Electrical and Mechanical Engineers. He is also a member of the New York Academy of Sciences. He is listed in "Who's Who in the World" and in "Who's Who in Science and Engineering".

He is the National Representative of Greece in IFIP General Assembly, a member of the CEPIS Network on Legal & Security Issues, a member of CEN TC251 (Medical Informatics) - WG6 (Security, Privacy, Safety), a member of IMIA (International Medical Informatics Association) - WG4 (Security, Privacy), the chairman of IFIP TC11 (Information Systems Security) - WG 4 (Network Security), the chairman of the Greek Computer Society Special Interest Group on IT Security and the secretary of the Greek Computer Society Special Interest Group on Software Reliability, Quality and Safety.

PART SEVEN

Privacy and Education

12

A Taxonomy and Overview of Information Security Experiments

E. Jonsson
Department of Computer Engineering
Chalmers University of Technology, S-412 96 Göteborg, Sweden
T: +46 31 772 1698, fax:+46 31 772 3663
email: erland.jonsson@ce.chalmers.se

L. J. Janczewski
School of Business and Economics, The University of Auckland
Private Bag 92 019, Auckland, New Zealand
T: +64 9373 7599, fax:+64 9373 7430
email: l.janczewski@auckland.ac.nz

Abstract

In July 1995 the Erasmus Bureau published a review of university programmes on Information Security followed by a proposal for an Information Security curriculum. These publications represent the first systematic attempt to review the Information Security discipline and to develop a common university program in the arena. The aim of the research presented in this paper is to bring this work one step further by means of surveying and systematising the role of experiments and practical project work in the discipline. We have thus made a world-wide inquiry to gather information on existing experiments. A few of these are presented in some detail, to give the reader a feeling for what is available. Furthermore, on the basis of the replies, we suggest a taxonomy for such experimentation and we classify the existing experiments accordingly.

Keywords

Security, experimentation, education, action learning, classification, taxonomy.

1 INTRODUCTION

In July 1995 the Erasmus Bureau published a review of university programmes on Information Security (ERASMUS 1995) followed by a proposal for an Information Security curriculum (ERASMUS 1995b). This set of publications is very important as it is the first systematic attempt to review the discipline and develop a universally accepted university program in the Information Security arena. For obvious reasons such publications do not define the delivery methods. It seems logical that the research phase to follow the set of ERASMUS publications should deal with the method of delivering the Information Security topics. An analysis of the ERASMUS project's publication (ERASMUS 1995) brings us to several quite interesting conclusions. One is the following:

The review of the existing programmes in the field was based mainly on what is offered at one Australian and seven European universities. It shows that these universities are using over 140 different textbooks. Among the publications listed, only one textbook, (Pfleeger 1989), is used at four institutions, one publication, (Muftic 1989), at three locations and 12 publications are used at two universities. The rest of the texts are limited to only one university institution. It is obvious that at the present there is not a great deal of coordination or exchange of information about contents and method of delivery of Information/Data Security subjects. Research on some aspects of delivery methods would be useful.

Therefore, during the 1996 IFIP SEC'96 conference, the IFIP WG 11.8* discussed an interesting topic: to what extent is the data security education at university level supported by practical activities, demonstrations, experiments or projects? This discussion, along with the other factors above, became a launching pad for this research, which discusses the possible ways of enhancing Information/Data Security presentation with practical experiments. The present paper covers the rationale behind conducting the experiments, introduces a classification of experiments and lists examples of experiments that might improve the quality of the teaching of the subject.

In the following, section 2 explains the scope of the topic and section 3 gives a framework for the experimental approach. The aim of the research presented is to systematise the role of experiments in teaching data security topics. Such a subject can not be dealt with without presenting experiments already introduced by various university organisations. We therefore contacted about 30 universities on five continents and asked about the contents of such experiments. The result is summarised in section 4. A brief evaluation of the data is made in section 5, and section 6 suggests possible directions for future work. Section 7 concludes the paper.

2 SCOPE

2.1 The action learning approach

In recent years there has been a growing interest in the *action learning* approach to education. Since 1990, International Congresses on Action Learning, Action Research and Practical Management (Brisbane 1990, Brisbane 1992, Bath 1994, Bogota 1996) have been held on this topic every two years, where scholars from all over the world discuss this approach to education.

---

* Working group WG 11.8 operates under the auspices of the Technical Committee TC11 of IFIP and concentrates on issues of data security education.

According to (Revans1992), (Revans 1984), action learning is a process by which groups of people (whether managers, academics, teachers, students or 'learners' generally) work on real issues or problems, carrying real responsibility in real conditions. The solutions they come up with may require changes to be made in the organisation and they often pose challenges to senior management, but the benefits are great because people actually own their own problems and their own solutions (Zuber-Skerritt 1990).

The action learning approach seems to be ideally suited to studying data security problems. While this discipline does have some highly theoretical parts (such as cryptography), in the majority of cases data security issues are very practical, and are implemented in the real life situation by the developers themselves.

Action learning is based on the Experiential Learning Cycle develop by (Kolb 1994). See Figure 1.

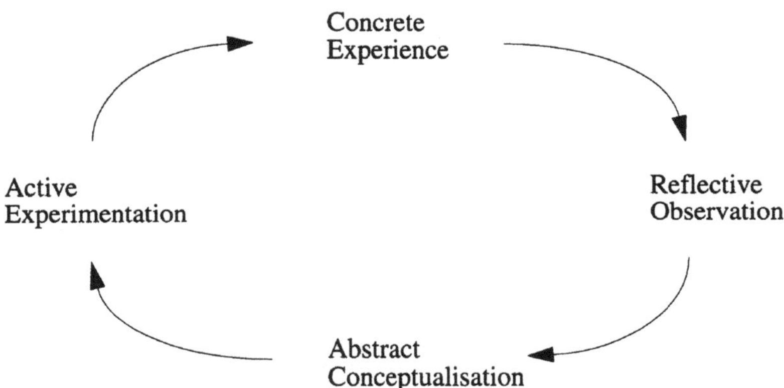

Figure 1 The Experimental Learning Cycle.

This cycle indicates the importance of active experimentation, and as a logical extension, significant parts of data security teaching should be based on experimental learning.

2.2 Difficulties with security experimentation

There are several reasons why conducting experiments in the field of data/information security is difficult. The discussion below gives the most important factors supporting that statement:

Information/data security is a rapidly changing discipline. In most cases experiments require lengthy preparation and academics investing great effort in preparing them wish to run them for several years. In the case of data security, this is almost impossible. On the contrary, the development of an experiment increases the effort required to deliver the topic. A good example would be the issue of viruses. Almost all dogmas about them have been changed in recent years. For instance, the arrival of macro viruses invalidated the well known statement that viruses are limited to one platform, i.e., PC viruses do not spread into the Mac world and vice versa. Hence preparation of a demonstration on virus properties requires a careful following of developments in this field and proper updating of the experimental content every year.

Data security experiments generally deal with very sensitive issues. A data security experiment may reveal weak spots in the security armour of an organisation and it might be used against an organisation in many ways: through direct attack or public exposure. Business organisations are well aware of that, and a great deal of persuasion is usually necessary to involve them in a data security experiment. Some time ago, when the issue of data security was relatively new, participants were generally more eager to be involved than they are today. In 1991 the University of Auckland conducted a survey of data security arrangements among local community enterprises. Approximately one hundred organisations were approached and the response rate was 56%. The same research group wished to perform a follow-up of that survey in 1995. Unfortunately the project had to be abandoned, as the response rate was about 5%(!). It was clear that Auckland's business community was alien to this research.

Data security research, by definition, probes the proper functioning of a system. Thus it may happen quite often that an experiment that is "successful" from a researcher's point of view may have quite a disastrous results on an evaluated system. For example, students examining the efficiency of a password system may accidentally gain access to sensitive data or suspend the functioning of the whole system by their actions. Data security experiments should be well protected against these types of calamities.

2.3 Legal issues

Apart from being familiar with technical problems, a data security researcher should be aware of the legal problems resulting from the experiments he/she is conducting. Legal problems focus on the possible violation of privacy laws or similar legislation. An example would be: during a workshop on eavesdropping techniques the students tap highly confidential information. Using that data for any purpose outside the data security research is, of course, forbidden. However, in many countries, permission must in any case be obtained to listen or tap such transmissions.

3 A TAXONOMY FOR SECURITY EXPERIMENTS

Under the terms of this research, an *experiment* is defined as any activity which is outside the typical lecturing environment, in which a lecturer tells the audience about the theory or practice of the subject. This section suggests a classification of such experiments along three axes: *degree of applicability, degree of innovation* and *level of generalisation.* These are explained in the following.

In terms of ***degree of applicability,*** or distance from reality, the experiments may be of three types, denoted *D, L* and *F,* for *DEMONSTRATION, LABORATORY* and *FIELD WORK,* respectively.

D. Conducted by the staff (DEMONSTRATION).

This type of experiment assumes the audience to have a passive role. The lecturer or guest speaker demonstrates the practical side of the addressed course item being addressed. For instance, a lecturer would present (during a lecture) the practical functioning of the reference monitor by connecting to a server and demonstrating various access rights. This type of presentation might take place at any location: it could be arranged during lecturing time, during a session in a university laboratory or at a real business/industrial organisation.

The common denominator is the same: students are passive and demonstrators are active during the conducting of the experiment.

L. Conducted by students in an artificial environment (LABORATORY)

This type of experiment assumes that the students have an active role and are asked to investigate a problem by themselves. The role of the staff is to explain the background, help in case of difficulties etc., but to stay away from the actual experiments. Experiments might be aimed at confirming some theoretical aspects of information security, for instance investigation of the time required for encryption/decryption of a text, or to solve some practical problem, for instance design of an access mechanism.

F. Conducted by students in the real environment (FIELD WORK)

Field Work experiments assume that students are asked to study a problem in a real-life organisation. Such an activity might, for instance, be investigation of the perimeter controls or design of a data security policy for an existing organisation.

The above classification is based on the distance between the participants, i.e., students, and the reality investigated; from a totally passive role (DEMONSTRATION) to dealing with very real problems (FIELD WORK). It implies that DEMO exercises could generally be presented without special preparatory work by students, while FIELD WORK is impossible without that.

The second way to classify experiments is to evaluate the ***degree of innovation*** of the ***object(s)*** of a particular activity. Examples of objects are hardware and software tools, mechanisms, protocols, set of rules etc. The most general classification would include the following classes:

U. Use of the object

These exercises are confined to normal use of the object. The goal might be to learn how it functions and in what situations it could be utilised. An example would be a lecturer that, during a class, is using an authentication and verification procedure to access the system in question.

E. Evaluation of the object

Here the exercises are aimed at presenting the object of the existing information security systems in such a way that its function and use can be evaluated and perhaps rated against other similar objects. A good example of such an activity would be a data security audit.

R. Redesign of an object

The purpose of these experiments is to make a new design of an existing object in order to learn about its basic functionality. The intended result is a better understanding of the security problems related to the design of the object as well as to the integration of it into its intended environment.

N. Design of new or improved objects

These exercises are the most difficult in the classification system. They require in-depth knowledge of the problem area investigated, which could result in new, improved designs of existing objects or recommendations aimed at enhancing the security of the installation. In more advanced cases, this class would also include the development of entirely new (and hopefully more secure) objects.

A step from the U to the N class requires an increased amount of knowledge in and experience of the domain.

The final way of classifying experiments is to define their ***level of generalisation.*** At this stage, we suggest the introduction of three classes:

M. Managerial level

Experiments of this class deal with an overall, organisational level of data security issues. A data security audit of a business unit, as mentioned before, may be example of such an activity. Security policy issues also belong to this level.

S. System level

This is the level of the system administrator as well as the level of abstraction experienced by the normal user of the system. It deals with the direct behaviour of the hardware and software system and with the implementation and use of security mechanisms, logging features etc.

T. Technical level

Experiments in this class deal with the low-level design issues of operating systems and data security mechanisms, such as the internal structure of a reference monitor or an authentication protocol.

Taking all the above into consideration, we suggest that all the experiments in the field of teaching data security should be classified by a three-tuple
{X,Y,Z}, where:

- *X* denotes the degree of applicability (possible types: *D, L* and *F*)
- *Y* denotes the degree of innovation required (possible classes: *U, E, R* and *N*)
- *Z* denotes the level of generalisation of the experiment (possible levels: *M, S* or *T*)

This way of classifying the experiments allows us to generate 36 different classes of experiments. Introduction of a classification of this type is a necessity. Each of the classes requires different preparation and different backgrounds among students and lecturers. For example an experiment of a class *{D,U,S}, "demonstration of the use of an object on a system level"*, does not require students to have a great deal of knowledge, whereas participation in the *{F,N,T}* class, *"design of new technical tools in a real environment"*, demands a thorough knowledge of the discipline in order to yield substantial results.

4 EXAMPLES OF DATA SECURITY EXPERIMENTS

4.1 Introduction

The aim of this research is to systematise the role of experiments in teaching data security topics. Such a subject cannot be treated without presenting experiments already introduced by various university organisations. To do this we contacted about 30 universities on five continents, North America, Europe, Africa, Asia and Australia/Oceania, and asked about the contents of such experiments at their institutions. Our questionnaire is presented in Appendix 1. In this way we received information of about 15 - 20 different exercises/projects, which we believe is only a small part of the existing ones. Still, this may serve as a sample that can be used for illustrating the principle and give an idea of the range of experiments.

In this section we present examples of these experiments, apply the suggested classification terminology and make comments about them. All the experiments described below are currently being conducted at various universities.

Each experiment is classified, not only according to the taxonomy suggested in section 3, but also with respect to educational level, duration and the effort required (in man-hours) to perform the experiment:

{X,Y,Z}, educational level, duration, required effort

4.2 Experiment No 1: Eavesdropping techniques

Classification: {D,U,M}, graduate, 2 hours, 2 hours

This experiment aims to demonstrate problems related to eavesdropping techniques: measures and countermeasures.

Students have an opportunity to inspect real "bugs", i.e., "hidden" microphones of various types, and how they may be planted in office and home environments. Live demonstrations of devices that listen to analog and digital cellular phones and to pagers are parts of the demonstration.

On the countermeasure side, a non-linear detector is presented in action. A non-linear detector is a sensor that informs the operator as to whether there is a p-n junction (or semiconductor device) hidden within a radius of about 30 cm around the probe. The operation of a frequency analyser is also demonstrated. This device detects all radio transmission, and hence the presence of any radio-transmitting bugs. No preparation is required of the students prior to the demonstration.

4.3 Experiment No 2: Virus hunt

Classification: {D,U,S}, graduate, 2 hours, 2 hours

In this class, laptops are used to demonstrate typical virus activities (boot sector, stealth, polymorphic, macro etc). An analysis is conducted of the system's resources that demonstrates the existence of a virus. Virus detection and cleaning of software are also demonstrated.

Prior to the demonstration, students must attend a two-hour lecture on viruses and virus software, in which virus mechanics and various types of virus scanners are discussed.

4.4 Experiment No 3: Evaluation of system security by means of synthetic intrusions

Classification: ranging from {L,U,S} to {L,R,T}, undergraduate, about 4 weeks, 40-80 hours

The idea behind this project is to increase students' awareness of security by means of letting them find out for themselves how insecure a system can be, which unfortunately is true for many "normal" systems, i.e., systems in which security is not enhanced and thoroughly managed. The students start the project with no special security knowledge. In many cases they do not even know very much about the object system. Their task is to perform as many intrusions as possible and to report *how* they made them and *how much effort* was required in order to achieve the intrusions.

The results of the experiment are also used for research purposes, in particular to investigate methods for modelling and quantifying the intrusion process. Thus, owing to the requirements of this research, no specific time limit for the duration of the experiment is given, but it is implicit that the expected number of man-hours should normally fall in the range of 40 to 80 hours. The experiment requires careful supervision by a supervisor who must ensure that the experiment is carried out in a realistic way, but without disturbing other users or attempting something that would be illegal or unethical.

The outcome of the project is very dependent on the students involved. An interested and skilful student may very well start to develop new program tools, whereas some students may limit themselves to finding and using existing tools for the attempted intrusions. This is the reason why the classification would include classes such as *{L,U,S}*, *{L,E,S}* and *{L,R,S}* to *{L,U,T}*, *{L,E,T} and {L,R,T}*.

Each student (or group of students) summarises the results of the work in a *final report,* in which all successful intrusions are listed together with the expended effort. The students may also give their personal comments to the experiment, suggest improvements to the system as a result of their experience etc.

4.5 Experiment No 4: Demonstration of cryptological weaknesses

{L,U,T}, undergraduate, 4 hours, 4 hours

The students are presented with encrypted texts and a list of encryption methods, together with some tools for statistical analysis. Each text is encrypted with a different algorithm, but the students have no prior information about which algorithm is used on a specific text.

Statistical tools and other relevant methods, such as the Berlekamp-Massey algorithm, are used to perform a cryptanalysis of the text. The students are supposed to return the key and plaintext to show that they have been successful in the cryptanalysis.

4.6 Experiment No 5: Implementation of cryptographic algorithm

Classification: {L,R,S}, undergraduate, 4 weeks, 32 hours

The students are given the task of writing a program that implements a known cryptographic algorithm, such as a poly-alphabetic one or columnar transpositions. Furthermore, a brief user's manual is written. The function of the program developed is proven by means of demonstrating its function to the teacher and submitting the user's manual.

4.7 Experiment No 6: Data security audit

Classification: {F,R,M} or {F,E,M}, graduate, 3 months, about 100 hours

In this experiment students are required to perform a security audit of a real business organisation. The work is very closely supervised by the staff. In practice the supervisor is a member of the working team. The experiment is divided into three phases:

I. Preparation

Students undergo intensive training on how to perform a security audit. The exercise is the capstone of their two year study of Information Systems. The training includes familiarisation with the auditing methodology and method of conducting an interview.

The management of the organisation to be audited is contacted and permission is obtained to do the audit. Also, if necessary, security formalities are completed (e.g. issuing of badges, signing of nondisclosure certificates etc)

II. Data collection

Data is collected in three ways: personal interviews, reading related documents and observation. All personal interviews are presented for authorisation after the collection.

III. Data analysis

The data analysis usually contains two types of evaluation: consequences and recommendations. In the first part the team states what could happen if the discovered threat were not eliminated and an attack was launched against the organisation. The second part discusses ways of eliminating the security hole.

The final report has a professional appearance and is signed by the members of the research team, including the supervisor. The report is presented to the company as an official university document. The recipients of the reports normally treat them very seriously and in many cases try to implement the recommendations.

5 A PRELIMINARY EVALUATION OF THE DATA

Even though the received material is not large enough to be statistically significant, we have made a brief evaluation of it to see whether there is a tendency towards specific classes of experiments. One of the problems in this work is that some of the larger experiments contain elements of more than one class, e.g., experiment numbers 3 and 6, and may thus be regarded as multi-class experiments. In general, the distribution over the classes will be different if all the classes in a multi-class experiment are considered instead of identifying only one class, e.g., the most common one, in each experiment. However, a good correlation was found between the two ways of calculating, at least with the material available so far. The results below are thus valid for both cases.

In the applicability class, it turns out that laboratory experiments, coded *{L,*,*}*, are by far the most common. Three experiments of four belong to this class. This may not be very surprising, since the laboratory is the traditional place for conducting experiments, although it could have been thought that security experiments might have been an exception to this.

As regards the innovation class, there is a tendency towards an even spread between "use of" or "redesign of" the object, i.e., *{*,U,*}* or *{*,R,*}*, whereas "evaluation of" the object, *{*,E,*}*, is less common and "design of new improved objects", *{*,N,*}*, is quite infrequent.

The most common level of generalization for the experiments is the system level, *{*,*,S}*, which is as common as the two other groups, *{*,*,M}* and *{*,*,T}*, together. Obviously, it is easier or more natural to develop experiments which are on the system level, and thus more or less directly referring to the user, than to go up or down in the hierarchy. The management level would require an overview and the technical level a knowledge of details not shared by all students. A plausible interpretation of this fact is that business and management educations have a focus on the management level and vice versa.

In summary, the most "typical" experiment is an *{L,U,S}* or *{L,R,S}*, and these two classes together amounted to almost half of the total number.

Another completely different observation may be made. Although it may not be entirely evident from the above examples, we can conclude, on the basis of the full material received that this type of experimentation is very much in line with present trends in engineering education. Not only is it a good example of action learning, as mentioned in section 2, but it also incorporates substantial elements of innovative teaching and interdisciplinary approaches, as discussed in (Smith 1991) and (Yngström 1996).

6 DISCUSSION AND FUTURE WORK

While the present analysis covers most of the classes introduced in the taxonomy - from demonstrations conducted during regular lectures to substantial field work involving close co-operation with industry or other external organisations - it is not surprising that a vast majority of the experiments were performed in laboratories and aimed at redesigning or using well-known objects. Here, an interesting question is whether this outcome reflects an optimal set-up of experiments or is the result of some other condition, e.g., that the experiments carried out are simply those that were easiest to organise. We suggest that future investigations attempts to clarify this issue. Another related issue would be to establish the results of the experiment, preferably in quantitative terms, such as student satisfaction or learning effect. It is clear that there are a number of factors that might influence the result and that must be considered.

Examples are:

- attitude of students and staff towards conducting the experiments.
- quality of the experimental leader (e.g., staff, students, expert, tutor etc.)
- level of studies and the number of IS papers offered in the programme.

Finally, we would like to point out that the descriptions we received of experiments carried out at various universities are very interesting and should be made available to all information security educators. We suggest establishing a databank for the collection of descriptions of such experiments.

7 CONCLUSIONS

This paper is a first attempt to present a rationale behind enhancing data security studies with experimentation. Also, a classification method was developed and typical experiments presented and classified. The results so far are quite rewarding. Still they call for further research to be undertaken, both to gain a better understanding of the experimental process as such and to put it into an educational context.

8 ACKNOWLEDGEMENT

We would like to thank all of our contributors without whose help this research would not have been possible. The page limit of the paper prevented us from incorporating all experiments.

9 REFERENCES

(ERASMUS 1995) Gritzalis, D. (Ed), *University Programmes on Information Security, Dependability and Safety*, European Commission, Erasmus ICP, Projekt ICP-94(&95)-G-4016/11, Report IS-CD-3c, Athens, July. 1995.

(ERASMUS 1995b) Katsikas, S., Gritzalis, D. (Eds), *A Proposal for a Postgraduate Programme on Information Security, Dependability and Safety (Syllabus)*, Version 2.2, European Commission, Erasmus ICP-94(&95)-G-4016/11, Report IS-CD-4a, Athens, Sept. 1995.

(Kolb 1994) Kolb, D. Experiential Learning, Experience as the Source of Learning and Development, Prentice-Hall (1984).

(Muftic 1989) Muftic, S.: Security Mechanisms for Computer Networks, Ellis Horwood Ltd, England, ISBN 0-7458-0613-9, 1989.

(Pfleeger 1989) Pfleeger, C. P.: Security In Computing, Prentice Hall International, Inc. ISBN 0-13-799016-2, 1989.

(Revans 1984) Revans, R., The Sequence of Managerial Achievement, MCB University Press, Bradford (1984).

(Revans1992) Revans, R., The Origins and Growth of Action Learning, Chartwell-Bratt Lty, Bromley (1982).

(Smith 1991) Smith, R. A. (Ed.), "Innovative Teaching in Engineering", Ellis-Horwood (1991). ISBN 0-13-457607-1. pp. 3-40, 253-294.

(Yngström 1996) Yngström, L., IT Security and Privacy Education. In Proc. of the 12th International Information Security Conference, IFIP/SEC'96, Samos, May 21-24, "Information Systems Security: Facing the information society of the 21st century". Chapman&Hall. ISBN 0-412-78120-4. pp. 351-364.

(Zuber-Skerritt 1990) Zuber-Skerritt, O., Action Research For Change and Development, Centre for the Advancement of Learning and Teaching, Griffith University, Brisbane (1990).

Appendix: Questionnaire.

To: Teachers of Computer Security and other interested parties,
RE: Request for data on practical security experiments

[General information on the research project - not included]

```
*********************************************************
                DATA SECURITY EXPERIMENT

University...............................................
Faculty..................................................
Department...............................................
Course name..............................................
Course level (undergraduate, graduate, etc)..............

Experiment type (please circle)  DEMO   LAB   FIELD

Experiment duration (in min, hours, days, etc)...........

Experiment goal..........................................
.........................................................

Experiment description...................................
.........................................................

Assessment method (if appropriate).......................
.........................................................

*********************************************************
```

13

Pseudonymous Audit for Privacy Enhanced Intrusion Detection

Michael Sobirey[1], *Simone Fischer-Hübner*[2], *and Kai Rannenberg*[3]

[1] *Brandenburg University of Technology at Cottbus, Computer Science Institute, PO 10 13 44, D-03013 Cottbus, Germany, Phone: +49-355-69-2101, Fax: +49-355-69-2236, E-Mail: sobirey@informatik.tu-cottbus.de*

[2] *University of Hamburg, Faculty for Informatics, Vogt-Kölln-Str. 30, D-22527 Hamburg, Germany, Phone: +49-40-5494-2225, Fax: +49-40-5494-2226 E-Mail: fischer@rz.informatik.uni-hamburg.d400.de*

[3] *University of Freiburg, Institute for Informatics and Society, Telematics Department, Friedrichstraße 50, D-79098 Freiburg, Germany, Phone: +49-761-203-4926, Fax: +49-761-203-4929 E-Mail: kara@iig.uni-freiburg.de*

Abstract

Intrusion detection systems can serve as powerful security audit analysis tools. But by analysing the user activities, they are affecting the privacy of the users at the same time. Pseudonymous audit can be the basis for privacy enhanced intrusion detection. In this paper, the concept of pseudonymous audit for privacy enhanced intrusion detection and its prototype realisations are presented. Furthermore it is discussed whether IT security evaluation criteria cover pseudonymous audit and the respective changes are suggested.*

Keywords

Pseudonymous audit, privacy enhancing technologies, intrusion detection systems, IT security evaluation criteria

1 INTRODUCTION

IT security mechanisms can be technical data protection measures and are therefore required by most western data protection acts. On the other hand, they require

*Parts of this work are funded by the Gottlieb Daimler and Karl Benz Foundation (Ladenburg, Germany) as part of its Kolleg "Security in Communication Technology".

the collection and use of specific personal data of users and usees† especially for access control and audit. This results in the conflict where security mechanisms can both help to protect the privacy of the data subjects and can be used to invade the privacy of the users and usees [De+87, Schae91, Fi+92, Fi94].

Audit provides the recording, analysis and review of data related to security relevant events. It shall deter and detect penetration of computer systems and forms a last line of defence against many kinds of security violations which cannot be prevented by authentication and access control. But audit generates personal data about the activities and behaviour of users. These data provide detailed information about: *Who* has accessed *when, where* and *how, what* and *whose* resource?

Up to now, the large amounts of audit data have caused no true privacy problems due to the lack of powerful analysis tools. The increasing use of intrusion detection systems is chanching this. Recent systems are capable of detecting intrusive behaviour by monitoring the system usage for subversive, suspicious or anomalous, possibly security violating activities.

Pseudonymous audit can help to balance the conflict between accountability and privacy. It is a privacy enhancing security audit technique where user identifying audit data are pseudonymized. Intrusion detection systems which operate with pseudonymized audit data offer a more socially and legally acceptable approach.

In this paper, we first briefly discuss criteria for privacy enhancing technologies. Then we present the concept and the first realisations of pseudonymous audit and privacy enhanced intrusion detection. Finally, we discuss whether IT security evaluation criteria cover pseudonymous audit and privacy enhanced intrusion detection and we recommend the respective changes.

2 IT SECURITY TECHNOLOGIES AND PRIVACY

2.1 Privacy and Privacy Enhancing Technologies

Privacy can be defined (as it has been done by the German Constitutional Court in its Census Decision of 1983) by the term right of informational self-determination, meaning the right of individuals to determine the disclosure and use of their personal data on principle at their discretion. In order to protect this right, the Council of Europe's Convention 108, the EU directive on data protection [EU95] as well as privacy laws of many western states require basic privacy principles to be guaranteed when personal data are collected or processed, such as:

- Purpose binding (personal data obtained for one purpose should not be used for another purpose without informed consent);
- Necessity of data collection and processing (the collection and processing of personal data shall only be allowed, if it is necessary for the tasks falling within the responsibility of the data processing agency);
- Requirement of adequate technical and organisational safeguards to guarantee the confidentiality, integrity and availability of personal data.

†Usees are personally affected by the collection and processing of data about them, but lack control over these activities.

In a fully networked society privacy is seriously endangered. Data protection commissioners are therefore demanding that privacy requirements should be technically enforced and that privacy should be a design criteria for information systems.

For example, recently the Dutch Data Protection Authority (the Registratiekamer) and the Information and Privacy Commissioner for the Province of Ontario, Canada, have collaborated in the production of a report [ReIPC95] exploring privacy enhancing technologies that are providing anonymity or pseudonymity for the users.

Extended security criteria for systems with high privacy requirements should cover a diversity of privacy enhancing security aspects, such as:

- Anonymity, pseudonymity, unlinkability, unobservability of users;
- Anonymity and pseudonymity of data subjects;
- Purpose binding and necessity of data processing of personal data of users and data subjects.

The privacy principle of necessity of data collecting means that personal data should not be collected or used for identification purposes when not truly necessary. Consequently, information systems should guarantee that, if possible, users can act anonymously. Examples for anonymous communication systems can be found in [Chau85, Pfi$^+$91]. If storage is needed, personal data of data subjects should be anonymized or pseudonymized as soon as possible. Security mechanisms, such as inference control for statistical databases, can help to guarantee that personal data are usable for statistical purposes without revealing the data subject's identities. Furthermore, the privacy principles of purpose binding and necessity of data processing can be technically supported through an appropriate security policy and access control mechanisms (see e.g. [Fi94] for a formal privacy-enforcing access control model).

2.2 Intrusion Detection and Privacy Requirements

Security mechanisms, such as identification and authentication mechanisms, access control, audit or encryption, are necessary to protect the confidentiality and integrity of personal data. But, as mentioned above, audit and intrusion detection can conflict with privacy requirements for collecting and using as few user identifying data as possible.

Especially in Germany and in other Western European countries, data protection and labour legislation can restrict or prevent the use of intrusion detection systems in organisations, if the privacy of the users is not protected sufficiently. The privacy principle of necessity of data collection requires that personal data should not be collected or used for identification purposes when not truly necessary. Furthermore, according to Art. 6 of the EU directive on data protection, personal data must be kept in a form which permits identification of data subjects for no longer than is necessary for the purposes for which the data were collected or for which they are further processed. Consequently, according to these provisions, user identifying data shall not be used in audit data, if not truly necessary, and should be pseudonymized, as far as possible.

Furthermore, according to German labour legislation, the works council in a company has the right of co-determination, if a system shall be introduced, that can be used or misused for monitoring the employees performance. As intrusion detection systems could be easily used for monitoring the users' activities and performance, works councils are normally not willing to accept them. This is probably also one reason, why in Germany there are hardly any powerful intrusion detection systems in use so far. Pseudonymous audit for privacy enhanced intrusion detection can be a socially and legally acceptable solution.

3 PSEUDONYMOUS AUDIT AND INTRUSION DETECTION

3.1 Functionality of Pseudonymous Audit

Pseudonymous audit is a special security audit technique, where subject identifiers and further user identifying data in audit records are pseudonymized right after creation and analysed in this representation, e.g. by an intrusion detection system (see Figure 1). When analysing the audit data, the security administrator does not have to know the real user identities of the monitored users. It is sufficient, that the real identity of a user can be determined, when suspicious or obviously intrusive behaviour was detected. Ideally, the security administrator should unmask an intruder only in cooperation with a data protection officer.

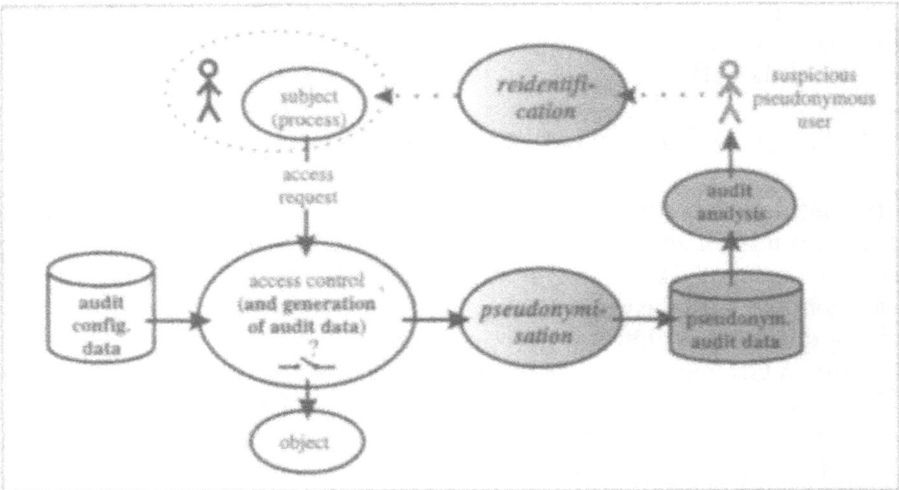

Figure 1 Functionality of pseudonymous operating system audit

By this way pseudonymous audit provides user accountability as well as pseudonymity. Regardless of the focus on operating system audit in this chapter pseudonymous audit is in principle also applicable to other kinds of audit, e.g. application audit [SoFi96].

3.2 The Raising Need for Pseudonymous Audit

Motivating the need for pseudonymous audit requires a short review of the developments in intrusion detection. Until recently the large amounts of audit data have caused no real privacy problems due to the lack of powerful analysis tools for a sophisticated, possibly abusing monitoring. With the gradually increasing usage of intrusion detection systems this situation is changing.

Many developments in this area were funded by government, military and intelligence agencies of the USA. Examples are the intrusion detection systems *Haystack* [Sma88] and *IDES* [Lu+92]. These systems monitored among others US Air Force mainframes and the in-house database system FOIMS (Field Office Information Management System) of the FBI headquarter in Washington D.C. Some research prototyps originated at universities and enterprises [BauKo88, Sna+91, Mo91, HaMa92]. With the beginning of the 90es first commercial intrusion detection systems became available, e.g. AT&T's *ComputerWatch* [DoRa90], *Stalker* [SmaWi94] from the Haystack Laboratories and *CMDS* [Pro94] from SAIC.

Privacy problems were discussed occasionally [De+87, DSL90], but they received nearly no technological consideration. The following statement in a product description [HLI95] demonstrates how some developers handle privacy: *"Stalker does not examine user's keystrokes, files, or electronic mail, so it does not violate user privacy."* However, the Haystack Labs recommend to inform the users with each login that they *"are subject to security monitoring and testing."*

The availability of commercial intrusion detection systems makes an efficient automatic network monitoring for "data intensive" enterprises, such as banks or insurance companies, possible. Large amounts of audit data, that have to be collected for intrusion detection, are getting more and more technically manageable and are at the same time sharpening privacy concerns.

Global networking, increasing numbers of incidents in enterprises and public institutions, and the previous unability to detect and ward off security violations seem to result in a gradual change in thinking of the people affected and the decision makers. For instance in Europe military and enterprises begin to build up own intrusion detection capacities. To deal with the increasing privacy risks, technical solutions for privacy enhanced intrusion detection have to be developed. Besides, IT security evaluation criteria have to be extended to cover this concept.

3.3 User Identifying Data in Audit Records

To support the understanding of structure and content of the audit data the following example of a Solaris 2.4 audit record is given. This record consists of several tokens (data lines) beginning with a token identifier. The *header* token contains general information, as the size of this record, the audit event and the time stamp among others. The *path* and the *attribute* tokens provide object related information, e.g. the object name, the corresponding access rights, owner and owner group.

The following *subject* token contains detailed information about the initiator of the recorded action, especially the audit ID[‡], the effective user ID, the effective

[‡]With each login a user gets a unique audit identifier that is unchangeable during his sessions regardless of temporary changes to other user identities, e.g. with the system command *su*. Each process runs under the audit ID of the user who initiated its start.

group ID, the real user ID, the real group ID and finally after some other data the host name. The last token contains the status of the audit event and a return value.

```
header,113,2,open(2) - read,,Mon Jan 22 09:34:32 1996, + 650002 msec
path,/usr/lib/libintl.so.1
attribute,100755,bin,bin,8388638,29586,0
subject,richter,richter,rnks,richter,rnks,854,639,0 0 romeo
return,success,0
```

In a simplified way the record can be interpreted as follows: On *22nd January 1996, 9.34:32,650002* user *"richter"* (see the audit ID) acted on his own account (audit ID and the real user ID are identical) and opened the file *libintl.so.1* successfully *(success, 0)* for reading *(open(2) - read)*. Owners of the program are user and group *"bin"*.

We distinguish concrete and conditionally user identifying data and data that can only be occasionally with additional knowledge used for reidentification. Concrete user identifying data are contained in the previously detailed interpreted subject and attribute token. Conditionally user identifying data are in the path token if a subject accesses own files or files owned by other users unlike system standard users *(e.g. daemon, bin or sys)*. In these cases the name of the *home directory*, often identical with the user name, is part of the complete recorded access path. Often the naming and the structure of subdirectories and the names of files/programs that are owned by regular users are user identifying in such cases. Similar path problems are caused by the recording of user account specific environment data (in certain audit records between the attribute and the subject token).

```
exec_args,2,
/usr/bin/sh,/home/fischer/my_special_subdir/xyz
exec_env,28,
DISPLAY=:0.0,GROUP=sec,HELPPATH=/usr/openwin/lib/locale:/usr/openwin/
lib/help,HOME=/home/schmal,HOST=hawk,HOSTTYPE=sun4,HZ=100, ...
```

Under certain conditions, especially if data on running processes of other users are available, the following data can be used for unwanted reidentification:

- Action in combination with date/time and the final action status;
- Action under consideration of the access rights, in combination with date/time and the final action status;
- Host identifier or name and host type.

For instance, if a file is writeable only for the object owner this action can only be successfully initiated by the object owner, the system administrator *root* or a masquerader who successfully hacked one of these accounts.

3.4 Pseudonymous Representations

The problem of the pseudonymisation is to find representations that provide optimal privacy for the audit based monitored users and that ensure on the other hand significant analysis results. Very extensively pseudonymized audit records provide no significant analysis results. Analysis problems will especially be caused if action, date/time (, access rights) and action status are pseudonymised. That is shown with the following example interpretation of a pseudonymous audit record.

A *certain user* acted on his *own account* (pseudonyms for audit ID and real user ID are identical) and refered *somewhere* (host), *sometime* (date, time), *somehow* (action, status) *an own file* (subject ID's and object owner ID are identical).

Our examinations have shown, that an effective pseudonymisation of audit records should cover:

- All concrete user ID's;
- Location ID's;
- Conditionally subdirectories and objects.

3.5 Technological Requirements

The analysis of pseudonymous audit data requires the *ability to link* the pseudonyms (to each other) that represent identical user identifying data. This is necessary to trace the actions back to the initiating user. Possible technologies for the pseudonymisation are pseudonym databases, secret key or public key encryption.

To minimize performance losses and especially to support real time intrusion detection and audit analysis, a fast technology for pseudonymisation is required.

3.6 First Example Realisations

The IDA Approach

The IDA (Intrusion Detection and Avoidance) system concept couples a reference monitor with a kernel integrated intrusion detection component. Before the reference monitor is performing a kernel request, it sends the corresponding audit record, which is pseudonymized by encryption of the subject fields[§], to the intrusion detection component for further analysis (see Figure 2).

If a subject acting under a certain pseudonym has initiated a suspicious action, the decision module sends a negative response to the reference monitor. Only kernel requests that pass the reference monitor and the intrusion detection component, will be performed by the reference monitor. The IDA prototype was realised as model implementation. The analysis module was tested for known DOS viruses using audit data that were generated on an MSDOS machine, see [Bru+91].

IDA can react in real time without *manual* interactions and reidentification of a suspicious subject by the security administrator. In the prototype implementation, only the subject ID of the audit records are replaced by pseudonyms. For the IDA concept it was also planned to pseudonymize also subject identifying data in the object fields as well as parameters that are unique for certain users (e.g. terminal ID's). To approach the problem of unwanted reidentification it was planned that pseudonyms for subjects should at least be replaced in certain time intervals.

[§] To realise the 4-eyes principle, the key for decryption could be split into two halves, which are given to the security administrator and to the data protection officer.

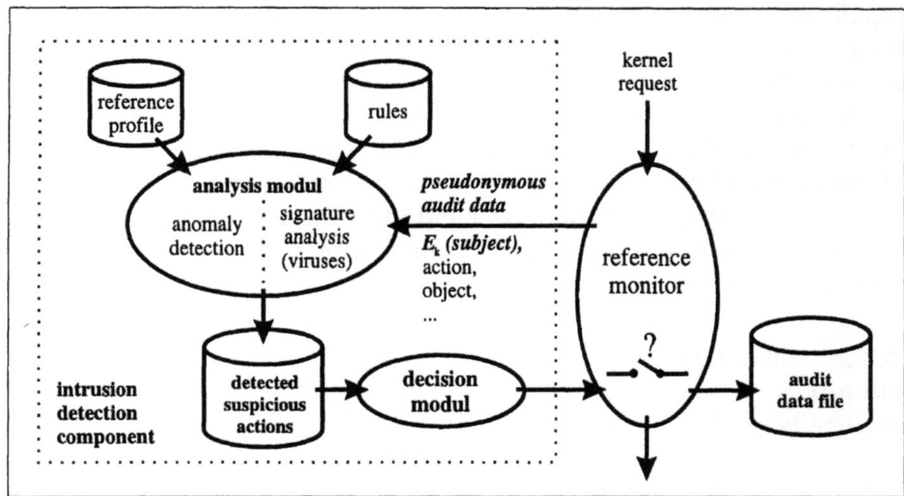

Figure 2 Architecture of the IDA system

The AID Approach

AID (Adaptive Intrusion Detection system) is a distributed intrusion detection system that monitors a local area network in real time. The system is based on a client-server architecture consisting of a central monitoring station and several *agents* on the monitored hosts. The central station hosts a *manager* and an *expert system* (see Figure 3).

The agents take the audit data that were collected by the local audit functions and convert them into an operating system independent data format. Then the data are transferred to the central monitoring station using secure RPC and analysed by an RTworks based real time expert system. The security officer can access the monitoring capabilities via a graphical user interface. In addition security reports are created. AID has been successfully tested in a Solaris 2.x network environment [So+96].

To provide a privacy enhanced audit based monitoring the audit data from the underlaying operating system are kernel internal pseudonymized before they are stored in the local audit data files. The pseudonyms are created by a *secret key* encryption. The audit functions of all monitored hosts use the same key that is changed from time to time. Only if security violations are detected, e.g. if an audit record and relevant context consitions match with (a part of) a certain attack signature, the user identifiers and other user identifying data (cf. 3.4) of the corresponding pseudonymized audit records are automatically reidentified respectively depseudonymized to enable countermeasures in time. That is required to support *real time* monitoring. In addition all depseudonymisations of audit records are logged. The implementation of this functionality in Solaris 2.4 and in AID is under way. The usage of *public key* encryption for pseudonymization is also examined.

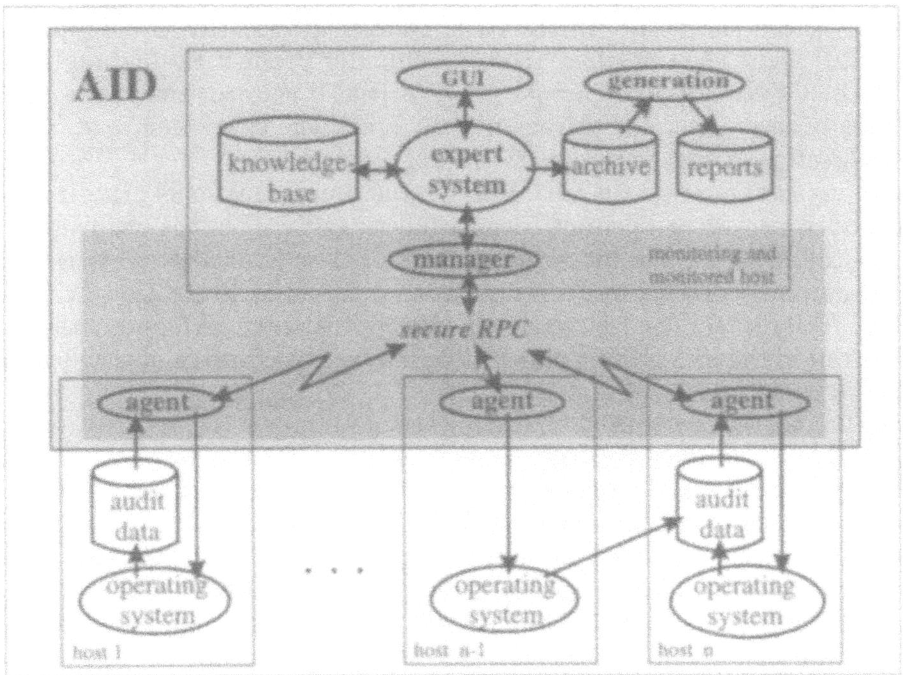

Figure 3 Architecture of the AID system

4 PSEUDONYMOUS AUDIT AND IT SECURITY EVALUATION

For over a decade now independent ("3rd Party") evaluation of the security properties of IT products and systems is considered as a relevant instrument to raise the level of IT security. The main idea behind this evaluation is, that users and procurs can place more trust into evaluation results or certificates of independent evaluators than into declarations just stated by producers or vendors.

A basic element for the evaluation results and the evaluation process is the criteria used. Therefore this chapter gives a short analysis whether the rather innovative security concept of pseudonymous audit is covered by the criteria in a way leading to meaningful evaluation results.

4.1 Evaluation Criteria and Privacy Enhancing Security

Most criteria differentiate the security properties of a *Target of Evaluation* (TOE; i.e. the IT product or system under evaluation) into *functionality* and *assurance* aspects. *Functionality* aspects describe what a TOE can do regarding IT security, e.g. audit, privacy protection or information flow control. *Assurance* aspects focus on how and to which extent the TOE has been evaluated, e.g whether just black box testing or a real code verification have been done. Consequently pseudonymous audit should be covered by the functionality part of criteria.

Early criteria are the US "Trusted Computer System Evaluation Criteria" [US_DOD85], the European "Information Technology Security Evaluation Criteria" [CEC91] and "The Canadian Trusted Computer Product Evaluation Criteria" (CTCPEC) [CDN_SSC93]. A former analysis [Ra94] showed, that none of these criteria really covers user and privacy friendly functionality, as their focus is biased on the protection of system owners instead of users or usees.

Despite its shortcomings the CTCPEC's structure of functional criteria was extendable to cover user and privacy friendly functionality. This was one reason, why it formed the basis for the functionality part of the "Evaluation Criteria for IT Security" currently drafted by Working Group 3 "Security Evaluation Criteria" of ISO/IEC JTC1/SC27. The last version of this approach can be found in the winter 1995/96 draft of the ISO-ECITS part 2 [ISO/IEC95]. Its coverage of pseudonymous audit is discussed in 4.3.

In parallel to the work in ISO/IEC, seven government IT security organisations (eg. the US National Security Agency and the German Information Security Agency) from six transatlantic countries (CDN, D, F, NL, UK, USA) started to develop an own set of criteria, the so-called "Common Criteria" (CC), whose draft version 1.0 [CCEB96] has been published in January 1996. The CC aimed to cover all the previous national and regional criteria. In April 1996 the CC replaced the previous working drafts in ISO/IEC JTC1/SC27/WG3, although they had caught hard criticism for their size, their structure and the fact, that they did not cover all the functionality from the previous drafts.

4.2 The Common Criteria and Pseudonymous Audit

According to the CC, the TOE IT security functional requirements (and consequently the evaluation results) are to be structured on the basis of *Security Functional Components*. These ca. 180 functional components are grouped into 76 *Families*, which are further grouped into 9 classes. *Dependencies* between functional components are listed in the components definitions.

Pseudonymity (FPR_PSE) is a family in the the class *Privacy* (FPR). Its component *Reversible Pseudonymity* (FPR_PSE.2) has a linkage to pseudonymous audit: it specifies, that aliases for user identities are provided and that only under certain conditions (to be defined before the evaluation) an authorised administrator can determine the user identity from the alias. So there is a partial coverage for pseudonymous audit, but the protection of user identifying data besides the user identities (cf. 3.3) is not covered.

The class *Security Audit* (FAU) consists of twelve families. Pseudonymous audit should be covered by those families, which specify requirements for the the generation and analysis of audit data:

- Security Audit Data Generation (FAU_GEN);
- Profile-Based Anomaly Detection (FAU_PAD);
- Penetration Identification Tools (FAU_PIT);
- Security Audit Analysis (FAU_SAA);
- Security Audit Review (FAU_SAR).

No component of these families considers pseudonymous audit or contains any declaration of dependencies to the Pseudonymity components. Only audit based on "classical" user identities (as described in component *Basic User Identification* (FIA_UID.1) is covered. Although the term "Identity" is not defined in the CC, the way in which it is used leaves no room for the interpretation, that pseudonyms are covered. To achieve this coverage via redefinition of "Identity" probably requires greater restructuring of the CC. An alternative [SoRa96] would be to modify the families listed above by:

1. Extension of the functionality to cover the use of reversible pseudonyms: This applies especially to FAU_GEN and its component FAU_GEN.2 (User Identity Generation);
2. Integration of a dependency statement to FPR_PSE.2 (Reversible Pseudonymity) into all components of the families FAU_PAD, FAU_PIT, FAU_SAA, FAU_SAR.

4.3 The ISO-ECITS Draft and Pseudonymous Audit

The basis for structuring the TOE IT security functional requirements are *Functionality Levels* (roughly comparable to the CC's functional components) of 29 *Security Services* (roughly comparable to the CC's families). *Dependencies* between functionality levels are declared in their definitions. Generally the description of the functionality levels as well as that of the security services is much broader and less detailed than that of the corresponding elements in the CC.

The *Pseudonymity Services* come in two functionality levels: "Pseudonymity for Partner Authentication" and "Pseudonymity for Third Party Authentication". They describe that users "may use a resource or service without disclosing their identity but can still be held accountable for that use". Depending on whether the audit analysis is done by the same party as the audit generation, the first or the second level can be used to specify the requirements. The rather general service specifications also cover the protection of user identifying data besides the user identities.

Five functionality levels are given for the *Audit Services.* The range of audit functionality described in this paper is covered by the highest level "Advanced Detection". As well as in the CC the declaration of dependencies to Pseudonymity Services is missing and should be added. Different from the CC the "Identity" management issue is handled in a way that makes it much easier to cover pseudonymous audit. This is achieved by a reasonable general specification, especially concerning the identity recoverage process.

All in all, the functionality descriptions of the ISO-ECITS Draft, though being much shorter than those of the CC, provide a more comprehensive basis for specifying the requirements for a pseudonymous audit TOE.

5 OUTLOOK

The concept of pseudonymous audit for privacy enhanced intrusion detection can help to approach the conflict between classical IT security and privacy by providing both accountability and pseudonymity. So far, privacy enhanced intrusion detection has been only implemented in two research prototypes. But it will probably become more relevant in future, because it can be a more privacy friendly and thereby socially and legally acceptable solution. In a networked society witzh increasing privacy risks it will be neccesary to develop and apply more privacy enhancing technologies as well as criteria for their assessment and comparison.

REFERENCES

[BauKo88] Bauer, D. S.; Koblentz, M. E.: NIDX - An expert system for real-time network intrusion detection, Proc. of the IEEE Computer Networking Symp., New York, NY, April 1988, 98-106

[Bru+91] Brunnstein, K.; Fischer-Hübner, S.; Swimmer, M.: Concepts of an expert system for virus detection, Lindsay, D.; Price, W. (eds.): Information Security, Proc. of the IFIP/Sec'91-Conference, Brighton, UK, May 1991, North Holland, Elsevier, 391-402

[CCEB96] Common Criteria Editorial Board: Common Criteria for Information Technology Security Evaluation, version 1.0, Jan. 1996, 4 of 5 parts

[CDN_SSC93] Canadian System Security Center: The Canadian Trusted Security Evaluation Criteria, version 3.0e, Jan. 1993, Communications Security Establishment, Government of Canada

[CEC91] Commission of the European Communities: IT Security Evaluation Criteria, V. 1.2, Office for Official Publications of the European Communities, Luxembourg, June 1991

[Chau85] Chaum, D.: Security without Identification: Transaction systems to make a Big Brother obsolete, CACM 28(1985)10, 1030-1044

[De+87] Denning, D. E.; Neumann, P. G.; Parker, D.: Social aspects of computer security, Proc. of the 10th National Computer Security Conference (NCSC), Baltimore, MD, 1987, 320-325

[DoRa90] Dowell, C.; Ramstedt, P.: The ComputerWatch data reduction tool, Proc. of the 13th NCSC, Washington, D.C., Oct. 1990, 99-108

[DSL90] Intrusion Detection: The State of the Art, Data Security Letter no. 22, Nov. 1990, 4-7

[EU95] Directive 95/46/EC of the European Parliament and of the Council of 24 October 1995 on the protection of individuals with regard to the processing of personal data and on the free movement of such data

[Fi92] Fischer-Hübner, S.: IDA - An Intrusion Detection and Avoidance System (in German), dissertation, Aachen, Shaker, 1992

[Fi94] Fischer-Hübner, S.: Towards a privacy-friendly design and use of IT-security mechanisms, Proc. of the 17th NCSC, Baltimore, MD, Oct. 1994, 142-152

[Fi+92] Fischer-Hübner, S.; Yngström, L.; Holvast, J.: Addressing vulnerability and privacy problems generated by the use of IT-security mechanisms, in Aiken, R. (ed.): Proc. of the IFIP 12th World Computer Congress, vol. II, Education and Society, Madrid, Sept. 1992, 245-257

[HaMa92] Habra, N.; Mathieu, I.: ASAX: Software architecture and rule-based language for universal audit trail analysis, Deswarte, Y.; Eizenberg, G. (eds.): Proc. of the 2nd European Symposium on Research in Computer Security (ESORICS' 92), Toulouse, Nov. 1992, 435-450

[HLI95] Haystack Laboratories, Inc.: Stalker version 2, product description, 1995

[ISO/IEC95] International Organization for Standardization /International Electrotechnical Commission, Joint Technical Committee 1, Subcommittee 27: Evaluation Criteria for IT Security, Part 1-3, Working Drafts Winter 1995/96; Documents ISO/IEC JTC1/SC27/N1269, ISO/IEC JTC1/SC27/N1270, ISO/IEC JTC1/SC27/N1271

[Lu+92] Lunt, T. et al.: A real time Intrusion Detection Expert System (IDES) - Final Report, SRI International, Menlo Park, CA, Feb. 1992

[Mo91] Moitra, A.: Audit Log Viewer and Analyzer, Proc. of the 7th Intrusion Detection Workshop, May 1991, SRI International, Menlo Park, CA

[Pfi+91] Pfitzmann, A.; Pfitzmann, B.; Waidner, M.: ISDN-MIXes: Untraceable communication with very small bandwidth overhead, Proc. of the IFIP-TC11 Sec'91 Conference, Brighton, UK, May 1991, 245-257

[Pro94] Proctor, P.: Audit reduction and misuse detection in heterogeneous environments: Framework and application, Proc. of the 10th Annual Computer Security Applications Conference, Orlando, FL, Dec. 1994, 117-125

[Ra94] Rannenberg, K.: Recent Development in IT Security Evaluation - The Need for Evaluation Criteria for multilateral Security; in Sizer, R. et al.: Security and Control of Information Technology in Society - Proc. of the IFIP TC9/WG 9.6 Working Conference, August 12-17, 1993, St. Petersburg, Russia; North-Holland, Amsterdam, 1994, 113-128

[ReIPC95] Registratiekamer, The Netherlands & Information and Privacy Commissioner/Ontario, Canada: Privacy-enhancing Technologies: The path to anonymity, vol. I, Aug. 1995

[Schae91] Schaefer, L. J.: Employee privacy and intrusion detection systems: Monitoring on the job, Proc. of the 14th NCSC, Washington, D. C., Oct. 1991, 188-194

[Sma88] Smaha, S. E.: Haystack: An intrusion detection system, Proc. of the 11th NCSC, Baltimore, MD, Oct. 1988, 37-44

[SmaWi94] Smaha, S. E.; Winslow, J.: Misuse detection tools, Computer Security Journal 10(1994)1, Spring, 39-49

[Sna+91] Snapp, S. R. et al.: DIDS (Distributed Intrusion Detection System) - Motivation, architecture and an early prototype, Proc. of the 14th NCSC, Washington, Oct. 1991, 167-176

[So+96] Sobirey, M.; Richter, B.; König, H.: The Intrusion Detection System AID. Architecture, and experiences in automated audit analysis, in Horster, P. (ed.): Communications and Multimedia Security II, Proc. of the IFIP TC6/TC11 International Conference on Communications and Multimedia Security, Essen, Germany, Sept. 1996, Chapman & Hall, London, 278-290

[SoFi96] Sobirey, M.; Fischer-Hübner, S.: Privacy oriented audit, Draft Proc. of the 13th Annual CSR (Centre for Software Reliability) Workshop "Design for Protecting the User", Bürgenstock, Switzerland, Sept. 1996, section 13

[SoRa96] Sobirey, M.; Rannenberg, K.: Remarks on the Coverage of Pseudonymous Auditing in the Evaluation Criteria for IT Security; Att. 2 to the German NB Reasons for disapproval of ISO/IEC CD 15408-2 (ISO/IEC JTC 1/SC 27 N 1402); Summary of Voting, ISO/IEC JTC 1/SC27 N1476

[US_DOD85] US DoD Standard: Department of Defense Trusted Computer System Evaluation Criteria, Dec. 1985, DOD 5200.28-STD, Supersedes CSC-STD-001-83, dtd 15 Aug. 83

BIOGRAPHIES

Michael Sobirey completed his diploma in computer science at the University of Technology "Otto v. Guericke" Magdeburg. Since April 1993 he has been scientific assistent at the Brandenburg University of Technology at Cottbus, Computer Science Institute. His research interests are real-time monitoring of heterogeneous networks and privacy-oriented security functions. He is member of the DIN working group NI 27c "Evaluation criteria for IT security" and of the National Expert Working Group "IT Security Criteria". He is leader of the research project AID.

Simone Fischer-Hübner studied Computer Science with a minor in Law at Hamburg University. She obtained her doctoral degree (Ph.D.) in July 1992. She is currently an Assistant Professor at the University of Hamburg, Faculty for Informatics. From Sept. 1994 - March 1995 she was a Guest Professor at the Copenhagen Business School, Institute for Computer and System Sciences. Her teaching and reseach has been focused on IT security and privacy. She is a founding member and secretary of IFIP WG 9.6, member of IFIP WG 11.8 and member of the National Expert Working Group on IT Security Evaluation Criteria.

Kai Rannenberg, Dipl.-Inform., TU Berlin 1989. 1989-1993 TU Berlin; 1990 Berlin Privacy Commissioner; 1993- University of Freiburg, Coordinator of the "Security in Communication Technology" Kolleg sponsored by Gottlieb Daimler and Karl Benz Foundation. Member of IFIP WG 9.6, IFIP WG 11.4, ISO/IEC JTC1/SC27/WG3 "Security Evaluation Criteria" and its German shadow group, GI "Privacy and IT Security Task Force", National Expert Working Group "IT Security Criteria"; Secretary of the CEPIS Special Interest Network Legal and Security Issues. Research focus: IT Security and Privacy for public and open communication systems, especially in standards and evaluation criteria.

Individual Management of Personal Reachability in Mobile Communication

Martin Reichenbach[1], Herbert Damker[1], Hannes Federrath[2], Kai Rannenberg[1]

[1] University of Freiburg, Institute for Informatics and Society, Department of Telematics, Friedrichstr. 50, D-79098 Freiburg, Germany

Phone: +49-761-203-4931, Fax: +49-761-203-4929

E-Mail: {marei, damker, kara}@iig.uni-freiburg.de

[2] Dresden University of Technology, Institute for Theoretical Informatics, H.-Grundig-Str. 25, D-01062 Dresden, Germany

Phone: +49-351-463-8470, Fax: +49-351-463-8255

E-Mail: federrath@inf.tu-dresden.de

Abstract

This paper describes a concept for controlling personal reachability while maintaining a high degree of privacy and data protection. By easy negotiation of their communication requests users can reach others without disturbing the called partners and without compromising their own privacy.

Reachability management can strengthen the called subscriber's right to self-determined communication without violating the callers' interests in protecting their personal data.*

Keywords

Security and Protection; Communications Applications

* Parts of this work are funded by the Gottlieb Daimler and Karl Benz Foundation (Ladenburg, Germany) as part of its Kolleg "Security in Communication Technology".

1 PERSONAL REACHABILITY MANAGEMENT AND MULTILATERAL SECURITY

Current opportunities for mobile communication increase the technical reachability of users. This, of course, endangers their right to self-determined communication. Persons, who need to be available for professional reasons, are particularly affected. Their need of personal mobility and technical availability rises. Frequently they are without a secretary's support. Some people even have to fear annoying and harassing calls in their private life.

The increased technical availability necessitates a new class of services in order to facilitate the self-control of one's personal reachability – **personal reachability management** (cf. 1.1).

As the interests of different parties participating in communications differ, personal reachability management is a telecommunication-area example for multilateral security (cf. 1.2 and 1.3). It's prototype implementation is going to serve as the basis for a trial to demonstrate the concepts of multilateral security and to examine their relation to the users' needs (cf. 1.4).

1.1 What is "Personal Reachability Management"?

Subscribers are able to control their personal reachability through the technical support provided by their personal Reachability Management System.

During the signalling phase of a call the caller transmits information concerning the nature and content of his communication request (cf. 2.1). Before the subscriber being called – the "callee" – is personally contacted, this communication request is evaluated and negotiated by his Reachability Management System.

Subscribers are able to configure their reachability easily for different situations. The situations may arise from daily life or requirements of the work environment.

By supporting these new services personal reachability management offers a high degree of security and privacy to the users.

1.2 Multilateral Security, Data Economy and Careful Allocation

A lot of the early security approaches (e.g. [USA_DOD85]) are focused on the protection of system owners and operators only. Frequently the security of users and subscribers has been neglected. The term **multilateral security** [Ranne94] is therefore used here to describe an approach aiming at a balance between the different security requirements of different parties.

In particular, respecting the different security requirements of the parties involved implies renouncing the commonly used precondition, that the parties have to trust each other, and especially renouncing the precondition, that the subscribers have to place complete trust into the service providers. Consequently, each party must be viewed as a potential attacker on the other and the safeguards have to be designed accordingly.

The following list gives some examples of different security requirements of different parties:

- Subscribers deserve protection from others, especially network operators or service providers, monitoring their communication activities (confidentiality, especially unobservability and message content confidentiality).

- Providers deserve protection from fraud, e.g. through unpaid and unaccountable calls, for which no subscriber takes responsibility (accountability, especially non-repudiation).
- Network operators deserve protection from sabotage, endangering the use of their systems (integrity and availability).
- Subscribers deserve protection from harassing calls, for which no one takes responsibility (accountability, especially non-repudiation).

The best design strategy to fulfil the confidentiality requirements is the **avoidance of data**, e.g. in communication protocols. In this context, data that do not exist or are not transmitted, need no protection from unauthorized use. Since identification data, for instance, are frequently needed for accountability purposes, complete data avoidance is rarely possible. Nevertheless the strategy of **data economy** (i.e. to avoid data, wherever possible) is worthwhile, because it reduces the expenditure for data protection.

Another helpful design strategy in order to reduce the risk of misuse is the strategy of **careful allocation**. This means especially to give the storage and the processing of data into the control of those who require the confidentiality.

1.3 Reachability Management as an Example for Multilateral Security

Personal reachability management can be viewed as an example for multilateral security as well as for the design strategies of data economy and careful allocation.

The need for multilateral security comes from the different interests of callers and callees. Callees are interested in avoiding a possible disturbance, e.g. by getting more information on an arriving call before answering it. On the other side callers are frequently interested in protecting their anonymity and in keeping their communication request confidential.

The following examples illustrate these issues and show which facets of security could be important in different situations:

- In order to avoid disturbance a medical woman or nurse in a nocturnal stand-by service is not interested in every call which might arrive at night. She wants to be reachable for emergency calls and perhaps also for near relatives or friends, for whom she would get up even at night. Potentially she wants to defend herself from annoying calls. Accordingly, her Reachability Management System will request the identity or function information from the caller before ringing the bell (and disturbing her sleep). Protection from transmission errors and from callers, pretending to be someone else, requires the integrity of the call information and the accountability of the call.
- The staff of a welfare centre as well as mobile social workers may use a Reachability Management System to ease their work during rush periods. The clients of welfare centres which handle socially taboo topics like AIDS, alcoholism, venereal disease or indebtedness generally want to stay anonymous. Often this anonymity is a prerequisite for an open and really helpful consultation. The client must therefore be able to contact the welfare centre anonymously. It must be guaranteed that, in fact, no identity information is transmitted. If the consultation can take place anonymously, but not free of charge, it must be possible to call under a pseudonym.

Providing a satisfying degree of both confidentiality and accountability of callers is not a simple task. Current caller identification mechanisms allow either, that callees protect themselves by forcing the callers to show their identity (to give some accountability to a call), or they allow, that callers stay anonymous (thus protecting their confidentiality).

Some systems allow calling users a per-call choice whether to show their identification or not, but even then the called users have no instrument to differentiate calls, before they are disturbed. Their only way to get some information about an incoming call is to look for the caller identification. This way the callers are forced to show this identification and lose their anonymity, even when other means would be more appropriate (cf. 2.1).

Personal Reachability Management is a more flexible approach allowing the caller and the callee to exchange only the information, that is really needed. This economical use of data enables the transmission of less personal data, which deserves to be protected.

The data arising in the context of personal reachability management are extremely sensitive: some of them describe callers' and callees' current situations, some (e.g. the programmed reaction to incoming communication requests) contain information on personal attitudes towards other people. Information like this may even be protected by the privacy regulations of some states. It must be allocated carefully and has to be protected from all potential communication partners as well as from third parties, such as service providers. The personal reachability data and programmes should therefore be located at a place, where those users, whose data are processed, can control them (cf. 2.2).

While the personal Reachability Management System can be seen as a prime example for the implementation of multilateral security both in a telecommunication terminal and on the application level, complementary work is needed on network and network infrastructure levels. Examples of techniques aimed at multilateral security on those levels can be found in [Chaum85, KFJP96, MS95, Pfitz93, PW87 and PPW91].

1.4 Demonstrating and Examining Multilateral Security

The personal reachability management prototype is currently being developed in the (virtual college) project "Security in Communications", mainly sponsored by the independent Gottlieb Daimler and Karl Benz Foundation, Ladenburg, Germany.

On one hand this prototype serves as an example demonstrator for the implementation of multilateral security in communication technology. On the other hand it will be examined in laboratory experiments and in trials. These trials are based on the simulation study method [KS95] and on cases occurring in the daily work of actors in the public health service, e.g. mobile nursing.

The trials will examine the subscribers' requirements for security and trustworthiness in the context of using telecommunication devices and networks. The prototype therefore has to contain additional security mechanisms (authentication, trusted services, user-to-user-encryption) or to provide at least a demonstration of their operation.

2 DESIGN OF THE REACHABILITY MANAGEMENT SYSTEM

According to the strategies aiming at multilateral security the main design aspects of the Reachability Management System are the communication context and the representation of urgency (cf. 2.1) as well as the secure data processing and storage (cf. 2.2). To ease the demonstration of multilateral security, a special effort has been placed into the usability and the user interface of the prototype (cf. 2.3).

2.1 The Communication Context and the Representation of Urgency

This chapter describes the central idea enabling multilateral security in a call situation - the careful modelling of the **communication context**. The communication context illustrates a communication request (respectively a proposal) or a currently existing communication between two (or more) partners. The communication context is transmitted as a whole or in parts during the signalling phase and is the object of the arrangement between the reachability managers involved.

The connection with the called subscriber will only be established if the negotiated communication context has fulfilled certain conditions. If not, the reachability manager is capable of offering a variety of reactions, for example storing a message, or diverting a call to another person.

A communication context contains information about:

- how the communication partners are acquainted with each other (anonymous, by a pseudonym, with their real identity);
- the intention of the communication request;
- the urgency of the communication request;
- the manner of communication (the kind of service involved);
- the existing security requirements;
- the mechanisms used to ensure the actual communication.

Of particular significance is the way the urgency of a communication request is represented. Consistent with the interpersonal negotiation of reachability, a technical system should provide a multitude of options. The subscribers to the Reachability Management System can provide details about the subjective urgency or a reference.

Possible options are:

- The **assertion of urgency**: The caller indicates a certain degree of urgency while he is trying to get hold of someone. This assessment may be very subjective.
- The **specification of a function**: The caller can give details about the reason for his call, about his position, or even his qualification. He may, for instance, call as a member of a particular project or company. This specification may be digitally certified.
- The **specification of a subject**: This specification may only be evaluated by the reachability manager when a prearranged list of possible topics exists.
- The **provision of a reference**: The caller mentions the recommendation of a third person. This might be accomplished by means of a certificate issued by this third person. If the called subscriber knows the third person, he may use this recommendation as a criterion for evaluating the communication request.
- The **presentation of a voucher**: The voucher differs from the reference in that it has been issued by the called subscriber himself. It may increase the chance of a return call.

- **Offering a surety**: In order to emphasize the seriousness of his communication request and his statement of urgency, the caller may remit to the called subscriber a (possibly negotiated) amount as a surety. If the called subscriber does not agree with the caller's evaluation of the urgency of his call, he has the potential to withhold this amount or remit it to a public welfare institution, or a similar organisation.

In the personal configuration of his Reachability Management System the subscriber determines the different kinds of reactions to incoming calls (respectively communication requests). He defines, which information the Reachability Management System will request from the caller in order to evaluate the communication request. A likely example will be that the called subscriber's Reachability Management System requests the identification or a surety from an unidentified caller.

2.2 Secure Data Processing and Storage

The configuration of the Reachability Management System demands a high degree of confidence. The user entrusts very sensitive personal data to a technical system, e.g. the information when he can be reached and which persons he wants to communicate with.

This requires:

- Processing and storage in a trustworthy and personal environment: Because the data should also be protected against third parties, such as service providers and network operators, the Reachability Management System can't be implemented as a purely network service (cf. 1.3).
- Protection against malicious investigation: The process of negotiation between the reachability managers should be arranged such that even repeated requests reveal no information about the personal configuration of any subscriber's reachability. It should be possible to discover attempts to gain such information.
- Protection from unintentional revelation of personal information or financial values such as sureties: This requirement should particularly be considered while designing the user interface of the Reachability Management System.
- The user's ability to audit the system: At all times the user should be able to control, change or delete all the information stored in his Reachability Management System. In particular, there should no data be stored in the Reachability Management System which would allow third parties to reconstruct the subscriber's communication behaviour if the reachability manager is lost.

It is essential to secure the communication and negotiation between two Reachability Management Systems according to the objectives of multilateral security. The confidentiality of transferred data can be guaranteed by point-to-point-encryption. Anonymity and unobservability may only be achieved by an appropriate underlying network infrastructure (cf. 1.3 and [KFJP96, Pfitz93]). In order to support these tasks, the Reachability Management System fulfils security functions, like managing information regarding the subscriber's location in a mobile communication network [Hetsc93, MS95].

Reachability managers have to function correctly even in the case of abuse or attack: The integrity and, if necessary, the accountability of the data transferred with a communication request have to be guaranteed. In order to fulfil these requirements the user has to supply evidence of the authenticity of his identity information by delivering a digital signature or a certificate.

To a certain extent the topic is related to access control systems (controlling the access to a called person's private sphere) and to value transfer systems. A value transfer system passes on values like "Reachability Rights", e.g. references and vouchers in a secure way. In order to confirm the declaration of urgency by means of a surety the transfer of a value is also needed.

2.3 Usability and the User Interface

Reachability management constitutes an extension to the service offered by a normal telephone. Some additional effort is required in usage, because the user has to assign additional specifications about the urgency of his call (over and above the information regarding which communication partner he wants to get hold of).

Standardized call templates reduce this effort by delivering default values, e.g. "normal" urgency, or the delivery of a small surety. As the Reachability Management System gives the opportunity to access a subscriber directory the effort may be reduced even more.

Furthermore, each subscriber is reachable under exactly one address, no matter where or in which situation he is.

The task of the user interface is to support the user while formulating his communication requests, presenting the actual communication context and configuring his reachability. It should also be possible to change the user's status.

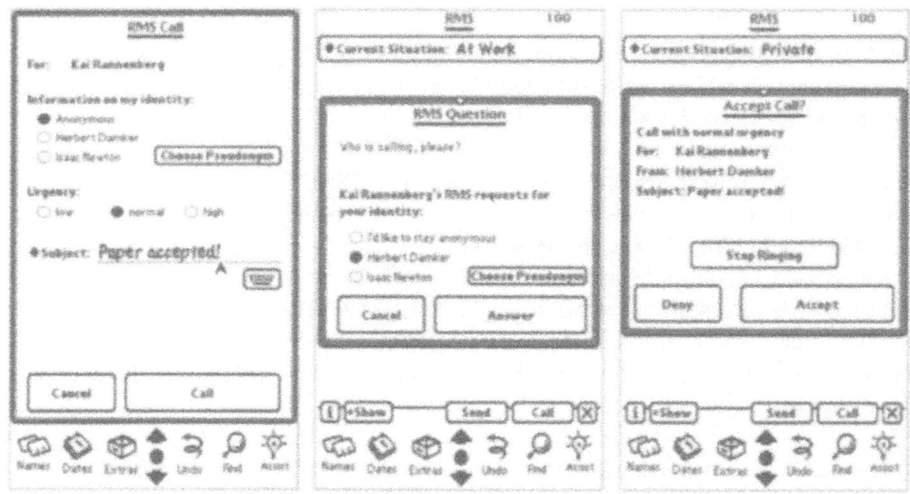

Figure 1 Reachability Management Dialogues on the Newton MessagePad™

Figure 1 shows three of these dialogues on the Newton MessagePad™(formulating a communication request, a question from the called subscriber's Reachability Management System and the display of an incoming call).

3 TECHNICAL IMPLEMENTATION OF THE REACHABILITY MANAGEMENT SYSTEM

3.1 Hardware Architecture

The implementation of the Reachability Management System involves two components.

The "personal communication assistant" serves as a trustworthy personal environment. While building communication requests it supports the caller by delivering a subscriber directory. On the other side it signals incoming calls and messages to the called subscriber. The sensitive reachability information is stored in this component.

The mobile part of the reachability manager is complemented by a "stationary subscriber station". This component is localized, for example, at the subscriber's home or office, accepting all the communication requests for the user and, should the occasion arise, forwarding them to the user's personal communication assistant. The stationary subscriber station performs additional functions of the Reachability Management System, which can't (yet) be implemented by a mobile device, for example, the recording of speech messages.

Within the scope of this project the personal communication assistant will be based on a Newton Message Pad™ with demonstrator functionality.

The stationary subscriber station is being implemented on a Personal Computer, connected to the fixed network via ISDN (Integrated Services Digital Network). The communication between the personal communication assistant and the stationary subscriber station takes place over the cellular mobile communication network GSM (Global System for Mobile communication).

3.2 Functional architecture

Figure 2 shows the functional structure of the Reachability Management System (both personal communication assistant and stationary subscriber station). The Reachability Management System consists of three functional units: the user interface, the core machine and the communication services.

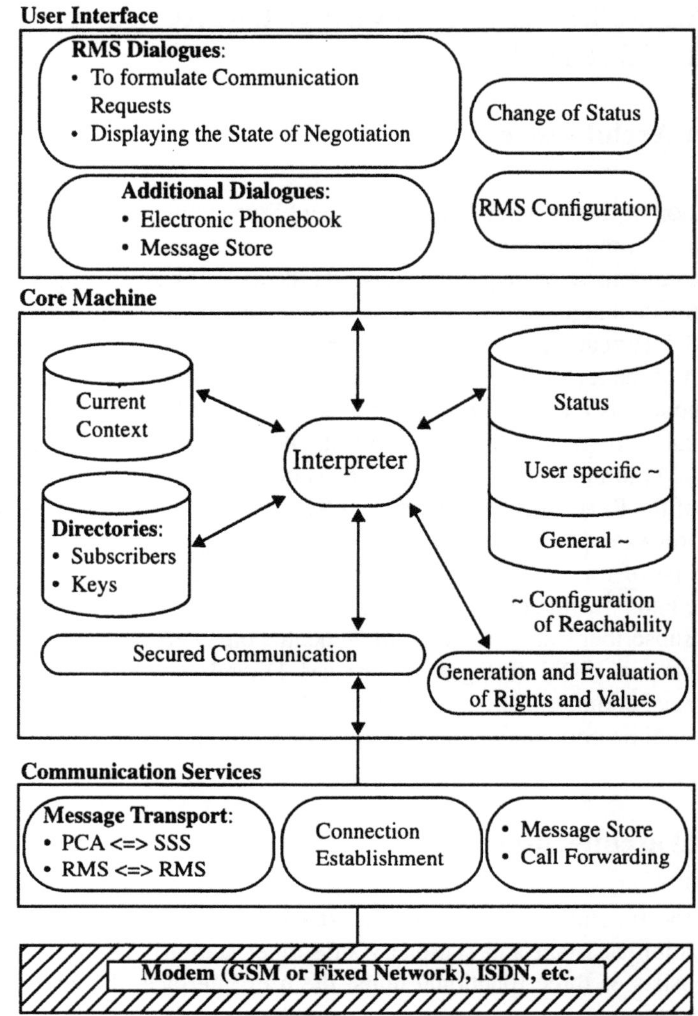

Figure 2 Functional Architecture of the Reachability Management System (RMS - Reachability Management System, PCA - Personal Communication Assistant, SSS - Stationary Subscriber Station).

4 THE CORE MACHINE

The core machine is the central technical part of the Reachability Management System. It evaluates the current communication context. This context is set up using the subscriber's specifications, as well as the data transmitted from the communication partner. The rules of evaluation come from three different areas:

- The status describes the user's current situation (e.g. "private", "at work", "meeting"). This information changes frequently and determines which part of the rules will be applied.
- The user specific configuration is defined in the Reachability Management System's configuration dialogue. In this dialogue the subscriber uses individual evaluation rules to define how the reachability manager should react to incoming communication requests.
- The evaluation rules are complemented by common reachability rules which can't be changed by the subscribers (for example the definition that emergency calls should always be put through).

As a result of the evaluation, the interpreter updates the communication context and decides whether the communication request will be accepted or denied. The interpreter may also require further information (from the user or from the caller) to make the final decision. Subsequently, appropriate messages will be sent to the user of the reachability manager (or rather to the user interface) resp. to other components of the user's or the caller's reachability manager.

5 REACHABILITY MANAGEMENT IN FUTURE NETWORK INFRASTRUCTURES

To receive the full benefit from multilateral secure reachability managers in future network infrastructures, the networks have to support the concept of multilateral security.

The network's support is necessary for anonymous and pseudonymous, or even better, unobservable communication. Broadcast signalling and implicit addressing [KFJP96, Pfitz93, PW87, PPW91] is a part of this. Even if many of these features might seem to be unrealistic today because of the networks narrow bandwidth, they should be easier to implement with the help of future broadband networks. Then the reachability manager could be addressed via temporarily valid implicit addresses, which the subscriber hands out to a circle of well chosen persons.

The limited possibilities of the today's signalling channels indicate an additional problem. They only allow the transmission of absolutely necessary signalling information. In future it will possibly be better to deviate from the strict separation of (free of charge) signalling and (subject to charges) data communication. If universally available services like "Universal Personal Communication" (UPT) are to be established it will be obligatory to extend the signalling networks.

Features like "offering a surety" inevitably call for the integration of systems for electronic payments or the transfer of values. However, in these systems the subscriber's anonymity and unobservability have to be guaranteed.

6 REFERENCES

[Chaum85] Chaum, D. (1985) Security without Identification: Transaction Systems to make Big Brother Obsolete; Communications of the ACM 28/10 (1985), 1030-1044.

[Hetsc93] Hetschold, T. (1993) Aufbewahrbarkeit von Erreichbarkeits- und Schlüsselinformation im Gewahrsam des Endbenutzers unter Erhaltung der GSM-Funktionalität eines Funknetzes. GMD-Studien Nr. 222, Oktober 1993.

[KFJP96] Kesdogan, D.; Federrath, H.; Jerichow, A. and Pfitzmann, A. (1996) Location Management Strategies increasing Privacy in Mobile Communication Systems; in Information Systems Security. Facing the information society of the 21st century. Proc. IFIP/SEC '96 - 12th International Information Security Conference 21-24 May 1996, Island of Samos, Greece, Chapman & Hall, 1996.

[KS95] Kumbruck, C. and Schneider, M.J. (1995) Simulation Studies, a new method of prospective Technology Assessment and Design; Working Paper, No. 190, provet, Darmstadt, September 1995.

[MS95] Müller, G. and Stoll, F. (1995) The Freiburg Communications Assistant Enabling Decentralization and Privacy in Mobile Communications Systems. Speaker's Papers, 7th World Telecommunication Forum, Technology Summit "Convergence of technologies, services and applications" Vol. 1, ITU Telecom 95 Technical Forum, Geneva, 3-11 October 1995, International Telecommunication Union, October 1995, 245-249.

[Pfitz93] Pfitzmann, A. (1993) Technischer Datenschutz in öffentlichen Funknetzen; Datenschutz und Datensicherung DuD 17/8 (1993) 451-463.

[PW87] Pfitzmann, A. and Waidner, M. (1987) Networks without user observability; Computers & Security 6/2 (1987), 158-166.

[PPW91] Pfitzmann, A.; Pfitzmann, B. and Waidner, M. (1991) ISDN-MIXes - Untraceable Communication with very small Bandwidth Overhead; Proc. IFIP/SEC '91 - 7th International Information Security Conference Brighton, UK, May 1991; North-Holland; 1991; 245-258.

[Ranne94] Rannenberg, K. (1994) Recent Development in Information Technology Security Evaluation – The Need for Evaluation Criteria for multilateral Security; in Richard Sizer, Louise Yngström, Henrik Kaspersen and Simone Fischer-Hübner: Security and Control of Information Technology in Society – Proceedings of the IFIP TC9/WG 9.6 Working Conference August 12-17, 1993, onboard M/S Ilich and ashore at St. Petersburg, Russia; North-Holland; 1994, 113-128.

[USA_DOD85] DoD Standard (1985) Department of Defense Trusted Computer System Evaluation Criteria; December 1985, DOD 5200.28-STD, Supersedes CSC-STD-001-83, dtd 15 Aug 83, Library No. S225,711.

PART EIGHT

Assessment and Evaluation of Secure Systems

15

New vistas on info-system security

Willis H. Ware
RAND
1700 Main Street
Santa Monica, California 90407, USA
310-393-0411 x6432, 310-451-7038 FAX, willis@rand.org

Abstract
This paper traces the history and evolution of the various criteria efforts associated with computer system and network security. It notes several new security requirements arising from new system architectures, intense networking, different operational environments, and evolving online services. Finally, it speculates on the continuing role of the Common Criteria.

Keywords
Security, system security, computer security, network security, criteria, Common Criteria, security requirements, future security, vendors.

INTRODUCTION

This paper first reviews history, chronology and background of various criteria efforts* which collectively will be considered the 'criteria movement' and indicates how they have fitted into the overall scheme of secure systems. It then considers the future, offers suggestions for aspects of security that have yet to be addressed, and considers what role criteria might play.**

The scope of this paper is that of the information systems we encounter in our daily lives; namely, those of commerce and industry, those of government and those that serve

**Criteria* is used in this paper in the sense that it has appeared since the early 1980s in the computer security community. Typically, it is a document containing sets of functional and/or technical attributes that define and characterize safeguards used in secure information systems. Hence, it serves both as design guidance and also as a test standard. The *criteria movement* includes not only the several criteria themselves, but also their influence and the involvement of government bodies, academic researchers, and commercial organizations.

**The historical review portion of this paper is based in part on the author's paper (Ware, 1995).

and control us personally. This discussion does not address problems that are unique to what are commonly called embedded systems; namely, computer-based systems that are an integral part of (such things as) process control and automation, of computer-based management of power grids, of flight controls in aircraft. They collectively are part of the operational infrastructure of the country but not directly of the information infrastructure.

HISTORY

In the late 1960s, remote access systems were entering operational status, and organizations became interested in sharing them among many users, sometimes for revenue. The US Government (namely, the Department of Defense) realized that it had no policy in place for the security of such an operational environment; and among other actions, sponsored a study group to examine the issue and make recommendations.

The outcome of this effort was the well-known (at least in the United States) 'Defense Science Board report' (Ware 1970). Since the time was the early 1970's, it is not surprising that the report said little about software.

At that time, except for one defense project (Peters, 1965), no one had really examined the software issue in regard to security safeguards, nor had the computer science research community addressed it. Other aspects, now well understood to be a part of the comprehensive computer security environment, were covered though: the communications, administrative, management oversight, personnel, and physical aspects of overall system security. Hardware, as is still true today, was not addressed. Again, because of its calendar timing, the report also reflected the environment of the period: pre-LAN, pre-explosion of microcircuits, pre-small computers, pre-intense networking, pre-Internet.

Subsequently, the Department of Defense [via the United States Air Force and the Advanced Research Projects Agency] sponsored research throughout the 70s, including three major efforts to build secure versions of then popular operating systems.*

Toward the end of the 70s, the government realized its dilemma. Industry was not producing secure software, and was not likely to commit the required investment because commercial demand for it was not perceived. The government concluded that if it wanted secure system software, it would have to fund it under special development projects, which it felt could not be afforded.**

---

*These were known by the acronyms KSOS, PSOS and KVM.

**As the DoD moved ahead in its computer security thrust, Stephen T.Walker (founder and president of Trusted Information Systems) played a prominent role. First at ARPA and later in the Office of Secretary of Defense, he convened some of the early discussion groups, sponsored the writing of earliest drafts of a criteria document, sponsored workshops which included the earliest discussions with industry, and formulated a program that later became known as the DoD/Computer Security Initiative. He later brokered the discussion that lead to the formation of the DoD Computer Security Center at NSA which is now known as the National Computer Security Center. He is credited with introducing the phrases 'trusted computer system' and 'trusted computer system evaluation criteria.'

A quid pro quo arrangement was culminated in late 1980. Industry was asked to invest its resources to develop secure operating systems; and in return, the government would test, examine and evaluate the resulting products at no cost. Products that successfully passed evaluation could be sold to the government without further qualification. An organization was created to preside over this effort; namely, the DoD Computer Security Evaluation Center.*

The Technical Computer System Evaluation Criteria

The implication of the arrangement was that a specification would be established against which vendors could design, build and be tested. There had to be a common target for such efforts; and in addition, there had to be a common understanding between government and industry as to what performance features the government would test to.

A series of workshops were convened to create the document which eventually became known as the 'Criteria'; and with it, the 'criteria movement' was born and acquired public visibility and awareness.

The people involved in the workshops had some or all of these characteristics: generally defense oriented, researchers that had been funded by the defense community during the 1970s, people who understood and were familiar with the historical defense threat and defense operations, and computer scientists. In particular, there was essentially no representation from nondefense government or from the commercial-user sector.

The Technical Computer System Evaluation Criteria (later nicknamed the Orange Book) was first published 15 August 1983 (NSA, 1983). It was a very difficult document to read. Its language, its constructs, and the attempt to make it very general combined to present a very alien technical discussion even to well-informed people. As it gained visibility, there developed a belief, by its promulgators, that it would apply not only to the defense part of government, but in fact to all of government and to the extra-government commercial sector as well.

Later additional items, each with a distinctively colored cover, were published. Collectively they became known as the 'Rainbow Series' of documents. Among them were:

- Yellow Book--a guide for applying the TCSEC, but strictly in terms of defense constructs (NSA, 1985).
- Puce Book--Database Management Systems (NSA, 1991).
- Red Book--Trusted Networks - By the time of its appearance, wide area networks, the Arpanet, and similar approaches had become the contemporary technology, but only an appendix addressed them. Most of the book spoke to the older mainframe-oriented network serving its own community of users (NSA, 1987).

*This was done under the authority of DoD Directive 5215.1, Computer Security Evaluation Cemter. October 25, 1982.

Some documents were called 'interpretations' which implied that they were a ministerial elaboration derived from the Orange Bible. They did not address an issue de novo but simply related the constructs and content of the Orange Book to the particular issue at hand.

TCSEC ANCESTRY

Thus, looking back over history, we can conclude that the ancestry of the Orange Book and derivative documents reflect the following heritage:

- It was defense driven ab initio;
- The defense threat was the implicit focus of concern;
- A defense concept of operations was implicitly assumed;
- The defense personnel environment was implicitly assumed;
- The defense operational environment was implicitly assumed;
- Main-frame oriented, reflecting the calendar time;
- Oriented to stand-alone systems--they were the environment of the time; and
- Little treatment of networks--in particular, LANs, WANs, Internets, client-servers and modern architectures were not addressed.

Other criteria efforts

The TCSEC triggered a number of other efforts. In the United States, there followed:

- *The Minimum Federal Security Requirements*
  Started in early 1991; a final draft appeared August 1992.
- The Federal Criteria Working Group
  The agreement to create it was signed December 1990; its first meeting took place January 1992; a final document was released January 1993.

There were concurrent efforts in other countries.

- *The Canadian Trusted Computer Product Evaluation Criteria*
  Begun August 1988; version 1.0 appeared in May 1989; version 3.0e was published in January 1993.
- *The UK Security Evaluation and Certification Scheme*
  The decision to undertake it was announced December, 1989; the first document, version 1.0, appeared 1 March 1991; Issue 2, UKSP 01 was published April 1994.
- *The Information Technology Security Evaluation Criteria*
  A joint effort of four ITSEC countries: UK/Germany/France/Netherlands.
  The Provisional Harmonized Criteria, version 1.2 appeared 28 June 1991.

- *The Common Criteria*
  The most recent and current effort; a worldwide effort of prior players in the criteria movement: ITSEC group plus Canada and the US. The agreement to undertake it was signed February 1993. The final draft has been disseminated for wide comment prior to final publication. In its present version it is an enormous volume approximately 800 pages.

It should be noted that, like the TCSEC itself, most of the people involved in other criteria efforts came from, or were closely related to, the various national defense establishments. Moreover, the Common Criteria group was formally called an 'Editorial Group' and it clearly stated that its mission was only to harmonize the content of the several national documents. Specifically, the group was not chartered to deal with new substantive concepts, to add new kinds of safeguards, etc.

FEATURES AND ASSURANCE

Recall that all criteria have (what are called) features and assurance.* Features are the security safeguards expected of the system or software; assurance is a measure of the confidence with which one knows that the features are present, work as intended, are themselves safe from circumvention or modification; and do not introduce a new basis for a penetration attack. Indirectly, assurance also implies that the software or system (in a security sense) does not do what it is not supposed to do.

It is well understood now that assurance is and has been the big stumbling block, although it is unlikely that its true difficulty was foreseen in the earliest days. The process of establishing assurance (called evaluation) has proved to be so complex that the time to complete it has often exceeded the market lifetime of the product. Moreover, it has proved to be costly for the vendor to prepare for it, an aspect that was certainly not foreseen in the initial quid pro quo agreement between vendors and government.

(Un)bundling

The TCSEC bundled the two aspects; certain levels of assurance were bound to certain sets of features. Knowing of the assurance experience with the TCSEC, the European efforts opted for unbundling. The Common Criteria has followed the unbundling decision and has emerged as a very complex document, one with many different sets of features, many different levels of assurance, and allowing them, in principle, to be pairwise coupled as a product vendor sees fit.

The Common Criteria, as structured, allows anyone to propose a product, affiliate his choice of features and assurance levels with it, indicate its intended use, define its threat environment, get it evaluated, and offer it to the market. The Common Criteria, in fact, even includes a claims language which the vendor is to use in describing his product and making security assertions about it.

---
*Assurance is also referred to as 'quality' and 'correctness' in some documents.

The generality of the Common Criteria is both a plus and a minus. It permits great freedom by vendors to offer a wide variety of security-containing products. On the other hand, if vendors do exploit its flexibility widely, end-users could be faced with building systems from components which have little in common, certainly with regard to assurance; and maybe, with regard to features also. Conversely, if an end-user wishes all components to have a common level of assurance, he might not have enough choice of products with required features.

DEFENSE vs. OTHER ENVIRONMENTS

Such is the history and current status of the criteria movement. Consider now the differences between the defense and other environments, notably the private sector. In particular, what consequence will the criteria movement have for civil government and for the private commercial sector? As the document certainly to be most widely adopted, can the Common Criteria provide an adequately broad foundation for the specification, design, and implementation of secure systems and networks for the future?

Evaluated products do exist and more are appearing over time. They are being used of course and to that extent, so are criteria. The assurance component stipulated by criteria has improved and will continue to improve software quality in operating systems and in other major software packages. The assurance requirement has helped to drive good software engineering practices, as well as the evolution and adoption of good software development environments.

The criteria movement has indirectly sparked attention to computer security as an issue, has instituted important conferences, has provided forums for discussion, and in general has been a guiding model for people putting security safeguards into products. Criteria documents and their related standards have been a forcing function to help maturation of the security field.

Clearly these are all major pluses and important advantages derived from some 25 years of addressing security safeguards in software. Might there be characteristics inherent in criteria that collectively could be of especial consequence for their future effectiveness? Consider these things, some of which are in the process of changing:

- The defense heritage stresses the wrong paradigm; namely, protect the system and data at any cost vs. the commercial view of protecting the system and data at acceptable cost. It is the question of risk-avoidance vs. risk-management, but defense organizations are now concerned about costs and are revising attitudes accordingly.
- Criteria have been based on the defense threat. They have assumed the well-funded, diligent, persistent, technically smart foreign opponent, whereas the commercial threat is that of the insider, the cracker, daily operational mistakes, or employee misbehavior.
- By ancestry, criteria assume the defense operational environment and the defense personnel environment implicitly; namely, the physically protected and possibly classified enclave populated by either cleared people or ones under military discipline. By contrast, the private sector environment is one of commercial machine

rooms populated by people of unknown trustedness, functioning under civilian law and sometimes hired in response to national social policies.
- Criteria, with its defense heritage, inherently reflects different management motivations: laws/agency rules/regulations drive defense managers, whereas cost/losses/P&L statements drive the commercial manager. Even though military managers have become more cost conscious, governmental fiscal procedures still emphasize traditional motivations.

PERSPECTIVE ON CRITERIA

Components vs. systems

While criteria can in principle be applied to a combined hardware-software entity, the dominant focus has been on software products. Similarly, while criteria might be applied to systems, especially small ones, the focus has been on components--driven largely by the difficulty of performing the assurance evaluation. Thus, criteria are most likely to yield components with known safeguards and defined levels of assurance, much less likely to yield entire secure systems.

Threat

Criteria as they exist today are not intended to address those collateral aspects of security which arise on a daily basis from (such things as) operational glitches, personnel mistakes, or anomalous situations not anticipated in the system design. Yet such things are of high importance to commercial installations, and they are regarded within the scope of security. They are likely to become also of importance to defense support systems, especially as military forces get involved in regional operations and may depend on an indigenous infrastructure.

Integrity

Even more importantly, criteria do not address the integrity issue satisfactorily, although there was an abortive attempt in the beginning to do so. Considering 'integrity' as 'meeting expectations' or 'freedom from surprise,' the business enterprise is unavoidably concerned with integrity of components, of people, of systems, of networks, and of software processes. These are far broader concerns than ever envisioned by the TCSEC.

Reality

The commercial end user must be responsible for the design, implementation, and operation of a secure system. The commercial end user must establish his view of the threat and create a system design that includes security safeguards as appropriate. The commercial end user has to be concerned with other dimensions of security that defense people generally can ignore. The end user must do a design that is balanced between expected loss and cost of security.

However large the inventory of evaluated products ever becomes, assembling them into a system, providing special software and/or hardware for requirement voids that such products do not consider, and assuring that the end result meets security expectations against the perceived threat in the given operational environment must collectively be an unavoidable obligation of the end-using organization.

WHAT ABOUT THE FUTURE?

In trying to judge whether the future of computer security is adequately founded on (notably) the Common Criteria or whether there are some essential gaps, two different thrusts become of concern; namely:

- How will vendors behave under the Common Criteria?
- Are there technical issues that have not been, or perhaps cannot be, or might not be, addressed under the Common Criteria?

Common Criteria, vendors and products

To date, vendors have participated in the criteria process (via evaluation) partly through persuasion, but also partly to be assured of being able to compete for governments' business. To the extent that an 'evaluated product'* becomes a commercially viable one, then it replaces a prior product and finds its way into systems of the commercial and nondefense sectors.

Since the Common Criteria document is just coming into final publication status and we have little experience with it, it is not at all clear how its flexibility will be used and the future will evolve. What are vendors likely to do? They might do business as usual and follow the past, considering the Common Criteria to be simply a generalized extrapolation of prior criteria; and react to the government as strong influence. But there is a slightly different new option; namely, to target products especially at the security needs and threats of the private sector business base, as they are perceived by the vendor.

It is often argued that the classes of the TCSEC and similar criteria overkill some aspects of the risks as perceived by industry and business, and do not address others that are important to them. To the extent that vendors can guess at or define or anticipate

*This phrase implies a product that has been through a formal process of testing/measuring/examining its features and design against its claimed security attributes. Commonly the process is called 'evaluation' and includes not only technical matters but also review of (1) design documentation, (2) the software development process with emphasis on management oversight and control, (3) possibly the quality and experience of the development vendor. Historically, such evaluations were first conducted by the US National Security Agency, sometimes with contractor assistance; but more recently (especially under the Common Criteria) private certified laboratories conduct them.

what industry really wants as evaluated products, the Common Criteria will have opened an important new direction.

THREAT DIMENSIONS

There is almost certainly more to providing system and network security than the state of knowledge today. Consider some possibilities for a future far, far away. We really do not know what the threat will be in detail, but it is easy to imagine all manner of scenarios. The Information Warfare community has excelled at the last. We can also understand that the security threat in the commercial world may well be more demanding than in the defense world.

The world of threats has not stood still since the defense threat motivated most of the adopted criteria. System designers and implementers have tried to adapt the safeguards of the 1970s to the environment of the 1990s with some success but only so much can be done. While there has been some evolution of safeguards, mostly it has been repackaging them into new ensembles.

Phenomena inherent in the defense threat shaped the TCSEC and other criteria; and to the extent that commercial circumstances resemble those of the commercial world, there is no question that extant criteria are relevant, useful, and can lead to desirable products. One such example is that of the firewall whose security task is essentially that of access control--something that is an intimate part of the defense threat and of ensuing criteria.

The safeguards in common use today are largely the ones identified in the 1975-1985 era. They reflect such characteristics as the following.

- They were conceived to counter the defense threat;
- They emphasize access control as the central issue and then in the context of the end-user of a system and its data;
- The threats of the day were not very rapidly changing, especially as they related to sophisticated thievery of assets;
- Safeguards were correspondingly slow to react; and hence, were intended, designed and implemented for a quasi-static operational environment.
- Monitoring activities are often off-line and hence, occur after any opportunity to counter an attack has passed.

Operational environment

The commercial environment differs from the defense one on such aspects as:

- Characteristics of the user base served by a system;
- Expectations of the user base served by a system;
- The cultural diversity of the user population;
- The depth with which such a user base enters into a system during normal operations;
- The motivations of penetrators;
- Discipline and authority oversight of the operating entity;

- The operational physical environment;
- The intensity of networking, either standing dedicated arrangements or on-demand connectivity.

APPLICATIONS AND THREATS

Observe what is happening in the commercial world already. Airlines offer ready access to their databases of flights and reservations; anyone with a personal computer and modem is interactively welcome. One can scan and select flights, and then book or cancel reservations. Similarly, banks are offering extensive on-line financial services, again to anyone with a personal computer and modem. As one executive of a major bank put it: 'We're inviting the public into our systems.'*

To be sure, such systems must implement security safeguards but how stalwart they are to imaginative attacks remains to be established. There have been incidents** and there could be more. And who can speculate what sort of attacks might be conceived against such publicly available systems?

Application-based safeguards

A point of concern. In computer security as traditionally practiced, the safeguards are concentrated largely in the operating system software, either of the central processor(s) or of subsidiary processor(s). In an environment that supports many applications, each with its own coterie of databases, it is relevant to ask: 'Is this an adequate posture for the future?' Or the collateral question: 'Is it feasible or even possible for the operating system to detect any and all attacks that might be mounted against the system?' In terms of a World War II imagery, is a Maginot Line philosophy satisfactory for the future? Is a single line of defense sufficient, or must there be defense in depth?

The answer to all three questions is almost certainly 'no.' There are bound to be attacks, especially fast developing and rapidly executed ones, that the operating system even with reasonably dynamic (say) audit trails and monitoring of them could not catch. One class of insidious attacks will be those that closely resemble the normal activities of authorized system users; perhaps worse, attacks that can be hidden within normal activities of authorized users.

The conclusion has to be (using the words of a colleague in the financial industry): 'Applications will have to take care of themselves.'*** Therefore, there will have to be safeguards which are peculiar and unique to an application and which function within it. Moreover, care will have to be taken that an application in responding to an attack does not inadvertently pass consequences along that might compromise others. The security interface among applications, and between each and the system software, will be very crucial.

---

*From a private conversation with Colin Crook, Chief Technology Officer, Citibank, New York City.

**For example, the well-publicized attack on New York's Citibank which resulted in major movement of funds to the penetrators' accounts.

***Private conversation, loc cit.

Why must applications protect themselves? Only the application will be able to recognize some attacks. Only the application will be able to perceive patterns of normal user behavior and have a chance of detecting misbehavior of authorized insiders. While in principle the operating systems could do such things, it would increase the complexity of the system software and it might be very difficult to conceive centralized safeguards that could oversee a variety of applications. It makes much more sense to distribute safeguards to the points at which detection is most likely, counter-actions taken most rapidly and effectively, and the current processing context exists.

Consequences of application-centered safeguards

There are consequences of putting safeguards into applications, especially if the threat is visualized as being very dynamic, perpetrated by or hidden under the actions of authorized users. For example:

- Safeguards must be responsive to fast developing threat actions;
- Safeguards must be effective in a dynamic environment; otherwise, a successful penetration, attack, or foray will be over before the system knows about it;
- Safeguards must capture reams of data and analyze them to establish normal behavior patterns and its variations with such parameters as time-of-day, event, workload scheduling, other processes concurrently functioning;
- Analysis packages must run continually, not periodically or when the system administrator feels like it;
- Analysis packages must be able to track events over time and make correspondingly astute decisions;
- Applications, if some or all of the audit information is to be archived in the operating system, must be able to perform trusted write-actions to centralized trusted audit trails.

Vendor application software

While such points are technical in nature, there are business aspects. Will vendors design and market application packages with self-contained security features and anti-penetration safeguards? Under a regime of the Common Criteria, might a vendor propose, claim, have evaluated and market (say) an accounting package with internal safeguards to counter a defined threat? We obviously do not know; it is a new mode of behavior for a criteria-centered environment.

For shrink-wrapped mass-market software, the answer might well be 'yes.' For the corporate market whose systems are built around larger centralized mainframe systems, the answer is less obvious. It could well be 'no,' which implies that the corporate world will either be forced toward the world of mass-market software--which might well not have the capability for a large corporation--or corporations will find themselves in the software development business with its associated cost and management obligations. It need not be individual corporations, each for itself; there could arise consortiums to do specialty secure application development for a community of like businesses; e.g., banks, other financial institutions, local governments.

The insider threat

The discussion above is clearly relevant to the insider threat, a threat about which little has been done although many reported incidents are in fact of this origin. Such threats come in at least two kinds:

- Direct unauthorized actions of authorized system users; or
- Leaks or assistance from insiders to outside penetrators.

Either is difficult to deal with and in fact, the second may prove almost impossible to handle, depending of course on just what the attack might attempt to achieve. Obviously, if the system is to detect aberrant behavior, it must know what normalcy is. The only way is to collect data and carefully analyze it for patterns by individual, by calendar date, by time of year, by time of day, by day of month, by the operating schedule for applications, etc. It argues again for application-centered security guards.

INTEGRITY

As previously noted criteria-based approaches have done little to assure integrity of software, process, data, results. Business is beginning to consider even integrity of the overall business processes embedded in their information systems.* While integrity does not equate, to be sure, to security, nonetheless the two are closely related. Security failures or penetration successes, even attempts, can intrude on the normal and expected functioning of business processes and hence will result in an integrity infraction. Thus, as integrity becomes more important to the commercial community, and to the auditing community as well, many aspects of security will have to be attended in its behalf.

Are vendors, doing business in a Common Criteria regime, likely to pay attention to the integrity issue with appropriate products?

NETWORKS

Networks certainly need much attention. The dominant security driver has been first, the development of the Internet, and more recently the emergence of the World Wide Web

*The integrity of an information process in the business world is an end-to-end concern. For example, an accounting process must take in the proper data, manipulate it in the correct way, and produce correct results; and it must do so according to the expectations of the business that designed it and had it implemented. Similarly, extraction of a subset of data from a master database must provide the expected result. Each such business process--data plus processing software plus operational procedures--must behave as expected from day to day. Hence, process integrity becomes of importance. This has been a little discussed dimension of integrity but is an emergent concern, not as yet widely examined.

with its intense evolving orientation toward the conduct of business. A lot has been learned about the security of Net-connected systems, but much has yet to be done.

Some unique threats have materialized; e.g., sniffers that monitor traffic for network addresses, worms that attack multiple machines, viruses that are spread by attractive downloadable software. Countermeasures exist and have been installed. While some are network specific (e.g., firewalls), others amount to closing software loopholes in the attached systems, loopholes that can be exploited by a penetrator to gain access to parts of a system that should be off-limits.

In effect, the Internet acts as a remote channel via which to mount an attack; but it also provides opportunities to mask the attack through intermediate systems, and it offers opportunity to attack a large number of like systems. While these phenomena are new in a sense, in another they are extrapolations or extensions of known technical problems, but they arise from the connectivity provided by the network.

There can be phenomena that are truly network security issues, as opposed to a security issue of the systems attached to a network. For example, Internet architecture utilizes so-called Domain Name Server machines to support routing of traffic. While any one is normally backed up by an alternate, subversion or collapse--incidental or intentional--of one or more of them can affect many connected systems. In truth, for the Internet overall:

Security of the many depends on the security of each.

Internet connectivity is at the mercy of well-behaved and secure name servers--a genuine security issue of the network per se.

Are there others of like kind? Probably so; certainly the vulnerability of routers is understood; actual incidents which brought down major portions of the Internet demonstrated the point. Are there central points of vulnerability? Probably; for example, in a Network Control Center which, among other things, manages and downloads software to routers.

How will the Common Criteria fit into this dimension of security?

ENSEMBLE SECURITY

There can be security issues that transcend a stand-alone machine because it is connected to other machines, either permanently or on demand. Such a security problem is a consequence of connectivity, but connectivity of any kind, not just through the Internet. Although this is an issue that has been latent in some parts of the defense community but has received little attention, it is likely to become a major concern for commercial systems as interconnections proliferate, especially on-demand ones.

It is straightforward to state the central issue. When two systems connect, how does each know with certainty who the other is? And, equally important, how does each know what the other is authorized to send or receive?*

Mutual identification and authentication

The first question can be sidestepped, and often is in the commercial environment, by dedicated intersystem connections or by connecting only to single-purpose systems. For example, the checkstand at a food market (while interconnected on its internal network) typically connects externally only to a check verification service or to bankcard services. Hence mutual identity is assured by the nature of the interaction. The financial or check service, in effect, assumes that the connecting system is legitimate because it poses the correct query in the correct format, is connected through a known and possibly fixed communications arrangement, and may have other protocol standards. There is a de facto authentication hand-shake implicit in the technical arrangements. An intruder of course could do a spoofing attack that mimics the food market although details of the query, identification of the questioner, interconnection protocol, etc. would have to be known.

In contrast, the telephony network demonstrates an environment of general connectivity; i.e., anybody can connect to anybody. Such behavior already exists in the Internet environment. People dial into online services such as various database servers. One system queries another in behalf of a user such as a web browser following hyperlinks. Sometimes (e.g., anonymous ftp) prior identification and authentication is not prearranged but required at the time of connection. Other times there are more explicit and formal arrangements; for example, a registration procedure has captured an identifier and a password.

Relative to how it is handled today, mutual identification and authentication are likely to become much more important as online services proliferate. Good intersystem security would demand that mutual distrust be the default condition when two systems initially connect. An any-system-to-any-system connection via a network must be untrusted until mutual trust has been established, either dynamically or by some a priori standing arrangement.

Dynamically, there is an elegant technical solution; namely, cryptographically based handshaking plus cryptographically based digital-signature identity. Prior arrangements might include such things as dedicated place-to-place communications, simple access control mechanisms based on a list of acceptable system identifications with which to connect, call-back schemes on dial-up connections.

Authorized data interchange

What about the second question: how do interconnecting systems know what each is allowed to receive or send? There are technical solutions but they might not work for all

---

*Just after this paper was being completed, a series of Internet messages raised just this point in the context of a browser (running in a workstation) and connected to a web-site with which a secure exchange of data was to take place.

situations. One would be to require each system, after mutual identification and authentication have been established, to transmit to the other whatever parameters are appropriate to establish the boundary or scope of a session. This would probably be an application-to-application exchange of security factors. Another might be to use cryptography to isolate various aspects of a session; e.g., one set of keys for type-A data, another set for type-B material. The authority to exchange information would then be governed by the specific crypto-keys that each system holds.

Both of these issues will clearly require that each party in a connection contain trusted* processes that conduct the handshaking, crypto-key management, session-parameter establishment, etc. with high confidence.

To illustrate this point in a commercial setting, consider a comprehensive corporate database. Each operating department (e.g., personnel, accounting) will be restricted to certain parts of each record. But, now distribute such functions geographically; each communicates with the server maintaining the master database through a dial-up modem. For each connection, the querying workstation would assure itself that it is connected to the proper server, and the server would assure itself that the query is from an authorized source. Moreover, the server must know just what data each source is authorized to receive, and what new data it is authorized to post.

In current systems, it typically is assumed that incoming data to a database is legitimate as to intent (although it might be software edited for format, completeness, etc.). Access to integrated databases is controlled by conventional database access control mechanisms, perhaps just simple name lists of authorized users or in more rigorous environments, by software systems that contain labels or even trusted labels and have been evaluated.

Such issues rarely surface in today's operational environments, yet they should. For example, the system upgrade for the US Social Security Administration has just the characteristic suggested here. There will be a central facility with massive database servers which connect through dial-in modems to the thousands of workstations in the hundreds of field offices. Good security will demand that such connections are authenticated as legitimate and appropriate controls will have to govern the flow of data back and forth. Otherwise, some aspects of system security will depend only on the trustworthy behavior of many employees.

Consider another example related to personal privacy. The trend of events is to create dossier-quality records of personal information in extensive databases and then to use it for decisions about people; e.g., eligibility for a social entitlement, granting of a financial loan. Because of past practices and technical inheritance, it is common practice to answer a query by returning the entirety of an individual's record. As the completeness of such databases increases, it is clear that a given query (and corresponding subscriber organization) is entitled to only parts of the record. It becomes just like the integrated database matter technically. At some point privacy law will awaken to this subtle detail and require that only data relevant to the query be released. Security safeguards will then

---

**Trusted* is used here as it is in criteria documents; namely, a trusted process executes its intended procedures with high confidence, and does not, with equally high confidence, execute spurious other procedures.

be required to authenticate connections, establish the legitimacy and boundary of a query, and control the data flow.

And the Common Criteria

Will a regime that is governed by the Common Criteria provide the kinds of features that have just been implied? Possibly, but not assuredly. Vendors might include trusted processes in evaluated operating system software for verifying session parameters, for conduct of cryptographic operations, or for other intersystem arrangements. But they are not likely to do so unless there is a perceived market for such products, but such a market might not develop if the products are not already available.

INTRASYSTEM SECURITY

Architectural advances, either for LAN-based geographically centralized systems or for widely spread systems with arbitrary interconnectivity, raise yet other security considerations. Consider the popular client-server architectures which need not have all system components geographically colocated. A software process called from one server by a workstation might well be expected to execute under the system software in some second system chosen from a collection of available systems and using relevant databases that, in principle, can be resident in yet another place or in several places.

A given application might not run under the same copy of the system software every time, or it need not run against the same database(s) each time; for example, processing a particular personnel database selected from those of all corporate divisions, each alike in structure but situated at different locations with different data. When process integrity is important or just when well-behaved functioning is expected, there must be assurance that the right process executes against the right database(s) under system software that contains no anomalous or unexpected features.

How do the interacting software components mutually assure themselves that all the participants are the proper ones? We now have an intrasystem mutual identification and authentication problem that can be important as systems become more and more distributed for legitimate operational or economic advantage, and even transcend national boundaries.

Considering a 'system' as an entity that has been designed and implemented as a whole and is expected to operate in a coordinated fashion, then we conclude that we may well need intercomponent handshaking procedures within it. Depending upon circumstances, such arrangements might be relatively simple (e.g., verifying the presence of certain expected parameters or certain expected software features or even just component identities or meeting the standard of an application programming interface) or as complex as cryptographically based handshaking with digital-signature authentication.

In terms of our prior construct, the relationship among an application, its database(s), and the system software in general will have to initiate in a state of mutual distrust, to be resolved by appropriate security mechanisms and procedures or processes.

And the Common Criteria?

The same question again: can a Common Criteria regime produce the security safeguards and evaluated products for complex circumstances as just outlined? The same answer: we do not know how vendors will behave under it, or whether there will be market demands to drive them. The other choice of course is for corporations and businesses to be in the system- and software-development business directly.

SINGLE POINTS OF FAILURE

This notion is well understood in system design; it implies that there can be places in the system which, if they fail or misfunction, can lead to major or catastrophic system collapse. It is a useful construct also for security.

To illustrate, if cryptography is used for some security purpose in a system, then the trust in the protection that it provides is vested in the secrecy of the crypto-keys. Similarly, if the interconnection assurance of identity depends on some software process, then the trust in that security requirement is vested in the integrity of the software.

The point is that for each security thread or function, there comes a point at which the security analogue of Harry Truman's sign* is posted: 'Trust stops here.' In complex systems, which is the way that the international World Wide Web and other systems of the Global Information Infrastructure are steadily moving, such trust-stops will have to be identified and great care taken to assure their own security and integrity, possibly with kinds of safeguards yet to be imagined. Such points at which trust is vested will surely be both global and local which makes the issue even more difficult with which to deal.

There are obvious current day examples. The so-called Trusted Third Party concept presently being discussed as the safe-haven repository for encryption keys and from which such keys can be obtained under emergency circumstances is an obvious single point of failure. A penetrated Trusted Party would eventuate in major damage to its clients. Hence, it becomes a trust-stop and requires extraordinary security by the nature of its role.

Or consider digital signatures, affixed perhaps to 100-year contracts. For the parties in question, the keys involved in creating the digital signatures are a very clear single point of failure. Moreover, they must be safely stored throughout the life of the contract, in part because no one can ever predict when legal proceedings might involve the contract and its signators.

There is a collateral operational issue: for how long can we assume or believe that trust arrangements are valid? Do we need to establish a subsidiary means to test, or verify, or examine, or validate them from time to time? And perhaps do so on an unscheduled basis, or possibly prior to some unusually sensitive interaction? A question, to be sure, for a time far, far away; but one that needs to be in our thinking.

---

*Former US President Harry Truman is famous for the prominent sign on his desk saying: 'The buck stops here.'

SUBTLE THREAT ISSUES

Denial of service

A denial-of-service threat is understood in principle; but in our future it must be addressed more pointedly and deliberately than does our present inclination. It becomes of increasing importance as dependence on computer-based infrastructure enlarges, expands geographically, and supplants traditional paper-based methods. Such threats are clearly very situation dependent. For example, a power outage can be tolerated for minutes, even hours, but for logging of high speed data even a brief period of intrusion could be disastrous.

Personnel trustworthiness

With security safeguards generally concentrated in geographically compact locations today (e.g., a computing facility, a protected physical structure), an organization can take some steps to assure that its people can be trusted. As systems become more complex and widely distributed, and especially as service outreach increases, the number of people who might undertake malicious actions grows rapidly. But worse, there is little that an organization can do to screen them or limit their numbers.

The implication is that system security safeguards will have to operate continuously, be very dynamic in their ability to adapt to circumstances, be very sophisticated in terms of operational data to be assessed, ..., in general have to be very smart.

Will such things emerge under the Common Criteria? Perhaps, but not for a while because there would appear to be some necessary very basicresearch done first. And there is always the chicken-and-egg problem; which drives the other?

CONCLUSION

This discussion has ranged over a wide variety of security things; some are for a future far, far away, but others are closer in time. We have touched on emergence of threats, sophistication of the threat, technical cleverness of system designers, motivations of system managers, exposure of the system to public use. We have imagined plausible situations and scenarios which raise potentially demanding security arrangements. Which become fact, which emerge before others, which become important or even when, depends on many things. Overall, we have imagined many things and we have pondered the role of the Common Criteria in responding to them.

How successful the Common Criteria proves to be will depend very sharply on how vendors respond to it, how vendors judge market needs for security products, how ingenious a vendor might be in finding a market niche and providing a product for it, and probably other things as well.

The Common Criteria has great flexibility, but it cannot motivate the vendor. It can only provide him with a framework in which to describe a product and its application, get it evaluated, and give the system user a consistent basis for judging the features and quality of products. As the discussion has suggested, though, there can easily be requirements for security products or components whose market demand is small. How will we get such things? Will the organizations requiring very specialized things unavoidably be in the system-development business? Will the security environment be provided by the organizations known as system integrators? And if so, what will be the process for establishing the appropriateness of the features provided and their levels of assurance? Do such questions become irrelevant in some cases? Can the specialized organizations now emerging to do criteria-oriented evaluations become significant players for special system-level investigations?*

The criteria movement began as a government-sponsored thrust, and the U.S. government was proactive in encouraging the spread of the ideas and adoption of the approach. Other governments had similar interests, in part to assure that products for themselves would be available. Over 15 years though, market forces have become increasingly important although government interests still are drivers.

Throughout the criteria movement but especially now with the Common Criteria, the info-security business has been moving gradually into a market-driven posture. There could still arise forces to intrude on such a drift, and move the industry back toward a government-influenced position. For example, laws could mandate threats or system performance obligations, or impose legal responsibilities with penalties for system downtime or malfunctioning. Or the information-warfare syndrome might prove so serious that governments will mandate security controls for some or all of the infrastructure. Is the info-security business likely to become dominated by market-driven forces?

My inclination at the moment is to answer the question: 'yes, we will see information security as a market driven industry.' Perhaps that is the best of all endpoints. It puts info-security, as the term that seems most categoric, on a par with just about anything else that societies undertake. That is an advantage because society and its institutions plus business and its organizations understand market forces; we might weave our way into the proper balance between threat and safeguards.

If these thoughts and conjectures about the future are valid, then it is reasonable to suggest that the eventual role of the Common Criteria is that of a meta-standard, one that provides a framework for spawning more specific standards, each in turn leading to security products of particular characteristics. And it is reasonable to conclude that such a structure will be most successful when the security requirements can be bundled together and assigned to a particular functional component; for example, the handshaking, authentication, and session parameter aspects of intersystem connectivity implemented within a communications processor.

REFERENCES

DoD Computer Security Center, National Security Agency (15 Aug 1983) *Department of Defense Trusted Computer System Evaluation Criteria*, CSC-STD-001-83. While the

*In Europe these organizations are often called CLEFs.

document is characterized in its preface as 'a uniform set of requirements and basic evaluation classes,' the TCSEC really filled the role of a standard and was later adopted as a USG/DoD standard.

DoD Computer Security Center, National Security Agency (23 June 1985) *Guidance for Applying the Department of Defense Trusted Computer System Evaluation Criteria in Specific Environments,* CSC-STD-003-85.

National Computer Security Center, National Security Agency (31 July 1987) *Trusted Network Interpretation*, NCSC-TG-005.

National Computer Security Center, National Security Agency (April 1991) *Trusted Database Management System Interpretation,* NCSC-TG-021.

Peters, Bernard (1965) Security Considerations in a Multi-programmed Computer System, *AFIPS Conference Proceedings,* **30**, 283 ff.

Ware, Willis H. [editor] (1970) *Security Controls for Ccomputer Systems,* Report of Defense Science Board Task Force on Computer Security, R-609-1. Published by RAND Corporation for the Department of Defense in February 1970 as a classified document and republished as an unclassified document in October, 1979.

Ware, Willis H. (1995) *A Retrospective on the Criteria Movement.* Presented at the 18th National Information Systems Security Conference, October 10-13, 1995, Baltimore, MD.

BIOGRAPHY

Willis H. Ware [PhD, Elec Engr, Princeton 1951] was with the engineering group at Princeton's Institute for Advanced Study (1946-1951) and then joined the RAND Corporation (1952-). His career has included all aspects of computer technology--hardware, software, architectures, software development, networks, government and military applications, management of computer-intensive projects, public policy and legislation. For 35 years, Dr. Ware has worked on various aspects of information security and personal privacy, and still actively contributes to both.

He is a member of the National Academy of Engineering, a Fellow of the Institute of Electronic and Electrical Engineers, a Fellow of the American Association for Advancement of Science, and a Fellow of the Association for Computing Machinery. He was first president of the American Federation of Information Processing Societies and is the US representative to the IFIP/TC11 committee.

He has received many awards and honors including IFIP's Silver Core Award (1995). He currently chairs the statutory (US) National Computer System Security and Privacy Advisory Board.

A *Common Criteria* framework for the evaluation of Information Technology systems security

R. Kruger, J.H.P. Eloff

Rand Afrikaans University

PO Box 524, Aucklandpark, South Africa,
+27 11 489 28 42, eloff@rkw.rau.ac.za

Abstract

In this paper is expanded a process of evaluation by means of which to determine the functional security requirements of an Information Technology (IT) system. The said process of evaluation has been developed on the bases of two sources currently used to determine the functional security requirements obtaining to an IT system; the first being the new foundation for information security, namely a framework that defines information security as a whole, and the second being the *Common Criteria* which are used to place information security functions within a framework. These two frameworks are used conjointly to determine the functional security requirements of an IT system. The two frameworks are also defined in such a way as to enable automation of the evaluation process.

Keywords

Information security, Common Criteria, new foundation for information security, functional security requirements, security functions, information security evaluation

1 INTRODUCTION

Why do we need to evaluate the information security of any IT system? The evaluation of an IT system determines the level up to which the system and its resources are protected. This knowledge, in turn, not only creates confidence in the users and owners of the system, but also in third parties, such as clients. Knowledge about the level of security may also uncover possible shortcomings or flaws in the information security make-up of the IT system. Shortcomings which could prove costly (Murray, 1995).

Currently, there are two ways in which to evaluate the security of an information system. The one way is to rate the information system on the basis of current evaluation criteria such as the ITSEC, TCSEC, CTCPEC and the *Common Criteria* (CSE, 1993) (CC, 1994)] (Pfleeger, 1989). The other way is to use one of the many risk-management or risk-analysis techniques.

The principal aim of the process described in the present paper is to determine the security needs of an IT system or **T**arget **Of** **E**valuation (TOE), as it would be referred to hereafter. In other words, it is used to evaluate a TOE on the basis of its information security. An important aspect of information security is security functionality. The term security functionality refers to that collection of implemented security functions that are concerned with information security. The process described hereafter determines the security functionality by determining the security aims of a TOE.

1.1 Scope

In order better to understand the scope of the process of evaluation described in this paper, it will be compared to other common evaluation methods.

The first common method of evaluation is risk management. Risk management is a cyclic, continuous process (Eloff 1995). The most important part of risk management is risk analysis, which includes the following steps (Pfleeger, 1989):

1. Identification of assets.
2. Determination of vulnerabilities and hot spots.
3. Estimated likelihood of exploitation.
4. Computation of expected annual loss.
5. Survey of applicable controls and the costs involved.
6. Projection of annual saving of control.

The process of evaluation described in this paper may also serve as a tool that will facilitate in the process of risk analysis, as it may facilitate steps 1,2 and 5. The process of evaluation described in this paper, however, adopts a different approach to determine suitable controls (security functions). The focus of the process is on the security objectives of the TOE rather than on the risks mentioned above.

The second common method of assessing the functional security requirements of a TOE is with the evaluation criteria. Most modern evaluation criteria are a combination of functional as well as assurance criteria. The ITSEC and CTCPEC, as well as the *Common Criteria*, distinctly distinguish between the functional and assurance criteria (CC, 1994) (CSE, 1993) (Strous 1994). The *Common Criteria* define the level of security enjoyed by a TOE, using a protection profile. A protection profile contains, among other things, a functional package consisting of a collection of security functions designed to meet the information security needs of a TOE. Predefined functional packages have been created with specific environments in mind, an example of which is a commercial organisation that relies heavily on the communication of electronic information. Every TOE has, however, specific needs that might not be met by any of the predefined functional packages. The aim of the process of evaluation described in this paper is to define a functional package according to the specific needs of the TOE under evaluation. The *Common Criteria* provide a way of defining a framework that could be used for this purpose during the process of evaluation. The latter framework will, henceforth, also be referred to as the function structure.

2 THE PROCESS

Figure 1 depicts the evaluation process in its entirety.

The process can be divided into the following three main steps:

1. Determine all applicable security functions.
2. Choose a subset of functions from the complete list in Step 1.
3. Compare the subset of functions to the functions that have been implemented already.

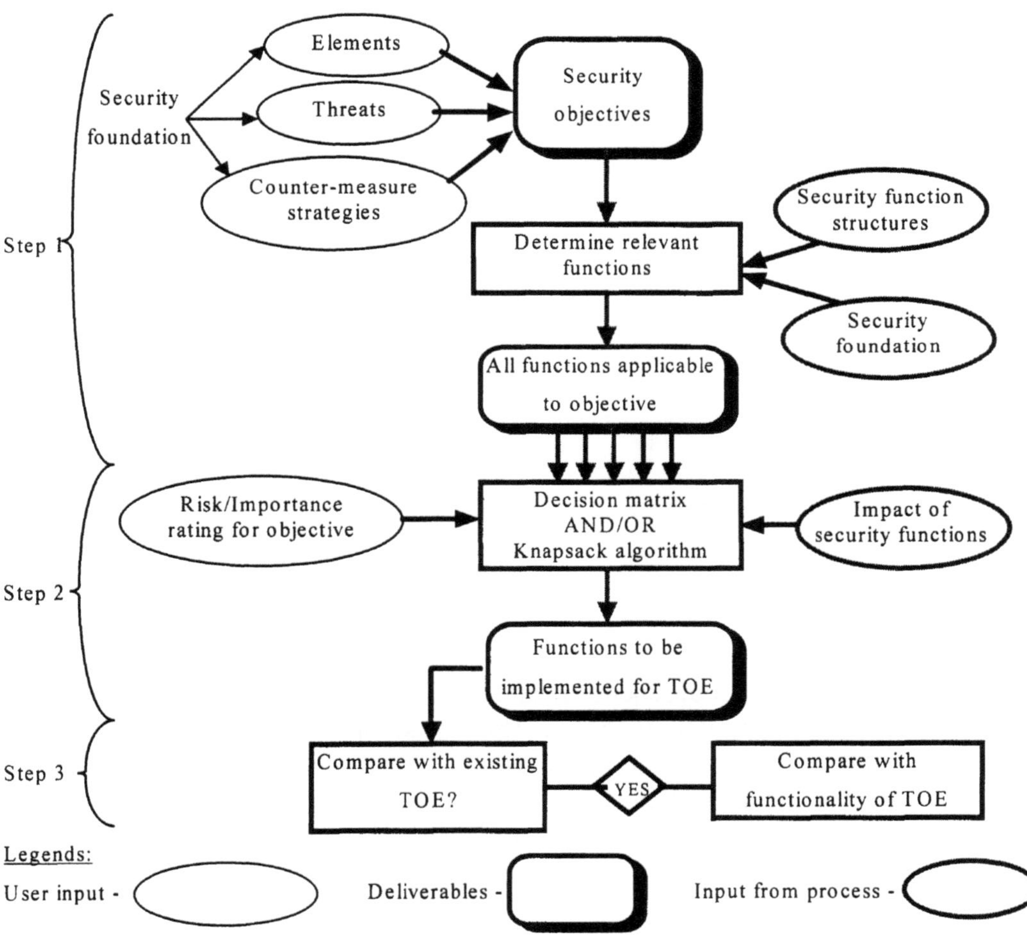

Figure 1 Process of evaluation.

Step 1

The aim of the first step is to find all the security functions that would have an effect on the security of the TOE under evaluation. This step is depicted in Figure 2 and involves the following smaller steps (the letters (a) to (e) referred to in the step are depicted in Figure 2):

- This step involves the definition of the security objectives (c) that would address the security concerns for the TOE under evaluation. The security objectives are defined according to the framework provided by the new foundation for information security (b), which will be expanded upon later.
- For each security objective, a short-list (a) of high-level security functions is defined, using additional information contained in the framework provided by the new foundation for information security.
- The short-list of security functions is then expanded into a list (e) of all the security functions that support the security objective. This is done for all of the security objectives. Finding all the security functions that are part of the complete list is done through the determination of all the security functions that are related to those contained in the short-list. Finding the related functions is done by using the function structure (d) that has been derived from the *Common Criteria*. The *Common Criteria* will be expanded upon later in the paper.

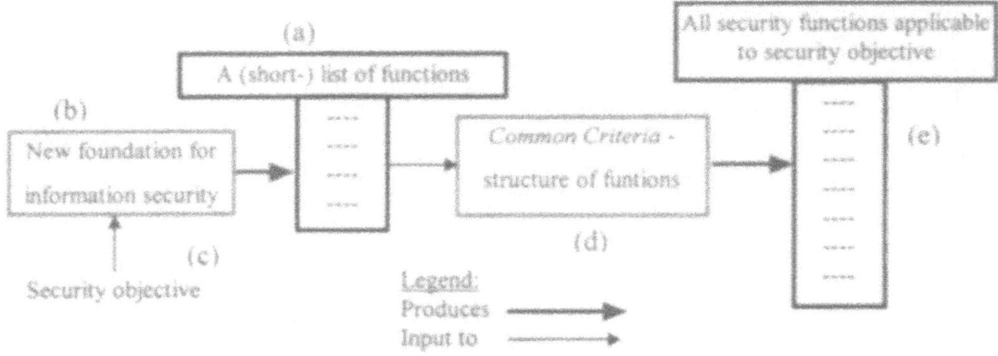

Figure 2 Process of evaluation - step 1.

Step 2

The first step produces a list of functions that contains all the functions that could have an effect on the defined security objective. This, the second step, is aimed, in its turn, to shorten the list of functions. The functions in the list produced in the previous step all have an effect on the defined objective, but the effect or impact these functions have are not all of the same magnitude. The most effective functions are chosen. This step culminates in a list of functions that will, henceforth, be referred to as the preferred functional package.

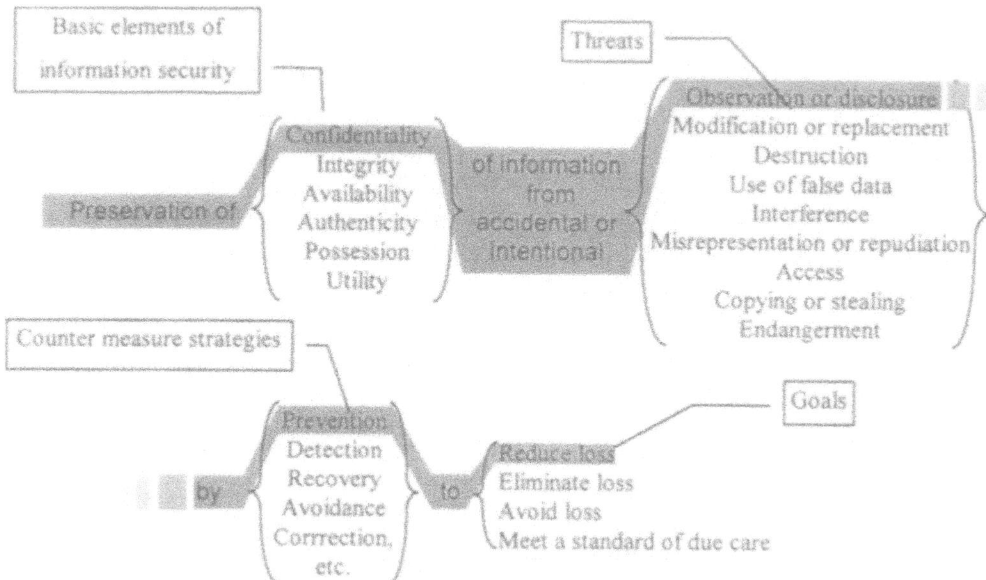

Figure 3 New foundation for information security (reproduced from Parker D. (1995), A new framework for information security to avoid information anarchy, in *Proceedings of the IFIP/Sec '95*, 1995.)

Step 3

In this step, the preferred functional package (i.e. the output of step 2) is compared to the functionality of the existing TOE for which the security objectives have been defined. This comparison gives an indication of how well the TOE is protected and also serves to highlight hot spots.

2.2 STEP 1 - The selection of all possible functions

This step can further be divided into three smaller steps, the first of which defines the security objectives that would address the security concerns of the TOE under review.

The second produces a short-list of high-level security functions that are gleaned from the security objectives. The source that is to help with the completion of the first two steps is the *new foundation for information security,* as described by (Parker, 1995), which will, henceforth, be referred to as the *foundation.*

During the third step, the above-mentioned short-list of functions is expanded by a consideration of the inter-relations among the different security functions. Details of these inter-relations are gleaned from the *Common Criteria* (CC, 1994).

The following two paragraphs will serve further to describe the role of these two sources, i.e. the new foundation for information security and the *Common Criteria.*

The new foundation for information security

The new foundation (Figure 3), as described by (Parker, 1995), consists of four parts, namely the basic elements of information security ('basic elements' for short), threats, counter-measure strategies and the goals.

These parts can be combined to form a sentence describing a 'security situation' or 'wish', for example: Preservation of *Confidentiality* of information from *Disclosure* by *Prevention* to *Reduce loss*. The example is highlighted in Figure 3 with the faded areas. According to this example, the aim is to reduce the risk of possible loss by protecting the confidentiality of information by preventing possible disclosure. This can be done by introducing security functions such as access control and the protection of the information whenever it is being transmitted. The first three parts would still culminate in the same result, for example: Preservation of *Confidentiality* of information from *Disclosure* by *Prevention.*

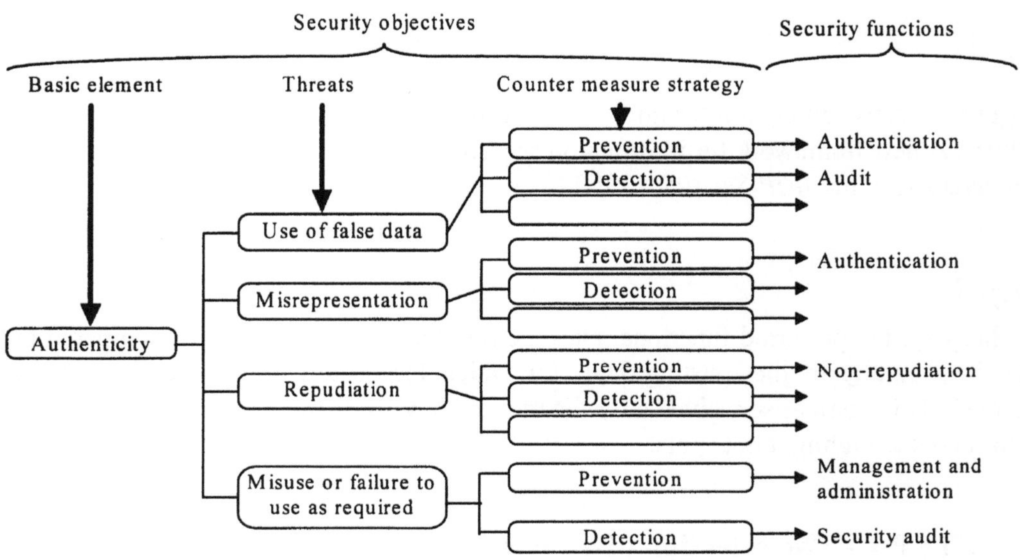

Figure 4 Authenticity - tree structure.

The role of the new security foundation in the evaluation process

The new foundation will be used as a basis for the first step in the process, namely the selection of security functions that would be used to compile the preferred functional package. The combination of the first three parts of the foundation (namely elements, threats and counter-measure strategies) will, henceforth, be referred to as a *security objective*. In short, an objective is compiled in the following way: element + threat + counter-measure strategy ⇒ security objective. For example: Preservation of **Confidentiality** of information from accidental or intentional **Access** by **Prevention**.

The combination of the elements, threats and counter-measure strategies points to certain security functions, for example the following security objective: Preservation of *Confidentiality* of information from accidental or intentional *Access* by *Prevention,* points to Access Control. In this example, Access Control is that security function that would help to achieve the stated objective. Thus, each security objective is associated with one or more security functions. The structure of the foundation and the way in which a security objective is compiled make it possible to represent the association between a security objective and a function by a tree structure. The new foundation organised into a tree structure is as follows: each basic element of security has a number of child nodes which represent (possibly) all the threats. Each threat, in turn, compasses (possibly) all the counter-measure strategies as child nodes. These nodes are then associated with the security functions. In this way, a tree associates a security objective with one or more security functions. Figure 4 illustrates the tree structure.

In conclusion, the foundation provides the basis for the partial determination of those functions needed in a TOE. The following sentence summarises the role of the foundation in the process: Element + threat + counter-measure strategy $\Rightarrow$ security objective $\Rightarrow$ (basic) function(s) applicable to security objective.

The following paragraph will show how to expand this basic list of functions that are applicable to the objective into a complete list of functions.

The Common Criteria

The *Common Criteria* define all of the functional requirements (CC, 1994). The functional requirements, in their turn, cover all of the security functions. An in-depth study of the functional requirements shows that there are, indeed, many inter-relations between the various security functions. The combination of all of the functions and inter-relations into a framework provides a function structure. The use of this function structure will be explained in the following paragraph.

The role of the Common Criteria in the evaluation process

The *Common Criteria* also provide a basis for the selection of functions. The new foundation provides a limited list of high-level functions needed for the TOE under evaluation. Because security functions are interrelated, not all of the possible functions (for a specific objective) can be derived from the new foundation alone. Thus, the limited set of functions is expanded upon with the use of the functional requirements specified by the *Common Criteria.*

Derived from the functional requirements specified by the *Common Criteria* is a set of structures that shows the relationships between the different security functions. These structures were gleaned by the author from his study of the functional requirements of preliminary draft of the *Common Criteria* as the *Common Criteria* do not directly show these relationships. These inter-relations are used to identify other functions that also contribute to the same objective as the function(s) derived at on the basis of the foundation. This expands the limited list of functions given by the new foundation.

The following paragraph describes the second step, which shows how to choose the functions that should be implemented from the complete list of functions produced by step 1.

2.3 STEP 2 - trimming of functions

Step 2 in the evaluation process takes all of the functions produced by the previous step and identifies the unnecessary functions. Unnecessary functions are functions that do not have a big enough impact on the security of the TOE to justify their implementation. In step 2, the remaining functions are, therefore, selected and combined to form a functional package.

A functional package is a collection of security functions that should be implemented. The motivation for the creation of a functional package is to limit the number of functions to be implemented to effectively protect the TOE.

Strength of association

It is also necessary to consider the fact that each function does not contribute to each objective with the same magnitude.

The degree to which a function addresses an objective will be referred to as the 'strength of association' between the function and the objective. It will also be referred to as the 'impact the function has on the objective'. Thus, the magnitude or degree of the strength of association (SOA) determines the effect the function will have on the objective. The SOA would, for the sake of standardisation, be taken as ranging from 0 to 10.

The previous paragraph illustrated the fact that each function has a SOA with a certain objective. Determining the SOA, however, presents us with a two-fold problem. Firstly, we have to determine the degrees of strength between the objective and those functions produced by the new foundation, namely the high-level functions. Secondly we have to determine the degrees of strength between the objective and those functions produced by the *Common Criteria*.

2.3.1 SOA - Foundation

The SOA between the security objective and the functions gleaned from the foundation will be given a standard value of 10 out of 10. The reason for this being that all the functions that are directly associated (in other words through the foundation) with the security objectives have very strong associations with these security objectives.

2.3.2 SOA - Common Criteria

The structures that are gleaned from the *Common Criteria* produce additional functions that contribute to the defined objectives. The information, strengths of association (SOAs), within structures, is static, however, and should be reviewed from time to time. This means that the (SOAs) should be defined beforehand in a knowledge base. For example, the SOA between Access control and User authentication is very high, because the latter is a prerequisite for the former. In other words, the objects of a TOE cannot be protected (by Access control) against unauthorised users if the users are not known to the TOE.

The next paragraph shows which of the functions should be kept for the functional package by virtue of their (SOAs) with the objective.

Creating the functional package

The SOAs between the functions and their related objectives provide the information needed to choose functions for the preferred functional package. Not all of these functions have to be included in the functional package. The next paragraph introduces a method by means of which to determine which functions to include.

The functions with the higher SOAs naturally have a bigger impact on the objective. If not all of the functions are to be used in the functional package, it would be better to choose the ones with the bigger impact on the objective. Two alternative means could be employed in deciding upon which functions to include in the functional package, the one being the Knapsack algorithm and the other the decision matrix.

2.3.1 The Knapsack Algorithm

One of the restraints imposed upon the functions chosen is cost. The importance of the objective dictates the cost that may be incurred when choosing its relevant functions.

The importance of an objective is directly proportional to the cost an institution is willing to incur in order to reach it. The variables that need to be considered when determining which functions to choose are: the cost of a function, the effectiveness of a function and the total cost allocated to achieving an objective.

Analogous to the Knapsack problem is the problem of choosing the correct combination of functions. Thus, by using the Knapsack algorithm, the most profitable combination of functions can be chosen and those functions that are deemed unnecessary can be left out. Unnecessary functions are all those functions that appear not to represent good value for money. There are, however, limitations implicit in the use of the Knapsack algorithm. The Knapsack algorithm only discriminates between functions based on their impact-cost ratio. A security function such as Authentication, that has multiple support functions, might, therefore, wrongfully be deemed unnecessary in terms of the Knapsack algorithm. Thus, only functions that are leaf-nodes in the function structure should be considered by the Knapsack algorithm. 'Leaf-nodes' in the function structure are functions that are not supported by any other functions.

2.3.2 Decision matrix

The decision matrix combines the following information:

- Each objective and all of its applicable functions.
- The risk rating of each objective, indicates the importance of the objective in terms of the security of the TOE. This is provided by the person/persons that defines/define the security objectives.

- The impact of each function on its relevant objective.

This information is combined and organised in the decision matrix to produce the following (useful) information:

- The impact of each function on the TOE (risk rating of objective incorporated).
- The total impact of the functions applicable to a specific objective (with or without risk rating being incorporated).
- The impact of each objective on the TOE (risk rating incorporated).
- An overall rating for the security of the TOE.

This information gives an idea of which functions to implement. Not only does the user of the matrix know the effect the function would have on the objective, but also what the effect will be on the TOE as a whole. Thus, a person can see the effect a function would have if the function were to be removed from the matrix.

2.4 Conclusion - step 1, step 2

All the objectives should be examined in the manner described above. This exercise would culminate in a list of security functions for all of the objectives. These lists can be combined to form a functional package for the TOE. In order to evaluate the information security of a TOE, the functional package created should be compared to what is currently installed in the TOE.

2.5 STEP 3 - Comparison

The previous step produces a functional package that will be used in this, the third step. If the TOE already exists, this step would be used to compare the functionality of the existing TOE with the functional package that was created during the previous steps. The functional package consists of the functions the TOE needs to achieve its defined objectives. Together with each security function, there would be a maximum level of implementation. The maximum level of implementation is the highest level of implementation a function could have. The level of implementation shows the degree to which the function is implemented. The functional requirements of the *Common Criteria* define various levels of implementation for the security functions (CC, 1994).

A simple table can be used to compare the relative level of implementation of each function, per objective. The relative level of implementation is the current level of implementation divided by the maximum level of implementation This would highlight functions that could be implemented to a higher level, especially functions that support more than one objective.

3 EXAMPLE

This example will look at a security concern, and take it through most of the process. The concern is: The existence and contents of an electronic transaction. Keeping in mind the definition of authenticity, the security objective that reflects the wishes of this security concern is: Authenticity + Misrepresentation or Repudiation + Prevention.

According to the tree structure, which is not given due to the lack of space, this objective leads to **Non-repudiation**.

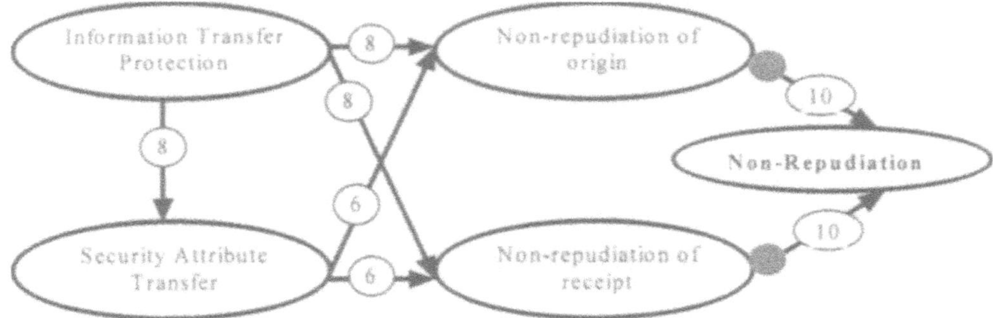

Figure 5 A Functions structure with Repudiation.

The function structure gleaned from the *Common Criteria* (in which Repudiation is involved) is depicted in Figure 5. Both the proof of origin and the receipt are necessary according to the security concern. Non-repudiation, however, is not a real security function; it is merely used as a collective descriptor for non-repudiation of receipt and/or origin. The following functions, therefore, all support the objective: Non-repudiation of origin, Non-repudiation of receipt, Information transfer protection and Security attribute transfer. Other functions are also associated with Non-repudiation but they will not be shown here due to lack of space.

Figure 5 depicts functions that are inter-related, and it also shows the SOAs between the functions. Information transfer protection has a SOA of 8 (out of 10) with both non-repudiation of origin and receipt, and therefor a SOA of 8 with the objective. Which is calculated as follows 80% × 100%. Using the same calculation for Security attribute transfer gives it a SOA of 6 with the objective, which, in turn, has a SOA of 8 with Security attribute transfer, which, in turn, has a SOA of 6 with the objective. Information transfer protection, therefore, has a SOA of 4,8 (60% × 80% × 100%) with the objective. This means that Information transfer protection has two different SOAs with the objective, namely 4,8 and 8. The higher of the two will be used. To summarise; Information Transfer Protection has a SOA of 8, Security Attribute Transfer 6, Non-Repudiation of origin and receipt both have a SOA of 10.

The impact of every function on the objective can be calculated and tabulated by the decision matrix to see their respective effects on the objective. If their costs are known the Knapsack algorithm can be employed to choose the most cost effective functions.

4 CONCLUSION

It will be important for many organisations to evaluate their IT systems in terms of the *Common Criteria*. The process of evaluation (in this paper) uses a framework derived from the *Common Criteria*. Using this framework in the process described in this paper hopes to give a starting point that would accommodate diversity of products by placing special emphasis on the specific needs of the IT system.

This paper expounds an alternative and new approach to the evaluation of the security functionality of a TOE. The main objectives of the process of evaluation are to help the user of the process to

- define formal security objectives
- identify all of the security functions that would support the defined security objectives
- facilitate the choice of a subset of functions to be implemented.
- illustrate ways and means in which to compare the functionality of the TOE to the suggested functionality the process provides.

The main focus, however, is the first three items on the above list. The process of evaluation described in this paper has been implemented into a workable prototype. There are, however, certain refinements and improvements that could, through further research, be made to the process described in this paper. They are:

- Further refinement of the function structures to include implementation issues.
- The alignment of the functional packages produced by the process of evaluation with the functional packages contained in the protection profile of the *Common Criteria.*

5 REFERENCES

CSE (1993), *The Canadian Trusted Computer Product Evaluation Criteria.*

Eloff, J.H.P et al. (1993) A comparative framework for risk analysis methods, *Computers & Security*, **12** 597-603.

Badenhorst, K.P (1994) *A formal approach to the optimisation of information technology risk management, 1994.*

CC (1994), *Common Criteria (preliminary draft).*

Pfleeger, C.P. (1989) *Security in computing.*

Murray, W.H. (1995) Security should pay: It should not cost, in *Proceedings of the IFIP/Sec '95*, 1995.

Strous, L. (1994) Security Evaluation Criteria, *Computers & Security*, **13** 379-384.

Parker D. (1995), A new framework for information security to avoid information anarchy, in *Proceedings of the IFIP/Sec '95*, 1995.

Curriculum Vitae

Jan Eloff holds a Ph.D (Computer Science) specialising in Information Security. He worked for a number of years in industry, since 1988 he is a Professor in Computer Science at the Rand Afrikaans University, South Africa. He has published widely on various aspects of information security. He delivered papers at leading information security conferences on an international level. He is chairman of the South African Special Interest Group in Information Security which is affiliated to the Computer Society of South Africa. He is also chairman of an international working group on Small System Security.
He serves as a professional advisor on variuous apsects on information security to industry.

Riaan Kruger is currently studying towards his Ph.D (Computer Science) specialising in the field of information security. He works for Nanoteq, a leading information security concern in South Africa.

A methodology for accrediting a commercial distributed database

J.H.P. Eloff and R. Körner
Department of Computer Science
Rand Afrikaans University, P.O. Box 524, Auckland Park, Johannesburg 2006, South Africa
Eloff@rkw.rau.co.za, Korner@iafrica.com

Abstract
This paper proposes a process through which a commercial distributed database could be accredited. The said process could be executed in order to ensure that the database product used in the operational environment, of an organisation is best suited to provide security safeguards and countermeasures to meet the unique security requirements of such environment. In addition, the framework of accreditation evaluation could provide a basis for the comparison of security criteria implementation in various commercial distributed database products.

Keywords
'information security', 'Common Criteria', 'accreditation framework', 'replicated distributed database environment', 'operational security environment' and 'certification'

1 INTRODUCTION

Buying off-the-shelf products, each with its own security classification, is all very well, but what do you have to show at the introduction of your computer system? Are you sure that you are fully utilising all the security services provided by these products? Are you confident that you are aware of all the features the certified products have to offer? Is the classification of your most important data product, the DBMS, relevant to you? The answers to these questions may even give rise to more pertinent questions, such as: 'Do you know which security services you need in your database environment?', and 'Do you know how to fully utilise the services provided by your suite of products in order to meet your needs?'.

The increasing use of client-server driven computer systems, as well as the geographic distribution of branches, has led to many companies' implementation of distributed database systems. In this paper, the authors will endeavour to provide all developers, database administrators and managers of distributed databases with a high-level framework for security. In the first section an overview will be given of the certification and accreditation processes. The second section will be devoted to the identification of all the security needs and requirements for your distributed database in your own operational environment. After having identified your needs, you may want to determine to what extent your current (or potential) distributed database meets these needs. The evaluation framework is set up in a very generic way, using the security functions specified in the 'Common Criteria' (Common, 1994). Oracle 7.2 will be evaluated in terms of the security services it provides for a symmetrical replication distributed database. Although Trusted Oracle 7 is classified as an NCSC B1 product, and Oracle 7.2 as an NCSC C2 product (Oracle 7, 1994), the authors believe in using a widely used commercial product to illustrate the workings of the framework.

The evaluation framework may also be used to accredit non certified products, or to compare the same product in two different operational environments. It is the generic nature of the framework, that contributes to making it a very important tool when evaluating and comparing products for a specific operational environment. The scope of this paper restricts the authors to accrediting one product (Oracle 7.2) in one environment (symmetrical replicated distributed database).

2 CERTIFICATION AND ACCREDITATION

Currently, there are many definitions for the processes of certification and accreditation. The following constitute the definitions selected by the authors for the purpose of this paper. Certification is the process of classifying a product according to a standard, generally known as Security Criteria, like the ITSEC, CTCPEC and NCSC standards. Accreditation is the process of certifying a product according to the specific needs of the operational environment in which it will be used. In this paper, Oracle 7.2 will not be certified (as it has already been certified by the NCSC as a C2 product, and by ITSEC as an E3 product), but rather accredited in terms of the security needs of a commercial symmetrical replication distributed database environment. The authors hold the view that the certification of a commercial product is very useful for the prospective buyer comparing database products, but that it is only once the buyer has gone through the accreditation process, as suggested in this paper, that the most suitable database product for his/her specific operational environment could be selected. A strong case will be made out for this view throughout the paper.

One of the weak points of or hot spots in the existing certification criteria (Pfleeger, 1989) is that the criteria are focused on commercial *products*, especially operating systems, at the expense of application systems. It might, however, be unfair to blame the standards, as this perception may have been created owing to the fact that the standards are currently only being applied to products (by the industry). The reality is that several computer products combine to form an operational computer system. These products may work in such synergy that the effect the security functions provided by a product, may be far more profound than anticipated merely from its certification classification. On the other hand, the product may behave very differently in its operational environment and in combination with other products than in clinical tests during its certification period. Used as a case in point is the example of an Oracle 7.2 database and the UNIX operating system combined with a front-end development tool such as SQL*Windows to form an operational environment. The Oracle 7.2 database and the UNIX operating system may be jointly responsible for the identification and authentication of users. The combination of the Oracle 7.2

database with the UNIX operating system enhances the function of identification and authentication of users in that true synergy is created. The user in such an environment, therefore, receives a better identification and authentication service from the combined products than from either product on its own. It may, however, also be possible that the SQL*Windows applications do not require the user to provide a password, but keeps a flat file containing passwords, against which it matches the user's log-on ID and password, and sends this information to the database. The identification and authentication service provided in the Oracle 7.2 database will, therefore, only be cosmetic, for any user may gain access to the client PC and log into the database by supplying a user log-on ID only. The uniqueness of an operational environment is, therefore, of vital importance when it comes to security services and their importance in the operational environment. The challenge for all of those managing an application system is to identify the best security services provided by the products and the optimal combinations of these services to act as safeguard for the application system as a whole. This process is known as accreditation.

The authors would, therefore, define the term accreditation as the assurance the user of an application system will have that the products combined in the application system are individually suited to the specific operational environment, and that they combine in an optimal manner to provide the best possible security safeguard for the system. The accreditation process will involve the evaluation of the potential products in terms of the security needs in the specific operational environment. In this paper, the core of the application system, i.e. the database, will be evaluated against the security needs of a distributed database environment, using the proposed accreditation framework. Some of the functional security services of the 'Common Criteria' (Common, 1994) will be used in the next section to act as a guideline for the identification of the security needs and requirements of a distributed database. These needs and requirements will help to define an ideal operational security environment for a distributed database system. Only five of the nine security functions of the 'Common Criteria' (Common, 1994) are used in this paper. The security functions were selected because they are, in the authors' minds, the most relevant to a distributed database system. The security criteria are used not to certify the database product, but to accredit the product in the operational environment of the organisation. The accreditation process can be seen as complementary to the certification process, and will be the responsibility of the organisation aiming to provide a secure computer system.

The long term goal of the research currently conducted by the authors, is to be able to accredit a database application, consisting of many products, for a specific operational environment. In order to complete such a methodology, additional criteria to the ones used for the purpose of this paper, will be developed. The said criteria may include aspects influencing the security policy, for instance the ownership of data. In this paper the first step towards accrediting a database application is taken in accrediting the database management system.

The authors will endeavour to use existing commercial products to illustrate the workings of the proposed accreditation framework. Although Trusted Oracle 7 boasts more security features than most other database products currently available, Oracle ver 7.2 has been chosen as an examplar because of its widespread commercial use. Whilst all the examplars used and all the technical information given may also be applicable to other commercial products, the focus of this paper will be on Oracle 7.2. Oracle 7.2 (Oracle 7 (TM), 1995) provides mechanisms for various types of data replication, depending, of course, on the need of the organisation implementing it.

3 IDENTIFYING SECURITY REQUIREMENTS

von Solms et al. (von Solms, et al, 1994) defines the operational security environment (OSE) of a computer system as the operational environment plus the countermeasures provided by the computer system. The ideal OSE will depict the ideal security environment for the computer system. This will be the environment that the system owner will endeavour to establish throughout the life-cycle of the system (von Solms, et al, 1994).

The very first step in evaluating a product for accreditation is, therefore, to identify security requirements and to weight them in the operational environment. The authors would suggest that an ideal OSE must first be compiled and evaluated for each component of the application, and then for the application system as a whole. When product evaluations are done, strong and weak points will be identified, where after the component evaluations could be used to combine these strong and weak points to produce a strong synergy in the application system. In this paper, the authors will define an ideal OSE for a traditional distributed database environment, as well as the symmetrical replication distributed database environment. This is done to illustrate the differences in the ideal OSE for different environments. The proposed framework will only be used to accredit Oracle 7.2 in the symmetrical replication database environment.

3.1 The ideal OSE for a distributed database

When administrators, users or managers want to assure themselves of the security provided by their computer system, it is logical to start at the core of the system, which is the database. The first step in accrediting a database application in a distributed environment, will be an attempt to identify the ideal operational security environment (OSE) for a distributed database.

In Table 1, the applicability of five of the main security functions, as defined in the 'Common Criteria' (Common, 1994), is plotted against the two main types of distributed database environments, namely the traditional and the replicated environment. The former criteria were chosen because of their applicability to the database environment, and in particular to the distributed database environment. The scaling method, as developed by Eloff (Eloff, 1983), will be used throughout this framework (Appendix A). This method weights the identified security requirements in terms of the relevance to the considered environment, as well as the degree to which they are implemented by the product to be accredited.

Table 1 The importance of security criteria in a distributed database environment

Security requirements	*Traditional distributed database environment*	*Replicated distributed database environment*
Trusted path	4	4
Identification and Authentication	3	4
Audit	2	4
Communication	4	3
Privacy	3	4

Where:
- 0 - Not applicable
- 1 - Necessary
- 2 - Important
- 3 - Very important
- 4 - Of critical importance

As it can be seen from Table 1 the ideal OSE for a traditional distributed database environment differs slightly from that of a replicated database environment. Only the ideal OSE for the replicated environment will be discussed in this paper. The generic accreditation framework may, however, be used to evaluate the same product in both environments.

Some of the high-level security requirements can be broken down into more specific security services that need to be provided in the operational database environment. In the following sections, the authors will break down these requirements and evaluate to what extent Oracle 7.2 provides these services in a replicated database environment. Only the security mechanisms provided in Oracle 7.2, and not all possible mechanisms, will be used for the evaluation.

3.1.1 Trusted path

The concept of a trusted path is that communication between a user and the database will be trusted in the sense that the user will be sure that he or she is talking directly to the database, and that the database is sure that data will be returned only to trusted applications (Common, 1994). The trusted path is used to ensure that the information used for authentication supplied by the user will be protected at all times (Common, 1994). Symmetrical replication supports updates on any and every copy of the data, as well as the distribution of such an update through to other copies, therefore, there should also be a trusted path between the various copies of data. The master table must be sure that it is sending data across the network to a trusted node to keep copies of the data. Both of the aforementioned security services are of critical importance to the secure implementation of a trusted path in the replicated distributed database environment. Table 2 shows the degree to which Oracle 7.2 implements this criteria.

Table 2 Oracle implementation of trusted path

Trusted path security services	*Log-on protocol*
Trusted path between client and server	0
Protecting user authentication data	2

Where: 0 - Not applicable
1 - Partially implemented
2 - Fully implemented

Oracle 7.2 does not have the ability to ensure a trusted path between client and server, or between server and server (Harris, et al, 1994). This means that there is no way in which the client could be certain that he/she is responding to the trusted server when passing user IDs and passwords in an attempt to log onto the database. It is, therefore, also not possible for the server to be sure that it is passing a result set back to a trusted client. There is also no way in which any one server could be certain that it is sending data to be copied onto another server (as in the case of a snapshot) to a trusted server.

Oracle 7.2 provides encrypted password-passing across the network. A special log-on protocol is used for communications between the client and the server. This protocol makes use of a different encryption key for each session. Every session the client opens with the server will, therefore, have the same password encrypted to different values (Harris, et al, 1994), making it very difficult for an eavesdropper to try and decrypt the encrypted password.

It may be argued that the log-on protocol should be seen as an implementation of the secure communication function and not of the trusted-path function. A possible solution may be to include the log-on protocol as an implementation of both the trusted path and the communication functions. In this case, the authors chose to keep the log-on protocol as part of the trusted-path function, for this arrangement satisfies one of the most important trusted-path security requirements as specified in the Common Criteria, namely that of protecting user authentication data.

3.1.2 Identification and authentication

Table 3 Oracle implementation of identification and authentication

Identification and authentication security services	*User log-on Ids*	*Password verification*
Identification	2	0
Authentication	0	2

Where: 0 - Not applicable
1 - Partially implemented
2 - Fully implemented

As is shown in Table 3, Oracle 7.2 implements identification and authentication through the use of user log-on identifications and passwords. Oracle 7.2 provides the facility of twofold identification: either the identification can be left up to the operating system or every user requesting a session with the database will have to provide a username and password. In case the identification and authentication process is left up to the operating system, users' IDs and passwords will be validated by the operating system mechanisms, and database roles may be mapped to operating system groups (Harris, et al, 1994). The user will, therefore, receive the database privileges associated with the operating system group for which it was authenticated. This means that access will be granted to a user to use applications without having to provide a separate database ID and password (Oracle 7, 1994). This will be done where it can be ensured that all users requiring access to the database will have only one path to the database, namely through the operating system. In case of database authentication, every user or program trying to gain access to the database will have to supply a user ID and password (Oracle 7, 1994). The latter case would probably be more often used in a replicated distributed database environment.

In the authors' minds, the mechanisms Oracle 7.2 provides fully satisfies the identification and authentication security service requirements. There are, however, some deficiencies in the current password mechanisms Oracle 7.2 is using. Oracle does not manage a minimum password length and suitable time periods requiring password changes (Harris, et al, 1994). This may, however, be overcome by educating staff members to keep their passwords secret, to choose them carefully and to change them regularly.

3.1.3 Security audit

The security audit of a database involves the recording, storing and analysis of information recognised as information regarding security-related activities (Common, 1994). Oracle 7.2 (Oracle 7 (TM), 1995) does provide an automated audit trail facility that will record information on relevant actions. The audit trail may be kept on database activity, prompted by a user using a system privilege, or only of actions relevant to certain objects or attributes, or actions performed by individual users (Oracle 7, 1994). A specific database activity may be audited through Oracle's audit facility without the additional overhead that is normally associated with audit keeping (Oracle

7, 1994). The audit trail may be switched on or off, and the scope and granularity of the trail may be changed, as the administrator sees fit. The audit trail records are kept in an Oracle table, available for viewing (Oracle 7, 1994). This table will be seen as a normal access control object, and rights to this table will be granted to users. The audit trail table is, therefore, protected against malicious changes.

All of the above is true for each and every node in the replicated database environment, the audit functions on each local database will function separately. Oracle 7.2 does not provide a distributed audit function that will allow a central audit function to manipulate audit functions on various geographical nodes. Every node will have full control of the audit function at local database level, but no control over the audit function at another node. The audit trail of a specific object will, therefore, be scattered over as many nodes as there are copies of the object. Database triggers and stored procedures may be used to partially implement a consolidated audit trail for an object (Oracle 7, 1994).

Table 4 Oracle implementation of audit criteria

Audit security services	*Audit trail*
Audit	1

Where: 0 - Not applicable
1 - Partially implemented
2 - Fully implemented

The extensive audit facility offered in Oracle 7.2 satisfies the audit security service requirement but, ideally, the database containing the master object should be able to manipulate audit trails on the various local databases where copies of the object occur. As indicated in Table 4, the implementation of the audit function in Oracle 7.2 is only partial, as it lacks the distributed option that would be required in a replicated distributed database environment.

3.1.4 Communication

Secure communications should support mechanisms to prove that data was either created, transmitted or received by a specific party (Chii-Ren, 1995). This service will be provided by implementing proof of sender, submission, delivery and receipt. These services form part of a secure communication system and do not fall within the scope of a database. The distributed database should, however, provide data protection on the communication of the data object itself. Trusted communication services regarding data objects ought to provide non-repudiation of origin and receipt (Common, 1994). Proof of origin and receipt will supplement the normal secure communication non-repudiation services. Proof-of-origin mechanisms will provide acceptable proof regarding the originator of the data object. The originator will not be able to deny preparing or creating the data object. The originator and sender of a data object need not be the same party. On the other hand, proof of receipt mechanisms will provide acceptable proof that the data object was received, and that the receiver will not be able to deny the receipt of the data object (Chii-Ren, 1995).

In the replicated distributed database environment, proof of origin and receipt should be implemented between the servers housing various copies of the data. In this way, the replicated database will have proof that the master database was the originator of the replicated data, and the master database will have proof that the replicated database had received data transmitted to it.

Oracle 7.2 does not provide any mechanisms to ensure proof of origin or receipt. This is the one component in which Oracle 7.2 does not even begin to achieve what is expected of it in terms of security services provided.

3.1.5 Privacy (confidentiality)

In the replicated distributed database environment, there are many copies of the same data stored over many geographical nodes, thus increasing the risk of an unauthorised subject (user or program) reading data. The implementation of access control in the replicated distributed environment is, therefore, of critical importance to the security of such a system. Another critical component is to ensure that the data that is read will not be tapped into covert channels. This environment also requires a more complex implementation of object re-use mechanisms than other database environments. Object re-use deals mainly with memory protection mechanisms in the operating system (Pfleeger, 1989). The mechanisms of the operating system will ensure that each user's program runs in a specific piece of memory, inaccessible to unauthorised users (Pfleeger, 1989). In the replicated distributed database environment, each geographical node may run on a different hardware platform, leading to diverse implementations of the object re-use, or memory protection, mechanisms in this environment. The unobservability and unlinkability of communication events are not that important for the implementation of security, but protect the privacy of users.

Table 5 Breakdown of privacy criteria

Privacy security services	*Symmetrical replicated distributed database environment*
Read control (access control)	4
Unobservability of communication events	1
Unlinkability of communication events	1
Object re-use	3
Covert channel handling	4

Where: 0 - Not applicable
1 - Necessary
2 - Important
3 - Very important
4 - Of critical importance

The access control mechanisms provided by Oracle, as discussed earlier, are well defined and implemented (Oracle 7 (TM), 1995). Oracle provides insert and update privileges up to attribute level. It does not, however, provide row level access and selective select privileges. These can be achieved through snapshots on horizontal or vertical subsets of tables. Row level access is the responsibility of the developers and administrators of the database schema, and may be implemented through application-specific database triggers. A database encryption facility is offered by Oracle 7.2 to supplement the access control measures when it comes to read control. Access to sensitive data may be limited by encrypting such data. The decryption privileges may then only be granted to the functional user of the sensitive data. This will ensure that developers and users in other functional areas cannot read the sensitive data in clear text format. At this point in time, table encryption facilities are provided and not column or row level encryption (Oracle 7, 1994).

Plotted in Table 6 are the security services and corresponding mechanisms through which the services are achieved .

Table 6 Oracle implementation of privacy

Privacy security services	*Access control (discretionary)*	*Database encryption*	*Snapshot*	*Deleted objects*
Read control	2	2	2	0
Unobservability of communication events	0	0	0	0
Unlinkability of communication events	0	0	0	0
Object re-use	0	0	0	1
Covert channel handling	1	1	0	0

Where: 0 - Not applicable
1 - Partially implemented
2 - Fully implemented

Oracle 7.2 does not provide for the unlinkability and unobservability of communication sessions with the database. This is not critical for the secure working of the replicated distributed database system. Object re-use will be achieved when Oracle only allocates space for use by an object (memory) once all traces of deleted data have been removed (Oracle 7, 1994).

This discussion has clearly shown how interdependent some of the security criteria are. The *Privacy criteria* is dependent on the *Identification and authentication criteria,* as are the *Communications* and *Trusted Path criteria.* Not only are the criteria interrelated, but some security mechanisms may satisfy security services in more than one criteria. The mechanism of access control, for instance, implements security services both in the *Identification and authentication* and *Privacy criteria.* In the following section, Eloff's (Eloff, 1983) model will be used to give Oracle 7.2 an accreditation score on each of the criteria, as discussed.

The five criteria used for the illustration of the model are by no means the only criteria applicable when doing accreditation. Two other criteria contained in the 'Common Criteria' (Common, 1994), namely *Protection of user data* and *Resource utilisation* may be included. The model will be extended ultimately to award Oracle 7.2 a global accreditation score for providing the security services needed in the ideal operational security environment of a replicated distributed database.

4 MEASURE OF ACCREDITATION

After identifying and discussing the security requirements of the ideal OSE in section 3, Oracle 7.2 can now be accredited in the symmetrical replicated distributed database environment. Each criterion will be evaluated separately using the formula as shown in Appendix A. The accreditation score will be determined by taking the product of the importance of the requirement and the degree of implementation thereof, multiplied by a constant value of 50, all divided by the weighted importance of the requirement. The calculations for the accreditation score achieved for the *Privacy criteria* is shown as an example.

Table 7 Accreditation score for the privacy criteria

Security services	*Implementation Scale*	*Importance of Requirement*	*Product (implementation and importance)*
Read control	2	4	8
Unobservability of communication events	0	1	0
Unlinkability of communication events	0	1	0
Object re-use	1	3	3
Covert channel handling	2	4	8
		13	19

Evaluation for privacy:

S Privacy = (50.19) / 13 = 73,08 %.

Table 8 Accreditation scores

Security requirements	*Accreditation score*
Trusted path	*S* Trusted Path = (50.8) / 8 = 50%
Identification and authentication	*S* I & A = (50.8) / 4 = 100%
Audit	*S* Audit = (50.4) / 4 = 50%
Communication	*S* Communication = (50.0) / 3 = 0%
Privacy	*S* Privacy = (50.19) / 13 = 73,08 %

The accreditation scores obtained by Oracle 7.2 for the five security criteria used are summarised on a high level in Table 9.

Table 9 High level accreditation scores

Criteria	*Accreditation score*	*Implementation scale*	*Importance of requirement*	*Product (implementation and importance)*
Trusted path	50%	1	4	4
Identification and authentication	100%	2	4	8
Audit	50%	1	4	4
Communications	0%	0	4	0
Privacy	73%	1	4	4
			20	20

Where: 0 - 49% = 0
50 - 89% = 1
90 - 100% = 2

Overall evaluation for Oracle 7.2:

***S* Oracle 7.2 = (50.20) / 20 = 50%.**

The accreditation model we used indicates that Oracle 7.2 achieves an accreditation score of 50% of the security services required in a replicated distributed database environment, based on the five chosen criteria. The framework makes it possible to determine what percentage Oracle achieves for each criterion, making comparison between products easy. It can be derived that Oracle 7.2 is very strong on the *Privacy* and *Identification and authentication criteria.* This enables the prospective database manager to evaluate several products with the same model and to obtain scores for each product. The accreditation scores for each product may then be compared to support a decision on which product to buy. It may be possible that the overall score is lower than that of other evaluated products, but its score obtained in one of the criterion is much higher than that of other products. If the specific criterion is very important to the potential database manager, the product may even be chosen over a product with a higher aggregate score. This framework, therefore, supports business orientated information systems decisions.

5 CONCLUSION

Every organisation serious about its data and application systems, should strive towards accreditation and peace of mind (regarding the security safeguards provided by their company). In this paper, the emphasis was placed on understanding how operational security needs and requirements for a distributed database can be satisfied by the mechanisms provided in the database. The proposed accreditation framework may be seen as an exciting development in achieving a better understanding of accrediting products for a specific operational environment. Distributed database managers can use this framework first of all to help answer the question: What security needs exist in the immediate operational environment of the distributed database, and how important are they? The second question that will have to be answered is: How well, if at all, does the current database mechanisms satisfy these security needs.

This framework will help the manager of the database system to identify the current security needs existing in the database's environment, and to evaluate the current or potential database's ability to satisfy these security needs. The framework also provides the manager with a yardstick with which to compare various database products in the same manner, so as to reach the best possible decision regarding a database product for the organisation. Although the framework provided primarily focused on the distributed database, it is sufficiently generic to allow for the evaluation of any component in an application system.

6 REFERENCES

Chii-Ren Tsai (1995) Extending Distributed Audit to Heterogeneous Audit Subsystems, in *Proceedings of the IFIP Sec '95* (ed. J.H.P. Eloff, S.H. von Solms).

Common Criteria (1994) *Preliminary draft.*

Eloff, J.H.P. (1983) Selection Process for Security Packages. *Computers & Security*, **2**, 256-260.

Harris, D. and Sidwell, D. (1994) Distributed Database Security. *Computers & Security*, **13**, 547-557.

Kaijser, P. (1995) Data Protection in Communication and Storage, in *Proceedings of the IFIP Sec '95* (ed. J.H.P. Eloff, S.H. von Solms).

Oracle 7 (1994) Database Security in Oracle 7 (Release 7.1).

Oracle 7 (TM) (1995) Server Distributed Systems, Volume II: Replicated Data, Release 7.2.

Pfleeger, C.P. (1989) Security in Computing. Prentice-Hall, Inc., London.

von Solms, R., van de Haar, H. ,von Solms, S.H. and Caelli, W.J. (1994) A Framework for Information Security Evaluation. *Information & Management*, **3**.

BIOGRAPHY

Jan Eloff holds a Ph.D (Computer Science) specialising in Information Security. He worked for a number of years in industry, since 1988 he is a Professor in Computer Science at the Rand Afrikaans University, South Africa. He has published widely on various aspects of information security. He has delivered papers at leading information security conferences on an international level. He is chairman of the South African Special Interest Group in Information Security which is affiliated to the Computer Society of South Africa. He is also chairman of an international working group on Small System Security. He serves as a professional advisor on various aspects on information security to industry.

Renita Körner is currently studying towards her Ph.D (Computer Science) specialising in the field of database security. She works as a Computer Consultant for Q Data Consulting, one of South Africa's leading consulting firms. In her capacity as a computer consultant she is often called upon to advise clients in the intricacies of computer security, and more specifically database security.

A comparison of schemes for certification authorities/Trusted Third Parties

A. van Rensburg
IBM Park Private Bag X9907
2146
Sandton
South Africa
Tel: +27 11 302 8619
Fax: +27 11 302 8778
E-mail: alicem@johic1.vnet.ibm.com

Prof B. von Solms
Rand Afrikaans University
Johannesburg
South Africa
Tel: +27 11 489 2843
Fax: +27 11 489 2138
E-mail: basie@rkv.rau.ac.za

Abstract

A comparison of schemes employed by certification authorities or trusted third parties to generate certificates.

Keywords

Certificate, certificate authority, cryptography, digital signature, key, security, trusted centre, trusted third party, public key

1. Introduction

1.1 Background

The application of information technology rapidly evolved from stand-alone centralised computer systems, where no or very little interaction with other computer systems was required, to distributed computing environments, establishing communication among different institutions using different computing systems, to the current trend of open systems and world wide accessibility via the internet and intranet.

As the need for interconnectability increased, information shared over these networks have become more and more exposed to misuse. Therefore it has become increasingly important for information security to address:

- Information privacy.
- Information integrity in term of:
  - origin of data.
  - destination.
  - content.
  - and ultimately non-repudiation.
- Identification and authentication between communicating parties

The requirements listed above can only be provided by applying cryptographic methods. Cryptography is the only known mechanism which can provide information confidentiality and data integrity economically within the information technology environment.

There are two general forms of key-based cryptographic algorithms known as symmetric and asymmetric. Symmetric algorithms are characterised by the ability of the enciphering key to be calculated from the deciphering key and vice versa. In most cases both encryption and decryption keys are the same. The security of a symmetric algorithm rest in the key and therefore the key needs to be kept secret. When two entities need to communicate private information, the same key has to be loaded into both systems with secrecy as well as with integrity. In most systems this application is performed by specially assigned security personnel.

Public-key algorithms are designed so that the key used for encryption is different to the key used for decryption with the additional proviso that the decryption key can not be calculated from the encryption key. The encryption key can therefore be made public. When two entities need to communicate private information between each other the public key of the receiving entity needs to be loaded into the sending entity's system. Since there is no risk in divulging the public key, this eliminates the need to load keys in secret. The loading of the public key however still needs to be done with integrity.

Public-key cryptography and symmetric cryptography work best together. The strength of public-key cryptography resides in key distribution and providing authentication. Symmetric cryptography is orders of magnitude faster and very suitable for the protection bulk information.

By applying these cryptographic algorithms in various ways, solutions for the above mentioned problems can be found in particular:

- Encryption and decryption to provide data privacy.

- Message authentication codes and digital signatures to provide integrity. Message authentication codes and digital signatures are equivalent to a cyclic redundancy check value except that the process involves a secret key during generation and verification cycles. Digital signatures have an additional advantage in that non repudiation can be achieved since only the entity which owns the private component of the public-key pair could have produced the digital signature. This is equivalent to a person hand-signing a document.
- Digital certificates to aid identification and authentication. A digital certificate is an electronic credential issued by a trustworthy organisation. The digital signature vouches for an entity's (an individual's, business's or organisation's) identity and authority to conduct any transaction over a network. The digital certificate can be seen as equivalent to an ID book, passbook or driver's license.

  More specifically: a public key certificate is a public key together with other unique identification which is digitally signed by a trustworthy authority. The objective is to certify that the information of the holder of the public key is valid and that the public key really belongs to the holder.

  Certificates are the result of an arbitrated protocol that utilises a third party to ensure authentication between communicating entities. These third parties may be referred to as certification authorities, trusted centres or electronic notaries.

1.2 Purpose

This paper examines the entities which create these certificates and the methods employed by these entities to achieve a trusted environment where these certificates can be used.

The purpose of this paper is to analyse the functionality of these certification authorities with the purpose of building a reference model.

A common minimum level of trust is required for open certification services provided by certification authorities interconnected in the network. A common framework for certification authorities can be useful with the accreditation of certification authorities, contribute to open standards for multiparty protocol and enable greater interoperability in an open environment.

2. A reference framework for certification authorities

2.1 Introduction

Certificates are used for the identification and authentication of a wide variety of entities in a wide variety of applications such as:
- Users, merchants, payment gateways, card issuers and aquirers for the purpose of performing financial transactions over a network.
- Point-of-sale devices for the purpose of establishing a secure channel for the interchange of keys.
- Users for the purpose of exchanging documents over the network.

Several certification authority applications have been developed to address the certification of public keys in each of these applications. These certification authority applications provide a specific set of functions within a specific framework of trust. This section first addresses some of the different trust models already implemented in order to meet certification requirements, followed by a breakdown of functions implemented by a certification authority and is structured as follows:
- 2.2 Trust models.
- 2.3 Functions.
- 2.4 Critical success factors.
- 2.5 Conclusion.

2.2 Trust models

Certification of public keys means that some trusted third party assures the binding of a public key and related person or entity. There are several possibilities how this trust can be realised:
- **Unstructured trust model.** Each certificate is self-certified and distributed with some personal assurance of validity. This provides bilateral end-user-to-end-user certification in that it trusts only in bilateral assurance.

  Pretty Good Privacy (PGP) (reference: Schneier) is an example. PGP uses a distributed approach to key management. There are no certification authorities. Each user generates and distributes their own public key. Users can sign one another's public keys, adding extra confidence to the key's validity. An entity which signs another's public key becomes an introducer for that entity. The user of the public key examines the list of introducers who have signed the key, if one of the introducers is trusted by this user, then the new public key can be accepted. If two introducers are marginally trusted then the key could also be trusted.
- **Single trusted arbitrator** such as Kerberos (reference: Schneier). **Kerberos** is a trusted third-party authentication protocol based on symmetric cryptography where a Kerberos server acts as a trusted arbitrator for each transaction.
- **A set of certification authorities** which are committed to certain security policies and operation modes. These certification authorities receive their trust from a broad user community due to their commitment to their certification behaviour and public control.

  Privacy-enhanced mail (PEM) (reference: Schneier) is an example. PEM adopted a very rigid hierarchical trust model. Each certification authority had to ensure that it certified only certificates subordinate to it in the name space. The resulting tree structure had only one root - that of the Internet Society.

- **Cross-certification model.** An intermediate model which again consists of a series of certification authorities but some certification authorities can cross-certify each other. Such a model was implemented by TESTFIT (reference: TESTFIT).
- **A hierarchy of certification authorities,** where each certification authority is certified by a certification authority at a level higher to achieve a hierarchy of trust. Each certificate is validated by traversing through the signature chain, verifying each certificate up to the root. **Secure Electronic Transaction (SET)** (reference: SET 96) is an example.

The usage of public-key based security services depends on a common set of rules that determine the security behaviour of all participants. This is especially important for the relationship between users and the certification authorities where the relationship is based on trust. These security policies govern the behaviour of certification authorities and the communication rules between the certification authorities and their clients as well as the characteristics of the security services between the users. The security policies are reflected in the trusted model and are eventually implemented as a series of security protocols or functions.

2.3 Functions

Independence of hardware, software and operating system specifics is a prerequisite for any generic model. The reference framework needs to adhere to the above criteria and also specifically address independence of security policies, cryptographic algorithms, cryptographic protocols and trust models as discussed in the previous section.

In its simplest form the certification process may consist of the association of a public key with the user's unique identifying details, followed by the structuring of this information together with an expiration date, into a formal structure and finally signing this structure with the private key of the certification authority. A more complex process may include aliasing, authentication with the use of time windows and initialisation services. The reference framework specifies a super set of functions which supports any certification process, from the most simple to the most complex.

In order to understand the requirements for a certification authority, some implementations of certification authorities were studied. Two of these case studies are described in subsequent sections of this document.

By studying a number of different implementations of certification authorities, it became clear that the certification procedure may be divided into the following sub-processes. Depending on a number of factors, the certification authority may perform all or only selected of the following sub-processes:

Certification practise statement

A certification practise statement should be generally accessible to all potential participants of a networking group so that business conduct of the certification authority and the client is understood. The security policies employed, different types of certificates provided and other general information required for certification should also be accessible.

Synchronisation

This step allows the requester and the certification authority to synchronise their cryptographic working environments. Details of the security environment such as cryptographic algorithms supported, preferred cryptographic protocols for certification and key exchange can be communicated during this phase. In many certification authority applications the cryptographic methods and protocols have been pre-arranged and are not negociable.

This step may also establish a secure communication channel between requester and certification authority so that the registration request may be transmitted securely to the certification authority.

Registration

A requesting entity needs to subscribe to a specific network group it wishes to join. Every user wishing to participate in a specific networking group must register with a certification authority. The registration process is initiated when the requester sends a registration request to the certification authority. The certification authority replies by stipulating the required information for the requester to join an exclusive application group. A registration form as used in SET (reference: SET 96) is an example of such an information list.

A section of the registration form will also request some uniquely identifying information relevant to the requesting entity. This unique information will eventually be tied to the public key during the certification process. The content of the uniquely identifying information depends on the entity being certified and the purposes for which the certificate will eventually be used. The registration form can also include policies which must be signed by the requester and which will serve to bind the requester to certain conduct within the group it wishes to join.

The following describes some of the information sent by the requester for registration:

- The requesting entity's public key if the entity is capable of generating its own public secret key pair.
- Unique identifying information.
- The purposes for which the public key will be used. Usage of keys may be separated into keys exclusively used for signing and keys exclusively used for encryption.
- The current state of the certificate - if it is a new certificate or an existing certificate to be renewed.

The registration process may be conducted personally or by correspondence. Alternatively, electronic registration may be considered for convenience.

Authentication

Once an entity registered, the application form is evaluated to ensure the integrity of the requesting party.

Authentication can be defined as consisting of those procedures an mechanisms that allow a computer system to ensure that the stated identity of some external entity is correct. Authentication approaches generally involve some sort of validation approach to produce evidence or confidence that a reported identity must be valid.

Once a certification authority receives a request for certification, the credentials of the requester are inspected to evaluate the request. The authentication process can be compared to a credit check and depends on the purposes for which the requested certificate will be used. The extent to which authentication is performed also depends on the grading, strength and value of the certificate requested. The authentication process may range from a manual to fully automated process depending on the authorisation policies agreed beforehand.

A variation of the process may pre-authenticate entities where sponsors introduce potential requesting entities to the authentication authority before the requesting entity approaches the certification authority. A white list may be compiled containing all entities which are expected to request certification and which may be positively identified. Such a variation is only useful where the number of requesting entities are low and the identity of these requesters can be determined with a high level of certainty.

Authentication of an entity is best done face to face but this is not always practical. Therefore the authentication authority may need further communication with the requesting entity to ensure the positive identification of the requester. Such communication may include some challenge to the requesting entity to prove that the requesting entity is not impersonating another. Challenges may vary and may include pre-defined operations executed on request such as the calculation of a modification detection code of the microcode contained in a device.

Time window intervals can also be used to prevent one entity from impersonating another. A time interval is agreed between the authentication authority and the requester during which the requester is expected to send a certification request containing the unique identity of the requester. If only one such request is received during the window, the authentication authority may assume that the requester is authentic, if two or more requests are received in the same interval the certification requests are denied. The time interval mechanism needs to be used in conjunction with other means to ensure that the certification request was not intercepted and an impostor's certification request accepted instead.

The authentication authority may operate a chain of authentication authorities, each of which examine an applicant's credentials, verify the applicant's identity and authorise the issuance of the certificate.

Key generation

The process of generating a public key pair is a resource intensive process. Not all entities may be capable of performing such a task. Especially some POS devices may have limited public key capability. For these cases the certification authority may generate a public key pair and send the key pair to the requesting node over a secure channel. Some cryptographic protocols rely on the generation of the keys by the certification authority.

Naming and aliasing

Each participant in the network needs to be identified by a unique name. If the number of participants is high, the use of a name may not be sufficient. A service is required which will guarantee unambiguous names or aliases which can be used to uniquely identify a participant in the network.

The unique user information also depends on the entity to be identified. For a user an identity number could be considered and for POS devices an internal unit number could be used. In some cases a pseudonym needs to be generated since the original user identification number may lead to misuse of the user's information as is the case in credit card transactions as explained in SET (reference: SET 96).

Key personalisation

The process of associating a particular public key with specific user information, is key personalisation. One and only one registered entity must be identified with a particular public key pair. This is especially important in the case where the requesting entity has to rely on another entity to generate the public key pair.

Certificate structures

X.509 is a standard for the structuring of certificate data which includes both the public key, unique identifying information and authentication for the key. Imbedded in the certificate are the validity dates as well as the identifying information of the authorising authority which enables signature chaining.

Extensions to the structure allow other information such as certificate policies, key usage restrictions and other application specific information to be imbedded in the certificate.

Certificate generation

Digital certificates are created by applying the private key of the certification authority to the personalised key. Key separation should be implemented, differentiating between keys used for signing and keys used the encryption of other keys.

Certificate revocation lists

A compromised certificate is revoked and listed in a certificate revocation list (CRL). This list has to be readily available within the environment where the certificate was active.

It is therefore very important that the integrity of the CRLs are maintained throughout the network. Certification identifiers can be employed as a mechanism to check the integrity of a CRL. This identifier is used in communications and ensures end users screen certificates against the latest revocation information.

Certificate directory management

On-line directories may be provided which contain the public keys and associated certificates for public access. X.500, a global directory service standard is an example of such a mechanism. These on-line directories may act as an electronic telephone directory and can be of great use in a large network where it is impossible for everybody to have all potential partner's addressing details and also serves to shield the users from complicated addressing details. These directories may however also be distributed for use in an off-line environment.

Although certificate directories are not an essential component in the certification process, the certification authorities would be the ideal hosts for such facilities due the trusted nature of the certification authority.

Distribution of certified material

This step allows two entities to exchange any other information required for the requester to actively participate in the network group once the requester has been certified. Some of the data required, excluding the certificate, may even be distributed before or during the registration process. This process would require an additional step after certification to complete the data required for an entity to actively participate in a network group. Alternatively the distribution of certified material may be performed once certification has been successfully completed. In an off-line environment, the distribution of this operational material may be more economical when distributed together with the certificate. Off-line distribution may employ the use of a PIN protected smart card for the distribution of this material.

In an on-line environment the initialisation process may be started when an entity sends an initialisation request to a certification authority. This request includes information reflecting the current operational state of the requester and may include:

- Identification check values or thumbprints of the certificates of other entities which may be required such as the certificate of the root certification authority. The list of certificates required for a particular user could be defined as a subset of the public key directory.
- Identifiers of certification revocation lists. These identifiers provide an economical way for the certification authority to validate that the requester operates on the current revocation lists.

The certification authority inspects the operational state of the requester and responds to the initialisation step with certificates, revocation lists and identifiers which where either stale or absent from the request.

The purpose of this step is to ensure that the requesting entity establishes a relatively trusted working environment. In addition, this step allows the requesting entity and the certification authority to synchronise their working environments with regards to the objects required by the particular application.

Integrity of the root public key.

Special attention needs to be given to assure the integrity of the public key of the certification authority at the top of the trust hierarchy since the integrity and the trust of the whole certification process hinges on this public key. One of the popular schemes is to publish the public key in publications. However, when the root public key needs to be renewed, some additional mechanisms need to be employed to ensure all entities will use the new root public key. In addition, methods need to be employed to ensure that the replacement of the root public key is indeed authentic and not an attempt to impersonate the certification authority.

SET (reference: SET 96) implements a mechanism which generates a renewal key at the same time the root public key is generated. The hash of the renewal key is already present in the self-signed root certificate when shared with subordinates. When the root key is to be renewed, users can validate that the new root key is indeed a relation of the old root key.

Miscellaneous functions

The certified authorities are trusted entities and therefore may provide additional services which require a high level of integrity. These services may include initialisation functions, date and time stamping services and key repository services. In cases where sensitive information needs to shared with entities not capable of communicating over a network or where a secure protocol can not be established, the certification authority may provide facilities to provide keys and certificates directly to the entity for example by injecting this information into POS devices. Such services may be offered by an initialisation service.

Date and time stamping services may be supplied where an authentic time and date is required.

A service for archiving keys can be useful where specific keys need to be shared among members of a selected group, especially when some participants are not capable of using public key functions. Such a service would be responsible to validate users requesting specific keys, ensure that the keys are communicated to the requesting users in a secure manner and ensure that users only access keys they are entitled to. The convenience offered by such a service must be weighed carefully against the potential risks involved in keeping secret keys in a central repository.

Critical success factors

- Certification authorities need to adhere to some common set of rules that will establish trust of the users in the certification authority. Accreditation of certification authorities would reassure users of a proper trusted environment.
- User software needs to be verified to ensure that cryptographic protocols are adhered to.
- End user applications must check for expired certificates. This would require that the end user systems would have to date and time synchronise with some entity in the network trusted to keep the proper date and time.
- Ensure all users use the current revocation lists to prevent unauthorised access.
- Certification authority root key revocation and renewal. The trusted chain hinges on the integrity of the root public key. Special care needs to be taken that the root key can be distributed with integrity.

Conclusion

The certification processes may be performed by one single entity or processing may be distributed among several entities, each specialised to perform a subfuntion or a group of subfunctions.

The following list includes some suggestions for some possible arrangements with variations on distribution within the SET (reference: SET 96) environment.

- One entity performs all subfunctions for its clients.
- One entity receives, processes and approves certificate requests and forwards the information to the appropriate entity to issue the certificate.
- Certificate requests are received by an independent registration authority which processes the certificate application and forwards the requests for approval to an authentication authority which in turn forwards all approved requests to a certification authority for

certification.

The following two chapters describe the certification process for SET and for TESTFIT. Each certification authority is described in detail to provide information for the last chapter where a reference model and both case studies are compared. In addition two well known certification schemes, Pretty Good Privacy (PGP), described in paragraph 2.2 on page 4, and VeriSign are also compared with the reference model.

3. Certification authority of the Secure Electronic Transaction (SET).

3.1 Overview

Secure Electronic Transaction (SET) (reference: SET 96) protocol was designed by Visa and MasterCard as a method to secure bankcard transactions over open networks. Transactions are performed on-line or store-and-forwarded such as electronic mail. Various certificates are used in SET including:

- Cardholder certificate which is an electronic representation of the bankcard and the customer signature for the transaction. The certificate binds the public key to an account number which is effectively protected using a blinding technique so that only the certification authority, the issuer and the cardholder know the account number and the name of the cardholder
- Merchant certificate which functions as an electronic substitute for the payment brand decal which appears in the store window.
- Payment gateway certificates which authenticate the payment gateways to users and merchants.
- Issuer certificates.

3.2 Hierarchy

Since a bogus certification authority could be set up to create certificates that would contain the same information as that contained in a valid certificate, it is essential that the signature of the certification authority itself be certified as authentic by a higher level certification authority. The highest level certificate is called the root and will is self-signed, distributed and verified by a number of independent methods.

Certificates are verified through a hierarchy of trust. each certificate is linked to the signature certificate of the entity that digitally signed it. The public signature key of the root is known to all SET software and may be used to verify each of the certificates in turn. The path through which the certificates are validated is called the signature chain.

3.3 Functions of the certification authority

Registration authority

Registration is performed on-line with the use of electronic registration forms. This process is initiated by the user requesting a registration form. As part of this request the user also includes a thumbprint for every certificate and certificate revocation list in the user's secure cache.

The certification authority identifies the financial institution from the request and sends the relevant registration form together with any certificates and revocation lists either absent or identified as out of date.

The user's trusted cache is updated to contain the latest certificates and revocation lists in preparation for when the user receives its own certificate. The details requested in the registration form differ depending on the entity requesting certification. In the case of a cardholder, the account number which would be used to uniquely identify the cardholder, is protected with a blinding technique to prevent the account number from being misused. The user submits the registration form and receives a receipt from the certification authority against which the user may query progress of certification.

Authentication authority

The processes and mechanisms involved in authorising certification is not part of SET and these are governed by policies as determined by the issuers.

Certification authority

Each entity must generate its own public key pair. Separate key sets are used for digital signatures and encryption purposes as well as for on-line and off-line processing. Catalogues are an example where a separate set of keys need to be used for off-line processing since the expiry date of the keys need to reflect the expiry of the catalogue offering.

The certification process associates the unique identification with the public key as provided during the registration process. This information such as with expiry dates, identity of the certification authority creating the certificate and other extensions is formatted into a X.509 structure which is signed by the certification authority.

Each certificate is linked to the signature certificate of the certificate issuing entity. The signatures are validated by following the trust hierarchy to the root. This path is referred to as the signature chain. The following list is also checked when a certificate is validated.

- Certificate association.
- Current date is within validity period.
- Intended key usage is valid.
- Key usage restriction is valid.
- The certificate is an end entity.
- Certificate type corresponds with the context in which the certificate is being used.

Special provision has been made for the generation and renewal of the root key. A replacement key is generated at the time when the root key is generated. The replacement key is stored securely until needed and the hash of this replacement root key is contained within the current self-signed root certificate. When a user receives a root key renewal, the user is obliged to verify the new root certificate by comparing the hash of the new root key with the hash contained in the current root key to ensure that the new root key is indeed the replacement of the current root key. This implies that the replacement root key is always pregenerated.

Revocation lists

Revoked certificates are added to a certificate revocation list. For each revocation list a check value is calculated which may be used to ensure that a user always uses the current revocation list. Different lists are maintained for different user groups for example, separate lists are maintained for the different card brands.

Certified material distribution

Material such as the certificates of other entities and revocation lists are distributed during the registration process. Special provision has been made to ensure the integrity of the root key.

- Root key distribution. The root key is initially distributed with the SET software. This distribution channel must be trusted. Some validation of the root occurs as a result of its initial use during contact with the certification authority.

  An alternative mechanism for initial distribution is provided by open distribution of the root key by some other channel and distribution of the hash of the root via another channel. The hash would be entered by the user to verify the root.

  The root key is distributed in a self-signed certificate. The root key certificate is available to software vendors to include with their software.
- Root key validation. Software can validate the root key by requesting the hash of the root key from the certification authority. If the software does not have the root key or the root key is found to be invalid, the root key may be requested from the certification authority. In this case the user will have to enter a string which corresponds with the hash of the root certificate. This string needs to be obtained from another reliable source. The replacement root key is validated by comparing the hash of the replacement key with the hash of the of the replacement key previously distributed.

4. Certification authority of TESTFIT - TTP and Electronic Signature Trail For Inter-modal Transport

4.1 Introduction

This project established a pan-European network of interworking Trusted Third Parties (TTPs), to provide services to support the electronic signing of documents which are used for the transport of freight across Europe. The TTPs specifically provide services to allow users to exchange electronically signed documents in a secure manner. As far as security is concerned, the participants in this pilot to a large extent rely on the inherent features of the communication media used, such as voice recognition, written signatures and stamps on paper documents.

The primary objective of the TESTFIT (reference: TESTFIT) project was to demonstrate the feasibility of establishing a pan-European network of interconnecting TTPs.

4.2 Hierarchy

The Trusted Third Party (TTP) environment consists of a number of TTPs connected together in a non-hierarchical network. Each TTP provides services to subscribers within its own domain. Interworking between users served by different TTPs is facilitated by interconnected service providers.

4.3 Functions of the TTPs

The services offered are the basic services required to support electronic signing of documents by users, such as :

User registration

Users register for the TTP service by filling out a registration form. A section of the form requests the name with which the user's key is to be personalised, addresses for billing purposes and other application related data.

Naming and aliasing

The naming format needs to provide for the unambiguity of names. This may be achieved by using information such as passport numbers, addresses and other information.

Key generation

The TTPs are responsible for the generation of all secure key pairs. The keys are issued to the users on PIN protected smart cards.

Key personalisation

This procedure is responsible for assigning a public key pair to the registered name of one user.

Key certification

Each TTP signs the public keys of the users within its own domain. TTPs also cross-certify keys between each other to allow users from different domains to communicate with each other.

Certificate revocation

When a certificate is revoked an immediate black-list stamp is associated with the relevant certificate. This information is also published on the public key directory.

Public key directory services

The TTPs provide a continuous updated directory of all certified keys issued by the TTP. The history of the lifetime of each key is also recorded. The directory service also includes revoked certificates as well as cross-certified public keys for users from different domains to be able to communicate.

Key distribution

Keys and certificates are distributed using smart cards. The smart card contains the user's secret key, certified public key, and the TTP's public certification key. The user's public key, certificate as well as the TTP's public key can be read from the smart card but can not be altered. The user's secret key can not be read from the smart card.

Revocation lists and the public key directories are distributed on-line via data modems and are also available on the request from the user.

5. Comparison of case studies

The following table compares both study cases with the list of functions as described in the reference model. This table of comparison is implemented primarily to test the reference framework against established implementations of certified authorities.

The following describes the table layout:

- Where the case study complies, the details are added into the table in **bold** text.
- Processes which are not implemented are left blank.
- Processes not implemented by the certification authority but supplied by other means are written in *italics* and details are added to the table.

Reference framework	**SET**	**TESTFIT**
Information	*Prearranged*	*Prearranged*
Synchronisation	*Prearranged - cryptographic protocols based on RSA and DES*	*Prearranged - cryptographic protocols based on RSA and DES*
Registration	**Electronic registration**	**Registration by mail**
Authentication	*Not prescribed and performed by issuer*	**Performed by certification authority**
Key generation	*End user generate own keys*	**All keys generated by certification authority**
Naming and aliasing	*Determined by end user*	*Determined by end user*
Key personalisation	**Performed by certification authority**	**Performed by certification authority**
Certificate structures	**X.509 standard supported**	**Proprietary structure**
Certification	**Certificate chaining implemented**	**Single hierarchy with cross-certification**
Revocation lists	**Seperation of CRLs implemented**	**Implemented**
Public key directory		**Public key directory implemented**
Certified key distribution	**On-line**	**Off-line on smart cards and on-line**
Certification authority public key integrity	**Pre-generated replacement**	**Certification authority public key distributed via PIN protected smart cards**

Reference framework	**PGP**	**VeriSign**
Information	**Informtion published on the internet**	**Information published on the internet**
Synchronisation	*Prearranged - cryptographic protocol based on* RSA *and IDEA*	*Prearranged - cryptographic protocol based on RSA*
Registration		**Electronic registration**
Authentication	**Self authentication**	**Authentiation depends on grade of certificate requested**
Key generation	**End user generate own keys by executing specific PGP command**	*End user generate own keys with own software/hardware*
Naming and aliasing	**Self determined**	**Performed by crtification authority**
Key personalisation	**Self determined**	**Performed by certification authority**
Certificate structures	**Proprietary**	**X.509 standard supported**
Certification	**Self certification**	**Certificate chaining implemented**
Revocation lists		**Revoked certificates are published in the VeriSign repository**
Public key directory		**Repository provided**
Certified key distribution	*Communicating parties exchange relevant information as required*	**Certificates are collected via the internet by providing a PIN**
Certification authority public key integrity	**Pass phrase protected**	**Integrity ensured**

References

Abad Peiro, J Asokan, N Waidner, M (1996) Payment Manager - Overview. SEMPER Activity Paper 212ZR054 <http://semper:zurich.ibm.com/info/212ZR054.ps.gz>

Amorosso, E (19XX) Fundamentals of computer security technology

Burton, S Kaliski, Jr (1993) An Overview of the PKCS Standards. RSA Laboratories < http://www.rsa.com/pub/pkcs/doc or http://www.rsa.com/pub/pkcs/ps/ >

European Commission DG-XIII.B.6 Infosec 94 - Phase II (1995) TESTFIT - TTP & Electronic Signature Trial For Inter-modal Transport

Europay International (1994) IC Card Specifications for Payment Systems - Part 3

IBM (1996) Internet Security Policy and Directives

IBM (1992) Transaction Security System Concepts and Programming Guide: Volume I, Access Controls and DES Cryptography GC31-3937

IBM (1992) Transaction Security System Concept and Programming Guide: Volume II, Public-Key Cryptography GC31-2889

Janson, P Waidner, M (1996) Electronic Payment Systems. SEMPER Activity Paper 211ZR018 <http://semper.zurich.ibm.com/info/211ZR018.ps.gz>

MasterCard Visa (1996) Secure Electronic Transaction (SET) Specification Book 1: Business Description

MasterCard Visa (1996) Secure Electronic Transaction (SET) Specification Book 2: Programmer's Guide

Schneier, B (1994) Applied cryptography. John Wiley & Sons, Inc

Tsudik, G (1996) Zurich iKP Prototype (ZiP): Protocol Specification Document. IBM Zurich Research. <http://www.zurich.ibm.com/Technology/Security>

VeriSign (1996) Certification Practice Statement. VeriSign < http://www.verisign.com/repository/CPS/intro.html >

Zimmermann, P (1993) Pretty Good Privacy Public Key Encryption for the Masses: PGP User's Guide

19

How to trust systems

A. Jøsang, F. Van Laenen[@]*, S. J. Knapskog and Joos Vandewalle*[§]
Department of Telematics
The Norwegian University of Science and Technology
N-7034 Trondheim, Norway.

Abstract
The owners and users of distributed systems need to trust components of the system from a security point of view. In this paper we investigate the possible methods for establishing trust in the security features of an IT product or system.

Keywords
Trust, security, trusted systems, assurance, security evaluation

1 INTRODUCTION

Security evaluation is an example of a well established method for establishing trust in implemented system components. The method is based on a set of evaluation criteria like e.g. TCSEC (USDoD, 1985), ITSEC (EC, 1992), CC (ISO, 1996) or similar, and accredited evaluation laboratories which perform the evaluation under supervision of a national authority. A successful evaluation leads to the determination of an assurance level which shall reflect to which degree the TOE or system component can be trusted. It must be recognised that evaluation assurance does not represent the users own trust in the actual system component, but rather a recommendation from a supposedly trusted authority. The evaluation assurance is thus only one of several factors supporting the user´s trust in the product.

In this paper we will discuss methods to establish trust in systems. Our goal is to

---

[@] A part of this research was done while the author was student at KUL, Belgium, and visiting NTNU, Trondheim.
[§] Department of Electronics, Katholieke Universiteit Leuven, Belgium

determine the most relevant factors which can contribute to the establishment of trust, and to find out how these factors can be combined to produce an overall perception of trust. Further, we will look at the ISO evaluation criteria (ISO, 1996) and suggest new elements not yet included in the present version. There is a slight distinction to be made between simply determining the most correct level of trust and wanting to increase it, and we will briefly describe how these aspects are related.

When studying IT security one is forced to take the human psychology into concideration. The traditional purpose of IT security is to prevent breaches of confidentiality, integrity and availability by implementing threat countermeasures expressed as technical aspects of the IT-system. The purpose of the countermeasures is to generate trust which is a human phenomenon. Trust would allow users to use a system in ways which they otherwise would avoid, so that in practice the system becomes more valuable and a more powerful tool.

2 DEFINITION OF TRUST RELATIVE TO IT SECURITY

Trust is a very general concept which can be used in almost any context. For the purpose of IT security, it is desirable to give trust a more specific meaning which may be useful in formal modelling of security.

The main rationale behind IT security is that some agents in a given situation may attempt an attack on the system, and security is supposed to prevent such attacks to succeed. The existence of malicious behaviour in general is not only the reason to have IT security, but in fact also as a necessary condition for trust (Jøsang, 1996).

Malice is here defined as a combination of dishonest and crooked behaviour, which implies both lying and breaking the rules (law, contract etc.). Similarly we define benevolence as a combination of honest and straight behaviour, which implies telling the truth[1] and respecting the rules.

A human would be trusted if believed to be benevolent, and distrusted if believed to be malicious. It may be true that there is a finite number of factors which determine whether a human will behave in a benevolent or malicious way, but it is extremely hard to determine all these factors, and therefore the behaviour of a human is hard to predict. For all practical purposes, whatever the underlying mechanism may be, we will call the human mechanism which decides between benevolent and malicious behaviour *the free will*, and we designate agents possessing this type of free will as *passionate*. We define trust in a passionate agent as *the belief that it will behave without malicious intent.*

Algorithms, protocols, software, hardware can hardly be characterised as passionate or having a free will, but they can still be trusted. We will call this type of agent *rational* as opposed to passionate. Because a rational entity has no free will, it is not expected to be malicious or benevolent. What exactly is being trusted is that its behaviour can be completely and uniquely described, and that it will resist any attempt

[1] In the sense: doing what you say you will do

of malicious manipulation by an malicious agent. Thus there is a third party involved in addition to the trusting party and the trusted rational entity, namely the possibly malicious agent. We therefore define trust in a rational entity as *the belief that it will resist attacks from malicious agents.*In the rest of the paper we mainly focus on the second type of trust because it applies to systems.

Even with the narrowing of the meaning of trust in systems through the definitions above, trust still has a broad meaning. In order to give it an even more precise meaning we use *trust purpose* which expresses what exactly the trusted system is being trusted for. The security of a system may consist of several components, such as integrity and confidentiality on a general level, and key generation and certificate verification on a more detailed level. The trust purpose can reflect these components.

3 ADEQUATE TRUST OR MAXIMUM TRUST

Trust should be based on objective evidence. Irrational trust is not based on objective evidence, but for instance on faith or a vague and fuzzy feeling which can not be rationally justified, and sometimes this trust can persist despite evidence of the contrary. This type of trust may be valuable in other situations, but can be risky for IT security. Even if trust ultimately is subjective, it will be an advantage if as many users as possible have a common trust based on the same objective evidence. One would normally expect the manufacturers to trust the systems they produce in the same way. However, there are indications that this is not always the rule.

A manufacturer which knows about vulnerabilities in the system it produces may not want to reveal this information for several reasons. A more or less legitimate reason can be that by publishing this information, the potential attackers may learn as much about the system's vulnerabilities as the legitimate users. After all, if nobody knows about a vulnerability, it will not be exploited. However, this strategy can be very dangerous, and if an attacker can discover and exploit a weakness which already was known by the manufacturer, the consequences can be serious.

Recent successful attacks on smart cards have shown that the cards can be very vulnerable. (Boneh *et al*, 1996), (Andersen and Kuhn, 1996). The manufacturers must have known about some of these vulnerabilities because of the extreme secrecy with which they have surrounded the manufacturing process. The security of smart cards depends to a large extent on the confidentiality of the hardware design and the supposed difficulty of physical inspection or manipulation. This was made very clear when an attempt to perform a security evaluation of a smart card failed due to the manufacturers' "fear" of having their products evaluated (EC, 1994), (Jøsang, 1995).

Humans are often irrational, and so is trust. This may be a minor problem for the user himself, because at least to some degree it is his own choice. On the other hand, this situation can be dangerous for the manufacturers because they may no longer be able to repair damaged trust with objective evidence. One good example of this phenomenon is the fuss surrounding the FDIV flaw in Intel's Pentium microprocessor during 1994. This flaw would only cause extremely sparse errors but the general public's trust in the processor and also in Intel as a manufacturer dropped dramatically. Only when Intel announced a no-questions-asked return policy did the company manage to regain the public's trust, and interestingly, even though everybody could have the old Pentium version replaced, many chose not to do so, which indicates that simply knowing that they could have their processor replaced was enough to restore the trust in it.

System manufacturers naturally wish to generate the highest possible public trust in their products whereas the users real trust may not always be based on objective evidence. For the general benefit of both the users and the manufacturers, it would be desirable if manufacturers always revealed, if necessary in a controlled way, all security relevant evidence which the users objectively should know, and users should try to base their trust mainly on objective evidence.

4 THE KNOWLEDGE PARADIGM OF TRUST

Many professions provide services in an environment of relative ignorance, and Smithson (Smithson, 1988) describes civil engineering and justice as two such examples. Civil engineering is very explicit when it comes to error in the estimations of load and structural strength. The practice of justice on the other hand has extensive relevancy criteria for the evidence presented in court. These two approaches reflect the different types of evidence which these two professions work with. IT security professionals also have to deal with relative ignorance, and for this purpose it will be useful to determine the nature of the evidence at hand and then determine the best practical way to use it. The two next sections give a general description of the types of evidence relevant for trust.

4.1 Direct evidence

A user of a system can never obtain perfect knowledge of the system he uses, nor of the external or internal threats, and he is therefore unable to exactly determine the system's security. By gathering as much knowledge as he can about the system he will get an idea or a belief about the security, or in other words, he will gain a certain trust in the system. In this perspective, security can be understood as an idealistic goal for the system designers, whereas trust represents the users' actual imperfect knowledge about how successful the designers have been in reaching their idealistic goal. This situation of less than complete knowledge will always persist, and the problem we are facing is how to handle it.

A good assessment of a system's security in its environment will be based on evidence from many different sources. A distinction can be made between direct and indirect evidence. By direct evidence we mean the evidence resulting from an investigation of the system through for instance a security evaluation, and through direct experience with the system. By indirect evidence we mean mediated evidence such as for instance recommendations and advice. The direct evidence can be grouped into system evidence, environment evidence and security incident evidence. This grouping fits well with a typical model of risk analysis like for instance the model employed by CRAMM[2] (CCTA, 1991). This is illustrated in Figure 1.

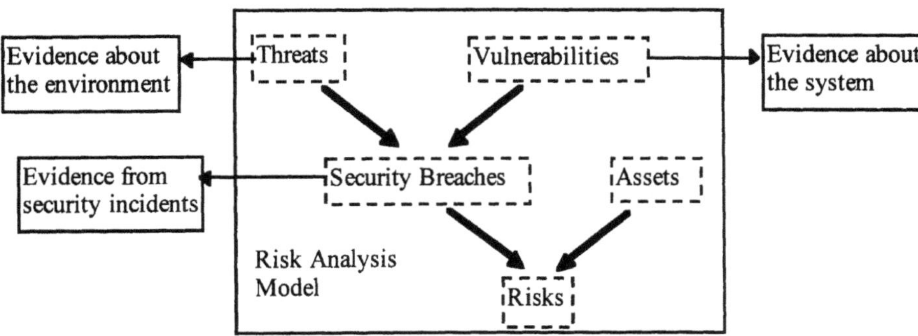

Figure 1 Direct security evidence.

According to the risk analysis model, the analysis and combination of evidence about the threats (environment) and about the vulnerabilities (system) generates likelihoods of security breaches, but only the operation of the system can show whether any of these breaches will materialise as security incidents. A materialised security breach is the worst that can happen, and it is considered better for an IT system to have too high security than to suffer from breaches. However, one of the purposes of the risk analysis is to be able to balance the cost of security with the losses due to security breaches. A direct consequence of this is that "sufficient" trust is the actual goal for a practical system.

4.2 Indirect evidence

We intuitively tend to trust somebody if he is trusted by others whom we already know and trust. This principle is extensively used, also for security services, e.g. when an entity must rely on trusted third parties, key distribution centres or certificate issuers to establish trust in IT- systems.

When a user is unable to collect direct evidence to form his trust in a system, either because he does not have access to it or because he does not possess the expertise to evaluate it, he depends on indirect evidence. A mediating agent can recommend in a backward direction that the following entity in the chain can be trusted, and so forth

[2] CCTA Risk Analysis and Management Methodology)

until the intended target entity is reached. This kind of recommendation can be formal and explicit like for instance the issuing of an evaluation certificate, or implicit like when a user simply trust a system because other users whom he trusts are using the same system and seem to trust it.

Figure 2 is an illustration of one possible way for a user to view a system of which he is unable to obtain direct evidence. The evidence he has direct access to may come from other users, a certification authority, consultants, experts etc. Their evidence may in turn come from the evaluators or the manufacturers who have access to the direct evidence.

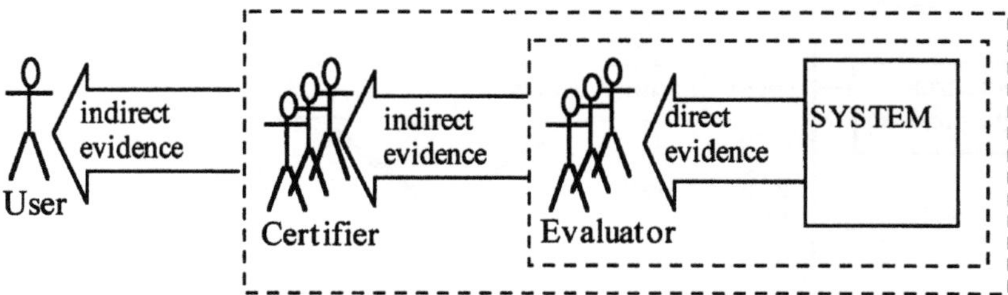

Figure 2 Indirect security evidence.

Figure 2 is not supposed to be a general model, but simply to illustrate the flow of evidence in the case of security evaluation. As a matter of fact, the user will usually have access to various types of both direct and indirect evidence. He may for instance obtain direct evidence from security incidents during operation and from assessing the threats in the system's environment. In addition to the security evaluation report, he may receive indirect evidence through security advisory reports. The difference between direct and indirect evidence is that the first is obtained by direct observation of the system and its environment, and the latter is mediated through passionate agents which can be humans, human organisations or the public in general. The user must therefore take into account potential malicious or irrational behaviour on the side of the mediating agents.

Strictly speaking, it is not correct to consider trust itself as flowing between the mediators. A recommendation from a trusted party to trust a particular system is in reality a piece of evidence which the user himself has to consider together with other relevant pieces of evidence, resulting in a subjective belief which constitutes his trust in the system.

5 HOW TO PRACTICALLY DETERMINE TRUST IN SYSTEMS

We will here try to describe a suitable framework for using the types of security relevant evidence described in section 4 in order to determine trust in systems. Like in civil engineering and in justice, where structures are modified and verdicts are changed if they are proven wrong by new evidence, the methodology for determining trust should be dynamic and take into consideration new evidence such as security incidents and new threats.

5.1 A measurement unit for trust.

Risk analysis methodologies usually operate with a quantifiable measure of risk. In case of CRAMM (see section 4.1) this is obtained by assigning a value to each threat and vulnerability and from this determine some sort of probability for each type of security breach which can occur. The probability value is finally multiplied with an asset value to produce a measure of risk. In practice the risk levels obtained after the first round of analysis are often outside any reasonable measure. For that reason, a second round of analysis is often necessary where the threat and vulnerability values are adjusted to give a more reasonable result. The reason for the abnormal results from the first round of analysis is that it is in fact difficult to determine a level of threat or vulnerability by a single value. Risk analysis methodologies were partly developed because it seemed a logical thing to do, partly also because a measure of risk is a managerial requirement. One purpose of risk analysis is to give the management an impression of quantifiable knowledge.

The idea of formally determining trust in computer systems was first developed within the military community and later spread to the commercial sector. TCSEC (USDoD, 1985) which were the first security evaluation criteria, defined a grading of 7 assurance levels, and when other criteria followed, they also tended to use 7 assurance levels as an attempt to maintain compatibility with TCSEC. When considering the large amount and the complex nature of the evidence which an evaluator must consider, there is nothing which logically indicates that this can be translated into a discrete value such as an assurance level. Again, it must be recognised that the idea of determining an assurance level for systems is as much a managerial requirement as it is a natural characteristic of a system. For this reason it should be recognised that the definition of 7 assurance levels is very ad hoc. On the other hand, a more rich and thereby complex classification of assurance could easily become useless because users would not be able to understand it. That is in reality the dilemma we are facing: The simpler the classification of trust becomes, the less it is able to reflect the diverse aspects of security, but on the other hand, the richer the classification, the less useful it becomes.

Evaluation assurance can not be directly translated into trust and only provides indirect evidence of a system's security. We argued that a single assurance level, attractive as it may be, in fact may blur the total picture of a system's security more than it clarifies it. The picture does not get any simpler when in addition other types of evidence have to be considered, thus indicating that trust can not be reasonably measured as a single value. Approximations may be used if a particular situation requires it and if users find it convenient, and for that purpose the problem is to find the most appropriate way of doing it.

5.2 A framework for determining trust based on objective evidence

Four sources of objective evidence which a user should consider for determining the security of a system are listed below:

1. **Evaluation assurance.** Whenever this type of evidence is available it will reflect a thorough analysis of the system. This can be very valuable, but can also generate unjustified trust if other types of evidence are ignored.
2. **Assessment of environment and threats.** The user or owner of a system should always make an assessment of the security threats present in the system environment. The system security should be reconsidered each time new threats are discovered,
3. **Security advisory reports.** This type of evidence gives up-to-date information about newly discovered security vulnerabilities, and should be closely monitored, even more so because also attackers usually have access to these reports.
4. **Security incidents.** A long period without security incidents does not necessarily lead to increased trust, but a security breach should directly influence the trust, overruling all other evidence including evaluation assurance.

The four types of evidence are quite different, and it may not be evident how they can be combined. We will suggest a method or framework which we believe suitable for the operators of a system. It assumes trust to be dynamic in function of new evidence, and takes the evaluation assurance level as a basis for the highest reachable trust level under normal operation conditions. Degradation of trust can for instance be caused by new evidence such as advisory reports on vulnerabilities. The elimination of the vulnerabilities may re-establish the trust. A distinction can be made between trust in the correctness of a system and trust in its effectiveness in the actual environment, in order to reflect the corresponding two types of evaluation assurance. Evidence of a fault in the system will for instance lead to degraded trust in the correctness, whereas evidence of a new threat may lead to degraded trust in the effectiveness. On a general level there should be defined grades of degradation from the normal security level, and on a more detailed scale, how much degradation each particular evidence type should cause. Upgrading of the security level may be done by eliminating or countering the factors which caused the degradation. By careful collection and consideration of evidence in this way, a system operator can keep a good overview of the system's security level which should be directly reflected in the operators' trust in the system. If their actual subjective trust deviates from the assessed security level, it can only mean that the operators consider factors or evidence not included in the assessment method.

Any mediating agent must be considered to be passionate. The case is different from trusting the security of a rational system which means trusting its ability to resist malicious attacks. The possibility that the evaluation facility itself is subject to malicious attacks in order to undermine the ongoing security evaluations is remote.

6 ASSURANCE COMPONENTS IN THE COMMON CRITERIA

6.1 Pedigree and credentials to ease evaluations

The concept of pedigree in IT Security (Van Laenen, 1995) can be useful in the sense that both direct and indirect experience with the security of the products from a given manufacturer may influence the final trust that the user will have in the security of future products from the same manufacturer. In the commercial market oriented world, this kind of trust building is probably even more common than the more formal product evaluation activities. Still, there may be a role to play for an evaluation facility, but not as evaluator of the security features of every single product, but as a process evaluator, checking on the manufacturer's security credentials in analogy to a quality assurance (QA) process. Several aspects may be included in a manufacturer's security credentials, e.g. the company as a whole, the development processes used within the company, what QA mechanisms are implemented, and the credentials of the individuals making up the company. Some of these aspects may be objective, and readily evaluateable, while others may be more subjective, quite subtle distinctions between trustworthy and non-trustworthy companies or organisations.

An experimental Assurance Class, called Credentials and Pedigree (ACP) is proposed. It contains (for now) only one Assurance Family, named Process Quality Label (ACP_PQL). The assurance components and their elements are described along the guidelines given in (ISO, 1996). The Assurance Family consists of 5 assurance components, one of which is covering the fact that the developer has earned an ISO 9000 certificate, and the other four covering the developer's consistent use of the Capability Maturity Model, in four hierarchically ordered levels.

Table 1 shows what an assurance component built on ISO 9000 may look like. The description does not pretend to be all-encompassing.

Assurance element ACP_PQL.1.1D states that the developer has to have an ISO 9000 certificate before the start of the development of the product (TOE).

Table 1 **Assurance Component ISO 9000 Certificate.**

ACP_PQL.1 ISO 9000 Certificate

Objectives This component makes sure that the plants of the manufacturer have a process with the proper quality, according to the ISO 9000 family, thus inferring that they are capable of producing a secure TOE with the specified level of assurance.

Threats Not all the plants of the manufacturer have the capability to produce a TOE with a good quality assurance.

Dependencies The ISO 9000 family

Developer Action Elements

ACP_PQL.1.1D	**The developer will have an ISO 9000 certificate before the start of the development of the TOE**
ACP_PQL.1.2D	**The developer will register all the plants that are involved in the development of the TOE**
ACP_PQL.1.3D	**All the subcontractors involved in the development of the TOE will have an ISO 9000 certificate**
ACP_PQL.1.4D	**The plants of the developer and all the subcontractors will be certified against all relevant parts of the ISO 9000 family**

Content and Presentation of Evidence Elements

ACP_PQL.1.1C	**The evidence elements will contain the ISO 9000 certificate for all involved plants**

Evaluator Action Elements

ACP_PQL.1.1E	**The evaluator will check that all the involved plants of the developer were certified before the start of the development of the TOE**
ACP_PQL.1.2E	**The developer will check that all the involved plants are certified to all relevant parts of the ISO 9000 family**
ACP_PQL.1.3E	**The evaluator will check that all subcontractors are certified to all relevant parts of the ISO 9000 family**

6.2 Flaw Remediation

Trust will be influenced by the presence of known flaws in the IT product you buy. The quick and appropriate remediation of found flaws therefore is of major importance. (On the other hand, flaw remediation can be made redundant if a perfect flaw avoidance scheme is invented.)

Not-the-First Version

It is quite common to have more trust in an existing system that already proved itself, than in a new system. The reasoning behind this is simple: newly added functionality will probably also mean newly added flaws.

Nevertheless, it is healthy not to automaticly regard the next version to be better simply because it is the next version, since the danger of adding a new flaw while remediating an old flaw is real. Also, if the next versions follow to quickly, this may indicate that the first version of the product was badly designed. Nevertheless, a next version will in general be better because the known flaws are removed from the product and the product has already proven itself through its use.

Time to Remediation

In some areas of IT, only known flaws are dangerous. As an example, a covert channel which cannot be exploited because it isn't discovered yet by any user, will not cause much harm. But as soon as one user knows how to handle the covert channel, it does become dangerous, and actually, a fortiori if the covert channel isn't known to the victim. If the covert channel is known to the public, the users can take precautions against the exploitation of it.

So, for some flaws, the time to remediation is most important. There are two ways to deal with this time to remediation: you can impose a maximum or a mean time to the IT producer. The maximum time is interesting to the user of the product, but may be very restrictive to the IT producer, and in the case of very severe flaws, may be seen as unreasonable. On the other hand, mean time to remediation may be to weak for the user.

6.3 Legal Aspects

Legal aspects can convert flaws into money loss for the IT producer, and therefore do have influence on the trust one can put in an IT product.

Liability and Guarantee

In most countries, it is possible to sue the producer if a product harms you in any way. Usually, the company will have to restore the damage, or pay for it. Damage may often not be restorable, like for example when data is lost or made public. If the IT manufacturer can be held liable for any damage the IT product does to the user, this will increase the users trust in the IT product.

If one tries to apply this in practice, several problems occur. First of all, this kind of assurance lies outside the traditional area of IT. Also, the laws may differ in different countries. This complicates the problem, and may restrict the use of this trust component.

Internal Liability

It may be a problem that the person responsible for a certain development project is transferred soon after the project is finished, so that in practice, no one can be held liable for any occurring flaws. It would be better to keep the person in charge responsible for the project, not only as long as its is being developed, but also after it is launched onto the market.

7 CONCLUSION

Trust expresses a belief and will always be a subjective notion. It is therefore meaningless to speak about solely objective trust. However it is possible to require trust to be based on objective and carefully collected evidence. We have described what it means to trust a system and suggested how trust should be determined and what it should be based on. Formal security evaluation may play an important role for determining trust in systems, and we have given some comments on the Common Criteria which possibly constitute the latest and most modern criteria for that purpose.

8 REFERENCES

Anderson, Ross and Kuhn, Markus (1996). *Tamper Resistance - a Cautionary Note. http://www.ft.uni-erlangen.de/~mskuhn/tamper.html*

Boneh, D., DeMillo, R. A. and Lipton, R. J. (1996). *On the Importance of Checking Computations*. BELLCORE. *http://www.bellcore.com/SMART/index.html*

CCTA (1991). *CRAMM User's Guide (Version 2.0)*. The UK Central Computer and Telecommunications Agency.

EC (1992). *Information Technology Security Evaluation Criteria*. The European Commission.

EC (1994). INFOSEC investigation S2108: *Security Project for Evaluating* Smart Cards. The European Commission.

Van Laenen, F. (1995). *Pedigree and Credentials, Remediation and Legal Aspects to Gain Assurance in IT Products and Systems*. Master Thesis, KUL.

ISO (1996). *Evaluation Criteria for IT Security* (documents N 1401, 1402, 1403, 1404). ISO/IEC JTC 1/SC 27.

Jøsang, A. (1995). *The difficulty of standardizing smart card security evaluation.* Computer Standards & Interfaces 17(1995), pages 333-341.

Jøsang, A. (1996). *The right type of trust for distributed systems*. In Proceedings of the New Security Paradigms Workshop 96. ACM.

Paulk, M. C. (1994). *A Comparison of ISO 9001 and the Capability Maturity Model for Software*. Technical report, Software Engineering Institute, CMU/SEI-94-TR-12.

Smithson, M. (1988). *Ignorance and Uncertainty.* Springer Verlag.

Swaelens, G.J. (1992). *ISO 9000 Quality Standards in 24 Questions*. ISO 9000 News, 1, January 1992. Interview with MR J. E. Ware, Managing Director of BSI Quality Assurance and Chairman of ISO/CASCO

US DoD (1985). *Trusted Computer System Evaluation Criteria*. US Department of Defence.

PART NINE

Management of Information Security and Risks (II)

Integrating information security in the development of telematics systems

O. Tettero, D.J. Out, H.M. Franken, J. Schot
Telematics Research Centre (TRC)
P.O.Box 589, 7500 AN Enschede, The Netherlands
+31 53 4850485; {Tettero, Out, Franken, Schot}@trc.nl

Abstract

As organisations become aware of their vulnerability to threats to their information and telecommunication systems, this often results in the ad-hoc addition of safeguards to those systems. This causes operational problems, because information security requirements were never an issue during the development of these systems. In this paper we propose that requirements for information security should be integrated in the development process in an early phase. The benefit of the integration is that information security will become an integral part of the system. We discuss the complications and some preliminary guidelines, assuming that system developers are used to a 'traditional' development process.

Keywords

Telematics systems, system development, design, requirements, information security

1 INTRODUCTION

Organisations using telematics systems[1] were generally unaware of their vulnerability to threats for a long time. For some the many incidents, public debates and governmental regulation have changed this. Unfortunately, information security requirements are difficult to effectuate in *existing* telematics systems. An example as illustration:[2]

[1] Telematics is the support of interaction between people and/or processes while bridging distance and/or time, through the integrated application of information and telecommunication technology.

[2] The example results from a study identifying the conditions for large-scale application of telematics systems in the Netherlands, sponsored by the Ministry of Economic Affairs, (Breed et al., 1995).

A Dutch University used an open network to exchange employee information between its central department and its annexes. To secure the information, crypto box-based encryption is used. The crypto-boxes are placed at strategic points in the network, to divide it in several secure and unsecure parts. The result was that the crypto-boxes caused a substantial loss of performance, both in the secure and especially in the unsecure part of the central hosts and servers. The key management system produced a large additional load for a network already plagued by heavy traffic.

In a number of similar cases, information security was added to existing telematics systems, which caused the following problems:

- Modification of an operational system may affect its *functionality*, resulting in a deviation from the desired functionality as defined in the user requirements of that system (Breed et al., 1995). The extent of the deviation is often unclear.
- Adding security to a system often causes changes in its *use*: organisational procedures surrounding that system should be changed as well, possibly causing all kind of changes within the organisation.
- The addition also results in huge costs (Mostert and von Solms, 1994). Often, the first addition of information security is unsatisfactory, and further additions must be made to deliver a secure system with identical functionality.

Tompkins and Rice (1986) and Booysen and Eloff (1995) foresee that taking information security into account from the start of the development process avoids problems later. However, we could not find a systematic description of a development process of telematics systems in the literature that actually has information security as one of its concerns.

Contributions of this paper

In this paper we investigate aspects of information security related to all stages of a traditional system development process. This process has a conceptual view of a system as input and the realisation of that system in an operational environment as output. We distinguish two viewpoints on the development activities: the *method of development* and the *problem solving* during the development. The method is a systematic procedure to obtain a real system (Dasgupta, 1989). This paper addresses the problem solving elements, like expressing the requirements. We focus on the development of safeguards as one of the concerns within the development process. Baskerville (1993) gives an analytical description of problem solving elements in the evolution of information systems. The authors are currently elaborating guidelines for several stages of the development process.

Definitions

A *telematics system* integrates information and telecommunication technology and consists of application software, system software, hardware and organisational procedures, Telematics systems contain *assets*, e.g. information, operate on assets or can be assets themselves. The system is operational in some *environment*. This environment contains a number of *threats* to the system. The assets are protected from threats by *safeguards*. *Vulnerabilities* in the system are weaknesses in the system or the absence of safeguards, whereas *attacks* are realisations of threats. Attacks that make use of the vulnerabilities are *risks* for the organisation and its systems (Ford, 1994).

Systems can be secured by applying information security[3], which is a complex of measures and procedures that meets the requirements of confidentiality, integrity, availability and authenticity[4] of systems in an adequate way, based on (Aalders et al., 1985), (BSI, 1994) and (OECD, 1996).

2 SYSTEM DEVELOPMENT ELEMENTS

To explore the incorporation of security in a development process, we need to understand its typical elements: the *phases*, the *actor roles* and *conditions*.

Phases

Several approaches to the development process are described in the literature, of which we used the common essentials, see e.g. (Mazza et al, 1994) and (Sommerville 1996). We have divided the process into phases[5], as defined in Figure 1. This approach is commonly recognised as a top-down, step-wise refinement approach. It is used because it facilitates reasoning at different levels of abstraction. There may be several loops within a phase and in the development process. Loops in the development process result from decisions made in a certain phase, that turn out to be unfeasible in a later phase: in that case the development process has to back up to the earlier phase and redo the unfeasible decisions.

Actors

Actors in the field of security are bounded by the prescriptions, prohibitions and constraints of government and branch organisations. The constraints of the government affect the products sold on the telematics market, both by regulation of distribution of certain products, or prescribing minimum levels of security. The various actors, actor roles and their influence on security are shown in Figure 2.

We identify two classes of actor roles, whose types of behaviour influence the development process, i.e. the *Telematics Market* and the *Organisation.*

- The Telematics Market consist of the actor roles System Architect and System Builder. The first is involved in the creation of the design of the SYSTEM. The second is involved when the SYSTEM is built and made operational.
- The Organisation is the purchaser of the SYSTEM and imposes requirements on the function and functioning of the SYSTEM. It can be a sole, autonomous institute, a part of a larger company or a consortium of several autonomous organisations. The Organisation consists of two sub classes, Management and Users.
  - The Organisation Management directs and controls the course of the Organisation. The functioning of the Management is established in a policy, of which the security

[3] For short we use the term security for information security in the remainder of the paper.

[4] As telematics systems are heavily oriented towards communication, we introduce authenticity as a separate requirement, defined as traceability of origin and ownership of data in a system or a process.

[5] In this paper we refer to the system that is designed in the design process as SYSTEM.

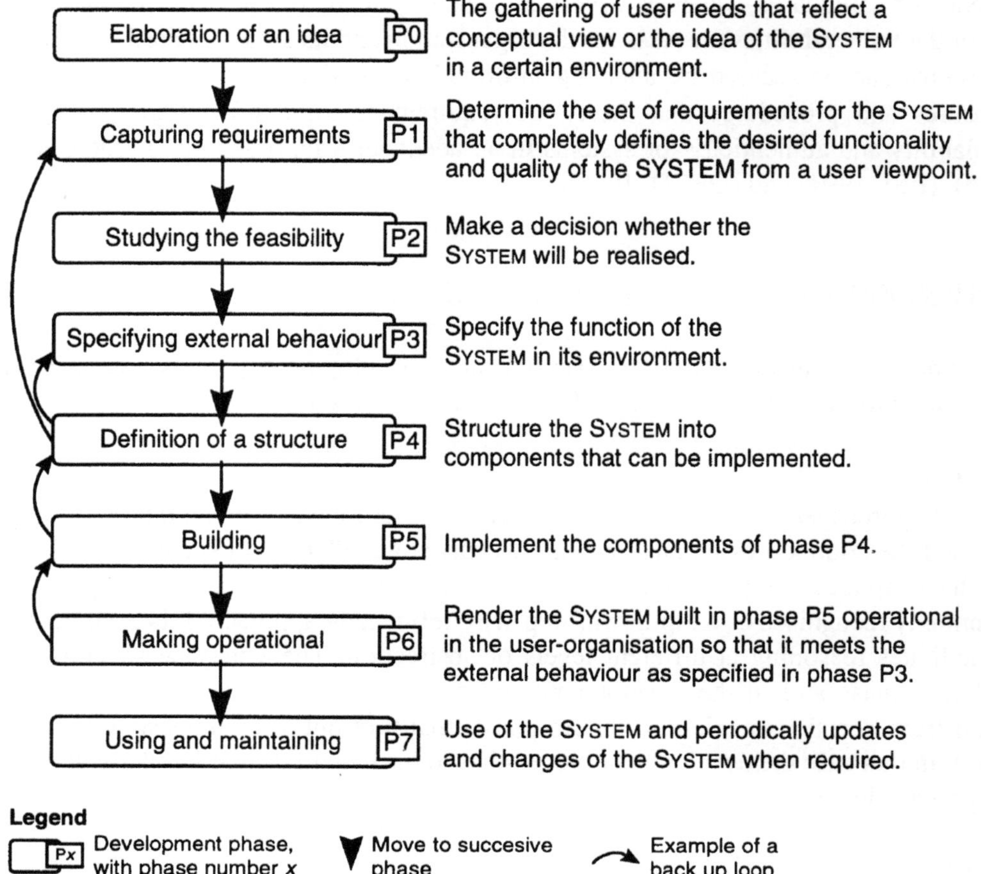

Figure 1 Phases and objectives of the traditional development process.

policy is a subset. The security policy is a set of rules to apply to all security-relevant activities (Ford, 1994). This policy therefore constrains the development. We identify two actor roles within the sub class Management of the Organisation, i.e. the Top level Manager and the Security Officer. The first is responsible for all matters related to information technology and telecommunication, and is part of the upper management. The latter is responsible for security matters.

- We identify two actor roles within the Users of the Organisation, the System Administrator, responsible for control, administration and maintenance of the SYSTEM, and the End User, who makes hands-on use of the SYSTEM.

Conditions

When developing secure telematics systems, it is insufficient to consider the SYSTEM separate from the Organisation. To develop a secure SYSTEM for an Organisation, an actor in the Telematics Market should fulfil at least the following conditions, see e.g. (Parker 1981), (Fisher, 1984), (Badenhorst and Eloff, 1989) and (Hitchings, 1995):

- Establishment of a security policy by the Management of the Organisation;
- Identification of the assets of the Organisation that need to be protected;
- Identification of the risks for the Organisation;

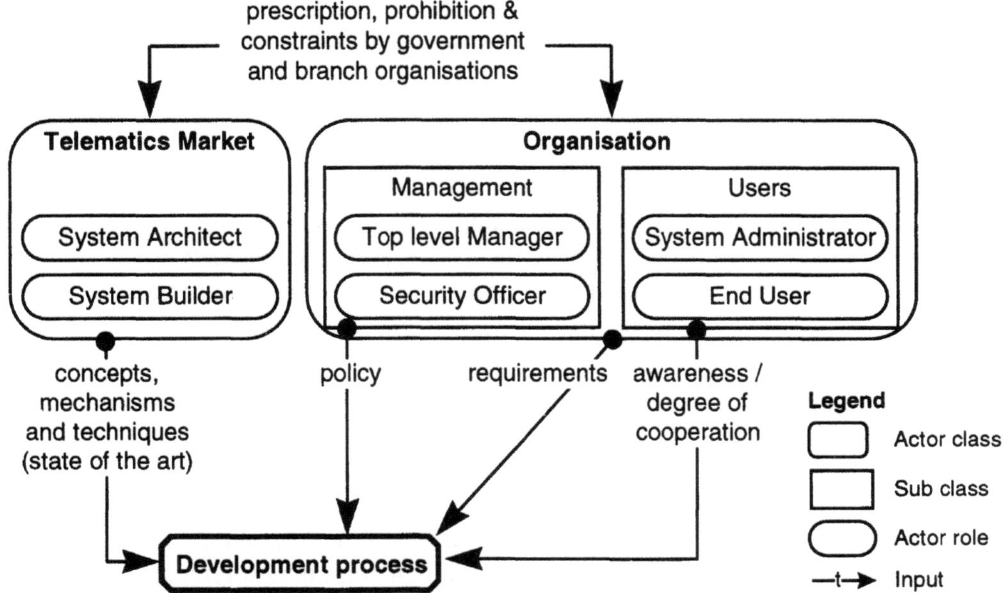

Figure 2 View on information security and a development process.

- Awareness of Management and Users of the need for security;
- Determination of which safeguards should be implemented where;
- Security is operational in an environment and therefore possesses not only technical dimensions, but economic, legal, organisational and human dimensions as well.

3 SECURITY AND THE DEVELOPMENT PROCESS

In this section we give an overview of the *goals* and *characteristics* of the phases in a traditional development process and we discuss the complications and preliminary guidelines of integrating security into this process (Tettero, 1996).

Elaboration of an idea

The goal of this phase is the gathering of user needs that reflect an idea of the SYSTEM capabilities in a certain environment. This idea can arise from many different situations, such as automating the communication process with another organisation, or the outcome of a business redesign process. The user needs are not yet clearly defined and precise. They express the purpose, scope and characteristics of the SYSTEM, and are laid down in a project proposal.

The idea of the SYSTEM can include security. However, this will not often be the case, because the core business of organisations is usually unrelated to security. In this paper we assume that the main purpose of a SYSTEM (we refer to this as to the 'must-functionality') is not related to security, and therefore not part of the original idea. An example of an idea is a ticket vending machine that issues tickets for train passengers.

The user needs are a first elaboration of the idea and should contain suggestions for security issues. The suggestions should at least indicate that Management is aware of the importance of security for this System. If security is not included in the project proposal it will be difficult to assign resources (e.g. personnel) to investigate security issues.

Capturing requirements

The goal of this phase is to determine the set of requirements for the SYSTEM that completely defines the desired SYSTEM functionality and quality from a user-oriented viewpoint. The requirements defines *what* the SYSTEM should do and not *how*.

In the example of the ticket vending machine the following requirements could be captured:

- Single and return tickets;
- Every railway station in the country can be entered;
- Only the destinations can be given, station of departure is station of vending machine location;
- Payments by means of coins or an electronic system.

Security requirements are functional or indicate the quality level of these functional requirements. Definition of these requirements involves the following three issues:

1. Government and branch organisations demand that certain requirements concerning, a.o., privacy, computer criminality and encryption, are incorporated in the SYSTEM.
2. Security requirements are derived from the Organisation's security policy.
3. Users connect security requirements and resulting safeguards with unlikely events and expected unpleasant work procedures.

The gathering of security requirements is complicated, because they are often implicit (Mostert and von Solms, 1994). Security awareness, although increasing, is still not at an adequate level. The Users are focused on the SYSTEM must-functionality. Mostert and von Solms (1994) proposed a method to gather implicit requirements in which requirement engineers have knowledge of both the security and the SYSTEM domain. However, the security requirements can only be defined if the definition of the must-functionality is stable, otherwise nothing can be secured.

In the ticket vending machine example the implicit requirements are, amongst others:

- Tickets cannot be issued without proper payment;
- Only the ticket that a passenger has asked for should be issued;
- Money should not be removable from the machine.

The security requirements are based on threats. A threat analysis can support this, see e.g. (BSI, 1994), by comparing the costs of safeguards for these threats with the costs of an attack it is possible to determine which threats should be taken into account. CCTA (1991) developed risk analysis and management methodology (CRAMM) which analysis the threats and asset groups and determines countermeasures.

The operational SYSTEM environment strongly affects the security requirements. In a military environment, confidentiality requirements prevail over other security requirements, while in a business environment the integrity requirements prevail (Clark and Wilson, 1987). Other environmental influences are e.g. use of public networks and the controllability of Users by the Organisation.

Studying the feasibility

The goal of this phase is decide whether the SYSTEM will be realised. The advantages, disadvantages, costs and benefits of the requirements are considered against the financial, organisational and technical possibilities of the Organisation and the Telematics Market.

Security is part of the requirements that are subject of the final negotiations between Organisation and System Architect. These requirements require insight in the possible safeguards and in their usage or nonusage once the SYSTEM is operational.

Specifying external behaviour

The goal of this phase is to (formally) specify the function of the SYSTEM in its environment. In contrast with phase P1 the function is specified from the SYSTEM viewpoint. The external behaviour only specifies *what* the SYSTEM should do within its environment.

The specification consists of the SYSTEM function, the (user) interfaces or interactions with the environment and the Quality of Service-measures (e.g. response times, throughput) delivered by the function. Contents of the specification are e.g. activities and services offered to the environment, SYSTEM boundaries and representation of data.

In the example of the ticket vending machine the following behaviour is specified:

- Clear all choices;
- Issue the ticket;
- Provide means for the input of the destination;
- Provide means for the input of the type of ticket;
- Provide means for the payment of the ticket;
- Show all possible destinations and possible tickets;
- Show the price of the selected ticket;

By specifying, the SYSTEM boundaries are defined by means of the interfaces with the environment and the knowingly allowed interactions. The term interface should be regarded in the broadest sense of the word. For instance, damaging the ticket vending machine with a hammer. The interface here is the outside plate of the ticket vending machine. The SYSTEM boundaries are defined as appropriate for this stage, however for a different development phase a different boundary can be appropriate. An example is the power supply for the ticket vending machine. In the current phase it could be regarded as an internal aspect of the SYSTEM, while in the building phase an external source is used. The introduced threat is: the power supply can simply be interrupted by pulling out the plug.

The main complication for security is that the SYSTEM is formalised and predictable whereas the SYSTEM environment is unpredictable. A solution is to view threats as actions in the environment, and attacks can then be viewed as interactions with the SYSTEM.

The traditional development process focuses on realising the must-behaviour of SYSTEMS. For security we also address misbehaviour of the SYSTEM or parts thereof, and exceptional behaviour of the SYSTEM environment. Normally, interfaces are precisely defined. However, it is impossible to define an interface when behaviour is not well known. The realised SYSTEM should be able to cope with behaviour that falls outside the prescriptive environment view in the specifications.

Definition of a structure

The goal of this phase is to structure the SYSTEM into components that can be implemented. The resulting structure is a hierarchical set of components, each of which is labelled with a function and its interfaces. Every component of the lowest level can be implemented by a System Builder. The whole of components and interfaces performs the function as specified in phase P3.

The SYSTEM structure supports the System Architect to keep track of the consequences of changes in the design. Especially for security a good structure is needed, because changes in the design can imply changes for all components or interfaces. The design of a good structure is based on a set of principles and techniques, which guide the process of decomposition regarding security (Muftic, 1994).

Security can be defined in the structure in two ways:

- *Independent component.* This component is fully dedicated to security, for example an authentication service. Other components can neglect the security components or can use its functionality.
- *Incorporated in all components.* Every component has some functionality, for example confidentiality functionality.

The International Standardisation Organisation has proposed standard services for a high level structure based on the OSI reference model (ISO, 1989).

Building

The goal of this phase is to implement the components of phase P4. Hardware components should be bought or physically built, while software components should be bought or programmed. Individual hardware and software elements must be connected and tested as a group. The SYSTEM has to be tested and documented.

To realise the security part of the components, safeguards are available, of which only the technical part is implemented in this phase. For proper implementations of safeguards the following should be considered:

1. *Impact on the organisation.* The characteristics of a safeguard determine the type of procedures in the Organisation that should be used. The impact can be the workload for End Users, changes in the organisational structure or extra costs.
2. *Legitimacy of the technical safeguards.* Some countries have stringent export controls. Products falling under these controls and produced in that country cannot be exported without government permission. Certain technical safeguards fall under these regulations and thus cannot always be freely used.

The System Builder can buy standard safeguards on the Telematics Market to realise the SYSTEM, such as a plug-in crypto card. Using standard elements can reduce costs of the SYSTEM. The standards elements have a certain function and interface and are meant to operate in a certain type of environment. The standard safeguard will probably not fully comply in function, quality and interface of the desired safeguard for the SYSTEM. To make the standard safeguard useful in a wide range of systems, its interface will be general and will thus include interactions that the SYSTEM does not need or that may introduce potential weaknesses.

Making operational

The goal of this phase is to render the SYSTEM built in phase P5 operational in the Organisation so that it meets the external behaviour as specified in phase P3. The SYSTEM from phase P5 is built and tested under 'laboratory conditions' and must be tuned to the Organisation and integrated into existing systems. In addition, new procedures in the Organisation should be set up, or existing procedures should be modified.

The technical safeguards of the SYSTEM are extended with organisational procedures. Procedures are needed because organisations change rapidly, while the technical SYSTEM is fixed. The SYSTEM must be used in the daily work of an End User, for which the daily work procedures should be adjusted.

The SYSTEM introduced to the Organisation should comply with the Organisation policies, including the security policy. However, the SYSTEM introduces new qualities which means that the security policy possibly has to be adjusted.

Using and maintaining

Once the SYSTEM is made operational in phase P6, it should be ready to be used for the goals of that moment in the organisation of that moment. Since both the goals and the organisation are susceptible to change, and no system is without bugs, the SYSTEM will have to be updated and changed periodically. Changes that affect the SYSTEM can be the cause of:

1. Predictable facts of life, e.g., the absence of people and career moves;
2. Organisation policies changes, e.g. introduction of EDI;
3. Environment changes, e.g. new laws or technology / policy changes of competitors.

Changes resulting from predictable facts of life should be anticipated in adequate organisational procedures. In this phase, the procedures and related data are carried out and kept up-to-date. An example is the provision of a password to a new employee, its removal when he leaves, its periodical update, and related events. Changes in the policies of an organisation could demand changes in the SYSTEM requirements and therefore cause adjustments. When the changes involve security these should be treated just as the other requirements. Changes in the environment should be studied carefully, since these could introduce new threats, requiring new safeguards in the SYSTEM. Changes could adjust the requirements and introduce other relations to the security requirements.

By using the SYSTEM, the End Users get to know the SYSTEM well and will discover deficiencies. End Users will become aware of security bugs. These bugs cannot be repaired immediately. The (multiple) causes of bugs can be found in indistinct procedures, malicious techniques and design flaws. Their consequences should be investigated carefully. To remove the bugs from the SYSTEM, the SYSTEM should be updated.

Guiding the whole development process

If the requirements include security, it is yet unclear how these additional requirements proliferate throughout the remaining development phases. For example, existing security evaluation criteria, such as ITSEC (Europe) and TCSEC (USA), could be incorporated as requirements for the development of a secure system. This means that the realised SYSTEM should pass a particular security level check as defined in these public criteria. The question is how these requirements translate into design and implementation decisions.

Landwehr et al. (1994) and Muftic (1994) recognise that maliciously introduced faults are not to be expected in the requirements, because they have been thoroughly reviewed. However, it is still possible to compromise the requirements in the remainder of the development process.

Specifications can be compromised unintentionally or intentionally. Unintentionally compromises follow from decisions made when filling in the degrees of freedom of previous phases or from too little insight in the consequences of the decisions. Examples of this kind of decisions are speed, simplicity and implement shortcuts. Intentionally compromises can be introduced by System Builders by putting backdoors in the SYSTEM, like Trojan horses (Landwehr et al., 1994). These compromises are far more difficult to avoid.

To escape from compromising the specifications, security should be maintained throughout all phases of the development process (Mostert and von Solms, 1994). Therefore, every phase should have additional, identifiable security conditions.

The tension between abstraction and completeness in different stages of the development can cause problems (Boswell, 1995). Every development phase represents the SYSTEM at a different level of abstraction. Sometimes knowledge of (technical) safeguards is needed in an early stage of the development process where this kind of knowledge normally is ignored. As a consequence a top-down development strategy alone will never be sufficient in practice.

4 CONCLUSIONS

Adding safeguards to operational telematics systems leads to operational problems and to systems that are not secure. To avoid these problems information security should be integrated in the development process of telematics systems. However, information security is not a common concern to take into account. Difficulties for the integration are the following:

- Traditional development focuses on the must-functionality of the SYSTEM;
- Current requirements capturing methods only gather the explicit user needs. Since information security requirements are often implicit, these remain hidden;
- Information security requirements are the first to be withdrawn in case of conflicting requirements;
- Prescription of the behaviour of SYSTEM environment alone is insufficient, because this behaviour is unpredictable, unknown and contributory to the SYSTEM behaviour;
- Design decisions can compromise information security specifications;
- The use of technical safeguards is constrained by the impact on the organisation and their legitimacy;
- It is unclear how information security requirements proliferate throughout the development process regarding potential malicious behaviour and selection of safeguards regarding the tension between abstraction and detail.

Considering the above difficulties we recommend the following:

- Decisions as to which requirements prevail over others should be guided by a strategy, based on the security policy of the Organisation;
- The SYSTEM environment should be taken into account in the definition of the development, because of its impact on the requirements;
- Development of methods or frameworks to translate a security policy to SYSTEM requirements, gather implicit requirements, include the behaviour of the environment (e.g. threats) in the specifications of interactions between the SYSTEM and its environment, reflect information security dimensions in the SYSTEM structure and define appropriate SYSTEM boundaries at every level of abstraction;
- Development of a set of information security principles to guide the structuring of a SYSTEM that helps to study the consequences of design decisions, to reduce complexity and supports comprehension of the interactions among parts of the SYSTEM;
- Definition of guidelines and techniques to map information security evaluation criteria onto practical guidelines for every development phase and to maintain information security throughout the whole development process.

Acknowledgements

This paper is partly based on research in the PLATINUM/MESH project (Lucent Technologies, TRC & CTIT), which is funded by the Dutch Ministry of Economic Affairs. PLATINUM/MESH aims at the design of a multimedia broadband ISDN platform.

5 REFERENCES

Aalders, J.C.H., Herschberg, I.S. and Zanten, A. van (1985) *Handbook for information security: a guide towards information security standards.* Elsevier Science.

Badenhorst, K.P. and Eloff, J.H.P. (1989) Framework of a methodology for the lifecycle of computer security in an organisation, in *Computers & Security*, **8**, 5.

Baskerville, R. (1993) Information systems security design methods: implications for information systems development, in *Computing Surveys* **24** (4).

Booysen, H.A.S. and Eloff, J.H.P (1995) A methodology for the development of secure application systems, in *Information security - the next decade : Proceedings of IFIP Information security.* (ed. J.H.P. Eloff, von Solms S.H.), Chapman & Hall, London.

Boswell, A. (1995) Specifications and validation of a security policy model. *IEEE Transactions on Software Engineering*, **21**, 2.

Breed, N.F., Out, D.J. and Tettero, O. (1995) *Informatiebeveiliging, een blik achter de schermen.* Samsom BedrijfsInformatie, Alphen a/d Rijn/Zaventem. [In Dutch]

BSI - British Standard Institute (1994) *Code of practice for information security management.*

CCTA (1991) *SSADM-CRAMM Subjectguide for SSADM version 3 and CRAMM version 2.* Central Computer and Telecommunications Agency, IT Security and Privacy group, Her Majesty's Government, London.

Clark, D.D. and Wilson, D.R. (1987) A comparison of commercial and military computer security policies, in *Proceedings of Symposium on Security and Privacy.*

Dasgupta, S. (1989) The structure of design processes, in *The structure of design processes.* (ed. M.C. Yovtis), volume 28 of Advances in computers.

Fisher, R.P. (1984) *Information systems security.* Prentice Hall, Engelwood Cliffs.

Ford, W. (1994) *Computer communications security: principals, standard protocols and techniques.* Prentice Hall, New Jersey.

Hitchings, J. (1995) Deficiencies of the traditional approach to information security and the requirements for a new methodology, in *Computers & Security,* **14.**

ISO/TC 97 (1989) *Information processing systems - Open Systems Interconnection - Basic Reference Model - Security Architecture. ISO 7498-2.*

Landwehr, C.E., Bull, A.R., McDermott, J.P. and Choi, W.P. (1994) A Taxonomy of computer program security flaws, in *ACM computing surveys,* **26**, 3.

Mazza, C., Fairclough, J., Melton, B., Pablo, D. de, Scheffer, A.. and Stevens, E. (1994) *Software engineering standards.* Prentice Hall/European Space Agency.

Mostert, D.N.J. and von Solms, S.H., (1994) A methodology to include computer security, safety and resilience requirements as part of the user requirement, in *Computers & Security,* **13**, 4.

Muftic, S. (1994) Security architecture for ODP systems, final results of the CEC COST-11 Ter "Security" project, in *Computer Networks and ISDN Systems,* **26.**

OECD - Organisation for Economic Co-operation and Development (1996) *Guidelines for the security of information systems.*

Parker, D.B. (1981) *Managers guide to computer security.* Reston Publishing.

Sommerville, I. (1996) *Software engineering.* Addison-Wesley, 5th ed.

Tettero, O. (ed.) (1996) *Security aspects of telematics applications, PLATINUM deliverable D3.2.* Telematics Research Centre, Enschede.

Tompkins, F.G. and Rice, R. (1986) Integrating security activities into the software development lifecycle and the software Quality assurance process, in *Computers & Security,* **5.**

6 BIOGRAPHIES

Olaf Tettero is associate member of scientific staff of the TRC. He holds an M.Sc. in computer science. His current research interest focuses on information security and design processes. He works on the design of a secure multimedia broadband platform.

Dirk Jan Out holds an M.Sc. and Ph.D. in computer science. He works as a member of the scientific staff of the TRC. His current research interest focuses on tele-education, information security and the design of multimedia broadband platform.

Henry M. Franken holds an M.Sc. and Ph.D. in Electrical Engineering. He works as a member of the scientific staff of the TRC. His current research interest focuses on applying systems engineering principles to telematics and business process (re)design.

Jeroen Schot is senior staff member of the TRC. He holds a BSc, MSc and PhD in computer science. His research interests are distributed systems design, and methods for supporting this. He has been involved in many projects in the health care, mobile telecommunications, space and aviation, logistics, and software development sectors.

21

Developing Secure Applications: A Systematic Approach

C. Eckert and D. Marek
Munich University of Technology, Department of Computer Science
D-80290 Munich, Germany, eckertc@informatik.tu-muenchen.de

Abstract

This paper presents parts of the SECREDS project which aims to bridge the gap between system modeling and implementation using a high-level programming language. Within SECREDS secure applications are developed top down starting with a top-level specification. Top-level specifications are given by our computational model and application-specific security policies are specified using our security requirement logic. To implement a top-level specification we developed a high-level programming language called INSEL$^+$ offering language concepts well adapted to our underlying model. We will present main features of INSEL$^+$ focusing on access control aspects and we will outline some guidelines to support the systematic implementation of a given top-level specification preserving specified security properties.

Keywords

Access Control, Security Policy, Programming Language

1 INTRODUCTION

The issue of developing secure applications is still a great challenge. Secure applications should be developed top-down starting with a formal top-level specification given by a security model comprising the security policy of the application. A lot of security models have been proposed in the literature focusing on confidentiality (e.g. Bell, 1975) or integrity (e.g. Clark, 1987) aspects. Besides their individual shortcomings existing approaches lack appropriate support to bridge the gap between system modeling and implementation using a high-level programming language. Hence, a framework is required offering features to model the behavior of a distributed secure application on a high level of abstraction as well as features to specify access properties as well as information flow properties adapted to the specific needs of the application. In addition, a high-level programming language is required offering language concepts adapted to the formalism used for top-level specifications.

This adaption enables to systematically transform a top-level specification into an executable program.

The paper presents parts of the SECREDS project which aims to bridge the gap between the formal specification of secure parallel and distributed applications and their implementation and execution in a distributed environment.

The rest of the paper will be organized as follows. In section 2 we give a short overview over the SECREDS project. Section 3 briefly introduces our computational model and the logic to specify application-specific security policies. Section 4 presents main features of the language INSEL$^+$. The development of INSEL$^+$ programs starting with a top-level specification is explained by means of an example. Section 5 concludes the paper.

2 SECREDS – AN OVERVIEW

Within SECREDS a framework to design and implement secure distributed applications is elaborated. An overview over the working areas of the project is sketched in figure 1. The paper focuses on the dotted parts.

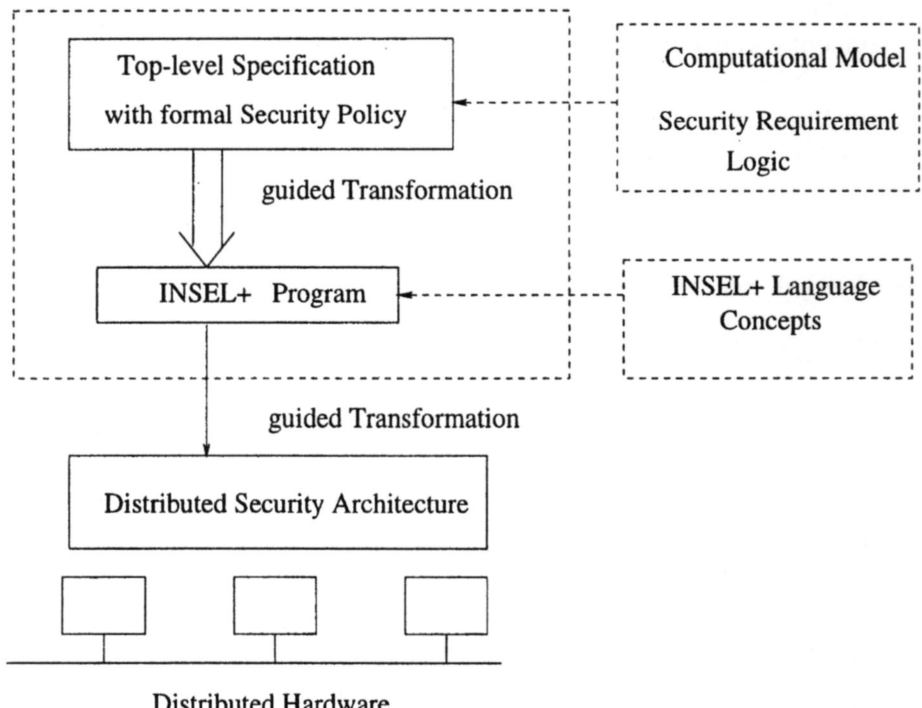

Figure 1 Overview over the SECREDS approach

In SECREDS the development of a secure distributed application starts with a top-level specification comprising a semantic model of application's behavior together with those attributes needed to capture security properties.

These properties (the security policy) are specified by allowed or disallowed information flows between users, as well as, access restrictions for users defined with application-specific granularity. The security properties are given by means of formulas of our security requirement logic.

A top-level specification is implemented by stepwise refinement. First, the specification is transformed into a program using the language concepts of our high-level programming language INSEL$^+$. Though desirable we are not able to perform a verified transformation from top-level specification to implementation within SECREDS. Formal verification requires great efforts (e.g. EHDM (Rushby, 1991)). Within SECREDS we pursue a less sound but more pragmatic approach. Instead of elaborating formal transformation rules we developed a programming language which offers language concepts that allow to express security properties in a declarative way. As the language concepts and the formalism to specify security policies are very closely related, major parts of the specification can be directly implemented using the adapted language concepts. In addition, we have elaborated guidelines which aid the application programmer in transforming a top-level specification into an INSEL$^+$ program.

INSEL$^+$ applications are executed in a distributed environment based on a tailored security architecture. The security architecture is part of the MoDiS distributed operating system (cf Eckert, 1996). Describing this architecture lies beyond the scope of this paper. The key feature of MoDiS is its distributed manager architecture. All resource management tasks including security services are cooperatively accomplished by a distributed reflective manager architecture. As INSEL$^+$ programs are realized by stepwise refinement it is the task of these managers to perform security services like access controls, authentication and encrypting messages sent across a network.

3 TOP-LEVEL SPECIFICATION

3.1 Computational Model

In this subsection we introduce the main features of our computational model to describe system behavior. A more detailed and formal description of the model can be found in (Eckert, 1995).

A distributed application is modeled by a set of **objects** and **subjects**. Objects are the protected entities which can be specified with fine-grained granularity. Objects are only accessible via well-formed **operations** comparable with well-formed transactions in the Clark-Wilson model (Clark, 1987). Operations define access rights for objects. Each operation invocation creates a distinct **instance** of the operation. The computational steps of an instance are defined by a sequence of **atomic actions** called action refinement of the instance. An action refinement starts with an initial action. During the execution of the initial action the input parameter association is performed. The last action of the refinement is the termination action which associates the output parameters if necessary. Executing an atomic action results in state changes mirroring the **effect** of the action.

Each user is represented by a set of subjects the so called **user representatives**, which execute operations on behalf of users. **Concurrency** between user activities is modeled by the interleaved execution of sequences of actions belonging to different action refinements of operations executed by the users' representatives. The sequence of states associated with a sequence of actions is called a **computation** σ of the model CS of a distributed application.

We introduce a **generic set of labels** and a labeling function to capture important object properties within our model. For instance, labeling associates a **role** with each user representative describing the role its associated user is playing. Introducing role-attributes allows us to grant access rights to roles rather than to individual users if required.

The computational model can be used to define the formal semantics of a programming language. Simple read and write operations on data objects of predefined types, like integer or boolean objects, can be modeled as atomic actions.

3.2 Policy Specification

User representatives execute operations on behalf of their associated users. Each execution of an instance may cause information flows between different user representatives and, therefore, between users. To describe these information flows we introduce two properties: the **influence** property and the **observation** property. The semantics of these properties (cf Eckert, 1995) is defined based on our computational model.

Definition: Influence
We say, that there exists an **influence between user representatives** ur_1 and ur_2 with respect to operations op_1 and op_2 in a given computation σ if the action refinement of at least one instance of op_1 executed by ur_1 contains an action a which influences the execution of an action b contained in the action refinement of at least one instance of op_2 executed by ur_2.

The execution of an action a **influences the execution of an action** b in computation σ if either executing b after a in computation σ provides different values for at least one object y compared with the value of y in a computation σ' where b is executed before a or a influences b if b is not enabled until a has been executed. $\triangle$

Restricting information flows based on allowed and forbidden influences turns out to be very restrictive as many applications just require that the information flows caused by influences may not be observable by other users.

Definition: Observation
We say, the activity of a user representative ur_1 executing instances of op_1 is **observable by a representative** ur_2 executing instances of operation op_2, if the value of at least one output parameter of at least one instance of op_2 executed by ur_2 depends on the effect of the execution of at least one instance of op_1 executed by ur_1. That is, observable information flows can be recognized via different values of output parameters of instances. $\triangle$

To specify disallowed influences and observations between users of an application we will define **conditional non-influencing** (*cninf*) requirements and **conditional non-observing** (*cnobs*) requirements. Disallowed and allowed accesses are specified by **access restriction** (*acc*) requirements.

Definition: Security requirement logic
Given a computational model CS of an application. The set of objects $\mathcal{K}$ of CS, the set of predicate symbols PS with $PS = PS' \cup \{cninf, cnobs, acc\}$, and the temporal operator $\Box$ expressing the usual 'henceforth' semantics form the syntactic basis of the logic. Let TFO be the set of all formulas over the basis. PS' contains predicates over $\mathcal{K}$ comprising logical and arithmetic operators and quantifiers.

Let $<$ define the linear ordering on states in a computation σ of CS.
$\omega : TFO \times \Sigma \longrightarrow \{true, false\}$ defines the semantics of formulas in a state.

Given two user representatives ur_1, ur_2, two operations op_1, op_2, an object k, a computation σ of CS and a predicate $Cond \in PS'$. The semantics of a formula $P \in TFO$ in state s of computation σ, denoted by $(\sigma, s) \models P$, is defined as follows*:

1. Let $P = cninf(ur_1, ur_2, op_1, op_2, Cond)$.
$(\sigma, s) \models P$ iff $\omega(P, s) = true$ whereby the **conditional non-influencing predicate** *cninf* is *true* in state s of the given computation, if either predicate *Cond* is *false* in state s or predicate *Cond* is *true* in state s and for each state s' with $s' < s$ holds, that no influence caused by user representative ur_1 executing instances of op_1 on user representative ur_2 executing instances of op_2 exists.
2. Let $P = cnobs(ur_2, ur_1, op_2, op_1, Cond)$.
$(\sigma, s) \models P$ iff $\omega(P, s) = true$ whereby the **conditional non-observing predicate** *cnobs* is *true* in state s, if either predicate *Cond* is *false* in state s or predicate *Cond* is *true* in state s and for each state s' with $s' < s$ holds, that no observation of the activities of user representative ur_2 executing instances of op_2 by user representative ur_1 executing instances of op_1 exists.
3. Let $P = acc(ur_1, op_1, k, Cond)$.
$(\sigma, s) \models P$ iff $\omega(P, s) = true$ whereby the **access restriction predicate** *acc* is *true* in state s, if either predicate *Cond* is *true* in state s or predicate

*Due to space limitation we focus on the *cninf*, *cnobs* and *acc* formula.

$Cond$ is $false$ in state s and user representative ur_1 does not execute an instance of op_1 in state s.

4. Given a formula $P \in TFO$:
$(\sigma, s) \models \Box P :\Longleftrightarrow \ \forall\, s' \in \sigma \ : \ s' \leq s \ : \ \omega(P, s') = true.$ $\triangle$

A conditional non-influencing predicate between two user representatives ur_1 and ur_2 with respect to two operations requires that, as long as the condition $Cond$ within the requirement specification holds, no influence from ur_1 on ur_2 executing instances of the specified operations exists. The meaning of a conditional non-observing requirement can be stated in a similar way. With an access restriction predicate the execution of operation op_1 of the specified object k is forbidden for user representative ur_1 as long as the condition $Cond$ within the requirement is $false$.

The condition $Cond$ may, for instance, contain a boolean expression concerning access rights or it may contain an expression concerning other objects of the system, for instance a timer to restrict access for a user to a limited period of time.

Based on the security requirement logic introduced a **security policy** for a secure parallel application is specified by a formula $P \in TFO$. Usually, a security policy is specified by a conjunction of conditional non-influencing, conditional non-observing and of access restriction predicates which must hold in every state of a computation, hence by a conjunction of $\Box acc(...)$, $\Box cninf(...)$, $\Box cnobs(...)$ formulas. As a computation of the model is given by a sequence of states associated with action executions the security policy P must hold in every state of the computation.

3.3 Example: Bank Scenario

Consider for example a simplified bank scenario. The set of protected objects comprises the customer accounts. For each account the set of operations is given by $OP(account) \supset \{read\_OP, enter\_rights\_OP, delete\_rights\_OP\}$. To distinguish between the operation itself and the access right we introduce the set of rights $\{read, enter\_rights, delete\_rights\}$. Users can act in different roles. Depending on the role a user currently plays a different set of access rights is granted. To keep the example simple we introduce only two roles: `customer` and `clerk`. Subjects in this scenario are for instance user representatives for customers and clerks. With each account we associate a unique owner and a clerk responsible for managing the account.

To manage access rights we introduce an object `access_matrix` M. M is a two-dimensional array, where columns are given by bank accounts and rows are given by users and roles and where each entry describes the set of access rights a user or role possesses with respect to a specific account (usual access matrix approach). Notice, that in our model possession of an access right is usually not a sufficient precondition to gain access permissions. M is itself a protected object which must be accessed in a protected and controlled way. $OP(M) = \{enter\_OP, delete\_OP, create\_account\_OP, delete\_account\_OP\}$. The access rights are given with $\{enter, delete, create\_account, delete\_account\}$.

Security requirements:

1. A user who possesses the *read* right and acts in the role customer is allowed to execute the operation *read_OP* on a specific account. A clerk may just read the balance of those accounts he is responsible for and this read access is restricted to office hours.
2. Each customer may only grant (*enter_rights_OP*) or revoke (*delete_rights_OP*) access rights concerning accounts he owns. Granting or revoking access rights concerning owned accounts requires the possession of the specific access right (*enter_rights, delete_rights*) by the customer. A clerk may only grant and revoke access rights concerning accounts he manages. As a clerk may revoke access rights a clerk can freeze an account by revoking all rights for the account owner.
3. The operation *enter_OP* of the access matrix to grant rights can only be executed in the context of the operation *enter_rights_OP* of account objects and the caller must possess the *enter* right. (For all other matrix operations similar context-dependent restrictions must hold.)
4. Activities of customers who do not share accounts may not be visible to each other.
5. Activities of a customer may not influence the activities of a clerk if the clerk is not responsible for managing the accounts of the customer.

To formalize the requirements using the logic formulas we first introduce the labels we need. A label l is given by a tuple ($user$, $role$, $account\_owner$, $resp\_clerk$). For each user representative ur, $l(ur).user$ denotes the user ur represents. $l(ur).role$ denotes the role of the associated user. The owner of an account k is given with $l(k).account\_owner$ and $l(k).resp\_clerk$ denotes the clerk being responsible for the account or for the user representative, respectively.

Security requirement specification in terms of logic formulas:

1. Access restriction formula for *read_OP* operations.

   $\Box\ acc(ur, read\_OP, account, Cond)$ with

$$\begin{aligned} Cond = \; & (read \in M[l(ur).user, account] \wedge \; l(ur).role = customer) \vee \\ & (l(ur).role = clerk \; \wedge \; l(account).resp\_clerk = l(ur).user \; \wedge \\ & 8 \leq CurrentTime \leq 16) \end{aligned}$$

2. Access restriction formula for *delete_rights_OP* operations.

   $\Box\ acc(ur, delete\_rights\_OP, account, Cond)$ with

$$\begin{aligned} Cond = \; & (delete\_rights \in M[l(ur).user, account] \wedge \\ & (l(ur).role = customer \; \wedge \; l(account).account\_owner = l(ur).user) \\ & \vee \; (l(ur).role = clerk \; \wedge \; l(account).resp\_clerk = l(ur).user) \end{aligned}$$

Access restriction formula for *enter_rights_OP* operations can be specified in an analogous way.

3. Restricting matrix accesses to specific execution contexts:

$$\Box \; acc(ur, enter\_OP(account, \ldots), M, in(enter\_rights\_OP(account, \ldots), ur))$$

The predicate `in(operation_name, user_representative)` describes context-dependencies. The predicate is *true* in a state s of a computation if user representative `user_representative` executes an instance of operation `operation_name` in state s.

4. Information flow restrictions are specified by conditional non-observable predicates. To identify users who share accounts we define:

$$\begin{aligned} set\_of\_accounts(ur) = \{account| \; & M[l(ur).user, account] \neq \emptyset \; \vee \\ & M[l(ur).role, account] \neq \emptyset\}. \end{aligned}$$

For all $op1, op2 \in OP(account)$ the predicate $\Box \; cnobs(ur1, ur2, op1, op2, Cond)$ must hold with

$$\begin{aligned} Cond = \; & l(ur1).role = customer \; \wedge \; l(ur2).role = customer \; \wedge \\ & set\_of\_accounts(ur1) \cap set\_of\_accounts(ur2) = \emptyset \end{aligned}$$

5. No information flows are allowed between clerks and customers not being correlated.
For all $op1, op2 \in OP(account)$ the predicate $\Box \; cninf(ur1, ur2, op1, op2, Cond)$ must hold with

$$\begin{aligned} Cond = \; & l(ur1).role = customer \; \wedge l(ur2).role = clerk \; \wedge \\ & l(ur1).resp\_clerk \neq l(ur2).user \end{aligned}$$

The security policy can be strengthened or weakened systematically by adding or removing information flow or access restrictions or by modifying the conditions within the requirement formulas.

4 IMPLEMENTATION

4.1 INSEL$^+$ Programming Language

Given a top-level specification we have to implement the specification using a programming language. Unfortunately, existing languages provide no or only insufficient languages features to support the implementation of security policies. Hence, application programmers have to deal with low-level security mechanisms (cf (Ancilotti, 1983, McGraw, 1979)) and security services offered by the underlying operating system like simple access control lists for files.

To bridge the gap between specification and its implementation programming language concepts are needed, that allow to specify security properties in a declarative fashion as far as possible and that are well adapted to the formal framework used for security policy specification. Our programming language INSEL$^+$ offers the desired features.

INSEL$^+$ is a strongly-typed, object-based language for programming secure parallel and distributed applications. INSEL$^+$ provides concepts for passive and active objects. An active object defines a separate thread of control. Each object is an instance of an INSEL$^+$-class. A class defines a set of operations that provide the only means for accessing objects of that class. One important feature of INSEL$^+$ is the principle of nesting. The principle of nesting enables to restrict the scope of objects according to visibility rules known from block-oriented programming languages like Ada 95 (cf Feldman, 1996). That is, access to objects can be a priori restricted. INSEL$^+$-objects may cooperate and communicate calling operations on other objects.

The object model of INSEL$^+$ is closely related to the object model of our formal framework. With the adapted object model, the principle of nesting and the well-known properties of object-based languages (e.g. information hiding by encapsulation) INSEL$^+$ provides an appropriate basis for implementing secure applications.

Security-related language features

Until now concepts for implementing access control policies that are specified with access restriction formulas *acc* have been elaborated and incorporated in INSEL$^+$. Language features to support the implementation of information flow restrictions (*cninf, cnobs* predicates) are still under investigation. As a lot of these flow restrictions can be expressed by access control restrictions as well, just needing appropriate object labeling, we are already able to implement a wide range of information flow policies. For instance, information flow restrictions comparable to the well-known multi-level security policy MLS (Bell, 1975) can easily be transformed into access control restrictions by introducing security classifications and clearances for objects. Within the *Cond* condition of an access control formula *acc* conditions expressing the 'no write down' and 'no read up' property of MLS must be specified to restrict access according to the MLS policy.

To support the implementation of *acc* predicates INSEL$^+$ provides the concept of **access-controlled objects** and **classes**. For each operation of an access-controlled entity we are able to formulate a boolean expression called **access restriction expression** that is evaluated at runtime on each operation call before operation execution. If the access restriction expression is true for the calling object the requested access is allowed and the operation is executed, otherwise access is denied. To handle denial of accesses we integrated a simple exception handling mechanism in INSEL$^+$.

Access Restriction Expression
An access restriction expression defined for an operation of an access-controlled entity is a boolean expression that may contain: (1) local objects of the access controlled entity including input and output parameters of the operation; (2) global objects, (3) special predicates `IN_ACL` and `ACCESSED` and (4) the attribute `Caller`.

The attribute `Caller` is defined for each operation call and describes the calling object. It contains the uid (`Caller.UserUid`) of the user who created the object, the identifier of the role this user currently plays (`Caller.Role`), the identifier of the calling object (`Caller.Actor`) and the execution context of the calling object given by the identifier (`Caller.Con`) of the operation.

With the components of the `Caller` attribute the application programmer is able to express access restrictions concerning specific users, roles, active objects or contexts, in which the active objects acts. Further components, for example containing a security label of the calling object to support the implementation of label based security policies, can be added to the `Caller` attribute.

`IN_ACL` Predicate
For each access-controlled INSEL$^+$-object an access control list (ACL) is implicitly defined which may contain a list of subject identifiers for each operation (right) of the object. A subject identifier may be either a user identifier or a role identifier. The list of subject identifiers in an ACL entry for an operation may contain positive and negative subject entries (= negative right). The ACL of an access-controlled object is initialized on object creation. The initialization of the ACL is specified in a special part of the class description of the object. To dynamically change the entries of an object's ACL, the operation `ChangeACL_OP(...)` is implicitly defined on each access-controlled INSEL$^+$-object. With `ChangeACL_OP(...)` the associated ACL of the object may be altered.

`ACCESSED` Predicate
The predicate `ACCESSED` allows to check if a subject has already accessed an object via a specific operation. With the `ACCESSED` predicate the application programmer is able to specify restrictions depending on the access history of subjects.

The INSEL$^+$ runtime system provides a range of mechanisms for implementing access-controlled entities in a distributed environment. ACLs are implemented and managed in a secure way using low-level mechanisms offered by the underlying security architecture. Objects must be authenticated by using appropriate authentication mechanisms. As sketched in section 2, SECREDS aims to provide a security architecture tailored to our language concepts for implementing application-specific security policies.

4.2 Guided Transformation

In this subsection we roughly explain some guidelines to systematically transform a model and its associated security policy into an INSEL$^+$-program. The guided transformation is explained based on the previously introduced bank example.

Given the set of objects defined in the top-level specification we identify classes of objects which have the same functionality and the same security requirements. For example the set of customer accounts in the bank scenario forms such a class. For each identified class the application programmer has to implement an INSEL$^+$-class which defines the set of operations (rights) specified for the objects. If users can act in different roles, the set of initial roles has to be defined in a special role part in the main program. Each role requires the implementation of an INSEL$^+$-class specifying user representatives for users acting in this role.

The labels of objects defined by the generic set of labels in the model have to be implemented. Some application-independent labels, like the user which is associated with an object and the role this user plays, are directly supported by the attribute `Caller`. Application-specific labels, for example the label *account_owner* of a customer account in the bank scenario, have to be implemented by local variables of the object and have to be managed explicitly.

To implement the access restrictions specified by *acc* predicates the *Cond* conditions of these predicates must be transformed into corresponding access restriction expressions. Consider for instance the implementation of the customer accounts. Each account is an instance of the access-controlled INSEL$^+$-class `AccountType`. The labels *account_owner* and *resp_clerk* defined for an account are implemented by the input parameters `AccountOwner` and `RespClerk`, i.e. these labels are initialized on creation of a new account. The `access_matrix` M is implemented by the ACLs implicitly associated with each account. The operations *enter_rights_OP* and *delete_rights_OP* defined in the model are implemented in INSEL$^+$ by the predefined operation `ChangeACL_OP`. As an account's ACL may only be accessed via the `ChangeACL_OP` operation the policy restrictions concerning the access matrix are implicitly implemented. The initialization of the ACL of an account is specified in the ACL part of the class `AccountType`. For each operation of an account an access restriction expression implementing the access restrictions for accounts specified by the *acc* predicates is given in the access restriction part of the class. The following program skeleton specifies the class `AccountType`.

```
PROTECTED DEPOT TYPE AccountType(AccountNumber  : IN integer;
                                 AccountOwner   : IN UserUidType;
                                 RespClerk      : IN UserUidType)  IS
 PROCEDURE TYPE Read_OP (Amount: OUT Real);  -- operations
      ...
```

```
 ACL                                                  -- ACL  part
  Read_OP :  AccountOwner;                            -- initialization of ACL
      ...
 ACCESS RESTRICTIONS                                 -- access restriction part
  Read_OP : (IN_ACL(Caller.UserUid,THIS,THIS) AND Caller.Role = Customer)
            OR (Caller.Role = Clerk AND Caller.UserUid = RespClerk AND
                 8 <= CurrentTime.Hour <= 16);
  ChangeACL_OP : (IN_ACL(Caller.UserUid,THIS,THIS) AND
                 Caller.Role = Customer AND Caller.UserUid = AccountOwner)
                 OR (Caller.Role = Clerk AND Caller.UserUid = RespClerk );
      ...
END AccountType;
```

THIS is the keyword for self-reference of an object or an operation. It strikes the eye that the gap between the *Cond* conditions of the *acc* predicates and the corresponding access restriction expressions is very small. Look for example at the *acc* predicate specified for the operation *read_OP*. The condition that an entry in the access matrix, ($read \in M[l(ur).user, account]$), has to exist for the calling user is implemented in the access restriction expression for Read_OP by the IN_ACL predicate IN_ACL(Caller.UserUid,THIS,THIS) and the condition that this user has to act in role *customer* ($l(ur).role = customer$) is implemented by Caller.Role = Customer.

The *acc* predicates for the operations *enter_rights_OP* and *delete_rights_OP* are combined and transformed into one access restriction expression specified for operation ChangeACL_OP.

As access and information flow restrictions may be specified for individual objects we are faced with the problem of specifying contradicting requirements. We have elaborated criteria to analyze access restriction formulas with respect to specific consistency properties. This analysis is incorporated into our INSEL$^+$ compiler. Discovering an inconsistency the compiler shows the two access restriction expressions and the kind of inconsistency caused by these expressions. Contradicting access restriction expressions then must be fixed by the application programmer. Hence, the programmer is offered support to strengthen or weaken parts of the security policy to gain an overall statically consistent policy as far as possible.

5 CONCLUSION

We have presented parts of our SECREDS framework to design and implement secure distributed applications. With our computational model fine-grained protected entities with access rights given by operations and application-specific user roles can easily be modeled. Our security requirement logic allows to specify fine-grained information flow restrictions, as well as, access restrictions customized to the individual needs of applications. As the SECREDS approach aims to bridge the gap between formal specification and implementation we presented main features of our programming language INSEL$^+$ offering well adapted language support to implement the top-level specification of a secure distributed application in a systematic way. Guidelines have been developed to implement access restriction formulas using the INSEL$^+$ features. Some of these guidelines have been demonstrated by means of an example. The development and implementation of our tailored security architecture to realize secure applications in a distributed environment is still on going. Future work is concerned with enhancing INSEL$^+$, and our compiler as well as our security architecture with features to implement a wider range of information flow policies, that is to implement information flow formulas which can not be transformed into access restriction formulas.

The SECREDS approach combining formal specification techniques and attuned programming language concepts and tools supports the application programmer in developing secure applications of high quality.

6 REFERENCES

Feldman, Michael B. (1996) *Software Construction and Data Structures with Ada 95.* Addison Wesley

Ancilotti, P. and Bowi, M. and Lejmaer, N. (1983) Language Features for Access Control. *IEEE Transactions on Software Engineering*, SE-9(1).

Bell, D.E. and LaPadula L. (1975) *Secure Computer Systems: Unified Exposition and MULTICS Interpretation.* Technical Report MTR - 2997.

Clark, D.D. and Wilson, D.R. (1987) A Comparison of Commercial and Military Computer Security Policies. In *Proceedings of the 1987 IEEE Symposium on Security and Privacy*,184 – 194.

Eckert, C. (1995) Matching Security Policies to Application Needs. In *11th International Conference on Information Security*, 237 – 254.

Eckert, C. (1996) Issues in the Design of Modern Distributed Computing Environments. In *Eighth IASTED International Conference on Parallel and Distributed Computing and Systems*, 188 – 192

McGraw, J.R. and Andrews, G.R. (1979) Access Control in Parallel Programs. *IEEE Transactions on Software Engineering*, SE-5(1), 1 – 9

Rushby, J.M. and von Henke, F. W. and Owre, S. (1991) *An Introduction to Formal Specification and Verification Using EHDM.* Technical Report, SRI International, Menlo Park.

22

Controlling Internet Access at an Educational Institution

W. Olivier and H. van de Haar
Department of Information Technology
Port Elizabeth Technikon
Private Bag X6011
Port Elizabeth 6000
South Africa
Tel: 041-5043279
Fax: 041-5043313
e-mail: wernero@iaccess.za helen@ml.petech.ac.za

Abstract

Internet usage is spreading as widely and as densely, as the personal computer which has settled in the homes of millions of people all over the world. As television created invisible glued threads onto children's eyes in the past, so the Internet and its weblike access to exciting opportunities and worlds, is sticking like glue to the minds of today's youngsters. The educational institutions are not immune to all of this, and especially not the computer studies students. All day and every day, one can walk into the laboratories and find groups of students glued to the screen, the browsing facilities, and the downloading activities. This is both good and bad for the students. Being late for classes, missing classes altogether, disrupting practical laboratory sessions, using workstations which could have been used by other students who wished to do valid practical work, chatting and gathering around the workstations and so on, are everyday occurrences due to the arrival of Internet. A friendly solution was deemed necessary, one that would still allow access at certain times, yet curtail such access during valid practical sessions in relevant laboratories.

Keywords

Internet, controllin g access, TCP/IP, firewalls, sockets, packet filters

INTRODUCTION

This paper attempts to define a solution to a particular problem, that of controlling access to the Internet at certain times of the day from certain computer workstations in the laboratories at a typical educational institution. The task of finding a solution to this problem, was given to a fourth year student, who subsequently delved into the intricacies of the Internet, the TCP/IP protocols, firewalls, sockets and packet filters. The result was, that for the particular problem, in the particular given environment, there could be at least four solutions, some better than others. This paper details the research and the suggested solutions as investigated by the student.

STATEMENT OF PROBLEM

The Internet is a global network of interlinked computers, allowing users all over the world to communicate with each other. It is constructed in such a way that the technology hides the details of network hardware and enables computers to communicate even though their respective physical network designs are different. Most educational institutions are obviously linked to the Internet to allow access to this wonderful resource. However, allowing the students access can become a problem due to the magnetic appeal of having such vast realms of information available on the Internet. The students tend to disrupt practical sessions in computer laboratories and use computer facilities for 'playing on the Internet', thus removing the capacity for other students to conduct their own valid practical sessions in order to complete assigned tasks.

A BRIEF LOOK AT THE INTERNET

The Internet itself is totally decentralized, in that the machines and networks taking part are managed and paid for locally. The Internet network itself, the mesh of dedicated telephone lines that connect all of these networks, is owned by no one, but used by all. The Internet Society (ISOC) is a voluntary non-governmental international collection of researchers, academics and users who determine the survival and future of the network. They cooperate and coordinate networking technologies and applications for the Internet and are bound by a common stake in maintaining the viability and global scaling of the Internet. Within the Society is the Internet Architecture Board, the IAB. The main function of the IAB is to maintain the Internet through the creation and enforcement of international networking standards, as well as to make sure that no two users have the same Internet address (Carvin) (Internet Society, 1995).

The Internet began with the birth of the ARPAnet in 1969. Commissioned by the U.S. Department of Defense, ARPAnet was a communications network which allowed computers at separate locations to communicate with each other in order to exchange military and national security data. With this new technology, the data from one computer could be formatted into an electronic bundle or packet and then addressed to another computer by way of the ARPAnet. This method of sending and receiving electronic information became known as the Internet Protocol, or IP for short. If a computer had the IP software implemented, it could in theory communicate to any other computer in the world, as long as that other computer had similar IP software and was on the ARPAnet (Carvin).

The rules formulated are officially named the TCP/IP Internet Protocol suite. This protocol is used by many organizations including the Department of Defence, National Aeronautics and Space administration (NASA) in America. After this initial development of the ARPAnet, additional networks branched out from defense research to general, scientific and academic use. Universities and research groups began to develop smaller networks specific to one site known as Local Area Networks, or LAN's. A LAN would have the ability to interconnect all the computers in a building using the correct network communication software. Using IP software, however, a LAN could connect with other LAN's, in other words a network within a larger network which formed the basis for the Internet. The National Science Foundation created another network, called the NSFNET, which would allow researchers and scientists to access their supercomputers by means of high speed phone lines. The NSFNET was so useful that very quickly other universities around the USA began to connect to the NSFNET. The BITNET is another network used by universities (Carvin). The building of networks throughout the country, using TCP/IP, in universities, government institutions and private industries, was happening at an unbelievable rate. TCP/IP was very popular, not because it was considered the best method for shipping data from computer to computer, but because of the fact that it was one of the first proven methods for delivering data. Today, this international network of networks is known as the Internet, and it is the most popular computer network in the world (Carvin).

A CASE STUDY NETWORK AND INTERNET SERVICE

Currently, the network setup for the case study problem at a South African educational institution, consists of multiple Novell 4.1 and Unix servers. All the workstations can access the network via DOS and Windows 3.1. Two of the Novell servers and one of the Hewlett-Packard unix servers, are used to house all the students' applications. To access Internet, the students may use Trumpet Winsock (written by Peter Tattum), which is available on any workstation. This Winsock software allows any Winsock compliant Internet software to access the Internet via Windows 3.1. The organisation connects to the Internet through UNINET, which is the local backbone network to which all universities and technikons in South Africa are linked. Routing on to the Internet takes place via a Cisco router.

The students may start telnet sessions to the unix machines, if they have a valid unix account. They have access to World Wide Web browsers, ftp, mail, chat, freetel and any other facilities that they manage to acquire. The main problem identified at the case study site, is in controlling the students' Internet access from the practical laboratories. The required level of control depends on the time of day and the type of access, since some practical sessions do require Internet access to continue. It is not viable to restrict access completely, because the students do benefit from the knowledge obtained by browsing the Internet. It is, therefore, envisaged that the restrictions will apply only to certain times of the day, and must be automatically and dynamically altered by some controlling mechanism.

A BRIEF LOOK AT TCP/IP

Transmission Control Protocol/Internet Protocol (TCP/IP) has become the standard communications protocol for the Internet since its creation by the US Department of Defence (DOD). For machine connectivity, one could call it the software solution. On the battlefield a communications network would have to sustain damage, so the DOD designed TCP/IP to be robust and automatically recover from any node or phone line failure. This design allows the construction of very large networks with less central management (Gilbert).

TCP/IP is not a single protocol as its name suggests, but rather it is a collection of related protocols designed to provide the ability to transfer information across a network and includes the provision of information about the network itself. The collection of TCP/IP programs (protocols) enables the user to send email messages, transfer and share files and the remote execution of applications across both LANs and WANs. One of the most important aspects of this software solution, is that it allows communications between heterogeneous computers and operating systems used on the Internet. Unix, VMS, Macintosh, Intel based personal computers and others can talk to each other, regardless of the differing hardware of the machine. The most common hardware solution is Ethernet, but TCP/IP will also run on Token Ring and Serial lines (modems, serial connections) and other systems as well. For a full installation of TCP/IP, one will need a hardware driver, a TCP/IP stack and the TCP/IP applications themselves (TCP/IP).

On Macintosh systems, the hardware drivers are built into the system or are provided by the board manufacturer. On a personal computer system, there are different types of hardware drivers available, both commercially and via public domain/shareware including the Packet driver specification by FTP Software, Inc., Microsoft's Network Device Interface Specification (NDIS), and Novell's Open Datalink Interface (ODI). Drivers for OS/2 systems are available from IBM and/or the board manufacturer (if they support OS/2).

The TCP/IP stack is package specific and usually comes with every product. Each such stack has its own requirements for hardware drivers. One has to find a combination of driver and TCP/IP stack which is compatible with the rest of the environment. Personal computer systems have something close to a standard in TCP applications called the Windows Sockets API (Winsock). (Note: This is not specific only to TCP/IP but it is a general standard for networking on personal computers irrelevant of the transport protocol.)

One would wish to have all the TCP/IP application programs such as Telnet, FTP, mail, etc. Just about every TCP/IP package has a corresponding set of applications but perhaps not every TCP/IP package contains all the different applications that are available.

The Transmission Control Protocol (TCP) part of TCP/IP treats the data as a stream of bytes. It logically assigns a sequence number to each byte because it is responsible for verifying the correct delivery of data from client to server. The TCP packet has a header that says, for example, that the packet starts with byte 532456 and contains 200 bytes of data. The receiver can detect missing or incorrectly sequenced packets. TCP acknowledges data that has been received and retransmits data that has been lost (TCP/IP).

Simply put, the Internet Protocol (IP) is the Internet's universal method of addressing and forwarding data from node to node. Every computer on the Internet has its own address, which is a series of four numbers each below 256, such as 101.231.03.56. This is called the IP number or IP address. The Internet authorities assign ranges of numbers to different organizations who in turn, assign groups of their numbers to departments. IP operates on gateway machines that move data from department to organization to region and then around the world. When a user sends data to another user, such as an email message, IP transmits the data in snippets of information known as packets (packet transmission is much faster than sending one's data as a single chunk). TCP/IP creates and uses what is known as a checksum to ensure correct ordering of packets (Internet Society, 1995).

Every time a message arrives at an IP router, it makes an individual decision about where to send it next. Traffic can be routed by the 'clockwise' algorithm, or the routers can alternate, sending one message the one method and the next by the other method. More sophisticated routing methods measure traffic patterns and send data through the least busy link. If one phone line in this network breaks down, traffic can still reach its destination through a roundabout path. This kind of recovery is the primary design feature of IP, and provides continued service though with degraded performance. The loss of a line is immediately detected by the routers, and somehow this information is sent to the other nodes. Each network adopts some router protocol which periodically updates the routing tables throughout the network with information about changes in route status.

There are three levels where knowledge of TCP/IP intrinsics become important. Those individuals who administer a regional or national network must design a system of long distance phone lines, dedicated routing devices, and very large configuration files. They must know the IP numbers and physical locations of thousands of subscriber networks. They must also have a formal network monitor strategy to detect problems and respond quickly.

Each large company or university that subscribes to the Internet must have an intermediate level of network organization and expertise. A half dozen routers may be configured to connect several dozen departmental LANs in several buildings. All traffic outside the organization will typically be routed via a single connection to a regional network provider.

However, the end user can install TCP/IP on a personal computer without any knowledge of either the corporate or regional network. Three pieces of information are required:

- the IP address assigned to this personal computer ;

- the part of the IP address (the subnet mask) that distinguishes other machines on the same LAN (messages can be sent to them directly) from machines in other departments or elsewhere in the world (which are sent to a router machine) ;
- the IP address of the router machine that connects this LAN to the rest of the world (Cedeno and Osborn, 1996) (Comer, 1991).

A BRIEF LOOK AT SOCKETS

Sockets is a name given to the package of subroutines that provide access to TCP/IP on most systems (Gilbert). WinSock is short for Windows Sockets. Today's most popular Internet applications for Microsoft Windows and IBM OS/2 are developed according to the WinSock standard. Berkeley Sockets is the standard programming model for TCP/IP networking under Unix. Windows Sockets was actually designed to be very similar to Berkeley Sockets so that those experienced in programming with sockets in Unix will be able to easily make the transition to Windows Sockets. WinSock is a .DLL (Dynamic Link Library) and runs under Windows 3.x, Windows for Workgroups, Windows NT, and Windows 95. The WINSOCK.DLL is the interface to TCP/IP and, from there, on out to the Internet. WINSOCK.DLL actually acts as a layer between the WinSock applications and the TCP/IP stack. The WinSock applications tell WINSOCK.DLL what to do, WINSOCK.DLL translates these commands to the TCP/IP stack, and the TCP/IP stack passes them on to the Internet (Cedeno and Osborn, 1996).

A BRIEF LOOK AT ETHERNET

Ethernet is one of the most popular network cabling schemes in use. The original ethernet specification was developed by Xerox. A second version (Ethernet II) was made with the efforts of Digital Equipment Corp., Intel, and Xerox. The Institute of Electrical and Electronics Engineers (IEEE) standardized a separate form of ethernet which has come to be known by the standards document number: IEEE 802.3. Both Ethernet II and IEEE 802.3 are compatible on the same wire so hardware utilizing either can work in the same network. Both these standards also specify a hardware protocol which describes each 'frame' of data. Ethernet hardware use CSMA/CD (Carrier Sense Multiple Access/Collision Detection) which says that only one machine on the ethernet can speak at any one time and if two or more try to do it at once, the packet frames sent will collide and the machine has to resend the frame of data at a later time.

Ethernet is a hardware and data link specification. Other software network protocols run above this such as IP, IPX and NetBEUI etc. In turn, other protocols can run over those: TCP & UDP over IP, SPX over IPX, etc. So TCP/IP will work fine with ethernet and this is also how the problem case study network is set up.

Personal computers and Macintoshes connect to an ethernet via a network interface card, which fits into the machine's bus (eg. ISA or PCI for personal computers) and require a network driver to function (Gilbert).

FIREWALLS

Packet filters are exactly what their name says: devices that filter the packets moving across a certain point in a network. Packet filter applications and mechanisms have become known as firewalls. A network firewall has the job of keeping unwanted visitors away from the network. Firewalls are therefore an excellent way to control Internet access on a network. The actual mechanism whereby this is accomplished varies widely, but in principle, the firewall can be thought of as a pair of mechanisms: one which exists to block traffic, and the other which exists to permit traffic. Some firewalls place a greater emphasis on blocking traffic, while others emphasize permitting traffic (Ranum, 1995).

A firewall can also act as the corporate voice to the Internet. Many corporations use their firewall systems as a place to store public information about corporate products and services, files to download, bug fixes, and so forth. Some firewalls permit only email traffic through them, thereby protecting the network against any attacks other than attacks against the email service. Other firewalls provide less strict protections, and block services that are known to be problems. More elaborate firewalls block traffic from the outside to the inside, but permit users on the inside to communicate freely with the outside (Ranum, 1995). Firewalls provide a single point where security and audit can be imposed. In a situation where a computer system is being attacked by someone dialing in with a modem, the firewall can act as an effective tracing tool.

There follows a definition of three basic types of firewalls: packet filters, circuit level gateways, and application gateways. Of course there are also hybrid firewalls which can be combinations of all three.

Packet filter gateways are usually comprised of a series of simple checks based on the source and destination IP address and ports. However, there is no way for the filter to securely distinguish one user from another. Packet filters are frequently located on routers and most major router vendors supply packet filters as part of the default distribution. Smart packet filters are really not very different from simple packet filters except they have the ability to interpret the data stream and understand that other connections which would normally be denied should be allowed. Smart packet filters, however, still cannot securely distinguish one user on a machine from another.

Circuit level gateways are much like packet filters except that they operate at a different level of the OSI protocol stack. Unlike most packet filters, connections passing through a circuit level gateway appear to the remote machine as if they originated from the firewall. This is very useful to hide information about protected networks. Socks is a popular de facto standard for automatic circuit level gateways.

Application gateways represent a totally different concept for firewalls. Instead of a list of simple rules controlling which packets or sessions should be allowed through, a program accepts the connection, typically performs strong authentication on the user which often requires one time passwords, and then often prompts the user for information about the destination host. However, for most environments it provides much higher security because unlike the other types of gateways, it can perform strong user authentication to ensure that the person on the other end of the IP connection is really who he/she says that he/she is. Additionally, one can perform other types of access checks on a per user basis such as what times they can connect, what hosts they can connect to, what services they can use, etc. Many people consider application gateways to be the only true firewalls, because of the lack of user authentication in the other two types.

Hybrid gateways are ones where the above types are combined. Quite frequently one finds an application gateway combined with a circuit level gateway or packet filter, since it can allow internal hosts unencumbered access to unsecured networks while forcing strong security on connects from unsecure networks into the secured internal networks (Ranum, 1995).

Application level or proxy type of filtering. The main principle of an application level filtering firewall is, that it blocks all IP level traffic between the internal network and the Internet. No IP packet from the internal network will ever reach the Internet and no IP packet from the Internet will ever travel the internal network. It therefore avoids much of the security related problems of the IP protocol which was not built with security in mind. The principle of a proxy based firewall is, that an internal client connects to the firewall and talks to a server on the firewall and not (directly) to the server on the Internet. This server on the firewall is called a proxy. The proxy on the firewall understands the client/server protocol and acts as an intermediate: when it decides that the client is allowed to do a certain type of operation, the proxy on the firewall connects to the server on the Internet and will execute that operation on behalf of the client. The filtering and screening of a proxy can be threefold.

- IP level information: source address, destination address, destination port, in fact the same type of information an IP level filtering firewall is filtering on.
- Additional authentication information: the client can be prompted for a user name and a password before the proxy allows a client to do something. Because user names and static passwords are dangerous to use on the Internet (passwords travel unencrypted on the Internet), more secure mechanisms can be used: challenge/response mechanisms using a dongle.
- Screening on the client/server protocol itself: sometimes the client is allowed to use the proxy in a limited way. For instance, the client may use an ftp proxy only to import files, or an http proxy which denies general clients access to private html pages and only allows privileged clients to get them (Bellovin and Cheswick, 1994).

The proxy type of firewalls are considered to be the most secure. However, there are complications and disadvantages. There is no general proxy: a proxy type of firewall runs a telnet proxy, an ftp proxy, an http proxy and so on. A proxy is, in general, a complex piece of software which is specifically designed for a certain type of client/server protocol.

There are advantages to be gained when using a proxy type of firewall. In principle they offer the highest level of security. It is not necessary to worry about security holes in the IP protocol since the firewall blocks all IP traffic between internal network and Internet. Also they allow for screening on application level. Sometimes a proxy can do more than offer security. In fact only a very limited Domain Name System (DNS) zone can be run (on the firewall).

Firewalls cannot protect against attacks that do not go through the firewall. Many corporations that connect to the Internet are very concerned about proprietary data leaking out of the company through that route. Firewall policies must be realistic, and reflect the level of security in the entire network. For example, a site with top secret or classified data should not be hooking up to the Internet in the first place. To set up a firewall, one has to first decide if it reflects the policy of how one's company or organization wants to operate the system.

DOMAIN NAME SYSTEM ISSUES

Some organizations want to hide Domain Name System (DNS) names from the outside. This approach is one of many, and is useful for organizations that wish to hide their host names from the Internet. The success of this approach lies upon the fact that DNS clients on a machine do not have to talk to a DNS server on that same machine. In other words, just because there is a DNS server on a machine, there is nothing wrong with (and there are often advantages to) redirecting that machine's DNS client activity to a DNS server on another machine.

First, one sets up a DNS server on the host that the outside world can talk to, such that it claims to be authoritative for one's domains. In fact, all this server knows is what one wants the outside world to know: the names and addresses of the gateways and so forth. This is the 'public' server.

Then, one sets up a DNS server on an internal machine. This server also claims to be authoritative for one's domains. Unlike the public server, this one is telling the truth. This is the 'normal' nameserver, into which one puts all the 'normal' DNS stuff. One also sets this server up to forward queries that it can not resolve to the public server (using a forwarders' line in /etc/named.boot on a UNIX machine, for example).

Finally, one sets up all the DNS clients (the /etc/resolv.conf file on a UNIX box, for instance), including the ones on the machine with the public server, to use the internal server. This is the key.

An internal client asking about an internal host asks the internal server, and gets an answer. An internal client asking about an external host asks the internal server, which asks the public server, which asks the Internet, and the answer is relayed back. A client on the public server works just the same way. An external client, however, asking about an internal host gets back the 'restricted' answer from the public server.

POSSIBLE SOLUTIONS

Possible solutions will be sought on the server side as well as the workstation side.

Non Centralized, Non Firewalling Solutions (Windows 3.1 / 95)

There is a non firewalling solution that can be implemented on each workstation that needs to be controlled. Almost 90% of all Internet software at the case study site is Windows based. With this knowledge, it is possible to create a small application that will close down the offending application depending on the time of day. Programming languages such as Visual Basic and Visual C have the capability to access the Windows Task list. The task list is a list of applications currently running on the workstation. If the list of running applications is available it is very easy to determine if any Internet applications, such as Netscape, are active and simply shut the application down depending on the time of day. There are, however, quite a few inherent problems with this solution.

Firstly, students will very soon realize that they can still access Internet by merely changing the system time within the control panel of windows itself. The solution is to update the time of the workstation from an Internet time server. This application connects to an Internet Time Server that has the correct time and updates the workstation's time accordingly.

Secondly, in Windows, nothing stops a student from merely closing down the application which checks what Internet software is running. The way to overcome this in the coding, is that there is a procedure saying that if the application is being shut down, to start up a new instance of the application. This is also very easy to accomplish in Visual Basic.

Thirdly, this Internet checking application must start up every time Windows is run. The normal way to do this is by creating an icon for it and placing a copy of the icon in the startup program group. Any program that has an icon in the startup program group will be run when windows starts up. Another place to start an application from within Windows is with a run command in the win.ini file.

However, a knowledgeable student may figure out which application is prohibiting him/her from accessing the Internet and from where it is being activated when Windows starts i.e. in the startup program group or win.ini file. Once this is known it is very simple to remove the icon from the startup program group or to edit the win.ini file and remove the run command starting up the Internet checking program.

To stop this from happening, it becomes a bit more complex and possibly more costly. A very secure method will be to have all necessary installed software on the C drive with a separate partition for space where the students can save all their files. The C drive then has to be secured so that no files can be deleted from there. This is done by special software that 'locks' the hardware so that only users with the right password will be able to change anything on the locked C drive. So Windows, its win.ini file and the Internet checking program are safe from deletion and tampering by students.

The current method of implementation forces each laboratory to have its 'version' of the Internet checking program since different labs have different requirements on time restraints and also different applications to terminate. All the information for each lab can be stored in a database on the Novell network. When Windows starts up, the Internet checking program will access the database on the network and from there read all the information pertaining to the laboratory. All the application needs to know is in which laboratory it is running and this can be stored in a file on the C drive which is locked.

This method will force the student to log into the Novell network in order for the Internet checking program to access its database and allow or disallow Internet access. Forcing students to log in will enable future monitoring and logging of what students are doing on the network.

Non Centralized, Firewalled Solution (based on server)
The case study site will probably migrate to a Windows NT network, leading to more possible solutions. Each laboratory can have its own dedicated firewall workstation set up to filter out its Internet connectivity depending on the time of day. The rules for the firewall in the laboratory will be simpler since one will have to restrict only a certain number of workstations at a time e.g. only the number of workstations that reside in that laboratory. This solution has a few drawbacks. If a student disables the controlling machine in a laboratory by switching off the workstation, then the whole firewall is shut down and the laboratory has full Internet access, thus implying extreme measures to secure physical access to each firewall machine in each laboratory.

Centralized, Firewalled Router Solution
The case study site uses a Cisco router to forward Internet traffic. Cisco routers can be used to do basic packet filtering. Since the router is the single entry and exit point for all Internet traffic, this is the natural point to install a firewall. As said previously, the Cisco router software is capable of basic packet filtering. The main problem with this solution is that at certain periods of the day the rules file or script for the Cisco router has to change, as the usage rights of different laboratories change during the day. The current Cisco software is unable to perform this function.

It is theoretically possible to enable the Cisco router to do the rules file updating procedure needed, but that entails the installation of remote management protocols not in use at the case study site. The installation of such protocols will increase the maintenance effort of the network of an already over stressed administration department.

Centralized, Custom Firewall Solution
The final option and probably the more popular one, is to install a central server solely and exclusively as a firewall. In other words, it has to be positioned in such a manner that all Internet traffic on way to the router or from the router will pass through the firewall. The firewall will have more than one rules file covering all the various periods of the day when different rules have to be enforced. The firewall server will have a timer running to trigger at the right time of the day to copy the correct rules file to the firewall. This way the correct rules will always be available to the firewall.

This firewall server can also be integrated with a proxy server. The proxy server will intercept all packets outbound on the Internet and change the packets' source address to that of the proxy server. When the return packet arrives the proxy will forward the packet to the original sender within the local network. This way all external networks will only see the address of the proxy server and in this way the rest of the internal network is hidden away from the outside world. The firewall to control the laboratories can then reside on the proxy server.

The Cisco router can also be brought into this solution. If, for instance there are a few unsavory sites to be completely banned from the network such sites that have previously initiated hacking attacks against one's network, the Cisco router's filtering capabilities can be used to filter out these unwanted sites completely, while the custom firewall keeps control on the laboratories.

This entire setup has one inherent flaw. The filtering of the firewall is based on IP addresses that are software generated addresses by Internet. A student may, however, change his/her workstation's IP address and in this way bypass all the security measures installed. This is a very serious flaw that needs attention. The student may have discovered one of the IP addresses of the administration or lecturing staff who perhaps have no limitations on their Internet access and usage.

Even though Internet uses IP addresses to establish a link between sender and receiver, these are merely logical addresses. In fact, these addresses are converted to the physical hardware addresses of the network cards themselves. So obviously in TCP/IP there already exists something that can translate an IP address to its hardware (MAC) address. It is in fact called the ARP protocol. One can use the capabilities of ARP to sample all the IP addresses and hardware addresses of the laboratories which must be controlled. The Internet firewall controlling the access to the laboratories will need a small customized add on facility to house a list of all the IP addresses and hardware addresses of the workstations in the laboratories. Once every half hour, for example, the ARP protocol will be used to query all the workstations in the labs and compare the addresses returned by the query to those housed in the table.

If the results do not match up, a student has most likely changed an IP address illegally. The network administrator must have access to the table housing the IP and hardware addresses to update the table if a workstation configuration changes, e.g. a network card is replaced. If an address does not match up, the custom ARP application can very easily notify the network administrator via email.

CONCLUSION

This last solution seems to be the best way to go for the particular case study site. Various alternatives have been suggested, but not all are viable, due to wastage of dedicated equipment, and decentralized control, which in turn places more burden on administrative staff. A centralized solution will allow for easier administration, and will cancel out the possibility of tampering by students. If the case study site replaces their network operating system with a Windows NT networking environment, then the first idea of a decentralized controlling mechanism may become popular, especially in view of the fact that it will then be possible to lock out certain sections and directories on the hard drives. Preemptive multitasking is a feature which can well by used in the Windows NT environment.

REFERENCES

Bellovin, S.M. and Cheswick, W.R. (1994). *Firewalls and Internet Security: Repelling the wily hacker.* Addison-Wesley Publishing Company.

Carvin, A. *EdWeb: Exploring Technology and School Reform.* http://edweb.cnidr.org:90./ibahn.int5.html

Carvin, A. *Network Wildfire.* http://edweb.cnidr.org:90./ibahn.int4.html

Carvin, A. *NSFNET.* http://edweb.cnidr.org:90./ibahn.int3.html

Carvin, A. *Paving the First Path: The Internet.* http://edweb.cnidr.org.90./ibahn.int1.html

Cedeno, N and Osborn, K. (1996). *The alt.winsock FAQ (Frequently Asked Questions).* http://www.well.com/user/nac/alt-winsock-faq.html

Comer, D.E. (1991). *Internetworking with TCP/IP*. Vol 1. Prentice Hall.

Gilbert, H. *Introduction to TCP/IP*. http://pclt.cis.yale.edu/pclt/comm/tcpip.htm

Internet Society. (1995). *What is the Internet Society?* http://info.isoc.org:80/whatis/index.html

Ranum, M.J. (1995) *Internet Firewalls Frequently Asked* Questions. http://www.greatcircle.com/firewalls/info/FAQ.html

TCP/IP - Short Description. http://www.webpress.net/ib/ibm/tcpip.htm

BIOGRAPHY

Werner Olivier is a full-time student at the Port Elizabeth Technikon, and is currently studying towards his Masters Technical Degree in Information Technology, in the field of Information Security.

Helen van de Haar began her computing career in 1972 as a computer programmer, and has been writing programs in various languages ever since. She has a B.Sc from the University of Port Elizabeth and a Masters Diploma in Information Technology from the Port Elizabeth Technikon where she is a Senior Lecturer in charge of Operating Systems. She is busy working towards a PhD at Rhodes University, in the field of parallel and distributed processing and debugging.

23

Analysis of JAVA Security and Hostile Applets

Dr. Klaus Brunnstein
Professor for Application of Informatics
University of Hamburg, Germany

Paper presented at SEC97 (Copenhagen, May 15, 1997)

Extended Abstract: **Rapid growth of Internet** was only possible when document description languages (esp. HTML), exchange protocols (HTTP) and **navigation tools** such as **Netscape's browser and Internet Explorer** were available for mass usage. Basic Internet features (protocols, esp. TCP/IP, domain organisation and routing concepts), navigation tools and document description languages have been specified **without observing relevant security requirements**, esp. concerning **confidentiality** of sensitive processes and data. Moreover, essential safety aspects - **availability, reliability, maintainability, functionality** - have also been **neglected**. As security and safety are „design-inherent" features (i.e. they must be specified in design and enforced in implemented systems), later enhancements (such as IP v.6 including authentication and encryption, protocols such as S-HTTP, SSL or SET) can **at best reduce risks, but they can NOT cure past design faults**.

Within this insecure and unsafe Internet environment, **„agent" technologies** develop, which perform net-"work" with usually small processes which interoperate at an **assumed benefit of users**. A multitude of agents applications has been discussed, including delegation of tasks, handling email, coordination of group work and scheduling, mobile knowledge robots, distributed searches and many others. Early examples of agent technologies (though not named as such) have been XEROXs **worms** (which materialized in several network experiements and attacks) and **chain letters**. Started either automatically or from a users desktop (or better: WebTop), **agents work in hidden manners**. Therefore, **security and safety aspects** as well as **mechanisms to control agents** must be carefully analysed from design to implementation and actual work.

JAVA was announced in 1996, by Sun Microsystems (in a „White Paper") as 4G-language for Internet applications. It supports development and execution of small agents, called **„applets"** which are executed upon a specific software engine (conceptually similar to Niklaus Wirth`s p-Code for Pascal).

According to Sun´s summary:

> **Java is a simple, object-oriented, distributed, interpreted, robust, secure, architecture neutral, portable, high-performance, multi-threaded, and dynamic language."**

The C++-like JAVA-language has several deliberate **restrictions,** which according to Sun shall guarantee **applet security**. Among such **restrictions**, **access to files and Internet address space** (URLs) is strictly **prohibited**, and memory management (including garbage collection) is automatic; user-manipulated **pointers are not supported** in JAVA. As manipulation of memory (e.g. via memory residence) and manipulation of files are regarded as essential means with which (traditional) viruses propagate, some experts and Sun assume that **JAVA viruses are „impossible";** in a counterposition, others (such as Bill Cheswick) have regarded **JAVA as „ideal virus writing language".**

Besides language restrictions, JAVA offers **more security features**. A special class of services **„security.java"** supports encryption, authentication (digital signatures), secure key exchange and integrity mechanisms (checksumming). On this basis, applets may be authorized and authenticated. This provides a secure channel to the manufacturer which is „secure" if and when the manufacturer is regarded trustworthy. An additional feature is that JAVA applets are executed upon ist own interpretor; JAVA code can then be verified for conformance with security prescriptions (byte-code verifier).

With these enhancements, JAVA is **much better** than almost all other language systems though it is **inferior to Secure ADA** which offers also formal methods for proof of specified features (this is not foreseen in JAVA which does not hide its medium-level origin: it is similar to C/C++). Nevertheless, **JAVA applets are far from being „secure".** First, any **hidden manipulation** within the scope of the language is possible; it is therefore no surprise that **„hostile applets"** have soon been demonstrated on Internet, ranging from rather „innocent" Noisy.Bear" which „only" consumes processor time and memory, to „Killer-java" which installs multiple threads and kills some browsers. These applets can be classified as **„malicious trojan horses";** they do NOT replicate but may nevertheless harmfully affect user data and processes.

More generally, **„security“ is a feature of a system whithin properly specified boundaries**. When JAVA applets **execute on insecure systems** (ranging from hardware to operationg systems to browsers and file systems), insecure use is possible despite JAVA restrictions. So far, **insecure interactions** of JAVA applets with browsers (esp. Netscape`s) have been discussed (Princeton University). So far, self-reproduction has not been demonstrated. Moreover, essential safety aspects - **availability, reliability, maintainability, functionality** - have also been **neglected in JAVA design.**

<u>Conclusion</u>: though JAVA has some security features, applets enlarges the risk of agent technologies. Based on insecure systems such as operating systems and browsers, risks of JAVA applets for sensitive information is significant.

New Organizational Forms for Information Security Management

Richard Baskerville
Copenhagen Business School and Binghamton University
Binghamton, New York 13902-6015, Tlf. +1 607 777 2337,
Fax +1 607 777 4422, Email rbask@binghamton.edu

Abstract

This paper contributes a functional analysis of current forms of information security management. This analysis is then applied in a discussion of organizational options for information security management including organizational location, organizational schemes (such as hierarchies, matrices and networks) and degree of outsourcing. Newer hybrid organizational forms are increasingly important for the development of distributed security management.

Keywords

Computer Security Management, Information Systems Security Management, New Organizational Forms, Disaster Recovery Planning, Contingency Planning

1 INTRODUCTION

The paradigm for organization and operation of the information security functions is typically centralized and rigid (*cf.* Forcht 1994). This has been reasonable in the past given the mission of information security management. However, newer forms of organizations are evolving in which the information systems (IS) function is distributed in various ways (Smithson *et al* 1994). Motives for such distribution include organizational transformation (Applegate 1994) and the rationalization of business processes (Hammer and Champy 1993). These newer forms of organization are placing demands for flexible and adaptive security management (Baskerville 1993). The need for distributed and flexible information security management is a considerable paradigm shift for most information security managers.

However, before we can discuss the different ways in which the organizational security function can be structured, we should first survey and analyze the major functional elements of this organizational component. After this functional survey, we will discuss organizational structures that might be used to plan, coordinate and control organizational information systems security in newer organizational forms. The exact activities related to each of these management functions are beyond the scope of this paper. Detailed discussions would require a book-length treatise, since these detail the complete IS security function. However, brief summary indicators are mentioned for each of these functions.

2 FUNCTIONS OF INFORMATION SYSTEMS SECURITY

The following analysis raises a hierarchical inventory of the essential functions of an organization's information systems security element. While an information systems security department could be structured in this manner, these functions are more often distributed across different organizational lines rather than concentrated in a single organizational department.

Operation Functions

The operation functions deal with the day-to-day, routine operation of security safeguards.

Media Backup Operation. This operation regards the routine writing of backup file tapes, the indexing of these files and tapes, and the shipment of these tapes to off-site storage locations.

Incident Monitoring. Monitoring is a routine security control function that captures information about both major and minor security incidents. Although most incidents have no connection with potential disasters, incident monitoring is a key coordination element in disaster recovery.

Anomaly Investigation. Systems anomalies may arise in the form of errors or unexplained erratic behavior in the information system. Usually these will lead to the discovery of errors or faults in the system hardware or software.

Information Classification. If the organization maintains a classification structure for sensitive information (*e.g.*, "secret" or "confidential"), a security function should exist to record and monitor the use of the structure.

Access Control. The access control function involves managing access accounts, data base access control, authentication token (*e.g.*, smart card) management, firewall and sucker trap operation and intrusion monitoring.

Safeguard Operation. The security operation function is also responsible for the operation of any other security safeguards such as management of cryptographic keys, logging computer room visitors or recording serial numbers of equipment on loan.

Security Development Functions

Another major functional area that should be coordinated by information security management is the development of security.

Policy Development. General security policies and procedures provide the framework for much of the non-computer-based information security, *e.g.,* rules for classifying information, storing types of documents, and the rewards and sanctions structure related to personnel involved in security incidents.

Safeguards Design regards the activities involved in analyzing and specifying the safeguards necessary in various application systems in the organization's applications portfolio.

Safeguards Implementation regards the activities involved in constructing, acquiring, installing and testing the safeguards necessary in various application systems in the organization's applications portfolio.

Security Operations Auditing. Audits of information systems usually involve an unannounced inspection of security safeguards in order to verify that these are being used correctly. Examples of such audit activities include EDP auditing and tiger team operation (a tiger team consists of security specialists who undertake the task of "attacking" an information system as if they were computer criminals).

Security Design Auditing. Auditing of general systems analysis and design processes and products determines the compliance of systems analysts and designers and their specifications with the organization's standard methods for conducting such projects.

Human Resources Functions

Many of the information systems security activities regard the people who are involved in processing organizational information, and using that information in their decision making.

Security Awareness and Training. A security training program has the goal of enabling people to use the systems safely by teaching them how to use the security features correctly.

Disaster Recovery Drills have two major goals. One is to test the technical feasibility of plan resources such as backup sites and media. This second goal is the development of disaster recovery competence in the potential members of a crisis management team and its support staff.

Security Clearance. If the organization has an information classification system, there should be a policy of clearance assignments for the people in the organization authorized to used classified information. IS security must manage these clearances or coordinate with other managers in charge of such clearances.

Electronic Employee Monitoring. Computer-based information systems have enabled a widespread number of electronic monitoring activities within systems applications. Some of these activities (*e.g.,* intrusion detection) may fall under IS security management.

Strategy and Planning Functions

Most of the other information systems security functions discussed above may be under the operational control of other departments, and may only be subject to coordination with the department tasked with managing information systems security. In contrast, the strategic and planning functions will fall squarely under the direct responsibility of security management.

Methodology Research. IS security involves specification of systems development and deployment methods that have sound security elements.

Risk Analysis. The security planning function will usually be responsible for evaluating the overall organizational IS risk profile.

Disaster Recovery Planning. The information system security management function usually takes direct responsibility for disaster recovery (business continuity or resumption) planning, since information technology (IT) is one of the most problematic elements of such recovery.

Assurance. Planning the general information risk posture includes adjusting the strategies regarding the organization's insurance portfolio. Coordination of the insurance portfolio with the security program is critical because changes in the insurance details will sometimes affect the degree of risk to information assets.

Security Program Planning. An organization's entire information systems security program must be coordinated and planned, and might consist of all of the coordinated activities outlined above. From this perspective, this analysis not only describes the functions that must be coordinated by the information security element, it also describes the possible components that might be developed by an information systems security program.

3 COORDINATION AND STRUCTURAL OPTIONS

In the previous section, we surveyed the various functions that must be coordinated by information systems security management. This section provides a survey and an analysis of ways in which the coordination of these functions might be structured. There are three dimensions used in this analysis: functional location, organizational scheme, and degree of outsourcing.

3.1 Locating The Information Systems Security Function

The information systems security function is usually considered a staff function unless the information system is producing the main (signal) output product of the organization. The location of the information security elements within the organization will probably be a function of how critical the information systems security needs are to the objectives and goals of the organization. Figure 1 illustrates a few possible locations for the IS security function. These are briefly discussed below, classified according to the related strength (risk) of information system hazards facing the organization.

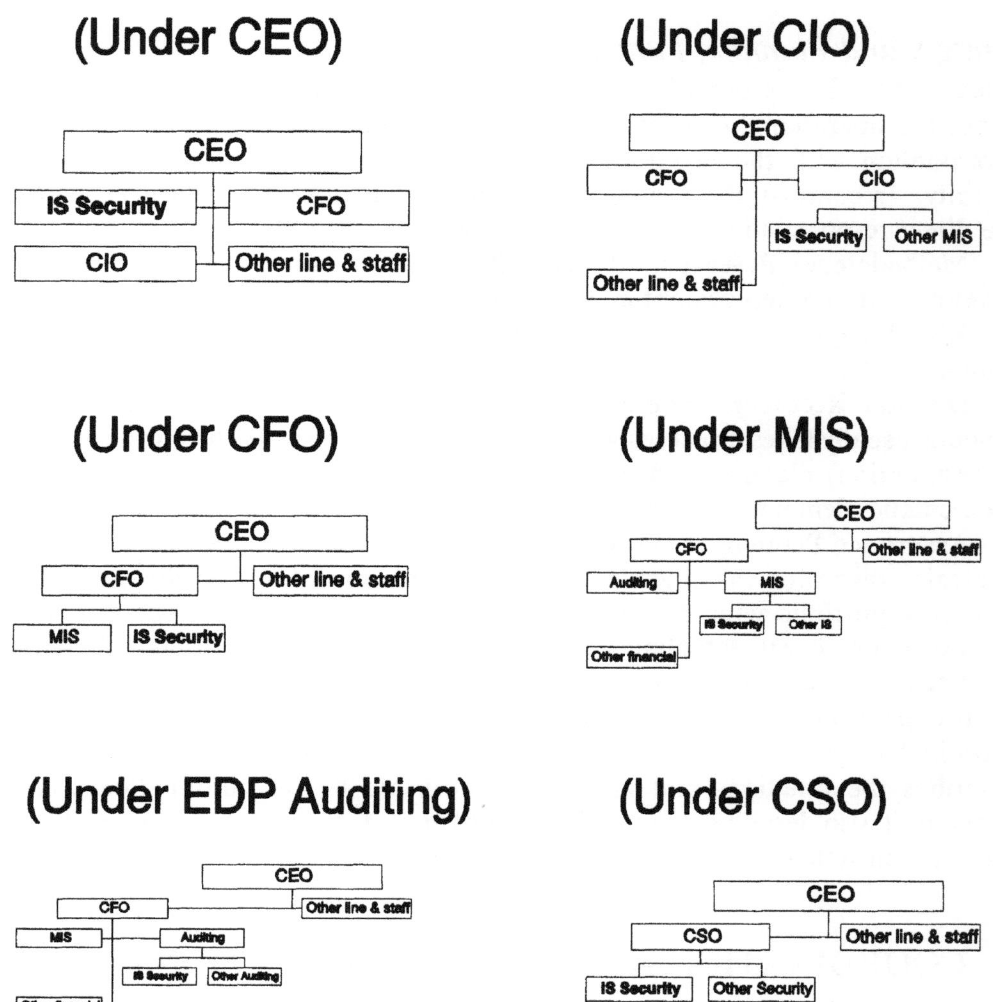

Figure 1. Some possible organizational locations for the IS security function.

Strong Hazard Level

If the security risks are high and the information systems are extremely important to the organization, as in military, diplomatic or financial institutions, then the security element may be located near to the chief executive officer (CEO). If the systems are somewhat less critical and the risks lower, then the function might be located on a parallel with the management information systems function (MIS), for example under the chief financial officer (CFO). These locations have the advantage of high visibility to senior management and represent an extremely strong organizational commitment to information security. The disadvantage lies in the separation of the functional IS management and security management, raising possibilities for fairly high-level strategic conflicts between IS and its security.

Moderate Hazard Level

If the information systems are not extremely critical and the risks are moderate, then the information security function will probably be placed under the chief information officer (CIO) or attached to the information systems department. The advantage of locating IS security within the IS group is the moderation of conflict between IS functionality and security, since the same management coordinates both elements. The disadvantage lies in the difficulty of preserving the rather transparent benefits of security safeguards under cost-overrun and behind-delivery-schedule pressures. Often the IS management rewards functional delivery above all other criteria, including (unfortunately) safety.

Weak Hazard Level

In low-risk settings, a possible alternative location groups the information security coordinating function with related security activities. For example, the IS security function might be grouped with the internal auditing function or under the chief security officer (*i.e.,* corporate security). The advantage in this location arises in the improved technical specialization of the security professionals and better efficiency in their tasks. The disadvantage lies in a strong emphasis on detection rather than prevention of the consequences of various information system hazards.

3.2 Organizational Scheme

Regardless of where the IS security organization is located, it should retain coordination responsibilities over the IS security functions analyzed earlier. However, with the possible exception of a few IT-intensive organizations with very severe security needs, it is unlikely that the IS security department would retain direct authority over all of the security functions. It is more likely that this department would retain direct authority over some part of these functions, with an appropriate staff, facility and budget to support these activities. The remaining functions would be distributed among other cognizant organizational groups, and the IS security department would retain only the authority to plan, monitor, evaluate and otherwise coordinate the necessary IS security activities of the other departments. As is the case for other modern organizations, there are three basic schemes (the hierarchy, the matrix, and the network) for organizing IS security.

Hierarchy

Figure 2 illustrates a possible IS security organizational structure as an hierarchical organization. This organization consists of five major functions much as described earlier in this paper. The human resources activities are focussed on disaster recovery drills and security awareness and training. (Other human resource activities are either not present in this organization, or directly managed by other organizational functions, *e.g.,* personnel or production management.) Similarly the security development activity is focussed on auditing designs and operations while safeguards design and implementation is not directly managed by the IS security function, and is probably under the direct control of other elements in the organization (*e.g.*, the MIS department). In this particular organization, the IS security department has grouped a select number of specialist activities under the rubric "special operations". These include investigations of system anomalies, incident monitoring, firewall programming and a tiger team activity. A staff operation, "security operations coordination", liaises with other departments to monitor and coordinate other elements in the security program and is likely to include most of the other missing activities (inventoried in the earlier functional analysis) that are not found in Figure 2.

The advantages of hierarchical organizations lie in their functional specialization and strong centralized control. The chief disadvantage is the rigidity that enables this specialization and control. These organizations are very efficient and reliable at performing routine functions over long periods, *e.g.*, a low-technology manufacturing industry with high volume manufacturing runs. These organizations are not very flexible when it comes to adapting to change. In the context of the information security function, hierarchical organizations are appropriate in stable settings because of their efficiency and strong emphasis on high standards of technical performance.

Matrix

Figure 3 shows an alternative scheme for organizing the IS security function based on a matrix, project or grid organizational structure. A matrix organization offers some opportunity for distributing the IS security function. In this type of organization, the IS security function retains only operational control of security program planning and strategy. The operational security work is housed in the various MIS departments, such as computer operations, data base administration, network management, *etc.* However, a member of the coordinating IS security staff activity is involved in project teams tasked to carry out work within the MIS departments. These project teams are represented by the dark lozenges in Figure 3.

The advantage of matrix organizations lie in their improved adaptability while maintaining some degree of centralized control and technical specialization. Their disadvantage lies in the goal conflicts that arise from split management directions, and the inefficiency of maintaining multiple management structures.

Matrix organizations may be good compromises for flexibility in moderate and high risk settings (even when the underlying organization follows a hierarchical model). Basically this matrix would be constructed by mapping the major functions from the IS security hierarchy onto the normal IS hierarchy. The matrix compromise enables the information security organization to recognize and adapt to changes in its encompassing host organization.

Network

A third example of a scheme for the IS security function organization is newer: a network, virtual or "spaghetti" organization. This is a relatively new scheme that is typically dependent on special computer groupware to provide on-line meetings, shared databases, ad-hoc data mining and electronic communication. There are two new aspects to the security function within network organizations: (1) the increased reliance on information technology as an essential organizational enabling factor

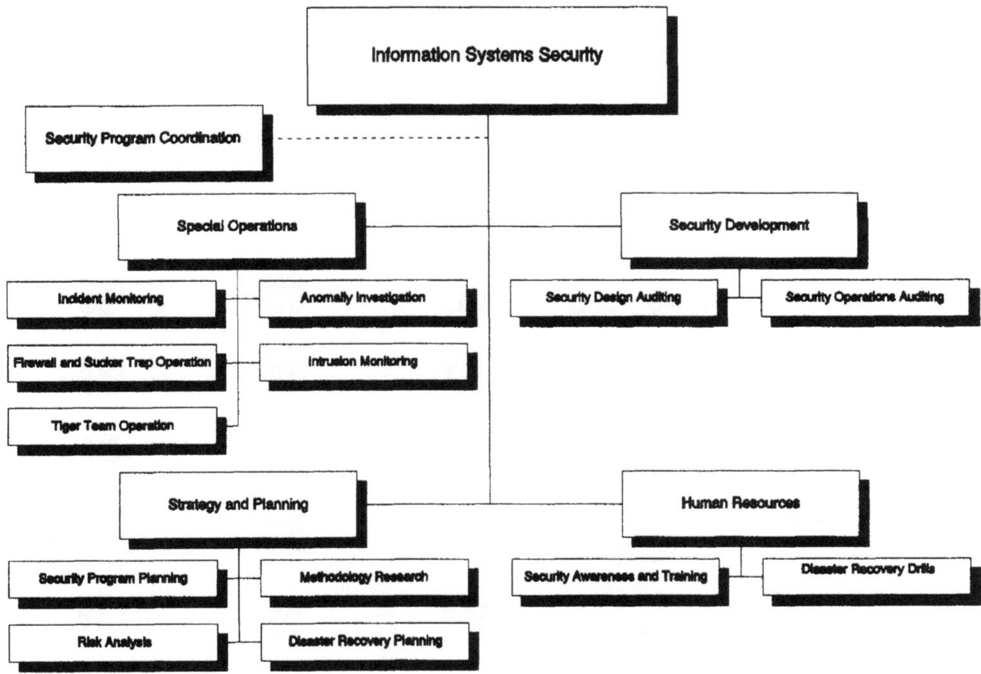

Figure 2. Example of IS Security Organization.

for such organizational structures; and (2) the devolution of organizational control from centralized management to entrepreneurial, cross-functional teams. The safety of the IT is more critical since these organizations are otherwise impossible. without newer IT. Totally centralized information security management is made problematic by devolved organizational control.

Network organizations focus on problem-solving accomplishments rather than routine tasks. While a hierarchical or network organizational outline may exist, the real form is kept fluid. When problems arise, ad-hoc groups form, solutions are implemented, and then the groups dissolve. Routine tasks are passed around cooperatively according to shifting group workloads. A network organizational form in security means that the roles of security professionals become blurred. Their tasks include attacking whatever problems arrest them, either by being brought deliberately to their attention by a co-worker, or by their own notice and interest. Importantly, the organization's departmental lines are also blurred. This means that security "outsiders" will be freely co-opted into the security organization according to interests and needs. Similarly, security specialists may get co-opted into "outside" tasks and problems.

The advantages of network organizations are their extremely high adaptability to change and their quick response to fast changing environments. The disadvantages include the heavy loss of efficiency and control, and the necessity for an expensive staff. Network organizations depend heavily on a well-motivated, creative and bright staff that seizes the initiative wherever necessary. Wherever the staff falter, the matter is difficult for management to detect and correct.

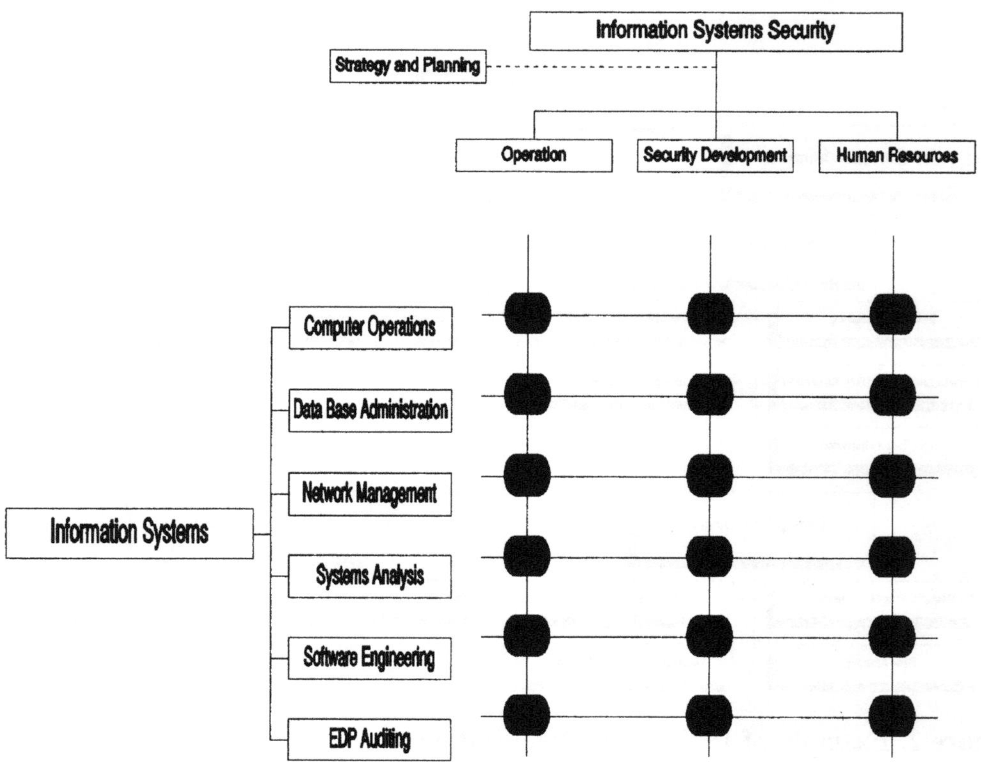

Figure 3. IS Security Management using a matrix organization.

Network organizations in information systems security are probably the only good response in an organizational setting that is network-based. This response is required in order to provide security support in a manner that is flexible enough to keep up with the shifting organizational requirements. However, if the organizational setting is highly volatile, a network organizational form may be suitable for the security organization, even if the host organization takes on a hierarchical or matrix form.

3.3 Degree of Outsourcing

Information security functions, and their underlying IS functions may be outsourced (contracted to an external organization) to a larger or smaller degree. The extent of this outsourcing has major effects on the organizational form of the information security element.

Outsourcing is not a new concept in information security management. Many organizations in moderate- or low-level hazard risk settings depend heavily on contractors and consultants for security expertise. While there may be a manager with security responsibilities in such organizations, virtually all of the security functions will be distributed among other departments. These organizations will bring in consultants for most specialist activities like security program planning, risk analysis and security design. In such settings, the chief operational duty of the IS security group will often be limited to security training and awareness programs.

The primary advantage of outsourcing is the high degree of technical expertise achieved at a low cost (compared to under-utilization of such expertise when maintained internally). The disadvantages revolve around the loss of control over outsourced functions. This loss raises such problems as the conflicting goals of contracted staff, varying availability of external resources, and the lack of internal expertise for strategy development.

The organizational security form must change if any part of the basic organizational information system has been outsourced. Essentially, all of the above-mentioned security functions must be coordinated with the external organization operating under the outsourcing contract. This will typically imply an underlying network or matrix organizational scheme that operates across the two organizations. The degree of overlap and coordination will vary according to the degree of outsourcing. For example, if there is total IS outsourcing, the amount of security coordination is minimal and the need for a network security organizational scheme would be unaffected by the outsourcing. Likewise, total insourcing of IS would minimize this motive for a network scheme. However, as the degree of outsourcing varies from zero to total the related demand for a network scheme would also vary (maximized, perhaps, around an even split between insourced and outsourced IS activity). A matrix organization might be more suitable for moderate outsourcing settings where technical expertise and review is critical, *e.g.*, settings where IS development is outsourced, but IS operation is insourced.

3.4 Hybrid Organizational Forms

The various elements of organizational forms discussed above are idealized to a large degree. It is unlikely that an information security organization will implement all of these functions using a pure form of the coordination and structural options as described here. Most information security organizations will be a hybrid that incorporates a subset of these functions (probably with some different delineations) with a combination of several locations, several schemes and several degrees of outsourcing. For example, the security organization may follow a hierarchical scheme regarding its insourced IS operations, a matrix scheme regarding its IS development activities and a network scheme regarding its outsourced IS activities.

Figure 4 diagrams the dimensional analysis presented above and can be used to illustrate the hybrid nature of today's IS security organizational forms. The horizontal axis of this diagram maps organizational schemes moving from less flexible schemes on the left to more flexible schemes on the right. The vertical axis maps organizational location moving from those suitable to less critically hazardous situations at the bottom of the figure to more critically hazardous situations at the top. Between these two axes the suitability of these forms related to the degree of outsourcing is shown as darker shading for moderately outsourced IS and lighter shading for less moderately outsourced IS. This illustrates the suitability of networked and matrix organizational forms for certain outsourcing settings.

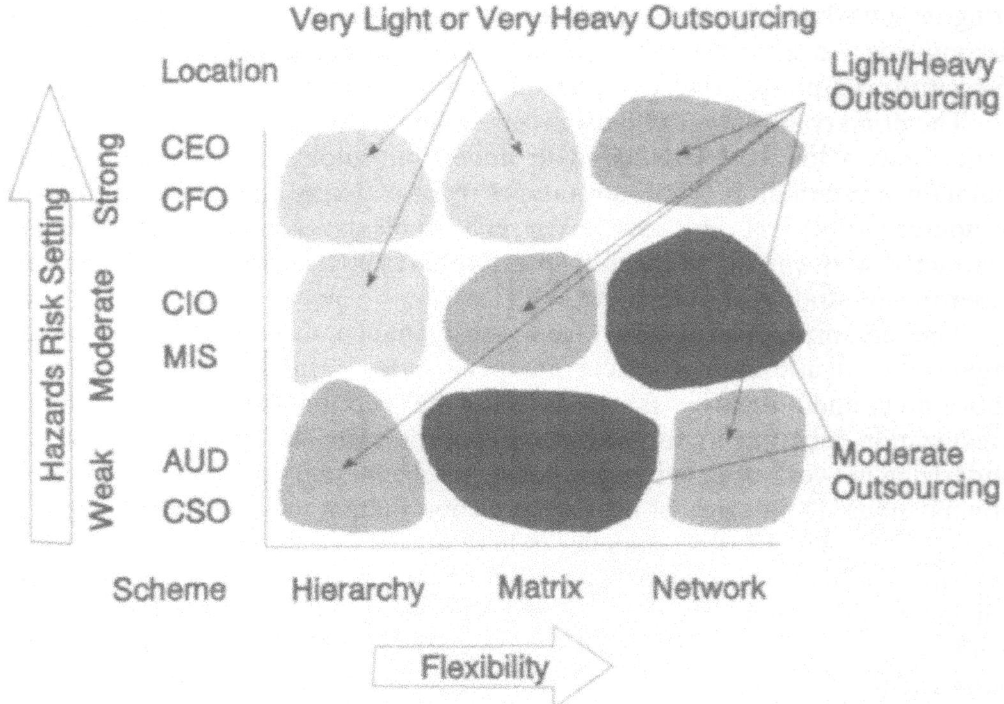

Figure 4. Dimensional analysis of hybrid IS security organizational forms.

There are two additional important notes about Figure 4. It would be unusual to plot an entire IS security organization as a single point intersecting the horizontal and vertical axes. It is more likely that the organization will be a hybrid of several different organizational forms. For example, the auditing functions might be characterized by the lower left-hand quadrant of Figure 4 while the program planning functions might be characterized by the upper right-hand quadrant. Our second note regards the shading. Figure 4 should not be read to imply that network and matrix forms are *only* suitable in outsourced settings. Rather, the shading only suggests that a best-practice characterization of an outsourced IS security function is motivated in part by the degree of outsourcing inherent in that function.

4 CONCLUSION

There are a large variety of ways in which an information systems security function might be structured. The most suitable solution is dependent on the organizational culture and its needs. But this does not mean that the various organizational forms are beyond analysis, and that there are no dimensions along which best practices might be positioned.

Examples of several important dimensions have been analyzed here: the functional inventory, organizational location, organizational scheme, and degree of outsourcing. Generalized advantages and disadvantages are distinguishable along each dimension. In addition, the importance of recognizing the hybrid nature of IS security organizational forms has been raised. While the discussion has been somewhat idealized, one major implication is that an IS security program cannot be fully developed, nor its full inventory of functions properly coordinated, until the nature of the IS organizational form is understood and planned. Without this understanding and planning, security functions cannot be properly managed and organizational information security will remain weakened. To this degree, proper IS security organizational planning and management is an important and high-priority IS security safeguard.

5 REFERENCES

Applegate, L. M. (1994) "Managing in an information age: Transforming the organization for the 1990s", in Baskerville *et al.* (eds) *Transforming Organizations with Information Technology.* Amsterdam: North-Holland, pp. 15-94.

Baskerville, R. (1993) "Information Systems Security: Adapting To Survive," *Information Systems Security* 2 (1) (Spring), pp. 40-47.

Forcht, K.A. (1994) *Computer Security Management*, Danvers, Massachusetts: Boyd & Fraser

Hammer, M. and Champy, J. (1993) *Reengineering the Corporation: A Manifesto for Business Revolution.* New York: Harper-Collins.

Smithson, S.; Baskerville, R. and Ngwenyama, O. (1994) "Perspectives on Information Technology and New Emergent Forms of Organizations," in R. Baskerville, S. Smithson, O. Ngwenyama and J. DeGross (Eds.) *Transforming Organizations with Information Technology.* Amsterdam: North-Holland, 3-13.

6 BIOGRAPHY

Richard Baskerville is an associate professor in the School of Management at Binghamton University. His research focusses on security and methods in information systems, their interaction with organizations and research methods. He is an associate editor of *MIS Quarterly* and *The Information Systems Journal.* Baskerville's practical and consulting experience includes advanced information system designs for the U.S. Defense and Energy Departments. He is chair of the IFIP Working Group 8.2, a Chartered Engineer under the British Engineering Council, and holds MSc and PhD degrees from the London School of Economics.

Security when outsourcing: concepts, constructs, compliance

E. Roos Lindgreen, H.R.D. Janus,
A. Shahim, G. Hulst, I.S. Herschberg

The authors can be reached at KPMG EDP Auditors, Burgemeester Rijnderslaan 10, 1185 MC Amstelveen, The Netherlands. Telephone: +3120-6567429. E-mail: roos.edo@kpmg.nl.

Abstract

As the ownership and management of information technology (IT) is increasingly put out at contract, information security turns out to be an essential issue to address in any outsourcing process. The authors analyse present concepts for both the demand side and the supply side of the market for external facilities management. They propose a cyclic approach related to British Standard 7799 allowing the service provider and his client clearly to define respective responsibilities in the construct of a formal security agreement, part of the general agreement between the service provider and his client. Such a security agreement stems from an assessment of the client's IT environment; compliance with the security agreement is tested by a formal review to be conducted by an impartial evaluator.

Keywords

Information security, outsourcing, security agreements

1 INTRODUCTION

It is a sad fact that many organisations are ill aware of the cost of ownership and the quality of service of information technology (IT), despite its many evident blessings.

According to recent surveys (see, for example, (Paans and Gianotten, 1994)), outsourcing some activities in owning and managing IT environments to a specialised third party, henceforward called the *service provider*, is believed to lower the cost and improve the quality, especially if the service provider has been chosen as one of several competitors. Acting in this manner, many organisations, henceforward called *clients*, are currently outsourcing their IT-related activities.

Typically, the client and the service provider unite to agree on the *quality* of the service to be delivered. In practice, the intangible notion of quality of service is carved up into disparate quality aspects, such as response times, throughput times and availability windows. Such individual aspects are usually specified in an overall *service level agreement*, part of the comprehensive agreement between the client and the service provider.

The present paper focuses on quality requirements to be imposed on information security in outsourcing, where information security is defined, in the present paper, as *the preservation of confidentiality, integrity and availability of information systems in the face of adversaries with malicious intent.*

As will be proved below, stipulating security requirements is beneficial to both the client and the service provider.

First, let us consider the benefits to the *service provider*. Typically, the service provider is under a contractual obligation to deliver a specified level of service. To the client, the obligation persists even when the service provider is confronted with inadvertent or intentional actions endangering compliance with the service level agreement. It follows that, to the service provider, taking proper security measures is a prerequisite for safeguarding any agreed quality of service.

There is another important reason for the service provider to take adequate security measures: the client relies on due care by the service provider, who has, in a manner of speaking, been entrusted with the client's vital organs. Note that, in the outsourcing market, reliability is seen as critical to success, and security incidents attributed to the service provider's negligence will dissuade customers from the service, rightly or not. Information security is thus essential to any outsourcing service.

Technical analysis shows that the security measures taken by the service provider ultimately depend on some minimal discipline by the client, ranging from the use of strong passwords to the proper reporting of security incidents. Only by explicitly agreeing on their mutual responsibilities, the client and the service provider can eliminate the vagueness threatening the effectiveness of the measures taken. Also, an explicitly worded agreement provides a framework for solving disputes on liability such as may arise after an incident.

In summary: to the service provider, taking appropriate security measures is necessary for risk management, which, in turn, requires the stipulation of security requirements in an explicitly worded agreement on the parties' mutual responsibilities.

Such an approach furnishes definite advantages to the client. First, security is set at a mutually acceptable level; and secondly, that level is visible to both contracting parties. An additional benefit is that, typically, the degree of security will be higher than it was before outsourcing, since the degree of security required by the service provider may well be higher than the degree of security achieved by the client beforehand. For a typical client, outsourcing will thus compensate for some part of a known security deficit.

Despite its evident importance, information security turns out to be an underrated item in many service level agreements. We propose a structural yet simple approach to remedy such underrating. Our approach has been applied successfully in a number of outsourcing projects. It is characteristic to our approach that conflicts between requirements are resolved, in the sense that the interests between opposing parties are agreed to have been uniformly victorious.

To quote one instance, business costs will be perceived to have prevailed whenever they are opposed to information security agreements; an objective discrimination is thus promoted.

The outline of the paper is as follows. Section 2 describes the basic requirements to be met by an information-security agreement between client and service provider. Section 3 describes the proposed approach for arriving at such an agreement. Section 4 discusses the practical applicability of the proposed approach. In section 5, conclusions and directions for future research are given.

2 BASIC REQUIREMENTS

In section 1, we have made our case that an *explicit* agreement on the mutual responsibilities for security is advantageous, both to the client and the service provider. The next step is to list the requirements to be met by such an agreement, without pretence to completeness.

Requirement 1 - Stipulation of mutual requirements and responsibilities

Above all, an approach should allow for a clear and unambiguous definition of mutual requirements and responsibilities. They must be able to identify which measures should be taken by whom or, at worst, be capable of inferring their mutual obligations.

Requirement 2 - Clarity

A security agreement should be worded so as to be necessary and sufficient for the goal envisaged; in other words, it should be clear. One important aspect of clarity is the *level of detail* of the agreement. A delicate balancing act must be performed. If stated in abstract terms only, the agreement will be ambiguous, leaving room for various interpretations when it is disputed. Yet, if overly detailed, it will be resented as rigid, confining and bureaucratic.

The ensuing optimisation problem is complicated by the fact that security requirements differ in kind from other quality requirements usually found in service level agreements. All other quality requirements have familiar schemata and are quantifiable. Typical examples could be performance requirements (e.g. *Performance of communication link: 2 Mbps sustained*), response times (e.g. *Response times for common commands: 95% within 2 seconds*) or availability requirements (e.g. *Availability of the system: 7 days, 24 hours, except for the second Wednesday of each month, when the system is unavailable from 17:00 to 19:00*). In contrast, there is no agreed way to quantify security requirements, and no agreed formalism for expressing them. Fortunately, it is proposed that the difference can be smoothed out by specifying security requirements in operational terms, viz. in terms of the measures to be taken. This brings security requirements in line with other conventional, customary quality requirements.

Requirement 3 - Completeness of measures

For want of a better approach, security requirements, we assume, have been stated in operational terms rather than in their ideal formulation, which would be in terms of business requirements. Granted this, completeness of those requirements is found to be essential. As an instance, the security part of the overall service level agreement should not only address technical security measures, but organisational security measures as well. Moreover, it should address *all* relevant technical and organisational measures.

The completeness requirement shows up the essentially negative character of information security. Moreover, it suffers from the defect that absence of security is provable experimentally, whereas positive security can never be proved: the tiniest flaw may leave an entire system wide-open to all potential adversaries (Herschberg and Paans, 1984). In this respect, security requirements are in the same unfortunate position as is testing of programs: flawedness is provable, correctness is not.

The completeness requirement is at odds with the clarity requirement. As above, we see that stipulating security requirements is an optimisation problem, and a non-trivial one at that.

Requirement 4 - Adherence to standards

If possible, an approach to information security should adhere to existing standards in order to improve efficiency and provide a sound basis for mutual confidence. A particularly appropriate standard is the Code of Practice for Information Security Management, promulgated as British Standard 7799 (BS 7799, 1995).

BS 7799 defines technical and organisational security measures, broken down as follows:

1. Security policy;
2. Security organisation;
3. Assets classification and control;
4. Personnel security;
5. Physical and environmental security;
6. Computer and network management;
7. System access control;
8. System development and maintenance;
9. Business continuity planning;
10. Compliance.

Although BS 7799 has been launched with much publicity, it has only met a moderate degree of acceptance. According to a recent survey in the United Kingdom (Bacon, 1996), about 2% of the organisations polled claimed to have fully implemented BS 7799, while another 11% stated to be seriously considering its implementation. Despite these mildly disappointing statistics, BS 7799 and its national adaptations emerge, at this writing, as the most widely accepted *de facto* standard.

Requirement 5 - Transparency

An approach to information security must be sufficiently transparent so as to be understandable to novices in the field of information security. Since any issue related to information security will constitute an interface between the client and the service provider, it will cross the paths of senior management, sales representatives, account managers and legal counsellors. It is most desirable that each party should be able to capture the essentials of the agreement without having to be an information-security expert.

Requirement 6 - Weighing by business value

Since different systems have different security requirements, no approach to information security should treat security requirements uniformly. Rather, those requirements should be weighed, whereas such differential weighing, it is widely accepted, is to be in harmony with the business value of the system under consideration.

Requirement 7 - Freedom of choice

The client, whenever outsourcing, must be the ultimate judge of the services he demands. It follows - as a complication to the service provider - that the client must be free to reject security measures, however much they may be desired by the service provider.

Requirement 8 - Flexibility

Information security is impacted by many external variables subject to continuous change, such as standards, legislation, the client's internal security policy and the state of the art in information technology. If it is to accommodate these external dynamics, any security agreement should have intrinsic flexibility, supple enough to adapt to any foreseeable changes.

Requirement 9 - Assessment of compliance

For mutual confidence, it is essential that an impartial evaluator should periodically assess to what degree the client and the service provider comply with the requirements agreed upon.

3 THE INFORMATION SECURITY CYCLE

In order to meet the requirements enumerated above, we propose a structured yet simple cyclically repetitive approach to the interaction between the client and the service provider when outsourcing.

This approach, termed the *information security cycle*, consists of six prescriptive consecutive phases as per table 1 and figure 1.

Table 1 Phases in the information security cycle

1	Classification	Classify IT environment based on business value.
2	Selection	Select proper security measures.
3	Quick security audit	Check which measures are in place.
4	Security agreement	Agree on security measures and mutual responsibilities.
5	Implementation	Implement unimplemented security measures.
6	Evaluation	Evaluate whether security agreement is complied with.

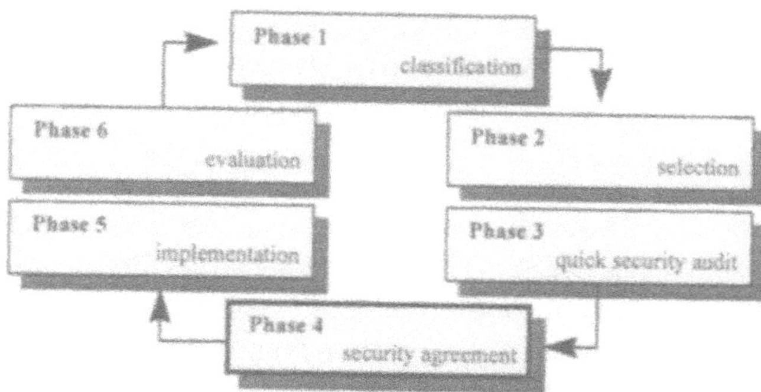

Figure 1 The information security cycle.

The phases above are to be traversed periodically. In the course of the cyclic traversal, there must be close co-operation between the client and the service provider. Since the security agreement will impact the service offered commercially, the information security cycle should be initiated as an essential part of pre-sales negotiations. Thereafter, a periodicity of a year is recommended, unless either party insists on a shorter time of traversal.

Below, the phases of the information security cycle are described in detail.

Phase 1 - Classification

In the classification phase, the client assesses the sensitivity of the IT environment to be outsourced, with due regard to the confidentiality, integrity and availability of the data and the applications.

Various methods for such a classification exist. There is a choice of a top-down approach and a bottom-up approach. In the top-down approach, the sensitivity of the IT environment is based on an inventory of business processes and applications. In the opposite approach, known as bottom-up, it is the IT environment which is primary to the classification. Since the IT environment is the better understood, one does do well to adopt the bottom-up approach. For this purpose, two stages are followed: first, a classification team inventories the data and applications stored and processed within the IT environment; second, the classification team inventories the business processes using these data and applications.

The next step is to identify the relative importance of these business processes, applications and data in a top-down fashion, taking each of the quality aspects (confidentiality, integrity and availability) into account. The resulting classification is set according to a high water mark; the most important data and/or application determines the classification of the entire IT environment.

In addition, the IT environment is categorised as being highly sensitive to negative publicity, should an incident occur or otherwise.

Phase 2 - Selection

In the selection phase, the client selects a set of security measures from a standard catalog based on BS 7799. The catalog comprises two sets of security measures: (1) elementary security measures considered necessary by the service provider from the viewpoint of due care; these measures are henceforward collectively termed the *information security baseline*; (2) additional security measures, henceforward termed *information security services.*

1. The information security baseline

In section 2, it was argued that the information security baseline should be derived from existing standards, most notably BS 7799. Unfortunately, BS 7799 is not fully fit for the purposes stated (Roos Lindgreen, 1996). In order to enhance its practical applicability, we propose to use a derived version of BS 7799 by modifying it in the following ways:

- to remove the standard's inherent redundancy;
- to remove measures aimed at special environments, such as traditional mainframe-environments;
- to remove measures that are way beyond due care;
- to remove measures that are application-specific, as opposed to generic;
- to remove unnecessary details.

The result is a "cleaned-up" version of BS 7799, preserving the overall structure, content and spirit of the standard. For purposes of reviewability, each deviation from the standard should be carefully motivated.

The resulting baseline is considered mandatory - respecting, however, the client's freedom of choice. Some of the measures in the baseline are to be taken by the client (e.g. stating an information-security policy or defining ownership for all information systems); some measures are to be taken by the service provider (e.g. installing a central desk for reporting security incidents or configuring the access-control mechanisms within the IT environment); and some measures are to be taken by both (e.g. stating security requirements in contracts with third parties and observing due care when using IT equipment).

2. Additional information security services

Of course, the client can have security requirements that surpass the information security baseline sketched above. In that case, the client should be able to pick his choice of security measures from an additional catalogue. Such a catalogue could describe information security services for each of the quality aspects confidentiality, integrity and availability; these services could then be implemented by tangible measures such as encryption, extended access control, extended physical security, data encryption for mobile PCs, or TEMPEST.

In any case, the selection of security measures should be based on the outcome of the classification phase; see figure 2.

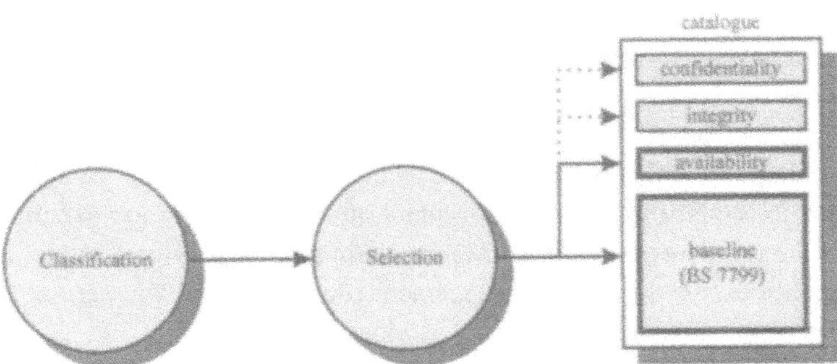

Figure 2 From classification to selection.

Phase 3 - Quick security audit

After a set of mandatory and additional security measures has been selected, the client and the service provider should perform an initial assessment in order to establish the degree to which the security measures selected have been put into place. This audit should be quick and clean; it should at least provide, to the client and the service provider, a first indication of information-security arrears. In order to speed up the audit process, an automated audit tool may be used.

Figure 3 Quick security audit.

Phase 4 - Security agreement

The client and the service provider then formally agree upon which security measures are to be taken by whom. The resulting *security agreement* is self-contained, referring to the corresponding paragraph in the generic service level agreement and vice versa.

It makes sense to model the security agreement after the information security baseline, so that for each of the measures in the baseline, the client and the service provider agree on their mutual responsibilities. In the security agreement, the client and the service provider also agree on the realisation of additional security services.

Phase 5 - Implementation

In the implementation phase, the client and the service provider implement the security measures agreed upon, especially those not already in place. The implementation phase should be performed according to accepted project-management principles. Prior to implementation, the client and the service provider should at least agree on the measures to be implemented, the procedures to be followed in the course of implementation and the conditions for acceptance.

Phase 6 - Evaluation

In this phase, an impartial evaluator assesses to which degree the client and the service provider comply to the security agreement. This assessment should not be limited to the mere presence of the measures, but rather should be extended to ensuring that any measure installed in turn is conformable to its specification. The assessment, which may result in some sort of certificate (Veltman, 1995), will expose any deviation from the security agreement and so contribute to the mutual confidence between the client and the service provider.

4 DISCUSSION AND CONCLUDING REMARKS

Supported by standard forms, automated tools, model contracts and security catalogues, the approach described above has been implemented by a large outsourcing company. It has been applied in practice on several occasions. Based on simple theoretical foundations, the information security cycle has proved a suitable basis for working out the complex issue of information security in real-life outsourcing processes. Nevertheless, some critical remarks can be made.

The classification phase should be traversed with caution. First, since the classification is based on a high water mark, it is not inconceivable that a relatively large IT environment is highly classified, although only a minor part of this environment contains truly sensitive data. In that case, the service provider can propose to carve up the IT environment into disparate compartments, each of which can be secured to fit. Second, the classification phase can easily lead to intensive and time-consuming discussions on details that may be less relevant in the scope of the information security cycle. This may lengthen the entire cycle's traversal time, which, in turn, will lessen its degree of acceptance. An efficient classification thus requires sufficient experience and expertise.

We have found that a formal security agreement may be highly appreciated by some clients, but will be perceived as unnecessarily bureaucratic by others. We feel that the security agreement should not degenerate into a goal in itself. The service provider should keep in mind that maintaining continuous contact and an open discussion with the client is far more important - and often far more effective.

A last point of criticism may be that the information security cycle as described is insufficiently detailed. Our defence is threefold. First, we feel that the simplicity requirement poses an upper bound to the level of detail of any approach that has "practical applicability" as its stated purpose, especially if non-experts are involved. Second, it is our experience that every client is unique, defying any attempt at designing a method that is highly detailed, yet generally applicable. And third, we argue that any approach to information security should offer sufficient leeway in order to deal with the dynamics of present IT environments.

Perhaps the most challenging aspect of the proposed approach - or, indeed, of any approach to information security - is to convince of its necessity all parties involved, observing the possibly conflicting interests of these parties. We have found that, especially at senior management level, security awareness may be raised by arguing that information security is an essential ingredient of general risk management, the latter, in turn, being an essential ingredient of responsible management, rather than dishing up scary stories about high-tech hacking.

5 REFERENCES

Bacon, M. et. al. (1996) *National Computer Security Survey 1996*, KPMG report, publication no. 4937.

British Standards Institution (1995) BS 7799, *A code of practice for information security management*, BSI, ISBN 0 580 23642 0.

Herschberg, I.S. and Paans, R. (1984) The programmer's threat: cases and causes, *Proceedings of the NGI Section EDP Auditing workshop "Beheer en controle van en in besturingssystemen"*, Noordwijkerhout, NGI, ISBN 90 706 9004 7, May 15-16, pp. 125-136.

Paans, R. and Gianotten, M.H.E. (1994) Data center management, *Getting order out of chaos*, Giarte Publishing, Amsterdam / Minneapolis, ISBN 90 74712 04 5.

Roos Lindgreen, E. (1996) A Sense of Secureness, *Approaches to information security*, Ph.D. Thesis, Delft University of Technology, Delft, The Netherlands, ISBN 90 900 9320 6.

Veltman, P. (1995): Third party review en -mededeling bij uitbesteding van IT-services, Compact 95/3, KPMG EDP Auditors en Samsom Bedrijfsinformatie, ISSN 0920-1645, pp. 20-37.

6 BIOGRAPHY

Edo Roos Lindgreen is audit manager at KPMG EDP Auditors, Amstelveen, The Netherlands. His current professional and research interests include corporate information security and the design, implementation and assessment of complex IT environments.

Hans Janus is business development representative at Communication Solutions Nederland (CSN), Leidschendam, The Netherlands. His professional interests include cryptography, information security and marketing research.

Abbas Shahim is consultant at KPMG Management Consulting, Amstelveen, The Netherlands. His professional and research interests include data warehousing, logistics, system development and information security.

George Hulst is security manager at CSN. He is responsible for corporate information security, coordinating and supporting the Information Security Cycle in outsourcing projects. George is a member of the project group Internet of the NGI, the Dutch computer science association.

Bob Herschberg is professor of the chair of Operating Systems and Distributed Systems at Delft University of Technology. His research interests are the penetrability of systems reputedly secure and the securability of systems reputedly sensitive.

PART TEN

Cryptopolicies

26

The IFIP TC11 Position on Cryptopolicies

(This proposal has been prepared by the special task force for voting on the TC11 meeting 1997)

a)IFIP TC11 recognizes the highly important role of cryptographic mechanisms. In the Global Information Infrastructure GII and in Electronic Commerce these mechanisms will influence acceptability, usage, and competitiveness.

b)IFIP TC11 takes notice that for the convenience of discussion it is helpful to distinguish between the differing objectives for the use of cryptographic mechanisms - presevation of confidentiality, provision of the ability to authenticate people/organisations, provision of the ability to prove the integrity/completeness of data, etc.

c)IFIP TC11 is fully convinced that a range of cryptographic mechanisms are required to meet the security needs of the GII. Users may select the most effective for their specific purposes.

d)IFIP TC11 recognizes that cryptography at the same time is prone to potential abuse by criminals. In this context law enforcement plays also an important role and we face the situation that different countries exhibit different attitudes.

e)Being aware that responsibilities for crime prevention and detection lies at national governments and that business is less and less related to national boarders IFIP TC11 recognizes that cryptographic services and cryptographic applications cannot be bound to a nation's territory.

f)IFIP TC11 recognizes the technical consensus that forbidding or restricting the use of strong cryptography is from a technical standpoint ultimately unfeasible.

Taking the above said into account IFIP TC11 takes the following position on the use and regulation of cryptography:

(I) Cryptography has equal impact and importance when data are stored or transmitted. A distinction is unrealistic in a world of networked computers.

(II) It is the prime goal that, whoever is involved in the process, cryptographic procedures and keys are handled in a way that full confidence of all partners, including the public at large, is assured.

(III) It is desirable that voluntary and free use be in place for all types of cryptography.

(IV) While a business will generally take precautions to protect itself against lost/forgotten/stolen keys, such considerations should be carefully separated from the law enforcement considerations, even though the mechanisms for each may be the same or overlap.

(V) When establishing key management and cryptography infrastructures this should be primarily driven by the users needs and not by regulatory requirements.

(VI) Law enforcement shall not establish methods in the cryptograhy context that infringe on a citizen's expectations of personal privacy and integrity within a country.

(VII) IFIP TC11 assumes that organised and major crime will successfully avoid or evade any requirement to comply with a key deposit scheme. Law enforcers must therefore not rely primarily on key deposit schemes when addressing the issue of criminal intelligence gathering. Research should be conducted, which results in a set of appropriate, acceptable, and well focused alternative methods.

(VIII) In cases where keys are deposited at third parties it is necessary that commercial and privacy interest as well as commercial liabilities must be guaranteed in all phases. This is particularly necessary if such systems allow law enforcement to access data in clear or keys, under proper legal constraint.

(IX) There is a great need that cryptographic methods and especially digital signatures be recognized by national and international law. Such recognition carries with it responsibilities for assuring availability of relevant keys throughout any legally specified retention period and liabilities for improper disclosure of or change to keys whilst they are being kept.

(X) Any legal or regulatory arrangement between two nations, in respect to cryptography and access to relevant materials, must be symmetric.

PART ELEVEN

Secure Commercial Systems (II)

Towards a Holistic View Of Security and Safety of Enterprise Information and Communication Technologies: Adapting to a Changing Paradigm

Dr. Klaus Brunnstein
Professor for Application of Informatics
University of Hamburg, Germany

Invited Paper for SEC97 (Copenhagen, May 16, 1997)

Abstract: When enterprises heavily rely upon proper working of Information and Communication Technologies (ICTs), they often experience shortcomings in programs and systems, failing availability and unreliable access through networks as major drawback in their operation, with possible effects on productivity and profitability. Traditional „security" addresses some of these aspects but, based on its military model (Bell LaPadula), essential requirements are seriously missing.

With view towards distributed enterprise work, the paper analyses why basic concepts of „traditional security" fail to meet these requirements. On this basis, it is postulated that holistic „sikerhet" combining traditional security and safety is needed for ICT based enterprises. This concept requires improved professional education and awareness, but will also need more user and public awareness.

1. Towards „Information Societies": Dependability of IT-based Enterprises

Roughly 50 years after James Watt`s basic patent on **steam-driven engines** (1765), the development of industrial technologies had gained sufficient momentum to subsequently change economies, societies and states into what was later called „Industrial Societies". With the deployment of „loco-motives", economies overcame local boundaries to develop mass transportation and thus produce industrial chains (though not net-works) from raw material to advanced products and customers. The original „steam-driven" engine was supplemented and later replaced by **more advanced engines**, based on liquid energy and electricity. Rather soon after their invention, as new enterprises and major branches of industrial economies developped, customers became significantly **dependent upon the proper work of industrial products and methods**.

Though industrial engines - driven by vapor, gasoline, or electricity - had their specific development cycles (Kondratieff`s cycles of industrial development), one common characteristic was concerned with **„quality“** of related products. At least in their early phases, industrial **products were rather „unreliable“ and often „dys-functional“.** Only **100 years** after their invention, when steam engines still tended exploding and producing significant damage, manufacturers developped **some quality measures in design, production and maintenance** of these engines to **reduce risks** for their users and environment. Only in those stages, quality measures were assessed and related organisations (dominated by the producers, rather than customers) developped to assess and assert „product quality“. Almost 100 years after the invention of gasoline-driven engines (N. Otto: 1867), cars were manufactured with inherent dys-functionalities. It was only when a customer attorney (Ralph Nader) publicly notified that such products were **„unsafe at any speed“**, that quality of these industrial products was improved, enforced by developping „customer protection“ (subsequently implemented in national laws). In similar (thoug sometimes shorter) cycles, other engines (such as nuclear reactors) were experienced to be unreliable.

Almost 200 years after the advent of the „industrial age“ (and roughly 20 years after its invention: e.g. Konrad Zuse, 1939), **the fast proliferation of computers into enterprises** lead some advanced industrial economies to new horizons of some **„Information Era“.** It is assumed that the engine governing this development - „the computer“ - is an implementation of „human reasoning“. One application was to introduce new production methods (e.g. early versions of Computer-Integrated Manufacturing), thus enriching traditional industrial production methods in design, production, distribution and market access. In another direction, traditional **information-related products** such as **monetarian services and insurances** were adapted to computers for „informational usage“. Early adaptors (e.g. banks, insurances) were limited by initial (main-frame) computing technologies. With the advent of small, cheap and easy-to-handle „Personal Computers“ (PCs) and with the development of computerized communication, **new „information products“** and related production methods developped, which required and stimulated **„Information Infrastructures“.** IntraNets and InterNetworking is postulated to require and enforce a new paradigm of **„distributed information work“** which subsequently leads to new information engines (e.g. „agent“ technologies) and more complex information products. These developments have even begun to change the world economic order into an ICT-supported **„global economy“**, and it has visible effects on vanishing abilities of national societies to enforce laws and maintain their values.

Only 60 years after the advent of „Computers“, and about 30 years after early developments of computerized enterprise communications (e.g. in inter-bank communication), **many large to small enterprises have become dependent upon availability, reliability and proper work of computers and networks**. Deficiencies in design, implementation, distribution and manufacturing of ICT-related products - esp. in their „soft“ forms - lead to **major losses in controllability, efficiency and values of information products and their ability to communicate**. Many forms of „risks“ materialize every day (see ACMs „Risk Forum“), and it is the „application side“, i.e. large enterprises and individual customers which have to pay.

As in related industrial phases, **ICT quality** in most areas is still under-developped. Even worse: **ICT experts too often do not sufficiently care for quality!** Though it is well known that contemporary PCs do NOT protect sensitive information and ICT processes, almost 100 millions are in daily enterprise use. Though it is well known that Internet is full of technical deficiencies (supporting hacking and massive scans, spoofing, sniffing and data hijacking, to name only few), ICT experts advise enterprises to communicate sensitive information via Internet and computerized telephone systems. New ICT products - e.g. script-based office systems - introduce and proliferate **new risks** (e.g. „macro viruses“, „malicious agents“ such as hostile JAVA applets and ActiveX controls) but almost no user cares. As in early industrial phases, „user requirements“ are NOT defined by users but included in the specifications of ICT manufacturers. User unawareness materializes in ubiquitous software „guarantee forms“ which every user must accept; such texts essentially say **that users are themselves responsible for any malicious side-effect** which the software produces, and that users at best get another copy of the deficitarian software which crashed their programs and data and destroyed results of hard work.

Many users tend to agree that it is high time to develop awareness among users about their dependency upon ICT, but users feel helpless. In a fatalistic approach quoting experiences of industrial evolutions, one could wait another 40 years until the problem is „sufficiently mature“ (that means: damages have become sufficiently serious and ubiquitous) to enforce changes. In a different approach, this paper argues for a rational solution: it is the **ICT profession** (including related manufacturers, and lead by professional bodies such as IFIP) which must **understand its shortcomings** and which must improve ICT quality by developing new visions of how to support the application side in mastering their problems.

2. „Security“: The Traditional Paradigm:

When potential shortcomings of new ICT products (to name some recent examples: JAVA and ActiveX) are discussed, manufacturers (such as SUN and MicroSoft) tend to argue that they have designed and implemented „proper security“. It is therefore worthwhile to understand security under the auspices of enterprises heading towards distributed information work.

Essential concepts of „Security“ can be illustrated using **the model of a military fortress** (generally: a system requiring some protection of sensitive proxesses and objects) **which is situated in an alien, foreign environment** (some books on security illustrate their object with pictures such as the „Tower of London“). Those in the fortress are the **„good guys“** which have to protect themselves and their „goods“ against the **„bad guys“ outside**. Anybody from outside requiring access to the fortress is regarded **suspicious**. According to this model (which is mathematically well described by Bell and LaPadula in their famous BLP-model), **adequate protection against attackers** (hackers, crackers) as well as **surveyal** (auditing) is essential. Consequently, **access control** (Identification and Authentication, I&A) is a major issue, which regards any individual as potentially suspect and therefore requiring positive authentication (e.g. by analysing bio-metrical personal characteristica). Any possibly **„covert“ access** through some hidden channel must be detected or, even better, excluded in the design of the fortress. **Authenticity** of outsiders must be visibly (e.g. by assigning „labels“) carried; to avoid risks of label manipulation, „label integrity“ must be assured.

Within the „protected environment“, there are **differences in „trust-worthiness“ of the good guys.** Lower levels are trustworthy in fulfilling special operations but they are not equally trustworthy concerning information and decision-making. Senior insiders (e.g. high officers) carry sensitive information which require more rights to access information and make decisions though not always to perform operations. Consequently, **„rights“** must be **administered**, and **proper usage must be enforced** (e.g. in design or by proper control) **and surveyed** (auditing). Strict rules **forbid to set-up information channels** where information may leak to less trustworthy insiders (in BLP-model: „no write-down“) or even outsiders; on the other side, the flow of essential information must be guaranteed to reach only responsible insiders (BLP: „no read-up“).

The model of responsibility and required trust is structured like a **pyramid**: **few persons on higher levels** require higher trustworthiness as they have access to sensitive information and decide about sensitive actions. On the basis of this pyramid, **many persons** act on a **comparably low level of required trust**. One beneficial aspect of this pyramid structure is that it is **easy to implement**: control for higher risks (which requires higher efforts) may concentrate on few persons, whereas the mass of control processes can be performed on lower levels of requirements. This beneficial characteristic **reduces the control overhead** and guarantees, to some degree, a **suitable performance/cost ratio**.

In **applying this model to ICT**, „security“ was somewhat formally described in National Computer Security Center`s „spectral series“, covering **single system security** („Trusted Computer Security Evaluation Criteria“, TCSEC alias Orange Book) and its „interpretations“ concerning **interconnected single systems**

(„Trusted Network Interpretation", TNI alias Red Book), **databases** („Trusted DataBase Management Systems Interpretation", TDBI alias Lavender Book) and others. For different levels of „required trustworthiness", systems can be evaluated and possibly certified to reach **specific levels of „security"** (ranging from C to B to A, with „beyond A1" reserved for adaptations to unknown requirements). Based on these criteria (and requests of some US institutions for their usage), this model of security is **implemented** in some **main-frame operating systems**, on higher levels (B) such as **MULTICS** with its central „reference monitor" controlling any access and action, or with less rigid mechanisms (C-level) such as IBMs **MVS** (with RACF). Compared to the mass of ICT products (esp. in office software areas), rather few systems and products have been evaluated according to TCSEC schemes, and even less apply TNI criteria. Recently, one client/server system used in many enterprises (Windows NT) has been quoted to be certified at C2, but only in its stand-alone facilities.

3. Shortcomings of the Traditional „Security" Paradigm:

Even in the 1980s when distributed information processing was somewhat „behind the horizon", it was argued that the inherent military model **was hardly applicable to enterprise computing**. Indeed, concepts of enterprise work seems to be rather different from military concepts. One major diufference **concerns access to and work with sensitive data**: work on design data (e.g. of a product), personnel data (e.g. of customers or employees) and market data is accomplished by the **lower-level employees**, on the basis of the pyramid of responsibility. On the upper side of the responsibility pyramid, senior managers have less access to operationally sensitive information but use, e.g. in enterprise decision, highly condensed information. An enterprise may significantly depend upon both kinds of information - the daily operational and the decision-oriented ones. In traditional terms, users on lower levels must therefore be **as intensely controlled** as higher levels; this implies either significant mass-problems in control mechanisms (e.g. zillions of audit data, performance problems in I&A) or reductions of control requirements. Usually, enterprises take the latter approach, e.g. in reducing authentication to low-level passwords, in switching audit trails off or in simply storing audit data without any evaluation.

Moreover, the **assumption that insiders are good guys** (if indeed applicable to the military) does not always hold for enterprises. Several case studies about computer crime have concluded **that damage from inside attacks was significantly higher than from outside attacks** (though this may change with developments of network-based „information war" between enterprises which exploit weaknesses of networks). In traditional terms, outsiders can simply be hindered in accessing sensitive data by proper physical, logical and organisation means. On the other side, insiders - esp. when operating on low levels of

„security“ - have many opportunities to access, manipulate or else misuse sensitive enterprise information. Moreover, unplanned damages e.g. by import and usage of malicious programs („computer viruses“, „trojan horses“) and documents („macro viruses“) are regarded as higher risks for enterprise computing than hacker attacks.

In an attempt to model **enterprise „security“ requirements** in a form comparable to the military fortress model, „integrity“ of processes and data was postulated. Related models have been developped, e.g. by Biba and Lipner which tried (though with differing assumptions) to build upon the traditional BLP-model. In another approach, the Clark-Wilson model attempted to describe the logical inter-dependency of enterprise transactions to develop some possibly formally provable model of integrity. Recently, Abrams and LaPadula developped a frame model which allows to import different - possibly incoherent - models into a „general framework“.

Following such suggestions, traditional security criteria have been somewhat enhanced. In one direction, four national European security government offices developped the **„Information Technology Security Evaluation Criteria“ (ITSEC)**. An essential merit of these criteria was to include integrity (though not clearly defined). Moreover, several aspects of communication (e.g. integrity and confidentiality) were added as new functions. Despite of the value of these further dimensions, IT-dependent enterprises have so far not experienced improved product quality in ITSEC directions. Indeed, one other innovation of ITSEC seems to produce major drawbacks in product quality. In TCSEC, specific security functions and the related assurance are closely bundled. ITSEC takes a different approach in **separating functions (F) from „quality“ (E)**. In ITSEC, each system or product can be described by a pair (F,E); it has not been properly analysed whether functional requirements and quality of products are sufficiently independent (mathematically: orthogonal) to serve as essential descriptions.

One beneficial effect of **„unbundling“ security funtionality from quality** of implementation could be that new functions (e.g. an AntiVirus functionality: F-AV) can easily be added. In reality, few such additions have been published over the last years. Moreover, breaking quality from functionality has now a dubious side-effect: products can receive an ITSEC certificate without any explicit functionality. So far, several products have certificates such as „medium quality“ which classifies a producers attitude and ability rather than making its products comparable to others. In several cases, US-based products have been certified which very probably would NEVER be certifiable according to Orange book.

Presently, another attempt - this time jointly by North-American and European state organisations - aims at developping **„Common Criteria“.** Fresh ideas such as „protection profiles" and a much larger set of functionality classes wait for being applied to relevant products. Though it will be interesting to observe whether this joint activity can lead to ICT products of higher quality, one native problem of all those criteria quoted (TCSEC, ITSEC, CC) is that they have essentially been **developped by government authorities** with long experience and strong interest in military models; **experiences in enterprise computing and networking** have rather **rarely been represented in related commissions**. This diminishes the likelihood that new approaches help understanding enterprise dependability problems.

All security models so far are essentially based on the assumption that ICT work is performed on a set of single installations whose characteristics and interdependencies can be informally or formally described. Clearly, this assumption is no longer valid when some dynamically adapting network replaces „the computers". To give one example: when some „agent" such as an „information broker" searches an Intranet for specifical information, it is neither possible nor feasible to know the actual network structure nor to control any information access on foreign systems; indeed, most users of such agents will never know whether this agent uses plug-ins in other systems to read local information. The complexity of the network and its associated production methods excludes „proper control", though the „quality" of the derived information depends strongly upon the quality of those production methods.

It should not surprise that **classical security concepts** (including certified products) are not highly relevant (if at all) in enterprise information work. Indeed, an ITSEC **certified product seems to have no advantage over non-certified products in enterprises** in general. One reason may be that manufacturers tend to declare their products as (e.g. C1 or F-C1/E1) secure though they are at best „designed at" that level. One other reason may be that certification strongly relies upon information presented from manufacturers; on such basis, one can hardly be surprised that certified products fail even in certified areas (one „nice" example was an AntiVirus product which, after having been certified by German Information Security Agency, was proven to distribute rather than detect viruses which it „improperly" handled; although this was made public, the certificate was NOT withdrawn).

Following the methodological inadequacies described, the state of „security" in many enterprises is also „inadequate". Many enterprises rely on software products which are - if working with some stability - D-level (TCSEC: „no security"). This applies esp. to Intel/Microsoft based „DOS/Windows" systems (with Windows NT fulfilling, in principle, C-functionalities, in local use) and Macintosh-OS, but also to most UNIX systems (IBMs AIX and Hewlett-Packards HP-UX are certified at C-level, but their network components are so buggy that Computer Emergency Response Teams have to distribute „warnings“ almost weekly). Generally, practice in I&A is as deficient as auditing.

Moreover, the situation in networks is even worse. Neither TNI nor communication-oriented functionalities in ITSEC have brought major improvements in security. Whereas **SWIFT** as inter-banking network had some built-in security mechanisms, **Internet banking** is based on a network with essentially **NO BUILT-IN security**. Indeed, original concepts of **ARPANET** (though financed and stimulated by military organisations) are **„insecure at any level“** (to adapt Ralph Nader´s decription of some industrial products); the only relevant design goal was that partial networks survive failures at other locations. When new information products such as Internet Commerce and Internet Banking are put on such insecure technologies, either additional means are needed or additional risks will unavoidably materialize.

Some security experts argue that **good encryption can overcome risks** in otherwise insecure networks. This approach assumes that encryption mechanisms can be made unbreakable (which is in principle achievable as such methods as RSA ciphers with sufficient keylength are practically unbreakable for some time); moreover, this approach would be successful **IF crypto-key management** can be **implemented with sufficient reliability and trustworthiness** (which is harder than just implementing a good algorithm), **AND IF keys can be protected against attempts of governments** to force manufacturers implementing methods that allow states to decipher encrypted messages. Discussions about „secure encryption“ of the European mobile telephone communication (A3/A8 algorithms being said to be unbreakable but now allowing deciphering) and successful requirements of European governments to break encrypted communication show **that users canNOT rely upon proper encryption**. Actual discussions about crypto-laws in USA and Europe point in the same direction.

Conclusion: neither the dominant understanding of „security“ nor its enforcement by criteria is adequate for IT-based enterprises.

4. Safety and Security: Adequate Paradigm for ICT-dependent Enterprises

Essential requirements of enterprises come from areas which have been overseen in security discussions. Apart from the inadequate dominance of military „security“, one reason is the **dominant Anglo-Saxon language** which distinguishes between „security“ and „safety“. In other European languages, such as Scandinavian (Denish, Norvegian, Swedish) and German, the central term („sikerhet“, „Sicherheit“) includes **BOTH Security AND Safety** which I subsequently call **„Sikerhet“.**

Generalized Sikerhet requirements include the following „dimensions" applied to „ICT objects" such as systems, programs, functions, services, data, structures, interdependencies etc:

Functionality: an ICT object perfoms its function always „as required",

Consistency: an ICT object is always consistent with its specification or definition,

Persistency: an ICT object is changed during its life-time only by explicitly permitted action,

Reliability: all functions performed on an ICT object are always equally performed under equal constraints,

Availability: all ICT objects are available when needed, and

Confidentiality: no illegal access to or use of an ICT object is possible.

Some of these aspects relate to „traditional security", such as confidentiality and integrity (which is generalized to persistency). Others have played major roles in other areas, such as control of industrial processes or application in high-risk areas such as medical ICT, control of infrastructures such as nuclear energy production, or control of life-sensitive transportation systems such a automatic vehicle control or Flight Management Guidance Systems (alias EFCS = Electronic Flight Control Systems). Related methodological requirements have been called **„Safety" or „Dependability"** requirements. Indeed, all these aspects - rather than the subset of „traditional security" - are relevant for ICT-based work. Therefore, a holistic view is needed (including a holistic name).

When one compares the methods applied in „traditional safety" (e.g. as used in developments of industrial application) with those in „traditional security", one finds that **formal methods** are applied in both areas, but with different sets of assumptions - and consequently with different success. The different approach can be condensed to the following **antagonistic positions**:

> Where users are **seriously aware of their mission and criticality** (as in many applications of safety), **users tend to prescribe what they require**. Formal methods are applied in modern applications to describe such requirements, which may also be used to assess whether actual products fulfil given requirements.

Where **manufacturers are more determined to bring their ideas and products to markets of many users**, they **tend to specify what users may find worthwhile to work with**. Such specifications are mainly for internal purposes, and they are rarely formally given or certified.

In a **holistic approach**, one must not only combine dimensions to yield a problem/solution space of higher order, but one must show that the holistic picture may seriously win from combining methods from the sub-spaces. Indeed, one **basic advantage** of **holistic „Sikerhet"** is that both views may well be combined to a sequential process, to the advantage of ICT quality:

Step 1: **Users** of Sikerhet-related products describe their **requirements**.

Step 2: **Manufacturers** of Sikerhet-related products **specify** what their **products offer** and what they can **guarantee**.

Step 3: On the **market** of Sikerhets-related IT products, users compare their requirements with manufacturer specifications. When they match (at least partially), the **manufacturer „guarantees"** the proper work of his product **„as specified" within agreed limits.**

This mechanism is somewhat comparable to methods of industrial quality assurance. It supports improved product certification such as developing **„sikerhets criteria"** which may eventually be **further developped from traditional security** (e.g. by properly enhancing confidentiality from single and conneced to distributed systems) **and traditional safety** (e.g. prescriptions of certifications of industrial products, air transport systems or nuclear power stations). Moreover, orientation towards production of „sikerhets products" based on ISO 9000 are also possible; some of these aspects (e.g. life-cycle orientation) are yet covered in ITSEC and Common Criteria.

4. Outlook: Implementation of Holistic „Sikerhet":

In order to **implement Holistic „Sikerhet"**, several processes must be started:

User awareness must develop to understand deficiencies of contemporary ICT. In some sense, this is an automatic process. With present InSecurity and UnSafety, it is just a matter of time that risks materialize to such a degree that customer protection becomes a matter of survival. The sad lesson (see 1) of industrial developments is that this may even happen at the expense of human lifes. One would hope that such serious con-sequences may be avoided in a technology which is based on human ratio.

Professional education will play an important role in planning, implementing and maintaining ICT on higher levels of „Sikerhet". Methods such as specification techniques and tools are available but professional education is still on the level of medium level programming as languages such as C/C++ and Visual Basic are major carriers of innovation.

In Security, only few universities offer coherent courses on Security and Safety; in Germany, Hamburg University`s related four-semester course (presently finishing its 4th cycle, with participation of over 60 students) is the only one in an Informatics faculty. Few other European universities (in Sweden, UK, Autria and Greece) are also offering related courses; in a joint European project (ERASMUS), several universities exchange both teachers and students to develop professional education. Within IFIP, a TC-11 working group also works on harmonising curricula.

Professional awareness must also be developped for experts which areactive in ICT industry to improve their previous - unsufficient - education.Apart from updating the professional knowledge at related conferences, national Computer Societies should play a major role.

Public awareness will probably only develop when the public realizes how insufficient contemporary ICT is to reach the publicly propagated goals of „Information Societies". Presently, politicians in USA and Europe assume that basic technologies such as PCs, multimedia and Internet work,as assumed". Only when writers and politicians experience themselves how unreliable and unavailable Internet connections often are, that data from Internet are often wrong and search engines produce misleading results, they will learn that their favorite technologies need „shaping". This will include legal regulations to enforce customer protection and reduce effects of failing ICT products.

In historical perspectives (which disregards individual and enterprise life stories), **concern about and requests for „sikerhet" will unavoidable grow**. Every new report about failing programs (e.g. when some network carrier becomes inoperable for hours or days) or forgotten characteristics (such as dropped century figures in dates) will add to **the public insight that present ICT does not perform what the public thinks**. This will **also diminish the respect for IT professionals**. Instead of observing how the information engines „explode", anticipatory action is the better advice.

5. References:

This paper re-evaluates concepts of traditional security which have been published in well-known literature, broadly available in SEC conferences. The paper is based on the authors book on „Information Technology: Inherent Paradigms and Risks for Future Information Societies“ (in preparation).

A Taxonomy of Electronic Cash Schemes

Ernest Foo, Colin Boyd, William Caelli, Ed Dawson,
Information Security Research Centre,
School of Data Communications,
Queensland University of Technology,
2 George Street GPO Box 2434,
Brisbane Q4001,
Australia

Abstract

A large number of electronic cash schemes have been proposed in the literature and several commercial ventures have started which claim to provide an anonymous payment protocol. These schemes have been designed to provide certain security properties.

Not all the schemes have proven to be practical and the precise security properties of the different schemes are difficult to compare due to their complex protocols. In this paper the key services required by electronic cash are identified and their provision in different electronic cash schemes published in the literature is compared. In addition to the security services, the mechanisms used to implement these services are isolated.

Keywords

Electronic commerce, electronic cash, security services and mechanisms.

1. INTRODUCTION

Electronic commerce can be described as any form of business transaction in which the parties interact electronically rather than by physical exchanges or direct physical contact. Within electronic commerce there are three distinct payment methods, namely: credit payments, cheques and electronic cash. These can be compared with their physical equivalents and are designed to provide similar properties.

Electronic cash schemes are anonymous payment schemes. As the potential of Internet commerce applications has started to be realised, the importance of electronic cash protocols has begun to be widely recognised. The possible number of uses for electronic cash is enormous. There are considerable benefits to consumers, merchants and financial institutions alike which result from the following fundamental properties of electronic cash.

- As for all electronic transactions, removal of the physical process leads to faster and more accurate processing.
- Electronic cash is of intrinsic value, allowing users immediate use of funds.

Most of the currently implemented systems rely on smart card technology. However, at present there exist only small experimental systems with a limited number of cards in circulation. One form of electronic card which is currently in wide-spread use is the telephone card; although a form of anonymous payment in its widest sense, these do not allow the user to refresh or refill the value of the card. Furthermore, such a system does not really encapsulate our design criteria since these cards cannot be used universally as an item of value. An electronic cash scheme should provide a secure payment system which allows a user to anonymously purchase, in principle, any goods and services.

1.1 What is Electronic Cash?

When trying to determine the required properties of electronic cash it is worthwhile to consider the usual properties of physical cash. Webster's Dictionary states that cash is:

1. ready money,
2. money or its equivalent paid promptly after purchase.

Physical cash has the following characteristics:

- "Value." It can be traded for goods or services.
- "Anonymous." Previous owners of the cash are not known by the current owners and the banks and government do not keep track of by whom, and where, the cash is spent.
- "Security." Cash currency is specifically designed to deter counterfeiting.

As mentioned above, it is the anonymous nature of cash that distinguishes it from other forms of payment scheme. Thus we are led to the following definition.

> Electronic cash is a payment system in which no information is retained such that the identities of the parties to a transaction may be deduced, after the successful completion of the transaction.

We would like to include within our definition of electronic cash any electronic payment scheme which has the same characteristics as physical cash. In addition there are other requirements of electronic cash which arise due to the electronic medium but which do not apply to physical cash. One of the properties of physical cash is that it is granted value by the local governing body. Currently electronic cash is not legal tender and is only granted value by the distributing body.

This paper classifies the properties of ideal practical electronic cash systems, which we term *electronic cash services*. These are considered in detail in section 2. Electronic cash services have been implemented in practice through many different specific processes or *electronic cash mechanisms*. Some mechanisms provide several services simultaneously. Section 3 details various mechanisms and how they provide the required services. Many electronic cash systems have been described in the literature and several have already been implemented, at least in prototype form. The final section compares which electronic cash services are provided in existing electronic cash payment schemes and what mechanisms are used.

1.2 Terminology

The following terms are commonly used in the literature:

Coin A unit of electronic cash. Coins can have different values.

Bank The warehouse and administrator of electronic cash. The bank monitors the electronic cash coins for security violations.

Customer The entity which spends electronic coins.

Merchant or Shop The entity which receives electronic coins.

To date, all electronic cash schemes include at least three types of transactions: withdrawal, payment and deposit.

1. *Withdrawal* occurs when a customer either converts some funds from an account in the bank or is granted an overdraft of funds from the bank. In any case the withdrawal transactions transfers some electronic coins to the customer.
2. *Payment* occurs when the customer spends electronic coins. The electronic coins are transferred to the merchant. This payment usually involves the reciprocal transfer of goods or services from the merchant, although such transfer is typically not part of the electronic cash payment schemes.
3. *Deposit* occurs when a merchant or customer transfers electronic coins back into real currency. This involves interaction with the bank or other similar authority.

Some schemes have an additional procedure usually conducted before any other transactions occur. This is often referred to as the *opening procedure* and is similar to opening an account with the bank. The opening procedure typically enables the bank to give the user a password which will identify the user to the bank as a valid user.

2. ELECTRONIC CASH SERVICES

A concise list of electronic cash services was introduced by Okamoto and Ohta (1992). These include privacy, security, transferability and divisibility. Additional services, more geared towards a wide scale practical implementation of electronic cash, include scalability and acceptability. The need for these properties was first described by in Medvinsky and Neuman (1993) in their NetCash specification. Of these services only the two properties of privacy and security are common to all electronic cash schemes and may be called *compulsory* services. The other services are termed *optional*.

2.1 Privacy ("Untraceability" or "Anonymity")

The privacy of the user should be protected. A fundamental property of physical cash is that the relationship between users and their purchases is untraceable. This means that even if all the banks and merchants colluded they would not discover the identity of the purchaser provided the purchaser has not breached security. This property causes many governments to be cautious about promoting anonymous payment schemes. Because electronic cash does not require physical confirmation (i.e. presence of physical coinage) it may allow any number of illegal transactions to occur without the possibility of tracing. For example, the ability to transfer funds over the Internet across international boundaries in an anonymous manner (and currently with no restriction) will be of great concern to national governing bodies.

2.2 Security

The aim of security in cash payment protocols, as in other payment protocols, is to prevent any party from cheating the system. This includes entities involved in the transaction as well as external adversaries. For customers and external adversaries the forms of cheating security which are specific to payment schemes are:

- double spending of coins.
- creation of false coins (forgery) during payment.

From the merchant's side it is essential that genuine coins can be identified. Similarly banks must be sure that merchants do not double deposit or create false coins during the deposit transaction.

In electronic cash schemes, the security services traditionally applied in financial transactions must also be maintained. For customers, banks and merchants authentication and non-repudiation are necessary across all transactions. During the withdrawal transaction the bank must be sure that the correct customer received the electronic coin and not an entity masquerading as the customer. All parties must ensure that the transaction has occurred legally.

2.3 Transferability

The transferability service allows the transfer of coins from individual to individual. Cash schemes which do not allow this service must return a coin to the bank after it has been spent; the coins are non-transferable and can only be spent once before being reset. Non-transferable cash systems can emulate a transferable system by having the electronic coins sent through the bank reset before being transferred to the intended recipient of the transfer.

It is feasible that transferable cash schemes may use coins which are *never* deposited back to the bank. This would mean that the coins are circulated constantly much like physical coins. This scenario is problematic in the case of electronic coins as the longer the coin is left in circulation the longer adversaries have to decipher the coin structure. Most schemes which offer the transferability service also include a "used by" date which requires the bank to refresh the coin after a period of time.

2.4 Divisibility

The divisibility service allows a coin to be divided into smaller denominations. Each subdivision is worth any desired value as long as all values add up to the original value. Without divisibility, a customer must withdraw a coin of the desired value whenever a transaction occurs or withdraw many coins of various values and conduct a series of transactions which total to the cost of the goods or services to be purchased. The divisibility service is not one which is specific to anonymous payment schemes; other electronic payment schemes also require this service.

The unrestricted ability to subdivide introduces the issue of minimum value. It is likely that using electronic payment schemes vendors will charge a small amount to access information on the world wide web. Is it valid to charge one hundredth of a cent for each page? If so what happens if the customer no longer wishes to use the remaining ninety-nine percent of the cent and attempts to deposit it at the bank?

2.5 Scalability

Scalability is the ability to handle the addition of users and resources without suffering a noticeable loss of performance. In a system where a wide circulation of coins and a large user base is anticipated this service is essential. Scalability ensures that the scheme can be easily expanded to handle more transactions. Most scaleable electronic cash schemes do not contain just one central server (bank) but rely on multiple servers.

2.6 Acceptability

Acceptability refers to the ability of banks to accept coins minted by other banks. In a cash system which has acceptability with multiple banks a customer may withdraw coins from a bank and transfer those coins to a merchant. At the end of the day the merchant should be able to deposit the coins at any bank.

Without acceptability coins can only be used between parties that share a common bank. This would not be practical in a cash system with a large number of potential customers and merchants. Ideally acceptability should occur automatically without loss of performance. Many theoretical payment schemes do not take into account the importance of this property.

3. ELECTRONIC CASH MECHANISMS

Electronic cash mechanisms are the protocols and procedures that electronic cash scheme designers have used to implement the services that their schemes provide. We identify several mechanisms which implement key services; it should be noted that several mechanisms provide more than one service.

- There are several mechanisms which are used to provide the security service. *On-line operation* may be used in place of cryptographic mechanisms to prevent double spending. Other mechanisms are *cut and choose, line method, single term coins, blind certification* and *electronic licenses* which detect double spending or forgery, and reveal the identity of the perpetrator. These cryptographic mechanisms are not essential for cash schemes which are dependent on *tamper-proof hardware* for security.

- *Blind digital signatures* provide aspects of the privacy service.
- The divisibility service is usually implemented by a *binary tree mechanism* or a *continuous hash* mechanism. These mechanisms also provide the transferability service.
- The scalability and acceptability services are usually provided through the use of *tamper-proof hardware* devices. No hardware independent electronic cash schemes directly address the issues of scalability and acceptability.

3.1 On-line Operation

In an on-line operation the validity of the transaction is verified while the transaction is occurring. When a cash scheme is on-line a coin being spent is sent to the bank and verified during the payment transaction. The bank is able to ensure that the coin has not been tampered with or previously spent. The bank then sends the coin to the intended recipient. The advantage of this system is that the bank can flag an attempt at an illegal operation as it is occurring and prevent it.

Most electronic cash schemes are off-line. In an off-line operation the validity of the transaction is verified a period of time after the transaction has occurred. Off-line schemes are more complex and are less secure than on-line schemes. Some authors, such as Simon (1996), argue that off-line operation is too risky whether tamper-resistant hardware is used or not. However, on-line schemes are widely regarded as too inefficient to be practical in most applications.

3.2 Tamper-Proof Hardware

Electronic cash schemes which do not use tamper-proof hardware do not rely on any physical properties (e.g. smart card, wallets) to maintain the security service, but rely only on cryptographic methods. This means that users will have access to the bit string values that represent the cash, but it must be infeasible, or at least unattractive, for the user to exploit this by copying the strings and using them multiple times. An advantage of hardware independent schemes is that they may be easily used for software implementation for Internet transactions.

In contrast, schemes dependent on tamper-proof hardware may employ both cryptographic methods and check physical conditions to ensure security. These schemes are usually more secure than hardware independent schemes. With hardware dependent observers off-line cash schemes can be as secure as on-line cash schemes with the obvious reduction in implementation complexity.

3.3 Blind Digital Signatures

Blind signatures were originally developed by Chaum (1983). The main aim of the blind signature mechanism is to allow a user to obtain another party's signature on a particular message without revealing that message. This is often compared to signing an envelope which contains a message on a piece of paper with a carbon paper backing. When the envelope is signed the pressure on the envelope combined with the carbon paper will cause the same signature to be impressed onto the message paper.

The mechanism is used to allow banks to validate coins by signing them, without knowing the coin details which would allow tracing. Customers choose randomised, but pre-formatted, coins which are then presented to the bank for signing. Any signed and properly formatted coin will be accepted as genuine. The customer usually selects a random number which is called the blinding factor. This number is multiplied with the message before sending it to the bank. The bank signs the hidden message and returns it to the customer. The customer can then remove the blinding factor and retain the signed message from the bank.

There are many variations on the blind signature theme. All the cash schemes surveyed for this paper use one of its forms to maintain the privacy service for the scheme.

3.4 Cut and Choose

Cut and choose was first introduced by Rabin (1978) as a zero knowledge proof technique. It was first used for electronic cash by Chaum, Fiat and Naor (1990) in conjunction with blind signatures to prove that a signature had been correctly formed. This technique was very popular with some of the earlier cash schemes and is still one of the most widely discussed mechanisms in the electronic cash scheme literature. The basic idea uses three distinct phases.

Withdrawal

The customer prepares a number of coins ready for signing by the bank. As well as randomising values and formatting, these must include some value which will be used to trace the customer in the event that he spends a coin twice. For example, it might contain the customer's identity split into two parts which are independently hidden cryptographically. All the coins are blinded and revealed to the bank. The bank chooses some (say half) and the customer 'unblinds' them which allows the bank to check that the customer is acting properly. Depending on the parameters used, there is a high probability that a cheating customer is caught and the bank then takes whatever action it decides. If the bank is satisfied that the customer is acting properly then the remaining coins are signed and returned to the customer, and the customer's account is debited.

Payment

This is an interactive protocol during which the customer presents a coin to the merchant and the merchant chooses randomly to see some of the customer information contained in it. For example, this information may be one part of the split identity. Double spending cannot be detected during payment.

Deposit

The merchant returns the coin to the bank where its random serial number is checked to see if it has been spent before. If so, then the two parts of the customer information are combined and, depending on the parameters used, the customer's identity is revealed with high probability. If the coin is spent only once, the information is not sufficient to find anything about the customer's identity.

Unfortunately cut and choose is a very inefficient method for proving that a customer has not breached security because it requires interactive protocols for both payment and withdrawal and only half of the coins prepared by the customer are used.

3.5 Line Method

The line method was developed by Franklin and Yung (1993) as a new mechanism which would decrease the amount of traffic. The line method uses a very similar mechanism to the cut and choose method called *oblivious authentication* which also uses blind digital signatures to provide the privacy service.

This mechanism requires a smaller amount of network handshaking than the cut and choose method but the size of the coins is still very large. This is because each coin must hold two points and the slope for several lines. The number of lines required to ensure a secure scheme determines the efficiency of the mechanism.

3.6 Single Term Coin

The single term coin mechanism was developed by Ferguson (1994). A similar mechanism was later used by Eng and Okamoto (1995). The single term coin is much more efficient than the cut and choose method because instead of using k coins to return $k/2$ useable coins, only one is required. This is similar to the line method in that only one challenge term is used, but here the challenge term is much smaller.

This mechanism uses a variation of the blind digital signature scheme called the *randomised blind signature scheme*. The randomised blind signature scheme requires both multiplicative and exponential blinding factors. The amount and size of the network traffic required is considerably smaller than that required by the cut and choose mechanism but the increased efficiency also results in increased complexity.

3.7 Electronic License

The electronic license mechanism was introduced by Okamoto (1995). The electronic license is a signed document authorising the user to spend coins issued by the bank and is used together with a bit commitment scheme and a binary tree representation of the coin to provide the security service. The electronic license and bit commitment prove that the customer has a valid coin from the bank and thus prevents forgery. A simple blind digital signature is used to provide the privacy service. The electronic license mechanism is more efficient than the original cut and choose scheme but like the single term coin mechanism it is more complex.

The electronic license mechanism is fairly efficient in its withdrawal, payment and deposit transactions. However, the opening transaction which issues the customer with an electronic license can involve the transfer of a lot of data, especially in the bit commitment section.

3.8 Blind Certification

The blind certification mechanism was first used by Yacobi (1995) and later used by Brands (1995) and Mao (1996). This security mechanism requires that each customer obtain a blind certificate. A blind certificate is similar to an ordinary certificate which contains a public key and the holder's identity but the identity of the customer is hidden using Chaum's blind signature technique.

The security of blind certification is dependent on Schnorr's one-time signature scheme (Schnorr 1990). This scheme was originally designed for the generation of signatures for use in smartcards. Schnorr's scheme uses a property of El-Gamal signature scheme which causes the identity of the customer in the blind certificate to be revealed if a customer attempts to sign two different messages using the same signature. Using this property double spending can be exposed.

3.9 Binary Tree

Divisibility may be implemented by using a binary tree. This mechanism was first used by Okamoto and Ohta (1992) and then used again in Eng and Okamoto's (1995) scheme with the single term coin mechanism. Lately the binary tree mechanism has been used in conjunction with Okamoto's (1995) electronic license mechanism.

The key to the binary tree method is the way the binary tree nodes are allocated values. If a cash scheme uses the binary tree mechanism, each coin of worth $w = 2^L$ is associated with a binary tree of $(1+L)$ levels and w leaves. Each node of the tree represents a certain denomination.

When dividing the value of the coin two rules are followed:

1. **Route Node Rule**: When a node is used, all descendant nodes and all ancestor nodes of this node cannot be used.
2. **Same Node Rule**: No node can be used more than once.

The divisibility service provided by the binary tree mechanism is implemented in the payment transaction.

3.10 Continuous Hash

The continuous hash divisibility technique was originally designed for micropayment schemes. It was first used in Rivest and Shamir (1996) for their *MicroMint* micropayment scheme. Mao (1996) adapted this mechanism for use in an anonymous payment scheme. Instead of using a binary tree to represent the coins, continuous hash consists of a series of coins chained together. The n-th coin is the seed number. The $(n - 1)$-th coin is the seed number hashed once. The $(n - 2)$-th coin is the seed number hashed twice, the $(n - 3)$-th coin is the seed hashed three times and so on. The following is a description of how Mao (1996) adapts the continuous hash mechanism for anonymous cash schemes.

Withdrawal

1. Hash a secret number n times, where n is the desired number of coins.
2. Link the hashed coins together in a chain as described above.
3. Get the bank and customer to sign the first coin.

Payment

1. The customer sends the chain of coins to merchant.
2. The merchant selects x-th coin and recursively hashes it x times.

3. Thus the merchant has computed the first coin.
4. The merchant now has the bank's signature.
5. The merchant signs the bottom coin and returns the chain of coins to the customer.

The customer can now spend the remaining coins. The merchant signed coin is now the top coin.

4. EXISTING ELECTRONIC CASH SYSTEMS

There are currently a number of electronic cash systems in use. The schemes with the widest circulation like CAFE (Conditional Access for Europe) (Boly et al. 1994) and Mondex depend on hardware devices to ensure security. Digicash, Cybank and VisaCash are three other companies providing an anonymous cash payment scheme. Unfortunately all of these schemes (except CAFE) have not published their protocols in the literature and so it is not possible to establish that these schemes are anonymous or secure.

We have classified thirteen electronic cash schemes, which have been fully described in the open literature, according to the services and mechanisms outlined in sections 2 and 3. Table 1 details the desired services for several electronic cash schemes. Table 2 indicates which mechanisms the electronic cash schemes in table 1 used to implement these services.

Mechanisms seem to be easily combined to form new electronic cash schemes. This is most easily demonstrated by looking at the use of the binary tree mechanism. This was first used with the cut and choose mechanism to form the cash scheme presented by Okamoto and Ohta (1992). Another combination using the binary tree mechanism is Eng and Okamoto's (1995) scheme which uses binary tree and single term coin mechanisms. Finally a third combination is Okamoto's (1995) scheme which uses binary tree and electronic license to present a new cash scheme.

		Services					
Designers	**Electronic Cash Schemes**	Anonymity	Security	Transferability	Divisibility	Scalability	Acceptability
Brands '95	Electronic Cash on the Internet	x	x	x		x	x
Chaum '89	Online Cash Checks	x	x		x		
Chaum, Boer et. al. '89	Efficient Offline Electronic Checks	x	x		x		
Chaum, Fiat and Naor '88	Untracable Electronic Cash	x	x				
Ferguson '93	Single Term Offline Coins	x	x				
Franklin and Yung '93	Secure and Efficient Offline Digital Money	x	x				
Hayes '90	Anonymous One Time Signatures and Flexible Untraceable Electronic Cash	x	x				
J.P. Boly et. al. '94	CAFE	x	x		x	x	
Mao '96	Lightweight Micro-Cash for the Internet	x	x	x	x		
Medvinsky and Neuman '93	NetCash	x	x	x		x	x
Okamoto '95	An Efficient Divisible Electronic Cash Scheme	x	x		x		
Okamoto and Ohta '91	Universal Electronic Cash	x	x	x	x		
Yacobi '94	Efficient Electronic Money	x	x				

Table 1 A Summary of Electronic Cash Services

Designers	Electronic Cash Schemes	Cut and Choose	Line Method	Single Term Coins	Electronic License	Blind Certification	Online Operation	Offline Operation	Hardware Dependent	Blind Digital Signatures	Binary Tree	Continuous Hash
Brands '95	Electronic Cash on the Internet					x		x	x			
Chaum '89	On-line Cash Checks						x			x		
Chaum, Boer et. al. '89	Efficient Off-line Electronic Checks	x						x		x		
Chaum, Fiat and Naor '88	Untraceable Electronic Cash	x						x		x		
Ferguson '93	Single Term Off-line Coins			x				x		x		
Franklin and Yung '93	Secure and Efficient Off-line Digital Money		x					x		x		
Hayes '90	Anonymous One Time Signatures and Flexible Untraceable Electronic Cash	x								x		
J.P. Boly et. al. '94	CAFE							x	x	x		
Mao '96	Lightweight Micro-Cash for the Internet					x		x				x
Medvinsky and Neuman '93	NetCash	x						x	x	x		
Okamoto '95	An Efficient Divisible Electronic Cash Scheme				x			x		x	x	
Okamoto and Ohta '91	Universal Electronic Cash	x						x		x	x	
Yacobi '94	Efficient Electronic Money					x		x				

Table 2 A Summary of Electronic Cash Mechanisms

The list of mechanisms in this paper is not complete. It is likely that new mechanisms will be designed to implement various services and be incorporated with some of the older mechanisms to develop new cash schemes. Designers need to be careful which mechanisms are selected. The advantages and disadvantages of specific mechanisms will also be included in the new cash schemes which contain them.

5. CONCLUSION

Electronic cash is an anonymous payment system which allows users to purchase goods or services electronically with privacy and security. This paper has identified some of the important services which a practical cash system should provide. These services include: security, privacy, transferability, divisibility, scalability and acceptability.

Once these required services were identified the paper investigated some of the mechanisms used to implement these services. The most common mechanisms used in the literature were: the cut and choose zero knowledge proof and off-line operation to provide security, blind digital signatures to provide anonymity and privacy, and the binary tree mechanism to provide divisibility of the electronic coin. Not all mechanisms were investigated in this paper. It is likely that new electronic cash scheme design will consist of a combination of existing mechanisms or of new mechanisms which provide the electronic cash services stated above.

There are a number of important issues that have not been covered in this paper but which must be considered in any practical electronic cash scheme. In particular the complexity analysis of the competing protocols and associated algorithms is a prime concern, especially because most schemes are implemented using smart cards. Other issues include interaction with legal and policy matters; recent schemes (Jakobsson and Yung 1996) have already suggested ways to limit anonymity with the cooperation of a trustee. We intend to cover all these concerns in future reports.

6. REFERENCES

J.-P. Boly et al. (1994) "The ESPRIT Project CAFE - High Security Digital Payment Systems", *Computer Security - ESORICS '94*, pp. 217-230, Springer-Verlag.

S. Brands (1995) "Electronic Cash on the Internet", In *Proceedings of the Internet Society 1995 Symposium on Network and Distributed System Security*, pp. 64-84.

D. Chaum (1983) "Blind Signatures for Untraceable Payments", In *Advances in Cryptology - Proceedings of CRYPTO '82*, pp. 199-203, Plenum Press.

D. Chaum (1989) "Online Cash Checks", *Advances in Cryptology - Proceedings of EUROCRYPT '89*, pp. 288-301.

D. Chaum, A. Fiat and M. Naor (1990) "Untraceable Electronic Cash", *Advances in Cryptology - Proceedings of CRYPTO '88*, pp. 319-327, Springer-Verlag.

T. Eng and T. Okamoto (1995), "Single-Term Divisible Electronic Coins", *Advances in Cryptography - Proceedings of EUROCRYPT '94 (LNCS 950)*, pp. 306-319, Springer-Verlag.

N. Ferguson (1994), "Single Term Off-Line Coins", *Advances in Cryptology - Proceedings of EUROCRYPT '93*, pp. 318-328, Springer-Verlag, 1994.

M. Franklin and M. Yung (1993) "Secure and Efficient Off-Line Digital Money", In *Proceedings of ICALP '93 (LNCS 700)*, pp. 265-276, Springer-Verlag, 1993.

B. Hayes (1990) "Anonymous One-Time Signatures and Flexible Untraceable Electronic Cash", *Advances in Cryptology - AUSCRYPT '90*, pp. 294-305, Springer-Verlag.

M. Jakobsson and M. Yung (1996) "Revokable and Versatile Electronic Money", *Third ACM Conference on Computer and Communications Security*, ACM Press, pp. 76-87.

W. Mao (1996) "Lightweight Micro-Cash for the Internet", *Computer Security - ESORICS '96*, Springer-Verlag, pp.15-32.

G. Medvinsky and B. C. Neuman (1993) "NetCash: A Design for Practical Electronic Currency on the Internet", *Proceedings of First ACM Conference on Computer and Communications Security*, pp. 102-196, ACM Press.

T. Okamoto (1995) "An Efficient Divisible Electronic Cash Scheme" *Advances in Cryptology - Proceedings of CRYPTO '95*, pp. 438-451, Springer-Verlag.

T. Okamoto and K. Ohta (1992) "Universal Electronic Cash", *Advances in Cryptology - Proceedings of CRYPTO '91*, pp. 324-337, Springer-Verlag.

M. O. Rabin (1978), "Digitalized Signatures", In *Foundations of Secure Computation*, Academic Press, NY.

R. L. Rivest and A. Shamir (1996) "PayWord and MicroMint: Two simple micropayment schemes", *RSA Security Conference*, January 1996.

C. P. Schnorr (1990) "Efficient Signature Generation for Smart Cards", *Advances in Cryptology - Proceedings of CRYPTO '89*, pp. 239-252, Springer-Verlag.

D. R. Simon (1996) "Anonymous Communication and Anonymous Cash", *Advances in Cryptology - Proceedings of CRYPTO '96*, Springer-Verlag, pp.61-73.

Y. Yacobi (1995) "Efficient Electronic Money", *Advances in Cryptology - Proceedings of ASIACRYPT '94*, pp. 153-163, Springer-Verlag.

Large scale elections by coordinating electoral colleges

A. Riera, J. Borrell, J. Rifà
Dept. d'Informàtica, Universitat Autònoma de Barcelona
Edifici C — 08193 Bellaterra — Catalonia (Spain)
Tel: + 34 3 581 17 77 — Fax: + 34 3 581 30 33
E-mail: andreu@ccd.uab.es

Abstract

In this paper we propose a truly very large scale voting scheme useful in national and international elections. We offer an implementable solution in which the voting authority is distributed among several voting centres. Each centre acts as an electoral college, carrying out a local scale ballot. The global tally is therefore computed by joining all partial tallies.

Our proposal consists on a hierarchical arrangement of the voting centres, strongly based on the use of X.500 Directory Service. Our scheme allows to solve many coordination problems: distribution of voters, coordination of the opening and closing times, management of the electoral roll, distribution of public keys, distribution of partial tallies, and computation of the global tally.

Keywords

Electronic voting schemes, X.500 Directory Service, wide area computer networks

1 INTRODUCTION

The first cryptographic scheme for secure electronic voting was introduced by Chaum (Chaum 1981). Many different proposals (over twenty) have appeared subsequently. Most of them consist in a set of cryptographic tools and protocols that are used together to fulfil the commonly accepted security requirements (Fujioka, Okamoto and Ohta 1992):

- *Completeness:* All valid votes are counted correctly.
- *Soundness:* The dishonest voter cannot disrupt the voting.
- *Privacy:* All votes must be secret.
- *Unreusability:* No voter can vote twice.
- *Eligibility:* No one who is not allowed to vote can vote.

- *Fairness:* The counting of ballots does not affect the voting.
- *Verifiability:* No one can falsify the result of the voting.

However, most of the proposals are designed without caring about the complexity of their possible real implementations. Consequently, the computation and communication costs usually prevent the development of a practical product.

Only four voting schemes have been implemented over a computer network. (Hassler and Posch 1995) and (Cramer and Cytron 1996) have been developed as simplifications of theoretical proposals —(Nurmi, Salomaa and Santean 1991) and (Fujioka, Okamoto and Ohta 1992), respectively—. However, such simplifications break some security requirements. A dishonest voter is allowed to disrupt the entire voting in (Hassler and Posch 1995), and a dishonest ballot collecting authority may break the fairness condition in (Cramer and Cytron 1996). In contrast, the proposals in (Hwang 1996) and (Borrell and Rifà 1996) were specially designed with practical implementations in mind. Furthermore, they adopt a conventional approach which has a better chance of gaining social acceptance. For example, (Borrell and Rifà 1996) uses an electoral board to administer the ballot.

Nevertheless, the designs of the four implemented schemes assume restricted environments involving a single voting centre. The number of voters is not expected to be large and the implementations are typically operated on a LAN. A single voting centre is clearly not enough when the number of voters is potentially very large. Even using simple protocols (as that proposed in (Fujioka, Okamoto and Ohta 1992)) a number of voting centres should be considered. Only (Hassler and Posch 1995) gives little directions on how to operate a hierarchy of voting centres, as an ampliation of the scheme, but without making more specific.

In this paper we present the design of an electronic voting scheme assuming a very large number of voters. It may be operated over a WAN or a group of interconnected networks (ideally the whole Internet). Our proposal is based on the concurrent operation of a set of electoral colleges (ECs), each of them carrying out a local ballot. We have adopted (Borrell and Rifà 1996) as the local voting scheme operated by the electoral colleges because it is specially concerned with the security requirements offered by the scheme.

The coordination of the set of electoral colleges poses several open questions that must be solved: distribution of voters, coordination of the opening and closing times, management of the electoral roll, distribution of public keys, distribution of partial tallies, and computation of the global tally. Our scheme offers mechanisms to solve these questions through a hierarchical arrangement of voting centres. We make extensive use of X.500 Directory Service (CCITT 1989a) to support the management of the whole system. We have adopted simplicity and efficiency as major requirements of our system, keeping in mind that the final goal is to practically implement the scheme.

The rest of the paper is structured as follows: In section 2 we show the overview of our model. Section 3 is concerned about the elaboration and use of the electoral roll by using X.500. Section 4 shows the policies related to key generation and key distribution procedures. Section 5 and 6 are devoted to the computation of the global tally from all partial results and its divulgation, respectively. Since all previous sections suppose an election that involves only one nation, section 7 discusses several questions that arise when an international voting has to be performed. Finally, section 8 contains the conclusions of the work, analyzing the security offered by the model.

2 OVERVIEW OF THE MODEL

The voting scheme presented in (Borrell and Rifà 1996) operates well in a restricted environment with a small comunity of voters, typically a LAN. However, it is not suitable for a large scale election. The ballot box and the electoral roll files could grow to unmanageable proportions. Even worst, the voting centre would easily become a bottleneck.

Clearly, in a wide area environment with a large number of users, voters must be distributed among many ECs. Such collecting centres should be operated concurrently, each caring only of a small number of voters. However, such point of view requires some mechanisms to assure the coordination of all ECs. It must be guaranteed, for instance, that a particular voter can only cast his/her vote to a unique EC. Moreover, this approach ends up with a number of partial tallies which should be joined. The protocols used to join the tallies must guarantee the security requirements of the ballot.

To solve these problems, we use a nation-wide hierarchical model in which the vertices represent different *voting authorities*. We call such hierarchy the *voting tree* (see Figure 1). The hierarchical arrangement is an effective way to distribute the voting authority among the members of the community. Moreover, the task of joining partial countings is extremely eased.

The leaves of the voting tree represent the ECs. Every EC carries out an independent ballot within a reduced group of voters. Intermediate nodes act as Counting Centres (CCs). Their main task is to join partial tallies from the nodes belonging to their corresponding subtrees. The outcomes are passed up through the tree until they reach the root, which performs the computation of the global nation-wide tally and publishes it. This last entity is not only a counting centre, but it also maintains the electoral roll and does some administrative tasks related to the elections. It is also responsible for publishing the valid voting options before the voting is initiated. We call it the National Voting Authority (NVA). The NVA is unique within its country and it has a permanent nature. It is intended to be the electronic version of the official organization that manages the electoral roll in conventional elections.

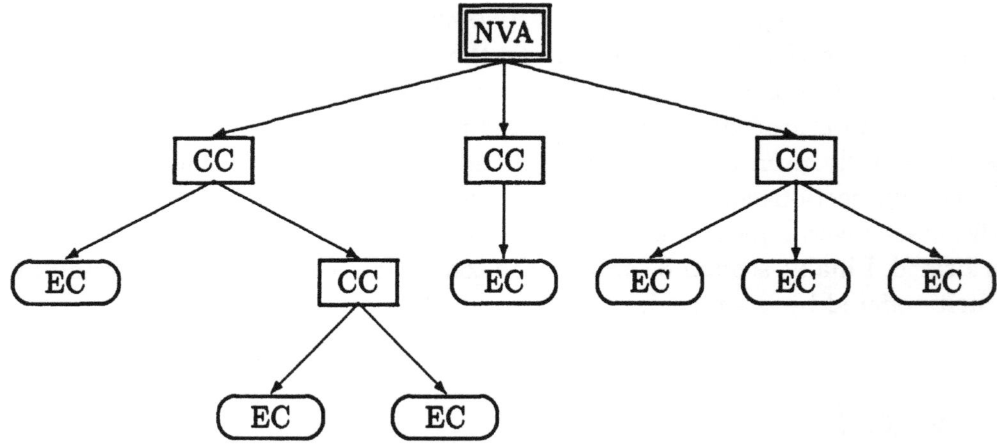

Figure 1 Hierarchical arrangement of voting authorities.

In Figure 1, we show an example of hierarchical arrangement of NVA, CCs and ECs. Any number of intermediate levels is possible. However, in order to simplify the discussions, in the rest of the paper we will suppose the voting tree has three levels: the root (NVA), an intermediate level (CCs), and the leaves (ECs).

3 MANAGEMENT OF THE ELECTORAL ROLL

In any election, the electoral roll must be used by the voting authority to determine whether a user is authorized or not to cast a vote. It can keep also a record of the voters who have already voted, to preserve the property of unreusability. Electronic voting schemes based on a single centre may use a locally stored file as electoral roll. In such case, any file format can be used. However, in a large scale scheme involving many voting centres, the electoral roll must be distributed and widely available on a commonly accepted format.

We plan to base the electoral roll on the CCITT X.500 Directory Service (CCITT 1989a). The main reasons are:

1. X.500 is an independent and totally distributed service which can be accessed from any point in the network. ECs do not need to care about it.
2. X.500 is standardized and therefore the uniformity of the operations on the Directory (consults, modifications) can be assured.
3. Access to the entries can be secured through strong authentication mechanisms (as described in X.509 (CCITT 1989b)).

We suggest the creation of a subtree on the X.500 Directory Information Tree (DIT), which should be used only for voting purposes. The NVA acts as the authority responsible for the allocation of names within this subtree (i.e., the naming authority). The shape of this subtree is determined by the naming structure chosen by the NVA. This structure reflects the relationships described in the voting tree introduced in last section. Therefore, the NVA must be represented by the root entry. Its immediately subordinate entries represent the CCs. Next subordinates represent ECs. Finally, leaves represent voters and, therefore, the electoral roll. The immediate superior of the NVA's entry should be the entry representing the country involved in the election. Figure 2 shows an example of a voting subtree on the DIT.

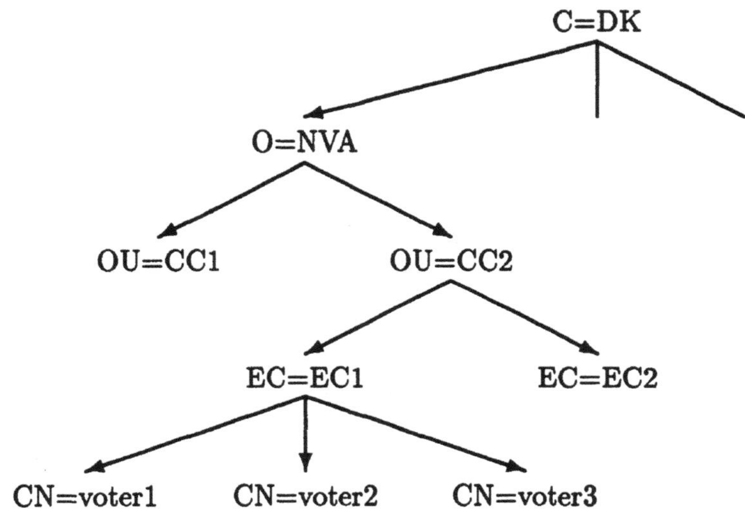

Figure 2 Voting subtree on the Directory Information Tree.

To create an independent subtree for the voting has the following advantages:

1. Duplicates are prevented if the naming structure of the subtree is carefully managed by the NVA. Each voter is assigned to only one EC only once. Note that every person may have different Distinguished Names disseminated across the whole DIT. Therefore, if already existing individual entries were used, mechanisms to solve the ambiguity had to be devised.
2. The shape of the subtree itself contains information about the hierachical relationship between the voting entities. This allows, for instance, to know which CC corresponds to a certain EC, just by examining the EC's Distingüished Name.

Concerning the electoral roll, there is besides a non-technical question that must be solved. It is related to the distribution of voters among the set of ECs. There are several alternatives to approach the problem. Each of them responds to a certain policy. It could be convenient, for example, to distribute voters on a territorial basis. In this way, each voter may be assigned to an EC depending on his/her locality.

In our model, we suppose that voters are users of a particular computer system that, in turn, is part of a local area network or group of interconnected local area networks (e.g., a company or university network). Such LAN environment is usually managed by an administrator. We assume every LAN will operate its own EC. The distribution of the software, tools and documentation required to operate the ECs is a task of the NVA. Letting voters cast their vote in their own LAN implies high efficiency at voting time. In addition, it is minimally intrusive to voters' normal behavior.

X.500 Object Entries

The NVA is represented in the Directory by an object of class *organization + strongAuthenticationUser*. The object class *strongAuthenticationUser* provides the attribute *UserCertificate*. The need for certificates will be discussed in section 4. In addition, the NVA's entry should support an additional attribute specific for our purposes: *talliesEncryptionKey*. The aim of this attribute will be explained in section 5. The ASN.1 definition of the Tallies Encryption Key is:

```
talliesEncryptionKey ::=  ATTRIBUTE
                          WITH ATTRIBUTE-SYNTAX
                               SignedKey

SignedKey ::=  SIGNED SEQUENCE {
                     votingDate             UTCTime
                     subjectPublicKeyInfo   SubjectPublicKeyInfo }
```

The entry of the NVA must be protected against creation and deletion of new components, updates, and naming modifications. Suck kind of access must be granted only to the NVA, after the proper authentication using cryptographically derived credentials (digital signatures). Detect, compare and read access to the attributes of the entry must be granted to anyone.

CCs are represented in the Directory by objects of class *organizationalUnit + strongAuthenticationUser*. The access rights of their entries follow the same phylosophy as that of the entry of the NVA. Only the CC represented by a particular entry is allowed to do writing operations on the attributes. The exception is the naming access category, which should be granted only to the NVA.

ECs are represented in the Directory by objects of class *electoralCollege + strongAuthenticationUser*. *electoralCollege* is a newly defined class with the following ASN.1 definition:

```
electoralCollege ::=  OBJECT-CLASS
                          SUBCLASS OF top
                          MUST CONTAIN {
                               electoralCollegeName,
                               alreadyClosed }
                          MAY CONTAIN {
                               organizationalAttributeSet }

electoralCollegeName ::=  ATTRIBUTE
                          WITH ATTRIBUTE-SYNTAX
                               caseIgnoreStringSyntax
                          (SIZE(1..ub-organizational-unit-name))

alreadyClosed ::=  ATTRIBUTE
                   WITH ATTRIBUTE-SYNTAX
                        booleanSyntax
```

As before, all the attributes in the entry must be protected against modification, addition and deletion by anyone except the EC represented by the entry. Detect, compare and read access categories may be granted to anyone. Again, the naming access category is reserved to the naming authority (the NVA).

Finally, voters are represented in the electoral roll by objects of class *person*. Note that we have not included the additive class *strongAuthenticationUser*, as before. It is not necessary to have a *UserCertificate* attribute in the entries of the electoral roll, because voters already own a public key certificate, held in another of their entries in the DIT. However, in order to easily find such entry from the electoral roll, a dereferencing attribute must be included in voters' entries: *voterIdentity*. This attribute can be used to identify and to find the corresponding user's entry. In addition a newly defined attribute must be present in the entry of a voter in the electoral roll: *voteAlreadyCast*.

```
voterIdentity ::=  ATTRIBUTE
                   WITH ATTRIBUTE-SYNTAX
                        distinguishedNameSyntax
                   SINGLE VALUE

voteAlreadyCast ::=  ATTRIBUTE
                     WITH ATTRIBUTE-SYNTAX
                          booleanSyntax
```

All attributes in a voter's entry may be compared, detected and read by anyone. Naming access must be granted only to the NVA. Addition and deletion of new components (attributes or attribute values) are also reserved to the NVA. The attribute *voterIdentity* must be updatable only by the NVA, whereas the attribute *voteAlreadyCast* must be updatable only by the corresponding EC.

4 KEY MANAGEMENT

In any cryptographic protocol involving public key cryptography, communicating peers must have knowledge of their partners' public keys. In this way, anyone is able to encrypt messages to every recipient and to verify any of their signatures. In our large scale voting model, asymmetric key pairs must be generated for each voter, each EC, each CC and the NVA. Public components must be properly certified by an independent infrastructure of trusted certification authorities (CAs). The X.500 Directory acts as a repository for the certificates.

The key generation and key certification procedures must follow different policies depending on whether the subject is the NVA, a CC, an EC or a voter.

The NVA must generate its own keys rather than allowing an independent CA to do it. The reason is the sensitiviness of such keys. However, the public key must be sent to a CA wich issues the corresponding certificate. The keys of the NVA do not have to be generated for each election but they may be used for several years (until the certificate expires). The certificate has to be published on the X.500 entry of the NVA.

The NVA generates also the asymmetric key pair formed by the Tallies Encryption Key and the Tallies Decryption Key. These keys are used when joining partial tallies (see section 5). The Tallies Encryption Key is not certified by any independent CA but it is rather directly signed by the NVA and placed on its X.500 entry. The Tallies Decryption Key must be stored in a safe local environment.

In contrast with the NVA, CCs are constituted just before each voting takes place. They may even be operated by different people each time. This suggests a new key pair must be generated for each ballot. As happens with the NVA, every CC generates its own keys and sends the public component to a certain CA which issues the certificate. After that, the certificate is published on the X.500 entry of the CC.

Every EC is operated by an electoral board of non-technical members. To guarantee the quality of the process of key generation, ECs' keys are directly generated by a CA. Note that ECs manage only a small number of voters and this makes their keys less sensitive than those of the CCs or the NVA.

Every CC orders to a certain CA the generation and certification of key pairs for all ECs which are under it on the voting tree. ECs must receive their key pairs by out of band means (at least the private component) from the CA. For instance, the members of the electoral board can physically pick up the keys at CA's site. Each EC is responsible for publishing the received certificate on its X.500 entry.

The case of voters is somewhat different from those of the other voting entities. The difference is that a voter, as a person, has many other roles not related with the elections. Consequently, it can be assumed that each voter will already own a public key, already certified and published on some entry on the X.500 Directory.

Such certificate is already used by the user for any purpose (e.g., contract signing or electronic commerce). If a voter does not have any key pair yet, it must be generated before the voting takes place.

It can happen also that a voter has several key pairs, under different Distinguished Names. In such case, only one of them must be used for the voting. The chosen Distinguished Name must appear on the voter's entry at the electoral roll, as we have seen in section 3. In this way, a second access to X.500 allows to retrieve the proper public key.

The NVA is who must choose the identity (in practice, the public key) which will be used for the ballot among all those owned by a particular voter. The criteria used to choose the identity must be settled according to the established voting policies. There must be a complaining period, after the elaboration of the electoral roll and before the voting is initiated. Voters can force the NVA to make the proper changes and corrections on the electoral roll. Note that if users were allowed to directly choose their public key and send their decision to the NVA, communication overheads could be much greater.

5 JOINING PARTIAL TALLIES

The main task of the set of CCs is to gather partial tallies from the corresponding ECs. Tallies are joined, resulting wider partial countings. The process of joining partial tallies should guarantee the following properties:

1. No partial tallies must be public before the last EC is closed.
2. ECs must be able to verify the treatment their partial tallies have received in the corresponding CC.
3. At the phase of outcomes divulgation, it must be possible to elaborate statistics on every EC and every CC basis.

When the electoral board of a particular EC closes the local ballot, the control is passed to a counting process which elaborates the tally from the contents of the ballot box. As in conventional elections, once the ballot box has been opened and all the ballot papers counted, they are destroyed and only the final tally remains valid. The tally has a much simpler format than the ballot box. It is just a list containing pairs of the form *(voting option, number of votes)*. To enforce the uniformity of all partial tallies, the NVA publishes (for instance, on the Web) the list of valid options before the ballot starts. Obviously, the list must be signed.

Any partial tally should be sent from the EC to the corresponding CC. Its simple format assures low communication overheads between ECs and CCs. Note that privacy of individual voters cannot be compromised at the CCs, since any personal information contained in the ballot box has been removed in the tally format.

A major threat to the property of fairness appears when the opening and closing times of the ECs are not simultaneous. If the geographic area involved in the election is totally included in a single time zone, then all ECs open and close at the same time. However, to accomodate the major number of scenarios, we have supposed that ECs are scattered over several time zones. No partial results must be made public before all ECs have reached their closing time.

Our model guarantees the fairness of the voting by means of the Tallies Encryption Key (TEK). This public encryption key is generated by the NVA at the beginning of each election. Every EC retrieves the TEK from the X.500 entry of the NVA, and uses it to encrypt its partial tally. Therefore, CCs always receive partial tallies which are encrypted. The Tallies Decryption Key (TDK) is private and known only to the NVA. This assures nobody (but the NVA) is able to decrypt partial countings.

When an electoral board closes its local ballot, it sets the flag *alreadyClosed* in the EC's X.500 entry. In this way, the NVA can monitor the state of all ECs by checking these flags. When all ECs have closed, the NVA reveals the TDK to the CCs, thus allowing them to initiate the joining process.

Knowing the TDK, every CC can decrypt all partial tallies it has received, and elaborate a wider count with them. Such outcome must be sent to the NVA, which performs the ultimate joining of partial countings. In this way the global nation-wide tally is obtained. Note that the countings sent from the CCs to the NVA do not need to be encrypted. They cannot affect the voting because all ECs are already closed.

The authenticity and integrity of the data that is passed up through the voting tree must also be guaranteed. Before encrypting and sending any partial tally to a CC, ECs must sign a hash of the tally with their own private key. In the same way, CCs must sign their countings before sending them to the NVA. These signatures are universally verifiable by using the public keys held in the corresponding X.500 entries. Since public keys have been certified by independent trusted third parties, no voting authority can tamper the signatures on the tallies of lower entities. Moreover, every electoral board keeps a copy of its partial tally after it has been sent to the CC. In this way, it is possible to replace the tally if it is damaged or lost.

6 DIVULGATION OF OUTCOMES

To allow statistics on every EC basis, not only the global tally has to be divulgated, but all partial tallies and countings have to be published too. Publication of outcomes can be done on the Web due to its wide availability and scope.

The NVA and the CCs are responsible for the publication of countings. Every electoral board can verify the correct treatment of its partial tally by verifying its signature on the published outcomes. Nevertheless, anybody can do this task since all signatures are universally verifiable. Figure 3 shows the format of the list of outcomes published on the Web by the NVA.

Date of the election	
List of valid options	
Global nation-wide tally	
Partial counting 1	Signature of CC 1
Partial counting 2	Signature of CC 2
Partial counting 3	Signature of CC 3
⋮	
NVA's signature on all fields	

Figure 3 Divulgation of outcomes by the NVA.

CCs publish on the Web a document containing a list of the same characteristics of that presented in Figure 3. However, the field corresponding to the global tally is concerned only with the partial counting of that CC, and all partial outcomes are from ECs and not from CCs. Partial tallies are accompanied by the corresponding signature from the EC. The whole data structure is signed by the CC. Such document allows statistics on every EC basis. Note that CCs do not have to wait for any authorization before publishing their partial countings. No data has to be kept secret after the revelation of the TDK by the NVA.

7 INTERNATIONAL ELECTIONS

Preceding sections have supposed that the election affected only one country. If several countries are involved (for example in votings carried out by the States of the European Union) some specifications have to be considered. In particular, it has to be expected that each country would want to have absolute authority over its partial tally and its electoral roll. Therefore, it does not seem logical to convert each NVA on a CC (although it is possible from the technical point of view).

The NVA of each country would still remain responsible for maintainig the corresponding voting subtree on X.500. It would also have to generate the TEK and TDK, and control their use within the country. Finally, it would elaborate the global tally for that country. In addition, an international voting authority (operated by an official organization like the European Commission) may act just as a counting centre to join all tallies from each country. We call such centre the International Counting Centre (ICC).

In each country the election takes place as it has been explained in previous sections. The only difference is that when all the ECs of a country have closed, the corresponding NVA does not reveal the TDK but it sends to the ICC a signed message indicating such condition. Once all the involved countries have informed the ICC about the closing of all ECs, the ICC authorizes the opening (decryption) of all partial tallies. This is achieved through the diffusion of a signed message from the ICC to the NVAs. The TDK for each country is then revealed by the corresponding NVA. Whenever a nation-wide tally is computed, the NVA has to send it to the ICC, signed but not encrypted. The signature removes any possibility of tampering. Divulgation of outcomes should follow the same scheme depicted in section 6. This allows the elaboration of statistics also on every country basis.

To allow reliable verification of the signed messages interchanged between the ICC and the NVAs, their corresponding public keys must be known to each other. The ICC can retrieve NVAs' public keys from X.500. The distribution of ICC's public key is made also through certificates and X.500. In addition (due to its sensitiviness), out of band means may also be employed. This would not imply great overheads since the number of out of band communications would be very low (it would equal the number of countries involved in the election).

Note that elections inside very large companies can also involve several countries because of their multinational nature. However, such elections can follow the national model (i.e., without ICC) since only one policy is used in the whole community of voters.

8 CONCLUSIONS

In this paper we have presented a realistic proposal for a large scale electronic voting scheme. The ballot process is distributed through the concurrent operation of a number of Electoral Colleges. Each of them carries out a small scale voting, controlled by an electoral board. Partial tallies are joined by means of a hierarchical arrangement of Counting Centres. The figure of the National Voting Authority, at the root of the voting tree, is a permanent entity which cares about all administrative and preparative tasks related with the elections.

The model requires the following tools and elements:

- X.500 Directory: The naming structure of the voting subtree reflects the hierarchical relationships between all voting entities. The electoral roll is maintained in voters' entries. Moreover, the Directory acts as repository of public key certificates.
- World Wide Web: It is used to publish the valid voting options before the election, and the outcomes after it.
- Certification infrastructure: A proper arrangement of Trusted Third Parties, independent from the election, issues the required public key certificates.

Assuming that the local voting scheme operated by each EC fulfils the commonly accepted security requirements (Fujioka, Okamoto and Ohta 1992), our proposal extends the security to wide area scope:

- **Privacy:** Every EC sends to the corresponding CC a partial tally, but not the ballot box in its original form (which is effectively erased when the local electoral board close the voting). The partial tally does not contain any information on individual ballot papers.
- **Soundness, eligibility and unreusability:** Secure access to X.500 is based on strong authentication mechanisms. They guarantee that each voter has a unique entry, and that only the authorized EC is allowed to modify the attribute *voteAlreadyCast.*
- **Completeness and verifiability:** Partial countings that are passed up through the voting tree are always protected by a digital signature. Such signature disables any corruption since all public keys are certified by an independent certification structure.
- **Fairness:** The TDK that allows to decrypt partial countings remains secret until all the electoral boards have closed. Only the NVA (which is a high-level entity) has to be trusted.

ACKNOWLEDGEMENTS

This work has been partially funded by the Spanish Government Commission CICYT, through a grant to the Combinatorics and Digital Communication Group.

REFERENCES

Borrell, J. and Rifà, J. (1996) An Implementable Secure Voting Scheme. *Computers & Security*, **15**, 327–338.

Cramer, L.F. and Cytron, R.K. (1996) Design and Implementation of a Practical Security-Conscious Electronic Polling System. *Technical Report WUCS-96-02*, Washington University, St. Louis.

CCITT (1989) Blue Book, Volume VIII – Fascicle VIII.8, Data Communication Networks: *Directory, Recommendations X.500–X.521*, Geneva.
ISO-9594: Information Processing Systems – Open Systems Interconnection – *The Directory.*

CCITT (1989) Recommendation X.509. *The Directory – Authentication Framework*, Geneva.
See also ISO–9594–8.

Chaum, D. (1981) Untraceable Electronic Mail, Return Addresses and Digital Pseudonyms. *Communications of the ACM*, **24**, 84–88.

Fujioka, A., Okamoto, T. and Ohta K. (1992) A Practical Secret Voting Scheme for Large Scale Elections. *LNCS, Auscrypt '92*, Springer Verlag.

Hassler, V. and Posch, R. (1995) A LAN Voting Protocol, in *Proceedings of IFIP SEC '95*, Ed. Chapman & Hall, 176–189.

Hwang, J. (1996) A Conventional Approach to Secret Balloting in Computer Networks. *Computers & Security*, **15**, 249–263.

Nurmi, H., Salomaa, A. and Santean, L. (1991) Secret Ballot Elections in Computer Networks. *Computers & Security*, **10**, 553–560.

BIOGRAPHY

Andreu Riera, Joan Borrell and Josep Rifà are members of the Combinatorics and Digital Communication Group at the Autonomous University of Barcelona.

Andreu Riera (Manresa, 1970) obtained the graduate degree in Computer Science in 1993 at the AUB. Since then he is working towards the Ph.D. degree in Computer Science in the field of Network Security.

Joan Borrell (Girona, 1965) obtained the graduate degree and the Ph.D. degree in Computer Science, in 1989 and 1996, respectively, at the AUB.

Josep Rifà (Manlleu, 1951) obtained the graduate degree in Mathematics at the University of Barcelona in 1973. He obtained the Ph.D. degree in Computer Science in 1987 at the AUB.

MVS-SAT : A Security Administration Tool to support SMF Protocol Data Evaluation

C. Eckert and Th. Stoesslein
Munich University of Technology, Department of Computer Science
D-80290 Munich, Germany, eckertc@informatik.tu-muenchen.de

Abstract

The paper presents a tool called MVS-SAT which supports extraction, off-line analysis and evaluation of security-related data recorded by the System Management Facility (SMF) running under MVS on IBM mainframe computers.

MVS-SAT consists of a PC and a MVS-host part. The PC part offers a simple user interface providing services to specify data sets which should be extracted from the SMF database by the host part of the tool. Furthermore, the PC-part offers services and databases to analyze and evaluate the extracted data via SQL-queries. Decoupling data extraction from its evaluation enables to implement the PC-part completely independent of any MVS version and to keep the tool extensible and adaptive.

Keywords

Security Management, Security Evaluation, Audit, Control, SMF

1 INTRODUCTION

Auditing of user activity usually serves as an effective preventive measure if a potential intruder is convinced that a security administrator will actually examine and analyze the audit data. Unfortunately, most audit logs maintain the recorded information in a format that is largely unreadable by a human being.

Automated intrusion detection tools (e.g. (Denning, 1986)) have been developed earlier to process and interpret the information that is recorded in audit logs. Intrusion detection is intended as means to identify potential malicious or undesirable activity. To accomplish this task intrusion detection tools need some kind of profiling describing typical and expected behavior of each user of the system. The main task of intrusion detection is to compare expected behavior with observed behavior. Hence, auditing mechanisms are required that record all information needed to perform this comparison.

Several utilities already exist to support audit and control of mainframe computers. SMF (System Management Facility) (cf SMF manual SMF, 1995) running on IBM mainframe computers under MVS (cf Johnson, 1991) is an example of such a utility. With SMF a huge amount of information is recorded. Usually, this data is used for tuning the operating system and for performing accounting. But the data gathered can be exploited with respect to security investigations as well.

Though a huge amount of security-relevant information is available intrusion detection tools just exploit a fraction of this information leaving worthy information uninspected. Hence, within many computing environments a great amount of a security administrator's daily work is still spent with off-line analysis and inspection of system log and audit files to detect potential security problems.

Faced with this situation in a computing environment running IBM/MVS we developed a simple tool offering some support for the security administrator to inspect SMF data logs with respect to security relevant entries.

In this paper we will present MVS-SAT (the acronym stands for Security Administration Tool). MVS-SAT supports extraction, off-line analysis and inspection of security-related data recorded by SMF. The tool has been developed in cooperation with an organization being responsible for checking the security of the computing environment of banking companies.

Note, that our tool has been neither developed to detect security holes within the underlying operating system nor is it a tool to evaluate a system according to security evaluation criteria like the TCSEC criteria (DoD, 1985). In contrast, our tool is designed and implemented to supports off-line investigations of a given system configuration, to analyze how the available security services are used and whether there is any evidence that security services can be circumvented by malicious users.

The rest of the paper is organized as follows. The next section gives a brief overview over MVS and SMF. Section 3 presents the main features of MVS-SAT and gives some examples to clarify how the tool can be used. Section 4 concludes the paper.

2 BACKGROUND

2.1 MVS

MVS (Johnson, 1991) is a mainframe operating system developed by IBM since 1974. Due to this long period of time MVS has undergone considerable changes while trying to keep compatible with existing versions of the operating system. As a consequence, MVS is by now a very complex software system. New system services have been continuously added to the existing kernel. These new features can be activated and configured via specific parameter values at system startup time or dynamically during the lifetime of the system. Hence, system services can be activated and configured through thousands of system parameters where each parameter value can influence other system components in an unforeseen way leading to a completely uncontrollable system. Paans (Paans, 1989) provides detailed insight in the internal structures of MVS.

Due to the complexity of the system (more than 10 million lines of code) no verified source code can be provided. To give a little impression of what we are talking about: 9 times a year about 1500 patches for MVS and IBM supported products running under MVS are delivered.

As verification is not possible we must at least test and analyze the system and its main components like the MVS-kernel comprising for instance SMF, the Job Entry Subsystem (JES), and system library programs APF (authorized program facility) running in privileged mode.

RACF (Resource Access Control Facility) (cf RACF manual (RACF, 1995)), the software to control accesses to critical resources, is not part of the MVS kernel and can be configured and installed separately. Hence, an evaluation of MVS security must comprise an analysis of the correct installation and integration of RACF (cf Conyers, 1991).

The prerequisite to perform security tests is an appropriate audit facility that records relevant system activities. Audit and control of MVS are for example addressed in (Conyers, 1991) and (Soper, 1989). MVS contains three major audit facilities: (1) EREP, (2) SYSLOG and (3) SMF. With the Environment Recording and Editing Program (EREP) faults of the underlying hardware are recorded. SYSLOG gathers all activities concerning the operator terminal. Examples of such activities are start and termination of jobs or messages from RACF concerning for instance access denials. SMF will be addressed in more detail in the next subsection.

2.2 System Management Facility (SMF)

System Management Facility is the most important audit facility of MVS. SMF offers services to record data about resource consumption and about access behavior of single jobs (users), i.e. which files have been accessed and so on. At system startup-time the operator can determine which data should be logged by SMF but this configuration can be changed dynamically during system execution. The data recorded is first stored in data logs maintained in main memory and these logs are then periodically written to disk.

SMF knows 256 different record types (cf SMF, 1995) which do not have a common structure. To access a specific information within a data record the start address of the required section is needed. The computation of this address requires loading of the whole data record. The heterogeneity and lack of uniformity of the SMF record types is very cumbersome, as a tool that tries to extract specific data from these records can not rely on any a priori information about position and length of the needed data being stored within a specific record.

Among other system components SMF audits RACF, RMF (Resource Measurement Facility), and JES. Information about SMF itself, that is about the selected values of the parameters to configure the facility are recorded in specific SMF record types as well. Depending on the selected parameter values different features of SMF can be activated or deactivated.

By now it should be evident that SMF records a lot of security related data like information about (1) all activities concerning system components being involved in performing access control. Especially, activities activating security related components or altering the configuration of security related components can be recorded. Recording data about which security services with which parameter values have been active during specific periods of time is very useful to detect potential security holes. (2) SMF gathers information about all actions concerning altering and management of access rights as well as (3) information about all unexpected accesses and access attempts.

Handling the amount of recorded data

A SMF log file stores in average 200.000 – 1.500.000 data records per 24 hours. Based on an average record length of 1Kbytes and an average amount of 500.000 records stored a day this results in memory requirements of 15GByte a month. The issue of system audit and control involves the task of inspecting and analyzing this huge amount of data.

To support the data evaluation only insufficient tools and facilities are available in MVS environments. One of the available facilities is the Dump Utility which allows to filter specific records and data sets. Major drawbacks of this facilities are that accessing an individual data field within a record is not possible and in addition, the output produced by the Dump Utility is nearly unreadable because it consist of raw hex representations.

Due to the huge amount of data the filtered data still contains an enormous amount of information. Even worse, most of this information is of no use for security evaluation, as it just records data concerning expected, that is, average behavior of users of the system. Using available filtering facilities a security administrator is still flooded with data which must be inspected 'by hand'. This is a time-consuming and error-prone task. Hence, the available utilities do not provide a pragmatic aid for the security administrator.

With respect to the evaluation of RACF data-sets the RACF Report Writer or other languages to query and evaluate RACF data sets can be used. Major problems with these facilities are that they are primarily directed towards tuning and that they are restricted to predefined record types and predefined evaluation criteria lacking flexibility needed with respect to more general security evaluations.

To summarize, depending on the given system configuration a SMF log may contain data concerning nearly all relevant system activities. The information is stored in an extremely complicated format, which aggravates evaluation considerably. SMF records enormous amounts of data per day which requires a proper filtering of the relevant from the irrelevant information where the amount of the latter preponderates the former considerably. Existing utilities provide just insufficient support to filter data according to criteria that can be specified dynamically and adapted to specific requirements of security audit and control. As security problems involve different components of a system it is necessary to combine information stemming from different data records, but as far as we know such a facility is not offered yet. In addition, existing utilities lack facilities to present the filtered data in a comprehensive and readable way.

3 MVS SECURITY ADMINISTRATION TOOL

3.1 Overview

We have designed and implemented a tool called MVS-SAT which supports the extraction and evaluation of security-related SMF-data. MVS-SAT offers a user interface which can dynamically be adapted to individual user requirements concerning the data to be extracted and analyzed.

A major issue in logging and auditing is to guarantee that all relevant data is actually gathered, i.e. that the log information is complete. As this requires detailed knowledge and deep insight in the complex relationships between different operating system components as well as knowledge about the features offered by audit facilities configuring the system appropriately can not be performed automatically by a tool. But an appropriate tool can offer means to facilitate this task in order to reduce the likelihood of overseeing important things due to the complexity of the task. A tool comprising certain security tests checking the security of a given configuration would be helpful. Such tools have recently been developed for network environments, e.g. SATAN. Unfortunately, those tools are not appropriate for mainframe configurations because they only offer a static set of test scenarios analyzing security holes stemming from well-known flaws within standard network services. Within our tool we decided to maintain a library of test scenarios which can be dynamically adapted and extended with user-defined security scenarios.

To check whether the selected configuration matches his security requirements the security administrator must investigate and analyze the audit data. This can hardly be performed automatically but the task can considerably be facilitated. In an average MVS installation the security administrator is typically faced with 10 - 30 million SMF-data sets per month filling hundreds of pages of a paper listings. The task of inspecting this huge amount of data is very time consuming and error prone. MVS-SAT offers means to reduce this huge amount of protocol data by extracting data according to conditions specified by the security administrator. The extracted data is made available for the administrator via a graphical interface. In addition, the tool aims to serve as online manual presenting all information needed concerning SMF data record's structures in an easy to use and in a comprehensive manner.

MVS-SAT comprises two main components: a MVS host part and a PC part. Figure 1 depicts an overview over the components of MVS-SAT. Below the dotted line the components of the host part and above the line the ones of the PC-part are depicted. The grey boxes describe the software routines being implemented on the host and the PC respectively. The various databases maintained by the tool are given by ovals.

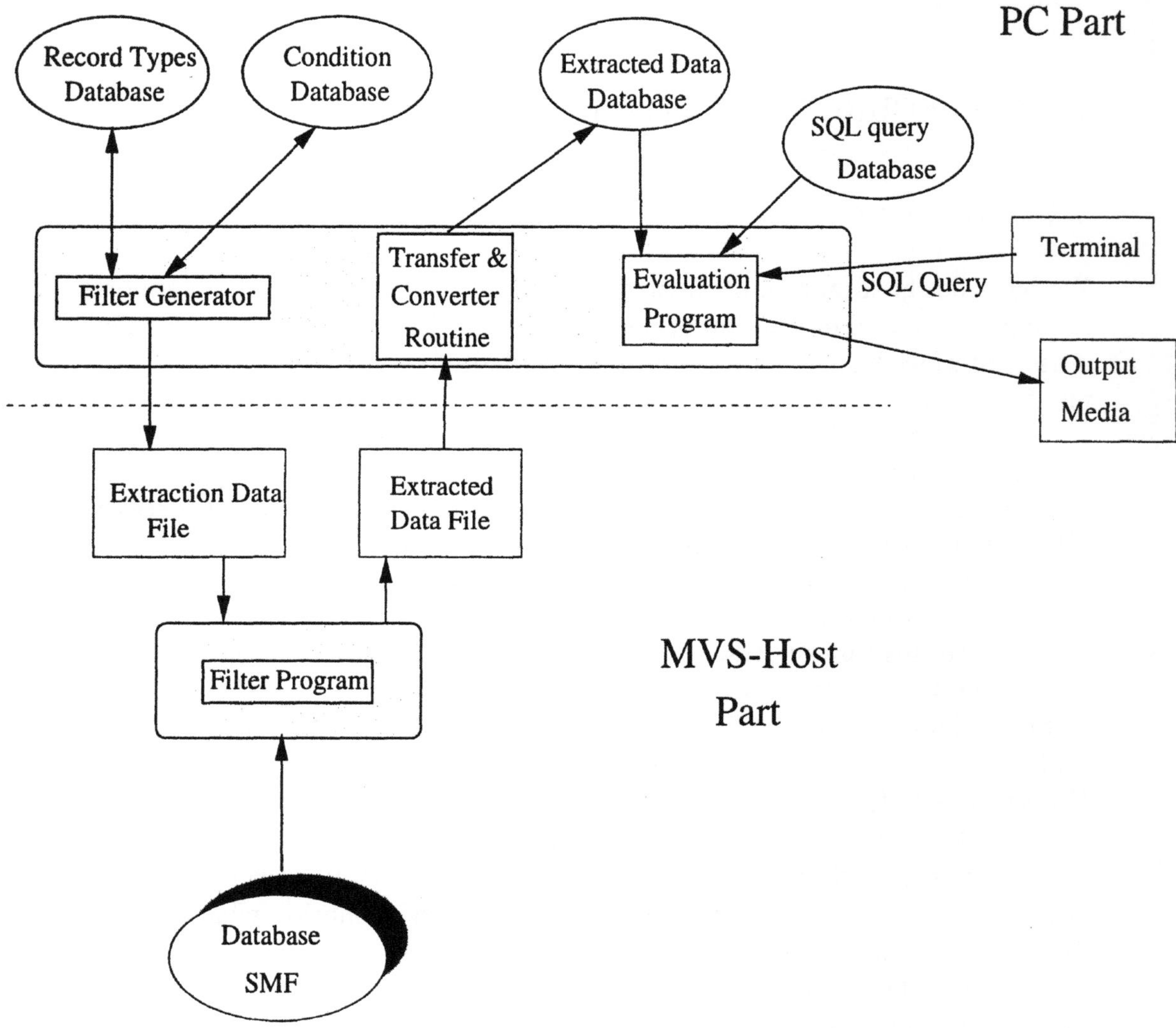

Figure 1 Overview over MVS-SAT

The main task of the host component of the tool is to extract desired data records out of the SMF database. The filter program reads the extraction data file, containing the information needed by the program to extract the required data items from the SMF-database. The extracted data is written into the extracted data file and then transfered to the PC.

The main task of the PC component is to generate the extraction data file based on user-defined extraction conditions and to send this file to the host. After receiving the extracted data file from the host it is the task of the PC part to convert the extracted data into appropriate database formats enabling a SQL-based evaluation where SQL-queries are specified by the user. Finally, the PC part offers means to support the evaluation of the extracted data. Decoupling data extraction from its evaluation enables to implement the PC-part completely independent of any MVS version and to keep it extensible and adaptive. That is, the PC-part can easily keep path with for instance changing SMF versions.

3.2 PC-Part

The PC part of MVS-SAT provides a user interface offering a simple menu which can be used to handle the tool. Figure 2 sketches the main structure of the PC interface menus.

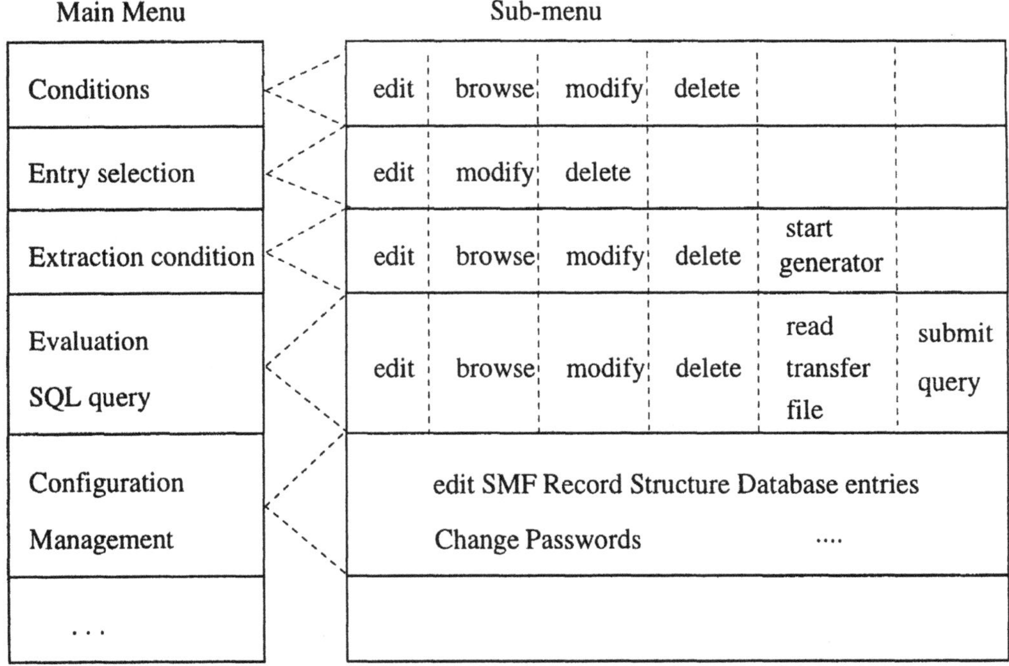

Figure 2 Menu structure of the PC interface

Usually, an evaluation of SMF audit data starts with the specification of the so called extraction conditions. To edit user-defined extraction conditions the security administrator selects the `extraction condition` button of the menu and then the `edit` button of the sub-menu. After the user has finished the specification of extraction conditions he clicks the `start generator` button. This activates the filter generator program which compiles the specified conditions into the extraction data file and automatically transfers this file to the host. The host executes the filter program and sends back the extracted data.

Via the menu button `read transfer file` in the menu `evaluation` the user can now select the option to convert the transfered data into database formats. As a result a conversion routine is executed which transforms each SMF record type contained in the transfered file into a type-specific database. The extracted data is now prepared to be used.

The user can evaluate the extracted data by submitting specified SQL queries to the PC evaluation routine. Within the menu `SQL query` several sub-menus are offered to edit queries, to browse through an existing query database, to select one of these queries and to modify it in a syntactically correct manner. SQL queries can be stored in the query database for later reuse by using user-defined names. Each such database entry describes the security problem being addressed with the specific query. Hence, the database contains a library of predefined security scenarios to evaluate a specific configuration. A user of MVS-SAT can browse through this library of existing queries taking advantage of the accumulated knowledge of previously performed security investigations. As mentioned above, the database entries can be altered and enhanced via the SQL query menu as well.

User-defined Extraction Conditions

As already mentioned, a menu is offered to specify extraction conditions in a syntactical correct way. Each extraction condition may comprise several conditions. Each condition may concern a different SMF record type. Hence, the first step in specifying extraction conditions is to specify these conditions. In a subsequent step the user has to combine these conditions applying logical operators AND or OR. As our tool offers a quite comfortable user-interface the user must not cope with translating its conditions into the format that can be understood by the filter program. During the execution of the filter program each SMF database entry is checked whether it meets the condition.

To edit a condition a specific editing-mask is provided via the menu button `conditions` and sub-menu button `edit`. In addition to edit a new condition a user can browse through a pool of previously defined conditions, can select one of these conditions and can modify it if necessary. New conditions or modified ones can be saved under a new user-defined name for later re-use.

Example:

If you want to analyze whether RACF has been active during Initial Program Load (IPL) you can specify a condition that extracts all record types number 81 being logged at a time that lies within a specific time interval because the information needed is held in type 81 records. $\triangle$

As mentioned above, each record type of a SMF data set contains different entries with a completely different structure. Hence, each condition must contain sufficient information to enable the selection of the required data items. To fulfil this requirement each condition contains the (1) **number of the record type** which should be analyzed, (2) **a list of record type entries** which should be checked against the condition, the specification of the condition itself consisting of an (3) **operator** (e.g. $=$, $\leq$) and of (4) a **comparison value** which specifies the criteria to be fulfilled.

Having specified the individual conditions, the whole extraction condition is created by composing conditions using logical operators. Again, condition composition is guided by a specific editing mask.

Example:
Imagine that a system administrator wants to know, who had initiated a specific job X in 1996. The required information can be retrieved from record type number 20. Job activation time is recorded in entry SMF20RSD of record type 20 and the name of the job is recorded in entry SMF20JBN.
The whole extraction condition specification consists of at least three single conditions:
C1 = SMF20RSD $\geq$ 0096001F; C2 = SMF20RSD $\leq$ 0096365F;
C3 = SMF20JBN = X;
The extraction condition is given by EC = C1 AND C2 AND C3. $\triangle$

Besides the conditions just explained each extraction condition specifies a list of record type entries which should be extracted from the SMF database. Whenever a recorded data set of the given record type fulfils the specified condition, the entries addressed with the entry list are extracted from the SMF database and stored in the extracted data file for later evaluation.

Example: (cont.)
Consider again the above example. The list of extracted entries comprises an entry SMF20UID recording the user identification UID of the user who had started the specific job X in 1996. $\triangle$

As it is very difficult for a security administrator to remember the meaning of the 256 different record types each comprising a lot of different entries our tool includes an online manual support describing every record type and its entry fields.

3.3 Host-Part

The MVS-host part of MVS-SAT comprises the filter program and a process which starts the program and creates the extracted data file. As our primary goal was to keep our tool compatible with as many MVS installations as possible we implemented the filter program in 370/Assembler. In addition, an assembler implementation seemed necessary to perform extractions which involves browsing through huge amounts of recorded data with acceptable performance.

The functionality of the filter program is very simple. First, the header information of the extraction data file is evaluated containing for instance information about the used SMF version. As the filter generator generates extraction data tailored to the structure of a given SMF version, this version information is necessary to verify that the SMF version used on the MVS host is the right one.

Second, the filter program reads every recorded data set from the SMF-database into main memory and checks the specified extraction conditions. The requested entries are written into the extracted data file converting all data into ASCII format. As the host part just uses standard MVS routines it can be ported to different MVS configurations and it does not require any special host support. The data transfer between PC and MVS host is performed using sequential files. Using simple and uniform formats (raw ASCII data) instead of a specific database format keeps the tool as compatible with heterogeneous MVS installations as possible and enables great flexibility with respect to evaluating and analyzing the data on the PC.

3.4 Examples

In this subsection we want to sketch how MVS-SAT can be used to support a security administrator in accomplishing his daily work. We give two simple but pragmatic examples of security scenarios by briefly describing the underlying security problem and the SMF record types required to investigate the problem.

Example 1: Time intervals with SMF being deactivated
We are interested in answering the question whether the SMF audit facility was deactivated or activated during a specific period of time, for instance during 6. p.m and 7 a.m. on Friday the 6th of September 1996. Moreover, if there was indeed a deactivation we are interested to learn how long this deactivation occurred. As we have learned in the previous section we first must specify appropriate extraction conditions to gather the required data from the SMF database.

Whenever all data logs are filled and all data buffers are exhausted SMF raises data lost status and recording of data is no longer active. As soon as a new data log is available SMF writes a dataset of record type number 7 containing information concerning the time (SMF7STM) and the date (SMF7STD) when SMF was deactivated. Hence, SMF record type number 7 records some of the information we need.

We specify an extraction condition concerning entries of record type number

7 for which the conditions SMF7STD = 9/6/96 and SMF7STM $\geq$ 6 p.m. and SMF7STM $\leq$ 7 a.m. hold.

Type 7 records just record the beginning of a deactivation period, hence, we need some more information to accomplish our evaluation. As each SMF database entry comprises a time stamp recording its logging time, the information we need is provided by the database entry following immediately after a record type 7 entry. Hence, our extraction condition specifies that such data items should be extracted as well.

Evaluation is now very easy. We just look at the extracted data to detect the periods of time during which the audit facility was deactivated. In a subsequent step we can perform further investigations to learn about the events that caused these deactivations. $\triangle$

Example 2: Evaluating access attempts
We are interested in information about unauthorized access attempts to the system or accesses to system resources controlled by RACF. The information needed is recorded in SMF record type number 80 which gathers information about for instance access attempts, access denials, modifications of user profiles etc. The structure of record type number 80 is very complex and can not be described here. We rather explain its relevance for security evaluation by means of a simple example. To be able to distinguish between different events recorded with type number 80 we must investigate several fields. An unauthorized attempt to gain access to the system is signaled by the record entries SMF80DES and SMF80EVT by setting the values SMF80DES=1 and SMF80EVT=1 (Event Code=Job Initiation, TSO Logon). This simply means, that the user-id used to login is unknown to RACF. If an invalid password is used the record item SMF80EVQ=1 is set or if an invalid terminal is used this is recorded in record item SMF80EVQ=4 .

It should be clear how to proceed. We must specify an extraction condition concerning record type 80 data sets with conditions testing the values of the fields SMF80DES, SMF80EVT and SMF80EVQ depending on our specific requirements. $\triangle$

These simple examples should demonstrate that MVS-SAT enables to evaluate a broad range of security related problems in a comfortable and efficient.

4 CONCLUSION

We have presented a tool that supports system administrators to evaluate the security of a given MVS configuration based on recorded SMF audit data. MVS-SAT offers a simple but quite comfortable user interface to specify user-defined extraction conditions and to evaluate extracted SMF protocol data via SQL queries. The tool has been developed in cooperation with an organization being responsible for checking the security of the computing environment of the members of the organization. The tool is in daily use since December 1995.

We tried to keep the tool as portable and independent of any specific MVS configuration as possible. This task was accomplished by our modular implementation, especially by separating the MVS-specific host part from the MVS independent PC part. Note, that our tool by no means is intended to replace a human being who is responsible to investigate security problems evaluating recorded SMF data. Our tool relies on the knowledge of its users. That is, the user must know the potential security holes of a system he wants to evaluate. He must have at least rudimentary knowledge of which information are stored within which SMF record types to investigate specific security problems. Our tool aims to support the user by offering databases and libraries maintaining as much information as possible a user needs to perform his evaluation. That is, previously acquired knowledge is kept in a quite comfortable manner for later reuse.

Though desirable, our tool does not yet support an administrator with hints how to improve his MVS installation. Future work will investigate this task. In addition, we intend to extend our tool by incorporating an on-line intrusion detection facility.

5 REFERENCES

Conyers, V.L. (1991) *Audit and Control of MVS.* EDP Auditors Foundation.

Denning, D.E. (1986) An Intrusion–Detection Model. *IEEE Transaction on Software Engineering,* SE-13(2):222 – 232.

Department of Defense. (1985) *Trusted Computer System Evaluation Criteria.* Technical Report CSC–STD–001–83, Department of Defense.

Johnson, R. (1991) *MVS Concepts and Facilities.* Intertext/McGraw-Hill.

Paans, R. 1989) *A Close Look at MVS Systems: Mechanisms, Performance, and Security.* North-Holland

RACF. (1995) *RACF1.9 Security Administrator's Guide.* Manual SC28-1340, IBM.

System Management Facility (SMF). (1995) *MVS/ESA System Management Facility.* Manual GC28-1628, IBM.

Soper, K.R. (1989) *MVS Top-to-Bottom: An Analysis of MVS and its Impacts on Audit and Security.* MIT Training Institute.

PART TWELVE

Security in Healthcare Systems

31

Security requirements and solutions in distributed Electronic Health Records

B. Blobel
Otto-von-Guericke University Magdeburg, Faculty of Medicine
Institute of Biometrics and Medical Informatics
Leipziger Str. 44, D-39120 Magdeburg
phone: +49-391-6713542, fax: +49-391-6713536,
e-mail: bernd.blobel@mrz.uni-magdeburg.de

Abstract

The healthcare systems in all developed countries are changing to labour-shared structures as *Shared Care*. Such structures require an extended communication and co-operation. Medical information systems integrated into the care processes must be able to support that communication and co-operation adequately, representing an active and distributed Electronic Health Record (EHR) system. Distributed health record systems must meet high demands for data protection and data security, which concern integrity, availability, confidentiality including access management, and accountability. Communication and co-operation in information systems can be provided by middleware architectures. For the different middleware architectures used in healthcare as EDI (HL7, EDIFACT), CORBA or DHE, the architectural principles and security solutions are shortly described in the paper. Supporting open information systems, these security solutions are independent of applications and transparent to the user. For trusted communication and cooperation, application-related and user-related security mechanisms are required. Such mechanisms have to fulfil the security policy of the application domain. They are using the basic security mechanisms of the underlying communication- and cooperation-supporting systems.

The discussed policy, threats, and countermeasures are referred to the first German regional distributed medical record, which is developed and step by step refined in the Clinical Cancer Registry Magdeburg/Saxony-Anhalt.

Keywords

Electronic health record, middleware, data security, security services, chip cards, TTP

1 INTRODUCTION

Due to the changed basic conditions of healthcare systems in all developed countries, which are characterised by the demographic development with an increasing number of elderly and multiple-diseased patients, rapidly growing and expensive medical and technical progress, and a generally increasing demand of health services, there is a substantial requirement for efficient and still high quality healthcare. The response of choice is the structural change of healthcare systems enforcing Shared Care, i.e. a continuous and coordinated activity of different care providers including the patient itself to give an optimal medical, psychological and social help to the patient (Blobel, 1996b; Blobel, 1996c). Such distributed, decentralised, labour-shared healthcare structure must be supported by an adequate information system structure, consisting of highly specialised and highly effective components enabled to optimal communication and cooperation. Therefore, these processes are accompanied with improving and extending electronic communication. The content and extent of communication as well as the used both services and communication infrastructure determine new threats, define the need for protection, and facilitate new measures for data security. The consideration here is restricted to issues related to middleware concepts as well as to services and threats within our distributed EHR (DEHR) solution. Communication in healthcare can be characterised by communication content, communication partners, communication infrastructure, and communication services. In a combinatorial way, different communication contents, partners, infrastructure, and services present different communication conditions and lead also to different security threats and requests for adequate countermeasures. A general approach to system security and a categorisation of architectures with respect to their threat models and trust models including an extended discussion of common communication services is given in (Blobel et al., 1996). The paper concerns especial advanced communication services, e.g., provided by middleware systems. Comprehensive guidelines on security of healthcare systems have been published in (The SEISMED Consortium, 1996).

2 SECURITY SPECIFICATION AND DOMAINS

Personal medical data are highly sensitive information. In this context, legal, medical, social, and technical aspects must be considered. For extended communication of such information in Shared Care systems and for trustworthy and non-repudiated cooperation, the basic security dimensions of data integrity, availability, confidentiality, and accountability of information and processes have to be ensured. The latter concerns also the non-repudiation of origin and receipt of data as a basic foundation of interoperability (Blobel, 1996b; Blobel, 1996c; Blobel et al., 1996).

We distinguish the globally manageable *communication security* from the locally managed *application security*, the former dealing with data transfer between two or more authenticated principals (users, processes, devices, etc.), the latter dealing with access of these principals to application resources (access control, management of rights or privileges) (Blobel, 1996b; OMG, 1995). Therefore, pure communication services as simple middleware services concern communication security, whereas application security is related to the requested and provided application functionality (data or service of the upper 7th OSI layer), but also to advanced middleware services (functionalities). Such services are e.g. the CORBA[1] common facilities. Differently to purely commercial domains (the customer takes something and pays for them), in healthcare only the rights of access to patient-related medical information can be given. The grant of access rights is provided solely in responsibility of the information owner or the application administrator. The basis of decision are singular facts (case-related patient-user relationship, patient's right of informational self-determination) as well as rule-based scenarios (roles) (Council of Europe, 1995). Figure 1 presents a scheme of that two security types and the related measures discussed below.

As information systems scale to regionally, nationally, and even internationally distributed systems, their complexity has to be reduced in order to remain manageable with respect to both the security specification and the threat model. This is usually achieved through collecting similar components into security domains, representing special scope to the system. Common features allowing grouping are, e.g., organisation, functionalities, responsibilities, obligations, technical basis, policy, application domain, jobs. According to (OMG, 1995) there are three major types of security domains:

- the *security policy domain*,
- the *security environment domain*, including *message protection domain* and *identity domain*,
- the *security technology domain* (Blobel et al., 1996).

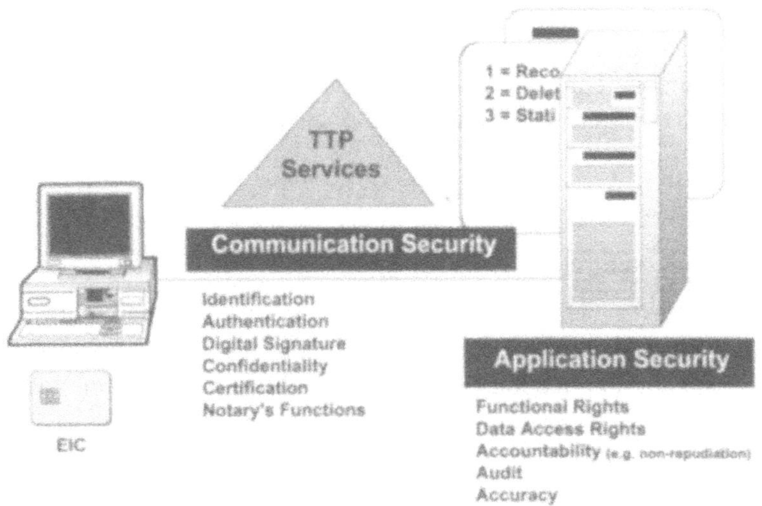

Figure 1 Security types

[1] Common Object Request Broker Architecture, the middleware concept of the Object Management Group (OMG)

The purpose of security domains is to form groups of mutual trust defining special level of risks and therefore demanding a set of countermeasures. Assuming adequate characteristics, departments, enterprises, institutions and even organisations can be considered as domains. These domains are assumed as trust environment, which must be only protected against external threats. Therefore, special security measures are required only for communication between different domains and are implemented at the domain boundaries. Nevertheless, the challenges and conditions of Shared Care, the use of widely spread and distributed middleware architectures, and the integration of many care and system providers require the consideration of current and future health information systems as open and distributed systems, accepting the untrustworthiness of the communication environment as well as involving several domains. Therefore, the communication partners and also the middleware system could belong to different technology domains, environment domains, or even policy domains.

3 MIDDLEWARE SERVICES AND THEIR SECURITY CONCEPTS

To meet the requirements of the future healthcare for efficient and interoperable healthcare information systems, some application-layer-specific advanced services were developed. These services, also called middleware, mediate the communication and the co-operation of application systems from different vendors on different platforms and with different application environments including also legacy systems. Related security requirements are discussed in section 7.3.5. The middleware architectures referred to below provide services on different levels involving EDI[2] and/or middleware products as CORBA, Microsoft's OLE/DCOM[3], or DHE[4].

Because information to the here only shortly discussed advanced services is published in a large number of standards and specifications, review articles are cited referring to the genuine sources. In this context the first comparative study of all the discussed architectural approaches should be mentioned (Blobel and Holena, 1996).

3.1 HL7

Architectural Approach

HL7 (Health Level Seven) is a communication standard for information interchange (electronic data interchange = EDI) in healthcare environments, supporting communication at the OSI application layer (level 7). The actual focus on hospitals will be extended within the next versions (V. 2.3, V 3.x) of the standard.

[2] Electronic Data Interchange; provides open communication, requiring specialised servers (communication servers) or standardised middleware products to serve interoperability

[3] Object Linking and Embedding / Distributed Common Object Model

[4] Distributed Healthcare Environment, the European Health Information System Architecture (HISA)

HL7 enables communication between any systems independently of their architecture and hardware basis. This is achieved by standardising the syntax and semantics of exchanged messages. HL7 interfaces realise the request/service procedure in the sense of sending and receiving these messages, including the transformation from the proprietary format to the standardised format and vice versa. The communication is managed by communication servers or by a standardised middleware architecture, which is not a part of the HL7 communication standard. Not HL7, but only the underlying middleware architecture as a very complex service system is able to provide interoperability between systems.

The basic principle of HL7 is a *point-to-point information interchange paradigm* (1:1 or 1:n in the case of broadcast). Communication is controlled either by *trigger events* (in the case of trigger event paradigm of process coupling, *unsolicited* or real time) or by *query/response interchange* (in the case of query/response paradigm of retrospective interchange or *solicited*). Therefore, HL7 enables healthcare information systems to manage concurrent processes and non-concurrent interchange of messages. Using unique object identifier, a controlled time order of messages is supported. HL7 provides both basic and enhanced acknowledgement paradigms.

HL7 has been widely introduced in the US healthcare sector and is increasingly used in some European countries, especially in Germany. The successful dissemination of HL7 will be promoted by the harmonisation of the different healthcare information interchange protocols, performed by the Joint Working Group for Common Data Model in Healthcare (JWG-CDM) and chaired by IEEE. The objective of JWG-CDM is to develop object-oriented models and specifications that are needed to support a generic messaging standard. In addition, interfaces to standard middleware architectures like ASN.1, CORBA, and OLE will soon be realised. Industry driven working groups like the HP-promoted AndoverGroup focus on JWG-CDM compliant products, starting with HL7 related procedures, followed by CORBA integration.

EDIFACT (Electronic Data Interchange for Administration, Commerce and Transport) is the European pendant of HL7, but is actually not achieving a similar significance in the healthcare domain.

Security Services

The similar security concept of HL7 and EDIFACT is based on separately useable services for identification, authentication, digital signature, certification/assurance, data compression, encryption, notary's office functions (e.g. time stamps) to ensure the above mentioned security dimensions. The services could be used at the level of functional groups or transaction sets. The security mechanisms could be provided exclusively or in combination as requested realising transparency and response to special technology and policy requirements or conditions. The services are provided between security originator and security recipient and certified by an assurance originator and recipient structure respectively.

3.2 CORBA

Architectural Approach

The CORBA of the OMG is a middleware standard, which provides an open generic concept including implementation tools for general and object-oriented interoperability of distributed applications. It realises all functions below the application layer using only some basic assumptions for simple transport protocols. CORBA consequently defines distributed objects, which are characterised by a set of methods and a set of attributes fulfilling all needs of environment for supporting co-operation. The objects are implemented using of *OMG-interfaces* in an open system involving all applications and providing all services needed for the communication and co-operation within the system aggregation. The interfaces are specified using an *interface definition language* (*IDL*). Different services have to be managed, which is performed by an *Object Request Broker* (*ORB*) giving that architecture the name *Common Object Request Broker Architecture* (*CORBA*). The CORBA services are separated into

- low level services
- common object services providing common functions for data handling (e.g. naming or transaction and time management),
- advanced services
- common facilities as well as application objects, both providing direct support of applications

The common facilities are divided into horizontal and vertical common facilities. The horizontal common facilities are related to functions needed in different application domains. Examples are user interface (connection to user environment, e.g. Microsoft's OLE or OpenDoc), information management (handling application data), system management, task management and others. Vertical common facilities are related to a specific application domain like healthcare (e.g., *Medical record object model framework* and *Master patient index framework*).

Using CORBA, the users (including application programmers) need no knowledge about its underlying architecture, available services, their location etc. In CORBA, the services needed can be implemented transparently. Via prepared interfaces, different CORBA implementations can be bridged together. In this way, CORBA enables even the collaboration of objects distributed in extended networks, such as Internet.

The intensity and quality of CORBA utilisation depends on the availability of vertical common facilities. DHE managers (see the next paragraph) could provide such application related services, provided they get compliant to the object orientation of CORBA.

Because of the short history, only a few healthcare projects are using the CORBA architecture. An important impulse to CORBA should come from the activities of the American JWG-CDM, including all organisations involved in healthcare communication standards. By these object-oriented solutions for communication standards, the healthcare applications will get access to CORBA services for optimal systems' interoperability.

Security Services

Domain-specifically, CORBA provides all important security services, such as identification and authentication, authorisation and access control, security auditing, security of communication including mutual authentication of clients and targets, integrity protection and confidentiality protection, non-repudiation, and administration of security (OMG, 1995). Basic principles for an object-oriented security architecture within CORBA are simplicity, consistency across the distributed co-operating systems, scalability and usability (transparency), flexibility of security policies, independence of security technology, application portability, interoperability, and sufficient performance. Security pertains to various components of the CORBA architecture. A considerable part of security functions is implemented directly through the ORB or through their bridging mechanisms. Others are confined to transaction services or to additional security services, implemented through specific security-related objects. Finally, security services are also provided by the underlying operation systems and communication services.

Identification and authentication of principals (users, processes, devices, etc.) requesting any object services is provided either by the outside system or by a Principal Authenticator object. The Principal Authenticator creates for each principal a Credentials object, containing the principal's privilege attributes, e.g. the access identity, groups to which the principal belongs, roles, security clearance, and capabilities concerning various groups of objects. A security aware target application may obtain attributes of the principal responsible for the incoming request, to make its own authentication-depending access decisions. The information contained in Credentials can be obtained either directly or through the Current, an interface of the Transaction Services, which holds reference to the current execution context at both client and target objects.

The privilege attributes are first needed for making a secure invocation, which is mediated by the ORB. Whether the invocation can take place, as well as the way in which it is mediated, depends on the client and target security policies. As mentioned above, security policies concern such issues as access control, establishing trust in client/target, protection of messages for integrity/confidentiality, time restrictions, or delegation of privileges. If a request initiates a chain of invocations, then the security policies of all objects in the chain are taken into consideration through delegation mechanisms, including all intermediate objects.

As far as access control is concerned, applications can enforce their own access policies. Typically, details of access control are isolated from the application itself, and are implemented through an Access Decision Object, specific to the access policy. In addition, there is an Access Decision Object associated with the ORB and used for the invocation access policy, which is enforced internally by the ORB. The decision whether to allow access to a given function or data depends on the privilege attributes of the initiator of the request, control attributes of the target, and on the execution context. Access policy can be actually shared by a whole domain of objects with similar security requirements. In that case, reference to the corresponding Access Decision Object is available via the Current interface.

Similarly, applications can also enforce their own audit policies, which can be again managed via a domain structure. Each application writes its audit records to an Audit

Channel object. One such object is created at ORB initialisation time and is used for all system auditing. Application can use different Audit channel objects.

Finally, CORBA supports optional Non-repudiation services, providing generation and later verification of evidence concerning performed actions and data associated with those actions. The evidence can be generated using either symmetric cryptographic algorithms requiring a trusted third party as the evidence generating authority, or asymmetric cryptographic algorithms assured by public key certificates issued by a certification authority. Keys or other information needed for generating or checking the evidence are available via Credentials.

3.3 DHE

Architectural Approach

DHE is an integration platform, which supports the development of new applications and their integration with existing legacy systems in a distributed hospital information system. This is achieved by providing a functional infrastructure composed of a set of healthcare specific services. Services are grouped into appropriate data managers (such as the Patient Manager, the Resource Manager, etc.) according to the type of information that is managed. Using the standardised services, openness and compatibility between different healthcare applications is achieved. The services have been defined and validated on top of a generic healthcare centre data model based on experiences and projects involving several European healthcare centres.

Essentially, the DHE is a healthcare specific middleware which supports the distribution of applications and the transparent interaction between them. It includes transversal functionalities such as the Act Management concept which defines a relationship between healthcare providers and requesting parties ensuring a permanent line of communication between them. In this manner full interoperability is achieved between completely independent applications, realised by the healthcare specific DHE middleware of services with its API. In contrast with CORBA, DHE provides only advanced services on top of a so-called 'bitways' layer ensuring a technical platform for supporting network and distribution requirements.

All issues concerning data and transaction management or distribution are managed at the DHE level, leaving the application developer free to concentrate on the actual needs of the users for which the application is being developed. The architecture does not dictate any specific organisational structure, to the contrary, it provides a flexible means for describing the systems so that the IT infrastructure may follow the adopted organisational structure, even if it evolves over the time. It also conforms to the pre-standard proposed by PT-013 of CEN TC 251 Working Group 1 describing the standard European architecture for Healthcare Information Systems.

The basic concepts of the DHE and its architecture not only support different types of healthcare centres, but also offer migration strategies for the future.

DHE is based on the RICHE architecture, also represented by a consortium. The differences consist especially in the availability of the corresponding managers for the various healthcare-related functionalities (Blobel and Holena, 1996).

Security Services

The DHE security concept is similar to that of CORBA, also regarding services for secure communication as well as services to provide application security of external systems and DHE managerial functionalities alike. Regarding DHE managers as common vertical facility type CORBA components, the integration of the different approaches can also be extended to the security concepts discussed in the next sections.

3.4 Architectures' Relationships

Each of the architectures HL7, CORBA and DHE/RICHE integrates components of distributed health information systems. The extent of integration, however, is different.

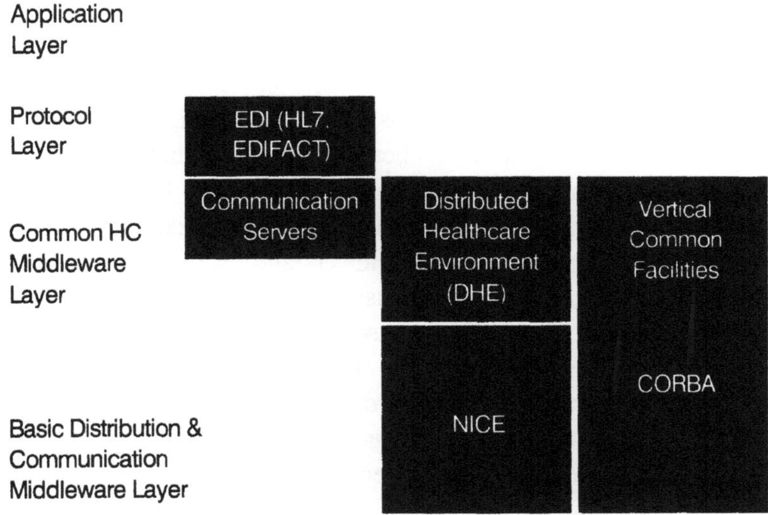

Figure 2 A joint architecture of essential middleware approaches (HANSA Consortium, 1996)

HL7 specifies standardised messages at the application level. DHE/RICHE provide complex healthcare-related services transparently supporting the co-operating applications. These services correspond to the vertical common facilities of CORBA. Apart from these facilities, CORBA defines general middleware services and facilities as well as implementation tools enabling transparently the interoperability of any systems in an object-oriented way. A joint architecture (figure 2) was proposed by (HANSA Consortium. 1996). For further details see (Blobel and Holena, 1996).

3.5 Common Security Aspects

The architectures considered above are a significant step beyond distributed cooperating systems. They provide not only communication services between security environment domains of end-users but they also provide application specific services to them. In addition to the service related threats, architecture specific threats caused by the advanced services need to be considered, which sometimes be provided by third parties with their own policy, environment, and technological domains in the sense of untrusted providers. Similarly to provided network services also the functional services of the middleware can be corrupt.

The above architectures vary considerably in the maturity of their security approaches. So far, HL7 respects security rather elementary whereas CORBA provides a mature and up-to-date security concept. Because the advanced security services of application-related communication protocols (EDI: HL7, EDIFACT) and of middleware architectures (CORBA, DHE) have to be

- transparent to the users or applications, ensuring security also for security unaware users or applications, and
- flexible for different domains requirements,

different security services must be provided. These services can be combined supporting authentication, confidentiality, accountability as non-repudiation, and access control on behalf of principals. CORBA uses credentials bearing corresponding attributes, which can be delegated or replaced in order to fulfil an HCE's policy. Furthermore, there are middleware-specific functionalities providing integrating services, such as system-wide identification of patients (Master Patient Index) and semantic tools supporting interoperability of heterogeneous systems consisting of different applications. For that purpose, the related security mechanisms must be provided independently of any application control.

Keeping in mind the combination of standardised middleware products (section 3.4), figure 3 outlines a structural model with essential security-related objects in distributed systems using middleware approaches. The scheme describes application visible objects and implementation security objects, controlled by advanced delegation and replacement mechanisms, assuming a scenario that an application A requests a service from an application B mediated by a (set of) middleware. Both applications as well as the underlying middleware could belong to different domains with respect to policy, environment, technology, mechanisms and services. Details of the presented structure are published in (Blobel, 1997).

In current security models, the service providers, including middleware services, are viewed as untrusted, following the basic concept to trust nobody and to organise security mainly by the communicating and co-operating partners (Blobel et al., 1996). Especially for distributed middleware architectures involving a number of hosts, Varadharajan proposed to install, on each of them, security functions (e.g., encryption/decryption, signatures), a security information base, secure factory objects (objects responsible for creation and deletion of other objects), and secure interfaces (Varadharajan and Hardjono,

1996). Most of these services can also be provided by functionalities specified in CORBA (OMG, 1995).

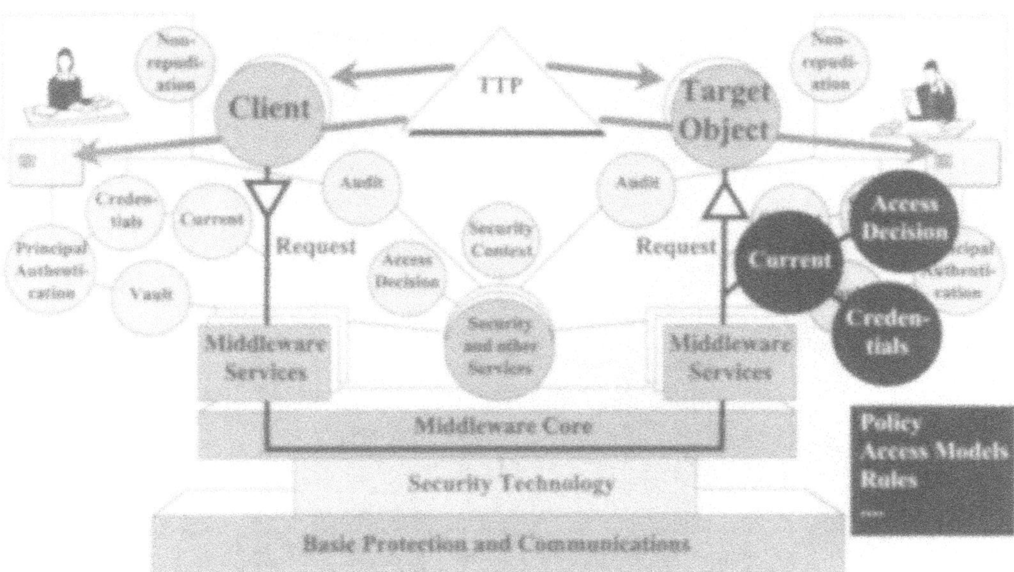

Figure 3 Structural model of a common middleware security

4 SECURITY ARCHITECTURE OF A ONCOLOGICAL DEHR

In the Clinical Cancer Registry Magdeburg/Saxony-Anhalt, the first German distributed EHR in oncology was implemented to support quality and efficiency of cancer care (Blobel, 1996b; Blobel, 1996c). For a catchment area with about 1.2 million inhabitants, more than 50 clinics and the Oncological Follow-up Organisation Centre are online connected to an extended patient-centred and case-oriented tumour documentation. The stored, processed, and cooperatively used information is highly sensitive. Therefore, our Cancer Registry was the first German healthcare application with advanced security mechanisms ensuring strong authentication of users as well as integrity and confidentiality of data. Improvement and further development of the system is embedded in several projects, related to both security and architecture and funded by the European Union. Currently, for communication and cooperation between a doctor's workplace and the registry middleware concepts (DHE, OLE, HL7) are being introduced. In coordination with the TRUSTHEALTH project (TRUSTHEALTH1, 1996a, 1996b), the system is also involved into the German Model Project "Health Professional Cards" (HPC) employing HPC for strong and certified authentication and additional communication security services mentioned in section 2 (Arbeitskreis, 1996). The task of providing a distributed oncological EHR is part of the telemedicine initiative of the German federal state Saxony-

Anhalt (Blobel, 1996a). An important challenge is the implementation of an adequate organisational and technical security infrastructure including Trusted Third Party (TTP) services. Figure 4 shows the Magdeburg TTP solution.

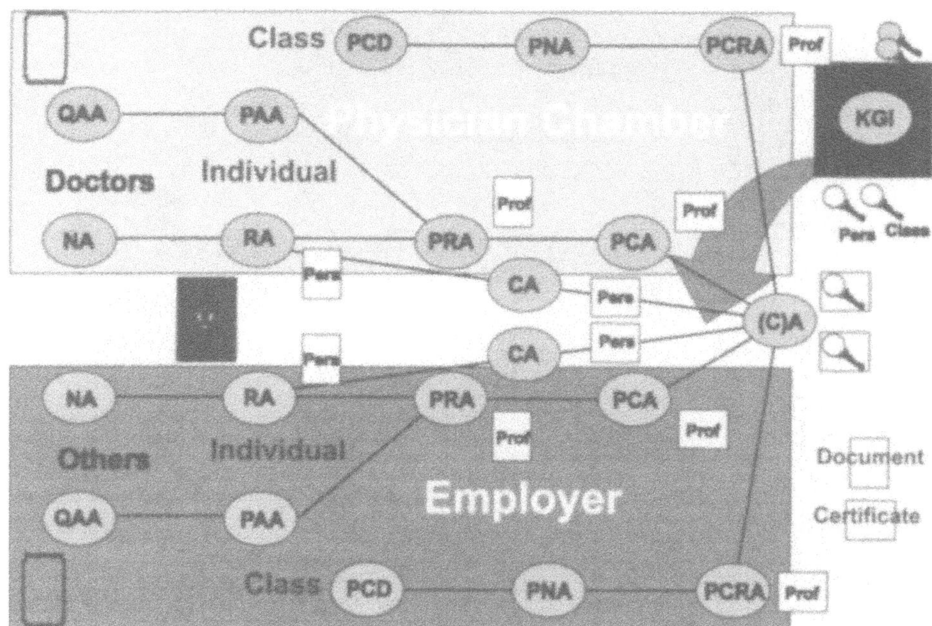

Figure 4 Magdeburg TTP solution

5 CONCLUSION

Currently, all industrial countries are trying to enhance the efficiency of their healthcare systems employing the Shared Care paradigm. Information technology plays a key role in these efforts. Information systems have to support decentralisation, communication, and cooperation by their own architecture. Numerous groups are pushing forward process-related and patient-centred open distributed and interoperable information systems developing and using middleware standards. Such systems are characterised by high requirements for data protection and data security. Important middleware approaches and their underlying security concepts are discussed. An interoperability trend of the different coexisting middleware architectures could been mentioned. On that basis, a structural model of a common security concept has been developed. The presented solution for an distributed EHR demonstrates need and feasibility of security solutions in open distributed heterogeneous health information systems supporting Shared Care.

6 ACKNOWLEDGEMENT

This work was supported within the "Telematics Applications Programme" framework of the European Union, and by the Ministry of Education and Science of the German Federal Sate Saxony-Anhalt. Furthermore, the author is obliged to thank the colleagues of the CORBAmed Task Force and the HL7 SIG Secure Transactions for kind cooperation.

7 REFERENCES

Arbeitskreis (1996) „Health Professional Card" der Arbeitsgemeinschaft „Karten im Gesundheitswesen": *Deutscher Modellversuch „Health Professional Card (HPC)"*, Göttingen, Stand Oktober 1996.

Blobel, B. (1996a) Konzeption für Telematikanwendungen im Gesundheitswesen sowie für ältere und behinderte Menschen. *Telematik-Initiative des Landes Sachsen-Anhalt.* Magdeburg, 19. Februar 1996.

Blobel, B. (1996b) Clinical Record Systems in Oncology. Experiences and Developments on Cancer Registers in Eastern Germany, in *Preproceedings of the International Workshop "Personal Information - Security, Engineering and Ethics"* pp 37-54, Cambridge, 21-22 June, 1996 (announced in LNCS, Spinger-Verlag).

Blobel, B. (1996c) A Regional Clinical Cancer Documentation System for an Optimal Shared Health Care in Cancer, in *Medical Informatics Europe '96* (edrs. J. Brender, J.P. Christensen, J.-R. Scherrer, P. McNair), pp 1019-1026. IOS Press, Amsterdam.

Blobel, B. (1997) An Object-oriented Security Approach Involving HL7, CORBAmed, and DHE Standards, *in Preceedings of the Conference „Toward An Electronic Patient Record '97"*, Nasville, April 26 - May 3, 1997 (submitted).

Blobel, B., Bleumer, G., Müller, A., Flikkenschild, E., and Ottes, F. (1996) Current Security Issues Faced by Health Care Establishments. *Deliverable of the HC1028 Telematics Project ISHTAR*, October 1996.

Blobel, B. and Holena, M. (1996) Advanced Healthcare System Architecture Using Middleware Concepts - A Comparative Study. *Deliverable of the HC 1019 Telematics Project HANSA*, July 1996.

Council of Europe (1995) EU Directive on the Protection of Individuals with Regard to the Processing of Personal Data and on the Free Movement of such Data. Strassbourg.

HANSA Consortium (1996) Middleware Approaches in Healthcare. A Presentation for the Healthcare Management (Draft). August 1996.

OMG (1995) The CORBA Security Specification. OMG Doc.No. 95-12-01.

The SEISMED Consortium (edr.) (1996) Data Security for Health Care, Volume I - III. IOS Press, Amsterdam.

TRUSTHEALTH1 (1996a) Selection of Security Services and Interfaces (Version 1.0). 1996-07-29.

TRUSTHEALTH1 (1996b) Functional Specification of TTP Services (Version 0.6). 1996-07-29.

Varadharajan, V. and Hardjono, T. (1996) Security Model for Distributed Object Framework and its Applicability to CORBA, in *Information Systems Security* (eds. Katsikas, S.K., and Gritzalis, D.), pp. 452-463, Chapman & Hall, London.

8 BIOGRAPHY

Dr Bernd Blobel is Head of the Department of Medical Informatics at the University of Magdeburg and chair of the first German distributed cancer registry. The department is involved in several projects, funded by the EU (e.g., HANSA, TRUSTHEALTH, ISHTAR, DIABCARD, EUROMED-ETS, MEDSEC). Dr Blobel is the German representative on the IMIA WG4 and WG13. He is cochair of the CORBAmed security group, represents the DHE Consortium within CORBA, and is involved in HL7 activities. Furthermore, he is chairing various German security groups as well as telemedicine initiatives with special responsibility to security aspects.

ODESSA
A new approach to healthcare risk analysis

by [1]M.J.Warren, [2]S.M.Furnell and [2]P.W.Sanders
[1]Business Security Group, Plymouth Business School
[2]Network Research Group, Faculty of Technology,
University of Plymouth, Plymouth, UK
Email: matw@pbs.plym.ac.uk

Abstract

The paper describes the development of a new security risk analysis methodology that can be used to determine the security requirements of organisations. The methodology has been developed for use within healthcare, but because of the generic nature of ODESSA it can be used to determine the security requirement of many types of organisation.

The paper describes the problems with existing automated risk analysis systems and how the ODESSA system can overcome the majority of these problems. The paper also presents example security scenarios.

Keywords

Security Risk Analysis, Baseline Security, Healthcare Security.

1. INTRODUCTION

The use of information technology (IT) has become more widespread in areas of business and society, and computers have now diversified into many types of applications. As a result, IT systems are used by all levels of staff within organisations, and relied upon greatly to such an extent that it would be difficult to operate without them.

The aim of risk analysis is to eliminate or reduce risks and vulnerabilities that affect the overall operation of these computer systems. Risk analysis not only looks at hardware and software, but also covers other areas such as physical security, human security, business and disaster protection.

In practice there are major problems with the use of risk analysis; the time taken to carry out a review, the cost of hiring consultants and/or training staff. To overcome these negative aspects a new methodology and operational system has been developed. This paper proposes a methodology that is able to simplify the identification of security requirements for individual systems, and to provide a means by which a system administrator or security officer can select the appropriate security countermeasures for their own system. The methodology also describes the impact that the implementation of security could have upon the organisation.

2. THE NEED FOR RISK ANALYSIS IN HEALTHCARE

Within the UK, National Health Service (NHS) there is a general lack of security awareness and security expertise, even though very sensitive and personal data is kept on computers and is communicated between computers. Medical computer security is primarily concerned with:

Confidentiality
Ensuring that unauthorised people (including staff) do not have access to the sensitive and/or personal healthcare data.

Integrity
Ensuring that the data produced by and used within a healthcare system can be trusted as being accurate and complete.

Availability
Ensuring that the computer systems are able to provide the necessary clinical data when and where it is needed.

From a medical point of view [1] perhaps the most important security problems are concerned with:

Physical security
The open nature of hospitals and clinics make them vulnerable to theft, damage and unauthorised access.

Risk to the patient
The failure of a healthcare computer system could affect the treatment given to patients with perhaps dire consequences.

<u>*Confidentiality*</u>
Medical data contains information that may be extremely sensitive to an individual, i.e. the person may be mentally ill or have the HIV virus. Disclosure of this information could be embarrassing for the individual in the extreme and could result in them being ostracised by society. Also any disclosure could destroy the trust between the clinician and the patient and possibly result in legal action being taken against the clinician or the health care organisation.

<u>*Data retention*</u>
Within some countries there is a legal requirement to retain healthcare data for a minimum period of many years. This raises problems concerning the long term storage of data, especially when it is converted between old and new systems, which could affect the integrity of the information.

Previous research resulted in a new medical risk analysis method being developed. The method is aimed at the enhancement of security in existing healthcare systems, with a key concept of the methodology being the use of security profiles. For example, using the assumption that a PC network system would require similar security countermeasures to be installed in similar environments. The method has been extended to develop a more generic methodology that can be used within most organisations, the major differences being the types of profile, types of data and organisational details. This generic system ODESSA (Organisational DEScriptive Security Analysis) [2], is being evaluated initially in the healthcare field to help overcome the lack of security awareness and act as a low-cost source of security expertise.

3. THE THEORY OF ODESSA

The rationale of ODESSA is that at a basic level, organisations will have similar security requirements, but beyond this basic level the security countermeasures are unique to each organisation.

Within ODESSA security is examined from the context of the whole organisation, with all factors that influence the organisation being considered, which may range from the location and age of buildings, to the sensitivity and type of data.

These elements have been incorporated into a framework as shown in figure 1. This illustrates the steps involved (at a theoretical level) in determining the security requirements for an organisation.

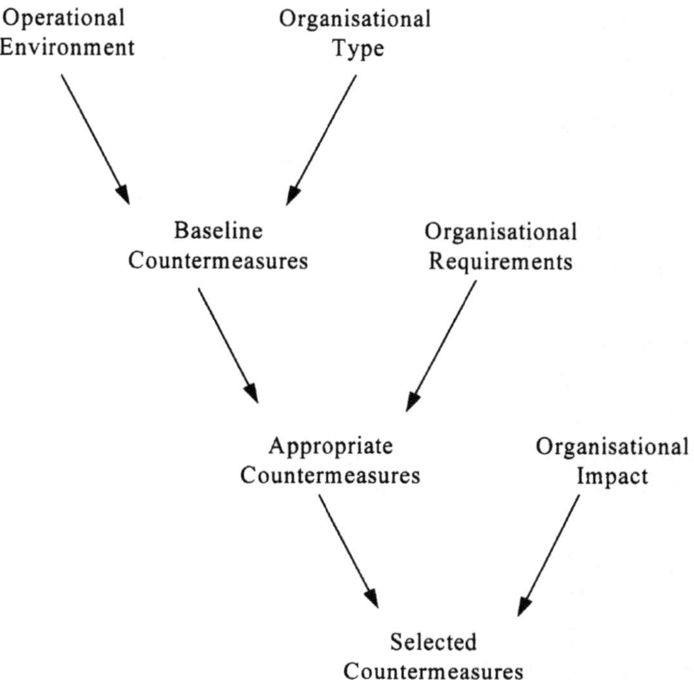

Figure 1. ODESSA methodology overview

The ODESSA system suggests three sets of security countermeasures.

- *Baseline Countermeasures*
  These represent the minimally acceptable security countermeasures for any organisational type.

- *Appropriate Countermeasures*
  These represent the unique organisational security countermeasures. They are based upon a series of questions from which data sensitivity profiles are formed.

- *Selected Countermeasures*
  These represent the selected countermeasures from 1) and 2) that have been applied against the SIM-ETHICS (see 3.5) impact criteria and then accepted by the user.

The main elements of the methodology are now considered in more detail:

3.1 Organisational Environment

This considers the environment in which the organisation's assets are located, which may affect the level of protection required. Table 1 gives examples of environmental considerations that have to be considered for a medical environment.

Table 1. Organisational Environments

Type	*Options*	*Comments*
Location	Inner City	Location may indicate risk of vandalism, theft.
	Urban	Location may indicate risk of theft.
	Rural	Location may be many miles from emergency services, i.e. fire station.
Old / Modern		Age of building may indicate risk of fire, disasters, etc.

3.2 Organisational Type

This relates to the different organisational types that exist within a business sector. The baseline security countermeasures are tailored to these different organisations. The research included a comparison of past healthcare security reviews, which helped to form the baseline security needs for the different types as shown in table 2.

Table 2. HCE Organisational Types

Type	*Description*
GP (Single)	A single doctor working among the community, location of surgery is within the community, i.e. in converted house.
GP (Practice)	A group of doctors working in the community, location of surgery is within the community, i.e. purpose built surgery, large converted house.
Community	Units used for specialist patient health care , i.e. speech therapists. Community units are based within the community, within a variety of different sites.
Hospital	Units used for the direct treatment of patients, i.e. specialised surgery, general surgery, radiotherapy, etc. These organisational types tend to be in very large units and based in one location or a variety of different sites.

3.3 Organisational Baseline Security

Previous research undertaken had shown that within a healthcare environment certain HCE's had the same countermeasure installed at lower levels. The concept of baseline within ODESSA relates to the minimal security levels requirements that an organisation should have installed [3]. These levels were determined by comparing results of different HCE security reviews and examining different HCE security guidelines:

- SEISMED Existing System Guidelines [4];
- SEISMED High Level Security Policy [5];
- NHS IM&T Security Manual [6];
- BS7799 [7].

3.4 Organisational Requirements

At this stage the use of the data is considered. Organisations use a cross selection of similar data types, which require similar countermeasures, i.e. encryption of personal data. The ODESSA system uses a set of HCE generic data types [8], as described below:

Table 3. HCE's generic data usage types

Data Use	*Description*
Patient identification	General information relating to patients.
Patient administration	Information used in patient day-to-day scheduling of non-clinical activities.
Patient care	Contains medical history, diagnosis care decisions and treatment information relating to patients.
Clinical services	Information used for planning of clinical services (not patient related).
Finance	Information relating to all aspects of finance that are involved in the operations of HCE.
Staff	Personal information relating to HCE staff.
Resource management	Information used in the management, monitoring and planning of HCEs.
Library and information	Details of existing medical knowledge that is used by clinical staff systems.
Expert Systems	Information used by decision support systems or neural networks used within the HCE.

Once the type of data has been decided, it's sensitivity has to be defined. The sensitivity impacts of the data are:

- **Denial** Denial of access to the information for different time periods.
- **Destruction** Destruction of the information.
- **Disclosure** Unauthorised disclosure of information.
- **Modification** Accidental or deliberate alteration of data.

The data impacts are determined as percentages, and rated as being low, medium or high, (low is equal to baseline security, and high the maximum protection that is offered). The sensitivity values and data types are determined from a series of questions to the appropriate staff of the organisation, which then are used to produce a security profile of the organisation under review. Figure 2, shows the steps involved in determining the organisational requirement.

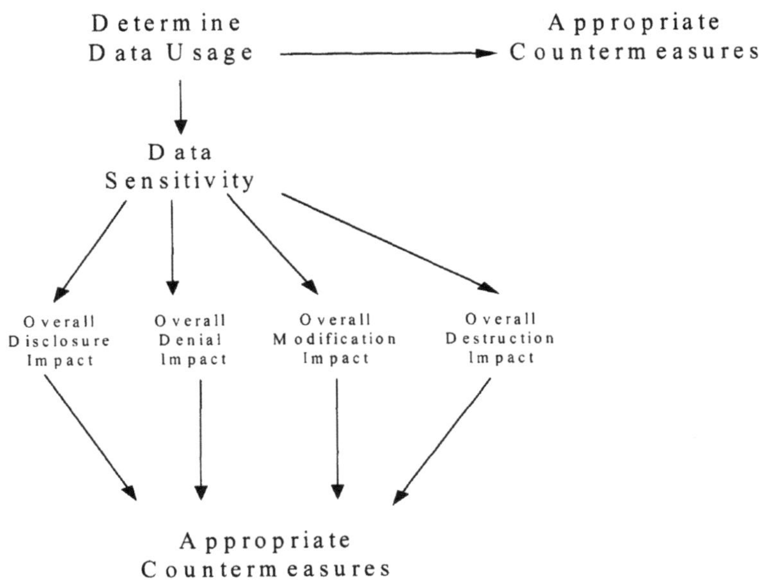

Figure 2. Organisational Requirement

The stages involved are:

Stage 1) Determine Data Usage
The user of the system picks the data types that the organisation uses, which are associated with certain countermeasures, i.e. levels of access, encryption.

Stage 2) Data Sensitivity
The user answers a series of security related questions. The replies determine the overall impact of disclosure, denial, modification and destruction. The countermeasures are generated from the answers and the overall levels of impact.

3.5 Organisational Impact

Any security countermeasure that is being implemented will effect the organisation as a whole. The impact is determined from a set of impact criteria that has been used as part of a change control methodology, SIM-ETHICS [9] (Security Implementation Method - Effective Technical and Human Implementation of Computer-based Systems).

The use of this criteria allows management to determine the impact of introducing security. It relates to:

Ease of Implementation
How easy can new security features be added to a system and/or new security procedures added to an organisation?

Training Issues
What are the training requirements needed by the staff to use new security features?

User Impact
What is the impact that security could have upon users, i.e. how does it affect user satisfaction, efficiency or effectiveness?

Organisational Impact
What will be the effect that security features could have upon the organisation, i.e. changing of the organisational culture?

Human Issues
What is the impact that security has upon a user from the human perspective, i.e. changes of peoples jobs, creating new management roles?

4. IMPLEMENTATION OF ODESSA

The ODESSA system has been initially developed as a prototype using Visual Basic and Access and is developed to work on PC machines. Visual Basic was chosen because it offered the quickest and easiest way to create the ODESSA prototype. Visual Basic allows a system to be developed that incorporates an easy to use graphical user interface (GUI) and on-line help facilities. The prototype system contains all the features of the methodology. Some of the features of the ODESSA system are described below:

Organisation Selection

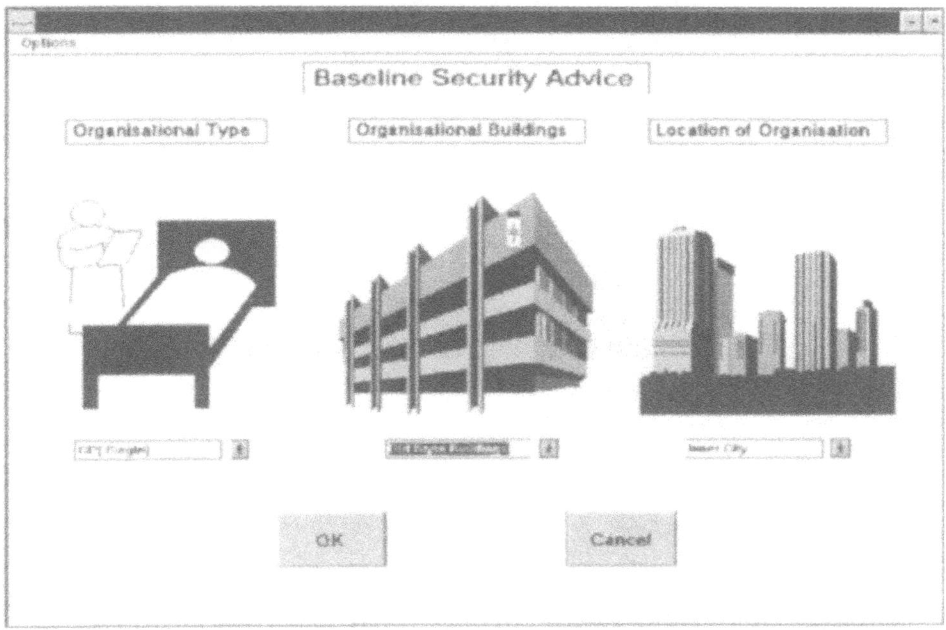

Figure 3. Organisational Requirements

Figure 3 shows the user selection of the different organisational types and organisational environments.

Baseline Security Selection

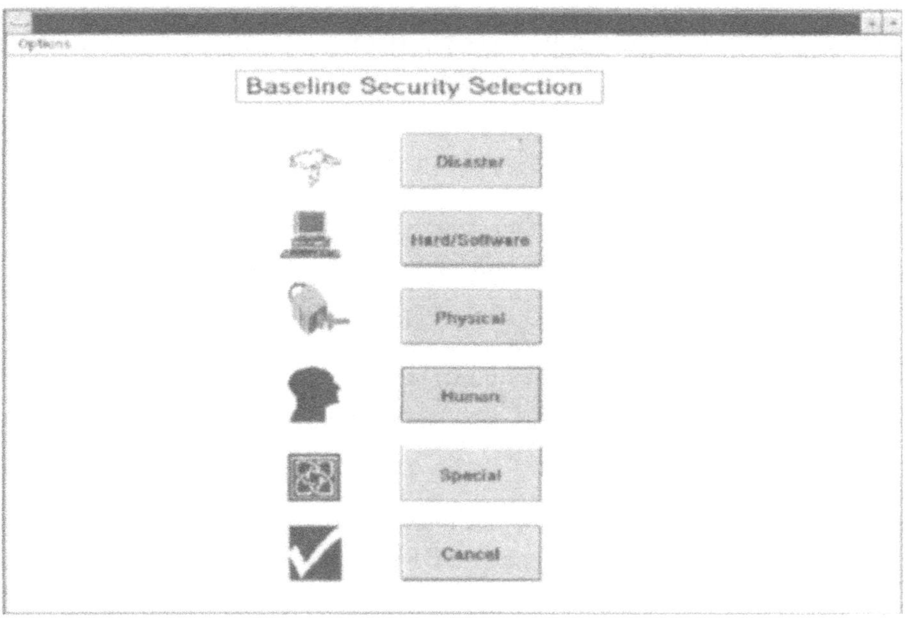

Figure 4. Countermeasure Groups

Figure 4 shows the selection option for Organisational Baseline Security. The security groups are broken down into several groups according to the aspect of protection being addressed (namely *Disaster, Hardware/Software, Physical, Human and Special*).

Organisational Impact

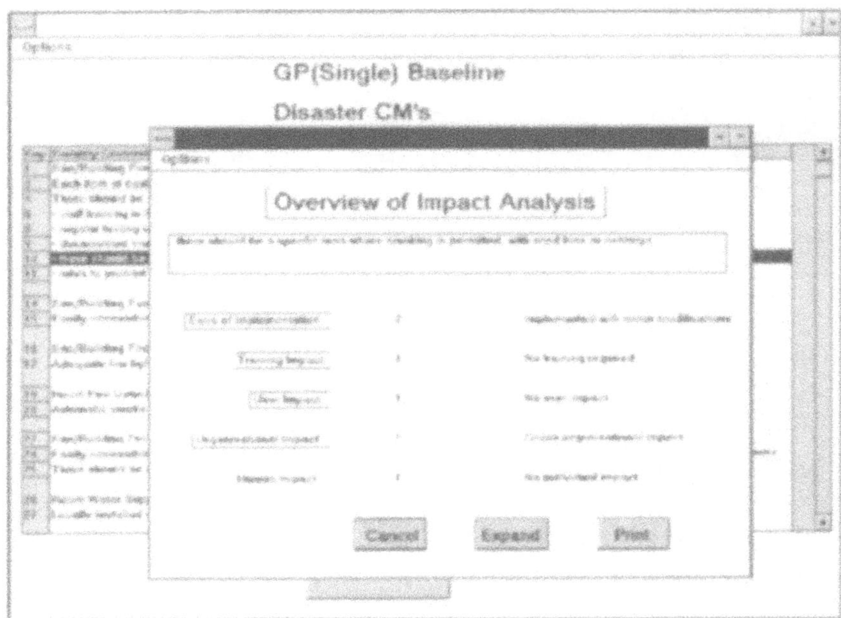

Figure 5. SIM-ETHICS analysis of countermeasure

Figure 5 shows an example of the SIM-ETHICS criteria being used in order to evaluate the selected security countermeasures.

Evaluation

The ODESSA methodology was evaluated by members of the AIM SEISMED consortium during its development. Once the prototype was developed it was sent to various healthcare security experts in order for them to evaluate the prototype. All of the results were very positive.

The SIM-ETHICS method was evaluated by a top UK soft systems expert and was also validated by using it within a HCE to help introduce security systems.

Future Development

At the moment the ODESSA system is just a prototype. The next stage is to develop it into a full system. A business prototype of ODESSA has also been developed.

6. CONCLUSION

The paper shows how by using ODESSA, the process of security reviews within healthcare can be simplified. The use of ODESSA is valuable where a security review has been denied on the grounds of budget or inconvenience. The paper shows the unique approach taken by the ODESSA method, that of using security profiling, data use and baseline security countermeasures. This is a major departure from traditional risk analysis methods.

It is the aim that ODESSA should be compatible with the majority of systems and that future versions of the system will be developed for different organisational types. In systems where extremely high levels of risk are identified, it is advisable that a more detailed security review should be undertaken.

7. REFERENCES

[1] Gaunt, P.N, and France, R.F. (1993), The need for security in health care information systems [A Clinical View], AIM SEISMED Internal Project Report SP11.02.A08.02, 1993.

[2] Furnell, S.M. Gaunt, P.N. Pangalos, G. Sanders, P.W. and Warren, M.J. (1994), A generic methodology for health care data security, *Medical Informatics*, **Vol 19**, **No 3**, 229 - 245, UK.

[3] Information Management Group (1992), Basic Information Systems Security, NHS Management Executive, UK.

[4] Sanders, P.W, Furnell, S.M. and Warren, M.J (1996), *Baseline Security Guidelines for Health Care Management,* Published in Data Security for Health Care, IOS Press, The Netherlands, ISBN 90-5199-264-5,

[5] Katsikas, S. and Gritzalis, D. (1996), *High Level Security Policy Guidelines,* Published in Data Security for Health Care IOS Press , The Netherlands, ISBN 90-5199-264-5

[6] Information Management Group (1996), The NHS IM&T Security Manual, NHS Management Executive, UK.

[7] British Standards Institute (1995), BS7799 - Code of Practice for Information Security Management, UK, ISBN 0-580-236420.

[8] Sanders, P.W and Furnell S.M (1993), Data Security in Medical Information Systems using a Generic Model, MIE 93 Congress, Israel.

[9] Warren, M.J, Sanders, P.W and Gaunt P.N (1995), Participtional Management and the Implementation of Multimedia Systems, UK.

8. BIOGRAPHY

Dr Warren is a lecturer at the Plymouth Business School. He is the head of the Business Security Group. At the moment he is working on a EU HCTA project called ISHTAR. This is concerned with the development of security training material transferable via the internet. Dr Warren has previously worked on the EU AIM SEISMED project, which was concerned with developing security guidelines for Health Care Establishments.

A Comprehensive Need-to-Know Access Control System and its Application for Medical Information Systems

R. Holbein,
S. Teufel,
O. Morger,
K. Bauknecht
Department of Computer Science
Winterthurerstr. 190, 8057 Zurich, Switzerland

+41-1-257 43 11

{holbein, teufel, omorger, bauknecht}@ifi.unizh.ch

Abstract

In this paper we present an access control system (ACS) that allows implemention as well as management of comprehensive need-to-know access control policies. The overall system is built around a role based ACS that has been extended by two additional components namely, a security design and a context autentication component which allow the overall system to cohesively implement and manage need-to-know policies. The security design component systematically generates access control information that is appropriate to initialise the role based ACS according to the individual need-to-know within an organisation. The context authentication component on the other hand, has been integrated with the access control decision facility of the role based ACS. It dynamically verifies if a need-to-know really exists at the particular point in time when users request access to information. Finally, we describe an application scenario that illustrates the benefits provided by our need-to-know ACS concerning privacy of patient data within a hospital environment.

Keywords

Access control, business process modelling, business transaction, context authentication, need-to-know, role based access control, security policy, security design, security modelling, medical information systems

1 INTRODUCTION

In this paper we introduce an access control system (ACS) that has been designed in order to prevent information misuse and therefore, allows to protect privacy of sensitive personal information. We also describe an application of this access control system for medical information systems within a hospital. The implementation of our system consists of a number of components that correspond to the concepts for need-to-know policy implementation presented in earlier papers [Holbein and Teufel 1995] [Holbein et al. 1995] [Holbein et al. 1996] [Teufel and Holbein 1996]. Therefore, our particular implementation and application area provide a synthesis of interrelated research results that realise comprehensive need-to-know access control for privacy of sensitive patient information in a hospital. There are two major aspects that must be considered in order to realise comprehensive need-to-know access controls [Holbein 1996]:

1. a task related specification of access rights that agents within an organisation must receive in order to fulfil their tasks;
2. a task related evaluation of access requests that considers the current business transactions within an organisation.

The task related specification of access rights is necessary to initialise an access control system according to the need-to-know within an organisation's business processes. This part of our overall system is called *security design* component. The task related evaluation of access requests on the other side, is called access control component. This part verifies if a task related access right that supports a particular request was defined during security design and furthermore, considers an organisation's current business transactions to ensure that the users' need-to-know is valid at the point in time when the particular access was requested. The latter is called *context authentication* [Holbein and Teufel 1995]. We have developed security subsystems for access control systems to adequately address these aspects comprehensively. Our subsystems allow a broad range of current access control systems which provide some basic features for need-to-know policy implementation to be enhanced for security design and context authentication. The result of this enhancement is called a comprehensive need-to-know access control system.

In our implementation we integrate the security design and context authentication subsystems with a role based access control system called Argos [Jonscher and Dittrich 1995] and apply the overall system to a mobile hospital bed unit (HBU) [Teufel and Holbein 1996]. The HBU is a hospital bed that includes a device for accessing a medical information system directly from a patient's bed within a hospital. This allows multiple medical, administrative as well as patient services and information to be used from widely distributed and commonly accessible sites. However, this also causes high sensitive patient information to be exposed and therefore, implies threats for privacy that require comprehensive need-to-know access controls.

The remainder of the paper is structured as follows: Chapter 2 continues with a conceptual overview and a description of the overall system architecture. Subsequently, in chapter 3 we focus on the major functionality of the security design and context authentication subsystems in some more detail. In chapter 4 we illustrate the benefits of our system within a hospital environment by means of an information access scenario. Finally, we point out some conclusions and further research activities.

2 CONCEPTUAL OVERVIEW AND SYSTEM ARCHITECTURE

From a generic point of view the conceptual overview of our comprehensive need-to-know access control system consists of two parts that correspond to the two major aspects as introduced above chapter (Figure 1): First, there is a *security design* subsystem that is connected to the access control system for administration of access rights according to a need-to-know policy. The security design system includes a number of interfaces that allow to import business models, e.g. business process models (BPM), to automatically derive security information and to establish need-to-know security models [Holbein et al. 1995] [Holbein et al.

1996]. These need-to-know security models can be exported to a number of access control systems. Again, there are interfaces that translate the security model to specific access control information that can be interpreted by the target system [IBM 1995]. Second, there is a *context authentication* subsystem which can be linked to different access control systems (ACS) on different platforms via corresponding ACS client modules. These modules are hooked up within the access control systems' procedure for evaluation of access requests and allow to verify if a current need-to-know concerning a particular access request exists [Holbein and Teufel 1995]. For that purpose it includes multiple server interfaces for different business automation systems with the capability to provide information concerning the state of an organisation's current business transactions, for example, workflow management systems[1].

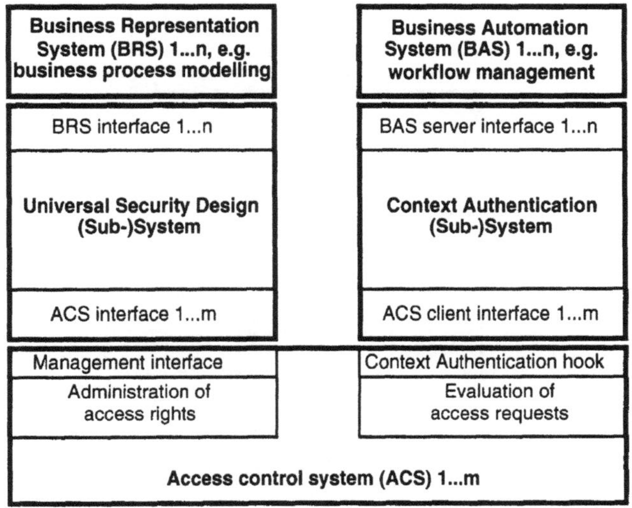

Figure 1: Conceptual overview

Our system implementation is based on the conceptual foundation above. It is constituted by the components shown in Figure 2. Below, there is a summarised description of all these components. The FELIX security design and CARDS context authentication components will be described in more detail in sections 3.1 and 3.2. The other components which are not for further consideration will be described as far as necessary in order to understand the overall architecture according to Figure 2:

- *ActionWorkflow Builder*: Business process modelling tool from Action Technologies which provides *transaction based BPM* as input for the FELIX security design system. The ActionWorkflow system is a software package from ActionTechnologies that provides tools for business process modelling and workflow control. One component within this tool set is called ActionWorkflow Application Builder (AW Builder). It allows transaction based BPM to be specified on a high level of granularity and detail. This tool runs on a Windows95-PC and communicates via a TCP/IP network connection with the BPM-definition database that runs on a OS/2-PC.

[1] In general, it is very useful when BRS and BAS are interrelated for example, workflow management systems that usually include a business process modelling component as well as a workflow control engine. However, this is not necessary in principle.

- *ActionWorkflow Manager*: Workflow management system from Action Technologies that controls an organisation's business transactions according to BPM definitions provided by the ActionWorkflow Builder. This system runs on a OS/2-PC with a proprietary database that can be accessed via a Lotus Notes interface.

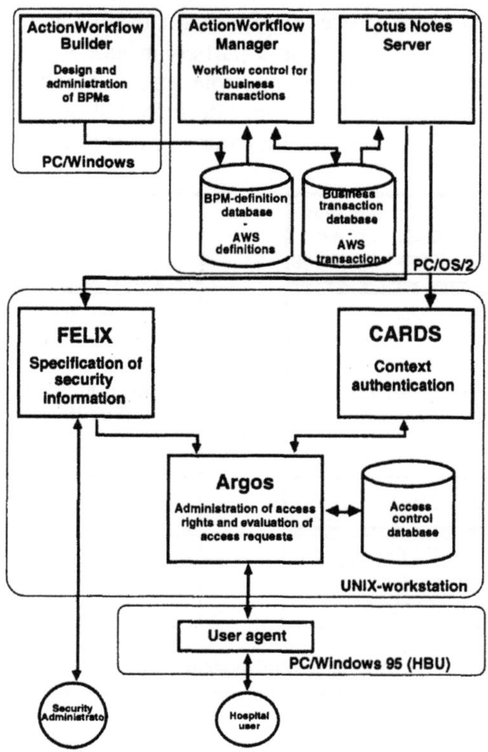

Figure 2: Overall system architecture

- *FELIX security design system*: Security design environment providing automation of our need-to-know security design method. This will be described in section 3.1.
- *CARDS*: Context Authentication service for Role based access control in Distributed Systems. This will be described in section 3.2.
- *Argos access control system*: Discretionary access control system providing role based mechanisms. This powerful ACS is highly flexible and configurable and was developed by Jonscher and Dittrich as a global access control system for heterogeneous database federations [Jonscher and Dittrich 1995]. Argos is founded on an object oriented data model [Jonscher and Dittrich 1993] and implemented on a UNIX platform as C++ application using an ObjectStore database[2]. Extensive customisation according to a security policy is possible due to a number of parameters that configure the reference monitor, e.g. closed/open world assumption. There are also capabilities to establish global controls, i.e. mandatory extensions according to an administration paradigm. The basic characteristics of

---

2 Argos was implemented as a prototype within the SPP-IF project CHASSIS [Jonscher and Dittrich 1995]. CHASSIS = Configurable Heterogeneous And Safe, Secure Information Systems; SPP-IF No. 5003-34355.

Argos and the mechanisms which FELIX uses to prepare for an implementation of individual need-to-know security models are summarised below.

Basically, Argos is characterised by discretionary specified rights which can be held by authorisation units. These authorisation units are represented by subject expressions. A *role* concept allows abstract subject expressions to be specified which represent users or sets of users according to their position - maybe a functional, organisational or social one - within a domain. Roles can be related to each other with a subordination relationship where permissions are inherited from subordinated roles and prohibitions from superior roles. Individual users can be associated with roles. Combinations of users and/or roles are also allowed to represent authorisation units. These combinations are called complex subjects. Consequently, access rights can be granted to subjects which may be individual users, roles or combinations of the previous ones, i.e. complex subjects. Furthermore, association as well as activation conflict relations can be used to establish restrictions for user-role association or simultaneous activation of roles during system operation.

A concept of *domains* is available for subjects as well as protection objects. Domains allow grouping and even nesting of sets of subjects and protection objects. Therefore, the definition of access rights refers to the whole set of elements belonging to a domain. Access rights define permissions and prohibitions concerning the execution of methods that belong to an object[3]. *Method classes* can be defined in order to group a particular set of object methods. Consequently, the object oriented approach with role hierarchies, domains and method classes allows extensive use of implicit rights to be made. Explicitly specified *rights* are represented as 7-tuples consisting of

(grantee, protection object, method, predicate, kind of right, grantor, grant flag).

Due to object orientation, access to the Argos services is realised by interface objects which provide methods for administration of the access control system and user interaction. A user is connected to the Argos system via a logon interface that provides a user interface or an administrator interface as the working environment in the case of successful user authentication.

- *User agent*: User related front end process to access the information system via the access control system directly from a HBU. This process runs on a Windows95-PC which is the HBU's IT device. The HBU front end will be further described in chapter 4.

In section 3.1 we will describe the FELIX part of our system which realises *need-to-know security design*, i.e. provides the security information which is necessary to initialise the Argos access control system. Subsequently, in section 3.2 we will describe the CARDS subsystem which realises *context authentication*, i.e. provides the task related information to the access control system which is necessary to evaluate the need-to-know concerning access requests at a particular point in time.

3 NEED-TO-KNOW SUBSYSTEM FUNCTIONALITY

3.1 Security Design

The first component that we have developed to enhance existing access control systems according to our need-to-know access control architecture (see Figure 2) is a security design

---

[3] This refers to the object oriented data model.

system called FELIX[4] which automates the generation of need-to-know security information according to the security design method presented in our earlier papers [Holbein et al. 1996] [Holbein et al. 1995]. Moreover, it allows interactive refinement and extension of the resulting security models. FELIX has been implemented using Ingres Windows4GL (W4GL) because W4GL provides extensive capabilities for human interface design and prototyping, hence it is suitable to implement FELIX as end user tool to be used by security administrators.

FELIX automatically generates security information from transaction based BPMs which correspond to the language/action approach [Winograd 1988]. At this point, we refer to the given literature for a detailed description of transaction based business process modelling. The transaction based BPM are provided by the ActionWorkflow Application Builder system [Action Technologies 1993] [Medina-Mora et al. 1992] [Action Technologies 1993, 1994]. FELIX allows to automatically generate security information which is suitable to initialise role based access control systems according to the individual need-to-know within an organisation's business transactions. Currently, FELIX is restricted to define administrator interface calls for the Argos access control system [Jonscher and Dittrich 1995], i.e. provides means for an individual application of Argos mechanisms. As Argos was developed within a parallel research project there was opportunity to prepare the system for integration within our overall system architecture.

From an overall security design viewpoint FELIX functionality consists of four parts: (1) the definition of security policy principles; (2) the definition of design principles, i.e. generic design constructs according to basic components of transaction based security design; (3) the generation of individual need-to-know security models according to BPM; and (4) manual specification and administration of security information.

The most powerful part of the FELIX functionality (3) provides automatic transformation of ActionWorkflow BPM onto need-to-know security models which can be implemented by Argos mechanisms via Argos administrator interface calls. This is embedded in an interactive environment for security design and administration of security information which also allows a manual refinement and extension as well as additional structuration of the security information that was automatically generated. The result of security design with FELIX are comprehensive security models that can be translated to the corresponding Argos administrator interface calls in order to initialise Argos according to these models.

In the following we give an overview of FELIX functionality. The basic screen of the security design environment is shown in Figure 3. It consists of two main areas: the BPM area and the security information area. The BPM area shows the BPM under consideration. It displays one business transaction construct belonging to a BPM with four lists of subtransactions assigned to its transaction phases and allows movement through all the business transactions belonging to the BPM. However, there are no means for modification of the BPM[5]. A mouse click on one of the subtransactions zooms into this transaction and provides a new arrangement of subtransactions listed around it. A "Task" button for both customer and supplier even allows observation of the task descriptions which belong to the displayed business transaction consisting of the corresponding business transaction activities. The security information area on the other hand shows the results of security design including the security policy principles, the generic design components as well as the need-to-know access rights which result from automatic or manual design activities. In this area a mouse click on a need-to-know access right

---

4 FELIX is a working name not an acronym.

5 Modification of BPMs is not a security design activity. It must be accomplished within business process (re-)engineering where ActionWorkflow provides appropriate tools to be used.

allows modification of its components (see also the description of the *Interactive design* item within the *Design*-menu below). A link between the security information area and the BPM area also provides for trace back from security design to an organisation's business processes. Whenever a mouse click is placed on a need-to-know access right within the security information area, the corresponding BPM will be loaded into the BPM area and the business transaction construct where the access rights has been derived from will be displayed with all its subtransactions listed around it.

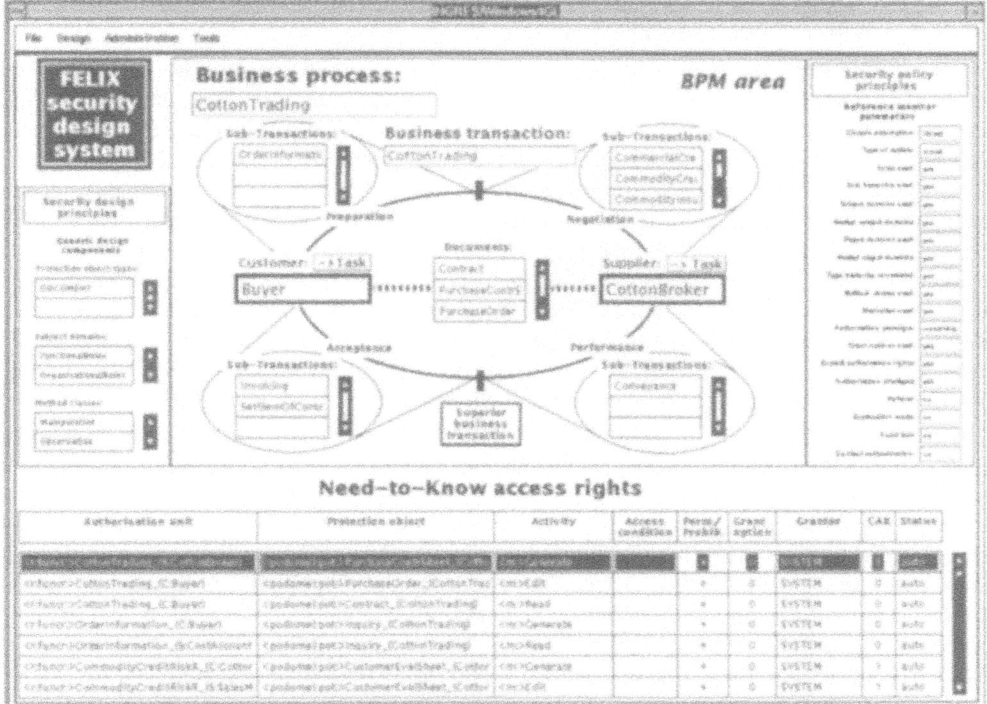

Figure 3: FELIX security design environment

The primary menu structure of FELIX consists of 3 pull down menus that offer file, design and adminstration functions. Unfortunately, the corresponding functionality cannot be explained in detail here. In summary, the *File*-menu basically provides import and export functions. Currently, import of ActionWorkflow BPM as input for security design and export of Argos administrator interface calls for initialisation of the ACS as output of security design (see Figure 2). The *Design*-menu provides the most important functionality that automates security design, i.e. *BPM transformation*, as well as the definition of security policy details, and a CAR-classification (Context Authentication Required) to control discrete CARDS service application (see 3.2). Finally, the *Administration*-menu allows for example, to define user-role associations and to analyse accumulations of rights etc.

3.2 Context Authentication

In this section we describe the CARDS service architecture (Figure 4). CARDS consists of a client part (C-function) that is linked to the access control system as well as a server part (Lotus Notes application) that provides access to the business transaction database (AW transactions) of the ActionWorkflow system. This database provides information on the actual state of an organisation's business transactions. The server part is realised as Notes-client application because Notes allows ActionWorkflow databases to be accessed in a comfortable way even across different platforms using Microsoft ODBC (Open DataBase Connect).

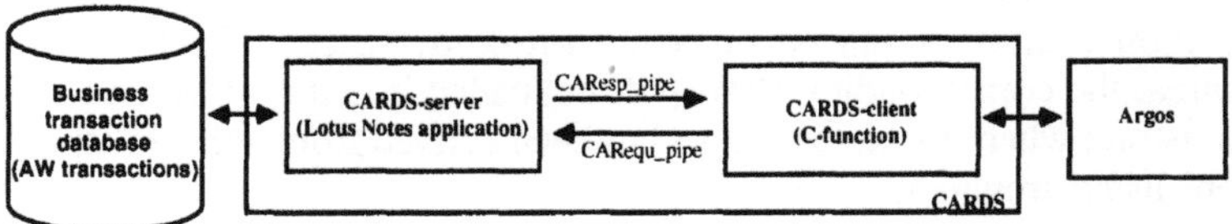

Figure 4: CARDS service architecture

It must be noted that this architecture neither includes an integration within a secure distributed system environment nor provides for high performance. However, this was not a goal of our first implementation which focuses on the context authentication procedure itself as a prototype. Hence, the CARDS-server part is implemented as a Notes-client application running under UNIX and providing an interface to the AWS transactions database running under OS/2. This interface is used to execute the database queries necessary to decide on context authenticity. The queries are specified by the CARDS-client and the query results are evaluated by the CARDS-client again. Communication between the client and server processes is realised by UNIX named-pipes where CARequ_pipe is used to pass database query specifications to the server and CAResp_pipe is used to return the results to the client(s). This architecture allows multiple clients to use the same CARDS server even if the clients are linked to different access control systems in a heterogeneous and distributed environment.

CARDS service access is realised via a CARDS-client which is a C-function that runs under UNIX. It can be called from any ACS that can link this function, exchange a number of parameters and receive a return value. This CARDS() function writes the role name that has been received from the ACS[6] together with the name of the requesting user as a database query specification to the CARequ_pipe. Now the CARDS-client function waits for the requested query result reading the CAResp_pipe. This result is a context certificate that specifies active business transactions and corresponding business process instances as well as the customers associated with these process instances which have been identified in the AW transactions database according to the query specification. The context certificate is signed by the CARDS server using asymmetric encryption techniques and can be verified by the CARDS client using the server's private key[7]. Success or failure of the context authentication finally depends on the following conditions:

- If no context certificate is provided, context authentication has failed (CAF) and a corresponding return code is passed back to the requesting ACS.
- Otherwise, the certificate together with a corresponding return code is passed back to the requesting ACS.

The CARDS-server is realised as Notes application that runs on a 'Lotus Notes workstation for UNIX' (UNIX Notes-client). This Notes workstation allows ActionWorkflow databases to be accessed via a Notes-server, both running on an OS/2 system. Communication between the Notes-client and Notes-server is based on the TCP/IP protocol.

The CARDS-server works as follows: During start-up of the Notes workstation a macro is invoked that calls a Notes function for import of data from the CARequ_pipe. If data comes through the pipe the import function inserts this data into the AWS transactions database using

---

6 Due to their construction these roles include the name of a business transaction which corresponds to workflow names in ActionWorkflow terminology.

7 Public key encryption facilities are provided by Lotus Notes.

a Lotus Notes form that has been defined to contain query specifications. Now, a second macro is started by the database insert event that selects business process instances from the AWS transactions database which includes active business transactions as specified by the inserted data, i.e. a workflow of the specified type with a customer or supplier as defined by the name of the requesting user.

The selected items are used to compose the query result which is a set of records consisting of a business transaction ID, the corresponding business process ID, customer and supplier name of the workflow as well as the customer name of the primary workflow that belongs to the business process. This data is organised in records and signed with the CARDS server's private key. The resulting context certificate is exported to the CAResp_pipe, the exported data as well as the query specification data is optionally deleted from or marked within the database and the macro that reads the CARequ_pipe is restarted to receive the next context authentication request.

4 HOSPITAL APPLICATION SCENARIO

In health care business it is very important to have simultaneous access to different patients data, e.g. health history, patient case data, administrative data etc. Additionally, the patient needs access to various hospital services and features that increase his comfort and safety. Further on, remote monitoring of the patients status (heart, respiration and chemical data) becomes more and more important with the evolution of patient surveillance. Finally, the introduction of Computer Integrated Services (CIS) in hospitals could have an enormous effect to reduce the health cost and enables introducing lean management techniques efficiently and effectively. In this context a project called MobiMed (Privacy and Efficiency of Mobile Medical Systems) was initiated [Fischer et al. 1995]. This project is part of the Swiss Priority Program for information and communication systems and co-operates with a project called EXODUS (EU-Project 00320, Programme ACTS).

The overall objective is to develop and install a Hospital Bed Unit (HBU), which includes a bedside terminal for access to a multimedia information and communication system including overall access to patient data anamnesis, clinical data, administrative and accounting data etc. One reason for that can be found in studies showing that bedside information technology decreased the time nurses spent in documentation activities and increased the time they spent in direct patient care.

In order to implement need-to-know access controls that protect the patients' medical data as described in the previous chapters, the first step is to examine and to model the internal hospital processes. Subsequently, we assume the following scenario: There is a hospital process called General Medicine which includes the phases Registration, Testing, Nursing Cycle, Treatment, Therapy and Discharge of the patient. For a definition of access rights according to the security design method that was implemented as part of our need-to-know access control system (FELIX) we consider these phases as the business transactions which are part of the General Medicine process. Consequently, a Nursing Cycle transaction will be activated as part of each general medicine process if a patient has to stay in the hospital. In this business transaction there is a Nurse who acts as a performer providing the following services to the patient: ordering prescribed medications, administering medications, recording vital signs etc. Service provision requires to have access to the patient's medical history as well as the medical report which is realised via the HBU user interface which has been designed as intuitive as possible, so that health care professionals can get very quick and easy access to patient information.

The following access right for example, results from the business transaction *NursingCycle* and is part of the need-to-know security model that has been automatically derived from the *GeneralMedicine* BPM: **(NursingCycle_(S:Nurse), MedicalHistory, read, , +, 0, SYSTEM, 1, auto)**.

We cannot provide an extensive and complete documentation here because the complete security model would be a vast and rather unreadable set of data consisting of several hundret security records. Therefore, we want to illustrate some practical insights that show benefits and deficiencies of our comprehensive need-to-know access controls within a medical information system. For that reason, we use the need-to-know access right above to explain a corresponding access control trial. The syntax includes the Argos 7-tuple. The access right consists of an authorisation unit representing a combined subject expression with an organisational role *Nurse* resulting from the organisational role of the service provider within the business transaction and a functional role *NursingCycle* according to the business transaction itself. The protection object within the access rights is represented by a protection object expression that corresponds to the *MedicalHistory* information unit which is specified as part of the business transaction. The activity corresponds to the information processing operation called read and was derived from the access type specification within the business transaction. The access right does not include an access condition. It is considered to be a permission (+) and not a prohibition. The receiving authorisation unit (grantee) is not allowed to grant the access rights to other grantees (0). The access right is global, i.e. it was created by a security administrator. This is represented by an artificial user named SYSTEM. Due to the sensitivity of the protection object there is a CAR classification defined for the access right, i.e. *MedicalHistory* has got a CAR classification which implies a CAR flag for each *MedicalHistory* related access right. Finally, the status of the access right is 'auto' because it was automatically generated.

Now we will explain an access control trial that illustrates how success or failure of access requests depends on the current state of the hospital's business transactions. For that reason, we consider a nurse's opportunity for misuse of *MedicalHistory* information. We explain the influence of business process states on the evaluation of an access request that corresponds to the need-to-know access right as explained in the previous section. A person who is assigned to the nurse role is also assigned to all functional roles that correspond to the business transactions where the nurse role occurs. According to our example this is the business transaction called *NursingCycle*. That means, a nurse's need-to-know access rights concerning a patient's medical history are restricted to the *Nursing Cycle* within the *General Medicine* process represented by the corresponding access right above.

We consider the following scenario: the user Petra Müller was assigned to the *Nurse* role as well as the functional role that was defined according to the *NursingCycle* business transaction. Now, we assume Petra Müller has activated the *Nurse* as well as *NursingCycle* roles and sends a request for read access concerning the *MedicalHistory_SamBrown* information object to the access control system. This object is an instance of class *MedicalHistory* where the information owner is a person named Sam Brown. Obviously, the first step of evaluating the access request succeeds because an appropriate role based access right exists. However, due to the CAR-flag within the access right there must be a context authentication for successful evaluation of the access request. In order to explain the possible evaluation results we consider the following four states of the AW manager system concerning the actual business transactions:

1. a *General Medicine* business process instance *GM1* exists, *Nursing Cycle* is the current business transaction within this process and a person named Sam Brown acts as customer within the *General Medicine* process.

2. a *General Medicine* business process instance GM1 exists and a person named Sam Brown is the customer but *Nursing Cycle* is not the current transaction within this process, i.e. must currently not be accomplished or has already been accomplished.
3. one or more *General Medicine* business process instances GM1,...,n exist but Sam Brown is not the customer within one of these processes.
4. no *General Medicine* business process instance exists.

Now it is important to note that although a role based access right exists *the only case where the access request succeeds is number 1 !* This is because the CARDS service provides a context certificate for *Nursing Cycle* and the customer of the business process is a person named Sam Brown which corresponds to the information owner of the requested protection object. In the second case, the access request fails due to a CAF that is provided by CARDS because there is no actual business transaction called *Nursing Cycle* that must be accomplished. The third case fails because even if there is a business transaction *Nursing Cycle,* this transaction is not part of a business process with a customer called Sam Brown. Obviously, the fourth case fails due to a CAF result provided by CARDS.

The access control trial shows that the nurse's opportunity for misuse of personal information can be restricted if the context authentication service is part of the evaluation procedure. The context authentication ensures that the access request succeeds in case of a current need-to-know but not at any time.

5 CONCLUSION AND FURTHER WORK

In this paper, we have introduced a comprehensive need-to-know ACS that is intended to prevent information misuse. However, prevention of information misuse by need-to-know access controls is limited. Our approach reduces the risk of information misuse but it cannot prevent information misuse at all because a user's overall access context is not restricted to his current task within an organisation and therefore, an information misuse risk still remains.

The practical application of our security approach clearly indicated that the security design method cannot be handled manually or in other words, a manual implementation of a need-to-know security model seems to be unfeasible. This is because even single BPM which are comparable to the *General Medicine* process in complexity require tremendous initialisation activities that must be accomplished for implementation of the need-to-know model. However, this security design procedure is necessary to prepare for need-to-know access controls with context authentication. For that reason, a computer based support for security design must be provided to a security administrator in order to apply our approach. The FELIX security design environment appropriately provides for this support by automation of the design process even if a few manual activities are required to complete the overall security model. It is possible to generate a security model consisting of several hundred commands for initialisation of the access control system within a few minutes. Additionally, FELIX allows the generated security model to be efficiently extended, modified and refined.

The CARDS prototype on the other hand allowed us to illustrate the shift from traditional access rights to the notion of rights of disposal concerning intended purposes that can be achieved by a context authentication service. However, the prototype implementation clearly indicated that efficient protocols are necessary in order to achieve system performance that will be suitable for operative use. Even in the case of a discrete and selective application of the context authentication service significant differences for evaluation of access requests will not be acceptable. For that reason, communication between the CARDS client and server components as well as the server database access procedures must be improved. In a first step, improvement will be possible by direct access to the transaction database of the AW manager, i.e. use of an ActionWorkflow API instead of Lotus Notes facilities. Furthermore, there must be efficient protocols to realise trustworthy communication between the participating communication partners in a distributed system environment.

REFERENCES

Action Technologies I, Ed. (1993). *ActionWorkflow Application Builder User's Guide.* Alameda, CA 94501, USA, Action Technology Incorporation.

Action Technologies I, Ed. (1993, 1994). *ActionWorkflow Analyst User's Guide.* Alameda, CA 94501, USA, Action Technologies Incorporation.

Fischer H-R, Teufel S, Muggli C and Bichsel M (1995) MobiMed - Privacy and Efficiency of Mobile Medical Systems. Project Proposal, Department of Computer Science, University of Zurich.

Holbein R (1996) Secure Information Exchange in Organisations - An Approach for Solving the Information Misuse Problem. Department of Computer Science. Dissertation, University of Zurich.

Holbein R and Teufel S (1995) A Security Service for Role Based Access Controls in Distributed Systems. Presented at the IFIP TC11 Eleventh International Conference on Computer Security IFIP/SEC95, Cape Town, South Africa, 1995.

Holbein R, Teufel S and Bauknecht K (1995) A Formal Security Design Approach for Information Exchange in Organisations. Presented at the IFIP WG11.3 Ninth Annual Working Conference on Database Security, Aug. 1995, Rensselearville, N.Y., USA, 1995.

Holbein R, Teufel S and Bauknecht K (1996) The Use Of Business Process Models For Security Design in Organisations. Presented at the accepted for presentation at IFIP SEC96 TC 11 Twelfth International Conference on Information Security, Samos, Greece, 1996.

IBM (1995) Distributed Security Manager for AIX, Concepts and Planning. IBM Entwicklung Deutschland GmbH, Information Development, Dept. 0446.

Jonscher D and Dittrich K R (1993) A Formal Security Model Based on an Object-Oriented Data Model. Technical Report, Department of Computer Science, University of Zurich.

Jonscher D and Dittrich K R (1995) Argos - A Configurable Access Control Subsystem for Interoperable Environments. Presented at the IFIP WG11.3 Ninth Annual Working Conference on Database Security, Aug. 1995, Rensselearville, N.Y., USA, 1995.

Medina-Mora R, Winograd T, Flores R and Flores F (1992) The Action Workflow Approach to Workflow Management Technology. Presented at the Proceeding of the ACM Conference on Computer Supported Cooperative Work, Toronto, 1992.

Teufel S and Holbein R (1996) Security Aspects of Mobile Medical Systems. Presented at the will be published in Proc. of IFIP TC11 WG11.2 Annual General Meeting on Small System Security, Samos, Greece, 1996.

Winograd T (1988) A Language/Action Perspective on the Design of Cooperative Work. In *Computer Supported Cooperative Work: A Book of Readings* (Greif R, Eds.), pp. 623-653. Morgan Kaufmann Publishers.

PART THIRTEEN

Secure Communications and Networks

The Future of Networks and Network Security

R. Nelson
Information System Security
48 Hardy Ave., Watertown, MA 02172, USA
(617) 924-9007 phone and fax; rnelson@cs.umb.edu

Abstract

Networks are evolving rapidly into huge, omnipresent, multiservice entities. They are connected worldwide into an Internet that has many different administrations, purposes, resource owners, and users. As the network grows, design parameters are exceeded and new vulnerabilities are introduced. Network security solutions must accommodate enormous changes in the network itself, in the network security requirements, and in the mechanisms and constraints that drive appropriate security mechanisms. As the network serves a larger and more diverse group of users, multiple, flexible security approaches will be necessary to meet their requirements.

Keywords

Internet, networks, security, denial of service, policies

1 INTRODUCTION

In its most general definition, security is the art of making a system behave according to its specification, even when there are forces trying to subvert its operation. Designing a secure system is never easy, but the problem is tractable for small, single purpose systems that are designed from the beginning with security in mind. The Internet is definitely **not** a system of this type. It is huge, constantly changing and under no single control. It was and is designed for flexible functionality rather than for security. This is our challenge as security professionals. How can we work effectively in such an environment?

We cannot secure the Internet. We cannot even secure an Intranet. We can certainly reduce the risk of putting our information resources on the network and of using the network for our various purposes. Network security must, however, be an ongoing process. We must understand the technology that we are trying to make safer, even as it grows, changes and becomes incompatible with our previous security approaches.

Security technology is also changing rapidly, so that we have new, more effective tools for our work. Cryptography is coming of age, and a public key infrastructure is being developed. Commercial tools can detect patterns of usage that may signal intrusions. Protocols are maturing and becoming more robust. Authentication mechanisms are more widely available, at affordable cost.

This paper looks at some of the rapidly changing network technology and at some recent network failures and attacks. It suggests some ways of restating and reinterpreting the Internet security problem so that we can apply security technology that is effective, flexible and adaptable to the changing environment.

2 THE CHANGING INTERNET

Today's Internet is almost unrecognizable to those who were involved in the early designs. It has evolved from a laboratory experiment to a business and household service, almost a necessity. All of the design parameters of the original network have changed by orders of magnitude. Growth has been explosive in capacity, services and number of users. The network is made up of many autonomous systems, with different administration, goals and services. No one, and no single country, is in control.

The size and scope of the current networks present challenging problems to those who need to manage and control network resources, including us in the security community. The network services and features vary from one provider to another and change from one day to the next. We cannot assume that a new behavior is a security problem; it may reflect a new, legitimate use.

The characteristics of the network affect not only the uses of the net and the expectations of the users, but also the vulnerabilities and the attacks. Many of the security approaches designed in the 1980s and implemented in the 1990s are independent enough of the new technologies to be effective. Some need updating and adaptation to the new environment; others have probably lost their usefulness.

In the complex Internet environment, users and providers have multiple, conflicting, changing goals and requirements. Security technology cannot possibly be effective without a clear specification of security policy and a clear model of anticipated threats and attacks. It is important that we security professionals understand the network technologies, how they are used, and how these uses can stress the system. This will allow us work with the network developers and providers on a realistic approach to security. We will be able to provide guidance about providing new services with a minimum of risk to the network, its resource owners and its users.

2.1 Integrated Services

The growth of the World Wide Web has brought integrated services into very widespread use. For some years, the major usage of the Internet was electronic mail, which is text data and typically small to moderate messages. This is still popular, but no longer dominant. Now the largest use may be transfer of web files using HTTP. Most of the information transferred is sound or image data; these are typically fairly large transfers. Another, growing, use is telephone conversations over the Internet; a popular toll-saving measure that can be done with cheap hardware and software. All of these forms of communications share common communications infrastructure, use IP, and traverse the heterogeneous Internet.

The integration of video and audio with the text and other data on the Internet has led to markedly different patterns of use. Transfers are more asymmetric than they were previously; requests to the servers are small and responses are large. It is interesting that packet voice was tried on the Internet in the 1980s and was basically a failure. The voice service worked on local networks, but the low bandwidth and high variability of delay on most paths made it impractical. The voice packets also required special handling by the routers: they were time sensitive and had to be delivered quickly or dropped. Voice and even video are now possible because of the vast increase in both communications bandwidth and network and end system buffer sizes.

A new initiative, called Internet II (Bradner, 1996), is addressing integrated services and new applications. This project is a collaborative effort among a number of universities, the US government, and private sector firms. Its goals include the extension of IP to support new applications and services while maintaining the concept of a single Internet bearer protocol. Significantly, this will be done by changing IP from a best efforts service to a differentiated service, with users able to specify guaranteed bounded delay, low data loss, and high capacity, for example. Current protocols, including IPv6, RSVP and RTP, will support this new structure.

From a security point of view, this user-selectable service presents both new vulnerabilities and new opportunities for control. Quality of service (QOS) parameters must be known to the routers on the route so that they can give the required service. Encryption protocols must permit this, requiring a larger bypass of data through the encryption process. QOS parameters must be authentic and protected from unauthorized change to protect against denial of service attacks on end users. Service providers must protect themselves against denial of service attacks by assuring authentication of QOS parameters and also by robust priority and throttling schemes.

2.2 High bandwidth and high usage

High bandwidth is a relative term. Rather recently, most home computers had modem connections to the local telephone company that ran at speeds from 2400 to 14400 bits per second. Current home computer modems double the previous top speed. Some subscribers are beginning to access the Internet through ISDN lines, at

T1 or higher speeds, and through cable television hookups at tens of megabits per second. Backbone speeds have also grown. When the ARPAnet, the early ancestor of the Internet, was begun, its backbone speed was 56 kbps. Internet access lines are often higher than this; backbone speeds may be 3 orders of magnitude greater.

It is estimated that by June 1996, there were 12 million Internet subscribers. Network users connected to their network service providers through telephone service have already overloaded local switches and caused some loss of telephone service. Telephone switches were designed for voice calls, lasting only a few minutes. Computer connections last much longer, using up the available connections.

Telephony communications models are used to predict load patterns and size systems. The applicability of these to the multimedia Internet world is now being questioned. William Stallings (Stallings, 1997) describes the phenomenon of self-similarity and how it affects buffers and links. The data traffic is not only burstier than voice traffic, but the bursts come in clusters. The effect is more overloading and more delays for the same network size and traffic. This fragility is a security vulnerability; denial of service attacks can be mounted with less effort if the network is overloaded.

2.3 Multiple services from multiple providers

The Internet is a large confederation of users and servers, with service providers of varying sizes and capabilities. Most data traversing the network crosses service boundaries. This means that servers must cooperate to provide end-to-end service. They also must protect themselves from unauthorized use of service and from denial of service attacks. The current protocol between domains is the Border Gateway Protocol (BGP), designed for limited cooperation and mutual protection of the domains. Quality of service negotiation will require a more complete protocol, and, probably more trust and cooperation between domains. Since not all providers can provide the same service, routing negotiations and computations will continue to increase in complexity, and complexity usually means less security.

2.4 Distributed Computing Power

One of the most significant changes in networks over the last 20 years is the distribution of computing power to millions of offices and homes. In the early days of networking, users had dumb terminals, network nodes were based on very small minicomputers, and processing was done by tine-sharing mainframes. Threat and attack models for the net are still based on this model. The distributed computing power has blurred the distinctions between terminals, communications components and processing servers. It allows integrated services to be offered and managed. It has also given attackers both more capability to attack and more accessible targets.

Today, there are no dumb terminals; essentially every terminal is at least a personal computer with more memory and programming capability than many old mainframes. Capable users now connect to the Internet via direct connections, essentially becoming Internet nodes with individual IP addresses for the duration of the connection. These user IP addresses are dynamically assigned, chosen either by the service provider or the user node. Assignment of IP addresses is a security concern, and there is no global policy or enforcement of this assignment. The user nodes should be network stubs, not carrying any through traffic, and should not participate as routers in network route computations. This restriction needs to be enforced by the service providers; there has been at least one incident where a major network was disrupted because a user node claimed its network number and this was not caught.

3 SECURITY ISSUES

Much of the security research and development over the last twenty years or so has been in the area of protecting confidentiality of information. This is clearly important, but it is not nearly broad enough. Network security must be address the multiplicity and diversity of network resources, services, providers and users. It must allow multiple policies and even the interconnection of systems with conflicting policies.

Ideally, a secure system should behave according to its specification, even when there are forces trying to make it do otherwise. That is, it should enforce all the policies specified for it, and it should do so in a predictable, robust fashion, resisting all attacks and misuses. However, in the case of the Internet, there is no specification; in fact, there is no single authority able to specify system behavior, system architecture or system security policy. This has been true for some time and it will continue and increase as the Internet gets larger and even more diverse.

If the service provider sets the policies, users can be informed of the rules when they subscribe to the network service. The resources of the system include information, of course, but also computing and communications capabilities. The difficult part of this is to define policies that can be enforced with the available technology, that are consistent with the network services of the system, and that can be explained and sold to users. Then, as the system changes and new technologies and services are added, the security of the system must be analyzed periodically for de facto changes in policies and also for new vulnerabilities to new attacks. This dynamic and local nature of network security means that rigid definitions and models cannot be effective, and yet we need clear models and definitions to build secure systems.

3.1 Local security to enforce local policies

There is a practical solution to this problem. Each system must protect its own resources according to its own policies. It is impossible (or at least unlikely) that any widespread agreements will be made about policies or resource usage. It is also unrealistic to assume that all the millions of users of the Internet will abide by any rules. The diversity of interests has already spawned techniques for local protection, including firewalls and now Intranets. These will probably continue to be necessary, along with more specific, server- and application-oriented defenses.

Local security can apply to a single physical system, to a client-server community or to a distributed system sharing a common management organization. The policies, mechanisms and techniques applicable to each system depend on the kinds of resources to be protected and the kinds of services provided.

3.2 Security to suit the purpose

It is important that the purpose of the system be considered. Most system policies deal primarily with the confidentiality of information. It is also necessary to consider integrity of information and fair allocation of processing and communications capability. Identification and authentication policies and mechanisms are critical for all of these protections. Some recent examples illustrate how current networks are being successfully attacked. The nature of these attacks may give some insight into the future. Some attackers are technologically sophisticated, and they will continue to learn.

Modification

Recently, hackers infiltrated a US Air Force computer at the Defense Technical Information Center (Schiesel). They modified the Air Force home page so that it contained material critical of the Air Force and also links to other web sites with hacker information. The hackers claimed major penetration of Air Force and Department of Defense computers, but this is questionable. It is clear that the successful attack caused embarrassment and loss of service; multiple web sites were taken off line. The computers at this site did not contain confidential information; their purpose was distribution of generally available information. However, the web site was clearly not sufficiently protected from a modification attack. The World Wide Web was designed to be very open and to offer free access to information; sites that are accessed are intended to be modified, at least to record the access. Security of the web site as a whole is not adequate; the policies and mechanisms must be much more specific to avoid embarrassment or worse.

Impersonation or spoofing is another type of modification attack. In this mode, the attacker simply creates a web site with an attractive title, implying that it belongs to a government, a vendor, or whatever. Users lured to the site may not only get spurious information; they may also be induced to give away their private information to the attackers.

Denial of Service

Denial of service attacks are very difficult to prevent. Attackers can find the limited resources in the network by understanding its technology. This happened with the TCP SYN flooding attack last fall (Graff, 1996). The attack aims at those server system that accept TCP connections from other systems on the Internet, such as Web servers, FTP servers or mail servers. TCP connections begin when the initiator sends a SYN message to the responder. The responder acknowledges the connection request with a SYN-ACK message. The initiator then sends an ACK message and the connection is established. While this sequence is in progress, the system receiving the

SYN must maintain information about the connection while it sends the SYN-ACK and waits for the ACK. Timers are set to allow for the delay of the communication. The attack is to send numerous SYN messages to a target system, forging the source addresses to be those of a system that will not respond with the SYN-ACK. The target system's space for maintaining connection request information becomes full, denying service to legitimate users who cannot open connections. If the system is not robust enough to deal with this flooding, the attack can even cause a system crash.

The limited resource is the list of connection initiations in progress. Since connections are opened quickly in normal circumstances, most systems have been designed for only a short list. The attack can be countered to some extent by enlarging the list size, shortening the time a request is kept before it is discarded, and other parameter adjustments. It is important to understand that these measures do not guarantee protection against denial of service. They do reduce the risk. This kind of attack is made possible by the fact that users have access to computing power and fast network connections, as described in Section 2. These connections were exploited by some hackers in the large Internet community. Designs that were effective in their original environment can fail when conditions change.

4 CONCLUSIONS AND CAUTIONS

Security concerns will not stop network growth and change, even when new services and features bring added risks for both users and service providers. The challenge to the security community is to develop and apply our technology with respect for the usefulness of the network, and knowledge of the communications and processing systems we are trying to protect.

If we try to consider the Internet as a single entity to be secured, the task is overwhelming. The diversity means that there is no single definition of security for the network and certainly no single architecture or set of mechanisms. Even if we could determine a security approach for the network, we would soon be overtaken by the introduction of new services and features that did not fit our solution. Attackers have ever greater processing power and network access. Network and security components and protocols are being used outside the environments for which they were designed.

However, there is much that we can do to reduce network risk and make the resources on the network safer to use. By taking a more specific, local approach, we can provide good security to many network subscribers and service providers for current uses. We can also be alert to changes in network technology and reexamine our security solutions as the environment changes.

Network designers, operators and users all tend to want the newest, fastest, most feature-filled systems. Vendors will continue to develop and provide new products and services, and they will often do it with no consideration of security at all. Security concerns do not drive the network; they restrict and constrain it. We often try to keep change from happening because we cannot make the new version secure (or even analyze it before it is fielded). This situation is likely to continue and to produce continued tension between the networkers and the security people.

The network providers and users are concerned about risk. And they need our help. We can be most effective if we understand that their primary interest is in the network functionality; we cannot stop the changes. We need to give them solutions for the changing network environment as it evolves. This means that our solutions must be flexible, modular, and functional. They must operate at the local system, where the service providers have some control. Most important, they must be consistent with the network services and architecture as they evolve.

We can develop useful network security strategies by working more closely with the system designers, understanding new network and computer technologies as they appear, and seeing the vulnerabilities of systems as they are revealed through attacks and misfunctions. Neither we nor the networkers have control of the Internet, but we do have some influence.

5 REFERENCES

Bradner, S. et al (1996) Internet II Architecture, distributed on the Internet as a working document. Project Director is M. Roberts, roberts@educom.edu.

Graff, M. (1997) Sun Microsystems Security Bulletin #00136, 9 October 1996.

Schiesel, S. (1996) Air Force Computer Invaded as Hackers Forge Web Page. *Boston Globe,* December 1996.

Stallings, W. (1997) Viewpoint: Self-similarity upsets data traffic assumptions. *IEEE Spectrum*, January 1997, 28-29.

6 BIOGRAPHY

Ruth Nelson is the president of Information System Security, a research and consulting company that she founded in 1993. She has been involved in network and computer security research since 1975, has participated in the design and security evaluation of many computer-based systems, has published numerous papers on security and is a frequent participant at security workshops and conferences. Ms. Nelson is a member of the Open Network Security Working Group, which meets to consider network security issues for US government and industry, and of a US National Research Council committee on Trustworthiness in Information Systems.

Securing communications over ATM networks

M. LAURENT - O. PAUL - P. ROLIN
Télécom Bretagne
rue de la châtaigneraie - BP 78 - 35512 CESSON Cedex - France
Tel: (33 2) 02 99 12 70 40
Fax: (33 2) 02 99 12 70 19
Email: {mlaurent, rolin}@rennes.enst-bretagne.fr

Abstract

This paper presents a survey of existing solutions aiming to secure communications over ATM networks. Different solutions are analyzed and compared. Details are given about the security services offered, their placement within the ATM Protocol Reference Model, the mechanisms to negotiate security services and the techniques to provide synchronization and dynamic key change during user data exchange.

Additionally, this paper proposes a new ATM security solution - the Solution For Frequent Communications (SFFC) - suitable to protect communications between ATM stations or companies that need to frequently communicate. An implementation outline is also presented.

Keywords

B-ISDN, ATM, security network, security services.

1 INTRODUCTION

To support near future multimedia services, each requiring specific needs in terms of Quality of Service (QoS), ITU-T defined the Broadband Integrated Services Digital Network (B-ISDN) and adopted the Asynchronous Transfer Mode (ATM) as the technology to implement B-ISDN. ATM is still under development and one issue is that ATM facilities emerge although some ATM specifications/standards are still unavailable. About security issues, current ATM facilities (e.g. ATM switches) have many restrictions which are not favourable to simple and reliable security services introduction. That is why, it is time to secure ATM since sooner security specifications will be defined, simpler and more reliable the chosen security solution will be and wider the security services will be implemented within ATM facilities.

In the literature many works introduce security services (in the sense of (UIT-T X.800, 1991)) into the ATM Protocol Reference Model described in section 2. Section 3 outlines and compares those schemes. Also a new scheme to make communications over ATM networks secure is proposed in section 4 and implementation details are given in section 5. Tables 2 and 3 resume those schemes' features and section 6 presents conclusions.

2 THE ATM PROTOCOL REFERENCE MODEL

As depicted in Figure 1, the ATM reference model (De Prycker, 1991), (CCITT I.321, 1991) includes three planes:

- the user plane to exchange user data,
- the control plane to monitor signaling information,
- the management plane to maintain the network operational.

User and control planes communicate over the ATM network through reserved virtual channels. The management plane may use the same channel as the user plane to exchange Operation And Maintenance (OAM) cells. All information is exchanged over the network in the form of 53-byte ATM cells.

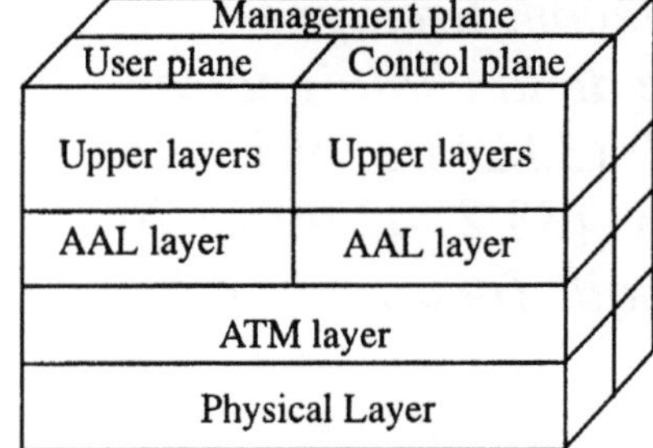

Figure 1 The ATM protocol reference.

The ATM reference model includes three lower layers, a physical layer mainly responsible for information transportation, an ATM layer mainly in charge of multiplexing and switching functions and an ATM Adaptation Layer (AAL) whose main function is to adapt services needs to ATM streams by performing segmentation into (/reassembly of) cells for instance.

3 SURVEY

Solutions to secure ATM communications are discussed in (Stevenson, 1995), (Deng, 1995), (Chuang, 1996) and (ATM Forum, 1996). As securing an ATM communication is based on firstly negotiating a security context and secondly applying negotiated security services on user data exchanges, these solutions' presentation is divided into two corresponding subsections. Along the sections, notations of table 1 are used.

Table 1 : Notations

A	calling entity
B	called entity
KAB	session key generated by A to protect flow from A to B
KsA {M}	encrypted M with A's private key
KpA{M}	encrypted M with A's public key
T_A	current timestamp generated by A
N_A	nonce generated by A
CA	certification authority entity
Cert_A	A's public key certificate generated by CA

Security IE Identifier 1 byte
IE instr. field
Length 2 bytes
Version
E/E | Signature Algorithm
Sequence number
Timestamp (4 bytes)
IE list lenth
IE list
Encrypted IEs
Reserved
Algorithm-specific information
Signature

The IE's fields include (for details, refer to (ATM Forum,1996)):
- *Authentication IE Identifier* identifies the authentication IE within signaling messages
- *Version* denotes the version to which the IE is compliant
- *E/E* indicates end-to-end (*E/E*=1) or hop-by-hop (*E/E*=0) authentication
- *Signature algorithm* identifies the code of the algorithm used for generating the signature
- *Sequence number/timestamp* allow each authentication IE to be unique
- *IE list length* and *IE list* contain respectively the number of IEs included into the IE list field and the list of IE's identifiers that specifies the IEs over which the signature is computed and the ordering of IEs during generation
- *Algorithm-specific information* includes parameters to be used for signature generation
- *Signature* contains the digital signature

Figure 2 Authentication IE format of the ATM Forum's solution.

3.1 Security services negotiation

ATM security solutions differ in that security services negotiation is done :

- during connection set up within control operations (ATM Forum, 1996), (Deng, 1995), (Chuang, 1996)
- along the connection within management operations (ATM Forum, 1996)
- over an auxiliary channel dedicated to security operations (Stevenson, 1995), (ATM Forum, 1996)

Note that ATM Forum's solution uses all these schemes to exchange security information.

3.1.1. Negotiation through signaling information

This scheme consists in inserting security information (session keys, security mechanisms, authenticator) into signaling messages such as SET UP* and CONNECT† within one or more Information Elements‡ (IEs).

3.1.1.1. The ATM Forum's solution

The ATM Forum limits signaling support to the authentication and access control services. Other security services are realized by other means presented in sections 3.1.2.1 and 3.1.3.2.

The ATM Forum defines a new IE whose format is given in Figure 2 and which allows to authenticate signaling messages' source. Authentication may be done end-to-end (between two end-entities) or hop-by-hop (between switches and end-entities) in connection set up messages (SET UP and CONNECT) and other signaling messages such as connection release.

Additionally to the authentication service, the IE ensures integrity of part or all the signaling message and replay detection with the *Sequence number* and *Timestamp* fields.

One access control specific IE is also defined to specify the sensitivity level of user data that need to be exchanged over the connection so that, for instance, the path selected over the network uses only links with appropriate sensitivity level.

---

*. SET UP is sent by A to initiate a call establishment.

†. CONNECT is sent by B in response to SET UP messages to indicate call acceptance.

‡. An Information Element is a structure within signaling messages that include one type of information useful for control operations. E.g. A and B's addresses are included within SET UP as calling and called entity number IEs.

Security IEs to be inserted by A into SET UP are:
IE#1: A's security association identifier
IE#2:Protection QoS: type of authentication, confidentiality and integrity levels
IE#3:Confidentiality operation parameters
IE#4: Integrity operation parameters
IE#9:A's certificate Cert_A = KsCA{serial number, validity period, A, KpA, CA}
IE#10: A's token = KsA{T_A, B, KpB{KAB}}

Security IEs to be inserted by B into CONNECT are:
IE#5: B's security association identifier
IE#6:Chosen protection QoS: chosen type of authentication, chosen confidentiality and integrity levels
IE#7:Chosen confidentiality operation parameters
IE#8: Chosen integrity operation parameters
IE#11:B's certificate Cert_B = KsCA{serial number, validity period, B, KpB, CA}
IE#12:B's token = KsB{T_A, A, KpA{KBA}}

Figure 3 Deng's solution IEs.

As it states in Figure 2, the authentication IE is inaccurate and flawed. Firstly, the IEs ordering that should be enforced when generating the signature is not specified in case signaling messages include repeated IEs (of the same type). Secondly, it would be more efficient to distinguish end-to-end authentication IE from hop-by-hop authentication IE by assigning each a specific IE identifier instead of using the *E/E* bit, since switches would no longer have to examin the Authentication IE fields up to the *E/E* bit to know if authentication is to be performed. Thirdly, the authentication IE enables stations authentication only. Fourthly, there is one scenario that results in a malicious station, say C, masquerading as A. Assume that A authenticates to B with an authentication IE whose signature is not computed over B's address. C (a station eavesdropping the network or even B) may retrieve the authentication IE and reuse it to authenticate to another station, say D as A. This assumes that the *Sequence number* is appropriate and C is quick enough so that the *Timestamp* remains valid.

On the other hand, the *Version* field makes this scheme flexible since it allows new authentication IEs to be defined and used simultaneousy on the same network.

3.1.1.2. Deng et al.'s solution

Deng defines twelve new IEs - six for each SET UP and CONNECT message - which allow entities A and B to authenticate mutually, exchange unidirectional session keys (2 IEs) and negotiate a security context (4 IEs).

Only confidentiality and integrity services to be applied on user data may be negotiated. The calling entity A proposes a set of security parameters to B within SET UP in four IEs (IEs #1 to #4 - see Figure 3). Parameters include its desired protection QoS and the lists of available confidentiality and integrity parameters. B replies with its chosen protection QoS and parameters in CONNECT (IEs #5 to #8). Then A accepts or refuses the connection depending on B's choices. Both A and B store the security context in the form of a security association identified respectively by A and B 's identifier (IEs #1 and #5).

Authentication and keys exchange are based on X509 two-way authentication protocol. The first X509 message within SET UP includes A's public key certificate (IE#9) that allows B to retrieve A's public key and a token KsA{T_A, B, KpB{KAB}} (IE#10) that allows B to authenticate A and retrieve A's session key KAB. The X509 message returned by B within CONNECT (IEs #11 and #12) is similar.

This scheme is rigid since the authentication protocol is imposed. Moreover using as many IEs as security parameters makes this scheme clear but not optimized in terms of modifications implied within UNI specifications (ATM Forum, 1994).

3.1.1.3. Chuang's solution

Chuang developed its solution within the MSN-CMA architecture (Multi-Service Network Connection Management Architecture) which is based on servers supervising all ATM network's management and control operations. That is, when A needs to set up a connection, A sends its signaling message to the appropriate server over the ATM network by the means of Remote Procedure Call (RPC) mechanisms. The server then finds the appropriate end-to-end path, informs B of the request and sets switches' routing tables appropriately.

Contrary to the ATM Forum and the ITU-T, a connection set up requires the exchange of three signaling messages instead of two so that two-way and three-way authentication protocols may be chosen for that solution to authenticate and exchange session keys. Since the three-way protocols usually based on nonces are more reliable than two-way protocols based on timestamps, Chuang's solution appears more reliable than those of the previous sections.

The three-way handshake connection set up enables to negotiate, amongst others, confidentiality, integrity and keys exchange mechanisms to be used for securing user data exchanges. Also Chuang suggests that security parameters renegotiation be done through signaling exchanges.

3.1.2. Negotiation through management information

This scheme consists in injecting security information in-band within the user data channel by the means of OAM cells (cf. section 2).

3.1.2.1. The ATM Forum's solution

The ATM Forum uses such a scheme when security information requires synchronization with the user data cells stream, for instance to exchange new session keys during a connection.

The ATM Forum defines new OAM cells dedicated to security in order not to confuse them with ordinary OAM cells and suggests to encapsulate security messages into the 45-byte OAM cells' function-specific field. To protect security messages exchanges, protocols based on symetric or asymetric algorithms are specified.

3.1.3. Negotiation through an auxiliary channel

Auxiliary channel notion is used here when security information is exchanged in the form of user data cells.

3.1.3.1. Stevenson et al.'s solution

Stevenson suggests to negotiate session keys at connection set up within the first data exchanged.

Figure 4 depicts such a scheme in a proxies context. Proxies A and B are usually on line cryptographic units located at LAN boundaries whose function is to protect communications over the public network.

As shown in Figure 4, A sends a set up request to its proxy which in turn forwards it to proxy B. Before completing the connection set up between A and B, proxies A and B negotiate session keys by exchanging firstly their certificates and nonces and secondly their tokens which include unidirectional session keys and serve as authenticator. After keys negotiation, proxies complete the connection set up between A and B which are then allowed to exchange user data.

3.1.3.2. The ATM Forum's solution

This solution is used in conjonction with the solution of section 3.1.2.1 to negotiate se-

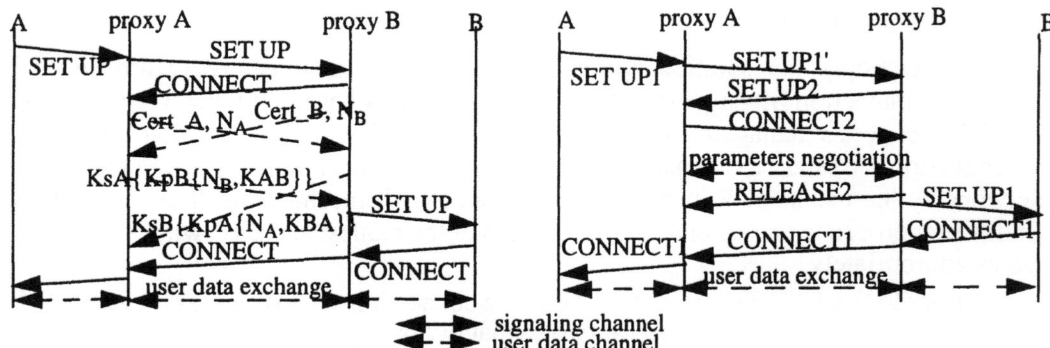

Figure 4 Session keys negotiation at connection set up via an auxiliary channel. Stevenson et al.'s solution.

Figure 5 Parameters negotiation via the auxiliary channel. The ATM Forum's solution.

curity parameters (security mechanisms). It may also be used to do mutual authentication during connection or at connection set up (in case a three-way authentication is required additionally to the two-way authentication realized within signaling messages in section 3.1.1.1).

This solution applies in a proxies context, however contrary to the Stevenson's solution, the auxiliary channel is a specific channel entirely dedicated to security parameters exchanges.

As shown in Figure 5, after receiving A's set up request (SET UP1), proxy A modifies the message into SET UP1' (by inserting security information such as a security services identifier) and forwards it to proxy B. Then proxy B detects the security services identifier and sets up a second connection with proxy A (SET UP2 and CONNECT2) over which all security parameters are negotiated. After the negotiation completion, proxies A and B release the second connection and complete the first connection between A and B.

3.1.4. Comparisons of the solutions

As shown in Table 3 (at the end of the paper), solutions may be compared in terms of modifications required within the ATM Forum's UNI 3.1 specifications (ATM Forum, 1994). Whereas Deng, respectively the ATM Forum, introduce twelve new IEs, respectively two new IEs and security OAM cells, Stevenson and Chuang require no UNI modifications since modifications are transparent for the ATM network. Stevenson modifies only the connection content and Chuang modifies processings within stations and servers (software).

All solutions include drawbacks listed hereafter.

The ATM Forum (section 3.1.1.1) and Deng's solutions expect intermediary public network equipments to transparently pass security information elements which may be used as covert channel (to pass data for free in case signaling is free). As a consequence, operators are reluctant to introduce new security IEs in signaling messages.

Both in-band and auxiliary channel schemes include flaws. The former is unsuitable for unidirectional communications and real-time applications. The latter is costly in terms of connections set ups (in ATM Forum 's implementation in section 3.1.3.2) or does not enable security parameters renegotiations during a connection (in Stevenson's implementation).

The environment of Chuang's solution is not compliant to ATM Forum and ITU-T's philosophy where management and control operations are distributed among network equipments so that his solution is not applicable to the current ATM standard environment.

3.2 Secure user data exchange

User data exchanges may be protected with the security services negotiated in section 3.1.

Solutions differ in that user data encryption is performed:

- at the ATM layer (Stevenson, 1995), (Chuang, 1996), (ATM Forum, 1996)
- within the AAL layer (Deng, 1995)

3.2.1. Confidentiality at the ATM layer

This scheme consists in encrypting user data on the cell-by-cell basis. However encryption algorithms are more or less error-extension sensitive. That is, cell loss occurrence may cause for instance at most one 64-byte block loss when encrypted with DES ECB (Electronic Code Book) and much more data loss when encrypted with DES CBC (Cipher Block Chaining), since in the ECB mode, blocks of data are encrypted independently whereas in the CBC mode, an encrypted block of data is dependent on the plaintext block that generated it but also all the previous encrypted blocks. To avoid too many losses to occur, encrypting/decrypting devices need to be frequently resynchronized. Hereafter each solution's synchronization mechanism is specified.

3.2.1.1. Stevenson et al.'s solution

Stevenson defines cryptographic units (proxies of section 3.1.3.1) which encrypt ATM cells with one session key per connection. He studies the "key agility" problem, i.e. the problem of switching keys quickly enough so that ATM cells streams from various connections can be encrypted independently. He also solves the synchronization problem by injecting synchronization information in-band within OAM cells or user data cells.

3.2.1.2. Chuang's solution

Chuang defines a cryptonode device encrypting user data at the ATM layer with one session key per connection. Synchonization is performed at the AAL layer by injecting AAL5 PDU tokens including new keys numbers and initialization vectors (IV) that should be used for decrypting the next block of data. Therefore when a key or IV change is detected at the decryption device (two consecutive tokens contain different keys or IVs), an interrupt is generated to the ATM layer decryption process, so that cells decryption is halted and temporarily controled by the AAL layer for keys or IV update. In such a scheme, a problem may occur since synchronization is realized at a different layer than encryption. Indeed when a synchronization token is received mixed up with user data cells of the same connection, during the token processing at the AAL layer, many user data cells may be decrypted at the ATM layer with the old security context (old keys or IVs).

Additionally to synchronization, tokens support user data integrity/authentication by the means of a signature appended to tokens together with integrity keys and IV.

3.2.1.3. The ATM Forum's solution

The ATM Forum supports user data confidentiality and integrity (with two independent keys) and optionally reordering/replay detection. Confidentiality may be realized end-to-end or switch-to-switch whereas integrity is only ensured end-to-end. Indeed, the confidentiality service is provided at the ATM layer but confidentiality at the AAL layer is also suggested for the end-to-end scenario.

The integrity and optional reordering/replay detection are supported at the AAL layer by the means of fields appended to the AAL SDU to protect: a signature computed over the AAL SDU, a timestamp and a sequence number. As mentioned in section 3.1.2.1, synchronization together with keys negotiation are realized in-band within OAM cells.

3.2.2. Confidentiality within the AAL layer

User data encryption is provided within the AAL layer prior to their segmentation into cells.

3.2.2.1. Deng et al.'s solution

Deng defines an additional layer called DPL (Data Protection Layer) which is placed between two AAL sublayers and supports confidentiality and integrity services and optional reordering. DPL SDUs are independently encrypted and signed with the keys negotiated at connection set up and the Initialization Vector (IV) specified within the DPL SDU's clear header. As a consequence no synchronization is needed.

During connection the DPL layer may update session keys by halting data transmission and sending repeatedly one DPL SDU containing a new session key (encrypted with its private key) until reception of a positive acknowledgement. This scheme appears unsuitable for unidirectional communications and real-time applications and is unsecure since no strong authentication protocols are used to exchange session keys.

3.2.3. Solutions comparisons

Solutions may be compared in terms of services supported. Stevenson's solution only supports the confidentiality service whereas all other solutions support confidentiality and integrity services.

We should note that the integrity service when offered is always placed at the AAL layer in order to avoid additional cells segmentations whereas the confidentiality service is placed at the ATM or AAL layer.

Encrypting user data at the ATM layer brings simplicity and performances improvements since encryption is realized on fixed-size cells and within hardware.

Benefits result also from encrypting user data at the AAL layer. Modifications within the ATM layered model are restricted to the AAL layer. Because of encryption realized on long-size block of data (up to 65535 bytes for DPL SDUs), no key agility problems raise. In Deng's solution, only session keys change requires synchronization with the user data flow and synchronization is easier to realize than in Chuang's solution since synchronization and encryption are done within the same layer like with ATM Forum and Stevenson's solutions.

However placing confidentiality at the AAL layer is less reliable than at the ATM layer since DPL PDUs and AAL PDUs' headers remain in clear.

It should be noticed that, contrary to ATM Forum and Chuang's solutions, the integrity and confidentiality services are not independent in Deng's solution since both of them use the same key. This results in algorithms choice restrictions and a weaker security level since in case the used key is broken, user data exchanged may be decrypted but also corrupted user data may be generated and signed.

4 SOLUTION FOR FREQUENT COMMUNICATIONS (SFFC)

We propose a solution which aims to protect communications between ATM stations but also ATM switches in case communications between ATM LANs need to be protected over the public network. This solution is especially suitable for ATM stations or LANs that frequently communicate and in particular, for companies needing to securely communicate with their remote subsidiaries. Later it is referred to as the Solution For Frequent Communications or SFFC.

SFFC enables security services introduction within ATM stations or switches, thus defining ATM security stations or ATM security gateway switches. Such security devices are noted A and B respectively for the calling and called security devices.

Hereafter our solution is described in the same way as previous solutions, i.e. it is divided into two parts: security services negotiation and secure user data exchange.

4.1 Security services negotiation

The solution proposed is close to the ATM Forum's solution (section 3.1.1.1) since one security IE is introduced to provide both signaling messages source authentication and integrity protection.

As illustrated in Figure 6, the security IE includes fields similar to these of the ATM Forum's IE but is organized into security elements, each of which supports either security services or security services negotiation.

Hereafter security services offered by the IE are described:

- authentication and integrity of part of the signaling message.
  Like with the ATM Forum's solution, the signature is computed over the security IE and part of the signaling message specified in the *IEs list length* and *IEs list* fields and the result is placed in the *Digital Signature* field. The repeated IEs' problem that raises in section 3.1.1.1 may be solved by introducing as many repeated IEs identifiers as repeated IEs to be signed into the *IEs list*. That is, if n repeated IEs' identifiers are introduced into *IEs list*, the signature is generated over the n first repeated IEs that appear within the signaling message. This is possible since repeated IEs' ordering is kept along the connection.
  Contrary to the ATM Forum's solution, the signature algorithm to be used can be chosen by the interconnected ATM security devices. Indeed when A sends a security IE, A specifies a list of algorithms (with their respective information) ordered according to preferences within the field: *List of algorithms to be used for signature*. The first instance in the list is the algorithm code used to generate IE's signature. As such if B does not support that algorithm, B can choose another algorithm among the list and sends it back within a security IE. A will then use that algorithm to authenticate in other messages. A may also specify available algorithms that B should use for generating its signature in the security IE within the field *List of algorithms to be used by the receiver if mutual authentication is required*.

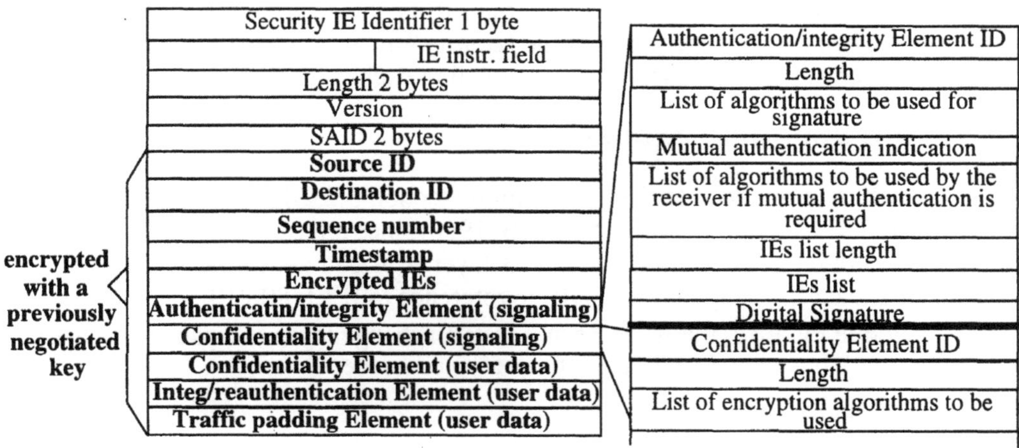

Figure 6 Security Information Element within SET UP messages.

Contrary to the ATM Forum's solution, A may demand B to authenticate by the means of the field *Mutual authentication indication*. Also authentication based on both stations addresses and users is allowed since the fields - *Source ID* and *Destination ID* - may be used to carry specific users or user groups identifiers (alternative use of such fields is described below).

- confidentiality of part of the signaling message.
  In the literature the signaling confidentiality service has never been studied since this assumes that a security context (i.e. session keys and encryption algorithms) has been previously negotiated. In the context where ATM security devices frequently communicate, we assume that a connection dedicated to security has already been set up between them to negotiate a list of session keys so that no keys exchanges are needed at connection set up. This security context is identified by a security association identifier (*SAID* field) so that when receiving such a security IE, the decrypting device needs to retrieve the appropriate key within the SAID security context to decrypt the security IE.
  The solution enables to encrypt part of security IE written in bold in Figure 6, i.e. security parameters included within security services elements but also ordinary signaling IEs that should not be analyzed by the public network and can be moved in the security IE in the *encrypted IEs* field to be encrypted.
  Also this confidentiality service may be used to hide information within the security IE such as stations' addresses. This scheme appears suitable for companies wanting to keep their own addresses mappings secret while communicating over the network with their subsidiaries. This is realized by defining one global address common to all company's stations. Thus when setting up a connection with that company, the only clear address within the SET UP message (in the called entity number IE) is the global one and the real stations' addresses are encrypted within the *Source ID* and *Destination ID* fields of the security IE. This assumes that the security gateway switch B decrypts the security IE with the context identified by the *SAID* field before forwarding the set up request to the appropriate station.
- replay detection by the means of the *Sequence number* and *Timestamp* fields
- confidentiality (signaling and user data), integrity/reauthentication and traffic flow confidentiality* services negotiation for the signaling and user plane
  Four security elements allow A and B to negotiate mechanisms and session keys numbers to be used to provide such security services. A specifies a list of algorithms ordered according to preferences and B returns its choice within the next signaling message. Then choices are stored as the security context (identified by an SAID) to be applied on subsequent user data and signaling exchanges.

4.2 Secure user data exchange

We propose a solution close to Deng's solution (section 3.2.2.1) and the IEEE 802.10 model (IEEE 802.10A, 1989), (IEEE 802.10B, 1990) since all user data security services are introduced into one additional layer. This layer is placed above the AAL layer and called Secure Data Exchange layer (SDE) in reference to IEEE 802.10.

As depicted in Figure 7, the ATM Secure Data Exchange layer encapsulates user data (*SDE SDU*) with one clear header and one encrypted header.

---

*. The traffic flow confidentiality service protects communications against traffic analysis by injecting spurious user data cells within user data flow

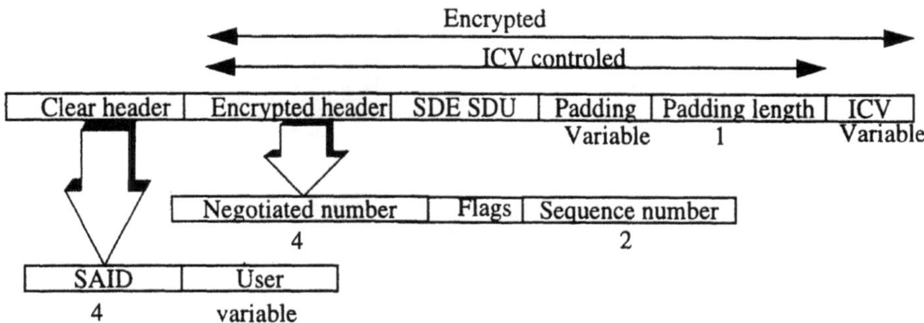

Figure 7 SDE PDU construction.

SDE offers the following security services:

- user data confidentiality. The *SAID* field identifies the security context (negotiated in section 4.1) used to encrypt user data (SDE SDU). *Padding* and *Padding length* fields are used to align data to be encrypted with a length suitable for the encryption algorithm.
- user data integrity/authentication. The Integrity Control Value (*ICV*) computed over the SDE PDU encrypted part may be used to both authenticate and check integrity. However in case the confidentiality service is offered, the ICV may be a simple Cyclic Redundancy Check (CRC) and the authentication service may be a secret number negotiated within the security IE and placed into the *Negotiated number* field.
- user data traffic flow confidentiality. Cells with no meaningful content may be injected into user data cells flow and recognized by the means of the *Flag* field.
- user data replay detection. User data unicity is ensured with the *Sequence number* field.

Like with Deng's solution, synchronization is realized on each SDE PDU by inserting into the *User* field synchronization information such as session keys numbers and initialization vectors to be used for encryption or ICV generation.

5 IMPLEMENTATION

We only implemented the security services negotiation part of our solution in SUN's ATM drivers environment (Paul, 1996). Since the ATM switch in our laboratory considers signaling messages with an additional security IE as error messages, our experimental network is limited to two SUN stations.

As depicted on Figure 8, we use TCP/IP stack on top of the ATM stack for testing purpose. Since SUN's ATM drivers use the concept of streams, our stack is divided into three streams:

- a first stream between TCP and IP
- a second stream one between IP and the ATM card's driver called SA. This stream is used to exchange user data and corresponds to the ATM model's user plane. The SA driver provides AAL5 services.
- a third stream between IP and SA including Q93B and SSCOP signaling protocols defined by ITU-T. This stream corresponds to the ATM model's control plane.

Signaling drivers include ONIP and Q93B. The latter checks signaling messages content to be compliant to the UNI specifications. We modified it, so it does not reject messages with a security IE.

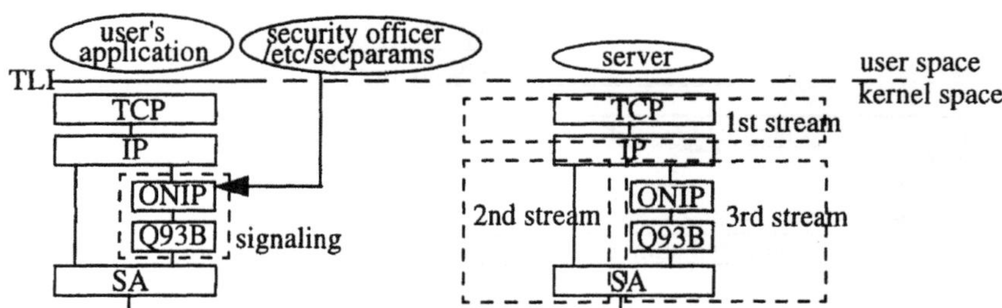

Figure 8 Our implementation.

Our implementation is based on another project "TCP Over Non-existent IP (ONIP)" realized at Télécom Bretagne which improves TCP performances by systematically causing an ATM connection set up for each TCP connection set up. This requires the following modifications: most of IP driver's functions are inhibited since they are realized in the AAL5 layer (e.g. cells segmentation/reassembly); an ONIP driver is created to monitor ATM connections and informs TCP of the identifiers of the connection being set up; TCP is modified in order to monitor ATM connections; the DNS server and its configuration files are modified to include ATM addresses.

Additionally to these modifications, we adapted cryptographic algorithms including DES, RSA, MD5 and keyedMD5 to the kernel space and created a cryptographic library. We modified the ONIP driver to build security IEs with the cryptographic library, i.e. compute fingerprints and encrypt part of the signaling message according to the security policy.

In order to retrieve the appropriate security policy when one TCP connection set up is requested, the TCP driver must send the appropriate SAID identifier together with its request to the ONIP driver. SAID can be buried in the user application thus allowing one security policy per application or computed at user login time. SAID is passed to the kernel by the means of a modified dynamically allocated TLI (Transport Level Interface) structure. Then ONIP driver can apply the appropriate security policy by consulting a kernel dynamically allocated structure which contains the SAID and the corresponding security policy. This structure can only be initialized or updated by the security officer with a root user program that reads a security policy file called /etc/secparams. After security services negotiation, ONIP driver has only to save the chosen security services and parameters with the user data connection identifiers in another structure.

One possibility to implement the SDE layer of section 4.2 is to place one additional driver CRYPT between IP and SA (along the second stream) which would provide user data security services. In order that CRYPT would retrieve the security policy negotiated at connection set up by ONIP, one solution would be that ONIP sends it to IP which would forward it to CRYPT.

6 CONCLUSIONS

In this paper, we present and compare solutions proposed by Stevenson et al., Deng et al., ATM Forum and Chuang to secure ATM networks. Thus, contrary to ATM Forum which meets both operators and users' security needs, Stevenson, Chuang and Deng focus on users' needs. That is, their philosophy is to ensure end-to-end communications security over an ATM public network considered as unsecure.

We describe also a new solution - the Solution For Frequent Communications (SFFC) - which aims to secure communications between ATM stations or ATM LANs switches where stations or LANs need to communicate frequently. This solution is close to ATM

Table 2 : Recapitulation of security services offered by ATM security solutions

a	Stevens on et al.	Deng et al.	Chuang	ATM Forum	Télécom Bretagne
security services established through signaling		A, KE, RD, SN:I+C	A, KE, RD, SN:I+C+KE	A, I, AC, KE, RD SN:I+C+KE +A for all signaling messages	(A, I, C, RD, SN:C+I+A+P +RD) for all signaling messages
security services established through management cells				KE	
security services established through the auxiliary channel	EC, A, RD			SN, A, KE	
user data security services	C within ATM S with OAM or user data cells	C, I, and (RD) within AAL S done for each DPL-PDU KE	C within ATM I, A within AAL S within AAL with a cryptotag	C rather within ATM I, A and (RD) within AAL S with OAM cells	(C, I, A, RD, P) above AAL layer S on each secure SDE PDU

a. Notations used:

A Authentication
AC Access Control
C Confidentiality
I Integrity
(XX) Optional service XX
KE Keys Exchange
P Padding
RD Replay Detection
SN:XX Negociation of service XX

Forum and Deng's solutions, however as described in Table 2, it integrates additional security services. Amongst others, it ensures confidentiality of part of the signaling, thus allowing interconnected LANs to keep their addresses mappings secret. It allows to perform security services negotiation within signaling and, contrary to Chuang and Deng's

Table 3 : ATM security solutions recapitulation

	Stevenson et al.	Deng et al.	Chuang	ATM Forum	SFFC
security parameters renegotiation	no	yes, keys exchange through DPL PDUs	yes, with three additional signaling messages exchange	yes, with management information	yes, via a secure auxiliary connection
authentication and/or keys negotiation protocol	protocols based on asymetric algorithms	X509 two-way protocol	two-way or three-way protocols	within the signaling flow: two-way protocols within the auxiliary channel: not defined	two-way protocols
modifications required within UNI	none (unless synchronization is realized through security OAM cells)	12 new IEs	none - software modifications only	2 new IEs and new security OAM cells	one new IE
distinction between confidentiality and integrity services		no, mechanisms are different but keys are similar	yes, mechanisms, keys and IVs are different	yes	yes, mechanisms, keys and IVs are different

solutions, that solution offers negotiated security parameters confidentiality. Moreover it enables both users and stations authentication. Additionally to the user data confidentiality and integrity services offered in Deng's solution, it offers user data reauthentication along the connection, replay detection and traffic padding.

7 ACRONYMS

AAL: ATM Adaptation Layer
IE: Information Element
IV: Initialization vector
OAM: Operation And Maintenance
QoS: Quality of Service
SAID: Secure Association Identifier
SDE: Secure Data Exchange
SDU: Service Data Unit
UNI: User Network Interface

8 REFERENCES

ATM Forum (1994) ATM User-Network Interface Specification, version 3.1.

ATM Forum (1996) ATM Forum 95-1473R3, Phase I ATM security specification, June 1996.

Chuang S.C. (1996) Securing ATM networks. *Third ACM conference on computer and communication security*, New Delhi, India.

CCITT I.321 (1991) B-ISDN Protocol Reference Model and its applications.

Deng R.H., Gong L. and Lazar A.A. (1995) Securing data transfer in Asynchronous Transfer Mode networks, *Proceedings of Globecom'95*, pp 1198-1202, Singapore.

McDysan D.E. and Spohn D.L. (1994) *ATM: Theory and application*, McGraw-Hill series on Computer Communications.

IEEE 802.10A (1989) Standard for Interoperable LAN security (SILS) - Part A: The Model.

IEEE 802.10B (1990) Standard for Interoperable LAN Security (SILS) - Part B: Secure Data Exchange.

Paul O. (1996) *Conception et implémentation d'un module de sécurité pour les réseaux ATM*, Report ME-96001, Télécom Bretagne.

De Prycker M. (1991) *Asynchronous Transfert Mode: Solution for broadband ISDN*, Ellis Horwood, New York.

Stevenson D., Hillery N. and Byrd G. (1995) Secure Communications in ATM Networks, *Communications of the ACM*, Vol. 38, No. 2.

UIT-T X.800 (1991) Data communication networks ; open systems interconnection (OSI) ; security, structure and applications. Security architecture for open systems interconnection for CCITT applications.

9 BIOGRAPHY

Maryline LAURENT obtained an engineering degree in electronics from the French graduate School ENSERB in 1993 and an advanced degree in Telecommunication Network Management from the Franco Polish School of New Information and Communication technology (EFP). Now she is a PhD student within the Networks and Multi-media Services Department (RSM) of Telecom Bretagne (a French Graduate School of Telecommunications Engineering), Rennes, France, since December 1994. She works on networks security, mainly in the ATM field, where her job consists in securing communications over ATM networks.

Non-intrusive authentication*

Daniele Alberto Galliano
Politecnico di Torino - Dip. Automatica e Informatica
corso Duca degli Abruzzi 24 - 10129 Torino, Italy, phone: +39-11-5647072, fax: +39-11-5647099, e-mail: galliano@athena.polito.it

Antonio Lioy
Politecnico di Torino - Dip. Automatica e Informatica
corso Duca degli Abruzzi 24 - 10129 Torino, Italy, phone: +39-11-5647021, fax: +39-11-5647099, e-mail: lioy@polito.it

Fabio Maino
Politecnico di Torino - Dip. Automatica e Informatica
corso Duca degli Abruzzi 24 - 10129 Torino, Italy, phone: +39-11-5647072, fax: +39-11-5647099, e-mail: maino@polito.it

Abstract

Available security solutions often are not widely used because the associated secure applications are awkward to use or they lack functionality when compared to standard insecure tools.

To avoid this dicothomy, we developed a non-intrusive (or external) client-server authentication framework which requires no modification to both the clients and the servers. In this way, full featured clients can be used to the satisfaction of the user community, and off-the-shelf servers can be used with augmented security to the happiness of the system administrators.

Our approach relies on software agents which use private keys and a challenge-response protocol to authenticate TCP/IP connection setup. The paper discusses the general framework as well as a sample implementation. Attacks and countermeasures are also outlined. The approach explicitly doesn't address data privacy during transmission, as we would rather see it placed at application level.

Keywords

Authentication in distributed systems, Trusted third-party, Network security

*This work was partially supported by project MURST 40% 'Metodologie e Strumenti di Progetto per Sistemi Distribuiti e Paralleli'

1 INTRODUCTION

Nowadays client-server is the dominant computing paradigm. It has brought many benefits, mostly in the form of flexibility and scalability, but it has also given rise to severe security problems because most client-server applications have retained the old centralized authentication schema: passwords. While passwords are adequate when authentication is performed over a private channel, they are completely inadequate when used in a open networked environment such as today's LANs and Internet. In fact, in TCP/IP all the data - passwords included - are sent in clear over the network, and hence they can be easily captured by eavesdroppers.

The problem is so general that several solutions have been proposed to overcome it.

OTP (One Time Password) methods (Haller 1994, McDonald *et al.* 1995) do not care about passwords being sent in clear because they are never reused: for every service request users have to provide a new password, usually extracted from a pre-stored list or generated on the fly by a crypto calculator. This solution is acceptable for those services that require authentication only few times a day (*e.g.* main session login), but it is completely unusable for short-life services (*e.g.* incoming e-mail checking) which require frequent authentication. Moreover, this technique is not easily applied to authenticate software agents acting on behalf of humans.

The most widely known and used network authentication system is surely Kerberos (Steiner *et al.* 1988). This is an excellent trusted third-party solution to provide user authentication, but it is rather complex. In fact, if it is to be applied to a network application, both the client and the server side need to be heavily modified (*kerberized*). As a consequence, a lot of maintenance is needed to upgrade the application to new versions of Kerberos or of the operating system. For certain services (such as the Network File System) support for Kerberos must be provided right in the kernel, and so it can be done only by the OS vendor. Another drawback is that, if a service has been protected with Kerberos, only kerberized clients can be used, and the user is forced to choose from a limited set of client applications. Last but not least, Kerberos requires the client host to be secure because the *tickets* are stored on the local disks, and thus can be easily stolen by anybody with system privileges; this can be a problem in open environments with public clients, as often used in an academic environment.

Client-server authentication can also be achieved by using public-key solutions, as is currently done when the SSL protocol (Freier *et al.* 1996) is adopted to secure WWW transactions. However, also this solution requires a safe storage for the private key of the user and the servers. In turn, this calls for use of smart cards, which are still expensive and require special hardware that is not always readily available.

All these solutions suffer from a common drawback: they require specially modified clients and servers to achieve their functionality. A quick look at the major USENET security newsgroups makes clear that people are eagerly looking for security-enabled applications, but they want them right on their platform and with the same user interface they are accustomed to. In other words, users want security to be added to their preferred applications, and they are unwilling (with few exceptions) to trade functionality for security.

2 NON-INTRUSIVE AUTHENTICATION

Based on the analysis of the problems encountered by the current distributed authentication systems, we propose a new one (GIANO) which complies with the following requirements:

- users must authenticate themselves explicitly only once when a new session is started (afterwards, it is the duty of a proper authentication agent to maintain a list of authenticated users for each client, and to transparently provide evidence of their identity to the servers queried by the user applications)
- standard client queries to servers will implicitly trigger the authentication agent (this allows the use of this authentication framework with standard vanilla client applications)
- user service keys are never transmitted in clear over the network (they are stored locally in encrypted format by the client authentication agent, which then uses a challenge-response protocol to prove the users' identity to the servers)

To satisfy these requirements, each client participating in the GIANO authentication framework runs a daemon, `gianod`, on a well known TCP port. This daemon talks both to local and remote processes to perform separate tasks.

Processes running on the client will make a local connection (normally during login) to the local `gianod` in order to subscribe the user to the authentication framework. Subscription requires `gianod` to get the user's key and to store it in a protected local memory area. To achieve an higher level of security, a different key for each service can be managed by the authentication agent, but it is also possible for a user to share keys across services.

When a server receives an operation request, it first contacts the `gianod` of the client. If the calling process (or one of its ancestors) is enrolled into the authentication framework, `gianod` provides to the server the proper authentication data, otherwise authentication fails and consequently access to the service is denied.

The proof of the user identity is provided by `gianod` to the authentication server via a challenge-response protocol, to prevent key transmission over the network. Basically, `gianod` acts as an electronic safe to which the user commits his service key upon login. Later, `gianod` will provide evidence that the keys are in the safe by answering to the challenges posed by the servers.

Since authentication takes place only upon request from the server, GIANO requires no modification at all of the standard client applications. Client machines have just to run the `gianod` authentication agent, which is the only piece of code that needs to be protected.

On the server side, few modifications to the application server code are needed to query the distributed authentication agent before providing the service. Even better, if we are allowed to manipulate the network tables (such as `inetd.conf` in UNIX) we can totally avoid to modify the server code by simply intercepting calls to the protected server ports. Services requests will be forwarded to the standard server behind the port only if the client is properly authenticated.

It is easy to see that in the most general case GIANO is able to easily add authentication to connection-oriented services which were not developed with security in mind.

3 IMPLEMENTATION

This section refers to the three fundamental kinds of interaction between the user and the authentication framework.

The GIANO daemon, as shown in figure 1, acts just as a safe meant to keep the ID data of each user subscribed: these data are the encrypted key, the expiration of the subscription, and the PID the user subscribed for. Comparing this approach to the Kerberos one, that uses file as the ticket repository, shows that GIANO, that maintain the authentication instances in main memory, provide an higher level of secrecy.

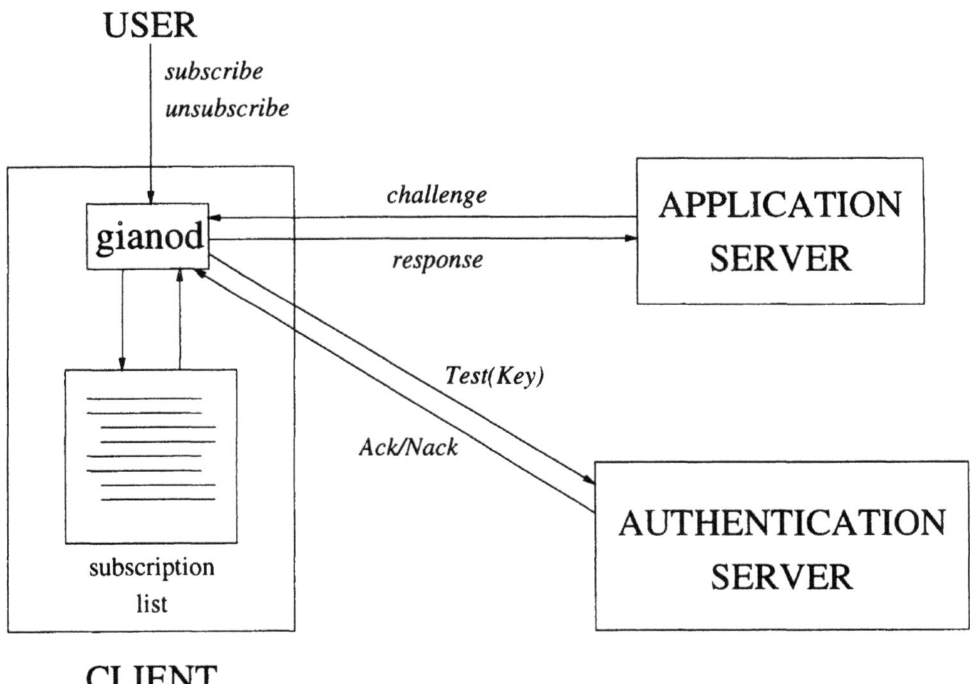

Figure 1 GIANO, a general view.

We assume that every server is physically secure and we assign a key to each service and to each user in the system. In this way we have a bunch of GIANO actors, that are not always real users, but just authenticated entities. Every key is known to the authentication server, so that it is able to check the response provided to any challenge.

3.1 User authentication

When a user wishes to get the GIANO service of authentication brokering, he should commit his keys to the `gianod` daemon. To do this, he must send to the well known port of the daemon a special packet, composed of the following fields:

`Subscr:USERNAME:KEY:PID`

`Subscr` identifies the message as a subscription;
`USERNAME` is the name by which the user is known to the authentication system;
`KEY` is an hex representation of the encrypted key made from the user's key;
`PID` is the PID the user wants to subscribe: the only values allowed are the PID of the calling process or its parent.

When the daemon receives the request, and recognizes it as a subscription request, it checks the key with the authentication server. If the user supplied the correct key, the authentication server will reply with an acknowledgment and the number of the seconds the subscription will be valid. Then the daemon detects from the kernel the PID of the process calling, hence only local processes are allowed to ask subscription. If all the conditions are satisfied, the daemon will add a new entry in its table for the process. The table will hold this data:

`pid` the pid of the process subscribed;
`login` the name of the user;
`key` the encrypted key;
`expiration` the last second this subscription will give a valid authentication.

Of course, this chain of events should take place at login, to be sure that every process the user will activate will be authenticated. It means that we shall have to modify only these two clients: login and xlogin; alternatively, a special application can be developed to perform GIANO subscription explicitly after a standard login.

3.2 Subscription of a new process

When starting a new application, the authenticated user will not have normally to subscribe the corresponding process to GIANO, because it will inherit the authentication from its chain of parents. However there are cases when an authenticated new process must be explicitly subscribed for itself:

- when the parent will die before the child, *i.e.* the child is launched as a background process, and will not end at user logout;

- when the new process should be authenticated with a new, or anyway different, authority (this applies either to a different user, or to the need of a longer lifetime).

3.3 Client and server authentication

As shown in figure 2 there are four processes involved in this task:

P, is the process the user executes: it is unaware of the authentication activity;
A, authentication agent (*i.e.* `gianod`) on the user machine, the same of **P**;
G, `cerere`, the master authentication server: it can be implemented by more than one server for redundancy, but it is represented as a single entity for sake of simplicity;
S, the application server process activated to answer **P**.

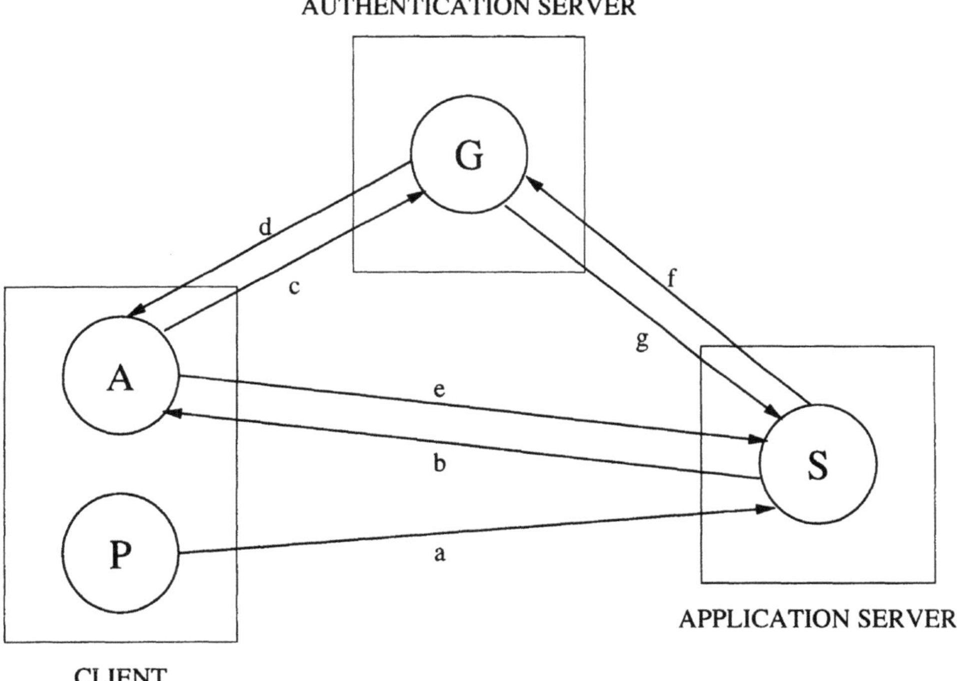

Figure 2 Service validation sequence: a) Service request; b) ID request; c) Server authentication by the broker for the user; d) Server authentication produced by the authentication server; e) User ID; f) User authentication; g) User authentication produced by the authentication server.

The packet that the actors involved into the process use to exchange messages has the following structure:

```
CRYPT:AUTHOR:TEXT:PEER:EDATA
```

Where:

- `CRYPT` is the encryption of `TEXT` by the `AUTHOR`'s key;
- `AUTHOR` is the user issuing the authentication request;
- `TEXT` is the challenge created by the server process;
- `PEER` is the user, which `AUTHOR` wants to authenticate;
- `EDATA` that contains a timestamp, the length of the message, and the message itself, all this fields are encrypted with a key owned by the `AUTHOR`.

The user starts the session by launching the client process **P**. This process is the execution of a program not modified in any way to accomplish authentication tasks. This allows us to use standard commercial products that may have optimizations we cannot reproduce easily.

Process **P** will contact the server host and try to talk to the server process **S** (Step a). This is a modified version of the program, which will be able to perform authentication issues. As a matter of fact we developed a general purpose server to authenticate the client, before starting server process itself: it avoids loss of performance and reduces the amount of work necessary to introduce this authentication.

The server process can easily discover the host who submitted the service request, and from which port: this is what the authentication is based upon. It now produces a challenge which, the user has to solve to have its request accomplished.

Challenge format is fixed, to provide further exchange of informations during the authentication procedure. Its structure is:

```
TSTAMP:PID$IP:PORT
```

Where:

- `TSTAMP` is the UNIX standard time of creation of the challenge, this prevents both replay and cut-and-paste attacks to the challenge;
- `PID` is the PID of the server process itself, and is introduced to increase the unpredictability of the challenge;
- `IP` is the IP address of the client host;
- `PORT` is the network port of the client host, from which the request comes. This field provide to `gianod` the clue to identify the process requesting the service.

The challenge is transmitted into a standard packet (Step b) to process **A**; the packet contains this information:

- `CRYPT` the challenge encrypted;
- `AUTHOR` the entity which represents the service;
- `TEXT` the challenge in clear that the service proposes to the user;
- `PEER` the string *unknown*, usually, unless an earlier transaction stated the identity of the user;
- `EDATA` a brief description for logging purposes.

In case the user is already known to the service handler, it can proceed to request the authentication without waiting for the user machine's answer.

Once **A** receives the request from the service process, it proceeds to search in the kernel itself which process holds the port from which the server machine was contacted.

The table of subscription is scanned for the process and all its ancestors. If none of them is found, the request is refused: **S** learns that **P** has no right for the service, and it should not be provided.

Otherwise, if it is found in the table, the authentication daemon **A** will have the ID data and the key, received when the family of processes was subscribed. Using these, it can produce its own solution of the challenge, and issue it to the authentication server, to check the server identity (Step c). The packet for process **G** will be composed of these fields:

`CRYPT` the user solution of the challenge;
`AUTHOR` the user;
`TEXT` the challenge received by the user;
`PEER` the server requesting the authentication;
`EDATA` a brief description for logging purposes.

G has two possible answers for this kind of requests: if `AUTHOR` authentication fails, an error message will be returned, encrypted with the `AUTHOR` key; otherwise, **G** will provide the challenge solution `PEER` should have computed, encrypted a second time with the `AUTHOR` key.

A will then receive the confirmation of **S** identity (Step d), so it will reply its own version of the challenge, in order to authenticate with the now trusted server **S** (Step e). The packet for process **S** will be:

`CRYPT` the user solution of the challenge;
`AUTHOR` the user;
`TEXT` the challenge received by the user;
`PEER` the server requesting the authentication;
`EDATA` a brief description for logging purposes.

G will then receive a symmetrical request from **S**, in order to authenticate the answer received from **A** (Step f); and symmetrically it will answer (Step g).

At this point all the actors are sure of the identity of each other, and **S** can carry on the normal transactions with **P**.

3.4 Status of the implementation

In order to test the validity of our authentication framework, we developed a GIANO environment under DIGITAL UNIX and HP/UX. The two main components of GIANO are:

`cerere`, the GIANO authentication server, which maintains all the knowledge about the authentication framework;

gianod, the daemon which performs all the authentication operations on user's behalf.

Some services that use the GIANO infrastructure have also been developed:

glogin, a secure login that subscribes a user to the authentication framework;
gexec, a secure exec to spawn a process that doesn't inherit the authentication state from the parent process, but gets a new one;
limen, a general purpose spawner for net services. It is a configurable general purpose interface for the usual net server **inetd**.

The functionality of these programs is detailed in the next sections.

Cerere

This application maintains the database of users, with all the related informations, and offers two services.

The main service, which covers the largest part of the activity, is the third-party authority, that confirms the mutual authentications between clients and servers. It can be easily replicated on several machines, using read-only copies of the database. Every transaction is logged, and is stateless. Since each request contains all the information needed, only one answer is needed to accomplish the task.

The secondary service that `cerere` must provide is related to administrative tasks: `cerere` is responsible for adding, deleting, and retrieving users from the authentication data-base, handled with **ndbm** routines.

Every entry has the key encrypted with the database master key, chosen at installation time. There is also a checksum, calculated with the same key: the database is, by these means, tamper-proof. To improve this security feature, `cerere` can be started in a conversion mode, that will ask for the old master key and a new master key, and then it will translate the database from one key to the other.

Giano daemon (gianod)

This daemon should be started at boot time to provide two main services: authentication and administration. The authentication service is the core project, and has been illustrated in the previous sections.

By administration, we mean process subscription. This occurs, when the daemon receives a packet starting with the string `Subscr` which cannot be the result of an encryption.

Glogin

This program covers two needs: user subscription and key change.

At login time, this program will generate the user subscription packet, send it to the well known port of `gianod`, and wait for the answer. The user subscription may fail for a few reasons:

- `cerere` installed in the system didn't accept the confirmation request issued by `gianod`

- `cerere` server replied saying that the user is expired
- `cerere` server replied saying that the key has expired

In this latter case, the program will ask for new key and its confirmation, and then it will issue an update request to the authentication server to change the key.

The user subscription can operate at two levels: it can be used to subscribe the parent process, asking in this way the brokering service to `gianod`; but it can also establish an interactive session in the host, updating the log files.

Gexec

To accomplish the task of spawning a new process that doesn't inherit the authentication state from its parent, a command named `gexec` has been developed.

Some special processes, such as the ones that perform a background computation, need an authentication instance different from that of their parent.

In its simplest form, `gexec` executes the new process, giving it a new authority in force of a precedent subscription. It does not request the key, since it comes from an already validated chain of processes. The result is that the subscription will be considered valid for a number of seconds specified in the authority database. This number is a data related to the user entry and retrieved at the moment of the subscription. It cannot be bigger than the amount specified at installation time. In this way a process can be executed for a very long time, without renewing its subscription. It can be useful for long unattended calculations, typically those launched at night or in the weekends.

Another use of `gexec` is the execution of a process authenticate by the means of a different user. This way an administrator can create a shell, in which he can issue commands to perform administration tasks, without interfering with his usual activity. We think this obviously better than having multiple authority files available on the system, as it was, for instance, in a Kerberos environment.

Limen

Since our major concern was the development of an authentication system to improve security in a standard distributed environment, we tried to reduce at a minimum the need to patch existing software. And since servers need to start the gianod authentication process, it was necessary to produce a general purpose shell to encapsulate server programs: this will provide authentication before executing the server program itself.

Born to be used with the standard UNIX network daemon `inetd`, `limen` is a configurable general shield for network servers.

Its use is very simple, and can be illustrated referring to the format of `inetd.conf` file:

```
service-name stream/dgram protocol mode user pathname argv
```

The complete pathname of `limen` will be put instead of the server's one, whose name will be replaced by the pathname itself. The usual arguments will follow; after those a string will follow, to introduce the `limen` parameters.

This way, `limen` will have in its argument vector all the informations needed to execute the program that will perform the service.

Currently the options available for `limen` are:

- `0`: it precedes the name to be used as argument 0, if different from the last part of the pathname indicated as argument 0 for `limen`;
- `a`: it precedes an option of the program to be executed, that in its syntax will precede the name of the user, which issued the service request; it should be left as the last, if no option is needed but the username itself;
- `b`: this option enforces security, preventing *limen* to execute the server program, unless the authentication was accomplished (it is disabled for default, but implied in the previous);
- `c`: it means that the server must be executed as a login session, so `limen` will update the log files, and open the pseudo-tty with the child;
- `d`: it introduces the name chosen for the log file; if absent, a default chosen at installation time will be used.

A practical example of the use of `limen` is the following one, by which an authenticated login was realized with minimum effort:

```
alogin stream tcp nowait root /Giano/bin/limen
    /bin/login -p #G# -a -f -c -d /Giano/logs/alogin.log
```

4 CONCLUSIONS AND FURTHER WORK

We believe to have designed an authentication system which is both simple and effective. Its main novelty lays in the fact that it doesn't require nearly any modification to the existing software, and this is really a big benefit for both users and system administrators.

So far there is only one problem we didn't cope with: shadow servers. It is possible for a malicious host to spoof the real server's IP address, and then the client will probably establish the connection with someone obviously not eager to trigger the authentication session.

Since the client itself is not aware that an authentication session should be performed, it will interact with the fake server as it would do with the real one.

Our solution to this problem is to rely upon the adoption of IPv6 with its packet authentication features.

Extension of the authentication mechanism to DOS/Windows based system is really easy. At boot or start time, a simple application will ask user's key, and then will act as a GIANO daemon, waiting for authentication requests. The system will be really simplified by the single-user environment, since all the requests will be for the same user. A trivial TSR or a WINSOCK application will fit this task.

ACKNOWLEDGEMENT

We want to thank Vic Abell, of the Purdue University Computing Center. His analysis of the kernel data structures (used in the development of `lsof`) was extremely valuable in the realization of `gianod`.

REFERENCES

Freier, A.O. and Karlton, P. and Kocher, P.C. (1996) The SSL Protocol Version 3.0. *IETF Internet draft.*

Haller, N. (1994) The S/key one-time password system. *The ISOC Symposium on Network and Distributed System Security*, 151-7.

McDonald, D.L. and Atkinson, R.J. and Metz, C. (1995) One Time Passwords In Everything (OPIE): Experiences with Building and Using Stronger Authentication. Proc. of *the Fifth USENIX UNIX Security Symposium*, Salt Lake City, UT, 177-86.

Steiner, J.G. and Neuman, C. and Schiller, J.I. (1988) Kerberos: An Authentication Service for Open Network Systems. Proc. of *Winter 1988 Usenix Conference*, Dallas, TX, 191-202.

BIOGRAPHY

Daniele Alberto Galliano is a young registered professional engineer, who took degree in Electronical Engineering from Politecnico di Torino. A former administrator of Athena based distributed system of that University, he is working now as a professional consultant in UNIX systems for universities and public administration. Strongly interested in multivendor distributed systems, he developes administration tools, with a massive advanced use of Tcl/Tk. From his interest in this topic comes the involvement in the field of security.

Antonio Lioy is an associate professor of computer engineering at the Politecnico di Torino. Professor Lioy holds a *laurea* (aka master) degree in Electronic Engineering *summa cum laude* and a Ph.D. in Computer Engineering from Politecnico di Torino. He is a registered professional engineer and a member of the IEEE and the IEEE Computer Society. His research interests are in the fields of computer security and CAD of digital systems.

Fabio Maino is a Ph.D. student in computer engineering at the Politecnico di Torino. He holds a *laurea* (aka master) degree in Electronic Engineering and he is a registered professional engineer. His research interests are in the fields of computer and network security.

Roaming security agents enabling intelligent access control and network protection

P.W.J. van Zyl and S.H. von Solms
Rand Afrikaans University, PO Box 524 - Auckland Park, Johannesburg, South Africa 2006, pietervz@nedcor.co.za

Abstract

This paper presents the concept of roaming security agents and shows how it can enable intelligent access control and transparent network protection in distributed computer environments. The security agents are called roaming because they accompany access requests and its resultant information throughout the distributed environment. The paths followed by, the access requests and its resultant information, are also logged by the security agent in an internal data store, called baggage. With the capability to refer to the baggage it is possible to define intelligent access control and network protection rules for access requests and its resultant information within the distributed environment. These access control rules and network protection rules are also held by the accompanying security agent. Protection is therefore transparent to the user, because the agents travel with the access requests and resultant information, and protects it on its path as the need arises (as specified by the protection rules). This paper describes the above concepts in more detail.

Keywords

Access control, access path, authentication, baggage, confidentially, integrity, network protection, non-repudiation, OSI, roaming agent, security agent, security architecture

1 INTRODUCTION

1.1 The distributed computer environment

We start the discussion by presenting a conceptual distributed environment, in which a user will access a remotely located file. The distributed computer environment, employs the concept of a distributed file system and therefore, the user is not aware of the actual physical location of the files. The user sees a logical view of all files in the distributed environment by way of a Global Directory Structure (GDS). The GDS, in turn, is responsible for mapping the logical file names to their physical location as illustrated in table 1.

Table 1 GDS mapping logical names to physical location in a distributed environment.

GDS entry	*Physical location*
Directory A\ File-C	Host-A\ Directory A\ File-C
Directory A\ File-D	Host-A\ Directory A\ File-D
Directory B\ File-G	Host-B\ Directory B\ File-G
Directory B\ File H	Host-B\ Directory B\ File H
File-A	Host-A\ File-A
File-B	Host-A\ File-B
File-E	Host-B\ File-E
File-F	Host-B\ File-F

For example, in the logical GDS, File-A resides on Host-A and File-E resides on Host-B. Examples of distributed file system implementations are, the DCE's Distributed File System (DFS) [15], and SUN's Network File Service (NFS) [16].

Figure 1 depicts the distributed computer environment. As defined in the GDS, the two hosts, Host-A and Host-B, respectively stores various files. The user (User-A) is signed onto Host-A and via the GDS selects File-E to be loaded into his application (WP-A). The user is not aware that the file is located on a remote host computer. The picture shows the steps (numbered 1 to 17) that would be followed to load File-E from Host-B to WP-A on Host-A.

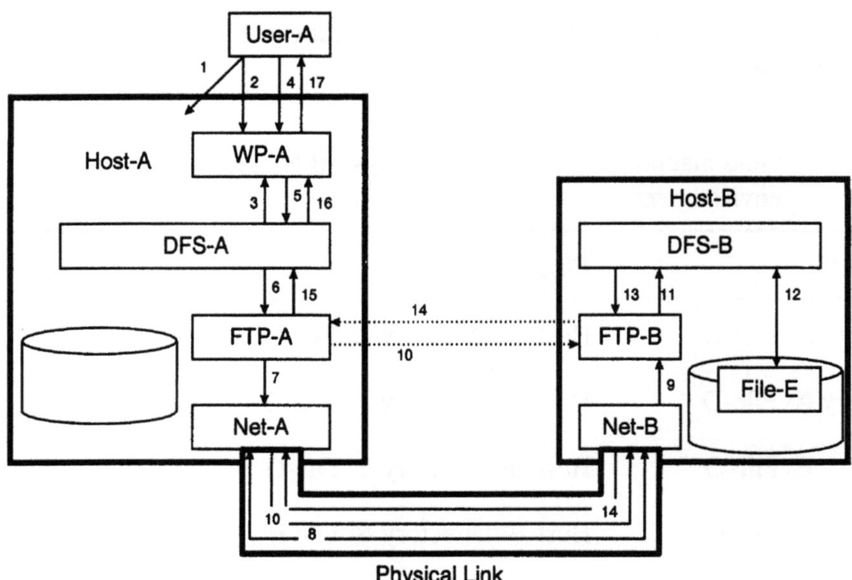

Figure 1 An example of a user accessing a file (File-E) on a remote system (Host-B), from his personal computer (Host-A).

Table 2 describe each of the acronyms used in figure 1.

Table 2 Descriptions of the acronyms used in figure 1

Acronym	*Description*
Host-A	Host-A, for example NT Workstation, OS/2, UNIX, etc.
WP-A	Application at Host-A, for example, MS Word, Word Perfect, etc.
GDS	Global Directory Structure
User-A	User at Host-A, for example Jack or Jill.
DFS-A	Distributed File System at Host-A, for example DCE's Distributed File System (DFS) [15] or SUN's Network File Service (NFS) [16].
FTP-A	File Transfer Protocol at Host-A, for example UNIX FTP, XCOM, etc.
Net-A	Network Sub system at Host-A, for example Microsoft (TCP) Sockets.
Host-B	Host-B, for example NT Server, AIX UNIX, MVS, etc.
DFS-B	Distributed File System at Host-B, for example DCE's Distributed File System (DFS) [15] or SUN's Network File Service (NFS) [16].
FTP-B	File Transfer Protocol at Host-B, for example UNIX FTP, XCOM, etc.

Each of the steps in figure 1 is now described in more detail. The step numbers and corresponding description are presented in table 3.

Table 3 Description of each step in figure 1.

Step	*Description*
1	User-A sign's onto Host-A
2	User-A starts up WP-A.
3	WP-A, retrieves the GDS from the DFS-A and presents it to User-A.
4	User-A selects File-E to be loaded.
5	WP-A requests DFS-A to load File-E in the GDS.
6	Based on the GDS, DFS-A notes that File-E resides on Host-B. DFS-A requests FTP-A to load File-E from Host-B. Note that the user may not be aware that the file is on a remote host, that is Host-B.
7	FTP-A would request Net-A to establish a link with FTP-B on Host-B.
8	Net-A establishes a connection with Net-B.
9	Net-A requests Net-B to connect to FTP-B. After Net-B establishes the connection with FTP-B, a logical connection, via Net-A and Net-B, exists between FTP-A and FTP-B.
10	Via the link, FTP-A requests FTP-B to copy File-E on Host-B.
11	FTP-B requests from DFS-B to load File-E.
12	DFS-B loads File-E.
13	DFS-B returns File-E to FTP-B.
14	FTP-B returns the file to FTP-A, via the Net-A to Net-B connection.
15	FTP-A returns File-E to DFS-A.
16	DFS-A returns File-E to WP-A.
17	WP-A displays File-E to the user.

1.2 Definitions

Access paths and baggage

In order to continue, it is important to define the concepts of an **access path** and **baggage**. An access path is the path that an access request follows, that are the components traversed, from the subject to the object. In the example above, an access path from User-A to File-E are defined by

User-A, WP-A, DFS-A, FTP-A, Net-A, Net-B, FTP-B, DFS-B, File-E (1)

An access path is also followed when an object moves from one point in the distributed environment to another, for example an access path for File-E, moving from its location to WP-A can be defined by

File-E, DFS-B, FTP-B, Net-B, Net-A, FTP-A, DFS-A, WP-A. (2)

If information is collected along an access path, such as (1) or (2), and the infomration is stored in a data store, then that information is termed baggage. Baggage is define by [1,2] as "*...the minimum amount of information that has to be collected and must accompany the access request on its route in order that responsibility and access authority checking can be performed even though various transformations or domain crossings may occur.*"

Subjects and objects

A subject refers to the users in the distributed environment, for example User-A. An object refers to the resources in the distributed environment that the subjects need to access, for example File-A.

1.3 Summary

In this section, it was shown how a user (User-A) can access a file (File-E) without needing to know what the file's physical location is. In the section, the concept of an access path, baggage, subjects and objects, were also defined.

In the next section, we will highlight some of the security problems that are experienced in such an environment.

2 PROBLEM STATEMENT

This section presents some of the security problems that are experienced within a distributed environment as described in the previous section.

2.1 Access control

Almost all access control systems and models today [6,7,10,11] make use of simple subject and object relationships to define access rules. In distributed environments, these simple subject and object relationships are sometimes inadequate in its ability to define access rules that take into account the access path followed [1,2]. For example, the security policy may state that the company executives (User-A, User-B, etc) may only access the corporate strategic plans (File-E) from a specific host computer, such as Windows NT Workstation (Host-A). Employing simple subject to object relationships, for access control definitions, are inadequate to implement such a security policy. Refer to Boshoff and von Solms for more detail about the above problem [1,2].

What therefore is required, is the ability to define access control rules that can take into account the access path followed from the subject (User-A) to the object (File-E). We will call this the requirement of *Path context access control for objects.*

2.2 Network protection

In the above example, there are two situations where network protection is needed. The one is the protection of the subject's (user-A) access request, that is transmitted across the network (step 10), and the other is the protection of the object (File-E), when it is transmitted across the network (step 14).

What is found in security systems today, is that it is not possible to specify network protection rules, for each access request and objects, that are directly associated to the respective subject and object. Typically, network security protocols are implemented, such as PCT [9], and all data that are transmitted across it will have the same protection services employed, that is the protection service to be employed are not linked to the actual subject or object. The result is that the protection services employed are usually "the same for all". Also note, that the user, as demonstrated in the example above, are not always aware that his request or his object (File-E) may traverse a network. This can be totally transparent to the user.

What therefor is required are

- The capability to specify network protection rules for access requests, that are directly related to the subject initiating the request. We will call this the requirement of *Subject linked, access path based, network protection for requests.*
- The capability to specify network protection rules for objects roaming the environment, that are directly related to the object. We will call this the requirement of *Object linked, access path based, network protection for objects.*

The network protection services referred to above, are those as specified by ISO 7498 Part 2 "OSI Security Architecture" [14]. OSI is a 7-layer architecture that defines peer to peer communications between open systems [13]. Table 4 presents the security services, and shows which are appropriate in which layer of OSI.

Table 4 OSI layers and the appropriate security functions per layer

Function \ Layer	*1*	*2*	*3*	*4*	*5*	*6*	*7*
Peer entity authentication			✓	✓			✓
Data origin authentication			✓	✓			✓
Access control function			✓	✓			✓
Connection confidentiality	✓	✓	✓	✓		✓	✓
Connectionless confidentiality		✓	✓	✓		✓	✓
Selective Field confidentiality						✓	✓
Traffic Flow confidentiality	✓		✓				✓
Connection Integrity with Recovery				✓			✓
Connection Integrity without recovery			✓	✓			✓
Selective Field connection integrity							✓
Connectionless integrity			✓	✓			✓
Selective filed connectionless integrity							✓
Non-repudiation, origin							✓
Non-repudiation, delivery							✓

2.3 Consistent protection

In most security modules and their implementations today [6,7,10,11], a situation exist that when an object moves in the environment, it losses the protection rules guarding it. For example when File-E is moved from Host-B and stored on Host-A, all the access control rules that guarded it on Host-B is not applicable any more on Host-A.

What therefore is required, is a mechanism that will ensure that the file does not lose its access control rules when roaming in the distributed environment. In addition, what is also required, is that the file does not lose its network protection rules when it roams in the distributed environment. We will call this the requirement of *Consistent protection of objects within the distributed environment.*

2.4 Summary

Table 5 present the security requirements identified for the distributed computer environment as presented above. Note, that the list of requirements presented below, are by no means exhaustive, but are those requirements that we would like to address in this paper.

Table 5 Security requirements for the distributed environment as depicted in figure 1.

Requirement	*Description*
1. Path context access control for objects	Objects must be able to reference the baggage collected for the access request, in order to make "intelligent" access control decisions. For example, only allow access to File-E if it is User-A AND the user is accessing it from Host-A using WP-A.
2. Subject linked, access path based, network protection for requests	The protection measures employed on a subject's request, must be linked to the subject. The protection rules must also be able to reference the baggage in order to make "intelligent" protection decisions.
3. Object linked, access path based, network protection for objects	The protection measures employed on an object, that are moved / copied over a network, must be linked to the object. The protection rules must be able to reference the baggage in order to make "intelligent" network protection decisions.
4. Consistent protection of objects within the distributed environment	The protection measures defined for an object must remain with the object, even if the object is moved or copied within the distributed environment.

3 PROPOSAL

In this section, we present the concept of roaming security agents, that will be used to demonstrate how it can address the security requirements identified above.

3.1 Definitions

In table 6, we define the subject security agents and object security agents.

Table 6 Definition of subject and object security agents

Security Agents	*Definition*
Subject Security Agents	Every subject has a security agent associated with it. This security agent will accompany all the subject's access requests and will be responsible for satisfying requirement 2. Subject security agents will be denoted by $SA_{Subject\text{-}ID}$, for example $SA_{User\text{-}A}$ is User-A's security agent.
Object Security Agents	Every object has a security agent associated with it. This security agent will accompany the object and is responsible for satisfying requirements 1, 3 and 4. Object security agents will be denoted by $SA_{Object\text{-}ID}$, for example $SA_{File\text{-}E}$ is File-E's security agent.

3.2 Security agent description

The following capabilities of security agents (subject and object) are defined.

1. A security agent will be able to collect baggage in the distributed environment along the access paths. The following baggage types can be collected:
   - Request information, for example the request to load File-E. This will be denoted by (request = load File-E).
   - Component only, for example Host-A, WP-A, Net-B, etc. This will be denoted by (component = WP-A)
   - Component as well as destination component, for example at FTP-A the destination component will be FTP-B. This will be denoted by (component = FTP-A, destination = FTP-B).
   - Component, destination component and the indirect component(s), for example from FTP-A, FTP-B is the destination, but via Net-A. This will be denoted by (component = FTP-A, destination = FTP-B, via = Net-a).
   - Result of a protection rule that was executed, for example the result of peer to peer authentication between FTP-A and FTP-B. This will be denoted by (result = **a**), where **a** is the result.
2. Subject security agents will hold the subject's protection profile that will govern the network protection of the subject's access requests.
3. Object security agents will hold the object's protection profile that will govern the access control to the object by subjects, as well as the object's network protection rules when it roams the distributed environment.
4. Subject and object protection profile rules will be able to refer to the security agents' baggage when making network protection decisions (subject and object) and access control decisions (object only). For example, If (component = FTP-B) AND (destination = FTP-A), then activate peer to peer authentication service.
5. When a subject's request (accompanied by the subject's security agent) reaches an object, then the subject's security agent and object's security agent will first "join". The subject's security agent then has to identify itself to the object security

agent, by exposing its baggage to the object security agent. The object security agent will use this baggage to authenticate the subject and to enforce the appropriate access control rules.

6. It is assumed that the security agent's themselves will be protected from unauthorized modification, interception or fabrication. Much research is being done on distributed objects (in the object oriented sense) and the protection thereof [5,8,12].

In the next section, the example used in the first section is referred, to demonstrate how the roaming security agent concept, as defined above, can address the security requirements 1,2, 3 and 4.

3.3 Example

In this section we define specific security rules for User-A's security agent and File-E's security agent. We then show how these are used to satisfy the security requirements as defined in a previous section.

SA $_{User-A}$ protection profile

The following protection profile rules are defined for SA $_{User-A}$, that is User-A's Security Agent.

At (component = FTP-A), if the (destination = FTP-B), then activate the peer to peer confidentiality and integrity services between FTP-A and FTP-B. (That is to protect the request against unauthorized disclosure, modification or fabrication between FTP-A and FTP-B). (Rule 1)

SA $_{File-E}$ protection profile

The following protection profile rules are defined in SA $_{File-E}$, that is File-E's security agent.

At "joining", if the subject is User-A (obtained from SA $_{User-A}$'s baggage) then, the request MUST be initiated from Host-A as well as via application WP-A, else do not allow access. (Rule 1)

Note that at the "joining" stage, as per point 5 in the security agent description section, the subject security agent, SA $_{User-A}$, will expose its baggage to the object security agent, SA $_{File-E}$.

At (component = FTP-B), if (destination = FTP-A), then activate the peer to peer authentication service. (To ensure that the peer host is authentic and not masquerading) (Rule 2)

The steps presented in the initial example are re-used to now show how the security agents will activate the security rules defined above (Please refer back to figure 1).

The baggage that is collected, by the security agents, in each step is presented in 6. Annex.

Table 7 Security agent action during each step of the access request

Step	*Description*	*Security Agent Action*
1	User-A sign's onto Host-A	SA $_{User-A}$ collect (component = User-A, component = Host-A)
2	User-A starts up WP-A.	SA $_{User-A}$ collect (component = WP-A)
3	WP-A, retrieves the GDS from the DFS-A and presents it to User-A.	
4	User-A selects File-E to be loaded.	SA $_{User-A}$ collect (request = load File-E)
5	WP-A requests DFS-A to load File-E in the GDS.	
6	Based on the GDS, DFS-A notes that File-E resides on Host-B. DFS-A requests FTP-A to load File-E from Host-B. Note that the user may not be aware that the file is on a remote host, that is Host-B.	SA $_{User-A}$ collect (component = DFS-A)
7	FTP-A would request Net-A to establish a link with FTP-B on Host-B. link with FTP-B on Host-B. <u>Security Note:</u> At this point Rule 1 of SA $_{User-A}$ is activated and will initiate the necessary peer to peer confidentiality and integrity services.	SA $_{User-A}$ collect (component = FTP-A, destination, FTP-B, via Net-A) SA $_{User-A}$ activate (result = a)

Step	*Description*	*Security Agent Action*
8	Net-A establishes a connection with Net-B.	SA $_{User-A}$ collect (component = Net-A, destination = Net-B)
9	Net-A requests Net-B to connect to FTP-B. After Net-B establishes the connection with FTP-B, a logical connection, via Net-A and Net-B, exists between FTP-A and FTP-B.	SA $_{User-A}$ collect (component = Net-B, destination = FTP-B)
10	Via the link, FTP-A requests FTP-B to copy File-E on Host-B.	
11	FTP-B requests from DFS-B to load File-E.	SA $_{User-A}$ collect (component = FTP-B)
12	DFS-B loads File-E.	SA $_{User-A}$ collect (component = DFS-B)
	Security Note: At this point Rule 1 of SA $_{File-E}$ is activated, which will check that the request is from User-A and that it was initiated from WP-A running on Host-A.	SA $_{User-A}$ join SA $_{File-E}$ (agents = SA $_{User-A}$, SA $_{File-E}$,result = b)
13	DFS-B returns File-E to FTP-B.	SA $_{File-E}$ collect (component = DFS-B)
14	FTP-B returns the file to FTP-A, via the Net-A to Net-B connection.	SA $_{File-E}$ collect (component = FTP-B, destination = FTP-A, via Net-B)
	Security Note: At this point Rule 2 of SA $_{User-A}$, is activated which will activate the peer to peer authentication services between FTP-A and FTP-B.	SA $_{File-E}$ activate (result = c)
15	FTP-A returns File-E to DFS-A.	SA $_{File-E}$ collect (component = FTP-A)
16	DFS-A returns File-E to WP-A.	SA $_{File-E}$ collect (component = DFS-A)
17	WP-A displays File-E to the user.	SA $_{File-E}$ collect (component = WP-A)

Table 8 contains the security requirements identified earlier, and it is shown where they are satisfied in the example above.

Table 8 Security requirements and how it is satisfied by the actions of the security agents

Requirement	*Description*
1. Path context access control for objects	At step 12, SA User-A joins with SA File-E. SA User-A exposes its baggage to SA File-E. SA File-E now activates Rule 1 in its protection profile and perform the necessary access control on User-A's access request. Note that the rule takes into account the context of the access path followed to make the access control decision.
2. Subject linked, access path based, network protection for requests.	At step 7, User-A's access request is accompanied by SA User-A, and as a result the appropriate network protection services are enforced according to Rule 1 in SA User-A's protection profile.
3. Object linked, access path based, network protection for objects.	At step 14, File-E is accompanied by SA File-E, and as a result the appropriate network protection services are enforced according to Rule 2 in SA File-E's protection profile.
4. Consistent protection of objects within the distributed environment.	Because every object has associated with it a roaming security agent that moves with it, its protection rules also moves with the object. The result is, that even if File-E moves back to Host-B, and then back to Host-A again, that the protection rules will still apply and be consistent.

3.4 Summary

This section defined the roaming security agent and described its associated concepts, such as protection profiles, its relationships to subject and objects, and certain assumptions that are made about the capabilities of the security agents.

The section then defined the protection profile for User-A's security agent $SA_{User\text{-}A}$, and File-E's security agent $SA_{File\text{-}E}$. By using the initially presented example, it was shown how the agents can address the four security requirements identified earlier.

4 CONCLUSIONS

In the paper certain access control and network protection problems, within distributed computer environments, were identified. Based on these problems, certain security requirements were identified to be addressed. The concepts of an access path, baggage, and roaming security agents were presented. It was then shown, by way of an example, how the security agents can satisfy the security requirements.

Considering the mechanism whereby World Wide Web servers access files, that is HTML (Hyper Text Markup Language) pages, with other HTML links within them, the same concepts could be applied. For example the following path

http://www.nedbank.com/File-E.html

refers to an HTML file, called File-E, on Nedbank's Web server. Within the design of this paper, these HTML files can be viewed as objects with associated roaming security agents, that will protect it within the distributed Internet environment. This still needs to be researched in more detail.

5 REFERENCES

[1] WH Boshoff and SH von Solms, "A Path Context Model for Addressing Security in Potentially Non-secure environments", Computers & Security, v8 1989.

[2] WH Boshoff and SH von Solms, "Application of a path context approach to computer security fundamentals", Security, Butterworth & Heinemann, v12 n2, 1990.

[3] P van Zyl and SH von Solms, "MOSS - A Model for Open Systems Security", Proceedings of IFIP Sec'94.

[4] ISO 7498-2, "Information processing systems - Open Systems Interconnection - Basic Reference Model - Part 2: Security Architecture", 1989.

[5] R Orfali, D Harkey and J Edwards, "The Essential Distributed Objects", Survival guide, John Willey & Sons, Inc, 1996.

[6] CP Phleeger, "Security in Computing", Prentice-hall International editions, 1989.

[7] http://www.microsoft.com/, "NT Workstation and NT Server Security", Sept 1996

[8] http"//www.microsoft.com/, "Cairo, Distributed Objects, OLE, COM, etc.", Sept 1996

[9] http://www.microsoft.com/, "Private Communications Technology", Sept 1996

[10] http://www.ibm.com/, "RACF Overview", Sept 1996

[11] http://www.ibm.com/, "AIX Security", Sept 1996

[12] http://www.ibm.com/, "CORBA", Sept 1996

[13] ISO 7498-1, "Information processing systems - Open Systems Interconnection - Basic Reference Model - Part 1", 1983

[14] ISO 7498-2, "Information processing systems - Open Systems Interconnection - Basic Reference Model - Part 2: Security Architecture", 1989.

[15] http://www.osf.org/, "The Open Software Foundation DCE (Distributed Computing Environment) DFS (Distributed File System)", Sept 1996

[16] http://www.sun.com/, "SUN's Network File Service (NFS)", Sept 1996

6 ANNEX: BAGGAGE VECTOR

In this annex, we provide the "baggage" as collected by User-A's security agent, SA $_{\text{User-A}}$, and File-E's security agent, SA $_{\text{File-E}}$,in the example.

Table 8 Baggage collected by SA $_{\text{User-A}}$ during its related steps in figure 1.

Step	*Baggage*
1	(component = User-A, component = Host-A)
2	(component = User-A, component = Host-A) ⇨(component = WP-A)
4	(component = User-A, component = Host-A) ⇨(component = WP-A)⇨ (request = load File-E)
6	(component = User-A, component = Host-A) ⇨(component = WP-A)⇨ (request = load File-E)⇨(component = DFS-A)
7	(component = User-A, component = Host-A) ⇨(component = WP-A)⇨ (request = load File-E)⇨(component = DFS-A)⇨ (component = FTP-A, destination = FTP-B, via = Net-A)(result = a)
8	(component = User-A, component = Host-A) ⇨(component = WP-A)⇨ (request = load File-E)⇨(component = DFS-A)⇨ (component = FTP-A, destination = FTP-B, via = Net-A)(result = a)⇨ (component = Net-A, destination = Net-B)
9	(component = User-A, component = Host-A) ⇨(component = WP-A)⇨ (request = load File-E)⇨(component = DFS-A)⇨ (component = FTP-A, destination = FTP-B, via = Net-A)(result = a)⇨ (component = Net-A, destination = Net-B)⇨ (component = Net-B, destination = FTP-B)
11	(component = User-A, component = Host-A)⇨(component = WP-A)⇨

	(request = load File-E)⇨(component = DFS-A)⇨ (component = FTP-A, destination = FTP-B, via = Net-A)(result = a)⇨ (component = Net-A, destination = Net-B)⇨ (component = Net-B, destination = FTP-B)⇨(component = FTP-B)
12	(component = User-A, component = Host-A) ⇨ (component = WP-A)⇨ (request = load File-E)⇨(component = DFS-A)⇨ (component = FTP-A, destination = FTP-B, via = Net-A)(result = a)⇨ (component = Net-A, destination = Net-B)⇨ (component = Net-B, destination = FTP-B)⇨(component = FTP-B)⇨ (component = DFS-B)(agents = SA$_{\text{User-A}}$, SA$_{\text{File-E}}$,result = b)

Table 9 Baggage collected by SA$_{\text{File-E}}$ during its related steps in figure 1.

Step	*Baggage*
12	(agents = SA$_{\text{User-A}}$, SA$_{\text{File-E}}$,result = b)
13	(agents = SA$_{\text{User-A}}$, SA$_{\text{File-E}}$,result = b)⇨(component = DFS-B)
14	(agents = SA$_{\text{User-A}}$, SA$_{\text{File-E}}$,result = b)⇨(component = DFS-B)⇨ (component = FTP-B, destination = FTP-A, via = Net-B)(result = c)
15	(agents = SA$_{\text{User-A}}$, SA$_{\text{File-E}}$,result = b)⇨(component = DFS-B)⇨ (component = FTP-B, destination = FTP-A, via = Net-B)(result =)⇨ (component = FTP-A)
16	(agents = SA$_{\text{User-A}}$, SA$_{\text{File-E}}$,result = b)⇨(component = DFS-B)⇨ (component = FTP-B, destination = FTP-A, via = Net-B)(result = c)⇨ (component = FTP-A)⇨(component = DFS-A)
17	(agents = SA$_{\text{User-A}}$, SA$_{\text{File-E}}$,result = b)⇨(component = DFS-B)⇨ (component = FTP-B, destination = FTP-A, via = Net-B)(result = c)⇨ (component = FTP-A)⇨(component = DFS-A)⇨(component = WP-A)

7 BIOGRAPHY

Pieter van Zyl received his Masters degree at the Rand Afrikaans University in 1991, cum laude. He is currently busy with his doctoral study, of which this paper is a result. During 1995/96 he worked in the technical architecture and strategic planning department of a major financial institution were he was responsibilities for designing the Information Security Architecture and Enterprise Systems Management Architecture for the bank. He now heads up the Network Management Support function for the Bank.

Prof Sebastiaan (Basie) von Solms is Head of the Department of Computer Science at the Rand Afrikaans University in Johannesburg, South Africa. He is also the South African representative on Technical Committee 11 [Information Security] (TC11) of the International Federation for Information Processing (IFIP), and is present Chairman of TC11.

Prof von Solms has published numerous research papers on Information Security, and had spent 1995 on a 12 month industry sabbatical at IBM Development Laboratory at Hursley in the UK. He is presently also a consultant on Information Security to IBM South Africa. He is also a member of the Review Panel of the journal Computers and Security, as well as a member of the Editorial Board of the South African Computer Journal.

INDEX OF CONTRIBUTORS

KEYWORD INDEX

GPSR Compliance
The European Union's (EU) General Product Safety Regulation (GPSR) is a set of rules that requires consumer products to be safe and our obligations to ensure this.

If you have any concerns about our products, you can contact us on

ProductSafety@springernature.com

In case Publisher is established outside the EU, the EU authorized representative is:

Springer Nature Customer Service Center GmbH
Europaplatz 3
69115 Heidelberg, Germany

www.ingramcontent.com/pod-product-compliance
Ingram Content Group UK Ltd.
Pitfield, Milton Keynes, MK11 3LW, UK
UKHW061831190726
13855UKWH00005B/1750
* 9 7 8 1 4 7 5 7 5 4 8 0 3 *